FIELDING'S
HAWAII

Fielding Titles

Fielding's Alaska Cruises and the Inside Passage
Fielding's Asia's Top Dive Sites
Fielding's Amazon
Fielding's Australia
Fielding's Bahamas
Fielding's Baja
Fielding's Bermuda
Fielding's Borneo
Fielding's Budget Europe
Fielding's Caribbean
Fielding's Caribbean Cruises
Fielding's Disney World and Orlando
Fielding's Diving Indonesia
Fielding's Eastern Caribbean
Fielding's England
Fielding's Europe
Fielding's European Cruises
Fielding's Far East
Fielding's France
Fielding's Freewheelin' USA
Fielding's Kenya
Fielding's Hawaii
Fielding's Italy
Fielding's Las Vegas Agenda
Fielding's London Agenda
Fielding's Los Angeles
Fielding's Malaysia and Singapore
Fielding's Mexico
Fielding's New Orleans Agenda
Fielding's New York Agenda
Fielding's New Zealand
Fielding's Paradors, Pousadas and Charming Villages of Spain and Portugal
Fielding's Paris Agenda
Fielding's Portugal
Fielding's Rome Agenda
Fielding's San Diego Agenda
Fielding's Southeast Asia
Fielding's Southern Vietnam on Two Wheels
Fielding's Spain
Fielding's Surfing Indonesia
Fielding's Sydney Agenda
Fielding's Thailand, Cambodia, Laos & Myanmar
Fielding's Vacation Places Rated
Fielding's Vietnam
Fielding's Western Caribbean
Fielding's The World's Most Dangerous Places
Fielding's Worldwide Cruises

FIELDING'S
HAWAII

By
Marael Johnson
and
Margie Nelson

Fielding Worldwide, Inc.
308 South Catalina Avenue
Redondo Beach, California 90277 U.S.A.

Fielding's Hawaii

Published by Fielding Worldwide, Inc.

Text Copyright ©1997 FWI

Icons & Illustrations Copyright ©1997 FWI

Photo Copyrights ©1997 to Individual Photographers

Some maps ©MAGELLAN Geographix, Santa Barbara, California, Telephone (800) 929-4MAP, www.magellangeo.com

FIELDING WORLDWIDE INC.

PUBLISHER AND CEO	**Robert Young Pelton**
GENERAL MANAGER	**John Guillebeaux**
MARKETING DIRECTOR	**Paul T. Snapp**
OPERATIONS DIRECTOR	**George Posanke**
ELECTRONIC PUBLISHING DIRECTOR	**Larry E. Hart**
PUBLIC RELATIONS DIRECTOR	**Beverly Riess**
ACCOUNT SERVICES MANAGER	**Christy Harp**
PROJECT MANAGER	**Chris Snyder**

EDITORS

Kathy Knoles	**Linda Charlton**
Catherine Bruhn	**Reed Parsell**

PRODUCTION

Martin Mancha	**Alfredo Mercado**
Ramses Reynoso	**Craig South**

COVER DESIGNED BY	**Digital Artists, Inc.**
COVER PHOTOGRAPHERS—Front	**C. Brad Lewis/Tony Stone Images**
Back	**Warren Morgan/Westlight**
INSIDE PHOTOS	**Hawaii Visitors Bureau, Maui Visitors Bureau, Molokai Visitors Bureau, Oahu Visitors Bureau, Sheila Donnelly & Associates, Corel Professional Photos**
3-D MAPS	**Paul Carbo**
TEXT	**Marael Johnson**
LISTINGS	**Margie Nelson**

Inquiries should be addressed to: Fielding Worldwide, Inc., 308 South Catalina Ave., Redondo Beach, California 90277 U.S.A., ☎ *(310) 372-4474*, Facsimile *(310) 376-8064*, 8:30 a.m.–5:30 p.m. Pacific Standard Time.

Website: http://www.fieldingtravel.com

e-mail: fielding@fieldingtravel.com

ISBN 1-56952-113-1

Printed in the United States of America

Letter from the Publisher

In 1946, Temple Fielding began the first of what would be a remarkable new series of well-written, highly personalized guidebooks for independent travelers. Temple's opinionated, witty and oft-imitated books have now guided travelers for almost a half-century. More important to some was Fielding's humorous and direct method of steering travelers away from the dull and the insipid. Today, Fielding's travel guides are still written by experienced travelers for experienced travelers. Our authors carry on Fielding's reputation for delivering travel experiences with a sense of discovery and style.

How do you truly experience America's most visited, most tropical getaway? Travel with Marael Johnson and Margie Nelson as they guide you to all of Hawaii's hidden corners—romantic beaches, friendly faces, dramatic scenery and sunsets that will make your jaw drop. They have worked tirelessly to take you past the crowds and beyond the tourist traps. I recommend this guide to anyone who wants to truly discover Hawaii the Fielding way.

Today, the concept of independent travel has never been bigger. Our policy of *brutal honesty* and a highly personal point of view has never changed; it just seems the travel world has caught up with us.

RYP

Robert Young Pelton
Publisher and CEO
Fielding Worldwide, Inc.

ABOUT THE AUTHORS

Marael Johnson

Marael Johnson is author of *Fielding's San Diego Agenda* and coauthor of *Fielding's Hawaii.* She is an award-winning freelance writer and poet who works and travels throughout the world. She's written travel guides to Australia, Louisiana and California for major travel publishers and has contributed to several other guidebooks. She is an active member of the Society of American Travel Writers.

Before and after taking up travel writing, the author designed and stitched clothing for rock stars, sold love beads outside American Express offices in Europe, worked as a barmaid in Spain, an artist's model everywhere and as a set dresser. She has lived in paisley-painted communes in Santa Cruz, elegant Victorians in San Francisco, squats in London, handmade tents in Spain, chateaux in France, and currently resides in San Diego County, California. She has completely disproven her mother's theory that "you can't run away," as well as Thomas Wolfe's, who swore "you can never go home again." She does both very successfully.

Margie Nelson

Margie Nelson, coauthor of *Fielding's Hawaii,* and a contributor to *Fielding's Europe,* was born and raised in Hawaii. She moved to California in her mid-20s and has become a specialist in writing about restaurants and cuisine. She has written travel articles and restaurant reviews for numerous magazines and newspapers. She lives in the country near Santa Barbara,California.

Fielding Rating Icons

The Fielding Rating Icons are highly personal and awarded to help the besieged traveler choose from among the dizzying array of activities, attractions, hotels, restaurants and sights. The awarding of an icon denotes unusual or exceptional qualities in the relevant category.

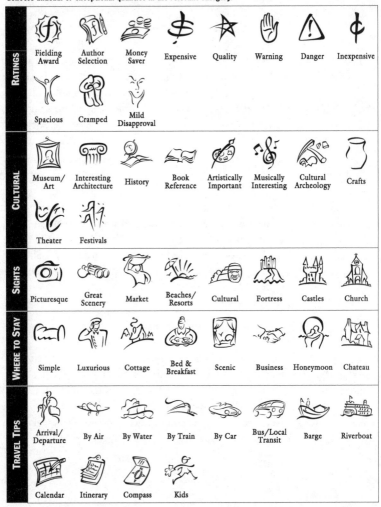

RATINGS
Fielding Award · Author Selection · Money Saver · Expensive · Quality · Warning · Danger · Inexpensive
Spacious · Cramped · Mild Disapproval

CULTURAL
Museum/Art · Interesting Architecture · History · Book Reference · Artistically Important · Musically Interesting · Cultural Archeology · Crafts
Theater · Festivals

SIGHTS
Picturesque · Great Scenery · Market · Beaches/Resorts · Cultural · Fortress · Castles · Church

WHERE TO STAY
Simple · Luxurious · Cottage · Bed & Breakfast · Scenic · Business · Honeymoon · Chateau

TRAVEL TIPS
Arrival/Departure · By Air · By Water · By Train · By Car · Bus/Local Transit · Barge · Riverboat
Calendar · Itinerary · Compass · Kids

ACTIVITIES

Downhill Skiing · X–country Skiing · Watersports · Sailing · Scuba Diving · Snorkeling/Diving · Deep-sea Fishing · Freshwater Fishing

Swimming · Hiking · Walking · Relaxing · Golf · Tennis · Horseback Riding · General Sports

Cycling · Workout

SPECIAL INTEREST

Nightlife · Singles · Romantic · Nude Beaches · Lecture · Spectacular Cuisine · Wine Tasting · Shopping

Cafe Stops · Gardening · Pro Sports · Mystery

Legend

Essentials

H Hotel
† Youth Hostel
✗ Restaurant
S Bank
C Telephone
i Tourist Info.
✛ Hospital
U Pub/Bar
✉ Post Office
P Parking
T Taxi
S Subway
M Metro
M Market
S Shopping
C Cinema
♥ Theatre
✈ Int'l Airport
✚ Regional Airport
★ Police Station
⚖ Courthouse
🏛 Gov't. Building

■ Attraction
✈ Military Airbase
🏃 Army Base
⚓ Naval base
🏰 Fort
🎓 University
🚩 School

Historical

∴ Archeological Site
⚔ Battleground
♜ Castle
🗿 Monument
🏛 Museum
▬ Ruin
🚢 Shipwreck

Religious

✝ Church
🛕 Buddhist Temple
🛕 Hindu Temple
☪ Mosque
🏯 Pagoda
✡ Synagogue

Activities

➢ Beach
▲ Campground
⊞ Picnic Area
⚲ Golf Course
🚤 Boat Launch
🤿 Diving
🐟 Fishing
🏄 Water Skiing
⛷ Snow Skiing
🐦 Bird Sanctuary
🦌 Wildlife Sanctuary
🌳 Park
🏕 Park Headquarters
⛏ Mine
🗼 Lighthouse
🌾 Windmill
⚓ Cruise Port
🏹 View
⬭ Stadium
🏢 Building
🐘 Zoo
🌻 Garden

Physical

——— International Boundary	🚶🚶 Hiking Trail
——— County/Regional Boundary	▬▬ Dirt Road
PARIS ◉ National Capital	✚✚✚ Railroad
Montego Bay ◉ State/Parish Capital	**RR** Railroad Station
Los Angeles ● Major City	⟿ Ferry Route
Quy Nhon ○ Town/Village	▲ Mountain Peak
⑤ Motorway/Freeway	⬛ Lake
⑯³ Highway	⟋ River
·········· Primary Road	◖ Cave
════ Secondary Road	⬯ Coral Reef
——— Subway	〰 Waterfall
ᘛ Biking Routed	♨ Hot Spring

©FWI 1995

TABLE OF CONTENTS

LIST OF MAPS

Hawaiian Islands

INTRODUCTION

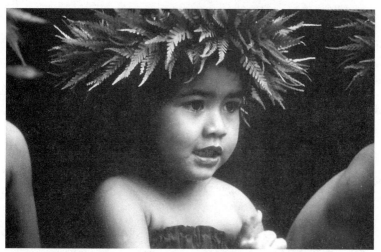

Children enjoy making traditional leis from ferns and flowers.

Every cliché and superlative you've heard of applies—sometimes nauseatingly so—to Hawaii, a chain of islands with palms, balms, breezes and leis—not to mention tourists galore (and many of them not a pretty sight). Reclaimed dreams of Paradise Lost—an Eden where every apple on the tree has at least one big old bite print. A place where sex and romance are all but written into the package deals along with tee times and "authentic" luaus.

Hawaii is where people—young, old or in between—come to live out their ultimate tropical dreams. The perfect honeymoon, the perfect wave, the perfect home video—choreographed around a turquoise sea of bikini-clad beach bunnies, muscle-bound native boys and dancing hula girls. Everyone is young again—or old enough—to live happily ever after. Life is tasty—one long romp with juicy pineapples and sweet sugarcane. No snakes anywhere. A reason to keep living after listening to the evening news. The Gaza what? Bosnia-where? Hamas, IRA, militias and gangs? Well, *aloha*, baby!

Hawaii is gorgeous—a blend of the exotic and the familiar, high-rising, fast-paced Honolulu juxtaposed against thatched-roof, yawn-a-minute villages. The U.S. military mixing with the tan-shouldered natives. Chinese cowboys galloping through McDonald's arches. Former resident Imelda Marcos' shoe collection just a stomp away from oodles of bare feet with callused soles. Some of the ritziest resorts and golf courses in the world bordered by neighborhoods ruled by low incomes and despair. Japanese honeymooners, well-to-do retirees, middle-class vacationers, surfers and hippies all doing their Hawaii thing. A string of some of the planet's most remote islands that are oddly enough part of the United States. In short, you'll feel as though you've died and gone to heaven but you didn't have to give up burgers, mai tais, or flush toilets to get there. And you probably didn't even have to pray.

What's your fancy? A hike down a remote canyon—or along a cliffhanger? Horseback riding through volcanic craters? Surfing 30-foot waves? Skiing down a slope in time to catch a rodeo? A leisurely stroll along beaches, through meadows—followed by a picnic beneath a waterfall? Cycling, diving, playing a round of golf on a championship course? Or being pampered like Hawaiian royalty and feasting on some of the finest international cuisine while surrounded by a horde of celebrities and Beautiful People?

Well then…*congratulations*! You have selected the ultimate no-hype, nonfluff guide to the Hawaiian islands. We are informative, sassy and opinionated. We don't insult your intelligence. We point things out, make suggestions, often get you all excited. It will be *you*, however, who makes the final choices for your journey. We are merely a companion—a companion that shuts up as soon as you close the cover. Could you ask for anything better?

HOW TO USE
THIS GUIDE

King Kamehameha Statue at Kapauu courthouse honors the king who unified Hawaii. Born in Kohala, he ruled until his death in 1819.

The "Hawaiian Planner" will send you on your way with useful info about how to actually *get* where you're trying to go, when to travel, what to pack, what to expect weather-wise and all manner of other useful tidbits—including a holiday and festival guide as well as a primer in the local lingo.

Flip to the "History and Culture" section to explore Hawaii's mythical past and cultural heritage. You'll bone up on everything from the legend of Papa and Wakea and Captain Cook's arrival (and demise) to traditional arts and crafts (including hula dancing and ukulele strumming). And exactly who *are*

Hawaiians anyway? And what about the pigs, the fish, the poi and the pupus? Not to mention the big deal about Spam! Keep reading.

The "Natural Wonders" chapter is an overview of the life-forms that make Hawaii such a drop-dead paradise—its plants, animals, birds, flowers and fruits. Scents, tastes and sights that you will want to take home—and some of them you will actually be able to.

"Island Snapshots" is a brief rundown on each island—little teasers to whet your already insatiable appetite after having read about the food and fruit. Then pick your island (or islands) and dive into the individual chapters with their expanded introductions, general information on how to get around and the skinny on attractions, accommodations, restaurants, sports, shopping and—of course—beaches. You'll find a broad range of prices and pickings. We aim to be eclectic. Price ranges are offered. Check out Fielding's "Five-Star Rating System" and "Rating Icons" chart for your built-in, every-thing-you-need-to-know quality control.

HOW TO USE THIS GUIDE

TRAVELER'S GUIDE

Mokolii Island, also known as Chinaman's Hat, is a good place to see octopi.

Fielding's Fascinating Fast Facts

Nickname	**The Aloha State**
Population	**1,108,200**
Highest point	**Mauna Kea (13,796 ft.), Big Island**
Lowest point	**Sea level**
State capital	**Honolulu**
State bird	**Nene (Hawaiian goose)**

State flower	Yellow hibiscus
State tree	Kukui
State gem	Black coral
State fish	Humuhumunukunukukuapuaa (trigger fish)
State mammal	Humpback whale
State anthem	"Hawai'i Pono'i"
State motto	"Ua mau ke ea o ka 'aina i ka pono," or "The life of the land is perpetuated in righteousness"

Hawaiian Planner

When to Go

Go whenever you like, whenever you can. The weather will always be perfect—especially if you're coming from some evil winter. Hawaii is body-and-mind friendly—like a permanent massage, facial and hair-conditioner combined with instant relaxation techniques (without even closing your eyes and humming a chant or affirmation). Days are sunny, humidity is low, pollution is practically nonexistent and—even on the hottest days—those blissful trade winds arrive to fan you.

Coolest months are December through March, when daytime temps are mid-70s and the evenings can drop down into the 50s (and 30 degrees is not unheard of over at Mauna Kea crater on the Big Island). August and September are usually the hottest months, with 90-ish highs during the day as well as higher humidity. Otherwise it's pretty much hum-drum 80s with the water temperature in the 75- to 80-degree range. The rainy season ordinarily falls December to March—though showers are relatively brief and bearable.

The worst tourist crunch (with the high-season prices) is roughly designated mid-December through mid-April, when many visitors are trying to escape their winter hell back home. If you come at that time be prepared for masses of snow-white flesh and flab vying for beach- and pool-chair space in the race to return to Minnesota or wherever with a to-die-for tan. December, however, is also the month when the perennially tan and hard-bodied surfers swarm Oahu's North Shore for competitions and other feats of daring.

TEMPERATURE CHART

	Jan.	Feb.	Mar.	Apr.	May	Jun.	Jul.	Aug.	Sep.	Oct.	Nov.	Dec.
Honolulu, Oahu												
Avg. High	80	80	81	83	85	86	87	88	88	87	84	81
Avg. Low	65	65	69	69	70	72	73	74	73	72	69	67
Kahului, Maui												
Avg. High	80	80	81	82	85	86	87	87	88	83	81	80
Avg. Low	63	63	65	66	67	69	70	71	70	68	66	64
Lihue, Kauai												
Avg. High	78	78	78	79	81	83	84	85	85	83	81	79
Avg. Low	65	65	66	68	70	72	73	74	73	71	70	67
Hilo, Hawaii												
Avg. High	80	79	79	80	81	83	83	83	84	83	81	80
Avg. Low	63	63	64	65	66	67	68	68	68	68	66	64
Lanai City, Lanai												
Avg. High	76	76	76	77	79	79	81	83	81	81	79	76
Avg. Low	58	59	58	61	63	63	65	65	63	63	63	61
Molokai Airport, Molokai												
Avg. High	79	77	79	79	81	83	85	85	85	85	81	79
Avg. Low	63	63	63	65	67	68	70	70	70	68	67	65

Fielding's Hawaiian Weather Watch

Rain

In the islands it usually occurs—if only a few drops—every day with the northeast (or windward) side of each island taking the most sop. December through March—visitor prime-time—tends to be the wettest period. Nonetheless the drizzle or soak rarely lasts all day and should not be a factor in planning your trip or other island outings. On the other hand, when a big storm *does* come in, it can be a whopper.

Hurricanes

Iniki, hurricane of 1992, blew through Kauai and Oahu's leeward coast, causing an estimated $1.5 billion in damages—not to mention scaring the shorts and sarongs off the huddled visitors and locals (everyone from housekeepers and taro farmers to Steven Spielberg and the assembled cast of *Jurassic Park*). Hurricanes are rare, but when they hit, watch out!

Fielding HAWAII

VOLCANOES

As the pacific plate moves slowly northwest it is passing over a hot spot that is now located below the Island of Hawaii. The hot spot creates volcanoes that become Islands. All eight islands in the chain were formed this way.

THE HOT SPOT

Plumes of magma rise from a "hot spot" deep within the mantle. This fluid rock pushes its way to the surface, erupting on the ocean floor. After several thousand years and eruptions, the volcano rises above sea level to form an island. The volcano remains active until the Pacific Plate carries it off the hot spot.

'Ring of Fire'　　N. American plate

HOT SPOT

Pacific plate

KAUAI　OAHU　MOLOKAI　MAUI　HAWAII

◀ PACIFIC PLATE MOVEMENT (4" per year)　ACTIVE

INACTIVE

HOT SPOT

NIIHAU
1,281 ft.

KAUAI
5,234 ft.

OAHU
4,020 ft.

HAWAIIAN RIDGE

All of Hawaii's eight major islands are actually the tops of huge volcanoes which make up the Hawaiian Ridge The ridge's slow birth began 25 million years ago when a fissure in the sea floor started spewing lava.

MAUNA KEA

Mauna Kea is the tallest volcano on Hawaii at 13,792 feet and has not erupted in 3500 years.

HAWAII

Mauna Loa

Hilo

HAWAII VOLCANOES NATIONAL PARK

Mauna Kea

Mount Everest

If Mount Everest was placed on the sea floor, it would not be as tall as Mauna Kea.

HALEMAUMAU CRATER

The Halemaumau crater is visible from the rim of the Kilauea caldera.

DEVESTATION TRAIL

Kilauea erupted in 1959 blanketing the area with volcanic cinders. Devestation trail winds through the area.

PU'U O'O

Pu'u O'o is a volcanic vent on the Island of Hawaii.

MOLOKAI
4,970 ft.

MAUI
10,023 ft.

LANAI
3,370 ft.

KAHOOLAWE
1,477 ft.

HAWAII
13,796 ft.

PACIFIC OCEAN

Trade Winds

We love the trades—they're what keep Hawaii breezy and balmy instead of sticky and oppressive. The trade winds billow throughout most of the summer and half of winter and are seemingly psychic—becoming blissfully strongest just when the sweat starts to bead. They lull you to sleep and gently kiss you when you wake.

Kona Winds

Kona winds are not quite as friendly as the trades. They blow, all right, but it's a hot, sticky, cloying feel—like a lover who won't go away. October to April is their big debut and they hang around for about half that time. Happily, the Konas are rare during the summer, when the combination of heat and intense wind can be abysmal.

Volcanic Eruptions

OK, so the Big Island has periodic eruptions. Contrary to what you might think, the islanders don't exactly run *from* these events—they rush *to* them. It's something like performance art. Bring a lawn chair. By the way, that post-eruption haze is known as "vog."

Earthquakes

They occasionally strike but the last Big One was back in 1975 (on the Big Island). And—due to all those volcanic jitters—it's hard to actually discern a bona-fide earthquake unless it's a *really* Big One. If you're on the beach when a quake hits, leave ASAP.

Before You Go

Getting to Hawaii by Air

The majority of flights set down at Honolulu International Airport, connecting with various international, domestic and interisland carriers. Some flights head directly for Maui or the Big Island. Nonstops from the mainland originate in Los Angeles, San Diego, San Francisco, St. Louis, Seattle and some other cities. International arrivals head in from Japan, Australia, New Zealand, Canada, the Philippines and other locations in Asia and the South Pacific. Flights from the mainland's West Coast take about five hours, with an extra 20 to 30 minutes to get from the airport to Waikiki hotels.

DOMESTIC CARRIERS	
American Airlines	☎ *(800) 433-7300*
Continental Airlines	☎ *(800) 231-0856*
Delta Airlines	☎ *(800) 221-1212*

DOMESTIC CARRIERS

Hawaiian Airlines	☎ *(800) 367-5320*
Northwest Airlines	☎ *(800) 225-2525*
Trans World Airlines	☎ *(800) 221-2000*
United Airlines	☎ *(800) 225-5825*

INTERNATIONAL CARRIERS

Air New Zealand	☎ *(800) 262-1234*
Canadian Airlines	☎ *(800) 426-7000*
China Airlines	☎ *(800) 227-5118*
Garuda Indonesia	☎ *(800) 826-2829*
Japan Airlines	☎ *(800) 525-3663*
Korean Air	☎ *(800) 421-8200*
Philippine Airlines	☎ *(800) 435-9725*
Qantas	☎ *(800) 227-4500*

Getting to Hawaii by Sea

Hawaii is a popular stop on the cruise ship circuit, but if you opt for this method, keep in mind your stay will most likely be a brief one- or two-day port o' call on the way to or from Mexico, Asia, Australia or other South Pacific islands. For a complete guide to Hawaiian cruises see *Fielding's Worldwide Cruises* by Shirley Slater and Harry Basch.

Cruise lines to contact for more details of their Hawaiian "expeditions" include:

Cunard	☎ *(800) 221-4770*
Holland America	☎ *(800) 426-0327*
Princess	☎ *(800) 421-0522*
Royal Caribbean	☎ *(800) 327-6700*
Royal Cruise Line	☎ *(800) 232-4666*
Society Expeditions	☎ *(800) 426-7794*

For cruises around the Hawaiian islands (you have to fly into Honolulu), sign on for a three-, four-, or seven-day interisland voyage with **American Hawaii Cruises** (☎ *(800) 765-7000*). Two luxury liners, the SS *Independence* and SS *Constitution*—holding 800-some passengers each—provide year-

Fielding **HAWAII**

HIGHLIGHTS

Oahu, Maui, Kauai and the Big Island continue as the biggest tourist draws. Molokai and Lanai are up and coming while Niihau and Kahoolawe are, for all practical purposes, completely out of the picture.

◀ **TOKYO**
3831 miles

KAUAI

Lihue ●

KAUAI   p. 435

Finally recovered from 1992's devastating Hurricane Iniki, Kauai has slowly snatched back its considerable chunk of tourism. The island has long been sought out by honeymooners and retirees who either bask on the beaches or hole up inside a resort or condo. As the "wettest place on earth," Kauai is perpetually lush, green and abloom—a true Garden of Eden. Less laid-back visitors will definitely want to explore the magical Waimea Canyon and the Na Pali coast. Other possibilities include swimming, surfing, waterfall-watching and running away from it all and doing nothing for the rest of your life.

NIIHAU

NIIHAU

Niihau is the really private island, so private that you won't be allowed to go there unless you're on a helicopter tour. Even then, you won't be able to see "the people." Owned by the Robinson family since the mid-1800s, Niihau is home to about 225 pure-blood Hawaiians who speak their indigenous language and live much the same way as their ancestors did. They have no plumbing, telephones, guns, alcohol or hotels, and few modern appliances. Most work on the Robinson ranch lands in exchange for anything they might need. The rare Niihau shells are fashioned by island women into extremely expensive leis that are sold on the other islands.

▲ **TAHITI**
2746 miles

Continued on next page ☞

OAHU   p. 185

Approximately 80 percent of the state's population calls this island "home." Oahu has more to offer than just the bustle of Honolulu and the tourist crunch of Waikiki. You'll still be able to find plenty of "real" Hawaiian feel and that pervasive aloha spirit. The North Shore has gorgeous countryside along with legendary waves. Oahu provides every visitor comforts and irritations plus an extraordinary range of activities such as golf, tennis, windsurfing, deep-sea fishing and some very serious surfing.

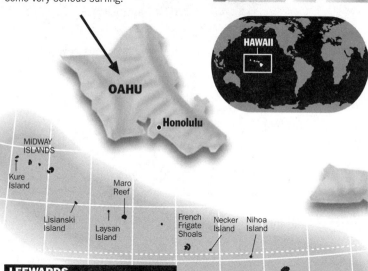

HAWAII

OAHU

Honolulu

MIDWAY ISLANDS

Kure Island

Maro Reef

Lisianski Island

Laysan Island

French Frigate Shoals

Necker Island

Nihoa Island

HAWAIIAN ISLANDS

LEEWARDS

The Leewards, or the Northwestern Islands, include Pearl, Hermes, Necker, French Frigate Shoals, Kure and Lisianski. They are the oldest Hawaiian islands (between 6 and 25 million years old). Most were discovered during the 1800s by passing ships. The islands stretch about 1000 miles between Nihoa Island (approximately 100 miles north of Kauai) and Kure Atoll, in the Midway chain.

The Leewards are all part of the Hawaiian Islands National Wildlife Refuge. Havens for seabirds, green turtles and myriad other wildlife, the Leewards can only be visited with special permission from the U.S. Fish and Wildlife Agency.

MOLOKAI
• Kaunakakai

MOLOKAI
p. 523

Known as the "most Hawaiian" of the islands, Molokai also gained fame as the home of a leper colony (which you can tour with a resident guide). Happily, the developers haven't (yet) destroyed Molokai and visitors will find lots of privacy and hidden hideaways. Gorgeous sea cliffs, waterfalls, views and trails beckon hikers, photographers and romantics, while fishers head straight for the bountiful coastal waters. There's only one main road on the island and it's nearly impossible to get lost—unless you want to.

LANAI
Lanai City

LANAI
p. 567

Lanai is the so-called "private island"—at least it used to be private. Once owned exclusively by the Dole family, the corporate heirs took a turn toward tourism in the 1990s when the future of their pineapple business wasn't looking so juicy. Now there's a posh resort, a couple of hotels, a four-finger handful of restaurants and pretty much nothing else except natural beauty and peace and quiet. You'll find only 22 miles of paved roads, cool pine forests, ancient petroglyphs and about 16,000 acres of pineapple plantation.

Kapalua
Kahalui

MAUI

KAHOOLAWE

KAHOOLAWE
This former bombing site just off the southeast edge of Maui was returned to the state in 1994. Considered a sacred island by the ancient Hawaiians, the U.S. Navy used it for target practice for almost 50 years. Some hope it will become a nature preserve, others would like to see it returned to the indigenous people, and many would happily turn it into a tourist resort. Some things actually did survive, such as ruins of ancient temples and settlements and, at least for now, Kahoolawe holds a place on the National Register of Historic Places.

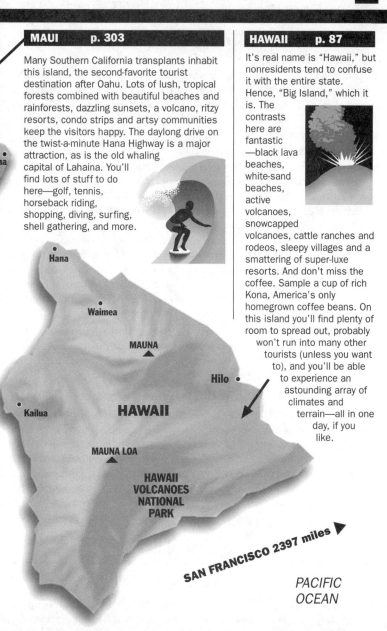

MAUI   p. 303

Many Southern California transplants inhabit this island, the second-favorite tourist destination after Oahu. Lots of lush, tropical forests combined with beautiful beaches and rainforests, dazzling sunsets, a volcano, ritzy resorts, condo strips and artsy communities keep the visitors happy. The daylong drive on the twist-a-minute Hana Highway is a major attraction, as is the old whaling capital of Lahaina. You'll find lots of stuff to do here—golf, tennis, horseback riding, shopping, diving, surfing, shell gathering, and more.

HAWAII   p. 87

It's real name is "Hawaii," but nonresidents tend to confuse it with the entire state. Hence, "Big Island," which it is. The contrasts here are fantastic —black lava beaches, white-sand beaches, active volcanoes, snowcapped volcanoes, cattle ranches and rodeos, sleepy villages and a smattering of super-luxe resorts. And don't miss the coffee. Sample a cup of rich Kona, America's only homegrown coffee beans. On this island you'll find plenty of room to spread out, probably won't run into many other tourists (unless you want to), and you'll be able to experience an astounding array of climates and terrain—all in one day, if you like.

TRAVELER'S GUIDE

ana

Hana

Waimea

MAUNA

Hilo

Kailua

HAWAII

MAUNA LOA

HAWAII
VOLCANOES
NATIONAL
PARK

SAN FRANCISCO 2397 miles ▶

*PACIFIC
OCEAN*

round itineraries at prices ranging from around $1000 for a cramped inside closet (er, *cabin*) up to the $4000-plus mark for an outside suite.

Getting into Hawaii by Any Means

Entry requirements for **U.S. citizens** are a joy—no passport or visa necessary. No need to change money. Hawaii may look like Shangri-La, but—gosh oh mighty—it's part of the United States. If you intend to drive, bring your driver's license. If you intend to drink or bar-hop, bring the license or an official picture I.D. **Canadian citizens** need proof of residence (passport, birth certificate, etc.) but don't require a visa.

Citizens of **other countries** must possess a valid passport, appropriate visa (check with your local embassy or consulate), enough money to keep them *on* the streets during the day and *off* the streets at night, and a ticket out of town. Also take the **customs regulations** *seriously*! Basic allowances are, per adult: one liter of booze, 200 cigarettes or 100 cigars (not your stash from Cuba) or three pounds of smoking tobacco, plus gifts totaling $100 or less. You have to spend at least 72 hours in the United States to qualify. Foreign visitors may also bring in or leave with $10,000 in United States or foreign currency without doing any paperwork. As for food, plants, and seeds—forget it. *Don't* forget, however, that Hawaiian customs and immigration officers are *extremely* zealous about their jobs (and pretty damn humorless, as well). Don't try anything funny.

All visitors should make sure they have adequate **health insurance**. You might also want to invest in a **comprehensive travel policy** that includes health and accident insurance as well as coverage for baggage loss trip cancellation, and other miscellaneous mishaps.

Getting Out of Hawaii

The dreaded time will come—unless you decide to abandon your life elsewhere (hey, *plenty* of visitors have). Leaving is a cinch. Your bags will go through **agricultural inspection**, where they'll be examined for forbidden take-aways such as fresh gardenias, live insects, sugarcane, soil and a few other verboten items. Don't worry about your fresh leis, pineapples, seashells, coconuts, etc.—they'll roll right through. Certain fruits, however (including the ambrosial avocado), might be subject to "pest control."

Say aloha, hop on the plane or ship, and you're out of there.

Getting Around Hawaii

By Car

Driving is by far your best option—often there's no other way to get around. Oahu's bus system is exceptionally good but that is an exception—

most of the islands have zilch in the way of public transportation. You can always get to the prime visitor spots by signing on to a scheduled tour coach, but for independent travelers, that mode can be depressing and unacceptable.

Major car rental companies are set up at the airports and many have desks in the larger hotels and resorts. Your best bet is to reserve ahead, especially during the high season, when your choices may be dismal—or nonexistent. If you're booking a package, a car usually is included in the deal. Check with your insurance or credit card company to see if you are covered for the collision damage waiver. If not, it's well worth the extra few bucks a day to not be paranoid about dents, dings or the financial ruin that might result from even a small collision. (*"Hey, Snookums—get a load of that black sand beach."* CRASH. Honeymoon's over.)

Hawaii's main highways and roadways are paved and in good condition. The back roads, however, are another story—you may need to four-wheel it to some of the more remote locations (check with the rental company for rules and regulations). Oahu's freeways (H-1, H-2 and H-3) can be confusing to navigate—somewhat like driving inside a big pretzel. Pay attention to signs, turnoffs and merges. And, while we're at it—traffic jams, alas, are common in and around Honolulu during rush hour (yes, that perversity of real life has followed you even here). Also, confused drivers are all over the place. Mostly they're visitors trying to find their way.

Fielding's Crash Course In Aloha Driving Etiquette

Do not honk unless it is a real emergency.

Do not speed up to pass a car. Hawaiians do not like being passed.

Do slow down when entering towns and villages.

Rental Car Directory

Alamo	☎ *(800) 327-9633*
Avis	☎ *(800) 831-8000*
Budget	☎ *(800) 527-0700*
Dollar	☎ *(800) 367-7006*
Hertz	☎ *(800) 654-3011*
National Interrent	☎ *(800) 227-7368*
Over the Rainbow	☎ *(800) 303-3750*

TRAVELER'S GUIDE

By Bicycle, Moped or Scooter

You can rent bicycles on all the islands—mopeds and scooters are a bit more scarce. Your ride depends on which island you're on and where you want to go. Pedaling around Waikiki, though congested, is pretty easy. Ditto for many of the well-paved coastal routes (especially on Oahu). Heading into the backcountry, on the other hand, can be more tedious. Many of the roads have narrow shoulders, some have no shoulders at all, and some of roads appear to be only shoulders. A mountain bike is advised for both safely navigating ruts and rivulets and allowing you to be more spontaneous. (See island chapters for rental agencies.)

By Taxi

Taxis are available on all the islands, but they are not for those on a tight budget. Fares tend to be hefty—$1.50–2.50 for the flag fall (which falls faster than a karate chop) and $.50–$1.50 per sixth- or eighth-mile, depending on where you are and where you're headed. Sometimes you can negotiate the price of long-distance trips, particularly between your hotel and the airport (work this out in advance, however). It's very difficult to hail a taxi (the drivers are supposed to be radio-dispatched only), but occasionally you'll luck out and grab the attention of a hungry renegade. To be on the safe side, call ahead from your restaurant or hotel—and remember, that cab most likely will arrive on "Hawaiian time" (late, sometimes *very* late). If you need to catch a plane, allow plenty of extra time, or ask your hotel if it provides airport shuttle service.

By Ferry

You'd think there would be ferries whizzing back and forth between all these islands, wouldn't you? Filled with shell-traders, native families and sun-soaking visitors? Wrong—there are only two, paltry ferry services. The **Maui Princess** (☎ *(808) 661-8397)* travels between Lahaina (on Maui) and Molokai, while **Expeditions** (☎ *(808) 661-3756)* runs a Lahaina-Lanai shuttle. Your only other "by water" choices are a luxury liner, a variety of scheduled water tours or your own boat with—perhaps—a pair of oars.

By Air

Interisland travel via airplane is by far the easiest and most practical way to move between islands. Major carriers are **Hawaiian Airlines** (☎ *(800) 367-5320 or (808) 838-1555)* and **Aloha Airlines** (☎ *(800) 367-5250 or (808) 935-5771)*, both long-established companies with frequent daily service between all the islands. Fares and deals seem to change at a dizzying speed—there are promotions, packages, advance purchases, coupon books, air passes, fare wars, rip-offs, lows and peaks. They are advertised, not advertised, tossed to and fro like dreadlocks in the trade winds. Check ahead (and good luck).

Island Air (☎ *(800) 323-3345 or (800) 652-6541)* and **Mahalo Air** (☎ *(800) 462-6256 or (808) 833-5555)*—newest challenger to the old guard—tend to offer better deals across the board, but maybe not for long. Also, both airlines have a slimmer selection of destinations. Island flies between Honolulu, Princeville, Molokai, Lanai and Hana, Kahului and Kapalua in Maui. Mahalo services Honolulu, Kahului, Kona, Lihue, Lanai and Molokai.

FIELDING'S GUIDE TO ISLAND TOURS

Not everyone likes to travel alone. Not everyone likes to plan his or her own journey. Even some intrepid Fielding guide readers might prefer to have an Experienced Other lead them by the hand for part, or even all of their Hawaiian odyssey. Following is a list of operators that conduct a broad range of island tours—everything from thrill-a-second kayaking and backpacking adventures to traditional luaus with apple-mouthed pigs and face-stuffing tourists.

Company	Phone	Comments
All Adventure Travel	☎ *(800) 537-4025*	Kayaking, diving, rafting, cycling and hiking adventures throughout the islands.
American Wilderness Experienced	☎ *(800) 444-0099*	Renowned adventure-tour operator with a variety of Hawaiian explorations on the books.
Backroads	☎ *(800) 462-2848 or* ☎ *510-527-1555*	Environment-friendly cycling, hiking and camping tours.
Crane Tours	☎ *(800) 653-2545 or* ☎ *818-784-2213*	Very popular kayaking and backpacking trips to Na Pali Coast, Waimea Canyon and the Big Island.
Elderhostel	☎ *617-426-7788*	Inexpensive and interesting learning programs for ages 60-plus.
Far Horizons	☎ *(800) 552-4575*	Cultural and archaeological journeys, led by experts, to petroglyph fields, museums and historic and archeological sites.
Globus	☎ *(800) 221-0090 or* ☎ *(303) 797-2800*	Top-class, all-inclusive, every-second-planned motor-coach tours.
Golftrips	☎ *(800) 428-1940 or* ☎ *(813) 324-2800*	The golfer's best friend—resort-based packages come complete with lessons, greens fees and confirmed tee times.

TRAVELER'S GUIDE

FIELDING'S GUIDE TO ISLAND TOURS

Hawaii Forest and Trail	☎ *(808) 239-1993*	Narrated naturalist-led day trips, via four-wheel-drive, around the Big Island, including Hawaii Volcanoes National Park and the Hakalau Forest National Wildlife Refuge.
Kayak Kauai Outbound	☎ *(800) 437-3507 or* ☎ *(808) 826-9844*	Challenging ocean kayak journeys along the Na Pali Coast and Kauai's south shore, plus backpacking tours and canoe/kayak/mountain bike rentals.
Kauai Mountain Tours	☎ *(808) 245-7224*	Four-wheel-drive day trips into Na Pali Kona Forest Reserve.
Maupintour	☎ *(800) 255-4266 or* ☎ *(913) 843-1211*	Deluxe fully escorted, we'll-do-everything-for-you motor-coach tours.
Nature Expeditions	☎ *(800) 869-0639 or* ☎ *(503) 484-6529*	Fifteen-day, four-island, natural-history tours emphasizing geology, flora and fauna.
Ocean Voyages	☎ *(415) 332-4681*	Seven- and 10-day yacht voyages throughout the islands, emphasizing the hidden nooks and crannies.
Outfitters Kauai	☎ *(808) 742-9667*	Cycling and kayaking—escorted or self-guided—for half-day or longer along Na Pali cliffs, backcountry Kauai and Hawaii's state parks.
Pleasant Hawaiian Holidays	☎ *(800) 242-9244*	Been-around-forever, mainstream tour company packaging air, hotel, car, and a variety of traditional "Hawaii vacation experiences."
Sierra Club Trips	☎ *(415) 776-2211*	The nature-lover's fraternity offering hikes, kayaking and camping trips to Kauai, Maui and elsewhere.
Tropical Adventures	☎ *(800) 247-3483 or* ☎ *(206) 441-3483*	Organized dive extravaganzas from live-aboard boats.
Walking the World	☎ *(303) 225-0500*	Hiking and backpacking tracks for the 50-plus crowd.
Whole Person Tours	☎ *(201) 858-3400*	Guided package tours around and about the islands for disabled travelers.

TRAVELER'S GUIDE

Alternative Accommodations

We know you probably wouldn't consider staying anywhere other than one of the super-luxe resorts or hotels that will spoil you rotten with room service, poolside bars, health clubs and spare toilet-paper rolls but—just in case—we've compiled a list of alternative housing. Maybe try a condo if you're with a group, or a hostel if you're on your own. A bed-and-breakfast for that cozy feel. A home exchange for that really homey feel.

Bed-and-Breakfasts	
All Islands Bed and Breakfast	☎ *(800) 542-0344 or (808) 263-2342*
Bed and Breakfast Hawaii	☎ *(800) 733-1632*
Bed and Breakfast Honolulu	☎ *(800) 262-9912 or (808) 885-4550*
Bed and Breakfast Maui Style	☎ *(808) 879-7865*
Hawaii's Best Bed and Breakfasts	☎ *(800) 262-9912 or (808) 885-4550*
Pacific Hawaii Bed and Breakfast	☎ *(800) 999-6026 or (808) 487-1228*

Condos, Apartments, Homes and Villas	
Affordable Accommodations	☎ *(800) 848-5567 or (808) 879-7865*
Hawaiian Apartment Leasing Enterprises	☎ *(800) 854-8843 or (714) 497-4253*
Villas of Hawaii	☎ *(800) 522-3030*

Home Exchanges	
Home Exchange Network	☎ *(407) 862-7211*
Trading Homes International	☎ *(800) 877-8723*
Vacation Exchange Club	☎ *(800) 638-3841*

Hostels and YMCAs	
Armed Services YMCA	☎ *(808) 524-5600*
Honolulu International Youth Hostel	☎ *(808) 946-0591*
YMCA Central Oahu	☎ *(808) 941-3344*
YMCA Kauai	☎ *(808) 742-1182*
YMCA Maui	☎ *(808) 244-3153*

FIELDING'S CAMPGROUND GUIDE

Ah yes—what would life be without an occasional night out under the starry skies? Lulled to sleep by the sound of tent flaps. Awakened by the sound of gentle breezes and a distant ukulele. Even for those who despise camping, you'll probably be able to pull off a night or two in the islands. The weather is ideal (none of those claustrophobic mummy bags to die inside), the natural settings can inspire even the most cynical camper, and the bears and snakes are on the other side of the world. Mosquitoes, however, are on the scene, so be sure to wear repellent.

State-run campgrounds require reservations and camping permits, but many of the islands allow camping at beaches and parks. Contact the Division of State Parks offices listed below for more information.

On Oahu

Division of State Parks: 1151 Punchbowl Street, Honolulu 96813 (☎ (808) 548-7455)

City Park	in Waimanalo, on ocean side of SR 83
Keaiwa Heiau State Recreation Area	three miles northeast of SR 720, at the end of Aiea Heights Drive
Malaekahana State Recreation Area	one mile north of Laie, off SR 83
Sand Island State Recreation Area	off SR 92, at the end of Sand Island access road

On Maui

Division of State Parks: 54 High Street, Wailuku 96793 (☎ (808) 244-4354)

Haleakala National Park	27 miles southeast of Kahului, accessed via SRs 36, 37, 377, and 378
Polipoli Spring State Recreation Area	about ten miles from Kula on Waipoli Road, off SR 377
Waianapanapa State Park	2.5 miles northwest of Hana via SR 360, then north approximately one-half mile on Waianapanapa Road

On Kauai

Division of State Parks: State Building, 3060 Eiwa Street, Lihue 96766 (☎ (808) 245-4444)

Kokee State Park	15 miles north of Kekaha on SR 550
Na Pali Coast State Park	get there by foot or boat through Haena
Polihale State Park	five miles north of Mana Village via a dirt road off SR 50

FIELDING'S CAMPGROUND GUIDE

On the Big Island:

Division of State Parks: 75 Aupuni Street, Hilo 96720 (☎ (808) 961-7200)

Hapuna Beach State Recreation Area
two miles south of Kawaihae on SR 19

Hawaii Volcanoes National Park, Kamoamoa
62 miles south of Hilo, via SR 11

Hawaii Volcanoes National Park, Kipuka Nene
42 miles southwest of Hilo via SR 11

Hawaii Volcanoes National Park, Namakani Paio
32 miles southwest of Hilo on SR 11

Kalopa State Recreation Area
five miles southeast of Honokaa on SR 19

MacKenzie State Recreation Area
10 miles east of Pahoa to SR 137, then go two miles south

Mauna Kea State Recreation Area
35 miles west of Hilo off SR 200

On Molokai

Division of State Parks: (same as Maui)

Palaau State Park
three miles north of Kualapuu, off SR 470

What Will All This Fun, Beauty and Romance Cost?

It doesn't have to cost a fortune. *Really.* You can do the whole luxury resort/trendy restaurant/fresh-lei-per-day number, or you can get by on an economical package deal that includes airfare, lodging, car rental and a bunch of tours or attraction tickets. Or you can camp, cycle, pluck a flower for your hair and feast on fruit for practically nothing. If you're a foreign citizen and need to change money, your budget may well depend on the prevailing exchange rate. Sorry, can't help you there—complain to the World Bank if you're on the losing end.

Luxury hotel room (double)	**$200–$450 (or more)**
Cheap hotel room (double)	**$40–$65**
Dinner for two at an expensive Honolulu restaurant (without wine)	**$50–$65**
Lunch for two at a moderate Maui restaurant (without wine)	**$16–$20**
Taxi ride from Honolulu International Airport to Waikiki	**$25**

TRAVELER'S GUIDE

The Don Ho cocktail show	**$28**
Cup of Kona coffee	**$1.50–$2.50**
Local telephone call	**$.25**
Fare on the Bus	**$1**
Bottle of beer	**$2.50–$3.50**
Movie ticket	**$5.50–$7**
Beginning dive course	**$75**
Dreaming on the beach	**free**
Half-day glass-bottom boat cruise	**$50**
Visit to USS *Arizona* memorial	**free**

FIELDING'S MONEY-SAVING TIPS

1. If you're a senior, child, student or a soldier (or even *look* like one of the four), use it to your advantage for applicable discounts on everything from airfare to museum admission.

2. Take advantage of all the great free stuff available—the beaches, for example. Isn't that why you've come *here*?

3. If you're traveling with a group or the family, renting a condo (and cooking some of your own meals) can save a bundle.

4. Cheap food in Hawaii doesn't necessarily translate to a Big Mac and a bag of fries. You can find a great assortment of ethnic foods on all the islands (try **Makai Market** *in Honolulu's Ala Moana Shopping Center*).

5. Keep an eye out for airfare deals. If your schedule is flexible, you'll often fly cheaper during mid-week.

6. Don't discard package deals with disdain. Many are an excellent value, especially when the rental car is thrown in.

7. Participate in local events—islander-sponsored concerts, arts-and-crafts fairs, etc. They're a lot of fun, cheaper and a lot more authentic than activities organized for the tourist trade.

8. Early bird dinners (or late lunches) can afford you a great meal in a top restaurant for a substantially lower-than-prime-time bottom line.

FIELDING'S MONEY-SAVING TIPS

9. If you're a golfer, consider swinging at one of the municipal courses rather than the posh clubs. Greens fees are much cheaper. Ditto for the tennis set—most public courts are free.

10. Don't get married just for the hell of it.

FIELDING'S FAVORITE FREEBIES

1. The Hawaiian Skyguide (☎ (808) 948-0759), recorded and updated weekly by astronomer Michael Chauvin, will tell you everything you need to know for sky-gazing into those starry island nights.

2. A variety of musical performances are presented by the Royal Hawaiian Band at Kapiolani Park Bandstand (Sundays at 2 p.m.) and Iolani Place Bandstand (Fridays at 12:15 p.m.).

3. View muumuus and aloha shirts in the making at Hilo Hattie's Garment Factory—turn your head and watch macadamias in progress. Extra bonus on Tuesdays, Wednesdays and Thursdays is a free hula show. Call ☎ (808) 537-2926 for information.

4. Don't miss a walking tour of Honolulu's circa early-1800s Chinatown, a vibrant and colorful area that encompasses 15 blocks and is now the commercial home of a number of Asian ethnic groups.

5. The USS *Arizona* Memorial in Honolulu's Pearl Harbor is a poignant exhibit and educational experience for all ages and cultures.

6. Catch a spectacular day or night view of Honolulu from the Tantalus and Round Top drives.

7. Friday nights in Maui's Lahaina are designated "art nights," when Front Street galleries are open for a browse, often serving up entertainment and complimentary refreshments.

8. In Maui, watch free Polynesian entertainment at Lahaina Center (Wednesdays at 2 p.m.), Wailea Shopping Village (Tuesdays at 1 p.m.) or the Lahaina Cannery (first Thursday of every month at 7 p.m.).

9. Whale-watch in Maui on the coast between Lahaina and Maalaea, in season.

FIELDING'S FAVORITE FREEBIES

10. Orchid-lovers shouldn't miss a visit to Hilo's Akatsuka Orchid Gardens (the Big Island), with an enormous range of colors and varieties.

11. Explore the petroglyph fields at the Mauna Lani Resort and royal Waikoloan Hotel (the Big Island).

12. See daily demonstrations of quilt- and lei-making techniques at Kapaa's Marketplace at Coconut Plantation (Kauai).

13. Strong and healthy hikers must hit the scenic trail along the Na Pali Coast (trailhead is in Haena).

14. On Lanai, explore the hundreds of well-preserved Luahiwa petroglyphs.

15. Watch the sun rise and set, and the lava formations change color in synch, at Lanai's Garden of the Gods.

Packing Your Hawaii-Bound Suitcase

If you're doing the whole stay-in-one-fancy-schmancy-resort trip or a deluxe escorted tour, you can probably get away with packing (and not carrying) anything you please. If you're like the rest of us, however, at *some* point you'll end up schlepping your own gear—and *hating every minute of it*! Packing light—especially for a trip to Hawaii—should be painless. After all, people wear hardly any clothes there.

Bring the obvious necessities: sunblock, insect repellent, camera, film, glasses, this guidebook, toiletries, bathing suits (and plastic bags for the wet ones), T-shirts, shorts, sandals (rubber flip-flops or jelly shoes will do), walking shoes, a lightweight jacket or sweater, sundresses for women, lightweight slacks and shirts for men (or women). Natural fibers are advised—those synthetics, wrinkle-less though they are, can be hideously uncomfortable in the tropics. Don't forget underwear (if you wear any). Women (or men) with big hair should probably toss in a scarf lest those trade winds turn your Hawaiian holiday into one long Bad Hair Day.

If you'll be dining rather than noshing, throw in some dressier gear for evenings out—a sport coat for men (forget the tie), something tropically chic for women—appropriately accessorized, of course. If you're heading for the hills or planning hiking and camping expeditions, bring along heavier pants or jeans, sturdy shoes and a weightier jacket and windbreaker. A pair of gloves might not hurt, either.

Don't forget to save room for your sure-to-be-purchased aloha shirts, muumuus, *pareus*, souvenir T-shirts, swimwear and *zoris* (Japanese flip-flops).

Your Fielding Fashion Statement

Now that you've packed it (or bought it), what do you wear, and when?

Hawaii is gloriously informal. Basically you'll be in T-shirts, shorts or swimwear most of the time. You'll be comfortable—no neck-strangling ties, or pantyhose run askew. This is what you've come here for.

Most business meetings require nothing fancier than an aloha shirt and lightweight pants for men and something *simpatico* for women. Dressier restaurants might require men to wear a jacket—but, blissfully, no tie. Women should invest in a *pareu*—a length of cotton (often a tropical print) worn sarong-like that serves as a beach cover-up, dress, skirt and variety of other creative wrap-and-go concoctions.

Watch your footsies: wear *zoris*, tennies or sandals but never white socks and dark shoes. Otherwise not even your new deep tan will fool locals that you're not really from Poughkeepsie.

Traveling with Children

Grab all the freebies and discounts you're entitled to. Start with the airlines—check on special fares (usually, alas, limited to children under age 2), meals, seats, bassinets and coloring books. The same goes for your hotel. Often kids (even up to age 18) can stay free in their parents' rooms. Check on age limitations before you book—you can save a bundle by switching to a hotel that will take your kids in for free or at sharply discounted rates. If you're staying at a large resort complex, chances are good there will be planned children's activities along with special pool and play facilities. Most hotels have a list of recommended sitters.

Once you're on the move, be sure to have whatever safety seats and seat belts are required for your child (these vary according to age). Some car rental firms toss the safety seats in for free (sometimes they're built into the vehicle so there's no choice!). Otherwise you'll have to bring your own or rent them at additional cost.

Almost every major attraction offers reduced (or free) admission for children and students, and often there are "family fares" that allow the whole gang in for one price. If you're a member of anything (especially an automobile association) bring along your identification card and see if it will get you a discount. Kids of all ages will be knocked out by all of Hawaii's free stuff anyway—volcanoes, waterfalls, canyons, pineapples, beaches, beaches and more beaches.

Fire dancers often entertain at the Polynesian Cultural Center in Laie.

Party in Paradise

The islands often seem like just one continual celebration. Choose from luaus, ethnic festivals, sports events and religious festivals. The following rundown is the *short* list.

January	
First Night (Honolulu)	The city streets are jumping (more than usual) with New Year's revelry and top local bands.
Hula Bowl Game (Oahu)	Aloha Stadium hosts the annual college all-star football game.
Molokai Makahiki (Molokai)	The last Saturday of the month (usually) launches the annual "time of peace" celebration with traditional games, native bands, a skin-diving tournament, and more.
Morey Boogie World Body Board Championships (Oahu)	Banzai Pipeline, on the North Shore, draws bodyboarders from around the world.

February	
Chinese New Year (Honolulu)	Chinatown's the scene for all the hoopla (also known as the Narcissus Festival), including fireworks, lion dances, a queen pageant, coronation ball and plenty of little white cartons to fill with delicacies.

Hawaiian Open Golf Tournament (Oahu)	Waialae Country Club is the scene for the big tees.
Makaha World Surfing Championships (Oahu)	Head for Makaha Beach for this major long-board competition that draws surfers from all corners of the world. Buffalo's Annual Big Board Surfing Classic (using the old wooden boards) is part of the event.
Mauna Kea Ski Meet (Big Island)	Watch (or join) this race down the volcano's slope (if there's snow).
NFL Pro Bowl (Oahu)	The annual pro football all-star game is held at Aloha Stadium.
Punahou School Carnival (Honolulu)	Lots of family fun at this yearly carnival, which features rides, local nibbles, arts-and-crafts booths and—at the end—a terrific White Elephant tent that dispenses the leftovers.
Sandcastle Building Contest (Oahu)	Hawaii's top architects vie with University of Hawaii architecture students for best sand sculpture at Kailua Beach Park.

March

Polo (Oahu)	Opening Day for the March-through-August season of Sunday polo play.
Prince Kuhio Day (statewide)	A day to honor Hawaii's first congressman (who probably would have rather been king). Ceremonies and events are held at various sites throughout the islands.

April

Easter Sunrise Service (Honolulu)	This veritable and venerable institution is held at the National Memorial Cemetery of the Pacific.
Honolulu International Bed Race (Oahu)	A charity fund-raiser (also known as the Carole Kai Bed Race) in which decorated beds on wheels are raced through the streets of Waikiki (yes, you read correctly). Grab your jammies and join the fun. A parade follows the race.
Merrie Monarch Festival (Big Island)	Modern and traditional hula feats are some of the islands' most popular events. The competition lasts a week and includes a parade, performances, workshops and lots of hip movement. Tickets sell out about a year ahead and televised broadcasts of each day's events are followed more closely than "All My Children."

May

Buddha Day (statewide)
Celebrate the birth of the Serene One at various island temples.

Hawaii State Far (Honolulu)
Two weekends' worth of state fair action over at Aloha Stadium—entertainment, exhibits, agricultural charms and lots of local food to sample.

Lei Day (statewide)
The great lei is celebrated with celebrations, pageants and competitions plus a Lei Day concert and crowning of the Lei Queen.

Molokai Ka Huia Piko (Molokai)
The birth of the hula is celebrated Molokai-style with music, dance, crafts and local taste treats.

Pineapple Festival (Lanai)
The "Pineapple Island" hosts a full-on event with music, dancing, tournaments, demonstrations, contests and arts and crafts.

Seabury Hall Crafts Fair (Maui)
The best prep school in town exhibits top artists at its annual fund-raising endeavor.

June

Hilo Orchid Society Show (Big Island)
Orchid-lovers descend upon Hilo's Civic Auditorium to catch whiffs and glances at hundreds of orchid varieties.

Japanese Festival (Oahu)
All kinds of Japanese cultural activities are held in Honolulu and Haleiwa, including dancing, candlelight ceremonies and a special Bon Odori tribute to the dearly departed.

King Kamehameha Day (statewide)
This is a state holiday in honor of King Kamehameha—Hawaii's first king who united all the islands. Festivities, parades, flowers and froufrou are all over the place.

King Kamehameha Hula Competition (Honolulu)
Hip-swingers and swayers come from near and far to compete in both traditional and contemporary hula contests.

Taste of Honolulu (Honolulu)
Eat your way around City Hall for this three-day pig-out that draws multitudes for tastings galore plus cooking demonstrations and entertainment.

Waiki'i Music Festival (Big Island)
Head for the Polo Field at Waikii Ranch (with about 10,000 other fans) for this two-day Hawaiian "Woodstock," where the state's top performers take to the stage.

July

Fourth of July (statewide)
Don't forget you're still in the United States. Celebrate Independence Day everywhere from rodeos on the Big Island to a parade of tall ships off the Oahu coast.

International Festival of the Pacific (Big Island)
Lots of Pacific and Asian food, music, floats, costumes, folk dancing and sports competitions.

Prince Lot Hula Festival (Honolulu)
And yet *more* hula merriment—both ancient and modern—performed *al fresco* at Moanalua Gardenas.

Volcano Wilderness Marathon (Big Island)
One thousand-plus runners do a rigorous wilderness circuit in Hawaii Volcanoes National Park. *Not recommended* for the out-of-shape.

August

Admission Day (statewide)
August 18th—the day the lucky United States officially claimed Hawaii as one of its own. Some jump for joy, others just sit and weep.

Establishment Day (Big Island)
A great family-type event that celebrates Hawaiian heritage. Learn ancient arts, crafts and traditional lore.

Hawaiian International Billfish Tournament (Big Island)
Head to the Kona shore to ogle the big fishers of Hawaii and the world compete in marlin-snagging tournaments.

September

Aloha Week (statewide)
It's an entire week of festivities to celebrate the "aloha spirit." You can't help but get caught up in the frenzy of parades, luaus, pageants and other entertainment.

Outrigger Hotels Hawaiian Oceanfest (Waikiki)
Ten days of ocean-oriented sports and to-do's including, a biathlon, lifeguard challenge and women-only windsurfing classic.

Seiko Super Tennis Tournament (Maui)
The leading pros compete at Wailea in this annual event.

Molokai-to-Oahu Canoe Race
A race using traditional canoes from remotest Molokai to Fort DeRussy in Honolulu. The women hit the Kaiwi Channel in September; the men race in October.

October

Ironman World Triathlon (Big Island)
Fabulous event seducing thousands of I'm-faster-than-you-are athletes to the cycling/swimming/running ménage à trois.

Kapalua International Championship of Golf (Maui)	A big-time, purse-heavy, international pro tournament.
Makahiki Festival (Oahu)	Waimea Falls Park is the site for this festival spotlighting traditional Hawaiian music, games, food and dance.

November

Hawaii International Film Festival (statewide)	Free showings throughout the islands of Pacific Rim films.
Hawaii Pro-Surfing Championships (Oahu)	Big waves and big money draw the big names in surfing to the North Shore's Banzai Pipeline.
Kona Coffee Festival (Big Island)	Move over, Starbuck's. Kona celebrates its coffee harvest with a week of tastings, bean-picking contests, parades, exhibits and tours.
Mission Houses Museum Christmas Fair (Honolulu)	A popular event with do-your-Christmas-shopping-here arts, crafts and specialty items.

December

Bodhi Day (statewide)	Hang around one of the Buddhist temples to join in the pomp commemorating Buddha's enlightenment.
Honolulu Marathon (Honolulu)	International runners, televised coverage...what more could you ask of a running event?
Christmas (everywhere)	White Christmas? You are dreaming!

Fielding's Guide to Wedding Bliss

We said "wedding," *not* "wedded." Hawaii is *so* hypnotically romantic you might pop the question to a complete stranger. No worries—have the wedding here, get the divorce back home. (OK, OK—we *know* it's the real thing, not just some fling in paradise.) Marriage and honeymoons are so popular here that the state even publishes a free information pamphlet. Hotels and resorts crowd each other in the quest to snatch your wedding and honeymoon biz. Wedding coordinators do everything except say "I do" for you. You can have anything your heart desires and your wallet can handle—a strange minister, helicopter spectacle, couples' massage, bathtub filled with champagne. Low budget? How about tying the knot in one of the national parks? Or on a secluded beach? For regulations and permits, contact the **State Health Department**, *1250 Punchbowl Street, Honolulu, HI 96813* (☎ *(808) 548-5862*).

Basic Rules

1. Both partners must be at least 18 years old (otherwise you have to ask Mom and Dad).

2. You must have a valid license from the State Department of Health, Marriage License Office (see address above).

3. There is no waiting period (i.e., no time to cool down and change your mind).

4. The license ($25, cash only) is valid for 30 days.

5. Bring identification when applying for the license (a driver's license will do).

6. Information about any previous marriages must be disclosed, as must names and birth places of each partner's parents.

7. The pre-marital rubella screening is a thing of the past (no cop-out there, either).

Most Popular Wedding Sites

Waimea Falls Park, Oahu

Fern Grotto, Kauai

Remotest Hana, Maui

Kilohana Plantation, Kauai

The Westin Maui, Kaanapali Beach

The Ritz-Carlton Mauna Lani, Big Island

Atop a horse in Kipahulu Valley, Maui

Fielding's Hawaii-Speak

Maybe Hawaii *is* part of the United States, but a lot of what you'll hear doesn't sound American. You'll pick up some real Hawaiian, and assorted bits of Chinese, Japanese, Portuguese, Korean and Samoan, as well as a very peculiar language known as "pidgin." Pidgin was actually born back in the plantation days when traders were trying to figure out a way to communicate with their laborers. Consequently, it's a blend of English, Hawaiian, Polynesian, Japanese, Filipino, Samoan and a few other languages to boot. It's a simple, very *non*-King's English dialect, somewhat akin to "jive" talk. The islanders simply adore their special pidgin and *don't* adore tourists who try to speak it—especially if they speak it poorly (and you thought the Parisians were sensitive!). Still, it's fun to try to decipher what you hear. And, it probably won't hurt to try out one or two well-chosen words. Check this guide's appendix for the English (*real* English) translation of common pidgin words and phrases.

Hawaii Traveler's Directory

Handy general information to lead you through a variety of day-to-day, where-is-it? how do I find it? *help me!* encounters. Also check the directories in individual island chapters for even more specifics.

Area Code

808 is the area code for all of the Hawaiian islands.

Business Hours

They vary. Hawaiians often begin their work day early (7–8 a.m.), wrapping things up by 3–4 p.m. so they can use the rest of the day to swim, fish or hang like the rest of the tourists. Postal hours are about the same as in the rest of the States, and banks are usually open until 6 p.m. on Friday with plenty of ATM machines to cater to you during the off-hours. Mall rats can get their fix on weekdays from about 9 a.m.–9 p.m., on weekends from about 10 a.m. until 4–5 p.m. Many shops and businesses in Waikiki and other high-profile tourist meccas stay open late all the time, ever ready to snag more visitor bucks.

Disabled Travelers

Disabled travelers might want to contact the **Commission on Persons with Disabilities** for accessibility and support services in the islands:

919 Ala Moana Boulevard, Room 101, Honolulu 96814, ☎ *(808) 586-8121*
54 High Street, Wailuku, Maui 96793, ☎ *(808) 243-5441*
1190 Waianenue Avenue, Box 1641, Hilo 96820, ☎ *(808) 933-4747*
3060 Eiwa Street, room 207, Lihue, Kauai 96766, ☎ *(808) 241-3308*

Electrical Current

It's the ordinary and usual American mode—110 volts AC, 60 cycles.

Emergency

Dial *911* (in a *true* life- or property-threatening emergency) to summon police, ambulance or firefighters.

Fishing and Hunting Regulations

Obtain permits and other skin-and-gills info from the **Hawaii Department of Land and Natural Resources, Division of Conservation and Resources Management**, *1151 Punchbowl Street, Honolulu 96813 (* ☎ *(808) 587-0077).*

Gay and Lesbian Travelers

Check in at the **Gay and Lesbian Community Center**, *1820 University Avenue, Suite 8, Honolulu 96822 (* ☎ *(808) 951-7000)* to find out about local events, as well as gay-friendly and gay-owned businesses.

Liquor Laws

Legal drinking age in the land of exotic cocktails is an ancient 21. Oahu and Maui bars mostly stay open until 2 a.m.; cabarets don't have to shut the doors until 4 a.m. Bars on the other islands are often locked-up-and-lights-off by 10 or 11 p.m. You can buy booze in supermarkets and liquor stores every day. Alcohol is off-limits in national and state parks.

Marijuana (aka *pakalolo*)

Yes, we know it's the state's biggest money-making crop. But—unlike pineapples and coffee beans—it's illegal to possess, use, grow or sell. Penalties are harsh—arrest, court, big-buck fines, property confiscation and *jail*. Never seen a narc wearing an aloha shirt and flip-flops? Just *wait*.

Money

Credit cards and traveler's checks are widely accepted, but some smaller establishments in more remote areas snub anything besides greenbacks. ATM machines are ubiquitous.

Park Information

For federal parks, contact the **National Park Service**, *300 Ala Moana boulevard, Suite 6305, Box 50165, Honolulu 96850 (☎ (808) 541-2693)*; for state parks, contact the **Hawaii Department of Land and Natural Resources, Division of State Parks**, *1151 Punchbowl Street, Room 310, Honolulu 96813 (☎ (808) 587-0300)*.

Publications

Honolulu's two dailies are the *Honolulu Advertiser* (morning) and the *Honolulu Star-Bulletin* (afternoon). *USA Today* and some mainland newspapers (usually a day or few behind) are also available. On Kauai, you can pick up either the *Kauai Times* or the *Garden Island;* on Maui, it's the *Maui News;* on the Big Island, look for either *West Hawaii Today* or the *Hawaii Tribune Herald*. Mags include *Honolulu, Spirit of Aloha, Hawaii, Hawaii Business, Waikiki Beach Press* and a dozen or so others. On every island, you'll find tourist rags galore.

Shipping Gifts and Souvenirs

Instead of hassling with packing those tricky coconuts and chocolate-covered macadamias, why not send them on home without you? Many tourist shops and hotels will provide this service for you—otherwise just pack 'em up yourself and throw some stamps on. You might even be able to get away with scrawling an address on an actual coconut and dropping it off at the post office. This has become such a cutesy idea, in fact, that vendors actually sell ready-to-address-and-mail coconuts purposely picked for ripe tourists. Most fruit won't be allowed out of the country via mail *or* packed luggage. One exception is the almighty pineapple. The easiest (though slightly more costly) method is to buy your pineapple at the airport—it will have been pre-inspected, pre-boxed and just waiting for you to take it home. Any edible souvenirs you mail should be wrapped discreetly—you never can tell who's going hungry at the post office these days.

Smoking

Forbidden in all public buildings, movie theaters and attractions. As for restaurants, smoking sections are becoming a rarity. Don't light up without asking first.

Taxes

Ouch! Sales tax is a measly 4 percent, but hotel occupancy tax is now *above* 9 percent.

Telephone

Pay phones require 25 cents for local calls (which include any place on an individual island), more for interisland talk. If you're calling from your hotel room, keep in mind that the surcharges can be astronomical. Ask the hotel operator *before* you dial—you might even be zapped for busy numbers or unanswered calls.

Time Zones

This can be a bit confusing as Hawaii does not conform to daylight-saving time—their daylight is always preciously saved. From the U.S. mainland, four time zones apply: Eastern Standard (five hours ahead of Hawaii), Central (four hours), Mountain (three hours), and Pacific (two hours). From April through October, take into account the daylight-saving factor.

Tipping

Tip 15–20 percent for restaurant servers, 15 percent for cabbies plus a buck per bag, $2–3 per bag for bellhops and a couple of dollars per day for the hotel maid (more if you're in a super-posh resort). Tour guides should get an extra 15 percent tacked on. And, if you ask the concierge for a special favor or a maitre d' for a special table, tip accordingly.

Travel Insurance

Some companies to contact for travel insurance coverage (including health, baggage loss and trip cancellation) are **Access America** *(☎ (800) 284-8300)*, **Travel Insured International** *(☎ (800) 243-3274)* and **Travel Guard International** *(☎ (800) 826-1300)*.

FIELDING'S ISLAND RADIO GUIDE (Not all islands receive all stations.)		
Station	**Frequency**	**Style**
KAIM	*AM 870, FM 95.5*	Contemporary music
KAOI	*FM 95*	Contemporary and other sounds
KCCN	*AM 1420*	Around-the-clock Hawaiian music
KDEO	*AM 940, FM 102*	Country music
KFMN	*FM 97*	Oldies and contemporary hits
KHLO	*AM 850*	Country tunes
KHPR	*FM 88.1*	News, classical and info
KIFO	*AM 1380*	Public radio, news programs
KIKI	*FM 94*	Contemporary hits and surf conditions
KIPA	*AM 620*	Contemporary sounds
KIPO	*FM 89.3*	Public radio, jazz and talk shows
KKON	*AM 790*	Contemporary sounds

TRAVELER'S GUIDE

FIELDING'S ISLAND RADIO GUIDE
(Not all islands receive all stations.)

Station	Frequency	Style
KKUA	FM 90.7	News and classical music
KOAS	FM 92.1	Contemporary sounds
KONG	AM 570, FM 93.5	Contemporary tunes
KPOA	FM 93.5	Mostly Hawaiian music, some jazz
KPOI	FM 98	Rock sounds
KPUA	AM 670	Contemporary sounds
KQMQ	AM 690, FM 93.1	Contemporary hits and surf conditions
KSSK	AM 590, FM 92	Easy listening, the Perry-and-Price show, weather and traffic updates
KUAI	AM 720	Surf reports and contemporary music

Fielding's Survival Tips

We know you've been lulled by the mesmerizing trade winds and hypnotic visions. You're wearing posies in your hair, running barefoot through the sand, you're already planning to sell the farm, become fluent in pidgin and live here forever. Forgive the intrusion, but it's time for the old reality check. Even the residents of paradise can be fallible (remember all those bite marks in the apples?). Heed some simple basics—then go back to dreaming.

- No matter how pretty those plants and flowers are, *don't* eat them—some of the loveliest are the most toxic.

- Don't discount the power of the ocean—no matter how calm and lovely it may seem. Regardless of how experienced a swimmer, surfer or diver you are, always ask lifeguards or locals about conditions. Be especially wary of riptides and undertows—and don't turn your back on the sea when rock-climbing or shell-collecting.

- Do we even have to tell you not to leave valuables in your car, whether it's locked or unlocked?

- Ditto for hotel rooms, no matter how fancy schmancy your digs are. Keep those valuables in the hotel safe. It's a lot less hassle than theft. Many hotels now have coin-operated in-room safes. Get some change and *use it!*

- We know you won't be out searching for marijuana but, lest you unwittingly stumble onto someone's garden, do not feign ignorance and help yourself to the interesting-looking weed. Don't touch a thing and leave *instantly!*

- Purses and cameras are on the theft hot list. Keep your eye (and hands) on both, especially in crowded tourist areas.

- Don't treat locals as second-class citizens (i.e., get rid of that *attitude*). Race problems do exist in the islands, and many of the natives are none too happy that *haoles* (white folk) have moved in and taken over. Hanging out in local bars while a lot of drinking is in progress might lead to a dicey situation.

- It's best to stay in well-lighted areas at night, and not to hike, jog or beach-walk alone in deserted or remote areas at any hour.

HISTORY AND CULTURE

The historic Sugarcane Train steams from Kaanapali to Lahaina.

Where Did Hawaii Come From?

Well, from Wakea and Papa, of course. At least *most* of the islands came from Papa, who was not a papa at all, but a mama—"earth mother," to be exact. According to legend, Papa hatched Hawaii, Maui and Kahoolawe, then went off to recuperate in Tahiti. Wakea ("sky father"), however, was not finished procreating and was still "in the mood." He took up with Kaula, who gave birth to Lanai, then with Hina, who bequeathed him with Molokai. Papa heard rumors of these other two hussies and returned *with a vengeance*. Taking up with Lua, she bore Oahu. So there, Wakea! Wakea—

contrite (and impressed!)—soon won Papa back and the reunited couple went on to round out their family with Kauai, Nihau, Kaula and Nihoa. Now you know.

When Did the Real People Get Here?

The Polynesians arrived somewhere between A.D. 500–900, but no one even seems to know that for sure—nor has it ever really been established where the mighty seafaring Polynesians came from in the first place. As far as can be determined, they originated in Southeast Asia, made their way through Indonesia, navigating their way around and about various island groups. They seem to have hung out in the Fiji islands for quite some time, mixing and melding their Asian/Caucasian/African traits into what became the distinctive Polynesian "look." Setting sail again, they continued on to Samoa, Tonga, Tahiti and the Marquesas and eventually—following the sun, moon, stars, currents, clouds, birds and fish—they landed at Ka Lae on the Big Island.

Quite possibly the Great Arrival looked something like a scene out of *Waterworld* (which, incidentally, was filmed in Hawaii). The Polynesians sailed in (having come some 2500 miles) on their fast, mega-huge outrigger canoes connected by large platforms. Everything *but* Kevin Costner was on board—entire families, household goods, plants, animals, religious forces, spiritual power and the all-encompassing aloha mystique.

Early Days with the "Caste Aways"

A peculiar dichotomy existed within early Hawaiian society. On one hand, the new Hawaiians were fierce, tattooed and rigid warriors who abided by a strict caste system. On the flipside of their breezy palm, however, they were nature-lovers, intrinsic environmentalists and artisans—a highly spiritual people who strung flowers in their hair and wound necklaces of shells around their necks *eons* before the hippies came.

The new settlers pretty much carried on with a simple Stone-Age-type existence. They erected grass huts, kept up their canoe-building skills and planted their claim-to-fame crops—coconuts, sugarcane, taro, breadfruit, bananas and such. Crops that would one day be boxed and hawked at the Honolulu International Airport, or stamped and sent through the U.S. mail.

The caste system worked like this: Each of the islands had its very own king; next step down were the *alii nui* (chiefs); next down were *kahunas* (high priests), courtiers, techies and artistes; and the *makaainana* (commoners) lagged below. Lowest of the low, however, were the slavelike *kauwa* (untouchables). All these life-levels were taken very seriously, and the whole scheme worked very much like feudalism. The king ruled the island, the chiefs ruled individual pie-shaped sections of each island, and the next rung down pretty much got to cruise as landowners, consultants and A-list party invitees. The commoners—like commoners everywhere in any era—did all the work. They farmed, fished and paid the piper (or, in this case, the chief) for protection by handing over a portion of their daily take. Not *so* different from the current method of taxation, is it? These days the ante just happens to be greenbacks instead of fresh fish or ripe coconuts.

Where Did God Fit Into Paradise?

The Polynesians' God (or *gods*) rode right in along with them on the humongous canoes. Religious beliefs were as perfectly laid out—and cut and dried—as was the caste system. And the two quite often worked together. The Polynesian belief system contained one supreme God and scads of underlings and stone temples *(heiaus)* were erected throughout the islands to worship these deities. And, since all of the gods seemed pleased by human sacrifice, those untouchable kauwas often became cornerstones down at the local temple.

Among the big names on the bow-and-scrape list were *Pele* (goddess of fire), *Ku* (god of war), *Lono* (god of harvest), *Kane* (father of living creatures) and *Kaneoloa* (god of departed spirits). *Mana*—or spiritual power—was embedded, in varying decrees, throughout all creation and *kapus* (a taboo system) applied to everyone and in every situation.

Kapus were strict and forceful. They were supposed to benefit everyone so, if someone screwed up, the consequences for both the individual and the group could be formidable. Some *kapus* included such no-no's as forbidden foods. For example, women weren't allowed to touch the sacred taro—that was left to the men. Women were forbidden to eat pork, bananas and coconuts, but hey—men weren't allowed to get *near* the dogmeat! Men, naturally, did all the construction and important fishing while the women hung out on shore with a line, made bark (or tapa) cloth, or else worked the gardens. One particularly nasty *kapu* was for a woman to intrude into the separate men's house and—horror of horrors—plop down and eat with them. And for the men—don't even think about having sex before going off to battle or to fish! *Kapu, kapu, kapu!* Break one itsy-bitsy, oh-just-this-one-time-*please* *kapu* and the punishment was severe—often death.

On the other hand, polygamy was not only allowed but practically cheered—and that went for both men *and* women! Incest was also pretty common—especially among upper-class brothers and sisters. Acceptance was less than warm, however, if a higher-up touched an untouchable. That "from the other side of the tracks" concept was on the books. Children born of such a *kapu* liaison were promptly killed (and, no doubt, offered to some god), whereas other "acceptable" offspring were raised by an extended family—polygamous or not.

"Hi, My Name's Captain Cook"

Life went on for about a thousand years. The Hawaiians cherished their environment and carefully planned their day-to-day lives so as not to endanger fish, fowl, posy or palm. The cannibals stopped eating one another. Comings and goings between Hawaii and Polynesia continued for some time, with each return trip introducing a new group of settlers. The arts flourished, children played, the Hawaiians chanted their legends and history through melodious tunes and their distinctive hula. The islands were left completely alone. And then, on January 20, 1778, along came intrepid explorer Captain James Cook.

Cook, who'd actually been trying to find the Northwest Passage across North America, ran smack into Kauai where he landed his two ships at Waimea. Since Cook was sailing under the patronage of the Earl of Sandwich, he decided to christen his newfound isles the "Sandwich Islands." He hung around for a couple of weeks, replenishing some of his supplies, trading brass medals for fish, and watching his crew swap venereal disease for fun times with the free-loving local women. Cook and his crew got on well with the natives. The locals were happy, welcoming, and genteel—they also teased the visiting *haoles* about the paleness of their skin. And the crew was, well, a hungry crew, up for a little teasing.

About a year passed before Cook and entourage returned to the "Sandwich Islands." That's when things turned ugly. Much of what transpired can simply be blamed on *really* bad timing. Cook's two ships eyeballed Maui, then continued on, finally anchoring off the Big Island near Kona. The date was January 16, 1779—day of the big rage (known as *makahiki*) to honor Lono, god of the harvest. The occasion was full of fun, frivolity, feasting, sex and the ongoing belief that Lono would appear on earth. *Voila!* Here comes Cook and his ships, bearing gifts yet! And, in the majestic sight of ships/masts/sails appeared pretty darn close to the natives' image of what Lono would look like if he showed up for the party. Best yet, Cook anchored in Kealakekua Harbor—the harbor that had been designated as Lono's! Oops!

At first everything was looking good. Natives descended upon the harbor and fell to their knees. Their beloved Lono had returned to earth! Cook was hastened away to his very own awaiting temple. He was honored, esteemed, ego-boosted and reprovisioned. The Hawaiians were fascinated by iron nails and other bits of metal and readily traded meat, fruit and their women for the nails and other tools. Cook and crew hung out for more than a month, quite enjoying themselves and the nothing-is-too-much-to-ask-of-us-holy-Lono (especially nonstop sex with our luscious brown-skinned women) natives.

The Polynesians became suspicious, however, when one of the crew members dropped dead. Huh? Gods don't *die*, not even those on the lower end of the heavenly ladder. These dudes were mortals like everyone else. The natives began to turn very irreverent and the Cook clan decided it was time to make a hasty departure. Unfortunately for them, stormy seas and a busted mast forced the sailors right back from where they came just one week later. Time had *not* healed all wounds—nor *any* wounds. The natives were *not* happy to see the phony-baloney "gods" back at their shore-steps. They threw rocks. The Cook-ies loaded arms. The natives snatched a boat (for its iron nails, of course). The Cook-ies attacked an *alii* on board. The Hawaiians waged fury. Cook and his boys wielded weapons. More theft (this time a small cutter), more ugliness, more fury—on both sides. The normally easygoing, egalitarian Cook suddenly became *very* angry! He gathered a group of his marines (armed, of course), went to shore and decided to take King Kalaniopuu hostage for the stolen cutter. Meanwhile the marines got a little too trigger happy and killed a chief. *Wrong!* The crowd swelled bigger and faster than a North Shore wave. Clubs were wielded, bullets spent and, alas, by the time the melee was over, the intrepid and seemingly invincible Captain James Cook was a hunk of dead meat. Actually make that a bunch of hunks. Trying to get the captain's remains back presented yet another series of mishaps. The Hawaiians—as was custom—had roasted Cook and took a nicely blackened chunk of him to his mates back on ship. Well, *that* didn't go over too well with the fish'n' chips Brits! Tensions mounted, yet again. For about a week the cannons fired, and bullets sprayed, and in the end about 30 natives had been killed. What remained of Cook was returned and buried at sea. The English sailed off, leaving behind venereal disease, measles and other marvelous souvenirs of Western civilization.

Kamehameha the Great— Queen Elizabeth Would Be Proud to Have *Him* for a Son

Hawaii's greatest claim to kin, Kamehameha I, was alive and kicking during the Cook era. It was his uncle, in fact, whom the captain had been trying to kidnap when he met his dismal demise. Born around Kohala in the Big Island, sometime in the 1750s, the six-foot, six-inch Kamehameha had actually met Cook, who'd been impressed by his intelligence, royal bearing and *very* formidable presence (though some diary entries say he was sort of ugly). Kamehameha had also been impressed with Cook or—more specifically— Cook's weaponry. Oh, yes—Kamehameha could certainly envision those cannons and muskets in his own powerful future!

King Kamehameha Statue is one of the sights on Honolulu's South King Street.

Anyway, the man was *born* to be a warrior. Besides the fact he was huge, fierce and into heavy artillery, Kamehameha had a thorough military training. His uncle Kalaniopuu—a great king of Hawaii and Hana and one tough warrior himself—had been the one to instruct his nephew in the art of military training. Just before Kalaniopuu died, he bequeathed Kamehameha as keeper of the family war god, Ku. Kamehameha took this duty seriously and, in fact, he had been a longtime worshipper of Ku, anyway.

Kamehameha easily took power—not just within the Big Island, but eventually over all the islands. First, though, Kamehameha had to see through a nine-year melee between his two cousins, which involved the islands of Maui, Oahu, Kauai and—potentially—the Big Island. Just when that affair had been settled (and one of the cousins killed), in came the Americans and a gruesome battle known as the Olowalu Massacre.

In 1790, Captain Simon Metcalfe cruised into Olowalu (somewhat east of Lahaina) on the merchant ship *Ella Dora*, followed by his son, Thomas, commandeering the *Fair American*. Their arrival—albeit pretty bloody at the onset—proved to be quite fortuitous for the shrewd Kamehameha.

Metcalfe the elder was an uptight jerk. Another of the natives' relatively harmless boat-stealing pranks turned into a major incident when one of the crew members was killed along the way. On the pretext of negotiating a truce, Metcalfe beckoned the Hawaiians near until their canoes were within firing range. Bang! The Olowalu Massacre. More than 100 natives were slaughtered. Metcalfe and mates sailed off, leaving not a whole lot of good will behind. He then cruised into Kealakekua Bay and angered one of the ruling chiefs, who swore he would reap revenge on the next white boy he laid his eyes on. Then along came young Thomas and his little *Fair American*.

Metcalf the younger—although he was a nicer fellow—didn't stand a chance. The ship became a heated battleground, and eventually it and Issac Davis, one of the more heroic crew members, were turned over to Kamehameha. Metcalf the elder, hearing of the plight, sent a bloke named John Young to save the day (as well as Thomas and the ship), but Kamehameha decided he liked this guy. He decided to keep Davis and Young (both smart and brave fellows) and turned them into chiefs. As for the *Fair American*, it was loaded with cannons and weaponry. *It* wasn't going anywhere. The unification of Hawaii was imminent.

By 1796, Kamehameha had control over the Big Island, Maui, Oahu, Lanai and Molokai. Kauai and Niihau—the two holdouts—were under his rule by 1810. He died nine years later.

HISTORY AND CULTURE

Oh No! Here Come the Missionaries— Fun's Over

Life had been relatively peaceful and prosperous for the Hawaiians as long as Kamehameha was alive. Then blatant as a fang mark in the proverbial apple, paradise—the *real* paradise sans outside interference—began its fall.

Before he died, Kamehameha designated his son, Liholiho, to be his successor, and his large wife, Kaahumanu (*not* Liholiho's birth mother), as queen regent or *kuhina nui*. Liholiho—aka Kamehameha II—at first was hardly on a par with his formidable father. Luckily he had the counsel of both Kaahumanu and Keopuolani (his natural mother). Perhaps the women's major input was inspiring the young king to abolish that rigid *kapu* system.

The Hawaiians were starting to get wind that the *kapus* were nothing but a bunch of meaningless rules. They'd been watching the incoming *haoles*—whalers, traders, ne'er-do-wells who came from Great Britain, Spain, Portugal, France, Italy and the Untied States. They drank, smoked, fought, caroused and often behaved very badly—yet nothing adverse seemed to happen to them! The gods ignored *their* misdeeds, so why exactly were the natives supposed to dance through hoops?

Kaahumanu advised Liholiho that it was time to do away with the old system if they were to keep Hawaii a peaceful and prosperous place. Liholiho was at first reluctant but even he felt like sowing a few wild oats and finally relented. Kaahumanu ate a banana. Liholiho chomped on dogmeat. The two renegades ate together at an A-list party attended by foreign dignitaries and high-level chiefs. No one died. No gods raged. Good-bye, *kapu!* Good-bye a whole lot of spiritual beliefs. Hello, missionaries.

Yes, it was perfect timing for the arrival of the missionaries—from Boston, no less! Led by the Rev. Hiram Bingham, they dropped anchor at Kona in 1820 and got right down to work. But if the Hawaiians had thought the *kapus* were tough, the uptight rules that the Protestants imposed were—in many ways—much worse. Had the natives not been floundering spiritually, the missionaries wouldn't have had a chance. Alas, the deeply religious Hawaiians were at that moment in need of some faith in *anyone's* god. After all, their own idols had just been teased and toppled.

Bingham and entourage were appalled by the natives' lifestyle—polygamy, incest, rampant sex, topless women, booze and tobacco all *had to go*. And they were not crazy about kite-flying, boxing, wrestling, leis or the hip-undulating hula, either. Introduction of the neck-to-ankle muumuus were at the top of the list of heathen reforms. Cover all that flesh—*immediately!*

So the conversions began, the churches were built and "proper" schools commenced. Hawaii was joining Western Civilization. Hurray! Kaahumanu and Keopuolani both converted, spurring the others to follow in suit. *Hurray, hurray!* Christian teachings and biblical references were bandied about, including those that let the Hawaiians know in no uncertain terms that they would never be white, but, being white, the missionaries decreed, was far superior to being Hawaiian. Oh great! "Bring back the *kapus!*" the Hawaiians were undoubtedly intoning under their newly Protestantized breath.

When Kamehameha II died in 1827, the throne was warmed by his nine-year-old brother, who became known as Kamehameha III. Thankfully, he also had the counsel of Kaahumanu—for a while anyway. There was a huge to-do about his love affair with Princess Nahienaena, who happened to be his younger sister. This arrangement was fine and dandy with the Hawaiians who remembered (and condoned) the old ways, but you can well imagine what the missionaries had to say about such a union! And, the missionaries were gaining in influence—not just religious, but political as well. The Kamehameha III/Princess Nahienaena tale was a sordid, sad and ill-thwarted one. They both were Christians, they both were teenage drunks, they slept with each other, they slept with *many others!* Eventually the princess gave birth to a baby boy. The baby (speculated to be Kamehameha III's son) lived only a few hours; the princess lived only a couple of months. The king, however, had the joy of living almost two more decades so he could pay regular visits to his sister-lover's mausoleum.

Kamehameha III had plenty of other concerns both during and after Nahienaena's demise. At Lahaina—site of the first mission (under the helm of the Rev. William Richards)—there was an ongoing battle between the prissy missionaries and the sexually insatiable and frequently drunk sailors and whalers. Pressure was being exerted by the Europeans, who wanted to claim Hawaii for their own individual countries—France and Great Britain, in particular. Why should this King Whatever-His-Name-Is have any authority over *them?* In short, the legitimacy of the monarchy was in question and it was looking as though the kingdom's autonomy was on rather shaky ground.

Eventually, with the counsel of his missionary mate, the Rev. Richards, Kamehameha III—in 1840—gave up his autocratic power and passed the Declaration of Rights and the Edict of Toleration. A short time later, Hawaii's first constitution was in place and, in 1842, the islands were officially deemed an independent nation by the independent nation—the United States of America.

Foreign Recognition Brought Recognizable Foreigners

The 1840s were memorable years for a variety of reasons. Kamehameha III decided to up and move the capital from Lahaina—soon to be recognized as the world's whaling capital—over to Honolulu, which had become a thriving commercial center.

In the late 1840s, the king activated sweeping land-ownership reforms—a startling tactic for these islands where all parcels had previously belonged to designated chiefs. The new scheme apportioned some land to the king, some to the chiefs and big chunks of property to commoners who worked their parcels. This more egalitarian system seemed wonderfully fair—maybe a little *too* fair, for the king eventually allowed foreigners to purchase cheap land. And we all know what *that* means—especially for a people who didn't really believe in the concept of property ownership in the first place. It was the beginning of the end for Hawaiian control of its "own" land.

To make matters worse, there weren't that many indigenous people left anyway—property owners or not. A majority of the Hawaiian population was dying out with frightening speed, thanks to the introduction of such Western-world delights as venereal disease, smallpox, cholera, measles and even colds and flu. The Hawaiians had absolutely no immunity to such strange illnesses. The population dwindled from a Cook-era estimate of 300,000 down to a shockingly low 60,000 by around 1850.

How Sweet It Is (Or Was)

Taking advantage of the foreign-ownership deal, whaler George Wilfong sweetened the islands even further by turning them into one of the world's leading producers of sugar. Wilfong set up a crude operation on his acreage in Hana (Maui) and—though this was certainly a boon to the economy—the Hawaiians who did the dirty work really became nothing more than disgruntled slaves. Time to find some new suckers who were more enthusiastic about raising cane. The solution? Import some cheap labor, of course!

Everything began to change in the once-isolated-from-all-mankind islands—the racial make-up, the economic structure, the exquisite simple-as-a-freshly-plucked-blossom life. The Chinese came in to work the plantations, served as domestic help to the rich whites, and eventually became small merchants in their own right. More planters came in, followed by Japanese laborers who, in turn, were shadowed by a mélange of international workers (with the white-skinned pulling rank for the better jobs). Catholic and Mormon zealots arrived to establish missions and convert all past and potential heathens. There were new foods, customs, religions, plants, animals and languages. Thus came about pidgin, the "island-speak" that enabled almost everyone to communicate. That, and intermarriage (particularly between Hawaiians and Asians) was on the rise.

The Beginning of the End of the Kamehamehas (And the Kingdom)

Kamehameha III died in 1854, no doubt believing he'd done a fairly decent job. He'd struck a deal with the United States, Great Britain and France that gave him reason to believe his nation's independence would be protected. His nephew, Alexander Liholiho, took over the throne as Kamehameha IV but only ruled until 1863. His reign was marked by two personal tragedies—the deaths of both his only son (and heir) and a good American friend. Kamehameha IV reportedly held the kid under cold water and shot the friend over jealousy.

Liholiho's older brother, Lot, became Kamehameha V and ruled until 1872. Not being particularly thrilled over all the *haeole* influence in Hawaii and the increasing prejudice against *real* Hawaiian citizens, Kamehameha V tried to restore some of the old ways, including absolute authority of the monarchy. Also weary of the whole foreign-controlled sugar power, the king decided to take a stab at tourism by building the Hawaiian Hotel. Still, sugar was the trump card and continued to be the islands' most powerful and sought after commodity—and particularly sought after by the Americans.

When Kamehameha V died heirless in 1872, the Kamehameha line also died. The next king, William Lunalilo (known as Prince Bill), was—for the first time in Hawaiian history—elected by popular vote. Prince Bill, who was known as quite a hard-drinking, skirt-chasing gadabout, died after only a year in office. His successor, David Kalakaua (known as "The Merrie Monarch"), also elected by the people, liked the United States (and its money). He lobbied enthusiastically for the Reciprocity Act of 1875, a long-awaited congressional bill that swapped a bunch of Hawaiian goodies (such as the right to use Pearl Harbor for a naval base) for import duty exemption on the much-coveted sugar crop. When The Merrie Monarch died in 1891, the reign was held by his sister, Lydia Liliuokalani, who would be Hawaii's final monarch. Unlike her brother, the queen preferred the Brits over the Americans and attempted to undo many of the concessions that had come about during his rule. In the process, the sugar industry began to slump. Do I even need to tell you how this went over with the powerful, sweet-toothy Americans and sugar barons? There ensued a bloodless and *fast* revolution. The queen was deposed, the monarchy was dead, and the U.S. Marines were in.

Dole Becomes President!

Make that Sanford B. Dole, and make that president of the provisional government of the Hawaiian Republic.

None of these goings-on impressed the Hawaiians. The *haoles* were racist, and had set up the natives' beloved queen (whom they continued to think of as their queen until she died in 1917). Hawaiians were being treated as second-class citizens in their own country, and the U.S. government—which had always *said* it would support Hawaii's independence—was selling her down the tubes.

The vote for annexation was absurd. Most Hawaiians (who would have voted against the measure) were prevented from voting at all for a number of ridiculous reasons (too naive, didn't meet income and property qualifications, etc.). Another factor was that the Philippine-based Spanish-American War had just broken out. And yet *another* factor was the growing nastiness between Japan and China. The United States *needed* its military boots in the Pacific, and where better than gorgeous and conveniently located-in-the-Pacific Hawaii? And the Hawaii-based American interests needed the U.S. military to protect them. Annexation passed easily and was signed into law in 1898 by President William McKinley.

Welcome to the Twentieth Century

Unfortunately we all kind of *know* what happened next, don't we?

No sooner had the flags changed, an event that was heralded by the *haoles* and mourned by many Hawaiians, the once-untouched island nation became more westernized than ever. Immigrants—who had already been brought in to do plantation duty—continued flocking in from all over the world, relegating the *real* Hawaiians to the status of strangers (and low-class strangers, at that) in their own land. The multiethnic jumble included Chinese, Japanese, Koreans, Russians, Spanish, Filipinos and African-Americans. The barely visible (or recognizable) Hawaiians became even less visible as they retreated to the most remote areas. A minority of rich whites pretty much ruled everything, while Asian immigrants performed the majority of labor. The Big Five companies (Alexander and Baldwin, C. Brewer and Company, Castle and Cooke, AmFac and Theo. H. Davies) maintained a huge stronghold in the islands, where they are still powerful today. The educational system (for all children) thrived, tourism was beginning to grow and the U.S. military had become an important force—especially to the Japanese.

From Pearl Harbor to Statehood— An Easy Leap on the Printed Page

The Japanese attacked Pearl Harbor and other parts of Oahu on December 7, 1941, thereby signaling the onset of U.S. involvement in World War II. Total casualties of the attack were 3,478—mostly servicemen, some civilians. Along with the flesh and blood, destruction and major damage on the U.S. side tallied 18 warships and 188 planes.

A period of martial law was instigated, but Hawaii's Japanese-Americans fared much better than did their compatriots over in California, who were being hauled off to concentration camps. Aside from the fact there were just too many Japanese Americans to lock away, they had no trouble proving their loyalty by forming the highly decorated *nisei* (American-born children of Japanese immigrants) contingent of the 442nd Regimental Combat Team. After the war, these patriots were welcomed as heroes who did much to champion the push for statehood.

It took awhile, and more than a few failed attempts, but finally—on August 21, 1959—President Dwight D. Eisenhower placed his John Hancock on the bill, officially decreeing Hawaii the 50th state.

What Happened After Statehood?

All the fun stuff, of course. The new Americans won the right to pay federal income taxes, among other things. The developers zoomed in. And the tourists zoomed in even faster—on Boeing 707 jets that streaked from California to Honolulu in just five hours. The first Hawaiian Open International Golf Tournament was held. James Michener published *Hawaii*.

After the we're-finally-a-legitimate-state celebrations had subsided, the developers lost no time in breaking ground with hotels, condos, shopping centers and freeways—particularly on Oahu which became *the* tourist mecca (almost 250,000 tourists had shown up by the end of 1959!).

There was a resurgence of proud-to-be-Hawaiian culture in the 1970s, an era that pretty much saw a resurgence of *many* things. Those upstart'70s were also the time when marijuana became Hawaii's most profitable crop—a claim to fame the plant still holds. Pineapple and sugarcane—though still major economic forces—just can't seem to muster the bucks that marijuana growers continue to enjoy. It's still illegal, of course—both to grow *or* use—but that obviously hasn't deterred either growers or users one bit.

Today's Hawaii offers a high standard of living, an even higher cost of living and continues to be the ideal image of paradise for a broad range of visitors (an estimated 6 million per year)—whether the search is for the perfect wave, the perfect honeymoon or the perfect retirement condo.

Fielding's Hawaiian History Time Line, or Exactly What Happened When

First things first	Sky-father Wakea and Earth-mother Papa find each other in the Big Darkness and conceive the Hawaiian islands.
A.D. 500–900	The Polynesians arrive from the South Pacific on their humongous canoes and begin their settlement of the Hawaiian islands.
1750s	King Kamehameha—future unifier of the Hawaiian islands—is born.

1778	Captain James Cook makes his first arrival, landing at Kauai and christening Hawaii the "Sandwich Islands" after the Earl of Sandwich.
1779	Captain Cook returns, gets into a dicey melee with the natives, and meets his end (and his end becomes barbecued meat).
1784	The Hawaiian islands are split into three separate kingdoms, each presided over by a different ruler, none of whom seem to be able to get along with each other (even though they're kin).
1788	Kamehameha I is named heir to uncle King Kalaniopuu's throne.
1790	The arrival of disagreeable Captain Simon Metcalfe sparks the Olowalu Massacre—Kamehameha I snatches Metcalfe's son's ship and grows fond of its powerful weaponry.
1810	After much bloodshed, Kamehameha I finally achieves domain over all the islands—the first time any Hawaiian king has done so.
1819	Kamehameha I dies, putting his oldest son in charge. Kamehameha II eats dogmeat with a woman chomping a banana, signaling the end of the ancient *kapu* system; the first whalers anchor at Lahaina.
1820	Protestant missionaries, led by the Rev. Hiram Bingham, arrive to set up missions and schools and to make sure the Hawaiians don't have any more fun.
1824	Kamehameha II dies, leaving the hot seat to his nine-year-old brother.
1840	Kamehameha III passes the Declaration of Rights and forms a constitutional monarchy.
1842	Hawaii is deemed an independent nation recognized by powers such as the United States, Great Britain and France.
1845	Hawaii switches its capital city from Lahaina, Maui to Honolulu, Oahu.
1846	Lahaina is known as the world's whaling capital.
Late 1840s	Kamehameha III instigates sweeping changes in land ownership and property rights.
1849	George Wilfong establishes the first sugar refinery in Hana, Maui.
1850	The Hawaiian population has dropped from about 300,000 to around 60,000, thanks to the introduction of Western germs and ailments; foreign workers are imported for plantation duty.
1854	Kamehameha III dies, handing the reigns to his nephew.

1863	Kamehameha IV dies, upping the Roman numeral for his older brother. Kamehameha V is the end of the Kamehameha line.
1872	Prince Bill takes over as the first elected monarch.
1873	Prince Bill dies and David Kalakaua, the "Merrie Monarch," is elected; the pro-American king pushes for stronger ties with the United States.
1875	The Reciprocity Act is signed, giving the United States rights to Pearl Harbor in exchange for exempting Hawaiian sugar from import duty.
1891	The Merrie Monarch dies and is replaced by his sister—and Hawaii's last monarch—Queen Liliuokalani.
1893	The queen (who is *not* pro-American) is deposed by those who are; a provisional government is established, headed by Sanford B. Dole, who is in favor of annexation.
1894	By popular vote (and one which excluded the majority of natives), Hawaii becomes a republic with Sanford Dole as its president. 1898: The Spanish-American War makes the US. think twice about Hawaii and its strategic position in the South Pacific; President William McKinley signs the official annexation papers.
1901	Sanford Dole is appointed the Hawaiian territory's first governor; the Sheraton Moana Surfrider (then just the Moana) is constructed on Waikiki Beach.
1903	Sanford's cousin, James Dole, gets the pineapple business going on the island of Lanai.
1919	The U.S. Navy formally inaugurates Pearl Harbor.
1936	Pan American World Airways begins commercial passenger flights from the United States, getting that tourist blood moving.
1941	The Japanese attack Pearl Harbor, marking the United States' entry into World War II.
1959	Hawaii becomes the 50th state in the union.
1997	On what island will you be making your *own* history???

HISTORY AND CULTURE

Government and Economy

A worker inspects coffee beans before packing.

Who's Running the Show?

As a bona-fide state, Hawaii has the pleasure of being ruled by the White House and the rest of the Capitol Hill gang. However, as the new kid on the block, Hawaii had the advantage of being able to learn from its governed-to-death siblings. State and county governments—along with some designated "special departments"—are the only in-your-face bureaucracies to be dealt with. Unlike the mainlanders, Hawaiians have decided city and town governments are complicated and unnecessary.

Hawaiians enjoy the political scene and take their voting privileges seriously, quite often coming in first in the national voting tally. Pre-World War II and statehood politics had a decidedly Republican bent, but then it was mainly the sugar barons and other corporate types who controlled things. Itinerant workers and others who would most certainly have given a nod in the Democratic direction were systematically ousted from the voting process via a long list of mark-the-ballot "qualifications."

In the 1930s, with the influx of unionization, Hawaii began steering its way to the Democratic side of the fence. After World War II, the returning Japanese servicemen exerted considerable clout and they—along with most of the rest of Hawaii's Asian population—turned into loyal Democrats. And, although the first post-statehood governor and lieutenant governor were Republicans (the first congressional seat went to Democrat—and Japanese-

American—Daniel Inouye), that was an isolated instance. Democrats have warmed the governor's chair ever since.

The state Legislature is made up of the House of Representatives (51 elected seats and two-year terms) and the Senate (25 elected seats and four-year terms). All 76 members hail from different electorates, all of which are based on population, leaving Oahu with the most representation. The Legislature meets annually for approximately 90 days, hashing out state laws, taxes and other issues. The governor and lieutenant governor (both four-year term holders) compose the executive branch. The governor has the power to appoint the five justices of the state Supreme Court, the appeals court and four circuit courts (all 10-year terms). The rest of the judiciary branch is composed of 27 district courts presided over by judges who are appointed by the chief justice of the Supreme Court and who serve six-year stints. In addition, Hawaii has a number of "special departments" (such as the Department of Education and Hawaiian Home Lands Department), the heads of which are appointed by the governor.

The people-elected Office of Hawaiian Affairs (OHA), created in 1979, seeks to protect and fight for the rights of native Hawaiians. Some of the issues OHA has become involved in include resolving native land-rights disputes, rescuing the island of Kahoolawe, and trying (in vain) to get the United States to admit its part in the coup against Queen Liliuokalani. Watch for this group's increasing visibility (and viability) in the Hawaiian political arena.

Where Is All the Money Coming From?

Simple answer: tourism, the U.S. military and agriculture.

How Many Tourists, and Who Are They?

More than 6 million visitors swamp into Hawaii every year. The tourist boom that began in the 1960s has just continued to boom. And boom. And boom.

Along with the tourists came all the things that tourists need when they escape to paradise—hotels, mega-resorts, golf courses, parking lots, shopping malls, rental cars, freeways and condos. And, of course, McDonald's—*many* of them, here, in McHeaven.

The majority of visitors are from the U.S. mainland, followed by visitors from Japan, Canada, Australia and Great Britain. Oahu (with super-crowded Waikiki Beach) remains the most popular island. Next are Maui, Kauai and the Big Island, with Molokai and Lanai lagging *way* behind. Many visitors come on package tours or honeymoon specials. Most tourists are pretty well-heeled financially and stay about 14 days. The Japanese stay the shortest time and spend the most money.

Economic factors aside, the locals are hardly crazy about all these "intruders," especially when their friendly communities suddenly turn into condo developments and shopping malls. Worse, the locals often end up working in the service industry, catering to what are often rich and demanding outsiders with little sensitivity for their land, culture and history. So what else is new?

Where Does the U.S. Military Fit In?

Plenty of places, and not just Pearl Harbor (where the U.S. Navy installed itself in 1887 upon the signing of the Reciprocity Act). More troops moved in for the coup to overthrow the monarchy in 1894, followed by more during the Spanish-American War years, followed by a never-ending slew (consisting of all five branches) since that little World War II mishap.

Oahu is base of operations for CINCPAC (Commander in Chief Pacific), the control center for more than half the Earth. Military personnel number about 60,000 and another 20,000 or so civilians are also employed by the big machine, which pumps billions of dollars into the local economy.

Despite those bucks, most locals are even less happy with the military presence than they are with the tourists. Many natives—still *very* unhappy over the overthrow of their feisty Queen Liliuokalani—feel as though the military has snatched away their traditional lands. Another hot issue is one raised by anti-nuclear groups, who are not thrilled with the irrefutable fact that Hawaii is a dead-on target for nuclear warheads.

Sugarcane, Pineapples and Other Edibles

Sugarcane—Hawaii's best-selling crop (aside from marijuana)—has been on the islands since the beginning of Polynesian settlement. The Polynesians, however, didn't get into its refinement, preferring instead to use the stalk and its juice. A couple of commercial plantations sprung up in the 1820s and 1830s on Oahu and Kauai. But it was whaler George Wilfong, who set up his crude refinery on Hana (Maui) in 1849, who really got the ball rolling. For refined sugar was what America (with a big gold-rush and war-era sweet tooth) *craved*. The refining process was upgraded a year later with the introduction of the centrifuge.

The really sweet action started up, however, in 1876 with the signing of the Reciprocity Treaty, which exempted Hawaiian sugar from U.S. import duty—an important move since the U.S. was (and still is) Hawaii's biggest customer. The sugar barons moved in and Claus Spreckels (who'd already hit it big with sugar in California) soon became *the* Sugar King, setting up large, modern refineries on Maui.

Pineapples were brought to Hawaii not by the Polynesians but, in the 1820s, by a visiting Spaniard. An "improved" version, arriving in the 1880s by way of Jamaica, is the juicy Hawaiian pineapple we know and love today.

Pineapples were brought to Hawaii in the 1820s.

James Dole (Mr. Pineapple) started up his Hawaiian Pineapple Company on his 60-acre farm on Oahu, later branched out into canning and shipping and, by 1922, had bought the whole island of Lanai for his mega-plantation, only to lose control in the 1930s to Hawaii's "Big Five" corporate stronghold. And, though the pineapple industry is still alive and thriving, there have been setbacks in the past decade with the closing of the Lanai plantation as well as plantations owned by Del Monte on Molokai, along with some prickly foreign competition.

Hawaii's superb soil and climate make it an ideal growing spot for everything from nuts to beef cattle (Parker Ranch, on the Big Island, is the largest independently owned cattle ranch in the United States). Heading the list of "lesser" crops are macadamia nuts, Kona coffee, exotic fruits, exquisite flowers and freshwater prawns. Oddly enough, fish are not given very high rank due to a rather skimpy fishing fleet. And, even odder, despite the bountiful cornucopia of delicious crops, Hawaii still must import vast amounts of food to feed its faster-than-they-can-grow-for-it visitor population.

Fielding's "The Big Five" Demystified

In order of appearance:

1. C. Brewer and Company (founded 1826)—chemicals, ranching, sugar

2. Theo. H. Davies and Company (1845)—investments, insurance, sugar, transportation

3. Amfac Inc. (1849)—sugar, land development, insurance

4. Castle and Cooke Inc. (1851)—pineapple, food packing, land development

5. Alexander and Baldwin (1895)—sugar, pineapple, shipping

The Big Five were—until statehood—*the* ruling power mongers who controlled the entire Hawaiian show. These five corporations consisted of old (white) Hawaiian family groups who also had links to the native nobility. They guarded their families and businesses zealously (often a tad *overzealously*) by keeping their hands and faces in every aspect of island life—from shipping, banking and commerce to utilities, merchandising and hotels. Anyone who crossed them would suddenly find that their lives and businesses were no longer running smoothly.

After the 1960s tourist boom, the Big Five lost some of their clout, but still are Hawaii's richest and most powerful landowners.

Fielding's Thrill-and-Amaze-Your-Friends Hawaiian Geographical Stats

- 6450 square miles of land
- 132 islands, islets, shoals and reefs
- The archipelago spans more than 1500 miles
- 2400 miles from the nearest continent
- More than 1000 miles of tidal shoreline
- The first islands emerged from the Pacific about 70 million years ago
- The Pacific Plate moves northwest about two-to-four inches per year
- Kauai is one of the world's wettest places
- Hawaii is the southernmost point of the United States
- The only active volcanoes are the Big Island's Mauna Loa and Kilauea
- The "Hot Spot" is not in Waikiki, but rests (for now) beneath the Big Island

THE PEOPLE OF HAWAII

Visitors receive a flowery welcome to Waimea Falls Park.

The Melting Pot

The term "melting pot" has long been used (and used and used) to describe the people of Hawaii and their society. Virtually every major race and more than 50 ethnic groups spice up the pot—along with their various traditions, customs, cuisines, languages and fashion statements. You'll find a rich mix that includes Hawaiians, Japanese, Filipinos, Koreans, Chinese, Portuguese, Irish and plain old Caucasians *(haoles)*—all immigrants who came

59

to the islands seeking work, riches or just a personal paradise. Even more interesting than the individual ethnic groups, however, are the amazing *mixtures*. Interracial marriage has been a long-established practice in the islands, with racial integration following hand-in-hand. Trying to sort out who is what and from where can be more challenging than *The New York Times* Sunday crossword.

This is not to say that all the ethnic groups live together in complete harmony. Depending on the island (and the location on the island) and the various groups, there are boundaries—not only along racial lines, but also among varying socio-economic levels. Public schools, however, have been integrated since the missionary days. This has led to a far more peaceful coexistence and cultural understanding than can be found at most mainland schools.

Hawaii's population numbers around 1.1 million with the largest segment consisting of Hawaii-born residents, followed by those born on the U.S. mainland, and next by foreign-born nationals. Permanently stationed military personnel and their dependents account for more than 100,000 in the population tally. Hawaii is the only state where Caucasians are not the majority race.

The Hawaiians

Sad but true—full-blooded Hawaiians (descendants of the original Polynesian settlers) are practically extinct in their own homeland. When Captain Cook arrived back in 1778 he tallied a population of around 300,000. By the time his men were through "enjoying" the uninhibited native women, they'd left a long trail of venereal disease that wiped out about half the Hawaiians in less than 50 years. Then came the whalers and other immigrants, coughing and sneezing, further infecting the natives whose immune systems just couldn't keep up with the germs. By 1850, the indigenous population had dwindled to about 60,000. Of those, some died out during wars, others went elsewhere, and the rest—well, with all that intermarriage—became blended with various other races.

The current estimate of pure-blooded Hawaiians is down around the 1000 mark, though about 135,000 residents claim to have at least some Hawaiian blood running through their veins. Niihau—a private island owned by the Robinson family—is home to some 250 pure-blooded natives, and almost one-half the population of Molokai can trace Hawaiian lineage. Oahu claims the largest number of pure- or mixed-blood Hawaiians—somewhere in the neighborhood of 90,000.

The ancestral blood may be running thin but, happily, the *aloha* spirit shows big promise of immortality, partly because of a number of Hawaiians' born-again cultural pride. Their precious love of the land and welcoming warmth are contagious to visitors—an appallingly unfair trade for the diseases the natives were given in exchange!

The Chinese

The Chinese began their big migration to Hawaii in 1852, beckoned to toil in the sugar plantations by the Masters and Servants Act. Like most itinerant laborers, they were exploited and exhausted. However they were *not* stupid. When their contracts were up (usually three to five years) they split the scene. Many moved on to become retail merchants and restaurant owners—and often were resented because of it. Their popularity certainly didn't take any leaps when both leprosy and smallpox epidemics were blamed on them (there was some legitimacy to the smallpox indictment). On the other hand, they imported rice, the water buffalo and interesting religions such as Buddhism and Taoism (which surely irritated the Protestant missionaries).

The Chinese were an enterprising group, no doubt about it. Although they numbered about half the plantation work force in the late 1800s, they were spinning many entrepreneurial dreams while sweating in those fields. By 1900, the Chinese laborers on plantation detail numbered a paltry 10 percent. This did not please the sugar barons, who needed a continual supply of slave labor. Thus, in 1886, the Chinese Exclusion Act was passed, prohibiting any more of those business-types from entering Hawaii. This was followed by other official acts and obvious deterrents that eventually caused many of the Chinese to sell their businesses and leave.

Luckily for the remaining Chinese, by the 1930s, it was the Japanese who were taking the heat. This allowed Chinese the opportunity to carry on with their lives and work, which they wisely did without making any waves. The current Chinese population is around 70,000, and all but a few thousand make Oahu their home. Many travelers pay a visit to Chinatown and some come for the Chinese New Year celebrations. For the Chinese, it's business as usual.

The Japanese

The Japanese also were given the opportunity to work themselves to death on Hawaiian plantations. There's some speculation that they actually visited Hawaii years before Captain Cook and his hungry crew blew in—the versions vary. Officially, however, a small band of laborers arrived in 1868, but it took almost 20 years before Japanese began coming to the islands in droves. The lag time was due to the Japanese government's desire to hang onto its hard-working citizens. The famine of 1886 changed matters, and the Japanese government finally sent over a shipload of farmers, as well as some of their "untouchables."

The Japanese contract workers earned a few bucks more than the Chinese had, plus they received bonuses for wives who were willing to work the factories or fields. Migration sped up and, by the turn of the century, the Japanese population numbered more than 60,000, ranking it Hawaii's largest ethnic group. Many workers eventually returned home, while others set up a permanent island existence with prearranged "brides" sent out by their families. Nonetheless their lives in paradise were, for a long time, hell. They were overworked, exploited and discriminated against, but managed to hang in longer than the Chinese had. Then they followed suit by becoming business owners, shopkeepers, fishermen and independent farmers. Achievement through education was highly stressed, particularly for the children.

By World War II the Japanese were firmly entrenched in the retail sector. The "old guard" (or first generation) still clung to its traditional ways, while the well-schooled children became "Americanized." After the attack on Pearl Harbor, Japanese loyalties were suspect by many—particularly the U.S. military—and martial law was instigated *just in case*. On the flip side, thousands of Japanese men formed their own combat units and fought for the United States in World War II, becoming war heroes. Returning as such, many opted for a college education under the GI. Bill, emerging as teachers, doctors, lawyers, businessmen and politicians. Currently, about 25 percent of Hawaii's population is Japanese, and Japanese Americans hold half of the state's political offices.

The "Haoles"

Hawaiians refer to any Caucasian—or *anyone* with white skin—as a *haole*. The word's actual definition is unclear (it was probably undefinable) but, basically, it means "white person." The intonation—and body language—with which it's said probably gives the best clue as to how it's meant to be taken at any given time.

Aside from the Hawaiians, white peoples' island roots go back further than any other group. The missionary bandwagon in the 1820s was the first significant settlement, though there had been a few immigrants back in the late 1700s.

Not surprisingly, the whites moved in and took control of just about everything. They ran the plantations, schools and, eventually, those all-empowered Big Five companies. They lost no time in making the natives feel like inferior beings in their own territory, a primitive group with some very bad customs. Before long, landowners were picking on and exploiting the Asian migrant workers who came to toil on their plantations. Worried that the increasing Asian population might turn on them—politically and otherwise—the land barons began recruiting white Europeans. In came Germans, Scandinavians, Russians, Scots, Poles and a huge number of Portuguese.

The white workers—surprise, surprise—were treated much better and paid higher wages than their Asian counterparts. Even so, most of them didn't take to plantation life and soon left for the mainland. The whites who stayed (particularly the Germans and Scandinavians) were soon elevated to higher status.

The Portuguese were in a separate category altogether. Because of their olive skin, the Hawaiians did not consider them *haoles* and they were welcomed with traditional aloha. Also the Portuguese weren't as picky as the other Europeans; both the men and women worked hard in the plantations, didn't give the owners trouble, and soon achieved top status as skilled laborers. Intermarriage occurred most often between Portuguese women and Hawaiian men, while the Portuguese men still fancied the women from back home.

The whites continued migrating to Hawaii during the Depression years, increasing their numbers in direct proportion to hotel and resort development. Currently the haoles make up about one-third of the population, are spread throughout the islands (with Oahu taking the brunt) and still control the state's economy.

The Filipinos

The Filipinos had the buck up on other Asians when they moved into the islands—they were already American nationals via the Spanish-American War of 1898. As such, they were exempt from any unpleasant immigration restrictions. Some 120,000 Filipinos made their way to Hawaii between 1907 and 1931, most of them coming from the northern Philippines. The plantation owners loved them—they took the worst jobs, didn't care about the conditions and didn't give a hoot about education (in fact, most of them were illiterate). The big problem was women: there were only a few hundred Filipinas to share among some 30,000 men. Lousy statistics.

The Filipinos were not at all keen on intermarriage—the idea had been to make some money and then return home. For most, that didn't happen. The Filipino population today makes up about 15 percent of Hawaii's total, most live on Oahu, many are on Lanai. Many are bachelors.

The Rest of the Melting Pot

The Koreans head the secondary list; they showed up between 1903 and 1905 and there probably would've been more if their government hadn't closed the doors. The Puerto Ricans came along about the same time as the Koreans.

Other Polynesians were lured over to Hawaii in the late 1800s; it was hoped they would beef up the rapidly dying native population. Good plan, but it didn't work. They all became homesick and went back to their own islands.

African-Americans, Native Americans and Vietnamese are all represented, and the number of inbound Samoans is growing quickly.

NATURAL WONDERS

The blowhole on Eastern Oahu is especially dramatic when the waves are rough.

Naturally, Hawaii lives up to the universal ideal of paradise: roaring water-falls, whispering palms, secluded beaches, succulent fruits, fragrant blossoms....Otherwise, probably no one would even go there, right? Well, hang on—today's paradise was at one time a big pile of dry-as-bone, palm-, posy- and birdless rock.

About 70 million years ago, the first Hawaiian islands popped out of the Pacific Ocean—2000-plus miles from any other landmass—the product of furious volcanic eruptions that, one day, would become one of the world's most sought-after tourist destinations. Maybe Mother Nature had a crystal ball. More volcano-spitting fury combined with formidable earthquakes, hurricanes, gales, tropical storms and tidal waves, all pounding, carving, niching, shaping, grinding, polishing and—*voila!* Welcome to Hawaii and its mini-world of diverse climate and topography.

As for the island's flora and fauna—so fantastic that they often co-star in such Hollywood big-budget films as *Jurassic Park* and *Waterworld*—they simply blew in with the wind or sailed in with the tides, then settled down, adapted to the new environment and thrived.

Unfortunately, humans had to come along, bringing in agriculture, tools, condos and the like. So, no, today's Hawaii does not have the same environment it did pre-human (what does?) but, on the other hand, it was the settlers and farmers who planted many of the trees (including coconut palms) as well as abundant flowers, fruits and vegetables. Not an altogether bad trade-off, is it?

Wildlife of Hawaii

Birds

Unfortunately, Hawaii's birdlife has dwindled horribly, down to less than 20 original species of the 70-plus native species that first made Hawaii their home. We can blame some of this on the Polynesian settlers whose farming endeavors forced them from their homes, but—again—we also have to point the finger at the big land developers. The depressing tally: 23 extinct species; 31 endangered species. And counting.

Ae'o

This skinny wading bird—or Hawaiian stilt—measures about 16 inches and hangs out in Kealia Pond and Kanaha Wildlife Sanctuary on Maui, and at Hanalei National Wildlife Refuge on Kauai.

Alae ke'oke'o

The Hawaiian coot has webbed feet, looks something like a duck and favors Maui and Kauai as its habitats.

Amakihi

A *not* endangered species, olive-green and lives on the high branches of koa and sandalwood trees.

Drepanidade

Known also as Hawaiian Honeycreepers. These fantastic birds can look like anything from a delicate finch to a hard-nosed woodpecker. They've been around so long that many of their species were probably extinct long before settlement occurred.

'Elepaio

An orange-breasted, gray flycatcher that dwells in the forest and can't resist checking out strange whistling sounds

'I'iwi

Bright red with a hooked bill that is found only in the higher elevations of Kauai, Maui and Big Island forests.

Moa

A red jungle fowl, relative to the chicken, first brought by the Polynesian settlers.

Nene

Hawaii's state bird—and kin to the Canadian goose—making a comeback after its near extinction. The goose-like bird stands about two feet tall and can be found only in Haleakala Crater on Maui, or on the slopes of Mauna Kea and Mauna Loa on the Big Island.

Pueo

The Hawaiian owl stands about 15 inches tall, can be spotted on most of the islands (with Maui being its favorite haunt) and was highly prized by the ancient Hawaiians.

Poouli

Saved from extinction and still highly endangered, this bird wears a black mask and is found in Maui's forests.

Other spotting possibilities include **wedge-tailed shearwaters**, **red- and white-footed boobies**, **frigate birds**, **red- and white-tailed tropic birds**, **Laysan gooney birds**, **egrets**, **doves** and **cardinals**.

Diving with manta ray, Big Island

Fish

This could be a book of its own. Hawaii *is* sealife and a veritable heaven for divers, snorkelers and fishermen who come to this land just to get at what's under water. Stunning coral reefs harbor myriad fish and crustaceans; some

HAWAIIAN FAUNA

Hawaii's diverse geography and its lack of predators has allowed both birds and mammals to flourish. Originally only 15 types of species, there are now over 70 types of birds unique to the Hawaiian Islands. The only mammals on land upon discovery of the islands were bats and seals.

KAUAI

Lihue •

NIIHAU

PACIFIC OCEAN

OAHU

Honolulu

MONK SEAL

The Monk seal, indigenous to the Islands, can be found nowhere else on earth. Not known to exist until 1905 there are more than 1000 seals throughout the Islands.

SOOTY TERN

These ground-nesters persist on flat, sandy areas with evenly spaced nesting territories.

THE HUMPBACK WHALE

The Humpback whales swim through Hawaiian waters between October and May. The waters off the Islands serve as both breeding ground and birth place for the whales.

MASKED BOOBIES

Nesting on rock and barren patches of ground, these birds live on offshore islets and other predator-free areas.

MOLOKAI

LANAI

MAUI

KAHOOLAWE

NENE, HAWAIIAN GOOSE

The Nene is the Hawaiian state bird. Nearly extinct in the 1950's, the bird has made a comeback, with human intervention. The Nene can be found on old lava flows on both Maui and Hawaii.

DOLPHINS

Dolphins abound year-round in the waters surrounding the Hawaiian Islands.

HAWAII

Hilo

700 fish species occupy waters around the islands and about 450 of them stay close to the reef area. Of these, approximately one-quarter are found exclusively in their native Hawaii, all part of that awesome evolution of flora and fauna to the new-born islands.

Among the colorful reef fishes apt to be swarming around are the sweet, shy **angel fish**; brilliantly colored **parrot fish**; gender-changing **wresses**; scalpel-spined **surgeon fish**; pro-relationship **butterfly fish**; and evil **scorpion fish**.

Hawaii is famous with the international angler set as the premier spot to hunt big game fish such as **marlin**, **tuna** and **swordfish**. The possibilities are daunting: **black**, **Pacific blue**, or **striped marlin**; **bigeye**, **albacore**, **skipjack** and **yellowfin tuna**; **gray**, **red** and **pink snapper**; **mahimahi**, **ono**, **trevally** and **sea bass**; **lady-**, **leather-**, **goat-** and **bonefish**. Or go for the freshwater fish in Oahu and Kauai reservoirs—**rainbow trout**, **catfish** and the like.

Forty or so **shark** species inhabit Hawaiian waters and, yes, one of them *is* the great white shark. You'll be happy to learn that attacks are *very* infrequent—only about 100 since 1779 (at least those were the ones recorded).

Animals, on Land and in the Sea

The only native animals (aside from birds) to greet the arriving Polynesians were the small **hoary bat** and the **monk seal**. Hoary bats are reddish creatures that migrated all the way from North and South America and now live mostly on the Big Island and Kauai. Monk seals—related to those in the Mediterranean and Caribbean—nearly disappeared into extinction during the 19th-century skin and oil slaughter. Now they enjoy a protected existence, mainly on the outer islands, though they sometimes make their way onto a tourist beach. If you spot one, leave it alone and stay clear at least 50 feet—via the Marine Mammals Protection Act, the seals have an enforced restraining order against humans (lucky them!).

Species brought in by everyone from the Polynesians to the Europeans still run wild throughout the islands today, and include pigs, goats, chickens, dogs, rats, deer, antelope and bighorn sheep.

The **mongoose** also can be found, often running in and out of traffic. Whoever introduced it to Hawaii back in the 19th century, for the purpose of eradicating the islands' rapidly growing rat problem, obviously did not do their homework. The mongoose likes to be out and about during the daytime, while the nocturnal rats are fast asleep. Consequently *both* creatures continued to multiply and the only thing that got eradicated was—thanks to the hungry mongoose—much of Hawaii's native bird population.

Other fauna include more than 1000 varieties of snails (how they arrived in Hawaii still remains a mystery), geckos (insect-eating lizards) and a small snake (that really looks more like an earthworm).

Between late November and early May, Hawaii's visitor population includes **humpback whales** that migrate over from Alaska. Year-round inhabitants are **sperm**, **beaked**, **pilot**, **false-killer-** and **pygmy-killer whales**, many of which can be seen off the Big Island's Kona Coast.

Flora of Hawaii

Trees

Hawaii's premiere native tree is the **koa**, a type of acacia. The ancient Polynesians used the prized wood (often measured 70 feet tall and more than 10 feet in circumference) to form canoes, spears, paddles and those big, long, royal surfboards. Today contemporary Hawaiians still use it to fashion furniture, ukuleles, building materials and tourist souvenirs. All this usage—along with logging, fire and foraging—unfortunately means the koa's existence has greatly diminished. You'll stumble across a variety of these majestic trees at the Big Island's Hawaii Volcanoes National Park.

The state's most common tree is the **ohia**, a hardy native that grows in an awesome variety of shapes and sizes (from mini up to 100 feet tall), and in a wide range of terrain (steamy swamps to cool hillsides). The ohia's fluffy, puffy, usually red flower was—according to legend—sacred to the volcano-goddess Pele. Pele's revenge, if her ohia blossoms were plucked, was *not* pretty.

Hawaii's state tree, the **kukui** (or candlenut), grows up to 80 feet and just about every inch—including flowers, bark and nuts—was put to good use by the ancient Hawaiians. Nuts became candles, condiments, lei ornaments and necklaces; bark was turned into dye for tapa cloth, tattoos, paints and preservatives; flowers metamorphosed into a drugstore of antibiotics and tonics; the oil was used for skin lotion; and the wood often turned up as someone's big, hollowed-out canoe.

Other island trees include the **African tulip** with its fire-alarm-red blossoms, sprawling **banyan**, majestic **monkey-pod**, striped-trunk **rainbow eucalyptus**, tangly-branched **hau**, scary-looking **baobab**, flowery-but-poisonous **angel's trumpet** and fragrant **kiawe** (or the **mesquite** under your grill). Among the plethora of fruit trees you'll find **banana**, **breadfruit**, **papaya**, **mango**, **macadamia nut** and **lychee**.

Flowers and Plants

The ancient Hawaiians, white settlers, and migrants from all over the world have been responsible for bringing in many of the state's to-die-for flowers and plants.

HAWAIIAN FLORA

Hawaii's moist tropical climate has made it an ideal habitat for colorful and rare flora.

KAUAI

Lihue •

NIIHAU

HIBISCUS

This colorful plant is abundant on Kauai and is Hawaii's state flower. According to Hawaiian tradition, if a woman wears the flower behind her left ear, she is committed.

OAHU

• Honolulu

PACIFIC OCEAN

KOA TREE

Originally from Africa, this tree adapted to and began thriving in the Hawaiian climate. The tree was important in the ancient Hawaiian culture, used for spears, canoes and surfboards.

PINK GINGER

Pink Ginger can be found in many forests in the island chain and is also used in leis.

MOLOKAI

LANAI

MAUI

KAHOOLAWE

FIDDLE-HEAD FERN

This fern is found in abundance in the high altitude rainforest of Volcano National Park.

PINEAPPLE

Lana'i is known as the pineapple island because James Dole planted it with 15,000 acres of pineapple trees.

HAWAII

• Hilo

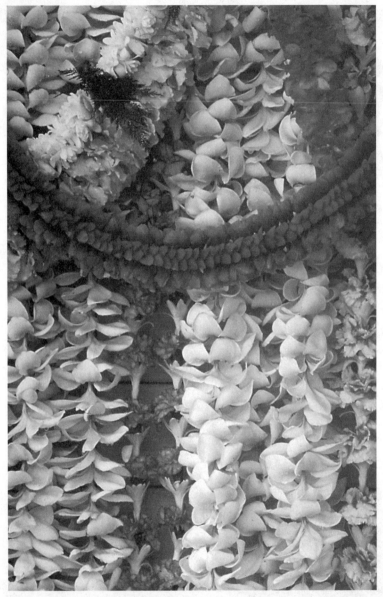

Most Hawaiian leis are made with plumeria, gardenias, carnations, ginger blossoms, ti leafs, ferns, kukui nuts and shells.

Some 700 species of **ginger** grow in the islands, ranging from tiny to tall, and in scads of shapes and colors. Fragrant gingers were used for leis, potpourri and air freshener; the edible root is a dominant flavor in Asian and Polynesian cuisine, and is also used as a curative for a long list of ailments; juice from the plant is still being turned into shampoo and other beauty products. The white-and-yellow ginger—brought from the Indo-Malaysia region in the 19th century—is some of the most aromatic. Other gingers are red, pink, pearly white and arrived from places such as Burma, India, the Caribbean and Malaysia.

Plumeria probably heads the list of this-smells-just-like-Hawaii flowers. Also known as **frangipani**, these are the blossoms commonly used for that traditional greeting lei. **Orchids** are way up on the I'm-really-here list as well, with the **vanda orchid** being the most widely grown.

Hibiscus also comes in thousands of varieties, sizes and colors (the state flower is the yellow hibiscus), and approximately 80 species of brightly colored **heliconias**—brought over from Central and South America and the Caribbean—continue to thrive. **Bougainvillea** grows profusely throughout the islands, joined by **gardenias**, **oleander** and **birds of paradise**. The rare **silversword**—related to the sunflower but not looking anything like it—is sighted only in Maui's Haleakala Crater and on the Big Island. Try to catch it during its July-to-September blooming season. Its happy-go-lucky reddish-purple stalks have a mysterious way of quickly turning into silver spindles.

Filmed in Hawaii

The islands have been used as film-shoot locations since 1913, when *Hawaiian Love* and *The Shark God* were filmed at Oahu's Liliuokalani Park (never heard of them, have you?). Yes, many of your favorite celebrities have spoken their lines *right* where you are standing! Perhaps some of their talent will rub off—or, maybe some of their makeup (didn't the pancake *drip* in the humidity?). Anyway, Kauai wins for most-used location site.

FILM	LOCATION	STARS
The Black Camel (1931)	**Waikiki and Kailua, Oahu**	Robert Young, Bela Lugosi
Curly Top (1935)	**Oahu**	Shirley Temple
From Here to Eternity	**Oahu**	Frank Sinatra, Burt Lancaster, Montgomery Clift, Donna Reed, Deborah Kerr
The Old Man and the Sea (1958)	**Big Island**	Spencer Tracy

NATURAL WONDERS

FILM	LOCATION	STARS
South Pacific (1958)	**North Shore, Kauai**	Mitzi Gaynor, Rozanno Brazzi
Gidget Goes Hawaiian (1961)	**Oahu**	James Darren, Deborah Walley
Blue Hawaii (1961)	**Kauai**	Elvis Presley
Papillon (1973)	**Molokai**	Steve McQueen, Dustin Hoffman
King Kong (1976)	**Kauai's Na Pali coast**	Jessica Lange
Islands in the Stream (1977)	**Kauai**	George C. Scott
10 (1979)	**Kauai, Oahu**	Dudley Moore, Bo Derek
Raiders of the Lost Ark (1980)	**Kauai**	Harrison Ford
Karate Kid II (1985)	**Oahu**	Pat Morita, Ralph Macchio
Black Widow (1985)	**Big Island**	Debra Winger
Throw Momma From the Train (1987)	**Kauai**	Danny DeVito, Billy Crystal
Lord of the Flies (1989)	**Kauai**	Balthazar Getty
Point Break (1990)	**Oahu's North Shore**	Patrick Swayze, Keanu Reeves
Hook (1991)	**Kauai**	Julia Roberts, Robin Williams
Jurassic Park (1992)	**Kauai**	Laura Dern, Sam Neill, Jeff Goldblum
Outbreak (1994)	**Kauai**	Dustin Hoffman, Rene Russo
Waterworld (1994)	**Big Island**	Kevin Costner

ARTS AND CRAFTS

Canoe Tour at the Polynesian Cultural Center details canoe history.

It's easy to see why arts and crafts have always played a big role in Hawaiian culture. Creative expression and inspiration are built into every shape, color and texture of the environment. The ancient settlers busied themselves with crafting practical items such as quilts, weavings and clothing, along with woodcarving, scrimshaw and lei-making. Hawaiian history and identity was uniquely expressed through the hip-swaying hula and its accompanying tunes. Later, in the 19th century, the ukulele became an integral part of the native act.

Contemporary artists capture the island spirit through media such as painting, sculpture, scrimshaw, jewelry and fabric design, exhibited at venues ranging from outdoor markets to trendy galleries. Souvenir hunters will be able to find a large selection of high-quality items to wow the family and friends back home and—for those less inclined—it'll be a cinch to find a bobbing-head hula doll and a good fake lei.

Tapa Cloth

Long before bolts of cotton and wool arrived from overseas, the Polynesians had perfected *tapa* cloth (cloth made from tree and plant bark) to use for their clothing (such as it was), blankets and various household items. Though the men sought out the appropriate plants, the actual weaving was relegated as "women's work." The whole process took *forever* and occupied a big part of those ancient days. There was the search for appropriate plants (*mamaki* and *wauke* made some of the finest cloth), then the bark had to be peeled, soaked, beaten on a log, flattened with a club, set out to sun dry and, usually, custom-dyed and block-printed. Only *then* was it ready to sew into loin cloths, bedspreads, room dividers or whatever. Today's tapa is, sadly, not quite the same and most is imported from other Polynesian islands.

Quilts

No surprise to find out it was those New England missionary women who brought over quilting techniques along with the Bibles. The Hawaiians watched and learned, then rolled with the needle. Obviously there wasn't match of a "rag pile" since woven cloth was still something of a novelty to the islands, and that woven tapa just wasn't going to cut it. Consequently the natives used whole lengths of fabric (usually white) and a one-color (usually bold) appliqué that was cut out much the same way as folded-paper dolls or snowflakes, and finished off with intricate free-form stitching. The quilters' imaginations ran wild with those appliqués, often pulling designs from dreams, events or the natural world around them—be it a flower or an octopus—developing their own sort of "copyright" system in the process. If one quilter wanted to use a design created by another, she was supposed to credit the originator. Unfortunately it didn't always work that way and "pattern theft" (today's "copyright infringement") became somewhat common. Antique quilts have become pricey (if not priceless) collector's items and museum pieces, with some of the splashier hotels and resorts hanging them up for display. Contemporary versions can be commissioned by island quilters, but be prepared to shell out some big bucks.

Featherwork

Bird feathers—particularly those of the *'i'iwi*, *'o'o*, *apane* and *mamo* birds—were like diamonds to the ancient Hawaiians. They were not only *the* most special commodity to possess, but they were also used to pay off taxes and other debts. And, if you owned a custom-made featherwork garment, you were *really* hot stuff. Yellow and red feathers were the favorites, with basic black sitting at the bottom of the list. After being plucked from the birds by professionals—who may or may not actually kill them—the feathers were stitched into helmets, cloaks, capes, staffs and idols. Only men were allowed to wear most of the plumage—particularly kings or high chiefs as they strutted to or from some war—though it was OK for women to wear a featherwork *lei hulu* around their heads and necks. Featherwork was found in some of the other Polynesian islands but, so far as anyone knows, the creation of such splendid garments was uniquely Hawaiian. You won't find a cape or cloak for sale at *any* price.

Scrimshaw

Whalers introduced the art of scrimshaw—carving and etching on ivory or bone—to the islands during the 19th century and, in fact, the state's scrimshaw "capital" is still based in Lahaina on Maui. Nautical and various other designs were worked onto whale bones and elephant ivory. Due to those mammals' precarious existence on this planet, the medium for contemporary scrimshaw has changed to walrus tusks. You'll be able to find jewelry, *objets d'art*, and other pieces in every price range from cheap to extravagant.

Leis

The Hawaiians have continued to make leis just like in the good old days. Throughout the islands, leis are made and presented for arrivals, departures, births, deaths, graduations, weddings and every other special occasion. The most common leis are made with plumeria, but gardenias, carnations, ginger blossoms, ti leafs, ferns, shells and *kukui* nuts are also lei-making materials. Connoisseurs eyeball the various stringing or weaving styles, which can run from simple put-togethers for mass airport arrivals to painstaking weaving and braiding techniques for a very special commemoration. Each island has its own home-style lei. You can buy perishable leis everywhere; the nonperishables (shells and seeds) are costlier.

Wood Carving

Koa was the wood favored by the old Hawaiian carvers who used to turn out furnishings, canoes, food bowls, sculptures and religious figures. And though koa is still the preferred material for contemporary woodcarvers, many have turned to less-scarce alternatives such as monkeypod. You can buy carved bowls, jewelry, tikis and other items in gift and craft shops but—if you care—beware of the cheap Asian imports, sold mainly in variety stores.

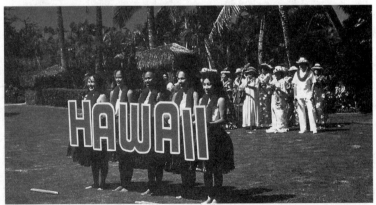

The Kodak Hula Show entertains visitors with demonstrations and background on the legendary Hawaiian dance, its music and costumes.

Hula

Surprise, surprise—the hula actually started out as part of the native religious cere-mony, it was performed only by *men* (with drum accompaniment) and it was more like martial arts or hand-to-hand combat. Eventually the women were allowed to take over the dance and *voila!*, it evolved into grace and elegance, though without the sensuous, jiggly quality of today's "tourist" version. The hula was much more than a dance—it was a vivid portrayal of Hawaiian history, culture and even some good gossip. Only the most poised and beautiful girls were selected for hula school, a life as strict and brutal as a serious ballet academy. As they emerged, each girl had developed her own individual "trademark" hula. This tradition continues on every island and, though the schools are no longer such an all-consuming endurance test, the dancers still take their art very seriously. Hilo's Merrie Monarch Festival each April is the *pièce de résistance* in hula competition and all the dancers await it with a passion. Traditionally the hula is accompanied by chants and the *ipu* (gourd drums), as well as various other drums and rattles. As to those grass skirts, they came from other islands; the Hawaiians only used ti leaves.

Ukuleles and Other Instruments

The translation of *ukulele* is "jumping flea," a term used by the Hawaiians to denote the fast-as-a-jumping-flea finger action of Portuguese immigrants as they adeptly played brought-from-home four-stringed *bragas*. The natives had already been strumming their own three-stringed *ukeke* and had other instruments such as the nose flute, shell trumpet and gourd whistle. During the latter part of the 19th cen-tury, the steel guitar (also known as the slack key guitar) was originated by 15-year-old Joseph Kekuku, creating a sound that would forever distinguish Hawaiian music from anyone else's tune.

Lava rock carvings (petroglyphs) depict animals and people.

ISLAND CUISINE

Honolulu's Ihilani Restaurant at the Manele Bay Hotel has a scenic view.

Again we're back to the melting pot—lucky us that all those ethnic groups brought their favorite recipes from home. You'll find every kind of cuisine (paradise, remember?), with a big emphasis on Asian (don't forget who the original restaurateurs were!). Then there are the local goodies—fresh fish, glorious fruits and exotic drinks served in coconut shells, as well as the trendier Pacific Rim (or Hawaiian Regional) cuisine. And yes, *of course*, there are plenty of McDonald's and Pizza Huts.

The Fabulous Luau

We know you wouldn't think of leaving Hawaii without having experienced a luau. The sight of hordes of aloha-shirted and muumuu-ed tourists panting over a whole pig *is* truly inspirational! Done to death or not, a luau is a good way to enjoy a broad selection of common Hawaiian dishes and to experience a slice of the traditional pie.

The cooking action is centered around the *imu* (or underground oven)—a hole in the ground that's filled with stones, then heated by fire and cooled. Into the *imu* goes that whole pig, its belly filled with wonderful ti-leave-wrapped packets of poi, fish, chicken, sweet potatoes, bananas and other dishes, with more ti and banana leaves layered in between. Then the entire meal is steamed (it takes about four hours), and that pig is transformed into the famed *kalua* pork (if you're thinking of the Mexican liqueur, that's *Kahlua—kalua* means anything cooked in the *imu*). Non-pork eaters can find alternative dishes buried in the hole: *lomilomi* salmon and chicken luau are common choices. Meanwhile, you'll be regaled with entertainment and those widely reputed tropical drinks. Expect to pay about $50 per person, but that includes all you can eat, and we *know* you will get your money's worth.

Believe it or not, luaus did not start off as tourist attractions. They were an actual part of native life, wonderful occasions to celebrate weddings, birthdays and special events, and were just for-the-aloha-of-it get-togethers. They're still held today, and with luck you will make friends with the locals and be invited to one! You might also keep your ears open or check the newspapers for community-sponsored luaus, which are more Hawaiian (and cheaper) than the tourist-specific events.

Hawaiian Foods

You'll find many of the luau favorites on the menus of Hawaiian restaurants. The purplish and pasty—but *very* nutritious—*poi* (crushed taro root) is, for many, an acquired taste. The Hawaiians, however, think it's fantastic (much like the Australians feels about their *vegemite*) and it has remained a household staple since the ancestral Polynesian farmers first planted it.

Plate lunches are a hot item for both locals and visitors. They're inexpensive, ready-to-go, paper or styrofoam plates heaped with a variety of goodies: two-scoop rice, macaroni salad, teriyaki chicken, lomi salmon, beef stew, breaded mahimahi and the like. You can find them all over the islands, either in restaurants or the lunch wagons (known as *kaukau* wagons), where they might be under an alias such as "Bento" or "box lunch."

A favorite island treat is **shave ice**—a cone-shaped paper cup filled with super-fine ice "shavings," soaked in your choice of syrup (strawberry, coconut, vanilla, guava, lemon, etc.) Slurp it with a straw, or suck it down with a spoon—just don't call it a "snow cone."

The **pupus** come out, usually when evening rolls around. These are appetizers, hors d'oeuvres, finger foods—call them what you will—customarily set out as **pupu platters** that may include tempura, chicken wings, crackers and seafood.

Trendier restaurants feature **Hawaiian Regional** cuisine, also commonly known to upmarket foodies as "Pacific Rim." The emphasis is on dishes that combine continental and Asian cooking artistry with super-fresh island produce, fresh-from-the-sea fish and locally bred meat. A meal done this way costs a lot more than the plate lunches and is served at fancier establishments.

Hawaii's magnificent bounty of tropical **fruits and nuts**, on the other hand, is practically yours for the picking (but don't unless you ask first). Some of the more delectable and famous crops include avocados, bananas, coconuts, pineapple, passion fruit, breadfruit, papaya, mangos, guava, macadamia nuts and litchi.

Or have your fruit and drink it too. Most of the **exotic drinks** are rum-based—mixed with juice, liqueur or other flavorings—and often come served in coconut or pineapple shells. You can also find a couple of locally brewed beers, as well as some Maui-produced wines. As for coffee, the Big Island's Kona is richer than Starbuck's.

Asian Foods

The Chinese, Japanese, Koreans and Filipinos have imbued the islands with the spices, flavors and concoctions from their homelands.

Chinese restaurants are ubiquitous throughout Hawaii. After all, they were the immigrants who couldn't wait to get off the plantations and open up shop. Chow mein, chop suey, fried rice and the like are inexpensive and—as everywhere—make great takeaways.

The Japanese put more flair into their meals—it must be perfect, it must be beautiful, it must be serene—even if it *is* going to be momentarily swallowed and digested. Teriyaki meats, tempura, sukiyaki and tofu dishes are all on the menu, and sushi bars are prevalent throughout the islands.

Korean cooking is flavorful and often very spicy. Especially popular is *kimchee*, a fermented cabbage slaw flavored with fiery red peppers (have plenty of ice water handy). Other favorite dishes include barbecued ribs and chicken, shredded veggies, thick noodle soups and hearty stews.

Exotic sauce and hot spice lovers will probably enjoy the Filipino flavors—meats simmered in garlic and vinegar, sour soups, whole suckling pigs and filled doughs.

Fielding's Guide to Hawaiian Delicacies

Unfamiliar names, strange shapes, slimy textures, too-vibrant-to-be-anything-but-non-FDA-approved colors. What does it all mean?

A'u	expensive and delicious broadbill swordfish or marlin
Adobo	Filipino specialty made with chicken or pork
Ahi	yellowfin tuna, one of Hawaii's best
Aku	skipjack tuna or bonita
Bento	Japanese box lunch
Breadfruit	high-carbohydrate (and somewhat bland) Hawaiian staple served baked, roasted, fried or boiled
Chicken luau	stew-like dish cooked with taro or spinach leaves and coconut milk
Crackseed	candy-like preserved, spiced seeds and fruits that originates from China
Dim sum	Chinese dumplings, steamed and with a variety of fillings
Guava	thirst-quenching, tangy tree fruit often made into juice and jellies
Hapu	Hawaiian sea bass
Haupia	a coconut pudding-ish dessert, especially popular at luaus
Imu	the underground oven used at luaus, especially to prepare the kalua pig
Kalua pig	the star of every luau—a pig steamed in the *imu*, or underground oven
Kaukau	general term for "food"
Kimchee	Korean dragon-hot slaw made from fiery peppers and fermented cabbage
Laulau	steamed ti leaves that have been stuffed with bananas, sweet potatoes, pork, taro shoots and other tidbits
Lilikoi	passion fruit—yellow and seedy, with a tart flavor—often made into juice, jellies or desserts
Limu	a seaweed garnish used in the islands since Polynesian settlement
Lomilomi salmon	raw salmon chunks mixed with onions, tomatoes and salt—a luau dish

Macadamia nuts	small, round, buttery-rich nuts found throughout the islands in many varieties—roasted, dry-roasted, chocolate-covered, salted—all irresistible and teeming with fat
Mahimahi	common island fish often served grilled as a fish burger, also called "dolphin" fish (don't spit it out, it is *not* a mammal)
Manapua	steamed dough wrapped around black beans or pork
Malasadas	hole-less Portuguese doughnuts, deep-fried and doused with sugar
Maui onions	also known as *Kula* onions, they are sweet and mild
Moi	big-eyed, shark-headed, superior eating fish
Ono ("delicious")	a flaky game fish, also known as "wahoo"
Papaya	small yellow or green melon-y fruit, high in vitamin C and widely eaten at breakfast
Pipikaula	beef jerky
Poi	superbly nutritious, pasty and purplish Hawaiian staple made from pounded taro root
Pupus	appetizers, hors d'oeuvres, finger foods—usually served on a "pupu platter"
Saimin	also *ramen*—those big bowls of long noodles in thin broth served with veggies, meat or fish
Sashimi	Japanese favorite consisting of thinly sliced raw fish, dipped in soy sauce
Spam	Is it *back*? No, it never *left* Hawaii! The tinned spiced-ham that was a staple for the military during the'40s is, for Hawaiians, a virtual love affair. They stick it in everything, and you'll find it on *many* menus throughout the islands.
Sushi	very popular Japanese dish concocted from vinegared rice and raw fish or other toppings, rolled together in seaweed.
Taro root	the starchy root, planted as a staple by the ancient Polynesians—baked, roasted, used for poi, or made into potato-like chips
Ti leaves	leaves from the Ti plant, often used to wrap food in; thought by the early Hawaiians to keep evil spirits away
Uku	gray snapper, a local favorite
Ulua	a type of jack crevalle with a steak-like texture

ISLAND CUISINE

ISLAND CUISINE

THE BIG ISLAND

Lava flowing into the ocean is a fascinating spectacle on the Big Island.

Its real name is "Hawaii" but, of course, this confuses a lot of people. Hawaii is a state and Hawaii is also the name given to the state's largest island—the Big Island. And it is big—at least compared with the other islands—about twice the size of all of them combined. Big and *young*. At just about one million years old, this island ranks as Hawaii's geological baby.

Historically, the Big Island is probably the most important of the Hawaiian Islands since it was, according to scholars, the first to be settled by the ancient Polynesians back around A.D. 500. After all, this southernmost island was the closest to Polynesia and the summits of its twin peaks must have seemed like beacons to the approaching travelers. According to legend, the

THE BIG ISLAND

mythical fire goddess Pele still lives there, rearranging things from time to time at her home atop Kilauea, one of the world's most active volcanoes.

The Big Island (also known as the "Orchid Island" and "Volcano Island") was the birthplace of the illustrious Kamehameha the Great, unifier and first king of all Hawaii, who was born in the northern region of the Kohala District around 1750. A tough and loyal warrior, Kamehameha easily won the respect of his uncle, Kalaniopuu, who also happened to be ruler of the Big Island. Upon Kalaniopuu's death, Kamehameha took over as the keeper of the family war god and eventually outwitted and out-fought his warring cousins, the chief of Maui and other legions of rulers and warriors. King Kamehameha ruled Hawaii until his death in 1819 at Kailua-Kona. Another big name had earlier met his death on the Big Island—Captain James Cook was killed in 1779 during a fracas at Kealakekua Bay.

About a year after King Kamehameha died, big changes began to take hold, changes that would see many of the ancient Hawaiian traditions disappear. In 1820, the first Christian missionaries sailed in—and you know what that meant in terms of fun, frivolity and hanging onto any non-Christian ways. The real clincher, however, was several years later when Chieftess Keopuolani climbed up Kilauea, ate some no-no berries, and shrieked testament to her new-found faith for all (including fire goddess Pele) to hear. Goodbye old Hawaii.

The Big Island is a compilation of "firsts," "mosts" and contrasts. It was the first Hawaiian island to be settled, and the most diverse. Its tip is the most southern point of any other state, and it's geographically the youngest Hawaiian island. It supposedly has the tallest mountain in the world (Mauna Kea, when measured from the ocean floor) as well as the largest privately owned ranch (Parker Ranch) in the United States. It boasts the world's most powerful telescope (at Keck Observatory), along with Hawaii's most tropical city (Hilo). Its two volcanoes are the largest in the world and the most active. And so on.

More like a miniature continent then a tropical isle, the Big Island presents dazzling contrasts within its borders. There are lava cliffs, jutting mountains, snowcapped peaks, sunbaked deserts, tropical forests, verdant valleys, crashing waterfalls, sleepy villages, fancy-schmancy resorts and green-, black- and white-sand beaches. And, of course, there are volcanoes.

The island economy is based primarily on agriculture—responsible for more than half of Hawaii's vegetables, more than three-quarters of the fruit (particularly papayas) and almost all the macadamia nuts. The 250,000-acre Parker Ranch is thought to be the largest individually owned cattle ranch in the United States, and beef production at Parker and the 300-odd other Big Island ranches makes up about 65 percent of the state's total. The strong, rich coffee grown in the Kona region is the nation's only commercial coffee plantation. Other contributors to the economy are the military machine and tourism—and all help to support the island's 120,317 inhabitants.

The Big Island gets fewer tourists (slightly more than 1 million per year) than any other island, and most who do come hole up in one of the ritzy resorts along the Kona-Kohala coast. Many visitors think the island is boring, full of lava, beachless and shopless. There are beaches—peopleless—enough shops and plenty of vegetation (as well as lava). True, you won't find the party, hype-and-schlock scenes you might over on Maui or Oahu, but that's what is wonderful about the Big Island. You can come here, explore a microcosm of a mini-continent, not be bothered by anyone and *really* feel as though you've gotten away from it all. In the 1960s, astronauts were sent over here to train on the moonscape of the Mauna Loa lava fields. Do you *really* need mega malls and hordes of tourists to have a good vacation?

Bird's-Eye View

The state's southernmost island is also its largest, a comparatively humongous 4038 square miles (93 miles long and 76 miles wide), which is about twice the size of all the other Hawaiian islands put together, and the only island with active volcanoes. The two most prominent volcanoes are Kilauea—erupting continually since 1983—and Mauna Loa, the world's largest active volcano (last eruption 1984). The two entry ports are Kailua-Kona on the west coast and Hilo on the east coast. The sunny, dry Kona District is where most of the condos and resorts (and tourists) are located, as well as the coffee plantations, the spot where Captain Cook was killed and a string of beaches. Hapuna Beach and some famed resorts (including Laurence Rockefeller's Mauna Kea Resort) are north of Kailua-Kona (the center of Kona) in South Kohala. North Kohala—the peninsula at the northern tip of the island—is an area of isolated beach parks, ancient *heiau*, the almost has-been sugar plantation town of Hawi, cattle ranch land, rolling hills, the powerful Pololu Valley and the birthplace of King Kamehameha. The Hamakua coast—on the island's northeast shores—offers sugarcane fields, the Waimea cowboy town (center of the Parker Ranch), lush valleys, ancient burial ground, taro plantations, a couple of small towns and Akaka Falls State Park with its stupendous 442-foot waterfall. Hawaii's most tropical town, Hilo, is also the island's main city, a rural delight surrounded by rainforests,

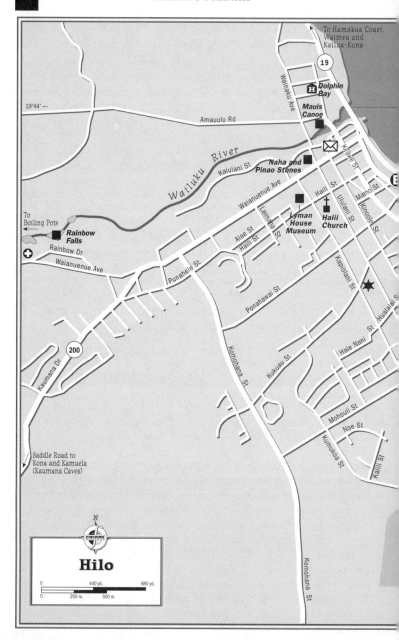

To Hamakua Coast,
Waimea and
Kailua-Kona

19

Dolphin Bay

Mauis Canoe

Wainaku Ave

Ikawe St

19°44'

Amauulu Rd

Wailuku River

Kaiulani St

Naha and Pinao Stones

Mamo St

Waianuenue Ave

Haili St

Kinoole St

Lyman House Museum

Halii Church

Alae St

Lanaela St

Ululani St

Kapiolani St

Hualalai St

To
Boiling Pots

Rainbow Falls

Rainbow Dr

Waianuenue Ave

Punahele St

Halii St

Ponahawai St

Hale Nani St

200

Kaumana Dr

Komohana St

Kukuau St

Mohouli St

Noe St

Saddle Road to
Kona and Kamuela
(Kaumana Caves)

Kumukoa St

Kalili St

Komohana St

N

Hilo

FIELDING

| 0 | 440 yd. | 880 yd. |
| 0 | 250 m. | 500 m. |

Hilo Bay

Coconut Island

Hilo Bay

Hilo Hawaiian

Hilo Naniloa

Hawaii Naniloa

Kuhio Bay

Waiakea Peninsula

Liliuokalani Gardens

Suisan Fish Market Auction

Bayfront Beach Park

Bayfront Hwy

Lihiwai St

Banyan Dr

Banyan Wy

Ocean View Dr

12

Reeds Bay

Kalanianaole Ave

Keaa St

Kamehameha Ave

Golf Course

Kuawa St

Kamehameha Ave

Pauahi St

Aupuni St

Kilauea Ave

Kaikoo Mall

Waianuenue Ave

Waiakea Pond

Park Rd

19

Waiakea Kai Shopping Plaza

Hoolulu Park

Civic Auditorium

Piilani St

11

Hualani St

Mililani St

Manono St

Orchid Gardens

Kekuanaoa St

Kanoelehua Ave

Kekuanaoa St

Kekuanaoa St

Leilani St

General Lyman Field (Hilo International Airport)

To Terminal

Leilani St

Mohouli St

Laniholi St

Kamana St

Lono St

Hilo Shopping Center

Kohola St

Iolani St

Leilani St

Hinano St

Laukapu St

Kalanikoa St

Tree Nursery & Garden

East Lanikaula St

Ululani St

Kinoole St

Kapiolani St

Kawili St

Railroad Ave

Auwae Rd

West Lanikaula St

East St

Hawaii Community College

Pookela St

Kukila St

Univ. of Hawaii at Hilo

West Kawili St

Kilauea Ave

Makaala St

Holomua St

E. Ohea St

11

High School

Lokahi Park

W. Ohea St

Kekela St

To Puna and Volcanic Area

Prince Kuhio Plaza

Hilo Municipal Golf Course

West Puainako St

123

West Puainako St

155°4'

plant life, heaps of orchids and other flowers. You can access Saddle Road either at Hilo or Kona to cut across the island right between Mauna Loa and Mauna Kea, the Big Island's highest point at 13,796 feet. The Puna District, southeast of Hilo, contains most of Hawaii Volcanoes National Park, some absolutely amazing lava fields, scads of hiking trails, small villages and the Chain of Craters Road—passage to Mauna Loa. The southern point of the island is mostly made up of the eerie Kau Desert, along with some state parks and dramatic beaches. Ka Lae, at the very tip, marks the most southern land in the United States.

Nature Guide

Vast numbers of birds inhabit most areas of the Big Island. Commonly found forest birds include the *'oma'o* (Hawaiian thrush), *apapane, amakihi, akepa, palila, po'ouli* and *'i'iwi*. Endangered coastal birds are the *'a'o* (Newell shearwater) and *'ua'u* (Hawaiian petrel), both breeders on the higher elevations of the volcanoes. Other indigenous species that are growing scarce are the *nene* (the Hawaiian goose, and Hawaii's official state bird), *alala* (Hawaiian crow), and *'io* (Hawaiian hawk).

Lobelia and gesneriad species are prolific in the Big Island—both come in a vast array of sizes, shapes and blossoms. *Panini* or prickly pear cactus is another common flora, found mostly in the North Kohala district. Many fern varieties as well as native koa and ohia trees can be sighted in the rainforests of Volcanoes National Park.

Introduced animals you might spot are feral cattle and sheep (both brought in by Captain Vancouver), feral donkeys, feral dogs and Mediterranean mouflon sheep. Migrating humpback whales can be seen from late December through mid-March along the South Kona coast, in North Kohala and off the Puna coast.

Fielding's Beach Finder

Hapuna Beach is considered not only the best beach in Hawaii, but one of the best in the world. It's ideal for sunning, hiking and a variety of watersports.

Rumor has it that the Big Island is devoid of beaches. Not true. More to the point, the beaches (more than 80) are devoid of people. Take your pick from white-, black- or green-sand stretches but—again—watch out for treacherous "rips," or riptides—ask locals for advice. The best beaches are up along the Kohala coast.

Kona Coast

Hookena Beach Park

About 25 miles south of Kailua-Kona, at the northern edge of Kauhako Bay.
Features dark gray sands and waters good for fishing, bodysurfing and swimming. Picnic facilities, rest rooms, showers.

Honaunau Beach

Adjacent to the Puuhonau o Honaunau National Historical Park.
A top spot for scuba diving and snorkeling, as well as whale watching. Facilities are available at the park.

THE BIG ISLAND

Napo'opo'o Beach Park

At Kealakekua Bay.

This was the last beach experience for Captain James Cook, who was slain here in 1779 (see the white obelisk memorial). The sand is black and the marine preserve is a great spot for scuba diving and snorkeling. Picnic facilities, basketball court, rest rooms and showers.

Kahaluu Beach Park

Between Kailua-Kona and Keauhou.

Once frequented by King Kalakaua, this beach is popular with locals for swimming, snorkeling and sunning. Watch the rips. Picnic area, showers, rest rooms, lifeguards, some parking.

White Sands Beach Park

In Kailua-Kona about a mile past the Kona Hilton.

A small area (often washed away in winter) with poor swimming and good board- and body-surfing. Lifeguards, showers, rest rooms.

Old Kona Airport State Park

At the end of Highway 11 north of Kailua-Kona.

Affords good surfing at the offshore break, tide pools for the kids and swimming, snorkeling and scuba diving for others. Rest rooms, showers.

Kona Coast Beach Park

Off Queen Ka'ahumanu Highway 19.

Here is where locals congregate for snorkeling, swimming, diving and winter surfing. Picnic area, but no potable water or flush toilets.

Kohala Coast

Kiholo Bay

Along a four-wheel-drive track off Queen Ka'ahumanu Highway 19.

Draws nude sun-seekers to black-pebble beaches with fish ponds at either end. No facilities.

Anaehoomalu Beach

At the Royal Waikoloan Resort.

Ideal for most watersports, plus there are petroglyph fields and fish ponds nearby. Rest rooms, showers, equipment rental and instruction.

Holoholokai Beach Park

Off Queen Ka'ahumanu Highway 19, near the Ritz-Carlton.

A good surf and snorkel area with adjoining petroglyph park. No facilities.

Hapuna Beach

Off Queen Ka'ahumanu Highway 19, between the Mauna Lani and Mauna Kea Beach resorts.

Not only the best beach in Hawaii but—according to various esteemed sources—the best in the world. Sparkly white sands, shallow tidal pools, and steep cliffs, combined with ideal conditions (in summer) for swimming, surfing, snorkeling, etc., make it a top choice of both visitors and locals. Showers, rest rooms, snack bar, cabins for camping, parking lot and crowds.

THE BIG ISLAND

Kauna'oa Beach

At Mauna Kea Beach Resort.
Another beauty, but beware the high winter surf. Rest rooms, showers.

Samuel M. Spencer Beach Park

Near Kawaihae Harbor.
Offers family frolicking with its white sands and safe swimming. Showers, rest rooms, picnic and camping facilities, tennis courts.

Mahukona Beach Park

Near the Port of Mahukona.
Good for summer snorkeling and diving. Showers, rest rooms, camping area.

Hamakua Coast

Keokea Beach Park

Near the end of Highway 270 and Upolu Point.
Has a kid-friendly protected cove, green lawns and black boulders, and very treacherous winter surf. On hand are rest rooms, showers, picnic facilities and a camping area.

Waipio Valley Beach

Off Highway 240, about eight miles from Honokaa.
Features nasty rips, but gorgeous viewing and picnicking. No facilities are available.

Hilo area

Reeds Bay Beach Park

Near central Hilo.
This is where the towns folk head for calm waters and safe swimming. Showers, rest rooms.

Leleiwi Beach Park

South of downtown.
Good for a variety of watersports such as swimming, snorkeling, board- and body-surfing and net fishing. Picnic facilities, rest rooms, showers.

Onekahakaha Beach Park

A few miles south of Hilo.
Another safe spot with white sands and protected waters. Picnic facilities, lifeguards, showers, rest rooms.

Puna District

MacKenzie State Park

Off Highway 137.
A shady area with dangerous winter surf. Rest rooms, parking, camping area.

Puala' Park

Southeast of Pahoa.
Sports a newer beach with pond swimming. Picnic facilities, portable toilets.

Punaluu Beach Park

On Highway 11, about seven miles past Volcanoes National Park.
A lovely black-sand beach with nearby ancient ruins and fish ponds. Rest rooms.

THE BIG ISLAND

Green Sand Beach (aka Papakolea Beach)

If you have a four-wheel-drive vehicle, head down to this beach and run your toes through green sand. No facilities, hazardous swimming, no protection from sun or wind. How can you resist?

Adventure Guide

The Kona Coast is a favorite spot for snorkelers and scuba divers.

Adventurers get to enjoy the true beauty of the Big Island's natural—and often otherwise inaccessible—attractions. **Hiking and camping** are especially superb, allowing close-up exploration of such sights as active volcanoes and Garden of Eden-like valleys.

In **Hawaii Volcanoes National Park**, the five-mile **Kilauea Iki Trail** leads you through the aftermath of volcanic eruption with not only views of the crater, but a cruise into the crater itself, past steam vents and through the **Thurston Lava Tube**. Other park trails take you to an astounding array of view points and—for those with health and stamina—up to the peak of 13,680-foot **Mauna Loa**. Before embarking on any hike, check in at park headquarters to register your itinerary and inquire about conditions, a precaution that might very well save your life. Also, keep in mind your elevation level. If you experience any altitude problems, start descending at once. For information and permits, contact **Hawaii Volcanoes National Park** *(P.O. Box 52, Volcano 96718,* ☎ *967-7311).*

An easy half-mile loop trail at **Akaka Falls State Park**, north of Hilo, lets you experience not only the 100-foot falls, but luscious rainforest and flora such as plumeria, ginger and birds of paradise. Only diehards should attempt the **Muliwai Trail** into **Waimanu Valley**, about 10 hours each way into an almost-surreal beauty filled with exquisite valleys, waterfalls, views and vegetation. Other trails will spirit you into the moonlike **Kau Desert**, or along remotest coastal regions.

The Big Island offers a huge range of **camping** opportunities. Choose everything from primitive sites to A-frame cabins, along the coast or up a volcano. Campgrounds are administered by the national, state and county parks, and require permits and reservations for overnight camping. For camping at Hawaii Volcanoes National Park, see address above. For information about state parks, contact the **Department of Land and Natural Resources** *(Division of State Parks, Box 936, Hilo 96720,* ☎ *961-7200);* for county parks, contact the **Department of Parks and Recreation** *(County of Hawaii, 25 Aupuni Street, Hilo 96720,* ☎ *961-8311).*

Superb visibility makes Big Island waters a joy for **scuba divers** and **snorkelers**. The Kona Coast affords calm waters, while advanced divers will probably want to drop down deep to explore some of the 60-plus miles of coral around the island. Top **dive sites** include **Red Hill**, south of the Kona Surf Hotel, with caverns, tubes and lots of colorful tropical fish; **Plane Wreck Point**, off Keahole Point, which lets advanced divers get close to a wrecked Beechcraft covered with abundant dish such as fantails and damselfish; **Manta Ray Village**, off Kona Surf Hotel and Keauhou Bay, is your friendly manta-ray feeding ground; and **Aquarium**, in Kealakekua Bay, is a best bet for beginners who can explore in an underwater park filled with friendly fish.

Snorkeling is a year-round sport on the calm western shores with its abundance of marine life. Try **Hookena, Honaunau, Kealakekua, Kahaluu, White Sands, Old Airport, Hapuna** and **Spencer** beach parks and **Kona Coast State Park**. Various operators and dive shops will organize your scuba, snorkeling and even "snuba" excursions, as well as provide equipment.

The Kona Coast is also ideal for year-round **ocean kayaking**. **Kailua** and **Kealakekua** bays are perfect for novices, though advanced types might want to try **Waipio Valley**. **Kailua Bay** is the departure point for soaring **parasailers** while **Anaehoomalu Bay** provides the setting for **wind surfers** with advanced wind surfers opting for **Puako** and **Hilo Bay**. Various **sailing excursions** depart from **Keauhou Bay, Honokohau Harbor, Waikoloa, Kawaihae Harbor**, and **Kailua Pier**.

HAWAII PARKS

From volcanoes to rain forests, Hawaii's geography is extremely diverse. The island chain's national and state parks, as well as its privately owned parks, make the region's diversity available to visitors by foot or car.

THIS SPREAD

NEXT SPREAD

KAUAI

● Lihue

NIIHAU

OA

NA PALI COAST

Kalaau lookout 4,120 ft.

Puu o Kila lookout

Kokee Lodge and Natural History Museum

KOKE'E STATE PARK

Waipao Falls

Puu Lua 3,475 ft.

Puu Hinahina 3,640 ft.

WAIMEA CANYON STATE PARK

Waimea Canyon lookout

550

0   1   2
miles

Waimea River

I'iwi bird

378

Park headquarters

Leleiwi lookout

Holua Cabin

Puu Ulaula Lookout

Kalahaku lookout

Haleakala Visitor Center

Puu Ulaula 10,023 ft.

Sliding Sands Trail

0   1   2
miles

KOKE'E STATE PARK

Koke'e State Park encompasses 4345 acres of rainforest. The park is home to many animals and birds including the bright red I'iwi bird.

MOLOKAI WILDLIFE PARK

Originally containing only antelope, the park now lists giraffe, oryx, eland and ostrich, to only name a few, as its inhabitants. The park now breeds its animals for zoos and is accessible for viewing through park tours.

U.S. Coast Guard Reservation

Kepuhi Beach

Kepuhi

Papohaku Beach

Kakaako Gulch

MOLOKEI RANCH WILDLIFE PARK

Lauhue

Wahiauhue Gulch

460

Maunaloa

0   2   4
miles

Honolulu

MOLOKAI
● Kaunakakai

Silversword

LANAI

Kahului

MAUI

KAHOOLAWE

Silversword Loop

Hanakauhi Peak
▲ 8,907 ft.

Halemauu Trail

■ Paliku Cabin

HALEAKALA NATIONAL PARK

Kaupo Trail

Cinder cone

HALEAKALA NATIONAL PARK

Haleakala is the world's largest dormant volcano. The road leading to the rim is the world's most rapidly ascending, 10,023 feet in just thirty-seven miles. The silversword plant dots the lunar landscape of the volcano.

Fielding THE BIG ISLAND

HAWAII PARKS

PREVIOUS SPREAD

THIS SPREAD

HAWAII VOLCANOES NATIONAL PARK

The park, established in 1916, encompasses two volcanoes—Mauna Loa and Kilauea. The rim of the Kilauea caldera is accessible by car while a trail leads down to the floor of the volcano. The park also contains a rainforest which houses rare birds and flora.

KILAUEA PROFILE

Magma from the earth's mantle rises to a reservoir beneath Kilauea's summit. As pressure builds in this reservoir of molten rock, earthquakes or inflation of the volcano create the possibility of an eruption at the summit or along the rift zone.

THE BIG ISLAND

WAIMEA

Mana Rd.

Kuhio
Village

190

Waimea
-Kohala
Airport

**PARKER
RANCH
VISITOR &
SHOPPING
CENTER,
MUSEUM**

PARKER RANCH

The largest family owned ranch in the U.S.,
Parker ranch is 225,000 acres, with 700
miles of fence enclosing it. In the heart of
Hawaiian cowboy country, the ranch holds
50,000 head of cattle, valleys, pastures
and rniles of sea coast.

KILAUEA

Lookout
shelter

Mauna Loa Rd.

**OLAA
FOREST**

11

130

Kilauea
Visitor
Center

Volcano
Village

Thurston Lava Tube

**PUNA
FOREST
RESERVE**

Jaggar
Museum

vastation
ail

Puhimau Crater

Napau
Crater

Pu'u O'o

Lua Manu
Crater

Pauahi Crater

Ko'oko'olau
Crater

Makopuhi
Crater

EAST   RIFT   ZONE

LAVA FLOW

Kalapana Trail

RIFT   ZONE

Chain of Craters Rd.

**Hilina Pali
Overlook**

Halap
e Trail

Keauho
u Trail

Puna
Coast
Trail

**Road closed
by lava flow**

**Pepeiao
Cabin**

**Ka'aha
Shelter**

**Halape
Shelter**

**Keauhou
Shelter**

PACIFIC OCEAN

THE BIG ISLAND

The Big Island is not especially noteworthy for great **surfing**—the reefs can be dangerous and the surf uninspiring. Try **Wailua** and **Kealakekua** bays, **Kahaluu**, **Lyman's** and **Palm Trees** on the Kona Coast; **Hilo Bay Front Park**, **Keaukaha Beach Park** and **Waipio Valley Beach** on the eastern shores.

What Else to See

Ancient Hawaiian trails along the Kohala Coast take hikers past scenic waterfalls, rain forests and volcanoes.

The **Kona coast**, on the western side of the Big Island, is where most visitors congregate. Aside from the sunny skies and good beaches, the seaside town of **Kailua-Kona** offers requisite tourist delights such as restaurants, cocktail lounges and a barrage of shops and boutiques—most of them centered along Alii Drive. Take a look inside **King Kamehameha's Kona Beach Hotel**, at Alii Drive and Palani Road. There's a shopping mall off the hotel lobby, as well as a small museum displaying Hawaiiana. You can take a tour of **Hulihee Palace** (behind the hotel), the restored 1838 home of Governor John Adams Kuakini and summer home of King David Kalakaua. Across from the palace, the 1836 **Mokualkaua Church** (also called the "Church of the Chimes") is Hawaii's oldest Christian church. **Kailua Pier**, across from the hotel, is the center of water activities and a great place to watch the returning fishing boats around sunset—or to sign up for an excursion on board the **Nautilus Semi-Submersible**, **Atlantis Submarine** or one of the cruises. Pick up high-quality, local arts and crafts at **Kona Arts and Crafts Gallery**, across from the seawall. South of Hualalai Road, **Waterfront Row** houses various popular eateries, including the Chart House, Palm Café and Under the Palm. Most afford spectacular views. **White Sands Beach**, off Alii Drive, is also known as "Disappearing Sands" beach, when late-autumn weather causes the sands to disappear. Nearby **Kahaluu Beach Park** stays put and offers protected swimming in its bay. **St. Peter's Catholic Church**, north of Kahaluu Beach, was built in 1889 and features a distinctive blue tin roof. Just north of Captain Cook, Napoopoo road leads to the **Captain Cook Monument**, where Cook was beaten to death in 1779. Continuing south, you'll reach **City of Refuge National Park**, near Honaunau, with ancient ruins and petroglyphs. At **Ka Lae**, down at the bottom of the island, you'll be positioned at the **southernmost point** in the United States.

Black lava marries glistening beaches up along the **Kohala Coast**, home to the island's very extravagant and expensive resorts. This is where you'll find—almost side by side—the one-more-fabulous-than-the-next mega-resorts such as Mauna Kea Beach Hotel, Ritz-Carlton Mauna Lani, Hilton Waikoloa Village, etc. You can take the inland route all the way up to **Hawi**, passing through some inspiring scenery that encompasses everything from lava fields to cattle ranches, or keep to the coastal (and resort) route. Stop for a tour of the **Natural Energy Lab of Hawaiian Authority**, near the Keahole-Kona Airport, or take a stroll at sunny **Wawaloli Beach Park**. Nearby **Kona Coast State Park** offers lava-field scenery, and **Anaehoomalu Bay** (near the royal Waikoloan) shelters ancient **royal fish ponds**. Near the Ritz-Carlton Mauna Lani, stop to explore the **Puako Petroglyph Archaeological Park** with its 400-year-old stone carvings. **Hapuna Beach State Park** is reputedly the most wonderful beach on the planet! In Mahukona, take a free tour of an ancient Hawaiian fishing village at **Lapakahi State Historical Park**. Rounding the Big

Island's northern tip and heading down the **Hamakua Coast**, you'll find a statue of **Kamehameha the Great**, in front of the Kapauu Courthouse. At the end
of Highway 270, in Makapala, don't miss the fabulous view from **Pololu Valley Lookout**. If you have the time, take the trail down to the black-sand beach.

In the ranching region of **Waimea**, you'll find "Parker Ranch" on just about
every building. Find out all about these illustrious Parkers at the **Parker
Ranch Visitor Center and Museum**, then do some shopping over at **Parker
Square**, then visit the 1897 **Hale Kea**, home of a past Parker Ranch manager.
Sick of the Parkers? The privately owned **Kamuela Museum** is filled with stim-
ulating, offbeat memorabilia.

In **Hilo**, you'll find the tourist-oriented hotels over on **Banyan Drive**, planted
with celebrity-planted banyan trees. Bask in garden glory at **Hilo Orchidarium**,
on Manono Street, and **Liliuokalani Gardens**, at the end of Banyan Drive.
More flowers, as well as fruit, produce and locally made goods, are for sale at
Hilo Farmers Market, at Kamehameha Avenue and Mamo Street. At **Wailuku
River State Park**, catch the sunrise over **Rainbow Falls**. Or hit Saddle Road,
and head up to **Mauna Kea**. Attractions south of town are **Nani Maui Gardens**
and **Panaewa Rainforest Zoo**.

North of Hilo, the **Mamalahoa Highway** highlights local color as you cruise up
the coast to sights such as **Hawaii Tropical Botanical Gardens**, **Akaka Falls State
Park**, **Kolekole** and **Laupahoehoe beach parks**, **Macadamia Nut Plantation** and—
finally—to **Waipio Valley**, just beyond Kukuihaele, where you can view exquisite natural beauty and ancient ruins.

Traveling down the island, south of Hilo, **Hawaii Volcanoes National Park**—
home of **Kilauea** (where the goddess Pele dwells) and **Mauna Loa** (the earth's
largest mountain, when measured from the ocean floor)—will capture your
attention. Continue south to run your toes in **Punaluu Black Sand Beach**, at
Punaluu, and **Green Sand Beach**, on Mahana Bay. A few miles more and
you're back at **Ka Lae**, that most southern point in the United States.

Hamakua Coast

Hamakua Coast

Hiking

Kalopa State Recreation Area   ★★★★

Five miles southeast of Honokaa, Hamakua Coast.

This recently renovated, scenic campground in a 100-acre native *ohia* forest preserve on the Hamakua Coast has reopened with improved camping and recreational
facilities. Now you'll find more parking, handicapped-accessible pathways and rest
rooms. Three new campsites take up to four people each. Nature trails, including a
circular trail through the koa and eucalyptus trees of Mauna Kea Forest, have been
upgraded, and a new two-mile horseback riding loop trail has been added. For
camping permits, call the Division of State Parks at ☎ *(808) 933-4200.*

Honokaa

Beaches

Laupahoehoe Point Beach Park ★★★

Highway 19 on the Hamakua Coast, Honokaa.

The "point" here is a lava finger jutting out over a crashing sea with a designated county camping area that's wildly beautiful but windy. Laupahoehoe is perfect for fishing, picnicking and woolgathering. Not so for swimming or snorkeling. A memorial at the ocean's edge was erected in memory of 20 children and their teachers killed in 1946 when a tsunami (tidal wave) destroyed their schoolhouse situated nearby. General admission: $1.

Tours

Paniolo Riding Adventures ★★★

P.O. Box 363, Honokaa, 96727, ☎ *(808) 889-5354.*

Paniolo Riding Adventures offers open range-riding on the 11,000-acre Ponoholo working cattle ranch in the Kohala Mountains. Depending on experience, riders can walk, trot or canter through lush pasturelands with breathtaking views. The company guarantees there will be "no mosquitoes." The 2.5-hour or four-hour rides include a 15-minute rest stop at the ruins of an ancient Hawaiian village or a native *ohia* grove. Bring your own snacks. Children must be eight years or older. General admission: $70–$100.

Waipi'o Na'alapa Trail Rides ★★★

P.O. Box 992, Honokaa, 96727, ☎ *(808) 775-0419.*

Experienced guides take riders on two-hour horseback rides through Waipio Valley, clip-clopping along waterfalls, jungle trails, taro patches and historical, spiritual places. Trips at 9:30 a.m. and 1 p.m. Reservations must be made by 4:30 p.m. the day prior to trip. Cancellations can occur due to rain. No children under eight or riders over 250 pounds. General admission: $75.

Papaikou

Parks and Gardens

Hawaii Tropical Botanical Garden ★★★

Rural Route 143A, Papaikou, 96781, ☎ *(808) 964-5233.*
Hours: 8:30 a.m.–5 p.m.

The Hawaii Tropical Botanic Gardens is a 45-acre forest preserve at Onomea Bay, a former sugar port. Visitors walk on scenic paths marked by palms, heliconia, bromeliads and fruit trees from around the world. A van shuttles visitors to the preserve every 20 minutes; purchase tickets at a converted yellow church seven miles north of Hilo. The coastal road to the church is well-marked. General admission: $12.

Waipio Valley

Hiking

Waimanu Valley ★★★

Highway 19 from Honokaa to Route 240, Waipio Valley.

Adjacent to Waipio Valley, it's a seven-hour hike (nine miles each way!) to this primeval valley. The trailhead starts from the Waipio Valley lookout pavilion and con-

THE BIG ISLAND

tinues and continues and continues through lots of difficult switchbacks up 1200 feet to Waipio's Northwest wall. The intrepid will be rewarded with the ultimate in seclusion. Rated as one of the three top hikes in Hawaii. Only for experienced hikers in good condition.

Waipio Valley   ★★★★

10 miles north of Honokaa, on Highway 240, Waipio Valley.

Hiking, unofficial camping and a broad, black-sand beach draw people to the historic, atmospheric Waipio Valley. The beach is the largest on the island, one mile wide and six miles long. Also referred to as the Valley of Kings, it was a favorite spot for Hawaiian royalty. Some 50 people still live here, raising taro, catching fish and running a couple of rustic hotels. Because of a stream entering the ocean here, you have a choice of fresh- or salt-water swimming. The beach has underwater boulders, and rip currents make ocean swimming dangerous, but fishing is great. The valley, reached by a narrow, steep, unpaved road, is subject to flooding and is accessible only to hikers or by those with four-wheel-drive vehicles. No facilities. Directions: Take Highway 19 north to Honokaa and pick up Route 240 to Waipio Valley State Park Lookout. If you don't want to drive or hike yourself, contact Waipio Valley Shuttle at ☎ *(808) 775-7121*. This company conducts excellent guided tours for $31.20 per person that leave every hour daily from 8 a.m.–4 p.m.

Tours

Waipio Valley Wagon Tours   ★★★★

Waipio Valley Lookout, Highway 240, Waipio Valley, ☎ *(808) 775-9518.*

Tour Waipio Valley in a covered mule-drawn wagon. Your guide will inform you about the history of the area, where thousands of ancient Hawaiians lived, raising vast amounts of taro and other crops. Royalty also loved to vacation here. Don't forget your video camera or camera. This company claims that "cushioned seats, spring suspension designed by the Amish combined with shock absorbers provided by GM make for a fabulously smooth ride." Tours last 1.5 hours and leave at 9:30 and 11:30 a.m. and 1:30 and 3:30 p.m. daily. Meet at the Waipio Valley Lookout and be transported via four-wheel-drive vehicle to the valley. Reservations required. General admission: $40.

Hilo

Wailoa Center   ★★

75 Aupuni Street, Hilo, 96720, ☎ *(808) 933-4360.*

Hours: 8 a.m.–4:30 p.m.

Special hours: Noon-4:30 p.m. Wed., 9 a.m.–3 p.m., Sat. Closed: Sun.

Revolving exhibits of Big Island art are featured in the gallery of this state-run cultural center.

Beaches

Coconut Island Beach Park   ★★

Hilo Bay, Hilo, 96720, ☎ *(808) 961-8311.*

Located over a bridge from Liliuokalani Gardens, Coconut Island Beach Park is a lovely setting for a family picnic or some low-key fishing. There's a diving tower and a naturally sheltered pool for kids. Facilities include a parking lot and pavilion with restrooms.

City Celebrations

Hilo Mardi Gras Festival   ★ ★ ★ ★

c/o Main Street Program, 252 Kamehameha Avenue, Hilo, 96720, ☎ *(808) 935-8850.*
Like its namesake in 'Nawlins, Hilo's Mardi Gras features a big parade with floats, crowning of a king and queen, music, decorative umbrella (yes), bicycle and costume contests, ethnic food booths and street fun held downtown every February. Each year a particular float stands out, such as one created by a local nursing home called "Heaven Can Wait." It all started as a neighborhood block party by New Orleans native Andre Oliver, the late owner of Roussel's restaurant, and local merchants. Unlike the Big Easy fete, this one is family-oriented, alcohol-free and "generally" unrowdy.

Merrie Monarch Festival   ★ ★ ★

Edith Kanakaole Auditorium, Hilo, ☎ *(808) 935-9168.*
An annual weeklong event, beginning on Easter Sunday, the festivities honor King David Kalakaua, a gifted musician who composed songs and created hulas. An impressive hula competition, which is the most prestigious in the state, is presented on the last three nights. Not surprisingly, the town is packed at this time. Call for prices and schedules of events.

Fun For Free

Suisan Fish Market and Auction   ★ ★

85 Lihiwai Street, Hilo, 96720, ☎ *(808) 935-9349.*
Hours: 8 a.m.–early afternoon
Watch famous chefs and restaurant suppliers bid for the day's freshest catches, including marlin, tuna and broadbill swordfish. Fishmarket for consumers next door.

Historical Sites

Palace Theater   ★ ★ ★

Corner of Kamehameha Avenue and Haili Street, Hilo, ☎ *(808) 935-8850.*
This gracious art deco building, built in 1925, was the first deluxe playhouse on the Big Island. It was owned by Adam Baker, son of the last royal governor of the island of Hawaii. The facade was restored in 1990, and at present work is continuing on the spacious interior, which includes an 800-seat auditorium. Ambitious plans are under way to use it as a movie theater and community performing arts center.

S. Hata Building   ★ ★ ★

Furneaux Lane and Kamehameha Avenue, Hilo.
Now a shopping, office and restaurant complex, this Renaissance revival building was constructed by the Hata family in 1912. Later confiscated by the U.S. government in World War II, it was returned to the family when one of the original owners' daughters bought it back from the government for $100,000 after the war.

Museums and Exhibits

Lyman Mission House and Museum   ★★★

276 Haili Street, Hilo, 96720, ☎ *(808) 935-5021.*

Hours: 9 a.m.–5 p.m.

Special hours: Sun. 1–4 p.m.

Descendants of David and Sarah Lyman, Hilo's first Christian missionaries, converted this 1830s home into a museum. The handmade furniture, quilts and other personal items evoke a sense of simplicity and self-sufficiency that is sorely lacking today. The house is on the National Register of Historic Places. Next door is a modern museum, opened in 1973, housing a valuable and extensive library of Hawaiiana and a worldwide collection of gems and minerals. General admission: $4.50.

Parks and Gardens

Akaka Falls State Park   ★★★

Highway 19, Hilo, 96720.

This well-maintained state park with a clearly marked trail encompasses 66 Eden-like acres, scented with wild ginger, tropical trees, plants and flowers. The circular trail loops past two falls: Kahuna and Akaka. Akaka falls 420 feet into a mountain pool. On the trail to the falls, you'll be dwarfed by the vegetation. Torch ginger plants can grow up to 15 feet. It's an easy but sometimes slippery walk for the whole family. There's a paved parking lot and public rest rooms.

Liliuokalani Gardens   ★★★

Banyan Drive, Hilo, 96720.

Located off of Banyan Drive, Hilo's main drag, this stately, 30-acre Oriental garden is the largest of its kind outside of Japan. The manicured walkways, pagodas and little bridges make a perfect backdrop for wedding pictures.

Nani Mau Gardens   ★★

421 Makalika Street, one mile off Highway 11, Hilo, 96720, ☎ *(808) 959-3541.*

Hours: 8 a.m.–5 p.m.

This 20-acre botanical garden in the middle of a rainforest bursts with color and about 100 varieties of tropical fruit trees, and 2000 varieties of ginger, orchids and anthuriums. A Hawaiian plant museum, ponds and waterfalls can also be explored on self-guided tours, although guided tours are available by reservation. Restaurants, gift shops and picnic pavilions. General admission: $5.

Rainbow Falls and Boiling Pots   ★★

Off Wainuenue Avenue on Rainbow Drive, outside Hilo.

The clearly marked trails to the falls are just a short distance out of Hilo. Best time for viewing the rainbows are on a clear morning when the sun shines on the water. If you turn left instead of right on the way to Rainbow Falls, drive to the lookout and see a remarkable series of pot-shaped depressions in the lava riverbed. When the river is high these "pots" seem to boil over with turbulent water. Absolutely no swimming.

The Shows

East Hawaii Cultural Center ★★★

141 Kalakaua Street, Hilo, 96721, ☎ (808) 961-5711.
Hours: 9 a.m.–4 p.m.

Both an historical site and a cultural attraction, the East Hawaii Cultural Center, completed in 1932, is on the National Register of Historic Places. Resembling a Hawaiian *hale* (house) of the 1800s era with a hipped roof, it served as headquarters for the Hilo County Police Department until 1975. Now home to Hilo Community Players, it's also an art gallery with regular exhibits by local and international artists. The Bard comes to Hilo in July when the HCP puts on "Shakespeare in the Park."

Tours

Mauna Loa Macadamia Nut Factory ★★★

Just outside Hilo off Highway 11, Hilo, 96720, ☎ (808) 966-8612.
Hours: 7:30 a.m.–4 p.m.

Learn how these delicious, fattening and hard-to-crack nuts are grown, harvested and processed. The road to the plant is lined with three miles of macadamia nut orchards, in all about 160,000 trees. After an obligatory video program, you look through large windows to observe workers cracking, weighing and eventually packing the nuts. Best of all is the chocolate-covering phase. Then you'll be ready for the free samples. A gift shop, snack and espresso bar provide further refreshment. Work it all off outdoors on the garden nature trail.

Ka'u

Naalehu

Beaches

Mahana Bay ★★

2.5 miles northeast of Kaulana Boat Ramp, Naalehu.

Three miles from the southernmost tip of the United States is this rare green-sand beach, made from crushed volcanic olivine crystals and lava. It's reached via a hot, three-mile hike from the nearest paved road. There's no fresh water or shade, and swimming can be treacherous because of a severe undertow. Yet it's a stunning, stark place to be alone. Directions: From Highway 11 (Hawaii Belt Road) take South Point Road. Near its end, take the left fork until the road becomes a rutted, dirt path. Use four-wheel-drive only, or walk 30–45 minutes.

Kona

Kailua-Kona

Beaches

Disappearing Sands Beach ★★★

Ali'i Drive, Kailua-Kona, 96740, ☎ (808) 961-8311.

So-called because the white-sand beach gets washed away in winter during periods of high surf, when all you will see is rocks. Good for swimming in summer months, intermediate bodysurfing. A lifeguard is on hand. Phones, showers, parking.

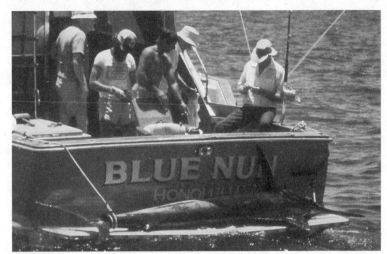

The Hawaii International Billfish Tournament held in early August reels in anglers from all over the world.

City Celebrations

Hawaiian International Billfish Tournament   ★★★

Kailua-Kona, various locations, Kailua-Kona, ☎ (808) 329-6155.

Late July-early August. This is the world's premier international marlin fishing tournament. Expect plenty of revelry, backslapping and camera clicking as the big ones are weighed in direct from the boats.

Kona Coffee Cultural Festival   ★★★

Various locations, Kailua-Kona, ☎ (808) 326-7820.

This two-week fest honoring Kona and the Big Island's most popular crop runs from late October through early November. Events and happenings include agricultural exhibits, a recipe and coffee-picking contest, parade, food and craft booths, hula festival and lively local entertainment.

Fun For Free

Hulihee Palace Concert Series   ★★★

75-5718 Ali'i Drive, Kailua-Kona, 96720, ☎ (808) 329-1877.

Hawaiian music concerts are held on the grounds of the historic Hulihee Palace in Kailua-Kona every fourth Sunday of the month, except June and December. A favorite local event.

The Kona Brewing Company   ★★

75-5629 Kuakini Highway, Kailua-Kona, 96740, ☎ (808) 334-1133.

Hours: 3–5 p.m.

Had enough coffee yet? Caffeine heads can chill out, at least briefly, by taking a free 15-minute tour of the island's first microbrewery, located in the old West Hawaii

Print Building. Afterward, purchase a six-pack or a case or more of the company's two handcrafted brewski varieties, Fire Rock Pale Ale or Pacific Golden Ale.

Historical Sites

Ahuena Heiau ★★★

At the end of Kailua Pier, Kailua-Kona.
This magnificently restored temple was the center of political power in the Hawaiian kingdom during Kamehameha the Great's heydey from 1812–1819. The king and his highest court advisers met here nightly; the monarch also died here on May 8, 1819. Shortly afterward, his son Liholiho (Kam II) abolished the ancient *kapu* system. The first Christian missionaries from New England were granted permission to come ashore here on April 4, 1820. Visitors are not permitted inside the temple.

Kaloko-Honokohau National Historic Park ★★★

73-4786 Kanalani Street, Building 14, Kailua-Kona, 96740, *(808) 329-6881. Hours: 7:30 a.m.–4 p.m.*
A settlement for Hawaiians until the 19th century, this 1300-acre park harbors more than 200 archaeological treasures, including Hawaiian gravesites, fishing shrines, canoe landings, petroglyphs, *heiaus* (temples) and achialine ponds.

Mokuaikaua Church ★★

Ali'i Drive, across from Hulihee Palace, Kailua-Kona.
This lava-rock and crushed-coral church located directly across Ali'i Drive is the first Christian church built in the state. Construction started in 1820 and was finished 17 years later by Hawaii's first band of missionaries. It boasts a stunning *ohia* and koa wood interior and is still used for services.

The Kona Inn Shopping Village ★★

75-5744 Ali'i Drive, Kailua-Kona, 96740. Hours: 9 a.m.–9 p.m.
Once a low-key old Hawaiian-style resort, the Old Kona Inn was built in 1929 and has been gentrified into a shopping and restaurant complex. Aside from its preservation of the past, the hotel was built on the grounds of the personal *heiau* (temple) and living quarters of King Kam II. Some say the rocks of the *heiau* can be seen on the large oceanside lawn. The seawall here is one of the best picnic spots in town. Pop into the restaurant for fish displays that include mako shark and Pacific blue marlin.

Museums and Exhibits

Astronaut Ellison S. Onizuka Space Center ★★★

Keahole-Kona Airport, Kailua-Kona, 96745, *(808) 329-3441. Hours: 8:30 a.m.–4:30 p.m.*
Launch a 12-inch model of a space shuttle, fiddle with the interactive displays or watch NASA space videos in this aerospace museum dedicated to Big Island native Ellison S. Onizuka, Hawaii's first astronaut, who died in the Challenger explosion. General admission: $2.

Hulihee Palace ★★★★

75-5718 Ali'i Drive, Kailua-Kona, 96740, *(808) 329-1874. Hours: 9 a.m.–4 p.m.*

THE BIG ISLAND

Hulihee Palace in Kailua, Hawaii is one of three royal palaces in the United States. It is constructed of lava rock, coral, koa and ohia timbers.

One of only three royal palaces in the United States, this two-story, modified Georgian style building was a vacation retreat for King Kalakaua and other royals until 1914. Originally built for Gov. John Adams Kuakini in 1838, Hulihee Palace is constructed of native lava rock, coral, koa and *ohia* timbers. It was restored in 1927 by the Daughters of Hawaii, who now operate it as a museum. The entry hall features photos, portraits and furnishings. Collections include beautiful Hawaiian quilts, tapa cloths, calabash bowls and featherwork. The palace is also a center of Hawaiian music, hula and culture. An award-winning hula *halau* rehearses on the grounds many weekday afternoons. The Hulihee Palace Concert Series, a free outdoor Hawaiian music concert, is held on the fourth Sunday of the month (except June-December). Open from 10 a.m.–3 p.m. on Saturday and Sunday. Senior admission, $3; $1 for children ages 11 through 18; 50 cents for children ages seven through 10; free for children ages six and younger. General admission: $4.

Tours

Atlantis Submarines   ★★★

Leaves from King Kamehameha's Kona Beach Hotel, Kailua-Kona, 96740, ☎ (808) 329-3175.

Hours: 10 a.m.–3 p.m.

Make like Captain Nemo and his crew and explore Hawaii's thrilling underwater world without getting wet. This 80-ton sub is air-conditioned and features bench seating with 26-inch "viewports." The crew narrates the action during the 45-minute ride. Two expeditions are offered; the Expedition Adventure is a 100-foot dive with entertainment provided by a scuba team. This extended coastal cruise has views and narration of Kona's historic sites. A special, low-priced Discovery Adventure is of shorter duration, and seating is limited. Children ages 12 and under; $39. Must be three-feet-tall to ride. General admission: $69–$79.

Benchmark Flight Center ★★★
Leaves from the Kona Airport, Kailua-Kona, ☎ (808) 969-2000.

If you always wanted to learn to fly but were too chicken or too cheap to get a license, try this "One Time" flight lesson offered by the Big Island's only FAA-certified flight school. The experienced pilots will run you through a preflight orientation in one of their four-passenger aircraft; once up in the air, you are handed the controls. The experience is guaranteed not to be boring: you'll be soaring above an active volcano, a pristine rainforest or a plunging waterfall. At the conclusion, you get a flight logbook and a "Flight Adventure" certificate; time goes towards your private pilot's license. Your instructor will also critique your performance. Bring a buddy. Cost is $139. Also offered are 45-minute to two-hour air tours from both Kona and Hilo. This company is permitted to fly at the lowest altitudes permitted by the FAA. The pilots claim a 100 percent accident-free record. Just thought you might like to know. General admission: $69–$169.

Big Island Air ★★★
Kona Airport, Kailua-Kona, ☎ (800) 303-8868.

This company specializes in flying over active volcanoes from twin-engine, 9-15 passenger aircraft. Flights leave several times daily from Kona Airport. Itineraries include the Super Saver; for $99, you'll fly directly to whatever is active, including the Pu'u O'o vent in Hawaii Volcanoes National Park. This one-hour tour leaves daily at 6:30 a.m. If you don't want to get up quite so early, the 1.5-hour Sunset Tour ($149) is much the same, but is dramatically accented by a brilliant Kona sunset. Also complete island flyovers, which include 266 miles of coastline. Private charters available. General admission: $99–$169.

Classic Aviation Corporation Biplane Tours ★★★
P.O. Box 1899, Kailua-Kona, 96745, ☎ (808) 329-8687.

Perform loops, rolls, figure eights and more in an open-cockpit biplane and live to tell the grandkids. Also go back to the golden era of aviation circa 1930, dressed in a white-silk scarf and goggles while you take the stick for some light stunts (the pilot does the takeoffs and landings). Or just take it easy, sit back and fly over the Kona or Kohala Coast, the Volcano area. Classic Aviation also takes you over the luxury resorts. Ride lengths vary from 25 to 60 minutes, minimum two passengers. Reservations required. General admission: $65–$250.

Hawaii Forest and Trails ★★★★
P.O. Box 2975, Kailua-Kona, 96745, ☎ (808) 322-8881.

Renowned naturalist Rob Pacheco leads guided birding expeditions to remote wilderness locations on the Big Island, where the sheer number of native forest birds is astounding. Most tours are on private lands, where individuals have no access. Highly recommended. Rates include transportation, continental breakfast, lunch and gear. Higher rate above is for a family or group rate, six maximum per party. Children 13–17, $95; four–12, $65. Ask about overnight expeditions and rainforest tours. General admission: $119–$549.

Hawaiian Helicopters   ★★★

Departs from Kona Airport, Kailua-Kona, ☎ *(808) 877-3900.*

These are no ordinary air tours. Passengers board luxury Astar touring helicopters that feature 180-degree views from all seats, a "total recall" video system, four independently mounted cameras, a CD-audio system and choreographed music. Everyone's "oohs and aahs" are recorded on video for a fond souvenir after each flight. Pickup is from Kona or Hilo Airport. Four tours are offered; the most expensive is the "Kona Island Special," which includes Hilo, the waterfalls along the Hamakua Coast and Kilauea Crater's Pu'u O'o vent, where molten lava flows along its surface. Reservations required. General admission: $115–$249.

Kenai Helicopters Hawaii   ★★★

P.O. Box 4118, Kailua-Kona, 96745, ☎ *(808) 885-5833.*

This experienced company (25 years) specializes in flight-seeing excursions over volcanic hotspots, currently the Pu'u O'o vent, the site of Kilauea's most-frequent eruptions. You may actually see new coastal areas forming on the island. Also offered is a tour along the less geologically active North Kohala coast. Adventures run from 45-105 minutes. Reservations from the mainland: ☎ *(800) 622-3144.* General admission: $129–$302.

Kona Walking Tours   ★★★

From the King Kam Hotel, Kailua-Kona, ☎ *(808) 232-2005.*
Hours: 8:30 a.m.–10:30 a.m.

Educational tours are led by longtime local residents familiar with the culture, color and history of Kona. The 1.5-hour tour begins on the grounds of the King Kam Hotel with its own archaeological sites, and restored *heiau,* and wanders through the Village along Alii Drive as far as Hale Halawai, ending on the grounds of the Hulihe'e Palace. Running commentary includes stories of King Kam's last seat of government in Kona, stories of the royal family's summer palace, the arrival of the missionaries and Kona's early cattle and coffee industries. The higher fee includes a tour of Hulihee Palace. Reservations can be made at the Historical Society from 8 a.m.–4 p.m., or at the Hulihe'e Palace Gift Shop at 75-5718 Alii Drive from 9 a.m.– 4 p.m. General admission: $10–$14.

Nautilus Semi-Submersibles   ★★★

57-5663 Palani Road, across street from Kailua Pier, Kailua-Kona, ☎ *(808) 326-2003.*

This 58-foot boat, unlike the submarine that it resembles, doesn't submerge. It's also a lot less expensive than a sub, and no one has to fight for access to a large viewing window. Guests can also ride topside. The show consists of professional divers leaping into the water and coaxing the fish to come to them, and bringing them directly to the windows. The most-popular critters, especially with kids, are the octopi and spiny sea urchins. Seniors, $28.95; children, $24.95. Ages three and under, free. Leaves daily at 9:30, 10:30 and 11:30 a.m.; and 1:30 and 2:30 p.m. General admission: $39.95.

NavaTrek Explorer Captain Cook Cruise   ★★★

Kailua-Kona Pier, Kailua-Kona, ☎ *(808) 326-2999.*

The NavaTrek *Explorer*, the largest American-made rigid inflatable boat, offers snorkeling tours of Kealakekua Bay and the Captain Cook monument, which can only be reached by sea. Operated by Royal Hawaiian cruises, the craft is staffed by a three-man crew and carries 49 passengers. Very comfortable for what it is, the boat features a shade canopy, rest room and freshwater showers. Seating is on raised bleachers, backseat rails or directly on the edge of the tube. It travels up to 30 knots and has great maneuverability. Passengers are picked up from various locations and transported to the reservation center near Kailua Pier for breakfast, followed by a four-hour snorkeling trip to Kealakekua Bay, with snorkel gear, lunch and return trip to hotels included. Admission for children ages four through 12 is $65. General admission: $85.

Paradise Safaris   ★ ★ ★ ★

P.O. Box 9027, Kailua-Kona, 96745, ☎ (808) 322-2366.
Hours: 7 a.m.–10 p.m.
Just before sunset, Pat Wright takes visitors on stargazing treks to the 13,796-foot summit outside the Mauna Kea Observatory via a four-wheel-drive wagon. There'll be ample time for photos before sunset transforms the area into an eerie, unearthly spectacle. After sunset, everyone moves to mid-mountain, where the night sky is explored with a large portable telescope and giant binoculars. A welcome supper of hot soup and sandwiches will be provided, as the average temperature is 30 degrees Fahrenheit, with high wind conditions. Warm, hooded parkas are also thoughtfully supplied. Pregnant women, people with heart or lung conditions, scuba or snuba divers and children under 13 are discouraged from taking the trip. No alcohol, please. General admission: $110.

Mauna Kea/Saddle Road

Mauna Kea State Park

THE BIG ISLAND

Waikoloa Beach Park stretches between ancient fish ponds and the ocean. The calm lagoon is safe for swimming when other beaches are not.

Parks and Gardens

Mauna Kea State Park   ★★★

Saddle Road, 33 miles out of Hilo, Mauna Kea State Park, ☎ *(808) 961-7200.*

There are seven cabins available at this park, which is 6500 feet above sea level. Bird-watchers love it. Contact the Department of Land and Natural Resources at ☎ *(808) 961-7200* for a permit. General admission: $8–$10.

Tours

Mauna Kea Observatory   ★★★★

Saddle Road (Highway 200) to 9200 foot elevation, Mauna Kea State Park, ☎ *(808) 961-2180.*

Special hours: hours vary. Closed: Tues., Wed., Thur.

Located 27 miles out of Hilo at the 9000-foot elevation of Mauna Kea Volcano, the Ellison Onizuka Visitors Center offers graphic displays of why the 13,796-foot sum-mit of the mountain provides the finest conditions for astronomical research. Open Friday from 1 to 5 p.m.; Saturday and Sunday from 8 a.m. to noon, 1 to 2 p.m., and 4 to 5 p.m. The Observatory, which can be visited on Saturdays and Sundays, is one of the island's greatest free attractions, if you can get to it. Meet the guide at the Onizuka Center at 1:30 pm. Four-wheel-drive vehicles are required for trips to the summit. People with heart or lung conditions and pregnant women are discouraged from making the trek. For information, contact **Mauna Kea Support Services**, at *177 Maka'ala Street, Hilo, Hawaii 96720.*

North Kohala

Kapa'au

Beaches

Keokea Beach Park   ★★

On the way to Pololu Lookout from Kapa'au, Kapa'au.

On weekdays you may have this beach that's on the way to Pololu Valley Lookout all to yourself. Decidedly unflashy, it's still a nice place to go for a picnic, with tables facing the ocean. Plenty of facilities, including showers and a covered pavilion.

Pololu Valley Lookout   ★★★★

At the end of Highway 270, Kapa'au.

This gorgeous vantage point overlooks a deserted valley that was once inhabited and lush with taro. It attracts fishermen and campers who want to be left alone. The hike to the valley and the black-sand beach takes about 15 minutes on a trail that can be slippery after recent rains. Not advisable for swimming, due to frequent rip-tides.

Historical Sites

Kalahikiola Congregational Church   ★★★

Highway 270, Kapa'au.

This historic white stone church was built in 1855 by Protestant missionary the Rev. Elias Bond, who is credited with bringing Christianity to Hawaiians living in the Kohala District. Bond served for 55 years as a teacher, postmaster, surveyor and supervisor of roads, something like Molokai's Blessed Damien. Nearby is Bond's home, constructed between 1839 and 1889, where he and his wife and 10 children lived. You can visit the carriage house, carpenter shop, tack room, stable, chicken house and washhouse. The estate also encompasses the old Kohala Girls' School, which Bond founded for native girls in 1874. It's now a ramshackle hotel that's on the National Historic Register.

Tours

Kohala Carriages, Ltd. ★★★

P.O. Box 1437, Kapa'au, 96755, ☎ (808) 889-5955.
Tour the back roads of North Kohala on a horse-drawn carriage. This low-key, romantic excursion ends with an outdoor picnic lunch in a secret spot. One- and 2.5-hour tours available. General admission: $15–$35.

Kawaihae

Historical Sites

Lapakahi State Historical Park ★★★

Highway 270, between Kawaihae and Mahukona, Kawaihae, 96743, ☎ (808) 889-5566.
Hours: 8 a.m.–4 p.m.
Take a self-guided tour to an ancient Hawaiian fishing village, which flourished long before the arrival of Westerners. The spot was chosen because the coral beach was one of the few places along this coast where canoes could be brought ashore year-round. Among the most interesting sights is a small shrine where fishermen sacrificed part of their catch to the fishing god, Ku'ula. It's easy to envision how villagers went about their daily lives; found among the stones are game boards that were used to play a native game of chess. The rock walls of the partially restored house sites enclose remnants of cooking pits and family shrines. Even if you're not an archaeology buff, the walk on the hour-long trail is a very pleasant one.

Pu'ukohola Heiau National Historic Site ★★★

P.O. Box 4963, Kawaihae, 96743, ☎ (808) 882-7218.
Hours: 7:30 a.m.–4 p.m.
Located a few miles south of Kawaihae on the Kohala coast, this temple honoring the war god Kuka'ilimoku was rebuilt by Kamehameha the Great in 1791. He was advised that doing so would guarantee his eventual domination of all the islands, which eventually came to pass. He personally led the work force of thousands who built the immense, lava-stone structure on top of Pu'ukohola hill overlooking the Pacific. Only the platform remains, but efforts are being made to preserve and restore the landmark. For two days in August, a cultural festival is held at the site, featuring Hawaiian food-tasting, arts and crafts workshops, ancient hula and other cultural demonstrations.

Kohala Ranch

Tours

Kohala Naalapa Trail Rides ★★★

Kohala Ranch on Highway 270, Kohala Ranch, ☎ (808) 889-0022.

This scenic horseback ride meanders through historic Kahua and Kohala ranches. You'll pass cinder cones, ancient Hawaiian ruins and lush pastures with sheep and cattle. Rides daily at 9 a.m. and 1 p.m. No children under eight or riders over 250 pounds. Reservations 24 hours in advance. General admission: $50–$65.

Puna

Pahoa

Parks and Gardens

Lava Tree State Monument   ★★★

Three miles down Route 132, Pahoa.

This ghostly state park was created after the 1790 eruption of Mauna Loa. Hot lava surrounded the fragile *ohia* trees that once stood here, leaving twisted, white molds that stand 12 feet high. You'll find a black-sand beach down a nearby lava rock trail. Turn your vehicle around about three miles back and explore Pahoa, a one-horse town with a raised wooden sidewalk and false-front shops.

Puna

Beaches

Cape Kumukahi   ★★★★

Highway 132, Puna.

A dramatic drive down Highway 132 to the easternmost cape in the state. Highlights include a series of relatively new lava flows, each marked with a date. At the end of the highway is a lonely lighthouse, the only thing left standing after a 1960 lava flow decimated the village of Kapoho. Legends say it was spared by Madame Pele (the goddess of fire), who had been well-treated by the keeper. You can see how the lava flow split to spare the lighthouse. All the buildings around it were destroyed. Continue on highway 137 to Kaimu for a series of black-sand beaches. The ebony grains are created by the fiery meeting of hot lava and cold ocean waters. The lava is broken into minuscule bits by steam explosions, then ground and polished to grains of sand by constant wave activity. The first is Isaac Hale Beach Park, which is well-serviced and has good swimming. Mackenzie State Park is next, offering excellent fishing but dangerous swimming. Kehena is a small, fairly inaccessible black-sand beach popular with nudists. Connect to Highway 130 from Kaimu Beach, a lovely, wild picnic spot (forget about swimming) to what was once Kalapana, site of a housing development and much-missed beach, which was covered over by lava and reclaimed by Pele in 1983.

South Kohala

Kamuela

City Celebrations

Parker Ranch Rodeo and Horse Races   ★★

Paniolo Park, Kamuela, ☎ *(808) 885-7655.*

Held in July, this authentic rodeo on one of the largest private cattle ranches in the country features bareback bronc and bull riding, plus Hawaiian Poo Wai U, or roping and tying wild cattle on the open range.

Waimea Cherry Blossom Festival   ★★
Church Row Park, Kamuela, ☎ *(808) 935-5068.*
Hours: 9 a.m.–2 p.m.
A lovely, low-key festival that takes place each February and March in Waimea-Kamuela, home of the Parker Ranch. It's known in these parts as "Hanami," which translates as "a viewing of the flowers of spring." Imported Formosan and Okinawan cherry trees bloom with light- and dark-pink blossoms at Church Row Park. Celebrations include Japanese tea ceremonies, ikebana demonstrations, and art and photo displays. Local specialties are prepared, including teriyaki, saimin, plate lunches and bento boxes, as well as mochi ice cream and manju (both made from azuki bean paste) for dessert.

Museums and Exhibits

Kamuela Museum   ★★
Waimea-Kamuela Junction, Routes 19 & 250, Kamuela, 96743, ☎ *(808) 885-4724.*
Hours: 8 a.m.–5 p.m.
Known for its collection of Hawaiian, European and Oriental artifacts, including royal Hawaiian treasures from Iolani Palace, this is the largest private museum in the state. Take a guided tour with owners Albert and Harriet Solomon (she's a direct descendant of the founder of the Parker Ranch), who are experts in Hawaiiana. The view of the surrounding ranchlands from the building are also outstanding. General admission: $5.

Parker Ranch Historic Homes   ★★★★
Parker Ranch Shopping Center, Kamuela, 96743, ☎ *(808) 885-5433.*
Hours: 10 a.m.–5 p.m.
Although Pu'u'opelu and Mana were both homes built in the mid-1800s by John Palmer Parker, founder of Parker ranch, they are two different structures. Mana (which means power), built of koa wood, is designed in a simple, New England-salt-box style, recalling Parker's Massachusetts origins. In contrast, Pu'u'opelo, an 8000-square-foot home with a sweeping lawn and flower gardens, was opulently furnished by Parker's great-great-grandson, Richard Smart, who sang and danced on Broadway stages. Smart lived up to his name and bought up a 100-plus-piece collection of fine French Impressionist art. The home, where Smart lived until he died on in 1992, features works by Renoir, Utrillo, Chagall, Corot, Degas and Dufy. In addition, there are originals by Maurice de Vlaminck, Henri Martin, Bonnard and Picasso. Among the rare glasswares and porcelains are five Ming Dynasty pieces. Mana, which was formerly located on a slope of Mauna Loa, was moved next to Pu'u'opelu in 1987. Children's admission: $5 for ages four to 11; free for children under three. This tour can be combined with the Parker Ranch Center tour for $10 for adults, and $7.50 for children. General admission: $7.50.

Parker Ranch Visitor Center   ★★★
Parker Ranch Shopping Center, Kamuela, 96743, ☎ *(808) 885-7655.*
Hours: 9 a.m.–5 p.m.
One of the largest ranches in the United States, the Parker Ranch grew over the years from two to more than 225,000 acres. Some 35 cowboys, or *paniolos*, are in charge of 60,000 head of cattle and 400 horses. Well-laid-out displays in glass cases

trace the history of the Parker Family from founder John Palmer Parker, an ex-sailor turned land baron and son-in-law of King Kamehameha I, to his great-great grandson, the late Richard Palmer Smart, who appeared on Broadway stages. Artifacts include a rare Hawaiian-language Bible, photos of various Parkers and an old tack room and saddlery dating from the late 1800s. A 25-minute video includes live footage of the workings of the 149-year-old ranch. General admission: $5.

The Shows

Kahilu Theatre　　　　　　　　　　　　　　　　　　★★

P.O. Box 549, Kamuela, 96743, ☎ *(808) 885-6017.*
An eclectic mix of entertainment is offered in a bucolic setting on Parker Ranch land. It was founded in part by Richard Palmer Smart, a Broadway actor and last descendant of the Parker family. The repertoire runs the gamut from spiritual ensembles to symphony orchestras to brass quartets. Performers have included Die Musik, a chamber quintet, and the Peking Acrobats.

Tours

Hawaiian Walkways　　　　　　　　　　　　　　★★★★

P.O. Box 2193, Kamuela, 96743, ☎ *(808) 885-7759.*
This well-established company specializes in custom hiking trips to volcanoes, rainforests, waterfalls and ancient Hawaiian trails along the coast. Hikes are rated easy, moderate and challenging and range from short day hikes to three-day, two-night camping trips or the 14-day, 150-mile treks across the entire island. These "Treks across Hawaii" combine walking with backpacking, mountain biking and sea kayaking. Hawaiian Walkways has been conducting tours since 1984. Included are light packs, lunch (for day hikes), support equipment, filled water bottles, and shared camp equipment and food for multi-day trips. Groups are kept small, but a minimum of two is necessary. General admission: $110–$425.

Mauna Kea Helicopters　　　　　　　　　　　　★★★★

P.O. Box 1713, Kamuela, 96743, ☎ *(808) 885-6400.*
If you'd like to experience helicopter flying the way pilots really like it, take one of this company's "Absolute Air Adventure" tours over the Kohala Valley. In this thrilling ride, all four doors of the 'copter are removed prior to flight, affording stomach-dropping vistas of remote valleys accessible only by air or sea. For safety reasons, no children under 10 are allowed. Also offered are flights over the active Pu'u O'o vent at Volcano National Park. Rides last from 30 minutes to two hours. All passengers are guaranteed a window seat. Flights leave from Waimea or Hilo Airports. General admission: $95–$285.

Kohala Coast

Beaches

Hapuna Beach　　　　　　　　　　　　　　　　★★★★

Highway 19, Kohala Coast, 96743, ☎ *(808) 882-7995.*
At 200 feet, this is the island's longest white-sand beach, except in winter when some of that sand recedes. Families and children love it, but it's big enough that couples and loners can eke out a spot for themselves. Swimming, unfortunately, can

be hazardous, and is extremely so in winter due to high surf and rip tides. There's no camping directly on the beach, but if you're lucky, you can rent yourself some of the cheapest accommodations on the island, complete with ocean view, for just $15. Situated less than a mile above the beach are six cute but spartan A-frame cabins that sleep four each. Facilities include covered cooking pavilions, enclosed showers and his-and-her rest rooms. Naturally, they're always booked up solid. For reservations, call or write to Hapuna Beach Services, *P.O. Box 5397, Kailua-Kona, HI 96745;* ☎ *(808) 882-1095.*

Spencer Beach Park ★★★★

Highway 19, past Hapuna Beach Park, Kohala Coast, 96743, ☎ *(808) 882-7094.*
Although not as famous or picture-perfect as Hapuna, its next-door neighbor, Spencer Beach Park is far safer, with a protected bay that assures fine swimming most of the year. The county-maintained facilities are superior, with barbecue grills, rest rooms that work, a volleyball net, basketball court, even tennis. The park is secured until closing, and there's a lifeguard. Kamehameha I's Pu'ukohola Heiau is a short walk away.

Waikoloa Beach Park/Anaehoomalu Bay ★★★★

Highway 19, Kohala Coast, 96738, ☎ *(808) 885-6789.*
Just south of Hapuna Beach and adjacent to the Royal Waikoloan Resort, this white-sand, half-moon-shaped beach stretches between ancient fishponds and the ocean. There's a calm lagoon that's usually safe for swimming when other beaches are not. Rest rooms, picnic facilities and services provided by the hotel.

City Celebrations

Aloha Festivals ★★★★

Mauna Lani Bay Resort and various locations, Kohala Coast, ☎ *(808) 326-7820.*
For general description, see Aloha Festivals, "Molokai" chapter. The organizers of the Big Island events try to top themselves every year with such wild happenings as the Ms. "Big" Big Island Contest, held at the Mauna Lani Bay Hotel on the Kohala Coast. To give you an idea, it's open to all *wahines* (women) weighing in at 200 pounds and up.

Winter Wine Escape ★★★

62-100 Kauna'oa Drive, Kohala Coast, 96743, ☎ *(808) 880-1111.*
Held at the Hapuna Beach Prince Hotel in November, this annual event includes food tastings, seminars showcasing the world's finest wines and a Grand Finale wine reception spotlighting Big Island farmers, aquaculturists and craftsmen. Meet and mingle with culinary and oenophilic celebrities. Hotel offers special room packages, some including golf. General admission: $50–$65.

Fun For Free

The Royal Waikoloan Historical Grounds Tour ★★

69-275 Waikoloa Beach Drive, Kohala Coast, 96743, ☎ *(808) 885-6789.*
Hours: 9 a.m. Tues., Thurs. only
Tour the grounds of this 543-room hotel with Armstrong Yamamoto, a "living Hawaiian treasure." Yamamoto has extensive knowledge about many uses of endemic plants.

THE BIG ISLAND

Historical Sites

Eva Parker Woods Cottage   ★★★

One Mauna Lani Drive, Kohala Coast, 96743, ☎ *(808) 885-6622.*

Located on the grounds of the Mauna Lani Bay Hotel, this cottage houses several interesting displays, including fishhooks, ti-leaf raincoats, feather leis and old photos of cattle shipments from Kawaihae. A free historical/ethnobotanical tour is also offered Tuesdays and Saturdays at 9 a.m.; and Thursdays at 3:30 p.m. Along with Kaniela Akaka, the hotel's resident Hawaiian historian, you'll visit shelter caves, a canoe landing, petroglyphs and natural fish feeding tour at the hotel on Tuesdays, Thursdays and Saturdays at 10:30 a.m.

Tours

Petroglyph Tours   ★★★

The King's Shops, P.O. Box 384330, Kohala Coast, 96738, ☎ *(808) 885-8811.*
Hours: 9:30 a.m.–9:30 p.m.

More than 12,000 well-preserved petroglyphs (primitive rock drawings) are located at easily accessible fields on the Kohala Coast. A knowledgeable, local guide takes visitors on 45- to 90-minute free walking tours through petroglyph fields along Anaeho'omalu Bay's Kings' Trail. Meet in front of food pavilion at Kings' Shops, which is adjacent to the Royal Waikoloan Resort. Historical and geographical dioramas of the coast can be seen within the shopping center itself. You can also explore the Puako Petroglyph Archaeological Preserve at Mauna Lani Resort any day of the week on your own. This 1.25-mile walk affords "up close and personal" views of more than 3000 petroglyphs. Wear broken-in footwear, and take along sun screen and drinking water.

South Kona

Captain Cook

Museums and Exhibits

Kona Historical Society   ★★★

P.O. Box 398, Captain Cook, 96704, ☎ *(808) 323-3222.*
Hours: 9 a.m.–3 p.m.

The Kona Historical Society's museum is housed in an old wood and stone store named after the Greenwell family, missionaries and ranchers who owned most of the land around Kealakekua from the 1850s to the early 1900s. When the museum was opened in 1985, the exhibits were original items sold in the store during its heyday. Today you'll see an antique bottle collection, photo displays, maps and manuscripts that explain the history of the Kona area. Guided tours available. Free for children ages 11 and under. General admission: $1.

Parks and Gardens

Amy B.H. Greenwell Ethnobotanical Garden   ★★

82-6188 Mamalahoa Highway, Captain Cook, 96704, ☎ *(808) 323-3318.*
Hours: 7 a.m.–3:30 p.m.
Special hours: hours may vary.

This agricultural research facility, an adjunct of the Bishop Museum, cultivates more than 250 rare crops that early Hawaiians used for food. New this year is an herbarium that consists of a mounted display of preserved Polynesian plants. Five of the 10 acres have been set aside as an archaeological site. On the second Saturday of the month, a 90-minute tour is offered at 10 a.m. Plant sales held in March and September.

Tours

Mauna Loa Royal Kona Coffee Mill & Museum ★★

P.O. Box 829, Captain Cook, 96704, ☎ (808) 328-2511.
An indoor-outdoor javarama, the Royal Kona Coffee Visitor Center gives out free samples of freshly roasted coffee to sip and displays and memorabilia relating to the Big Island's flourishing industry to look at.

Holualoa

Tours

Capt. Dan McSweeney's Whale Watch ★★★★

P.O. Box 139, Holualoa, 96725, ☎ (808) 322-0028.
Captain Dan McSweeney is Kona's only whale scientist, who has spent more than 30,000 hours observing the magnificent mammals, photographing their antics for such publications as *National Geographic* and *Audubon*. His trips are different in that they're conducted year-round, except for a two month summer break—he guarantees you'll see a whale or get your money back. Sightings are not limited to humpback whales, who only migrate to Hawaii in the winter months. Six other species are found off the Kona Coast, plus five types of dolphins. Two three-hour cruises leave daily in the winter from Dec. 20–April 30; from July 1–Dec. 19, tours leave three to five times a week. Captain Dan personally accompanies each trip, providing expert narration. A live underwater camera records whales and dolphins playing around the stationary boat, and with the aid of a hydrophone, you'll hear the whales communicate with each other. Included in the price is a professional, color guide to Hawaii's whales plus snacks and juices. General admission: $39.50.

Honaunau

Historical Sites

Pu'uhonua O Honaunau National Historic Park ★★★★★

Off Highway 11, Honaunau, ☎ (808) 328-2288.
Hours: 7:30 a.m.–5:30 p.m.
This 181-acre, national historic site on the Kona Coast, about 20 miles south of Kailua-Kona, is the best preserved example of a *pu'uhonua*, or city of refuge. *Kapu* (sacred law) breakers in ancient times had no recourse but to attempt to flee here or they would face certain death. Eventually absolved by a *kahuna*, or priest, the wrong-doer could return to normal life. During frequent outbreaks of war, the weak or the defeated could come here to wait things out. Sounds easy, right? Not quite. Those coming from the south would have to scale a 1000-foot-long, 10-foot-high lava rock wall (still partially standing); others coming north either had to swim or canoe their way in, as the high chief's home was placed on this side, and commoners were forbidden to set foot on royal grounds. Today, visitors can take a self-guided tour of *Hale O Keawe Heiau*, built in 1650 at one end of the Great Wall.

This sacred structure served as a temple mausoleum until 1818 and housed the bones of more than 20 chiefs. Other attractions on the site are canoe sheds and carved wooden figures called *ki'i*. Several cultural events are held at the park on an annual basis. For three days, on the weekend closest to July 1, the park throws itself a big birthday party. Revelers can attempt to use a poi pounder, make leis or *lauhala* (pandanus leaf) baskets, or help pull in the big fish net at a traditional *hukilau*. The festivities are presided over by a royal court, dressed in feather cloaks and helmets. On the first Friday in February and November, Hawaiian sports are the focus of the park's day-long La Pa'ani celebration (coming together for sports and games). Watch school-children compete in dart sliding, arm wrestling and spear throwing.

Parks and Gardens

Wakefield Botanical Gardens ★★★

City of Refuge Road, Honaunau, 96785, ☎ *(808) 967-7479.*
Hours: 10 a.m.–5 p.m.

This five-acre botanical garden and macadamia nut orchard offers refreshment and lush contrast to its nearby neighbor Pu'uhonua O Honau'nau National Historic Park. More than 1000 varieties of plants and flowers are labeled for your edification. Also a restaurant serving healthful sandwiches, soups and homemade pies.

Hookena

Beaches

Hookena Beach Park ★★★

Off Highway 11, adjacent to the City of Refuge, Hookena, 96704, ☎ *(808) 961-8311.*
The road to this beach is twisty, steep and narrow, and the area around it is slightly seedy, but the sea here is benevolent, making for usually ideal snorkeling and swimming conditions. Facilities are sort of wild and uncared for, with no water and iffy toilets, but there are picnic tables. Tent camping is available with a county permit.

Kealakekua

The Shows

Aloha Performing Arts Center ★★★

Highway 11, Kealakekua, 96750, ☎ *(808) 322-9924.*
This remarkable old theater with a tin roof was built in the 1920s. Recently, folks drove out to see the resident Aloha Community Players in a revival of Euripedes' *Medea*. By all reports it was wonderful. Call for current schedule. General admission: Varies.

Tours

Captain Jack's Charters ★★

P.O. Box 1018, Kealakekua, 96750, ☎ *(800) 545-KONA.*
Daily deep-sea fishing charters in search of wahoo, marlin, tuna and mahi are available on the *Notorious*, a 35-foot Bertram. Available on an exclusive or share-boat basis, full- or half-day. Novices as well as seasoned anglers and professionals are accommodated. The boat is also wheelchair-accessible. Captain Jack has 38 years in Kona waters and boasts that his record catch was five marlin in a single afternoon. Also overnighters for $1300. General admission: $85–$475.

Kings' Trail Rides O'Kona ★★★

P.O. Box 1366, Kealakekua, 96750.
Hours: 7:30 a.m.–5 p.m.
Kings' Trail Rides O'Kona offers a 4.5-hour horseback ride and snorkeling combo. You'll ride a gentle horse down a mountain trail to the Captain Cook Monument in Kealakekua Bay, followed by snorkeling and a picnic lunch. Some riding experience is necessary. Wedding packages and custom camping/hiking/swimming adventures can be arranged. The meeting point is at the 111-mile marker on Highway 11 in Kealakekua, 15 minutes south of Kailua village. Reservations required. General admission: $95.

Keauhou

Beaches

Kahalu'u Beach ★★★

Ali'i Drive, next to the Keauhou Beach Hotel, Keauhou, 96739, ☎ (808) 961-8311.
A salt-and-pepper (a nice term for gray) sand beach with shallow protected bay for excellent snorkeling, swimming, boogie boarding. Facilities include a lifeguard, picnic facilities, showers and phones. There's snorkel equipment rental and eateries nearby.

Volcano

Volcano Village

Hiking

Climb Mauna Loa–Sierra Club Outing Dept. ★★★

Hawaii Volcanoes National Park, Volcano Village, 96720, ☎ (415) 923-5525.
Adventurous travelers can make the difficult, three- or four-day, 18-mile hike to the summit of Mauna Loa with an experienced Sierra Club outing leader. Also available for booking through the Sierra Club is a "Hidden Hawaii" outing with the John Muir Society, usually held in summer. The various adventures include hikes into rainforests and snorkeling with sea turtles and dolphins on the islands of Lanai and Maui. For information, contact the Sierra Club's Outing Department, 730 Polk Street, San Francisco, CA. 94109.

Crater Rim Trail ★★★★

Hawaii Volcanoes National Park, Volcano Village, 96785, ☎ (808) 967-7311.
This loop trail begins at park headquarters and circles the summit caldera of Kilauea. An easy, 11-mile trail that's partly paved, it travels through cool rainforest and warm desert, all on the same day. Several other trails branch out from it, including Halemaumau Trail (see Hawaii Volcanoes National Park description). General admission: $5.

Mauna Loa Trail ★★

Hawaii Volcanoes National Park, Volcano Village, 96785, ☎ (808) 967-7311.
This strenuous trek starts at 6662 feet from its head, and takes two days to climb to the south rim of the Mokuaweoweo Caldera at 13,250 feet. Most hikers spend the night in a cabin with eight bunks at Red Hill (10,035 feet) and proceed to the summit shelter (12 bunks) on the second day. It takes another half-day to hike around

the caldera to the true summit at 13,677 feet. Catchment water for drinking and pit toilets are located at each cabin—but if others have been there before you, and were greedy, there may be NO water at all, so be prepared. Even hardy hikers (no neophytes here, please) have experienced severe headaches and nausea upon reaching the summit. Try to walk on smooth lava; those with humps or ridges have been known to collapse, fragmenting into sharp pieces. For guided hikes contact the Sierra Club's Outing Department, *730 Polk Street, San Francisco, CA 94109*, ☎ *(415) 923-5525*. General admission: $5.

Museums and Exhibits

Thomas A. Jaggar Museum   ★★★★

Hawaii Volcanoes National Park, P.O. Box 52, Volcano Village, 96718, ☎ *(808) 967-7643.*
Hours: 8:30 a.m.–5 p.m.

This museum, at the Hawaiian Volcano Observatory, is perched on the rim of the Kilauea caldera, and naturally its focus is on volcanology (you knew that!). One of the finest museums in the finest national park in the world, the Jaggar gives out eruption and volcano information through seismograph machines that measure the Earth's movement. Murals of Madame Pele, goddess of fire, by Big Island artist Herb Kane; rock samples; and videos of past eruptions round out the entertaining and informative exhibits.

Parks and Gardens

Akatsuka Orchid Gardens   ★

Highway 11, north of Volcano Village, Volcano Village, 96785, ☎ *(808) 967-8234.*
Hours: 8:30 a.m.–5 p.m.

This six-acre covered garden features one of the largest orchid collections on the island. Cattleya, vanda and other varieties can be shipped to the mainland. Also handicrafts and floral-related gifts.

The Shows

Volcano Arts Center   ★★★

Hawaii Volcanoes National Park, Volcano Village, ☎ *(808) 967-8222.*
Hours: 9 a.m.–5 p.m.

Plays, musical concerts and art exhibits are presented at this unique cultural center in the original circa 1800s Volcano House Hotel. Call for schedule.

Tours

Hawaii Volcanoes National Park   ★★★★★

P.O. Box 52, Volcano Village, 96718, ☎ *(808) 967-7311.*
Hours: 7:45 a.m.–5 p.m.

Some wags call this 229,000-acre national park a drive-in volcano. Hawaii Volcanoes National Park is the only park in the world where spectacular eruptions emanating from the perpetually active Kilauea volcano can be observed from its slopes. When that happens, the Chain of Craters road resembles rush hour at a well-known hamburger chain. What could also be said about the park is that its territory is constantly expanding—without benefit of permits.

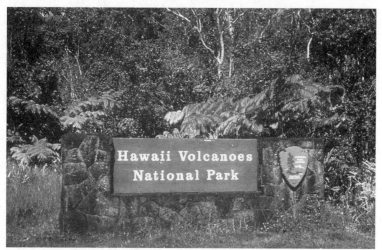

Mauna Loa and Kilauea volcanoes are in Hawaii Volcanoes National Park.
At present, the park encompasses the southern and eastern flanks of Kilauea Volcano, the slopes of Mauna Loa and the Kalapana coast. In 60,000 years, a new volcano, Loihi, now some 3,180 feet below sea level, located 30 miles southeast of the Big Island, will join her sisters. Of all the sights in the entire state, the park is one attraction that shouldn't be passed up. Besides the Earth-moving fire and lava show, there's an excellent museum of volcanology, an informative visitor center, an 11-mile circular loop around the Kilauea caldera (crater), hiking trails, camping, an art gallery and even a hotel, Volcano House, perched right on the crater rim. The Kilauea Visitor Center presents a film of spectacular past volcanic eruptions, and entertaining, educational displays of plants, animals and volcano lore. Check out the bulletin board for the latest volcanic activity and trail information. Adjacent is the **Volcano Art Center** ☎ *(808) 967-7643*, which features the work of Big Island craftsmen, photographers, woodcarvers and artists. Thomas A. Jaggar Museum (see listing) overlooks Halemaumau, Kilauea's steaming firepit. If you only have a day at the park, drive the Crater Rim Drive loop road to see the summit caldera, sulfur banks, steam vents, pit craters, recent lava flows and a "walk-thru" lava tube. If you've ever tried to imagine Dante's Inferno, don't miss the three-mile hike to **Halemaumau Crater**, Pele's legendary home—pungent sulphur fumes are emitted from the steaming cracks of the 3000-foot caldera. For those who have a week to spare, the park offers two drive-in campgrounds: Namakani Paio, three miles from the park entrance on Route 11; and Kipuka Nene, which is closed to campers from October to March due to nesting Nene geese. The former has free tent sites with eating shelters and fireplaces available on a first-come, first-served basis. It has flush toilets but no showers. Also, 10 housekeeping cabins sleeping four persons each are operated by the privately held Volcano House hotel. Fees are $24 a night and must be reserved at least a month in advance. The cabins, set a few yards away from the

campsites, have electricity (but no heater or outlets) and a separate facility with rest rooms and warm water showers. General admission: $5.

Volcano Winery   ★★

P.O. Box 843, Volcano Village, 96785, ☎ (808) 967-7479.
Hours: 10 a.m.–5 p.m.

Sample guava, starfruit and lilikoi blended with chablis and take a self-guided walk through a 14-acre vineyard bordering Hawaii Volcanoes National Park. Gift shop.

Sports

Among the Big Island's claims to fame are its renowned **golf courses**—rolling green blankets in the midst of parched lava fields. Most famous are the Robert Trent Jones Sr. course at Mauna Kea Beach Hotel and the Robert Trent Jones Jr. course at Waikoloa Beach Resort. Other top courses are Mauna Lani Resort, Waikoloa Village, Kona Country Club, Makalei Hawaii Country Club and Hapuna Golf Course. Low on bucks? Try Hilo Municipal Golf Course, Hamakua Country Club or Discovery Harbor. **Tennis** buffs will find plenty of courts around the Big Island. For high-class play, the Keauhou-Kona resorts are primo—nonguests might want to try the many free school- and county-operated courts around the island.

The Kailua-Kona waters are internationally famous for big-game **fishing**. You'll find tuna, mahimahi, wahoo and, of course, the highly prized marlin, which can be caught year-round. The **Hawaiian International Billfish Tournament**, the first part of each August, reels in anglers from all over the world. Hit the beaches, forests, valleys or ranch land via **horseback**. A variety of outfitters will guide you on escorted rides to scenic island sites—a ride down to the Captain Cook monument is one company's trademark excursion. Or how about **skiing**? This is the Big Island, remember? Expert skiers should bring their own equipment, rent a four-wheel-drive vehicle (no ski lifts!), and head for the slopes of Mauna Kea. Came unprepared? **Ski Guides Hawaii** (☎ (808) 885-4188) will organize your outing.

Hilo

Hilo Municipal Golf Course   ★★

340 Haihai Street, Hilo, 96720, ☎ (808) 959-7711.
Hours: 7 a.m.–5:30 p.m.

Popularly priced, this public course three miles from the Hilo airport was established in 1950. It has a nice, flat, wooded setting that might bore some hotshots.

Cart rental: $14.50. Facilities include a pro shop, practice green, driving range. General admission: $25.

Kona
Kailua-Kona

Eco-Adventures ★★★
75-5744 Ali'i Drive, Kailua-Kona, 96740, ☎ *(808) 329-7116.*
Offers diving adventures and instruction (from beginner to dive master) on board a 42-foot Seattle Delta dive vessel. Morning trips include lunch, beverages, tanks, weights and guides. Highlights include "Manta Mania" night dives, in which participants are taken to sites where rays come right next to shore to feed on plankton, encouraged by divers' bright lights. Ocean kayaking, snorkeling and custom fishing charters are available. The company also arranges hiking, bike/hike expeditions. General admission: $45–$1050.

Fair Wind ★★★★
78-7130 Kaleiopapa Street, Kailua-Kona, 96740, ☎ *(808) 322-2788.*
The Fair Wind II is a state-of-the-art 60-foot catamaran owned by a kamaainas Puhi and Mendy Dent. The Dents and their crew like to impart a special "local style" family feeling to their snorkel and dive cruises to historic Kealakekua Bay. There are other cruises to this marine sanctuary accessible only by boat, but this one seems to draw lots of repeat customers. Two cruises depart daily from Keauhou Bay. The deluxe morning excursion lasts 4.5-hours, and includes a yummy breakfast with Kona coffee from the Dents' farm, plus a lunch of barbecued cheeseburgers or gardenburgers. The 3.5-hour afternoon cruise includes snacks; both offer a no-host bar. *The Fair Wind II* has a 15-foot water slide and a high-dive platform. All snorkeling gear, plus instruction if needed, is provided. Scuba (certified and intro) and snuba are optional. General admission: $44–$69.

Makalei Hawaii Country Club ★★
72-3890 Hawaii Belt Road, Kailua-Kona, 96740, ☎ *(808) 325-6625.*
Hours: 7 a.m.–6 p.m.
Sprawled within the slopes of Hualalai Mountain overlooking Kona, this country club offers unbeatable weather and spectacular golf over terrain ranging from 2100 to 2800 feet. Higher greens fees are for out-of-state players; lowest rates for Big Island residents; $45 for Hawaiian island residents. Cart fee $25. Facilities include a restaurant and driving range. General admission: $45–$110.

UFO Parasail ★★
P.O. Box 5438, Kailua-Kona, 96745, ☎ *(808) 325-5836.*
Hours: 8 a.m.–4 p.m.
Leaves from Kailua Pier in downtown Kona. See UFO Parasail description in Maui chapter. General admission: $32.50–$48.00.

North Kohala
Kapa'au

Chris' Adventures ★★★
P.O. Box 869, Kula, HI 96790, Kapa'au, 96790, ☎ *(800) 224-5344.*

Hours: 8 a.m.–6 p.m.

Special hours: Saturdays, 8-10 a.m. Closed: Sun.

Chris and his associates offer on- and off-road cycling, hiking and snorkel adventures (or combos of the three) for small groups daily, morning or afternoon. The varied itineraries include a Kohala-Pololu Venture, in which participants bike "mostly downhill" to the coast, then hike the magnificent Pololu Valley and its black-sand beach. This tour is recommended for riders of all abilities. Tough dudes and dudettes can take the 50-mile "Mauna Loa Challenge" and bike 11,000 feet to sea level via challenging, seldom-traveled roads. The scenery changes from lava fields to lush ranchlands. For experienced riders only. Ask about "Inn-to-Inn" vacations, three- to eight-day biking and/or hiking trips for all levels, with options for the more advanced (or masochistic) participants. Included are all meals, transportation, equipment, lodging and all extras; price ranges from $200–$275 per day. Call Chris' Adventures tour planner for details, dates and trip itineraries. General admission: $110–$275.

South Kohala

Kamuela

Mauna Kea Mountain Bikes   ★★

P.O. Box 44672, Kamuela, ☎ *(808) 885-2091.*

Choose from eight scenic but hard-core mountain biking and/or hiking trips, although beginners are welcome. Pedal and hoof it through rainforests, downhill or coast trails. Gourmet lunch or snacks provided. Front-suspension bikes and rentals available. General admission: $75 and up.

Mauna Kea Ski Corporation   ★★★

P.O. Box 1954, Kamuela, 96743, ☎ *(808) 885-4188.*

Lofty Mauna Kea, an extinct volcano and the world's tallest mountain, isn't called "White Mountain" (translated from the Hawaiian) for nothing. From late November through May the 13,796-foot summit is usually covered with four to six feet of snow. Prime conditions are between the months of February and March. The world's highest cross-country ski race takes place up here in May, called "Pele's Cup." The area is not maintained for skiing, as its primary use is for observing the heavens. Only experienced skiers should tackle the slopes, as there are no lifts, lodges or medical services. The Mauna Kea Ski Corporation, formerly called Ski Hawaii, is the only company to conduct guided ski tours. It also provides transportation to the summit by four-wheel-drive vehicle (which also doubles as a ski lodge), lunch and portable toilets. Must be 14 years or older. Group tours are $150 per person (ski rental extra), or $250 for personal tours (includes equipment, clothing). Both include lunch. General admission: $150–$250.

Kohala Coast

Francis H. I'i Brown Championship Course   ★★★★

Mauna Lani Resort 68-150 Ho'ohana Street, Kohala Coast, 96743, ☎ *(808) 885-6655.*
Hours: 7 a.m.–6 p.m.

Composed of two courses, both of which look like they belong on an Irish moon. The dazzling, emerald-green fairways of the south course were built on rough lava from a relatively recent flow. This challenging course features ocean and mountain views. The famed 15th hole crosses crashing surf. The North Course, situated atop Pahoehoe lava (smoother and far older) is characterized by rolling terrain and thorny kiawe groves. Feral goats on the fairways present a hazard. Higher greens fees for nonguests, lower fees for guests of the Orchid at Mauna Lani and the Mauna Lani Bay Hotel. Facilities include on-course refreshment carts, bar and lounge, restaurant, pro shop, practice green, two driving ranges. Lessons and shoe and club rentals. General admission: $80–$150.

Hapuna Golf Course ★★★★

62-100 Kaunaoa Drive, Kohala Coast, 96743, ☎ *(808) 880-3000.*
Hours: 7 a.m.–6 p.m.

Situated next to the Hapuna Beach Prince Hotel, this 18-hole championship links-style course, designed by Arnold Palmer and Ed Seay, was named the "most environmentally sensitive in the state" and "course of the future" by the USGA. Shared cart and tax included in greens fee, higher price is for nonguests. Pro shop, driving range, practice green, restaurant, spa. General admission: $80–$130.

Mauna Kea Golf Course ★★★★

62-100 Mauna Kea Beach Drive, Kohala Coast, 96743, ☎ *(808) 880-3480.*
Hours: 7 a.m.–6 p.m.

Designed by the venerable Robert Trent Jones Sr., Mauna Kea is one of his best courses and possibly the best in the nation. The third hole is considered to be the most difficult, with the ocean between you and the green. Rental cart included in the fee. Facilities include a restaurant, lounge, snack bar, locker room, pro shop, driving range and practice green. General admission: $80–$130.

Waikoloa Village Golf Club ★★★★

P.O. Box 383910, Kohala Coast, 96738, ☎ *(808) 883-9621.*
Hours: 6:30 a.m.–6:30 p.m.

Established in 1972, this course, designed by Robert Trent Jones Jr., is situated on the slopes of the legendary Mauna Kea Mountain on Parker Ranch land. Rental cart included in greens fees. Facilities include a restaurant, lounge, snack bar, locker rooms, pro shop, driving range, practice green, pool, tennis. There are two other courses bearing the Waikoloa name; these cater to guests of the Hilton Waikoloa Village and Royal Waikoloan resorts, but off-property guests can play too. The Beach course, at *1020 Keana Place, Waikoloa, (* ☎ *(808) 885-6060)* was also designed by Robert Trent Jones Jr., who incorporated petroglyph fields, historic fishing villages and lava formations into the fairways of this par-71 course. Facilities: golf shop, driving range, practice green, restaurant, lounge. Tom Weiskopf and Jay Morrish designed the 130-acre Kings' Course, at *600 Waikoloa Beach Drive,* *(* ☎ *(808) 335-4647)* on natural lava terrain, with six lakes and 83 traps. It has a golf shop, and complete practice and golf school facility. General admission: $70.

THE BIG ISLAND

South Kona

Napoopoo

Kona Kayak Expedition   ★★★

Napoopoo, Napoopoo, ☎ *(808) 329-6411.*

Hours: 7:30 a.m.–noon

Paddle across Kealakekua Bay to the famous Captain Cook monument, accessible only by water. You can hike around the monument or take a dip in the fresh-water Queen's Bath. Rate includes a naturalist guide, lunch, snorkel gear and instruction. For more information, contact Royal Hawaiian Cruises, 2270 Kalakaua Avenue, Suite 708, Honolulu, HI 96815.

Volcano

Volcano Village

Volcano Golf and Country Club   ★★

P.O. Box 46, Volcano National Park, Volcano Village, 96718, ☎ *(808) 967-7331.*

Hours: 7 a.m.–5 p.m.

Located in Pele's back yard, this par-72, Jack Snyder-designed course is 4000 feet above sea level. It combines modern facilities with historic character and magnificent natural surroundings. Rental cart included in greens fees. Pro shop, driving range, practice green, restaurant, lounge. General admission: $50.

Where to Stay

It's easy to find accommodations in a wide range of price brackets on the Big Island. Occupancy rate is relatively low, so crowds and overbooking are usually not a problem—except during certain festivals (April's Merrie Monarch Festival, for example). Most of the hotels and condos are spread around Kailua-Kona—the sunny part of the island. The **luxury resorts** such as the Mauna Kea Beach Hotel, Ritz-Carlton Mauna Lani, Kona Village resort and Mauna Lani Bay Hotel are situated close to each other along the Kohala coast. Over on Hilo, there are about half as many rooms, but certainly a lot more rain. Or how about an A-frame cabin at Namakani Paio Campground, in **Hawaii Volcanoes National Park**? A **bed-and-breakfast** overlooking Waipio Valley? A **campsite** on a black-sand beach?

Hamakua Coast

Honokaa

Bed-and-Breakfasts

Paauhau Plantation House   **$75–$140**   ★★★

P.O. Box 1375, Honokaa, 96727, ☎ *(808) 775-7222.*
Single: $75–$140. Double: $75–$140.

It's on the wrong island, but Paauhau Plantation House could easily be mistaken for
Robin Masters' estate on the "Magnum, P.I." TV series. Guests can mix their own
drinks at the wet bar in the TV room, play billiards or select a book from the library
in the main house, which has 12-foot ceilings. The formal gardens are immaculately
maintained and overlook the ocean. At 1200 feet above sea level, the house is perpetually cooled by ocean breezes. Honeymooners (or other romantics) will appreciate the peach and white bathroom with an ocean view in the master suite with its
oval tub (large enough for two) surrounded by mirrors and candles. The suite has a
fireplace, color TV and a large private lanai. A continental breakfast is served at 8
a.m. or as requested. In addition to the main house, there are three cottages on the
estate for families or those who wish additional privacy. The entire facility can be
rented for seminars or meetings for $400 a day. One drawback is there's no laundry
service, and the only phone is in the office. Maid service additional. Amenities: tennis. 6 rooms. Credit cards: MC, V.

Waipio Wayside Bed and Breakfast Inn   **$65–$105**   ★★★

P.O. Box 840, Honokaa, 96727, ☎ *(800) 833-8849, (808) 775-0275.*
Single: $65–$95. Double: $75–$105.

The Waipio Wayside Bed and Breakfast Inn was built in 1938 to house executives
of a local sugar plantation and the building has been meticulously restored and furnished to retain the character of that period. Household furnishings are an astute
mix of wicker, Chinoiserie, lace and contemporary artwork. The neat garden surrounded by a picket fence and established plantings of palm trees, poincianna trees,
hibiscus and bananas adds to the feeling of Hawaii before Pearl Harbor. Three guest
rooms share baths and two have private baths. All rooms have windows that overlook adjacent sugar cane fields and the ocean. Several have private decks. If you're
an avid reader, book the Library Room; it has a cozy reading nook where you can
sit and browse through more than 400 volumes. Breakfast is an almost ceremonial
occasion, celebrated with mugs of Hamakua Coast coffee (half native Kona beans
and half locally grown Jamaica Blue Mountain beans). During the day, guests are
welcome to make themselves a cup of tea from the selection of Republic of Tea tins
in the reception area. Amenities: balcony or patio. 5 rooms. Credit cards: not accepted.

Kukuihaele

Apartments

Waipio Valley Artworks Vacation Rentals   **$65–$90**   ★★★

P.O. Box 5070, Kukuihaele, 96727, ☎ *(800) 492-4746, (808) 775-0958.*
Single: $65–$90. Double: $65–$90.

Waipio Valley Artworks functions as a workshop/gallery/coffee house. An outlet
for the work of more than 75 artisans, the majority of whom work in exotic woods,

it also offers two comfortable, reasonably priced apartments in this desirable area. Located in a private home, the most expensive one is a two-bedroom, two-bath unit on the top floor. It has a huge lanai with fantastic waterfall and valley/ocean views, and a complete kitchen with dishwasher and washer/dryer. You can park your car in an enclosed garage. The other apartment, on the ground floor, offers similar features, less one bedroom and one bath. Both have phones and color TVs. Check in at the art gallery beforehand, where you can peruse the creative offerings and sample the excellent coffee, sandwiches, ice creams and sorbets. Wapio Valley has an extensive collection of books on Hawaiiana. Units can be rented by the week or month. Amenities: balcony or patio. 2 rooms. Credit cards: MC, V.

Inns

Hale Kukui $85–$175 ★★★

Box 5044, Kukuihaele, 96727, ☎ (800) 775-7130, (808) 775-7130, FAX (800) 775-7130.
Single: $85–$175. Double: $85–$175.

The Hale Kukui guest cottage is a perfect destination for those of us who want to get close to nature. It's located in a pristine little postage stamp of a village called Kukuihaele, on bluffs overlooking Waipio Valley, which is only a mile away. It also looks out over the ocean and on a clear day you can see Maui. Hale Kukui is a perfect base for hiking in the valley. If you must get back to civilization, Honokaa is about eight miles away. The four-acre spread supports fascinating examples of local flora and fauna. Plumeria, bamboo, wild ginger, palms, bananas and avocados are just a few of the plants that have rusticated around the pools and waterfalls formed by a year-round stream. Even non-bird-watchers will be fascinated watching the cardinals, pheasants, doves and native Hawaiian hawks that make this garden their home. Non-native animals include a Waipio pony and two dogs who never fail to ingratiate themselves with guests. Accommodations consist of one studio, one 2-bedroom, and one 3-bedroom unit. All have living areas, kitchenettes, private full baths and lanais. Dividing walls are soundproof. The cottage is 150 feet from the hosts' property. Discounts of five percent are available for members of Greenpeace, the Sierra Club and other national environmental organizations. Smoking on lanai only. Amenities: balcony or patio. 3 rooms. Credit cards: MC, V.

Papaikou

Bed-and-Breakfasts

Our Place $55–$70 ★★

P.O. Box 469, Papaikou, 96781, ☎ (808) 964-5250.
Single: $55–$70. Double: $55–$70.

Our Place is a small, well-appointed bed-and-breakfast property with lots of cedar paneling and comfortable beds. Some rooms share baths. The master bedroom has a king-size bed and private bath, and decorating touches include a rolltop desk and a vintage wall clock. Guests are welcome to use the high-ceilinged great room with sliding glass doors leading to a covered, wrap-around lanai. Cozy wing chairs, a chess set and a grand piano give the feeling that you're really visiting a relative and not a commercial establishment. The surrounding hills are lush with greenery and

THE BIG ISLAND

City of Refuge, Big Island

Viewing lava flow, Big Island

Napo'opo'o Beach

Hawaii Volcanoes National Park

Rainbow Falls near Hilo

Mauna Kea Volcano

the front yard is fanned by palm trees. Hosts Ouida Trahan and her sister Sharon Miller serve a continental breakfast with such treats as homemade granola, fresh tropical fruit juices, home-baked breads and, of course, lots of Kona coffee. Our Place is four miles north of Hilo and six miles from Honomu, which makes it a good place to stay when visiting Akaka Falls. Children over 12 are welcome; no pets. There's a two-night minimum stay. Amenities: balcony or patio. 4 rooms. Credit cards: not accepted.

Waipio Valley

Guest Houses

Waipio Treehouse Waterfall Retreat $175–$225   ★★★

Waipio Valley, 96727, ☎ (808) 775-7160.
Single: $175–$225. Double: $175–$225.
Not for the fainthearted. Guests are met at the Waipio Valley Lookout (cars are left in a secret parking area) and transported in a four-wheel-drive vehicle over "Hawaii's steepest road" to the retreat. Getting there is half the fun and involves fording five streams and a river. Sometimes you won't be able to leave when you want, as the place becomes inaccessible because of high river water. Each of the guest houses has a different feeling. The Waipio Treehouse, as indicated by its name, is located 30 feet up in a monkeypod tree. The Hale has a spectacular waterfall view from the sleeping area in the loft. Shower and toilet are outside. The Kahu is the most traditional of the guesthouses and has a living room, full kitchen, dining area and loft with waterfall view. Activities offered to guests are deliberately low key—among them are listening to the fall of tropical rain, reading, swimming in tropical pools, soaking in an antique Japanese hot tub and watching the taro grow. It's suggested you bring reefwalkers or aqua socks and mosquito repellent (not the moisturizing types, please). Guests must provide their own food. Amenities: Jacuzzi. 3 rooms. Credit cards: not accepted.

Hilo

Hotels

Dolphin Bay Hotel $50–$85   ★★

333 Ilahi Street, Hilo, 96720, ☎ (808) 935-1466.
Single: $50–$85. Double: $55–$85.
The Dolphin Bay Hotel is a more than adequate no-frills establishment. It doesn't have a pool or restaurant, but it's only three blocks away from Hilo Bay and management is happy to make recommendations. Because of its location in a residential area, parking is not a problem. Guests can explore the grounds, set in the middle of a private "jungle" with banana trees. Four types of rooms are available, including superior studios with large Roman tubs; these units sleep up to four people. All have kitchens, color TVs and ceiling fans. Some have private lanais. The Dolphin Bay has a loyal clientele of repeat travelers who eschew glitzy resort living. Amenities: balcony or patio. 18 rooms.

Hawaii Naniloa Hotel $96–$144   ★★★

93 Banyan Drive, Hilo, ☎ (800) 442-5845, (808) 969-3333, FAX (808) 969-6622.

Single: $96–$144. Double: $96–$144.

The Hawaii Naniloa is Hilo's largest hotel, and may be the best in town—if you like plenty of on-site services, banquet rooms and restaurants. It also has a spectacular pool area. The entire hotel was given a thorough face-lift a few years ago, and it's quite popular with tour groups. If you have a choice of which wing to stay in, opt for the Waipio Wing; it has the best ocean views. Amenities: tennis, health club, Jacuzzi, balcony or patio, business services. 325 rooms. Credit cards: A, CB, DC, D, MC, V.

Hilo Bay Resort Hotel $77–$91   ★★

87 Banyan Drive, Hilo, 96720, ☎ *(800) 367-5102, (808) 935-0861, FAX (808) 935-7903. Rated Restaurant: Uncle Billy's Family Style Restaurant.*
Single: $77–$91. Double: $77–$91.

Operated by Uncle Billy's Resort Hotels, this is Uncle Billy's flagship location, and it's the kind of place they dream about in Lake Wobegon. The lobby sets the tone for the rest of the hotel—lots of dried grass skirts, tapa cloth, flowered material and white wicker. At second glance you notice that there are five or six coats of paint on the wicker and that the tapa cloth is a little tattered around the edges. That's because Uncle Billy is famous for never throwing anything out, which is one of the reasons he can run this place so cheaply. The hotel is also wedged in between two behemoths on either side and you may have to lean out the window to see the ocean from your room. Nevertheless, what the Hilo Bay Resort lacks in pizzazz it makes up for in an enthusiastic and friendly staff and good value. The restaurant is family-style buffet, cheap, and the free Hula Show is on of the great bargains of Hawaii. (Some of the dancers may be on the mature side, but by golly, they look like they're enjoying what they're doing!) All rooms have color TVs, fridge and private lanais. Some "condo-style" rooms have kitchenettes. Oceanfront swimming pool. Amenities: balcony or patio, family plan. 150 rooms. Credit cards: A, D, MC, V.

Hilo Hawaiian Hotel $99–$315   ★★★

71 Banyan Drive, Hilo, 96720, ☎ *(800) 367-5004, (808) 935-9361, FAX (808) 961-9642. Rated Restaurant: Queen's Court.*
Single: $99–$315. Double: $99–$315.

Renovated in 1992, the Hilo Hawaiian is a vintage 1970s hotel that has done its best to catch up. The good news is that some of the rooms have spectacular views over a lagoon, and glass louvers that you can open to let in fresh air. Decor is a non-committal beige and earthy blue with a judicious number of indoor ficus. I'm not at all sure that I really go for Berber carpets in this climate (tile or hardwood looks cooler) but the effect is pleasing to the eye. The Queen's Court Dining Room has a certain retro charm with naugahyde banquettes and booths, but I am of the firm opinion that this would have been an ideal place for wicker or wrought iron (it gets sticky sitting in those booths). The Wai'oli lounge features nightly entertainment. All rooms are air-conditioned and feature refrigerators, color TVs, coffee makers and radios. Some have lanais. Suites have kitchenettes. On-site services include a banquet facility for 450, laundry room, gift shop, beauty salon, massage and wake-up service. Golf across from the hotel, nearby tennis courts, two miles to the beach. Amenities: balcony or patio, business services. 283 rooms. Credit cards: A, D, MC, V.

THE BIG ISLAND

Ka'u

Naalehu

Bed-and-Breakfasts

Becky's Bed and Breakfast   **$50–$65**   ★ ★

P.O. Box 673, Naalehu, 96772, 64 miles from Hilo, 56 miles from Kona on Highway 11,
☎ *(800) 235-1233, (808) 929-9690, FAX (808) 929-9690.*
Single: $50–$55. Double: $50–$65.

Becky's is a cheerful green and white plantation house that was built before World War II. The front porch is crowded with potted plants, and a hot tub takes pride of place on the back. All rooms are simply furnished and have private baths. Breakfast is an all-you-can-eat affair, but it's served from 6:30-8 a.m., so if you want to eat, you can't sleep in. The village of Naalehu is located on the southern edge of the island, roughly halfway between Hilo and Kona. Sea Mountain, Discovery Harbor and Volcano golf courses are within easy reach of Naalehu, but a car is a necessity. Volcano Park is a scenic 35 minutes away and Punalu'u State Park—with its green sea turtles and black sands—is only 12 miles away. This place isn't fancy, but there are good reasons to spend a couple of days here. There's a 25 percent discount on stays of four days or longer with prior reservation. Amenities: Jacuzzi. 3 rooms.
Credit cards: not accepted.

Condos

Colony One at Sea Mountain Condominiums   **$85–$150**   ★ ★ ★

Highway 11, 28 miles from Volcanoes National Park, Naalehu, 96777, ☎ *(800) 525-5894, (808) 326-2252.*
Single: $85–$150. Double: $85–$150.

Colony One at Sea Mountain is a modern condo development overlooking a golf course and the ocean. The unusually attractive units are constructed of wood and local stone. Designed to be reminiscent of the long houses of Polynesia, they blend unobtrusively with the surrounding landscape. The main attraction for many visitors to this area is golf, and even those who are lukewarm toward the game will be impressed with the par-72 Arthur Jack Snyder golf course. Every hole has a spectacular ocean or mountain view. Hiking trails along the coast lead to hidden coves with black-sand beaches. Sea turtles often feed here and adjacent tidal pools present a wealth of marine life for the interested observer. (That means please look, don't touch.) Restaurant, conference center. Amenities: tennis, Jacuzzi, sauna, balcony or patio, business services. 76 rooms.

Kona

Kailua-Kona

Bed-and-Breakfasts

Adrienne's Casa Del Sol   **$60–$150**   ★ ★ ★

77-6335 Ali'i Drive, Kailua-Kona, 96740, ☎ *(800) 395-2272, (808) 326-2272.*
Single: $60–$150. Double: $60–$150.

Adrienne's enjoys an enviable location between historic Kailua and the modern Keauhou Resort and Kona Country Club and its famous golf courses. Plus, it's only a hundred feet from the beach. The two-story house looks like it was transported, tile by tile from the Costa del Sol. The common areas are decorated with antiques and Oriental rugs, plus a baby grand just waiting for guests to tickle its ivories. The guest-room decor is romantic-tropical, with ceiling fans and canopy beds in some of the rooms. From the deck surrounding the pool, visitors enjoy watching dolphins, surfers and the occasional whale. Host Reginald presides over the breakfast table, serving homemade breads (don't miss the macadamia nut pineapple muffins) and tropical fruits, washed down by pure Kona coffee, Hawaiian teas and fresh-squeezed fruit juices. Cable TVs, video library. No children under 16. Amenities: Jacuzzi, balcony or patio. 5 rooms. Credit cards: MC, V.

Hale Maluhia $55–$135   ★ ★ ★

76-770 Hualalai Road, Kailua-Kona, 96740, ☎ *(800) 559-6627, (808) 329-5773.*
Single: $55–$135. Double: $55–$135.

Located about 15 minutes from the airport and two and a half miles from Kailua-Kona, Hale Maluhia is a country inn/bed-and-breakfast that sprawls comfortably above the road to Holualua. It's actually a family compound that is composed of four buildings, so there's plenty of privacy and room for everyone. The architectural style is a sort of retro-plantation-Victorian, which means that there's lots of wood, and open-beam ceilings, with brass, marble and stained glass thrown in. Several small waterfalls in the garden provide a tranquil background sound. The elegant outdoor spa is made of Japanese slate and tile. The house takes great pride in its Breakfast Lovers Buffet. Breads are baked daily and Kona coffee is served in copious quantities. After breakfast and before exploring the Big Island, we especially enjoyed watching the koi in the lily ponds. The varied accommodations consist of four guest rooms (one with a private garden), an 800-square-foot cottage with a private Carrara marble Jacuzzi tub, kitchenette and entertainment center, and a gate house that's perfect for family gatherings. The gate house has two rooms and a kitchenette, two full baths and sleeps five. Two rooms are equipped for the physically disabled. Amenities include game room, book and movie library, portable massage table, beach gear, office facilities, even an art studio. The entire place can be booked for $500 a night. Smoking on lanais only. Amenities: Jacuzzi, family plan, business services. 8 rooms. Credit cards: A, D, MC, V.

Kailua Plantation House $145–$205   ★ ★ ★ ★

75-48 Ali'i Drive, Kailua-Kona, 96740, ☎ *(808) 329-3727.*
Single: $145–$205. Double: $145–$205.

Kailua Plantation House will appeal to the sybarite in all of us. Guest rooms have been meticulously appointed, many with queen-size canopy beds and ceiling fans; all have private lanais. Furniture makes ample use of rattan, wicker and netting. The top-of-the-line rooms, Pilialoha and Kai o Lani, feature luxurious platform tubs and glass-enclosed showers with ocean views. Most accommodations overlook the black lava boulders and foamy breakers a few feet from the front of the house. Sunset, with a glass of wine and a good companion in this setting, is a never-to-be-forgotten experience. Breakfast is served daily (7:30–9:30 a.m.) in the elegant living area on the shady lanai overlooking the ocean. Table settings are imaginative and as one might expect, the breads and muffins are prepared fresh daily. After a long day of exploring, the perfect nightcap is a moonlight dip in the oceanfront spa and triangular-shaped dipping pool. No children under 12 accepted. Amenities: Jacuzzi, balcony or patio. 5 rooms. Credit cards: A, MC, V.

Kiwi Gardens $50–$80   ★★

74-4920 Kiwi Street, Kailua-Kona, 96740, ☎ *(808) 326-1559, FAX (808) 329-6618. Single: $50–$80. Double: $50–$80.*
Kiwi Gardens lives up to its name. More than 100 exotic fruit-bearing trees and bushes dot the one acre estate located just a few minutes from the Kona airport and a short drive from the town of Kailua-Kona. One of the most enjoyable features of staying at the Kiwi Gardens is watching the tropical birds in the garden. Some are caged, but many more are free-flying. They are most active in the early morning and late afternoon. The house, built in an art deco style, is impeccably maintained, and the 800-foot elevation assures cooler temperatures and breezes. There are two standard rooms and a master suite within the house, two with lanais. A Hawaiian-style guest cottage has a queen bed, and from its lanai there's an outstanding sunset view over the ocean. Breakfast is included in the room charge, and consists of freshly baked breads every morning, plus fruit picked in the gardens. Amenities: balcony or patio. 4 rooms. Credit cards: not accepted.

Three Bears' Bed and Breakfast $65–$75   ★★★

72-1001 Puukala Street, Kailua-Kona, 96740, ☎ *(800) 765-0480, (808) 325-7653. Single: $65–$75. Double: $65–$75.*
A visit to Three Bears' Bed and Breakfast is like staying in a private home. A large common area opens out onto a covered terrace, which overlooks the lush gardens surrounding the house. Banana plants, papaya trees, hibiscus and the ubiquitous impatiens grow in profusion. During the winter, there's a telescope on the lanai for whale-watching. All year round, wild canaries and parakeets take advantage of a bird feeder (bring your binoculars). Both guest rooms have private baths, color TVs, coffeemakers, microwaves and a small fridge. Full kitchen privileges are available for longer stays. A superior breakfast is provided, much of which is produced on the premises. Papayas, pineapples and lilikoi from the garden are frequently served, as well as coffee from its own coffee farm. Hosts Anne and Nanette grow their own macadamia nuts and guests can eat all they want! Special mac cracker provided. Beach gear provided free to guests. German spoken. Amenities: Jacuzzi, balcony or patio. 2 rooms. Credit cards: not accepted.

Condos

Aston Royal Sea Cliff Resort $125–$400   ★★★

75-6040 Ali'i Drive, Kailua-Kona, ☎ *(800) 922-7866, (808) 359-8021, FAX (808) 326-1897. Single: $125–$400. Double: $125–$400.*
This meandering, terraced condominium property overlooks a dramatic, rocky stretch of ocean, but has no beach. The apartments, furnished in wicker and rattan, are BIG, especially the lanais; many have great views. One- and two-bedroom suites have kitchens with microwave, while lower-priced studios only have fridges, and

THE BIG ISLAND

you'll have to drive a bit to get to a restaurant. There's a sundry store, but it's definitely overpriced. Other amenities include an iron and ironing board, washer-dryer, in-room safe and voice mail. Large seawater pool, smaller freshwater pool, barbecue. Free parking, maid service. Amenities: tennis, Jacuzzi, sauna, balcony or patio. 146 rooms. Credit cards: MC, V.

Colony Kona Bali Kai — $88–$200 — ★★★

76-6246 Ali'i Drive, Kailua-Kona, 96740, ☎ *(800) 777-1700, (808) 329-9381, FAX (808) 326-6056.*

This four-story Colony condominium property overlooks a lava rock beach. Units consist of studio or one- or two-bedroom apartments with fully equipped kitchens, private lanais and color TVs. Not all rooms are air-conditioned, but all have louvers that can be opened to let in the sea breezes. Units are well-maintained and feature natural rattan furniture and light floral upholstery. Incoming guests receive a complimentary package of Kona coffee. Nearby attractions include golf courses, deep-sea fishing, snorkeling, scuba diving, tennis, horseback riding and shopping at the Kona Inn Shopping Center. If you tire of cooking, restaurants of all types and in all price ranges can be found nearby. Pool on premises. Amenities: Jacuzzi, balcony or patio. Credit cards: A, CB, DC, D, MC, V.

Hale Kona Kai — $75–$85 — ★

75-5870 Kahakai Road, Kailua-Kona, 96740, ☎ *(800) 421-3696, (808) 329-2155. Single: $75–$85. Double: $75–$85.*

The Hale Kona Kai is ideal for long-term travelers. All the one-bedroom apartments in this three-story building have some kind of ocean view and are equipped with full kitchens and color TVs. On those nights (or days) when cooking lacks appeal, guests can walk next door to the Royal Kona Resort with its restaurants and coffee shops, or walk to Kailua Town and choose from a number of interesting dining establishments. Nearby activities include deep-sea fishing, horseback riding, snorkeling, hiking, golf (five miles from the Keauhou Golf Course), sailing and hunting. Pool, laundry facilities. Maid service on request. No Sunday or holiday check-in. Amenities: balcony or patio. 39 rooms. Credit cards: not accepted.

Keauhou Resort — $90–$135 — ★★★

78-7039 Kam III Road, Kailua-Kona, 96740, ☎ *(800) 367-5286, (808) 322-9122, FAX (808) 322-9410. Single: $90–$135. Double: $90–$135.*

Keauhou Resort is a condominium development that caters to travelers who want to spend an extended period of time in the islands. One- and two-level townhouses are located in a landscaped, five-acre tropical garden. Almost all have an ocean view and all have at least one covered lanai. Amenities include full kitchens with microwave, dishwasher and fridge with ice-maker, washer-dryer and cable TV. Two championship golf courses are within walking distance (reduced rates on green fees offered) and two pools, shaded by coconut palms, are available for the enjoyment of those who would rather stay at home. Nearby attractions include snorkeling and/ or scuba diving, deep-sea fishing, ancient Hawaiian temples and shopping in the nearby town of Kailua-Kona with its boutiques, open-air cafés and historic buildings. A resident manager is on hand to solve any problems and give good advice as to what to do, where to go, and how to get there. Amenities: balcony or patio. 48 rooms. Credit cards: not accepted.

Kona Reef **$130–$285** ★ ★

75-5888 Ali'i Drive, Kailua-Kona, 96740, ☎ (800) 367-5004, (808) 329-2959, FAX (808) 329-2762.
Single: $130–$285. Double: $130–$285.
These one-, two- or three-bedroom condominiums overlook an attractive pool area and black-lava beach. Decor is a soothing beige with natural rattan, and sliding glass doors open out onto lanais. All have full kitchens with dishwasher, washer-dryer, cable TV, lanais and daily maid service. The Kona Reef has a good location within walking distance from the town of Kailua which offers a myriad of sights, shops and restaurants. Pool, barbecue area, sundeck. Free covered parking. Amenities: Jacuzzi, balcony or patio. 130 rooms. Credit cards: not accepted.

White Sands Village **$100–$150** ★ ★

P.O. Box 4466, Kailua-Kona, 96745, ☎ (808) 329-6402, FAX (808) 326-2401.
Single: $100–$150. Double: $100–$150.
White Sands Village is another good choice for families and travelers who want to stay in one place for a while. The two-bedroom, two-bath apartments in several low-rise buildings feature fully equipped kitchens and washer-dryers. The village has an attractive pool area with lush plantings and is across the street from a namesake white-sand beach. Adjacent to the pool is a game room with a pool table and gas-fired barbecue. Plan on renting a car, though, as it's four miles from Kailua. Amenities: tennis, Jacuzzi, sauna, balcony or patio. 10 rooms. Credit cards: A, MC, V.

Hotels

Keauhou Beach Hotel **$98–$415** ★ ★ ★

78-6740 Ali'i Drive, Kailua-Kona, 96740, ☎ (800) 367-6025, (808) 322-3441, FAX (808) 322-6586. Rated Restaurant: Kuakini Terrace
Single: $98–$415. Double: $98–$415.
The Keauhou Beach Hotel is a resort that's manageable. There's plenty to do but not so much that you feel guilty if you just relax and sit in one place. Tennis courts are located on the grounds and a free shuttle takes guests to the nearby Kona Country Club, where they can play on a world-famous 27-hole golf course. Guest rooms recently have been renovated. Most rooms have sliding glass doors that lead to a private lanai. The hotel is right on the beach with access to Kahalu'u Beach Park from the gardens. This is one of the best beaches in the area for swimming and snorkeling. If you go early in the morning, or late in the afternoon, you'll spot sea turtles. The grounds are extremely well-maintained, and the orchid and anthurium collections are quite well-known. History buffs will be interested in visiting the house, which was occupied by King David Kalakaua when he withdrew from the summer court at Kailua. There are also the remains of ancient temples and petroglyphs carved into the lava rock. On weekends, the seafood buffets are reputed to be the best on the island. Even locals eat here. Depending on the availability of local talent, there's usually a good musical show on weekends. Amenities: tennis, balcony or patio. 318 rooms. Credit cards: A, DC, D, MC, V.

King Kamehameha's Kona Beach Hotel $100–$500   ★★★

75-5660 Palani Road, Kailua-Kona, 96740, ☎ *(800) 367-6060, (808) 923-4511, FAX (808) 922-8061. Rated Restaurant: Kona Beach Restaurant.*

Single: $100–$500. Double: $100–$500.

This old-timer on the Kona Coast is practically self-contained. With a minimum of effort, guests can enjoy golf, tennis, twilight outrigger canoe rides, a stroll in the tropical gardens, a visit to an active volcano and shopping in 28 boutiques and specialty stores. Luaus on the beach are offered four times a week. If just relaxing is what you want to do, the hotel has its own stretch of beach right in front of the property. Casual meals are served in the poolside Billfish Bar, which comes alive with music after dark. Guest rooms are spacious and attractive wooden-louvered doors lead onto private lanais with either ocean or garden views. Amenities include refrigerators, safes and color TVs with movies. The King Kam is one of the only hotels to boast a national treasure on its grounds—the faithfully restored *Ahu'ena Heiau* (see "Historical Sights"). Amenities: tennis, Jacuzzi, balcony or patio, business services. 460 rooms. Credit cards: A, MC, V.

Kona Bay Hotel $77–$91   ★★

75-5739 Ali'i Drive, Kailua-Kona, ☎ *(800) 367-5102, (808) 329-1393, FAX (808) 935-7903.*

Single: $77–$91. Double: $77–$91.

You can take your cue from the fact that this hotel is operated under the name Uncle Billy's Hawaiian Family Hotels. This generic budget Polynesian-style property is sort of like going to visit your Uncle Billy, who's laid-back, awfully nice and not terribly hip. Atmosphere is achieved through the use of fake tapa cloth, some masks on the wall and a bit of fishnet hung in the corners. Encroaching civilization has taken its toll on the Kona Bay. It's located right in downtown Kailua and a shopping center now separates it from the beach. Rooms tend to be small and renovations seem to be limited to slapping another coat of paint on the aging rattan furniture. But all rooms are air-conditioned and contain private lanais, refrigerators and color TVs. Meals are buffets of the all-you-can-eat variety—filling but undistinguished. Nevertheless, the management is friendly and tries hard. The prices are right, too, which no doubt accounts for the fact that this place is still in business. Bar, pool, children's pool. Amenities: Jacuzzi, balcony or patio, family plan. 123 rooms. Credit cards: A, DC, D, MC, V.

Kona Tiki Hotel $59–$65   ★★

75-5068 Ali'i Drive, Kailua-Kona, 96740, ☎ *(808) 329-1425, FAX (808) 327-9402.*

Single: $59–$65. Double: $59–$65.

The Kona Tiki is a no-frills operation with an enviable location in a palm grove right on the (rocky) oceanfront. It's also close to golf courses and Kailua shopping and restaurants. The downside is that the rooms are small, yet they all face the ocean and have private lanais. No TVs or phones. Complimentary rolls and Kona coffee (natch) are served poolside in the morning. A good place to use as a base of operations for exploring the Kona coast. The management will be happy to arrange deep-sea fishing trips or boat cruises. Amenities: balcony or patio. 15 rooms. Credit cards: not accepted.

Royal Kona Resort   **$195–$1500**   ★ ★ ★

75-5852 Ali'i Drive, Kailua-Kona, 96740, ☎ *(800) 44R-OYAL, (808) 329-3111, FAX (808) 661-6150. Rated Restaurant: Tropics Café.*
Single: $195–$1500. Double: $195–$1500.

Your typical "Polynesian" resort, the Royal Kona boasts a private lagoon and a two-level swimming pool overlooking the ocean. The floral prints on the bedspreads are a trifle dated and the furniture runs towards '50s institutional Danish, but the units are well-maintained and can be forgiven when you step out on to the private lanai. Most of the rooms have at least a partial ocean view, and sunset from your own balcony is an unforgettable experience. Food in the Tropics Café is good and the bartenders in the Windjammer Lounge are especially creative—almost every evening there's a new cocktail to try. Tihati's "Drums of Polynesia" luau is the only oceanfront luau on the Kona Coast. It's a little bit touristy, but a lot of fun. Amenities: tennis, Jacuzzi, balcony or patio, business services. 454 rooms. Credit cards: A, D, MC, V.

Resorts

Kona Surf Resort   **$109–$555**   ★ ★ ★

78-128 Ehukai Street, Kailua-Kona, 96740, ☎ *(800) 367-8011, (808) 322-3411. Rated Restaurant: Pele's Court*
Single: $109–$555. Double: $109–$555.

The Kona Surf Resort and Country Club enjoys a spectacular setting on an ancient lava flow at the entrance to Keauhou Bay. The design of the hotel is stark and modern in the extreme, in dramatic contrast to the lush tropical surroundings. All rooms have views—either of the gardens, the ocean or both. The oceanfront suites with their view of the lava cliffs and pounding waves are especially impressive. All rooms have private lanais, mini-fridges and private dressing areas. Golfers are invited to play on Kona Country Club courses next door—36 challenging holes between volcanic mountains and the Pacific. Pele's Court restaurant serves steaks, prime rib and local seafood among waterfalls and flowering indoor plants. Dress is casual. Lighter meals and tropical drinks are served at the poolside Nalu Terrace. Karaoke sing-alongs are a nightly happening at the Puka Bar. A variety of watersports can be arranged. Volleyball, shuffleboard, botanical gardens, wedding chapel, meeting facilities. Amenities: tennis, balcony or patio, business services. 530 rooms. Credit cards: A, CB, DC, D, MC, V.

North Kohala

Kapa'au

Guest House

Hawi Farms Guest House   **$75–$95**   ★ ★

P.O. Box 640, Kapa'au, 96777, ☎ *(800) 889-0680, (808) 889-0007.*
Single: $75–$95. Double: $75–$95.

Hawi Farms Guest House is the place to get away from it all. Located in the hill country of North Kohala, it's 30 minutes from the Parker Ranch and 20 miles from beaches that offer surfing, deep-sea fishing and snorkeling. In other words, you can get there if you want to, but you'll probably prefer to sit on the guest house lanai and enjoy the scenery and sunsets. Closer to home are the back-to-back towns of

THE BIG ISLAND

Hawi and Kapaau (should be called Hawikapa or Kapahawi depending on point of view), which up to now have been overlooked by tourists, though they're slowly becoming gentrified. There are several interesting art galleries, restaurants (including the excellent Bamboo), an ice cream shop and a handful of worthwhile historical sites. Amenities: balcony or patio. 1 room.

North Kona

Resorts

Four Seasons Resort Hawaii at Hualalai   **$400–$600**   ★★★★★

8 Queen Kaahumanu Highway, North Kona, ☎ *(800) 332-3442, (808) 325-8000, FAX (808) 325-8100.*
Single: $400–$600. Double: $400–$600.

Always known for its attention to detail and comfort, the Four Seasons outdid itself this time with a complex of 32 beachfront and four golf-club bungalows situated on a secluded private beach on the North Kona Coast. Careful planning (each room has an exterior entrance—no corridors!) ensures that each room has an ocean view and a feeling of maximum privacy. Windows that don't look out over the ocean face onto artfully composed views of native vegetation, the Jack Nicklaus golf course or private plunge pools surrounded by black-lava rock. The resort has eight tennis courts and a pro staff to arrange tournaments and provide group or individual instruction. The 15,000-square-foot Health and Wellness center provides aerobics, massage, treatment rooms and indoor-outdoor showers in addition to a lap pool, whirlpool, Olympic free weights and cardiovascular training equipment. There's also a Kids for All Seasons program included in the room rate. Amenities: tennis, health club, exercise room, Jacuzzi, balcony or patio, business services. 243 rooms.
Credit cards: A, DC, MC, V.

Kona Village Resort   **$395–$680**   ★★★★★

Highway 19, North Kona, 96745, ☎ *(800) 367-5290, (808) 325-5555, FAX (808) 325-5124. Rated Restaurant: Hale Samoa*
Single: $395–$680. Double: $395–$680.

The Kona Village boasts 125 *hales* and a notable reputation for integrity and service. The *hales* have varying floor plans and their design and decor reflect various Polynesian cultures–Hawaiian, Fijian, Samoan, Tahitian, New Hebridean, Maori and Marquesan. All have private baths and almost all have lanais (with hammocks). By design, there are no telephones, TVs or clocks in the rooms. Amenities include in-room safes, minibars and coffee makers with Kona coffee. The "Do Not Disturb" sign is a coconut placed outside the door. Botanical and historical walks are always rewarding and often worth repeating. A children's program runs year-round (except September). Aside from arts and crafts, activities include night reef-walking with flashlights (a real winner). The high point of the week is the famous luau, which begins at 9 a.m. with the preparation of kalua pig in an underground *imu* (oven). Along with all the traditional dishes, a special *haupia* cake is prepared for dessert— this is a classic butter cake with a RICH coconut frosting. The resort is a popular wedding site. With advance notice, the hotel will help you select a site, issue the marriage license and arrange for a minister. Honeymoon packages and special-occasion packages also are available. Other services and features include watersports, use of sailboats, outrigger canoes and kayaks, two freshwater pools. Prices are based on an American Plan of three meals a day and airport transfers. Note: Children over 13 are charged $160 per day; six-12 years, $110 per day; two-five years, $55 per day; INFANTS (!) $25 per day. Amenities: tennis, balcony or patio. 125 rooms. Credit cards: A, CB, DC, D, MC, V.

Puna

Kalani Oceanside Eco-Resort   **$45–$95**   ★★★

RR2, Box 4500, Puna, 96778, ☎ (800) 800-6886, (808) 965-7828.
Single: $45–$85. Double: $75–$95.
The Kalani Oceanside Eco-Resort is for travelers who really want something different. Take your cue from the fact that it's operated as a nonprofit organization. Accommodations range from campsites (from $15) in the orchard to cozy, oceanfront cottages. Meals are vegetarian buffets. The Kalani also doubles as an educational facility and has an exceptionally active list of seminars and conferences. The 1996 offerings were as diverse as yoga retreats, a HeartPower Healing and Celebration, a workshop on Sculpture in Landscape, a retreat entitled Women and Sacred Transitions, or a study of Hula Heritage. Nearby attractions include beaches with dolphins, Hawaii Volcanoes National Park, thermal springs, snorkeling, cave climbing, hiking and fascinating tidal pools. Dress is casual in the extreme, and the management recommends cotton or rayon fibers. Bring your thongs and sneakers. Facilities include a 25-meter pool. Amenities: tennis, exercise room, Jacuzzi, family plan. 30 rooms. Credit cards: A, MC, V.

South Kohala

Kamuela

Bed-and-Breakfasts

The Kamuela Inn   **$54–$165**   ★★

P.O. Box 1994, Kamuela, 96743, ☎ (808) 885-4253, FAX (808) 885-8857.
Single: $54–$165. Double: $54–$165.
The Kamuela Inn is a well-established hostelry in Parker Ranch country; reservations have to be made far in advance. It offers varied accommodations, ranging from comfortable double rooms to third-floor "penthouse" suites. A newly completed wing houses the Executive Suites with full kitchens and private sunrooms; one has a carved rosewood antique bed. All rooms have private baths and cable TVs. A serve-yourself continental breakfast is offered daily on a coffee lanai. It's close to shops, museums and restaurants. 31 rooms. No credit cards.

The New Millennium Institute   **$65–$125**   ★★

Near Waimea-Kamuela ☎ (808) 593-2297, FAX (808) 593-2640.
Single: $65–$125. Double: $65–$125.
The New Millenium Institute concerns itself with studying the issues confronting our civilization in an "era of infinitely mutable knowledge and transient values." Weeklong sessions are scheduled twice a year, timed to coincide with the "equinoxes" and are led by "leading visionaries." As of this writing, sessions are sched-

uled in such areas as "Mind, Novelty and the Eschaton;" "Life after Life;" and "The Reinvention of Work." Sessions are held in a spectacular Frank Lloyd Wright-designed passive-solar hemicycle house near Waimea, which was completed in 1995. Unfortunately, only a limited number of students can live here, but those left out will be referred to other outstanding bed-and-breakfasts in the area through Hawaii's Best Bed and Breakfasts at ☎ *(808) 885-4550* or *(800) 262-9912*. The home can also be rented independently for $500 a day, or $3000 per week, with a minimum two-night stay. Attendees can expect breakfast, three hours of classes in the morning and a vegetarian lunch, yoga classes and a dinner celebration on Friday evenings. Afternoons are deliberately left free to enable participants to discuss material presented in morning sessions, explore nearby Hawaiian sacred sites, or simply hike along the coast. The complete package is $975; deposits of $375 are due 60 days before the programs begin. 4 rooms. Credit cards: A, D, MC, V.

Waimea Gardens Cottage $115

P.O. Box 563, Kamuela, 96743, ☎ *(800) 262-9912, (808) 885-4550, FAX (808) 885-0550.*

Single: $115. Double: $115.

Waimea Gardens Cottage actually consists of two adjoining wings of a restored historic cottage on a 1.5-acre estate in Parker Ranch country, only eight miles from Kohala Coast beaches and two miles from shopping, restaurants and museums. Both are meticulously decorated in a picturesque country style that Martha Stewart would approve. The older of the two, the Kohala Wing, is a large studio with a gleaming, complete kitchen. The Waimea Wing, with a kitchenette, has a romantic sleeping alcove, a sitting area with a fireplace, a koa-wood rocker and a comfy loveseat. Both have private baths, hardwood floors, wainscotting, lace curtains and French doors opening to brick terraces. Robes are provided. Guests cook their breakfasts from foodstuffs provided by hosts Barbara and Charlie Campbell, including eggs from their miniature hens. Amenities: balcony or patio. 2 rooms. Credit cards: not accepted.

Motels

Waimea Country Lodge $78–$98

Highway 19, Kamuela, 96743, ☎ *(800) 367-5004, (808) 591-2235, FAX (808) 596-0158.*

Single: $78–$98. Double: $78–$98.

Located within walking distance from the historic country town of Waimea, the Waimea Country Lodge (formerly the Parker Ranch Lodge) offers spiffy, modern accommodations at a reasonable price. High-ceilinged rooms are comfortably rustic, with knotty pine furniture and color TVs hidden in armoires; all have views of the surrounding mountains and horse meadows. Kitchenettes are available for those who want to set up light housekeeping on an extended visit. 21 rooms. Credit cards: A, D, MC, V.

Kohala Coast

Keokea Beach Park on the way to Pololu Valley Lookout on the North Kohala Coast is a great place for a picnic. On weekdays it's pleasantly uncrowded.

Condos

Elima Lani   **$89–$125**   ★★★

68-3883 Lua Kula Street, Kohala Coast, 96743, ☎ (800) 367-5004, (808) 883-8288, FAX (808) 883-8170.
Single: $89–$125. Double: $89–$125.
The Elima Lani is a good, reasonably priced option for golfers and their families. Special rates at Waikoloa Village course are offered, as well as to six other courses nearby. The one- and two-bedroom units feature full kitchens and two full baths. There are two swimming pools, jet spas and barbecue areas at various locations on the grounds. All units have lanais overlooking the Waikoloa Village course. Guests have complimentary use of the tennis courts. Recent redecoration of the suites included Berber carpeting and soft floral print upholstery for the rattan furniture. Ceiling fans keep the air circulating and high ceilings give a pleasant, open feeling to the units. Amenities: tennis, Jacuzzi, balcony or patio. 216 rooms. Credit cards: A, CB, DC, D, MC, V.

Mauna Lani Point   **$260–$520**   ★★★★

68-1310 Mauna Lani Drive, Kohala Coast, 96743, ☎ (800) 642-6284, (808) 885-5022, FAX (808) 661-1025.
Single: $260–$520. Double: $260–$520.
This is how the rich and famous live. One-, two- or three-bedroom units overlook either the Francis H. I'i Brown South Golf Course or the ocean. The fairway units are cheaper. The interior decorating schemes are done in a sophisticated blend of beige, pale peach and natural rattan. Large sliding glass doors open out onto covered lanais with more wicker furniture. Pools, artificial and natural, surround the

THE BIG ISLAND

buildings. At the beach in front of the hotel, hammocks are strung invitingly between palm trees for the less athletically inclined. The facilities of the Mauna Lani Resort are available to guests of the condominium at reduced rates, including some of the most sophisticated tennis facilities in the Pacific, and players have their choice of hard surface, clay or grass courts. Amenities: tennis, exercise room, Jacuzzi, sauna, balcony or patio. 116 rooms. Credit cards: A, D, MC, V.

The Islands at Mauna Lani $375–$475 ★ ★ ★ ★

2 Kaniku Drive, Kohala Coast, 96743, ☎ *(800) 642-MAUI, (808) 885-5022.*
Single: $375–$475. Double: $375–$475.

These independent luxury town houses are completely furnished (they even include a car during your stay). Luxury is the watchword, from the groceries in the kitchen to the glass-topped table in the dining room. The two- and three-bedroom suites are decorated in pastel colors with accent floral prints. French windows open out onto covered lanais off of every room. Plumeria, hibiscus, ti plants and palm trees all grow in the private gated courtyards and complement the five acres of man-made lagoons and waterfalls that surround the townhouses. Each unit has at least 2300 square feet of interior space, allowing guests to spread out and really relax. All have a full kitchen, wet bar and gas barbecue, laundry and central air conditioning. Arrangements can be made to play on the nearby, award-winning Francis H. I'i Brown golf course or the Mauna Lani Racquet Club. Amenities: Jacuzzi, balcony or patio. 41 rooms. Credit cards: A, CB, DC, D, MC, V.

Hapuna Beach Prince Hotel features spectacular ocean and mountain views.

THE BIG ISLAND

Resorts

Hapuna Beach Prince Hotel   **$325–$6000**   ★★★★★

62-100 Kauna'oa Drive, Kohala Coast, 96743, ☎ *(800) 882-6060, (808) 880-1111,*
FAX (808) 880-3112. Rated Restaurant: Hakone
Single: $325–$6000. Double: $325–$6000.

If location, location, location makes a resort, the Hapuna Beach Prince has it all. Its
350 rooms all overlook the Pacific and spill down the mountainside to the ocean,
providing unobstructed views. Better yet, the teak louvers and sliding doors allow
the option of eschewing air conditioning and enjoying the sea breezes instead. The
atrium lobby sets the tone for the entire establishment. It's open on all sides and displays a portion of the hotel's collection of Asian art, which is on display throughout
the building and grounds. The rooms themselves are on the small side and their
decor can best be described as opulent-minimalist. As for appointments, everything
you expect is there: the robes, the fluffy towels, the goodies in the bathroom. All are
equipped with TVs and VCRs. The golf course, consistently ranked among the best
in the world, was designed by Arnold Palmer and Ed Seay—a par-72 course, it rises
from sea level to 700 feet and wanders 6875 yards between the lava beds and the
ocean with dramatic views on every hole. It's no surprise to anyone that the restaurants at the resort are some of the best on the island. The most elegant (coat and tie
for gentlemen, please) is the Bistro. Mediterranean dishes made with local produce
are their signature offerings and these are truly outstanding. Nevertheless, we preferred Hakone and its Japanese chefs. Golfers tend to frequent Arnie's (named after
You-Know-Who). There are always deli sandwiches or salads. Don't overlook the
Reef Lounge. In the morning it's a coffee bar and in the evening it turns into an elegant cocktail lounge with signature drinks and a jazz trio playing in the background.
Other amenities include ocean sports, summer children's program, Hawaiian arts-
and-crafts classes, shuttle service to local hotels and shops, boutiques, beauty salon.
Amenities: tennis, health club, Jacuzzi, balcony or patio, business services. 350
rooms. Credit cards: A, CB, DC, D, MC, V.

Hilton Waikoloa Village   **$210–$3750**   ★★★★★

425 Waikoloa Beach Drive, Kohala Coast, 96743, ☎ *(800) HIL-TONS, (808) 885-*
1234, FAX (808) 885-7592. Rated Restaurant: Donatoni's
Single: $210–$3750. Double: $210–$3750.

Guests are housed in more than 1200 rooms spread out over three low-rise buildings. No one has to walk anywhere because trams and canal boats (on underwater
tracks, a la Disneyland) whisk him/her from place to place. Amenities include in-
room refreshment center, safes and cable TVs. All have private lanais with sliding
glass doors that make the already ample rooms seem larger. Concierge service is
provided in all guest towers. In what seems to have been an attempt to improve on
nature (the property faces the ocean), a seven-acre artificial lagoon has been constructed and stocked with tropical fish so guests can snorkel without having to leave
the premises. In another lagoon, the hotel sponsors Dolphin Quest, which allows
guests to experience direct contact with six of these marine mammals. The Dolphin
Discovery program (for children five-12) and the Teen Encounter (for teenagers)
require advance reservations. Demand for Dolphin Doubles, the adult dolphin-

encounter program, is so great that places are allotted daily in a random drawing. Children's activities get special priority at the Waikoloa Village, including the daily Camp Menehune program for children ages five-12. Adults have a choice of two championship golf courses. There are both clay and hard surface tennis courts. Workout facilities, aromatherapy, massage (Swedish shiatsu, and lomi-lomi Hawaiian), Jacuzzis, steam rooms, saunas, beauty salon, herbal wraps—it's all here. There are eight main restaurants and as many snack bars/sandwich shops. Amenities: tennis, health club, exercise room, Jacuzzi, balcony or patio, family plan, business services. 1238 rooms. Credit cards: A, CB, DC, D, MC, V.

Mauna Kea Beach Hotel $280–$500   ★★★★★

62-100 Mauna Kea Beach Drive, Kohala Coast, 96743, ☎ *(800) 882-6060, (808) 882-7222, FAX (808) 882-3112. Rated Restaurant: Batik*
Single: $280–$500. Double: $280–$500.
From 1965-1994, the Mauna Kea Beach Hotel was considered by many to be THE standard by which other resorts in Hawaii were judged. But... even the best hotels begin to show their age and in 1994 the Mauna Kea shut down for renovations. When the doors opened in late 1995, most changes to the guest rooms and public areas were so subtle that curious returnees hardly noticed the difference. Everything now has a larger and brighter look due to the lighter shades of marble and tile. Guest bathrooms, which were on the small side, have been upgraded with new marble floors and modern fixtures. The rooms themselves have been appointed with specially commissioned willow and rattan furniture and original watercolors. Six restaurants will serve you a meal at any time of the day or night. The famous and scrumptious buffet spread at the Terrace/Copper Bar is still going strong; there is also a nightly buffet in the vast Pavilion restaurant overlooking Mauna Kea Beach. If you want to dress up in jacket and tie, the Batik, the resort's premier dining establishment, serves classic Provençal French cuisine. Two special ál fresco dining events are the seafood buffet and clambake on Saturdays at the Hau Tree and the Tuesday evening Luau, featuring performances by Kumu Hula Nani Lim and her award-winning hula *halau* (school). Recreational facilities include the par-72 Mauna Kea Golf Course, which was named number-one golf course in Hawaii and among America's 100 Greatest by *Golf Digest* in 1995; guests can also play at the newer, "environmentally sensitive" Hapuna Golf Course, which is within walking distance of the Mauna Kea's sister hotel, the Hapuna Beach Prince. Amenities: tennis, horseback riding, health club, exercise room, Jacuzzi, balcony or patio, business services. 310 rooms. Credit cards: A, CB, DC, D, MC, V.

The Mauna Lani Bay Hotel and Bungalows $260–$3970   ★★★★★

68-1400 Mauna Lani Drive, Kohala Coast, 96743, ☎ *(800) 367-2323, (808) 885-6622. Rated Restaurant: CanoeHouse*
Single: $260–$3970. Double: $260–$3970.
This is a resort in the true sense of the word. The two golf courses, carved from a 16th-century lava flow, will be familiar to TV viewers as the site of the Senior Skins Game. The on-site Tennis Garden has been rated as one of the Top 50 Greatest Tennis Resorts by *Tennis* magazine. The 10 plexi-pave courts of varying speeds will suit the needs of players of all levels. The hotel lobby has a saltwater lagoon, two

waterfalls and full-sized palm trees in an open atrium. Ninety percent of the rooms have an unobstructed view of the ocean. The hotel takes a special interest in children's activities. *Keikis* have their own special beach with small cabanas. Kids lucky enough to be here in the summer can participate in Turtle Independence Day, July 4, when *honu*, or endangered sea turtles, that have been raised in the hotel fish ponds are released into the sea. Guest rooms at the Mauna Lani range from luxurious to downright opulent. If you can swing it, try for one of the five private bungalows, which are 4000 square feet, with private swimming pools, whirlpool spas, steam baths and round-the-clock butler service. Meals are a delight here, especially in the evening at the terrific Canoe House restaurant, made famous by now departed chef Alan Wong, serving inspired Pacific Rim cuisine. Sunsets from its terrace are spectacular. Amenities: tennis, health club, balcony or patio, family plan, business services. 350 rooms. Credit cards: A, D, MC, V.

The Orchid at Mauna Lani   **$285–$475**   ★★★★★

1 North Kaniku Drive, Kohala Coast, 96743, ☎ *(800) 782-9488, (808) 885-2000, FAX (808) 885-8886. Rated Restaurant: The Grill*

Single: $285–$475. Double: $285–$475.

A fixture on the Kohala Coast luxury resort scene since 1990, the Ritz-Carlton Mauna Lani became the newest member of ITT Sheraton's "Luxury Collection" in March 1996, and has been renamed The Orchid at Mauna Lani. A $14 million renovation is planned, and due to a new landscaping scheme, more guest accommodations and public areas will be exposed to the spectacular ocean views around the 32-acre property. New artwork (the beautiful collection of nautical art will be auctioned off) and furnishings will reflect a more Hawaiian theme, gradually replacing the impeccably beautiful baronial English country mansion ambience. At press time, all guest rooms feature sumptuous marble baths with separate shower, double vanities and an additional telephone, fully-stocked honor bar with refrigerator, plush terry robes, Crabtree and Evelyn toiletries, in-room safe, color TV, and a 24-hour in-room video service. The Club Level on the top floor, which is an excellent value, is entered via a special key, and guests are provided with a private lounge, continental breakfast, mid-morning snacks, a light lunch of sandwiches and salads, cocktails, pupus, chocolates and liqueurs. A "Beach Boys Club" features local boys who teach guests about tides, surfing, canoe paddling, celestial navigation, ancient land division system and more. The Orchid's "Spa without Walls" healing and wellness package is one of the finest on the island. The program includes t'ai chi classes under palm trees, power walks through ancient lava flows, aqua aerobics in the 10,000-square-foot pool, and yoga on the beach followed by snorkel dives in the Pacific. Traditionalists can huff and puff on the good ole' Lifecycle in the fitness center. Guests have privileges at the Francis H. I'i Brown 36-hole championship golf courses as well as five other courses in the vicinity. You might think about hosting a company function here; the resort has very impressive conference facilities. Amenities: tennis, health club, exercise room, Jacuzzi, balcony or patio, family plan, club floor, business services. 539 rooms. Credit cards: A, D, MC, V.

The Royal Waikoloan   **$184–$365**   ★★★

69-275 Waikoloa Beach Drive, Kohala Coast, 96743, ☎ (808) 885-6789, FAX (808) 885-7852. Rated Restaurant: Royal Terrace

Single: $184–$239. Double: $255–$365.

Located between the Mauna Lani Bay Hotel and the Hilton Waikoloa Village, two of the pricier destinations on the Big Island, the Royal Waikoloan, until just recently an Outrigger property, is a welcome oasis of mid-range pricing. You won't find as many restaurants in the resort as you will at its neighbors, but the ones it has offer fair value for the price. Rooms are a nice size and all have private lanais. If you want more pampering and frills, book a room at the Royal Cabana Club. This 15-unit, two-suite building overlooks the lagoons. Guests are treated to continental breakfast while meeting other guests. The hotel offers a popular all-inclusive package for $177 per person. All meals, the Royal Luau, beverages in bars and lounges, watersports (including whale watching and snorkel sails), taxes and gratuities are included. The luau is offered two nights a week, but between times, guests can watch torch-lighting and torch-dancing acts after dark in the beachfront lounge. Activities available to guests are year-round swimming on beautiful Anaeho'omalu Bay, a white-sand beach protected from high surf by a living reef. There's golf at the nearby King's Course and Beach Course (shuttle available), tennis, snorkeling, hiking, tours of petroglyph sites, Hawaiian crafts classes and shopping in the adjacent Waikoloa King's Shops. The helpful and cheerful staff make the establishment one of the best buys on the Big Island. Amenities: Jacuzzi, balcony or patio, business services. 533 rooms. Credit cards: A, D, MC, V.

South Kona

Captain Cook

Hotels

Manago Hotel   **$22–$55**   ★★

P.O. Box 145, Captain Cook, 96704, ☎ (808) 323-2642.

Single: $22–$55. Double: $22–$55.

The Manago is a bare-bones, no-frills operation that will appeal to the type of traveler who uses his/her hotel as a base of operations for doing something else. Rooms have balconies, are spotlessly clean and have radios but no telephones. The only TV is in the lobby. The original rooms are on the first floor of the old building and are Spartan in the extreme-linoleum floors, shared baths and minimal bedding. The rule of thumb is, the higher up the room, the more comfortable the accommodation, so the "best" rooms are on the third floor of the new wing. The most expensive, at $52–$55 per night, are the Japanese rooms, with tatami mats and furo baths. The dining room is popular with locals and serves home-style Hawaiian meals in copious quantities—pork chops, rice and lots of gravy is the house specialty. Amenities: balcony or patio. 42 rooms. Credit cards: MC, V.

Holualoa

Bed-and-Breakfasts

Holualua Inn   **$125–$165**   ★ ★ ★ ★

P.O. Box 222, Holualoa, 96725, ☎ (800) 392-1812, (808) 324-1121.
Single: $125–$165. Double: $125–$165.

This beautiful inn, set in a private country estate overlooking the ocean in the heart of the Kona Coffee Belt, is surrounded by 40 acres of gardens and coffee trees. Its location on the slopes of Mount Hualalai ensures that guests enjoy cool breezes year round. The sprawling, three-story house and each of the four rooms are paneled in polished cedar, the floors of eucalyptus wood. Each guest room has a different theme with platform beds. The Hibiscus suite has an oversize Japanese whirlpool bath. Doors and windows open directly into the surrounding gardens. A stunning pool in the shape of a bird's beak features a flower mosaic at its bottom. Guests are also welcome to lounge in the TV room, play billiards or cozy up to the fireplace in the sitting room. Continental breakfasts (with lots of Kona coffee) are included with the price of the room. Picnic coolers are provided for day trips. The inn prides itself on its pupu platter of fresh fruit and cheese, served in the late afternoon, on request. Guests are encouraged to bring home meals from nearby restaurants and enjoy dining ál fresco in the gardens or rooftop gazebo; later you can use the telescope to get a close look at the stars. No children under 13, please. Amenities: balcony or patio. 4 rooms. Credit cards: A, MC, V.

Honaunau

The Dragonfly Ranch   **$70–$160**   ★ ★ ★

P.O. Box 675, Honaunau, 96276, ☎ (800) 487-2159, (808) 328-2159, FAX (808) 328-9570.
Single: $70–$160. Double: $70–$160.

The owners of the Dragonfly Ranch describe the place as a "tropical fantasy lodging," and if your fantasies involve close contact with nature, then you won't be disappointed. The indoor-outdoor ambience means there's as little between you and the outdoors as possible; if you have a phobia of spiders (they're harmless) this might not be the place for you. The gardens surrounding the guest accommodations are lush with tropical vegetation, and the honeymoon suite features an outdoor waterbed with a mirrored canopy. Fantastic snorkeling is available just two minutes away from the ranch. An added treat is swimming with the dolphins residing in the bay. Besides the honeymoon suite, guest quarters include two rooms in the main house and a writer's studio attached to—but below—the main house, with a private entrance. Suites have wet bars with toaster oven, small fridge, coffee makers and utensils. Ingredients for a do-it-yourself continental breakfast are supplied. Other amenities include robes, CD player and stereo, color TV and VCR. Tapes, games and a library of Hawaiiana are available to guests. All rooms have private outdoor showers. Dragonfly Ranch is proud of its Hawaiian Experience Work/Play-shops held once per season. During this time guests learn about Hawaiian culture from native Hawaiians and explore the nearby Pu'uhonua O Honaunau National Historical Park. 4 rooms. Credit cards: MC, V.

Kealakekua

Dr. Boone's Bed and Breakfast Lodge   **$65–$65**   ★★

P.O. Box 666, Kealakekua, 96750, ☎ (808) 232-3231.
Single: $65. Double: $65.

There's something for everyone on the Big Island, and Dr. Boone's is a haven for bicyclists. The doctor and his wife (a weaver) are avid cyclists themselves who have led tours through China. As longtime residents, they have firsthand knowledge of the back roads of the island. For a nominal fee and with advance notice they'll pick you up at the airport and help you reassemble your bike. Hearty breakfasts are tailored to athlete tastes (hint: plenty of carbos). The Doc has three rooms with shared baths in his large but simply furnished home. The grounds include a pool and exotic fruit trees. The Boones are very sociable people, so if you vant to be alone, this isn't the place for you. 3 rooms. Credit cards: not accepted.

Merryman's Bed and Breakfast   **$75–$95**   ★★★

P.O. Box 474, Kealakekua, 96750, ☎ (800) 545-4390, (808) 323-2276.
Single: $75–$95. Double: $75–$95.

Merryman's Bed and Breakfast is in the heart of coffee plantation land in South Kona. It exudes the comfort and charm of a well-loved country home with views over the ocean as well as its own well-maintained gardens. Guests are encouraged to relax in the living room with its cathedral ceilings, hardwood floors and wicker furniture with lots of nice, soft cushions. The Rose Room and the Lanai Room have private baths; the latter has a covered terrace overlooking the garden. The Garden Room and Blue Willow Room share a bath. We especially liked the look of the Blue Willow Room with its ocean view and antique four-poster bed. All have luxury linens, fresh flowers and color TVs. A Jacuzzi sits outdoors on a large lanai in a park-like setting. Breakfast is served at the not-too-early hour of 8 a.m. Both Don and Penny Merryman will happily point you to all the prime snorkeling spots; complimentary gear and beach supplies are supplied to guests. Children are welcome if they're "well-behaved." Amenities: balcony or patio. 4 rooms. Credit cards: MC, V.

Volcano

Volcano Village

Carson's Volcano Cottage   **$75–$105**   ★★★

P.O. Box 503, Volcano Village, 96785, ☎ (800) 845-LAVA, (808) 967-7683.
Single: $75–$95. Double: $85–$105.

Each of the four rooms at Carson's Volcano Cottage has a different theme. The Kau Room's decor is inspired by the colors used at the Royal Hawaiian in Waikiki in the '40s. Unique collectibles from the period are used as accent pieces. Take a second look at the bedcovers, which were custom-designed for the room. The Kobayashi is named in honor of the family that planted the cedar, camellia, plum and maple trees surrounding the house. Authentic shoji screens exude peace and tranquility. Nick's Cabin 19 is a separate building dating from the 1940s, and was once the bachelor pad of the owner's son—hence the name. Our favorite room was the Kahau a'lea, furnished with antiques from the Hawaiian Monarchy period. Tropical Victorian may sound like an oxymoron, but it's right for this room. Guests are encouraged to make use of the hot tub in a gazebo in the garden. An ample breakfast is served in the rooms. Breakfast in bed by request. Ask about additional rentals in the area, including a beach house in Kapoho. Amenities: Jacuzzi. 4 rooms. Credit cards: D, MC, V.

Hale Ohia Cottages   **$75–$95**   ★★★

P.O. Box 758, Volcano Village, 96785, ☎ (800) 455-3803, (808) 967-7986.
Single: $75–$95. Double: $75–$95.

Once the estate of a wealthy kamaaina family, Hale Ohia maintains its tradition of hospitality in its present reincarnation as one of the better accommodations on the Big Island. The main residence, guest cottage, gardener's cottage and other buildings have been meticulously restored and provide guests with an exceptional level of comfort and privacy. The gardens of Hale Ohia can be considered a destination in themselves. No earth was moved in their development and they take advantage of the natural lava formations. The gardens have evolved over the course of almost 60 years. A favorite gathering spot is the Japanese soaking tub, or *furo*, behind the main house. The Hale Ohia Cottage is popular with families. It has three bedrooms, a large living room, sitting area and a fully furnished kitchen. The covered lanai is a favorite place for barbecues. Honeymooners are partial to the Hale Lehua and Ihilani Cottages. The Hale Lehua is the oldest of the cottages and is notable for its lava-rock fireplace. It is very secluded and visitors can use the limited housekeeping facilities—a microwave, fridge and hot plate. The covered lanai looks out over the gardens. Amenities: Jacuzzi. 7 rooms. Credit cards: A, CB, DC, D, MC, V.

Kilauea Lodge and Restaurant   **$95–$135**   ★★★

P.O. Box 116, Volcano Village, 96785, 27 miles from Hilo, Junction of Highway 11 and Highway 148, ☎ (808) 967-7366, FAX (808) 967-7367.
Rated restaurant: Kilauea Lodge Restaurant.
Single: $95–$135. Double: $95–$135.

The Kilauea Lodge is a comfortable example of pre-World War II Island bungalow construction. It was built in 1938 for the YMCA and thousands of islanders remember it with affection as the jumping-off point for their explorations of the nearby volcano. In 1986, it was purchased by Lorna and Albert Jeyte and completely refurbished to begin a new reincarnation as a country inn and restaurant. Accommodations are in four separate buildings. There are four rooms in the original building, Hale Maluna; all have fireplaces. Other units include a small, one-bedroom cottage with living room and woodburning stove. Tutu's (Grandmother's) Place is a two-bedroom cottage one block from the main lodge. It's equipped with a full kitchen, living room and fireplace, and has its own large garden and porch. All this for only $135 a night! Albert is also the chef, who presides over a dining room that enjoys a growing reputation for capitalizing on local produce and seafood; desserts are all homemade. His dining room staff is attentive and the wine list is well-chosen. All rates include a full breakfast served in the main lodge. Amenities: balcony or patio. 12 rooms.

Lokahi Lodge   **$75**   ★★

P.O. Box 7, Volcano Village, 96785, ☎ (800) 457-6924, (808) 985-8647.
Single: $75. Double: $75.

The Lokahi Lodge is an inviting pink building with a wide veranda and tropical white roof. It's presided over by Zipper, a distinguished collie, and his colleague, Giblet, the resident cat. Together, they encourage guests to enjoy the cozy parlor with its wood stove and antique pump organ, and join them for the ritual afternoon tea. The lodge also serves a hearty continental breakfast to prepare visitors for a busy day hiking, bird-watching, biking, golf and volcano watching in the nearby countryside. After all that activity, guests will want to relax in their individually appointed rooms, all featuring two extra long double beds, a private bath and private entry. Amenities: balcony or patio. 4 rooms. Credit cards: MC, V.

My Island Bed and Breakfast   **$40–$75**   ★★

P.O. Box 100, Volcano Village, 96785, ☎ *(808) 967-7216, FAX (808) 967-7719. Single: $40–$50. Double: $60–$75.*

My Island is owned by Gordon and Joann Morse and daughter Kii, who have been residents of Volcano for 30 years. The main house, Hale Ohu, with three guest rooms, is a century-old dwelling that was once owned by the Lyman missionary family (see Lyman House Museum). The Morses (he a former newspaper reporter, she an artist) have vowed to keep the house as it was, so you may have to suffer a few inconveniences such as a lack of closet space. There aren't any in the whole house. People in 1886 made do with a rod in the room, and so will you. None of the bedrooms have screens, due to the lack of creepy-crawlies. Stored rainwater is used for washing. Otherwise, the house is a cheerfully chaotic assemblage of rare Hawaiian art and family heirlooms. Guests can pore over a collection of magazines or books on the Volcano area in the library, or listen to more than 300 phonograph records. Other amusements include watching the eruption of Kilauea from your bedroom window. A botanical garden bursts with more than 150 varieties of blooms all year, including orchids and anthuriums. Three more units are available in a garden annex; all have private baths and separate entrances. Two share a covered patio. One offers a complete kitchen, cable TV and telephone. Breakfast is a "stuff yourself delight" served family style from 7–8:30 a.m. The Morses are knowledgeable, generous hosts who will be glad to answer your questions about what to see and do in Hawaii. 6 rooms. Credit cards: not accepted.

Cabins

Kilauea Volcano Kabins   **$45–$80**   ★★

P.O. Box 963, Volcano Village, 96785, ☎ *(800) 628-3876, (808) 628-3876, FAX (808) 967-8067. Single: $45. Double: $55–$80.*

Kilauea Volcano Kabins are a good choice for the budget minded family. The six cedar cabins, surrounded by tree ferns, are all self-contained and most of them can accommodate more than two people. Most have fireplaces, all have heaters (much appreciated in this chilly climate), refrigerators and coffee makers with complimentary coffee, tea and cocoa provided. The Lehua Kabin has two bedrooms and a full kitchen. The cabins are 30 minutes from Hilo and 45 minutes from the tide ponds, and hot pools at Kapoho. Trails lead from the "Kabins" into the rainforest for sensational hiking. Rates include all applicable taxes, which is something to consider.

Substantial discounts are available on stays of more than three nights. The last night of a week's stay is free. 6 rooms. Credit cards: not accepted.

Hotels

Volcano House   **$105–$131**   ★★★

On the north rim of Kilauea Crater, Volcano Village, ☎ *(808) 967-7321. Rated Restaurant: Volcano House Restaurant*
Single: $105–$131. Double: $105–$131.

The only hotel in the Hawaii Volcanoes National Park, a sprawling lodge with a dramatic setting, perched on the northern rim of Kilauea crater. The present structure was built in 1941 after a fire destroyed the original 1800s Victorian-style building; Mark Twain, Franklin D. Roosevelt and Queen Liliuokalani were among the most distinguished guests. Part of the original section escaped the flames, and is now the Volcano Arts Center, a nonprofit outlet for local artisans. Volcano House features 42 recently redecorated rooms, some overlooking the crater, outfitted with rare koa-wood furniture and Hawaiian-style quilts. One drawback is the rather cramped baths. The centerpiece of the lobby is the historic fireplace that's never allowed to burn out. The cocktail lounge and restaurant are often engulfed by tour groups during the day, but the hotel is quiet and peaceful at night, and the atmosphere is always casual and low-key. Gift shop. It helps to make reservations at least six months in advance in the winter and three months ahead other times of the year. You might try calling a day in advance to see if there are any vacancies. Amenities: balcony or patio. 42 rooms. Credit cards: A, DC, D, MC, V.

Where to Eat

Dining on the Big Island can range from putting a picnic together from neighborhood-type markets to fine dining. The resorts offer a range of dining options, including scheduled **luaus**. At **Kailua-Kona**, you'll find visitor-oriented **cafés**, **bistros** and **restaurants**. **Waterfront Row**, with its **Chart House**, draws heavy tourist traffic. Over on Hilo, dining tends to be more casual—and cheaper—with neighborhood eateries (and the ubiquitous fast food) the big rave. **Waimea** also offers a couple of good options for the inland crowd.

Hamakua Coast

Jolene's Kau Kau Korner   **$**   ★★

Corner of Lehua and Mamane Streets, Hamakua Coast, ☎ *(808) 775-9498.*
Specialties: Hamburgers, beef teriyaki, grilled mahi-mahi.
Lunch: 10 a.m.–8 p.m., entrées $3–$8.
Dinner: 10 a.m.–8 p.m., entrées $3–$8. Closed: Sun.

This cheerfully decorated, family-owned restaurant is located near the Hawaiian Holiday Macadamia Nut Factory. Jolene's is a convenient stop on the way to the Waipio Valley. Several different American and Hawaiian specialties are prepared daily, and everything is available for takeout. Open until 3 p.m. on Saturday. Reservations not accepted.

Hilo

Bear's Coffee $ ★★★

106 Keawe Street, Hilo, ☎ (808) 935-0708.
American cuisine. Specialties: Coffee drinks, espresso, Belgian waffles, sandwiches, bagels and lox, ice cream.
Breakfast: 6:45 a.m.–5 p.m., entrées $3–$8.
Lunch: 6:45 a.m.–5 p.m., entrées $3–$8. Closed: Sun.

For people who are grizzly bears until they have their first morning cup of joe, Bear's is ideal—it's open bright and early at 6:45 on weekdays (from 8 a.m. on weekends). If you're the type who brings your own coffee grinder wherever you go, there are some 30 kinds of fresh-roasted beans available, too. There are sidewalk tables outside so you can take advantage of the passing Hilo scene while chowing down on souffléed eggs made in the espresso machine, or Bear's famous "busters," sort of a genteel version of the greasy stuff you get at a well-known fast-food joint. If you don't like eggs, there are pastries and Belgian waffles or lox 'n' bagels. Soups, salads, sandwiches and hot dishes are served at lunch. Picnic lunches available on request. Features: outside dining, own baking. Reservations not accepted.

Broke da Mouth $ ★★★

93 Mamo Street, Hilo, ☎ (808) 934-7670.
cuisine. Specialties: Hawaiian vegetarian dishes.
Breakfast: 9 a.m.–2 p.m., entrées $4–$6.
Lunch: 9 a.m.–2 p.m., entrées $4–$6. Closed: Mon., Sun.

Non-greasy and absolutely meatless plate lunches are served at this downtown Hilo deli/takeout establishment that was once a fish market. Combinations are surprisingly complex, eclectic and inventive, and nothing is over $6. All produce is grown on a cooperative farm nearby. Even the mustards and salad dressings are homemade. Sample the manapua, traditional dumplings made here with whole-wheat flour and filled with Chinese eggplant or taro, sweet potato and green papaya salad. Features: outside dining, own baking. Reservations not accepted.

Café Pesto $$$ ★★★

308 Kamehameha Avenue, Hilo, ☎ (808) 969-6640.
Italian cuisine. Specialties: Fresh local seafood, gourmet pizzas, Pacific Rim pastas and appetizers.
Lunch: 11 a.m.–9 p.m., entrées $12–$22.
Dinner: 11 a.m.–9 p.m., entrées $12–$22.

The historic, meticulously restored circa 1912 S. Hata building is the site of this rather stark, contemporary restaurant with a centerpiece exhibition-kitchen that puts out an interesting combination of Italian and Pacific Rim cuisine. The original location is in a shopping center near Kawaihae Harbor, not far from Hapuna Beach. Expansion was possible due to the popularity of the mini-chain's specialty: delecta-

THE BIG ISLAND

ble, wood-fired pizzas and breads made from their own dough mix. The combinations put the California Pizza Kitchen to shame. Microbrewery beers, a decent wine selection accompany the sparkling cuisine. Espressos, lattes and homemade "chocoholic" desserts. The one sour note was the rather pushy service. Features: own baking. Reservations recommended. Credit cards: A, MC, V.

Don's Grill $$ ★★

485 Hinano Street, Hilo, ☎ (808) 935-9099.
American cuisine. Specialties: Saimin, loco moco, breakfast dishes, teriyaki.
Breakfast: 10:30 a.m.–11 a.m., entrées $4–$9.
Lunch: 10:30 a.m.–3 p.m., entrées $6–$13.
Dinner: 4–9 p.m., entrées $7–$15. Closed: Mon.

Don's Grill is as plain and no-nonsense as its name. It serves the kind of food that brings tears to the eyes of starving truckers hauling a load down an interstate highway. Only in this case, saimin, loco moco and teriyaki dishes are interspersed with hearty pork chops and liver and onions on the sizable menu. Rotisserie chicken and barbecued ribs are also big sellers, and the place is packed for breakfast on weekends. Credit cards: A, MC, V.

Ken's House of Pancakes $ ★★★

Corner of Highway 11 and Kamehameha Avenue, Hilo, ☎ (808) 935-8711.
American cuisine. Specialties: Pancakes, 24-hour breakfasts, Hawaiian dishes.
Breakfast: prix fixe $4–$9.
Lunch: entrées $4–$9.
Dinner: entrées $6–$10.

Providing "good, old-fashioned" service for more than 20 years at the same location, Ken's is also the only place in Hilo that offers this service 24 hours a day, rain or shine. It's ideal for folks who like to have their pancakes and eggs at midnight. The daily specials include local dishes as well as heart-healthy "lite" cuisine. Features: late dining. Reservations not accepted. Credit cards: A, DC, D, MC, V.

Lehua's Bay City Bar and Grill $$ ★★★

11 Waianeunue Avenue, Hilo, 96721, ☎ (808) 935-8055.
American cuisine. Specialties: Charbroiled teriyaki chicken burgers, country pork ribs.
Lunch: 11 a.m.–4 p.m., entrées $7–$14.
Dinner: 5–9:30 p.m., entrées $7–$14.

A collection of vintage signs, photos and memorabilia on loan from various businesses decorates the walls of this downtown Hilo eatery, situated in the 1930s Hilo Drug Company building. The menu is just as old-fashioned, with comforting dishes such as charbroiled chicken teriyaki sandwiches and country pork ribs with paniolo barbecue sauce. Spots of trendiness show up in the sauces; for example, a cajun fish burger is served with wasabi butter, and a sweet-chili basil sauce dresses a dish of Thai coconut shrimp. A good deal is the all-you-can-eat (but "no sharing or splitting") soup and salad bar for $7.95 at lunch, $8.95 at dinner. No lunch on Sundays. Reservations recommended. Credit cards: A, D, MC, V.

Restaurant Fuji $$$ ★★★

142 Kinoole Street, Hilo, ☎ (808) 961-3733. Associated hotel: The Hilo Hotel.
Japanese cuisine. Specialties: Japanese teishoku lunches and dinners, tempura, teriyaki.
Lunch: 11 a.m.–1:45 p.m., entrées $9–$25.

THE BIG ISLAND

Dinner: 5–8:45 p.m., entrées $9–$25. Closed: Mon.

Restaurant Fuji, a fixture in the Hilo restaurant scene, is a relaxing, fine-tuned old-timer with a genteel atmosphere, gracious service and traditional Japanese cuisine. The fish teppanyaki, cooked with assorted vegetables at your table, is the meal of choice. Reservations recommended. Credit cards: A, DC, MC, V.

Roussel's $$$ ★★★

60 Keawe Street, Hilo, ☎ (808) 935-5111.
cuisine. Specialties: Shrimp remoulade, blackened sashimi, soft-shell crab, Cajun prime rib, gumbos, fresh fish.
Lunch: 11:30 a.m.–1:30 p.m., entrées $12–$25.
Dinner: 5–9 p.m., entrées $15–$30.

New Orleans comes to Hilo via this swank Creole restaurant on the ground floor of a turn-of-the-century bank building, one of the first to be restored in an ambitious city gentrification program. Lights are low, ceilings are high and airy—even the bare wooden floors gleam. One of the founders, the late chef Andrew Oliver, was instrumental in getting the Hilo Mardi Gras Festival off the ground. Features: private dining rooms. Reservations recommended. Credit cards: A, MC, V.

Ting Hao Mandarin Restaurant $$ ★★★

Highway 11 at the Puainako Town Center, Hilo, ☎ (808) 959-6288.
Chinese cuisine. Specialties: Shrimp with lobster sauce, Kung Pao chicken, shredded pork with garlic sauce, vegetarian dishes.
Lunch: 10 a.m.–2:30 p.m., entrées $7–$12.
Dinner: 4:30-9 p.m., entrées $7–$12. Closed: Sun.

Ting Hao is a family-style restaurant that's usually packed with local Chinese, who obviously enjoy the trademark spicy Szechuan and Hunanese specialties served in this shopping-center location not far from the airport. Less-brave souls are treated kindly; they tone down the chilies on request. There's also a gentler menu of dishes from Peking and Taiwan. Veggie specials too. Another branch, Ting Hao Seafood Restaurant, is located in the lower lobby of the Naniloa Hotel, at *93 Banyan Drive* on Hilo Bay. It's open from 11 a.m.–2 p.m. for lunch and from 5 to 9 p.m. for dinner daily except Tuesday. Call ☎ *(808) 935-8888* for info. Reservations recommended. Credit cards: A, MC, V.

Ka'u

Naalehu

Naalehu Coffee Shop $$ ★★

Highway 11, Naalehu, ☎ (808) 929-7238.
American cuisine. Specialties: Banana bread, fresh fish.
Breakfast: 7:30–11 a.m., entrées $5–$8.
Lunch: 11–4 p.m., entrées $7–$9.
Dinner: 4–8 p.m., entrées $7–$13. Closed: Sun.

If you find yourself way down south Naalehu way, drop in to this down-home, linoleum-and-chrome, country restaurant that has surprisingly good food. There are some sophisticated fish dishes among the liver and onions and deep-fried items; the source is only a few minutes away in Ka Lae, the southernmost point of the United

THE BIG ISLAND

States. Take some of their famous banana bread with you for on-the-go munchies.
Features: own baking. Reservations not accepted.

Punalu'u Bake Shop   **$**   ★ ★

Highway 11, Naalehu, ☎ *(808) 929-7343.*
American cuisine. Specialties: Sandwiches made with Hawaiian sweetbread.
Breakfast: 9 a.m.–5 p.m., entrées $4–$8.
Lunch: 9 a.m.–5 p.m., entrées $4–$8.

A working bakery in a charming village that's conveniently placed between Hawaii
Volcanoes National Park and Ka Lae, the southernmost point of the United States,
Punalu'u Bake Shop has a picnic area where you can sample sandwiches made with
Hawaiian sweetbread. It's also the place to try chili made with macadamia nuts
grown by the Mauna Loa Macadamia Nut factory. Features: outside dining, own
baking. Reservations not accepted.

Kona

Kailua-Kona

Banana Bay Buffet   **$$**   ★ ★

75-5739 Ali'i Drive, Kailua-Kona, 96740, ☎ *(808) 329-1398. Associated hotel: Uncle
Billy's Kona Bay Hotel.*
*American cuisine. Specialties: Breakfast and dinner buffets with free hula show, Sunday
brunch.*
Breakfast: 7–11 a.m., entrées $6–$8.
Dinner: 5:30–9 p.m., entrées $10.

Uncle Billy, known for his mini-chain of affordable hotels (another in Hilo) also fea-
tures all-you-can-eat buffets for breakfast and dinner (no lunch). The restaurant
opens to a garden with fountains and banana trees (of course) ripe with fruit. There
are more than 20 items available for breakfast, including healthful things such as
oatmeal and fruit bars, and local kine chili, stew and mahi-mahi. Muffins are made
fresh daily and there's a river of Kona coffee constantly flowing. Dinner is a multi-
ethnic affair with Hawaiian, Chinese, Korean and even Mexican food (slightly dubi-
ous) to choose from. Also on the list are 14 homemade salads, ribs, fresh pasta, stir
fries and carved roast beef and loin of pork. Management swears you can eat here
seven days a week and always find something different. Desserts and beverages
extra. There's a free hula show on Saturdays and Sundays from 6–8 p.m. No buffet
on Sunday, when there's a brunch offered from 7 a.m. to noon at $6.95 per person.
Reservations for large groups only. Features: Sunday brunch. Reservations recom-
mended. Credit cards: A, MC, V.

Buns in the Sun   **$**   ★ ★

75-5595 Palani Road, Kailua-Kona, ☎ *(808) 326-2774.*
American cuisine. Specialties: Cinnamon buns, sandwiches, espresso.
Breakfast: 5 a.m.–4 p.m., entrées $1–$3.
Lunch: 10 a.m.–4 p.m., entrées $1–$3.

An indoor-outdoor deli, bakery and coffee shop combination, the saucily named
Buns in the Sun features nicely priced, tasty cinnamon rolls (even low-fat ones),
fresh-baked pastries, breakfast sandwiches, deli sandwiches, (try the island ono) and

soup or salad. Everything is available for take-out. Features: outside dining, own baking. Reservations not accepted.

Huggo's $$$ ★★★

Ali'i Drive, Kailua-Kona, ☎ *(808) 329-1493.*
American cuisine. Specialties: Fresh fish, barbecued ribs, steaks.
Lunch: 11:30 a.m.–2:30 p.m., entrées $10–$25.
Dinner: 5:30–10 p.m., entrées $10–$25.
Dreamy Kona sunsets, live music (different every night), fresh fish and prime rib ensures a steady stream of customers to this 25-year-old South Seas-style building that juts out over the Pacific. The fresh catch of the day is prepared in a Cajun, Mediterranean or Pacific Rim style. Barbecued ribs are the specialty on Tuesdays and Thursdays. No lunch on weekends. Features: outside dining. Reservations recommended. Credit cards: A, D, MC, V.

Island Lava Java $

75-5799 Ali'i Drive, Kailua-Kona, ☎ *(808) 327-2161.*
American cuisine. Specialties: Specialty coffee drinks, pastries, Tropical Dreams ice cream, sandwiches.
Breakfast: 6:30 a.m.–2:30 p.m., entrées $6–$10.
Lunch: 2:30–5 p.m., entrées $6–$10.
Dinner: 5–10 p.m., entrées $6–$10.
Although it's open late, Lava Java (great name) is particularly popular for breakfast pastries and an excellent imported dark-roast espresso blend. Treat yourself and top it with chocolate or cinnamon. Other menu items include sandwiches, croissants, soups and Tropical Dreams ice cream. Outdoor tables overlook Oneo Bay. Open until 11 p.m. on Fridays and Saturdays. Features: outside dining, own baking. Reservations not accepted. Credit cards: MC, V.

Jameson's $$ ★★★

77-6452 Ali'i Drive, Kailua-Kona, ☎ *(808) 329-3195.*
American cuisine. Specialties: Fresh seafood, steaks.
Lunch: 11 a.m.–2:30 p.m., entrées $10–$15.
Dinner: 5–9 p.m., entrées $10–$15.
Known for steaks and sunset views over Magic (or Disappearing) Sands Beach, Jameson's is, to some, one of the best places to eat on the Big Island. The newly expanded outdoor dining area is a big plus, so more folks can dine on well-prepared island fish and filet mignon while enjoying the sea breezes. At lunch, bring the kids to watch the feeding of the resident moray eels that live in the surf among the black-lava rocks below the deck. Excellent service from old Kona hands. No lunch served on weekends. Features: outside dining. Reservations recommended. Credit cards: A, MC, V.

Jennifer's Korean BBQ $ ★★

Luhia Street, Kailua-Kona, ☎ *(808) 326-1155.*
Asian cuisine. Specialties: Yakiniku.
Lunch: 11 a.m.–2:30 p.m., entrées $4–$8.
Dinner: 5–9 p.m., entrées $4–$8. Closed: Sun.
A second-story restaurant under a big satellite dish in an industrial section of Kailua-Kona, Jennifer lures a clientele primarily composed of local office workers. The spe-

cialty is *yakiniku*, where a little grill is set up on your table, and the server cooks your choice of marinated meat, chicken, veggies, shrimp and calamari while you watch. Entrées come with four or five small salads or vegetable side dishes, including fiery kim chee (pickled vegetables and chilies). Also noodle dishes, combination plates. Reservations not accepted. Credit cards: MC, V.

Keauhou Beach Hotel Buffets   **$$$**   ★ ★

78-6740 Ali'i Drive, Kailua-Kona, ☎ *(808) 322-3441. Associated hotel: Keauhou Beach Hotel.*
American cuisine. Specialties: Chinese, Hawaiian and seafood buffets.
Dinner: 5–9 p.m., entrées $14–$22.

Three different theme buffets are featured every week in the Kuakini Terrace at the Keauhou Beach Hotel in Kailua. The Hawaiian dinner buffet on Wednesdays and Thursdays is like a luau without the show. For $13.95 (children four–12 years, $7.95) it's an all-you-can-eat feast of traditional goodies such as lau lau, lomi salmon, tako poke, kalua pork and, of course, poi. Also included is a 25-dish salad bar. Chinese night is on Mondays and Tuesdays, while Seafood buffets are on Fridays, Saturdays and Sundays. Reservations required. Credit cards: A, MC, V.

La Bourgogne   **$$**

77-6400 Nalani Street, Kailua-Kona, ☎ *(808) 329-6711.*
French cuisine.
Dinner: 6–9 p.m., entrées $12–$15. Closed: Sun.

With only 10 tables, this is an intimate (some might say cramped) French restaurant, a little gem tucked away in a shopping center three miles from Kailua-Kona. The menu has been updated over the years to include some Pacific Rim-style dishes using fresh local produce. Try the delectable opakapaka in caviar cream sauce. You'll be treated like a special guest by the American chef and his wife, who work the room themselves with very little help and do an admirable job. A winner from the start and getting better all the time. Features: own baking, rated wine cellar, non-smoking area. Reservations required. Credit cards: A, DC, D, MC, V.

Mixed Plate   **$$**   ★ ★ ★

Palani Road, in Kopiko Plaza, Kailua-Kona, ☎ *(808) 329-8104.*
Asian cuisine. Specialties: Plate lunches, Korean dishes.
Breakfast: 10 a.m.–8 p.m., entrées $5–$15.
Lunch: 10 a.m.–8 p.m., entrées $5–$15.
Dinner: 4–8 p.m., entrées $5–$15.

This large, air-conditioned shopping center eatery is popular with local residents, but drop-ins get a warm welcome. The Kim family specializes in 36 lunch and dinner plates, ranging from vegetable tempura to a sizzling 10-ounce New York steak with shrimp. There's an emphasis on Korean dishes such as kalbi ribs, or short ribs marinated in ginger, soy, garlic, sesame oil and grilled. Also bulgogi beef, and teriyaki chicken and steak. Friday night is prime rib night, and it's served until they run out. All dishes are cooked to order. Reservations not accepted.

Ocean View Inn   **$$**   ★ ★

Ali'i Drive, Kailua-Kona, 96740, ☎ *(808) 329-9998.*
American cuisine. Specialties: Chinese vegetarian dishes, breakfasts, fresh fish, roast pork.

Breakfast: 6:30–11 a.m., entrées $7.
Lunch: 11 a.m.–2:45 p.m., entrées $8–$12.
Dinner: 5:15–9 p.m., entrées $10–$13.

The Ocean View Inn has been in the same location for more than 50 years, and looks it. No attempt has been made to yuppify it, to the relief of many faithful customers. Veteran waitresses (who may be a little ornery at times) take your order from a huge menu that encompasses Chinese vegetarian dishes, fresh fish, teriyaki steak, corned beef and cabbage (!) and the like. If you're the type who has to have rice with your breakfast eggs, this is the place to come. No outside seating, but there is an ocean view from across the sea wall, just like the name says.

Palm Café — $$$ — ★★★★

75-5819 Ali'i Drive, Kailua-Kona, 96740, ☎ (808) 329-7765.
Dinner: 5–10 p.m., entrées $15–$24.

Although Kailua town's main drag bustles below, you'd never know it at this sublime open-air, ocean-view restaurant outfitted in white wicker and crisp linens and cooled by ceiling fans. Some of the Asian-flavored dishes were inspired by the French chef's sojourn in the Philippines, including a signature item, crab lumpia. The mercurial menu changes frequently, but you can always count on the fresh fish, perhaps a gentle mahi-mahi malia with lobster and crispy noodles in a creamy coconut sauce. The service here is a perfect blend of unobtrusiveness and efficiency. A casual bistro, Under the Palm, is appropriately located under the Palm (you knew that). Breakfast is served from 7–11 a.m., and lunch and dinner from 11 a.m.–midnight. Preferred dining is on the open-air patio and sidewalk café, which is great for people-watching. Inventive pizzas, grilled dishes, mouth-watering sandwiches and desserts are all recommended. Features: outside dining, own baking. Reservations recommended. Credit cards: A, D, MC, V.

Sam Choy's Diner — $ — ★★★

Frame Ten Center, next to Kona Bowl, Kailua-Kona, ☎ (808) 329-0101.
Asian cuisine. Specialties: Plate lunches.
Breakfast: 9 a.m.–2 p.m., entrées $5–$7.
Lunch: 11 a.m.–4 p.m., entrées $5–$7.
Dinner: 4–10 p.m., entrées $5–$7.

Celebrity chef Sam's second Kona eatery is a diner situated in a shopping center next to a bowling alley in Kailua. In true diner fashion, there's both counter and booth seating. Open continuously for breakfast, lunch and dinner until 10 p.m., the fare consists of 25 plate lunches, including his signature fried poki, fresh fish in a special sauce, served with plenty of rice. Dishes are dressed with potato/macaroni salad or tossed greens with Sam's Oriental dressing. Reservations not accepted.

Sam Choy's Restaurant — $$$ — ★★★★

73-5576 Kauhola Street, Kailua-Kona, ☎ (808) 326-1545.
Breakfast: 6 a.m.–2 p.m., entrées $4–$8.
Lunch: 6 a.m.–2 p.m., entrées $5–$9.
Dinner: 5–9 p.m., entrées $17–$25. Closed: Sun.

Sam Choy's Restaurant is hidden away in the Kaloko Industrial Area near Kona Airport; unlikely neighbors include the Shooter's Choice indoor gun range and a bowling alley, among others. But local boy Sam Choy's creative variations on the humble plate lunch have made him number one with a bullet among his growing legion of fans. Entirely casual (and casually priced) at breakfast and lunch, you'll be served such items as Spam sushi (here called musubi), beef stew or Kaloko Noodle Mania—beef chow mein in a deep-fried noodle bowl. At dinner, though, the management pretties up the place with white linen and jacks up the prices accordingly. Patrons have to bring their own booze as Sam's has no liquor license; the restaurant passes out the corkscrew. You'll enjoy Sam's award-winning seafood laulau, with fresh fish instead of pork, wrapped in a ti-leaf. Entrées include soup, salad and fresh bread. Reserve in advance for dinner. Features: own baking.

Sibu's   **$$**   ★ ★ ★
75-5695 Ali'i Drive, in the Kona Banyan Court, Kailua-Kona, ☎ *(808) 329-1112.*
Asian cuisine. Specialties: Chicken satay, Gado-gado.
Lunch: 11:30 a.m.–3 p.m., entrées $8–$12.
Dinner: 5–9 p.m., entrées $12–$17.
Possibly the only eatery to serve Indonesian specialties (one of my favorites) on the Big Island, the open-air Sibu Café can be found behind a monstrous banyan tree in a mall populated by hungry felines waiting for a handout. It's been a local fixture for almost 10 years, and the exotic offerings—such as chicken satay with peanut sauce, or gado-gado salad with a mound of lettuce, cabbage, potatoes and sprouts with a peanut-lime dressing—have become old friends. Specify whether you want your meal mild or spicy. No MSG is used, and there's an extensive vegetarian menu. Features: outside dining, wine and beer only. Reservations not accepted.

North Kohala

Hawi

Bamboo Restaurant   **$$$**   ★ ★ ★
At the intersection of Highway 250 and Highway 270, Hawi, 96755, ☎ *(808) 889-5555.*
Hawaiian cuisine. Specialties: Chicken satay pot-stickers with sweet chili-mint dipping sauce, coconut milk clam chowder.
Lunch: 11:30 a.m.–2 p.m., entrées $8–$12.
Dinner: 6–9 p.m., entrées $22–$37.
The old Takata dry-goods store, which was also once a sugarcane workers' hotel in the early 1900s, has been transformed into this widely talked-about restaurant in sleepy Hawi. The interior decor recalls 1950s Hawaii, when homes were decorated with ukuleles and hula girl statuettes in grass skirts; the wicker chairs were rescued from the venerable Moana Hotel in Waikiki. The artwork on the walls is a skillful blending of originals by local artists and the currently in-vogue antique menus from the Matson-line passenger ships *Lurline* and *Matsonia*. This is the kind of place where customers call the warm-hearted, amply proportioned waitresses "auntie" and the chef comes out of the kitchen to sing and dance for guests. The inventive Hawaiian-Pacific Rim cuisine should be more expensive than it is. The menu tries to please everyone, including a separate section for vegetarians, and it usually succeeds. Make it a point to start your meal with a passion-fruit margarita and end it with a dual-chocolate lava mousse. Scrumptious. Afterward, check out the Kohala Koa Gallery within the restaurant for beautiful custom-made wooden furniture. No

dinner on Sundays. Features: own baking. Reservations recommended. Credit cards: MC, V.

Kapa'au

Don's Family Deli   **$**   ★★★

P.O. Box 1463, Kapa'au, 96755, ☎ (808) 889-5822.
American cuisine. Specialties: Deli sandwiches, vegetarian dishes, smoothies.
Breakfast: 8 a.m.–6 p.m., entrées $5–$8.
Lunch: 10 a.m.–6 p.m., entrées $5–$8.
With a landmark such as the King Kamehameha statue across from it, you can't miss Don's Family Deli. True to its name, deli sandwiches are available, as well as bagels and lox. But much of the menu is pretty healthful and darn incredible for these parts, including tofu burgers, mesquite chicken, veggie enchiladas, quiche, toasted crab or peanut butter and guava jam sandwiches, shepherd's pie, and Portuguese bean soup. The luscious banana-papaya-strawberry smoothies are a meal in themselves. Oh, and ask them about Blue Green Algae, if you dare. Open 10 a.m.–5 p.m. on weekends. Reservations not accepted.

Tropical Dreams   **$**   ★★★

Highway 270, Kapa'au, 96755, ☎ (808) 889-0505.
American cuisine. Specialties: Homemade ice cream.
Lunch: 11 a.m.–5 p.m., entrées $2–$3.
Just down the road from Don's Family Deli (see description) is this ice cream emporium with a factory behind it. It's owned by Diane and Warren Wulzen, former California ranchers who pulled up stakes two years ago and decided to fulfill their tropical dreams of trying to make a living in Hawaii. Some of the flavors they've devised will make you delirious—how about Tahitian vanilla, coconut cream, white chocolate ginger, lilikoi sorbet, pikake and papaya? There are usually 40 ice cream flavors available, as well as 25 sorbets and 10 low-fat yogurts. Wow. Also espresso drinks, Italian sodas, pastries and shave ice. Another location in downtown Hilo, in the historic Kress building, 961-4767. Open Sunday from 1 p.m. Reservations not accepted.

North Kona

Manago Hotel Restaurant   **$**   ★★

Highway 11, North Kona, ☎ (808) 323-2642. Associated hotel: Manago Hotel.
American cuisine. Specialties: Pork chops.
Breakfast: 7–9 a.m., entrées $6–$10.
Lunch: 11 a.m.–2 p.m., entrées $6–$10.
Dinner: 5–7:30 p.m., entrées $6–$10. Closed: Mon.
Located in a budget hotel owned by the same family since 1917, this restaurant is equally plain. Seating is on uncomfortable metal chairs that scrape the bare linoleum floors they're set on. But the food is generously proportioned, with all the rice and macaroni salad you can eat garnishing such hip-hugging specialties as fried pork chops. The fish is as fresh as can be. Reservations not accepted. Credit cards: D, MC, V.

Teshima's   **$$**   ★★★

Highway 11, North Kona, ☎ (808) 322-9140.
Japanese cuisine. Specialties: Sashimi, tempura, teriyaki.

Breakfast: 6:30 a.m.–1:45 p.m., entrées $7–$12.
Lunch: 6:30 a.m.–1:45 p.m., entrées $7–$12.
Dinner: 5–9:45 p.m., entrées $7–$12.
You won't find any rock-and-roll sushi chefs at this always reliable Japanese restaurant and small inn situated in the heart of Kona coffee country. Year in and year out, faithful diners can expect the same well-prepared set lunches and dinners of sashimi, teriyaki, shrimp tempura and all the trimmings, nestled in their own little compartments on a black lacquer tray. Yes, there is a Mrs. Teshima, and she's usually on hand to greet customers. A favored spot for local dignitaries.

The Captain Cook Inn   **$**   ★
Highway 11, North Kona, ☎ (808) 323-2080.
American cuisine. Specialties: Plate lunches.
Breakfast: 7 a.m.–8 p.m., entrées $4–$10.
Lunch: 10 a.m.–8 p.m., entrées $4–$10.
Dinner: 4–8 p.m., entrées $4–$10.
A good budget choice in a restaurant-poor area, Captain Cook Inn serves a mixed bag of cuisines, including Korean chicken served by the plate or by the bucket (this was, after all, an old Kentucky Fried Chicken outlet), and fresh fish, burgers, fries, sandwiches and salads. Reservations not accepted.

The Coffee Shack   **$**   ★ ★
Highway 11, North Kona, ☎ (808) 328-9555.
American cuisine. Specialties: Kona coffee, capuccino, espresso, latte, eggs benedict, pastries.
Breakfast: 7–10 a.m., entrées $1–$5.
Lunch: 10 a.m.–5 p.m., entrées $1–$5.
Connected to the Kahauloa Coffee Co., which has been in business for 20 years, this open-air café features a heady brew made from beans picked straight off the trees, and ground and roasted in-house. The house specialty is a dark-roast peaberry coffee as well as 100 percent no-foolin' Kona coffee. Decaf available. Accompaniments include eggs benedict, quiche, waffles or fresh pastries at breakfast or daily specials, pasta, salads and sandwiches at lunch. Ask for their mail-order brochure or inquire about shipping their product to friends in faraway places. Features: own baking.

South Kohala

Kamuela

Edelweiss   **$$$**   ★ ★ ★
Highway 19 (Kawaihae Road), Kamuela, 96743, ☎ (808) 885-6800.
German cuisine. Specialties: Sautéed veal, lamb, beef and bacon with wild mushrooms.
Lunch: 11:30 a.m.–1:30 p.m., entrées $16–$20.
Dinner: 5–9 p.m., entrées $16–$20. Closed: Sat., Sun.
Designed like an alpine chalet, Hans Peter Hager's Edelweiss has been crowded with regulars and the curious since its opening 14 years ago, despite newer and better restaurants opening in the vicinity. It has an annoying, "no reservations" policy and a cramped bar where you're supposed to cool your heels and down a few, but satisfied customers don't seem to mind. Frankly, I find the food here to be disap-

pointingly ordinary and way too salty. On the up side, the service is friendly and utterly professional. Features: own baking. Reservations not accepted. Credit cards: MC, V.

Hawaiian Style $ ★★

Highway 19, Kamuela,.
American cuisine. Specialties: Loco moco, Belgian waffles, plate lunches, sandwiches.
Breakfast: 6 a.m.–1 p.m., entrées $5–$7.
Lunch: 10 a.m.–1 p.m., entrées $6–$9. Closed: Sat.
This owners of this spotless, spiffy café took over Masayo's, an old-time greasy spoon, leased the building next door, and tore the walls down to create more space. The action centers around a circular wood counter, and when you enter, regulars may give you the once-over, but it's a friendly place. There are also four or five blond-wood tables, and decor features reproduction tapa-cloth curtains, paintings of local scenes, frosted glass fixtures and ceiling fans. The menu is chalked onto a huge blackboard. There's a list of weekly specials, including oxtail, shoyu chicken and the Friday luau plate of laulau, chicken long rice, lomi lomi salmon, kalua pig, rice and poi for $8.95. Among the regular plate lunches, served with rice and potato-mac salad, are kalbi ribs, teriyaki steak and broiled mahi-mahi. There are a number of sandwiches, served with fries or mac salad; the ground barbecued pork is huge and delicious. Open Sunday from 7–11 a.m. It's closed every last Sunday and Monday of the month. Note: Hawaiian Style often runs out of things before closing time. Reservations not accepted.

Island Bistro $$ ★★★

Highway 19 and Kawaihae Road, Kamuela, ☎ (808) 885-1222.
International cuisine. Specialties: Waimea sweet potato soup, tamarind roasted leg of lamb with pepper-papaya sauce.
Lunch: 11:30 a.m.–2 p.m., entrées $10–$18.
Dinner: 5:30–9:30 p.m., entrées $10–$18.
Former Merriman's chef Michael Neff has opened an indoor-outdoor restaurant of his own in Waimea that's giving the long-entrenched Edelweiss restaurant across the street some lively competition. The relaxed decor features an exhibition kitchen. Specials change nightly, but there's always something for vegetarians and pasta lovers. Come for an ál fresco lunch during the week (not served on weekends). The patio offers a majestic view of Mauna Kea, and soups, salads and sandwiches are mostly under $10. Features: outside dining, own baking. Reservations recommended. Credit cards: D, MC, V.

Maha's Café $ ★★★

P.O. Box 6960, Kamuela, 96743, ☎ (808) 885-0693.
American cuisine. Specialties: Smoked ahi with lilikoi salsa, Hawaiian style bread pudding with guava-ginger sauce.
Breakfast: 8 a.m.–10:30 p.m., entrées $4.
Lunch: 10:30 a.m.–5 p.m., entrées $7–$9. Closed: Tues.
This small but delightful country-style café is ensconced in the back of Cook's Discoveries, one of Kamuela's finest island craft stores. Open for light breakfasts, lunch and afternoon tea, selections are unusual and creative. Breakfasts include poi pancakes with coconut syrup and Maha's granola parfait with fruit, nuts and yogurt. At

lunch, hearty appetites might go for the fresh roast turkey on squaw bread with home-style mushroom stuffing and Ka'u orange and cranberry relish. Light eaters will appreciate the Waipio Ways platter—broiled fresh fish with sliced steamed Waipio taro and sweet potato on a bed of Kahua greens, served "nude" or with a gingered vinaigrette. Folks can drop in for dessert washed down by a cup of the featured Kona coffee flavor of the month. "Maha" is a caterer and pastry chef, so you won't go wrong with any of her old-fashioned sweets, such as Hawaiian-style bread pudding with guava ginger sauce. Maha's homemade honey-curry dressing, green olive pesto, poi bread, banana bread and papaya coffee cake are available to go. Afternoon tea ($12) served from 3–4:30 p.m. Features: own baking. Reservations not accepted.

Mean Cuisine   **$**   ★ ★ ★

65-1227 A Opelu Road, Suite 4, Kamuela, 96743, ☎ (808) 885-6325.

American cuisine. Specialties: Homemade sushi, turkey and mashed potatoes, chocolate cake with triple raspberry sauce.

Breakfast: 6 a.m.–8 p.m., entrées $5–$8.

Lunch: 11 a.m.–4 p.m., entrées $5–$8.

Dinner: 4 p.m.–8 p.m., entrées $5–$8. Closed: Sun.

The food is the only show at this unpretentious storefront eatery and bakery located just steps away from the highly praised Merriman's in the Opelu Shopping Center. Chef Ann Sutherland has much in common with Peter Merriman: each served as executive chefs at the Mauna Lani resort. Both are energetic overachievers; where Merriman dives for the shellfish on his table, Sutherland is up way before the 6 a.m. opening baking breads, muffins and pastries and rolling homemade sushi (!), which disappears quickly. But one striking difference is that nothing in the restaurant is priced over $8. All items are available for takeout. Features: own baking. Reservations not accepted. Credit cards: MC, V.

Merriman's   **$$$**   ★ ★ ★ ★

Highway 19, in Opelo Plaza, Kamuela, ☎ (808) 885-6822.

American cuisine. Specialties: Wok-charred ahi, Kahua ranch lamb, steak with Cabernet Sauvignon and Gorgonzola sauce.

Lunch: 11:30 a.m.–1:30 p.m., entrées $15–$25.

Dinner: 5:30–9 p.m., entrées $15–$25.

This is a surprisingly bright, tropical-romantic restaurant in a shopping center setting. The atmosphere is livened further by the goings-on in a wraparound, open kitchen, where celebrity chef Peter Merriman is usually seen orchestrating the proceedings. Merriman, an expert hiker and all-around athlete, has been known to dive under the sea for the shellfish on your plate. Anything he doesn't catch himself is obtained from local fishermen off Kawaihae harbor, and all produce is grown locally. You can't go wrong with anything, especially the inventive salads or the signature dish, wok-charred ahi. One wrinkle: the large wine list is a tad overpriced. No lunch on weekends. Features: own baking, rated wine cellar. Reservations required. Credit cards: A, MC, V.

Kohala Coast

Donatoni's   **$$$**   ★★★★

425 Waikoloa Beach Drive, Kohala Coast, 96743, ☎ (808) 885-1234. Associated hotel:
The Hilton Waikoloa Village.
Italian cuisine. Specialties: Pizza, osso bucco, cannoli.
Dinner: 6–9 p.m., entrées $18–$25.

Donatoni's is the star among the Hilton Waikoloa Village Resort's six restaurants.
The elegantly appointed room recalls a villa on the Italian Riviera rather than the
volcanic Kohala Coast, but it all works. And you can get here by gondola. Cuisine
is Northern Italian, and there's a dress code to match the decor. Try the delicious
pizzas, osso bucco, cioppino and fresh cannoli for dessert. Excellent wine list. Fea-
tures: own baking, rated wine cellar. Jacket requested. Reservations required. Credit
cards: A, DC, D, MC, V.

Hakone   **$$$**   ★★★★

62-100 Kauna'oa Drive, Kohala Coast, 96743, ☎ (808) 880-1111. Associated hotel:
The Hapuna Beach Prince.
Japanese cuisine. Specialties: Sukiyaki, nabemono, shabushabu, kaiseki dinners, sushi.
Dinner: entrées $18–$25.

You'll have to dress a bit to enjoy a wide variety of Japanese specialties at this tranquil, peaceful, yet elegant dining room in the Hapuna Beach Prince Hotel. In addition to a menu (buffet or a lá carte) of traditional sukiyaki, seafood in broth,
shabushabu (tabletop cooking) and Imperial court-style kaiseki dinners, there's a
separate sushi bar with its own kitchen. Ocean or garden views are included. Jacket
requested. Reservations required. Credit cards: A, DC, MC, V.

Roy's Waikoloa Bar & Grill   **$$$**   ★★★

250 Waikoloa Beach Drive, in the King's Shops, Kohala Coast, ☎ (808) 885-4321.
International cuisine. Specialties: Dim sum-style appetizers, imu oven pizzas, fresh fish,
dark chocolate souffle.
Dinner: 6:30–9:30 p.m., entrées $8–$27.

The fifth Roy's restaurant in Hawaii, Roy's Waikoloa Bar & Grill, opened in June
1996 at the King's Shops in the Waikoloa Beach Resort. The executive chef is Jac-
queline Lau, who recently helmed Roy's Nicolina on Maui. Straight out of a com-
munity college culinary school in California's San Joaquin Valley, Lau started with
Roy in 1988 at his original Hawaii Kai location on Oahu as a pastry chef. She was
his first chef de cuisine, eventually creating 20–25 new dishes per night! Like Roy's
other establishments, Roy's Waikoloa (or is it Jacqueline's?) will feature a regular
menu of appetizers, individual imu pizzas, pasta, fresh salads and entrées side by side
with a nightly special sheet. Some items might include Puna papaya and hibachi beef
salad with julienne veggies and hoisin sesame vinaigrette, "local style" Portuguese
sausage pizza with Maui onions and cheddar, or a mixed plate of lemongrass shu-
tome and blackened ahi. Among the desserts are Roy's signature original dark choc-
olate soufflé with a liquid center (a must for chocoholics), or Big Island style sundae
with tropical sauces and ginger candy. Are you drooling yet? Features: own baking.
Reservations recommended. Credit cards: CB, DC, D, MC, V.

The Bistro   **$$$**   ★★★★

62-100 Kauna'oa Drive, Kohala Coast, 96743, ☎ *(808) 880-1111. Associated hotel:*
The Hapuna Beach Prince.
Mediterranean cuisine. Specialties: Steaks, fresh seafood, chicken.
Dinner: 6–9 p.m., entrées $18–$25. Closed: Mon., Tues.

Renowned for a prodigious wine cellar, the luxurious, intimate Bistro is subtly dec-
orated in an elegant English hunt club style. Many dishes are prepared at tableside,
and patrons are expected to dress in "evening resort attire." The Bistro recently
switched from Mediterranean cuisine to a contemporary American menu of grilled
steaks, fresh seafood and poultry, enhanced by fresh local produce. Features: own
baking, rated wine cellar. Jacket requested. Reservations required. Credit cards: A, DC,
MC, V.

The CanoeHouse   **$$$**   ★★★★

68-1400 Mauna Lani Drive, Kohala Coast, 96743, ☎ *(808) 885-6622. Associated hotel:*
The Mauna Lani Bay Hotel.
Gourmet cuisine. Specialties: Fresh coriander crusted ahi with curried eggplant, kiawe
smoked five-spice duck with mango relish.
Dinner: 6–9 p.m., entrées $17–$25. Closed: Tues.

Even if the name of the restaurant is all stuck together, this gleaming, open-air,
beachfront dining room in the Mauna Lani Bay Hotel is one of the most beautiful
on the island. There is a fishing canoe suspended from the ceiling as well as ancient
native artifacts relating to boating unearthed on the grounds throughout the restaurant. Dinner here is pure romance, with magnificent views of the splendid sunsets,
twinkling stars and waves lapping the sand right outside. Try the signature rare peppered ahi (tuna) accompanied by a bottle of champagne. A must for a special-event
dinner, and definitely worth the price. Features: outside dining, own baking, rated
wine cellar. Credit cards: A, DC, MC, V.

The Coast Grille   **$$$**   ★★★★

62-100 Kauna'oa Drive, Kohala Coast, 96743, ☎ *(808) 880-1111. Associated hotel:*
The Hapuna Beach Prince.
Seafood cuisine. Specialties: Oyster bar, fresh seafood.
Dinner: 6–9 p.m., entrées $18–$25.

This circular-shaped dining room in the Hapuna Beach Prince allows almost all din-
ers a view of fabulous Hapuna Beach and the ocean; suffice it to say that sunsets can
be wonderful from this vantage point. Executive chef Corey White uses local ingre-
dients, such as tender ahi (Pacific yellowfin tuna) and fresh Big Island produce in his
Hawaiian Regional cuisine. Seafood is the star here, including a tantalizing steamed
whole fish wrapped in a banana leaf, but meat dishes are also served. Some people
linger at the oyster bar for the rest of the evening. Features: rated wine cellar. Res-
ervations required. Credit cards: A, DC, D, MC, V.

The Orchid at Mauna Lani   **$**

One North Kaniku Drive, Kohala Coast, 96743, ☎ *(808) 885-2000. Associated hotel:*
Orchid at Mauna Lani.

In March 1996, the Ritz-Carlton Mauna Lani officially became The Orchid at
Mauna Lani, with ITT Sheraton taking over the management reins of the hotel and
its restaurants. Chef Amy Ferguson-Ota is no longer the executive chef, replaced by

David Reardon, most recently the general manager and executive chef of the five-star Laurels Restaurant at the Sheraton Park Central Hotel in Dallas. Reardon will now oversee the resort's three restaurants and four lounges. At press time, with the exception of the Dining Room (now closed), new restaurant names and culinary themes will be developed for The Grill and The Café, now the resort's main dining venues. Currently, The Grill features grilled dishes (what else?) prepared with a light Mediterranean flair and Hawaii regional cuisine specialties. The ambience is club-like, and enhanced with koa wood embellishments; jackets are optional. The more relaxed, tropical Café is popular for a lavish Sunday brunch and serves Pacific Island specialties, local favorites and spa cuisine.

South Kona

Captain Cook

Aloha Café $$ ★★★

Highway 11, Captain Cook, ☎ *(808) 322-3383.*
American cuisine. Specialties: Breakfasts, baked goods, coffee drinks.
Breakfast: 8 a.m.–8 p.m., entrées $7–$9.
Lunch: 11 a.m.–4 p.m., entrées $7–$10.
Dinner: 4–8 p.m., entrées $8–$12.

Since good restaurants of any substance are few and far between in this area, this small but terrific indoor/outdoor café in the lobby of the Aloha Theater, a circa 1920s building and home to the Aloha Community Players theater troupe, is a welcome relief. Locals and tourists in the know head here to sit on the covered, wrap-around lanai for hearty breakfasts and steaming-hot Kona coffee sprinkled with chocolate. All pastries, desserts and muffins are homemade. If you're here for lunch and dinner, fresh fish is the best bet, prepared with light, healthful sauces. Sunday hours: 9 a.m.–2 p.m. Features: outside dining, own baking. Reservations not accepted. Credit cards: MC, V.

Holualoa Café $ ★★★

76-5901 Mamalahoa Highway, Captain Cook, ☎ *(808) 322-2233.*
American cuisine. Specialties: Kona coffee, pastries, smoothies.
Breakfast: 6:30 a.m.–5 p.m., entrées $2–$5.
Lunch: 11 a.m.–5 p.m., entrées $2–$5. Closed: Sun.

A charmer of a coffee house/cum gift shop with a garden for outdoor seating, Holualoa Café is in the heart of the Kona coffee belt. This café's house blend is served with whipped cream if you desire. Homemade pastries and friendly service, as well as live music on Thursdays from 7 p.m.–10 p.m. Features: outside dining, own baking. Reservations not accepted.

Kay's Kitchen $ ★★

Four miles above Keahole Airport, Captain Cook, ☎ *(808) 325-1086.*
Specialties: Loco moco.
Breakfast: 7 a.m.–11 a.m., entrées $5–$6.
Lunch: 11 a.m.–4 p.m., entrées $5–$6.
Dinner: 4–7 p.m., entrées $5–$6.

Primarily used for takeout, this family diner with four outdoor tables is in a somewhat out-of-the-way location next door to a small market. Locals don't mind making the drive for the familiar rib-sticker, loco moco, a freshly ground meat patty topped with brown gravy and served with an egg, or hamburger steak. Call ☎ *(808) 325-7797* for a recording of daily specials. Features: outside dining. Reservations not accepted.

Keauhou

Edward's at the Terrace   **$$$**   ★★★

78-261 Manukai Street, Keauhou, 96739, ☎ *(808) 322-1434. Associated hotel: Kanaloa at Kona Condominiums.*
Mediterranean cuisine. Specialties: Medallions of pork with prunes, Bastia, fresh fish, homemade desserts.
Breakfast: 8–11 a.m., entrées $15–$19.
Lunch: 11 a.m.–2 p.m., entrées $15–$19.
Dinner: 5–9 p.m., entrées $15–$19.
The poolside terrace of the Kanaloa at Kona condominiums, overlooking the ocean, is the setting for this lovely restaurant serving Mediterranean cuisine with a touch of the Middle East. Edward is Edward Frady, who manned the stoves at the Hyatt Regency Waikoloa before it became a Hilton; he then moved on to the Ritz Carlton Mauna Lani (now the Orchid) before setting up shop here. If you've maxxed out on Pacific Rim fare, sample Frady's Moroccan bastia, Cornish game hen wrapped tenderly in phyllo pastry. Features: outside dining, own baking. Reservations recommended. Credit cards: A, CB, DC, MC, V.

Volcano

Volcano Village

Kilauea Lodge and Restaurant   **$$$**   ★★★

Old Volcano Road (between Haunani & Wright Roads), Volcano Village, 96785, ☎ *(808) 967-7366. Associated hotel: Kilauea Lodge.*
European cuisine. Specialties: Broiled marlin with mango relish, game dishes, vegetarian specialties, macadamia nut pie.
Dinner: 5:30– 9 p.m., entrées $13–$27.
European specialties with a local touch are served in a baronial, high-ceilinged dining hall with polished hardwood floors and koa tables. A historic rock "fireplace of friendship" glows constantly in the center of the room. Located in the Kilauea Lodge, this is the favored choice for dining in the Volcano area, and chef-innkeeper Albert Jeyte (together with wife, Lorna) make all the soups, breads and desserts from scratch daily. Features: own baking. Reservations recommended. Credit cards: A, MC, V.

Nightlife

The Big Island doesn't offer a whole lot of heel-kicking action after nightfall. The resorts and large hotels feature lounge acts and various other entertainment, including **luaus** and **Polynesian revues**. Two **discos** to try on the **Kona coast** are the **Eclipse Restaurant**, in Kailua, and the **Second Floor**, within the Hilton Waikola Village. Don Drysdale's Club 53, Jolly Roger and Under the Palms are popular lounges for drinking and hanging out. Over at **Hilo** (which is *really* dead after dark), you can practice **country dancing** at Fiascos or Lehua Bay City Bar and Grill, **disco** at D'Angoras or do the **karaoke** thing at KK Tei's Lounge; the bar at the Hilo Seaside Hotel draws the locals who entertain themselves. There are **movie theaters** in Kailua-Kona, Hilo and Pahoa, and **legitimate theater** in Kainaliu, Hilo and Waimea.

Hilo

Fiascos ★★

Highway 11 near Banyan Drive, Hilo, 96720, *(808) 935-7666.*
Line dancin' in Hilo Thursdays from 8 p.m. to midnight; Live Hawaiian music on Friday and Saturdays from 9 p.m. General admission: Varies.

Kona

Kailua-Kona

Eclipse ★★

75-5771 Kuakini Highway, Kailua-Kona, 96740, *(808) 329-4686.*
Hours: 10 p.m.–2 a.m.
A Kona hot zone, with '90s style-disco dancing on weekends. Big-band and country-western the rest of the week.

Huggo's ★★

75-5828 Kahakai Road, Kailua-Kona, 96740, ☎ *(808) 329-1493.*
Hours: 9 p.m.–Closing.
Closed: Tues., Thur., Fri., Sun.
A "smorgasbord" of live music accompanies the good eats at this Kona bayfront institution. "Sound Effects" plays oldies from the '50s and'60s on Friday nights, slinky salsa by "Kona Blend" on Saturday nights, "island attitude" music (whatever that is) on Mondays. Tuesday, karaoke and dancing. Wednesday, contemporary; Thursday, jazz.

Island Breeze Luau ★★★

75-5660 Palani Road, Kailua-Kona, 96740, *(808) 326-4969.*

Hours: 5:30–8:45 p.m.
Closed: Mon., Fri., Sat.

Although most luaus have similar menus and entertainment, this one is special in that it's set at King Kamehameha I's restored Kailua Bay beachfront estate, Kamakahonu. The revue commences with the arrival of the royal court, replete with ceremonial headdresses and "feather" *kahili*. Among the 22 dishes served are some vegetarian items. It's also offered four nights a week and is reasonably priced. General admission: $49.

King Kamehameha's Kona Beach Hotel ★★

75-5660 Palani Road, Kailua-Kona, 96740, ☎ (808) 329-2911.

The poolside Billfish Bar at this beachfront hotel offers live music entertainment to accompany the gorgeous sunsets; it's relatively uncrowded, and pupus and cocktails are served. Warble to the karaoke machine on Friday and Saturday nights at Paddlers Grille, also on the hotel grounds.

Kona Bowl Lounge ★★

75-5586 Ololi Road, Kailua-Kona, 96740, ☎ (808) 326-2695.
Hours: 7 p.m.–2 a.m.

Karaoke with deejay "J.J." Kapele every evening; if you stink, at least the rolling balls will drown you out. On the other hand, if you're great, the room will be so quiet you can hear the pins drop (ugh).

The Puka Bar/Kona Comedy Club ★★

78-128 Ehukai Street, Kailua-Kona, 96740, ☎ (808) 322-3411.
Hours: 8 p.m.–2 a.m., Wed. only.

The nightly karaoke song fest is interrupted one night a week when the Kona Comedy Club takes over the bar on Wednesdays at 8 p.m. Good for a couple of belly laughs.

North Kona

Kona Village Resort Luau ★★★★

P.O. Box 1299, North Kona, 96740, ☎ (808) 325-5555.
Hours: 6:45–9 p.m., Wed. only.

The Kona Village luau, a tradition for 30 years, has been consistently judged by luau connoisseurs as the best all around. The exclusive resort opens up its guarded gates to anyone who can afford to attend the feast. Preparations start as early as 9 a.m. on Fridays when 20 hot cooking stones are put inside the traditional *kalua* pig. At 6:45 p.m., guests are invited to witness the unveiling of the pig at a special ceremony, when chefs remove the stones with their (gasp!) bare hands. The luscious menu features sushi, fresh crab and teriyaki beef as well as the usual Hawaiian dishes. The fiery Polynesian revue includes Hawaiian hula, rhythmic chants and a Samoan fire dance. No price.

South Kohala
Kohala Coast

Mauna Kea Beach Hotel Luau ★★★★

Mauna Kea Beach Hotel, Kohala Coast, ☎ (808) 882-7222.

Hours: 6 p.m.
Closed: Mon., Wed., Thur., Fri., Sat., Sun.
The newly reopened Mauna Kea Beach Hotel presents an authentic luau on the North Pointe Lawn every Tuesday at 6 p.m. The special entertainment is provided by Kumu Hula Nani Lim and dancers from her hula halau, winners of the prestigious Merrie Monarch hula competition. No price.

Petroglyph Bar   ★★★
69-275 Waikoloa Beach Drive, Kohala Coast, 96743, ☎ (808) 885-6789.
Hours: 4:30–10:30 p.m.
Located on the rooftop of the Royal Waikoloan Hotel, this relaxing spot offers uninterrupted views of gorgeous Anaeho'omalu Bay, ancient fishponds and Mauna Kea in the distance. A favored sunset sojourn, the tropical drinks are choice, and the Hawaiian music is live and romantic.

Shopping

Both Kona and Hilo have enough **malls and shopping centers** to please even the most fixated visitors. Waimea and Captain Cook also have their own—albeit small—shopping areas. The strip along **Alii Drive**, in Kailua-Kona, is geared toward visitors who crowd in to pick up souvenirs, resort wear, gift items and arts and crafts. Selections of **local arts and crafts**—jewelry, pottery, weavings, glasswork, carvings, beadwork, feather work, etc.—can be viewed and purchased at Volcano Art Center (within Hawaii Volcanoes National Park) and at galleries in **Holualoa**, **Kapaau** and **Kainalu**.

Hilo

Basically Books   ★★
46 Waianuenue Avenue, Hilo, ☎ (808) 961-0144.
Hours: 9 a.m.–5 p.m.
Specializes in books about the islands, including out-of-print vintage Hawaiiana. The adjoining map shop has a large selection of travel guides and maps of Hawaii.

Dan de Luz's Woods Inc.   ★★★★
760 Kilauea Avenue, Hilo, ☎ (808) 935-5587.
Hours: 9 a.m.–5 p.m.
Collector's-item wood bowls made by famed island artist Dan de Luz, who has a workshop in the back that guests are invited to tour. Visit his Waimea-Kamuela shop at *64-1014 Mamalahoa Highway, ☎ 885-5856,* daily 9 a.m.–5 p.m.

Panaewa Homestead Farmers Market   ★★
Puainako and Ohuohu Streets, Hilo, ☎ (808) 959-2726.

Hours: 6 a.m.–noon
Closed: Mon., Tues., Wed., Thur., Fri., Sun.
This market was established recently by local farmers from Hilo's Panaewa area. It's a colorful distribution point for a variety of produce and foodstuffs. Also check out Hilo's main farmer's market at the corner of Kamehameha Avenue and Mamo Street on Wednesdays and Saturdays from 6 a.m.–1 p.m.

Sig Zane Designs ★★★

122 Kamehameha Avenue, Hilo, 96720, ☎ (808) 935-7077.
Hours: 9 a.m.–5 p.m.
Sig Zane features locally designed, 100 percent cotton clothing, original fabrics to buy by the yard, bedding and gifts.

Kona

Kailua-Kona

Hula Heaven ★★★

75-5744 Ali'i Drive, Kailua-Kona, 96740, ☎ (808) 329-7885.
Hours: 9 a.m.–9 p.m.
This shop in the Kona Inn Shopping Village will assuage any pangs people have for the romantic era of mid-1900s Hawaii. Hula Heaven features Matson Line menu art (up to $500 for those in mint condition), and Aloha shirts worth as much as an Italian haute couture original.

Island Preservations ★★

75-5660 Palani Road, Kailua-Kona, 96750, ☎ (808) 329-7770.
Hours: 9 a.m.–5 p.m.
Located in King Kamehameha's Kona Beach Hotel, this unique shop uses real blossoms from the Big Island, including orchids, pikake and roses, and preserves them whole in a unique, dye-free, secret process. The flowers are then mounted and placed in a Plexiglass case to protect them from ultraviolet light, trimmed with copper foil and placed in a handsome koa frame (some back-lit). Amazingly, some of the orchids are more than 10 years old but look freshly picked. A lava-rock-like urethane foam is sculpted into a human torso to display leis. Prices range from $65 to $1250 depending on size and complexity. Shipping available worldwide.

Kona Farmers Market ★★★

Kona Inn Shopping Village, Kailua-Kona.
Hours: 6 a.m.–3 p.m., Wed., Sat. only.
Rare orchids and heliconias, papayas, Ka'u oranges and other tropical flowers and fruits as well as island-style food, coffee and macadamia nuts are featured at this lively market.

Noa Noa ★★★

75-5744 Ali'i Drive in the Kona Inn Shopping Center, Kailua-Kona, 96740, ☎ (808) 329-8187.
Hours: 9 a.m.–9 p.m.
All original, hand-painted batik clothing in natural fabrics from Indonesia for men, women and children. Also a fine collection of Pacific Island artifacts including Ikat weavings, basketry, masks and ceramics.

THE BIG ISLAND

North Kohala
Hawi

As Hawi Turns

Downtown Hawi 96719, ☎ *(808) 889-5023.*
Hours: 10 a.m.–6 p.m.
Vintage clothing, crafts and "wild things" all in the heart of downtown Hawi.

Hawaiian Moon Gallery

P.O. Box 1469, Hawi, 96755, ☎ *(808) 889-0880.*
Hours: 9 a.m.–5 p.m.
This eclectic gallery in rustic Hawi exhibits the works of talented local potters, artists, sculptors and jewelers. Also featured are handcrafted wood furniture by the owner's husband. Also distinctive, one-of-a-kind clothing.

Kohala Koa Gallery

Junction of Highway 250 and 270, Hawi, ☎ *(808) 889-0055.*
Hours: 9 a.m.–5 p.m.
Located within the Bamboo Restaurant, a restored old general store. Robin and Michael Felig have amassed a unique collection of locally crafted wall art, pottery, jewelry, baskets, koa clocks, boxes, bowls and custom furnishings and accessories made of Hawaii's native woods.

Kapa'au

Ackerman Gallery

P.O. Box 961, Kapa'au, 96755, ☎ *(808) 889-5971.*
Hours: 10 a.m.–5:30 p.m.
Owned by Gary Ackerman, a Paris-trained artist with a distinguished reputation, this restored old auto showroom and gas station features canvases, hand-blown glass pieces, wood sculptures, hand-painted silks and original works by Hawaii's leading artists, including Greg Pontius, Leimana Pelton, John Flynn and Wilfred Yamazawa, a Kapa'au resident famous for petroglyph jewelry displayed at the Bishop Museum. Also Oriental antiques, primitive artifacts.

South Kohala
Kamuela

Cook's Discoveries

Highway 19, in the Waimea Center, Kamuela, 96743, ☎ *(808) 885-3633.*
Hours: 10 a.m.–6 p.m.
Shopping here is truly a discovery: you get to explore several rooms full of genuine koa carvings, jewelry, clothing, toys, confections made by artists with taste. Cook's Discoveries is also an excellent location for authentic hula implements (sorry, no ukuleles). It's located in the restored Spencer House, an old general store built in 1850.

Kamuela Hat Company

Waimea Center, Highway 19, Kamuela, ☎ *(808) 885-8875.*

Panama, lauhala and Western hats are all made individually at this shop. Also a large selection of handmade feather leis, Western novelties and Australian oilskin garments.

Parker Square ★★★

Highway 19, one block past Edelweiss Restaurant, Kamuela.
Hours: 9 a.m.–5 p.m.

The eight shops and galleries in this rustic-chic shopping center in a country setting are fun to just browse through. Hawaiian, Polynesian, Asian and primitive art, antique baskets, jewelry, koa bowls at Gallery of Great Things, ☎ *(808) 885-7706*; Antique Japanese, Korean and Chinese furniture, porcelains, textiles from Silk Road Gallery; Gourmet kitchen accessories, gift cards, Hawaiian books, candles, blankets, linens, Crabtree and Evelyn products at Waimea General Store, ☎ *(808) 885-4479*; Kamuela Goldsmiths for gold and gemstones, country furnishings, teddy bears galore, woven throws and quilts; Christmas collectibles at Bentleys; and meditation supplies, beads, incense at Sweet Wind. Relax with aromatic coffee and a snack at Waimea Coffee Company, ☎ *(808) 885-4472*.

Princess Kaiulani Fashions ★★★

Waimea Center, Kamuela, 96743, ☎ (808) 885-2177.
Hours: 10 a.m.–6 p.m.

Don't think you can hide under these designer muumuus—the elaborate shoulders and scoop necklines recall the Victorian era of the real Princess Kaiulani. Also a full line of distinctive women's clothing. Opens at 9 a.m. on Saturday.

Upcountry Quilters and Topstich ★★★

Holomua Center, Kamuela, ☎ (808) 885-4482.
Hours: 10 a.m.–4 p.m.

Open since 1983, Topstitch features authentic Hawaiian quilts, kits, books and supplies.

South Kona

Holualoa

Kimura Lauhala ★★★

Mamalahoa Highway and Hualalai Road, Holualoa, 96725, ☎ (808) 324-0053.
Hours: 9 a.m.–5 p.m.

This shop, specializing in fine woven *lauhala* (split bamboo) work, began life as a general store in 1915. Mrs. Kimura, a loquacious octogenarian who still works in her shop, often comes out to talk with visitors, reminiscing about the old days. On display is a large selection of hats, purses, mats, baskets and more.

Studio 7 ★★★

Mamalahoa Highway, Holualoa, ☎ (808) 323-2877.

The old coffee town and art colony of Holualoa is home to Studio 7, where woodblock prints, paintings, sculptures and pottery by contemporary Big Island artists Hiroki and Setuko Morinoue are displayed.

THE BIG ISLAND

Keauhou

Alapaki's ★★★

Keauhou Shopping Center, Keauhou, ☎ *(808) 322-2007.*
Hours: 9 a.m.–6 p.m.

Enter this dramatic shop through a unique lava rock archway where Alapaki and Josie Tampos have collected Hawaiian crafts by more than 100 local artists. The woodwork is incredible, including bowls, jewelry and poi pounders. Feather *uli-uli* rattles, coconut *pahu* drums and other Hawaiian musical instruments make great gifts. Open Sunday from 10 a.m.–5 p.m.

Volcano

Volcano Village

Farmer's Market ★★

Cooper Center, P.O. Box 600, Volcano Village, 96785, ☎ *(808) 967-7121.*
Hours: 8:30–11 a.m.
Closed: Mon., Tues., Wed., Thur., Fri., Sun.

Fresh produce, herbs, flowers, and coffee grown by volcano farmers are the main attractions at this local-style market. Also used clothing, books and fresh from the baked goods, including *malasadas* (Portuguese donut holes).

Fielding's Fascinating Big Island Facts

A.k.a.	The Big Island
Main city	Hilo
Flower	Red lehua
Color	Red
Area	4038 square miles
Length	93 miles
Width	76 miles
Population	120,317
Highest point	Mauna Kea (13,796 feet)

The Big Island Survival Guide

Getting There

You can fly into either Keahole-Kona International Airport or Hilo International Airport. **Keahole-Kona International Airport**, the choice of visitors staying on the western side of the island—about seven miles north of Kona and serves some 50-or-so mostly interisland flights per week, plus United's San Francisco-to-Big Island run. You'll find basic airport amenities at the open-air terminal including snack shops, baggage lockers, concessions, visitor information and a number of car rental desks. Airlines are **United** (☎ *(800) 241-6522)*, **Hawaiian** (☎ *(808) 326-5615)*, **Aloha** (☎ *(808) 935-5771)*, **Island Air** (☎ *323-3345)* and **Big Island Air** (☎ *329-4868)*—for travel between Kona and Hilo. Car rental agencies are **Alamo** (☎ *(808) 329-8896)*, **Avis** (☎ *(808) 327-3000)*, **Budget** (☎ *(808) 329-8511)*, **Dollar** (☎ *(808) 329-2744)*, **Hertz** (☎ *(808) 329-3566)* and **National** (☎ *(808) 329-1675)*.

Hilo International Airport is about two miles from the city's hotel district on Banyan Drive. The modern two-story terminal features a restaurant, a slew of concessions, baggage lockers, an information center and car rental booths. Airlines are **Hawaiian**, **Aloha**, **Island Air**, **Big Island Air** (see numbers above) and **Mahalo Air** (☎ *(800) 277-8333)*. Car rental agencies operating out of Hilo's airport are **Alamo** (☎ *(808) 961-3343)*, **Avis** (☎ *(808) 935-1290)*, **Budget** (☎ *(808) 935-6878)*, **Dollar** (☎ *(808) 961-6059)*, **Hertz** (☎ *(808) 935-2896)* and **National** (☎ *(808) 935-0891)*.

Waimea-Kohala Airport (known locally as Kamuela Airport), located outside Waimea, is served by **Trans Air** (☎ *(808) 934-5801)*, out of Oahu, for interisland commutes. Upolu Airport, a remote airstrip at Upolu Point at the island's northern tip, serves private planes and small charter operations.

Getting Around

You'll either need to rent a car or catch a taxi from Hilo International Airport—there is no public transportation and no shuttle service, either. The situation is the same at Keahole-Kona International Airport, except that some of the big Waikoloa resorts (Hilton Waikoloa Village, Royal Waikoloan, Mauna Kea and Mauna Lani) offer shuttle service to guests.

Driving on the Big Island is relatively easy. One main thoroughfare, the Mamalahoa Highway, more or less circles the island, with Queen Kaahumanu hugging the Kona and Kohala coasts. Ali'i Drive is Kona's main tourist strip, while Hilo is an easy grid-designed town. Saddle Road, the byway that slices through the island, is usually verboten in the car rental contract.

In Hilo, you'll find **taxis** in front of baggage claim, otherwise call **A-1 Bob's** (☎ *(808) 959-4800),* **ABC Taxi** *(*☎ *(808) 935-0755),* **Ace One** *(*☎ *(808) 935-8303),* **Hawaii Taxi** *(*☎ *(808) 959-6359)* or **Hilo Harry's** *(*☎ *(808) 935-7091).* For Kona-based taxis, call **Aloha Taxi** *(*☎ *(808) 325-5448),* **Kona Airport Taxi** *(*☎ *(808) 329-7779)* or **Marina Taxi** *(*☎ *(808) 329-2481).* Don't forget to consider "Hawaiian time" when booking, especially for flights. Approximate fare between airports and town is $10, Hilo; $20, Kona; $45, Waikoloa.

The county-operated **bus service**, **Hele-On Bus** *(*☎ *(808) 961-6722 or (808) 935-8241),* provides transportation Mondays through Saturdays to a number of Big Island areas, including a run between Hilo and Kailua-Kona (about $8, one way). The Ali'i Shuttle goes the length of Kona's Ali'i Drive about every 45 minutes. **Chauffeured limo service** is provided by Robert's *(*☎ *(808) 329-1688, Kona, or (808) 935-2858, Hilo)* and Luana's *(*☎ *(808) 326-5466).*

Narrow or nonexistent shoulders on the roads, combined with tour-bus traffic, make the Big Island unfavorable for **mopeds** and **bicycles**. If you have your heart set on cycling, opt for a mountain bike. Rent mopeds and bicycles from **DJ's Rentals** *(*☎ *(808) 329-1700, Kailua-Kona).* Other outlets for bicycle rentals include **Dave's Bike** and **Triathlon Shop** *(*☎ *(808) 329-4522, Kona),* **Hawaiian Pedals Unlimited** *(*☎ *(808) 329-2294, Kona),* **Island Cycle Rentals** *(*☎ *(808) 329-7585),* **Pacific United Rental** *(*☎ *(808) 935-2974, Hilo)* or **Teo's Safaris** *(*☎ *(808) 982-5221, Keaau, south of Hilo).* Many of the rental agencies also lead guided cycling tours.

Visitor Information

Both airports have visitor information booths with brochures and helpful attendants. Otherwise call in to one of the **Hawaii Visitor Bureau** offices: *75-5719 Alii Drive, Kailua-Kona 96740 (*☎ *(808) 329-7787),* in Kona; or *250 Keawe Street (*☎ *(808) 961-5797),* in Hilo. For information **before you arrive**, write or call: **Destination Kona Coast** *(Box 2850, Kailua-Kona 96745,* ☎ *(808) 329-6748);* **Destination Hilo** *(Box 1391, Hilo 96721,* ☎ *(808) 935-5294);* or **Big Island Group** *(HCO 2, Box 5900, Kamuela 96743,* ☎ *(808) 885-5900 or 800-648-2444).*

OAHU

Oahu's Diamond Head is one of the island's most photographed attractions.

Many island-bound visitors no doubt believe Oahu *is* Hawaii. They land at Honolulu International Airport, shuttle over to Waikiki, crowd together on the sand, elbow each other in the shops, ogle Diamond Head in the distance, pay respect at Pearl Harbor, do a luau and see a real hula dancer, then go back to the airport and head home. Hawaii!

In many ways, Oahu is indeed the perfect island—a place with plenty of everything to do, as well as room to escape from it all—with contrasts that can't help but startle and amaze even jaded tourists. Yes, there is the tourist mecca of Waikiki with its crowds, malls, hotels, restaurants, street vendors, flash and fervor, schlock and gawd—all mesmerizing even if it is *not* your style. But blink hard, and you'll also be gazing at a booming city, overdevel-

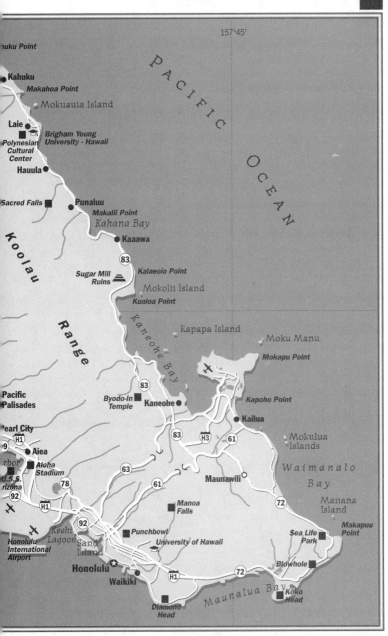

oped communities, rural villages, highly visible military power, sugarcane and pineapple fields, cultural presence and sinful practices, cranes and bulldozers, world-class surfing beaches and bubbling streams, claustrophobic beaches and wide-open spaces. Nicknamed the "Gathering Place," Oahu's 826,231 residents (about 80 percent of the state's population) are quite happy, thank you, with this "gathering" of elements.

Oahu more or less slipped through the cracks of the early settlement days, only becoming *really* noticed in 1795 when King Kamehameha the Great swooped in on his island-unification quest. It wasn't long before Honolulu, with its attractive harbor, became the islands' center of commerce, and Pearl Harbor, with its deep waters, became the focal point of U.S. military might.

Once King Kamehameha shifted the capital from Lahaina to Oahu, the island became something of a royal playground, with the kings and queens growing more and more enchanted with their new home *and* that strip of beach known as Waikiki. Many members of the royal family set up residence near the beach (Kamehameha's IV and V, Lunalilo, Kalakaua, Liliuokalani and Kaiulani). Did someone say, "island, beach, remote, paradise—women?"

Bring on the writers in search of solace! In came authors such as W. Somerset Maugham, Herman Melville, Jack London, Mark Twain and Robert Louis Stevenson.

The influx of royalty, writers and other significant visitors meant, of course, that they needed places to stay. *Voila!* The building began. First came a barrage of beach cottages but, come the turn of the century, a hotel just *had* to go up. The Sheraton Moana Surfrider (then known as the Moana) became Oahu's first hotel, followed in 1927 by the luxurious Royal Hawaiian Hotel (or the "Pink Palace of the Pacific"). It didn't take long before Waikiki became known as a visitor destination *par excellence*. But tourists weren't the only ones to visit Oahu—the Japanese made a surprise appearance on December 7, 1941, making their presence felt by bombing the brains out of Pearl Harbor.

Within a decade, the island was ready again to welcome the paradise-seeking masses. More hotels went up, followed by resorts, followed by condos, and today's visitors can now choose from about 130 hotels and condos, and approximately 34,000 rooms.

It probably won't surprise anyone that economic giant Oahu garners more visitors (about 3.5 million annually) than any of the other Hawaiian islands. The trend that began in the 1960s (and which completely usurped pineapple and sugarcane profits) has grown into a more-than-$2-billion-per-year industry, and shows no signs of slowing. The visitor profile includes such diverse groups as Japanese honeymooners, European backpackers, Australian surfers and U.S. military personnel.

Government spending tops tourism on Oahu's economic scale—easy to understand when you take a look at the statistics. More than 60,000 military personnel, plus an additional 20,000 civilians, help fuel the island's humongous military machine. The Navy, Marines, Army, Air Force and Coast Guard are all represented and, combined, make up some 65 percent of the state's federal jobs and control more than 240,000 acres of Hawaiian land. Agriculture ranks third (after tourism) in economic importance, with sugarcane and pineapple the big cash cows.

Bird's-Eye View

At 594 square miles (44 miles long, 30 miles wide), Oahu holds the position of third-largest Hawaiian island. The famous stretch of beach known as Waikiki (on the dry, sunny side of the island) measures about two miles—between Diamond Head and the Ala Wai Canal—and is filled with hotels, tourists, restaurants, tourists, malls, tourists, street vendors and tourists (hard to believe it was once filled with swamps and ducks!). Nearby Honolulu is the island's main city, the state capitol and the political, cultural and commercial heart. Few visitors miss a trek over to Pearl Harbor, west of Honolulu, home of the USS *Arizona* Memorial. The Koolau Range (highest point is 3150-foot Puu Konahuanui), behind Honolulu, runs north and south across most of Oahu, slicing the island into windward and leeward sides, and is traversed by the Pali Highway (Highway 61). The center of the island is planted with acres of sugarcane, pineapples, bananas, flowers and fruit trees. Main communities on the fairly uncrowded windward shore are Kailua and Kaneohe, suburban towns that break up the almost end-on-end run of gorgeous beaches. Continuing northwest, the area around Waiahole offers sleepy villages and taro fields and, beyond, more great beaches, Kahana Valley State Park, Sacred Falls and the Polynesian Cultural Center. Curving around Kawela Bay, the North Shore area features the world-famous Banzai Pipeline, Waimea Bay, Sunset Beach and Kaena Point, with artsy communities and Dillingham Airfield situated in between. The Waianae Coast, along the northwestern shores, is Oahu's last frontier, a region savored by locals who did not take well to the huge Koolina Resort recently built in Kapolei. More top surfing beaches sit along this coast (Makaha hosts

P

P

P

Round Top Dr

Oahu Ave

Manoa Rd

Manoa Stream

Pukele Stream

unchbowl
ookout

P

Round
Top

Manoa Rd

E. Manoa Rd

Woodlawn

Waiomao Stream

— 21°20'

Manoa
lley Inn

Vancouver

University Ave

University of Hawaii
Manoa Campus

Sierra Dr

Lurline Dr

Monterey Dr

Paula Dr

St. Louis Dr

Paiolo Ave

10th Ave

Koko Dr

Kapiolani Blvd

Waialae Ave

Sierra Dr

16th Ave

Date St

Kapahulu Ave

Lunalilo Fwy

Ala Wai
Golf Course

ai Canal

Ala Wai Blvd

Kuhio Ave

Kalakaua

6th Ave

H1

M

International
Market Place

Kilauea Ave

16th Ave

18th Ave

Pahoa Ave

Kahala Mall
Shopping Center

S

Hawaii
Visitors
Bureau

Ave

Kapahulu Ave

Alohea Ave

Kapiolani
Community
College

Kahala
Mandarin
Oriental

Honolulu Zoo

Paki Ave

Monsarrat

Diamond

Kilauea Ave

Esfepao St.

Hunakai St.

H

he New Otani
ana Beach Hotel

Ave

Kapiolani
Park

Head Rd

Fort Ruger

H

Waikiki
Aquarium

Nalaau
Hawaii
Arboretum

Diamond
Head
Crater

Kahala Ave

Kahala Beach

s Souci Beach

Kaimana Beach

Diamond Head Rd

Black Point
(Kupikipikio)

Diamond Head

OAHU

annual surfing championships), along with the towns of Makaha, Waianae, Maili and Nanakuli. Backdrop to the coast is the Waianae Mountain Range and 4003-foot Mount Kaala—Oahu's highest point.

Nature Guide

Flora and fauna on crowded Oahu? *Mais oui!* This island, in fact, is one gigantic tropical paradise endowed with almost every species of flower, fruit, tree and shrub that Hawaii has to offer.

Around the cities and beaches, you can spot such feathered friends as sparrows, bulbul and munia, plus upland forest game birds such as the Japanese quail, ring-necked pheasant and dove. Less visible are the marine birds—Laysan albatross and various species of tern. In the forests and mountain ranges you might sight native dwellers such as the *'i'iwi* and *pueo* (Hawaiian owl). True bird enthusiasts should visit one or both of Oahu's national wildlife refuges (Pearl Harbor National Wildlife Refuge, at Pearl Harbor, and James Campbell Wildlife Refuge, near the North Shore) which attract many introduced and endangered species.

Oahu's unique and prolific plant life can be enjoyed throughout the island, but animals are another story. You might hear the call of a feral goat or wild pig if you're hiking in the mountains; otherwise you'll have to be content with suburban puppies and kitties.

Fielding's Beach Finder

Most people, when they think of "Waikiki Beach," envision it as one distinctive stretch of sand. A misnomer! The two-plus-mile strip is actually a clump of beaches that stretch between the dramatic Diamond Head and the bustling Hilton Hawaiian Village Resort. The island of Oahu is laced with more than 100 different beaches, ranging from crowded tourist haunts to remote bays and international surfing haunts. Check with local authorities before you venture into the water, especially along the North Shore.

Kailua Beach is Oahu's prime windsurfing spot.

Waikiki

Kahanamoku Beach
> *In front of the Hilton Hawaiian Village.*
> A gentle lagoon that is favored by families with children and novice swimmers. Rest rooms, showers, surfboard rentals, volleyball, snack bar.

Fort DeRussy Beach
> *In front of Fort DeRussy and the Hale Koa Hotel.*
> Offers good snorkeling and is targeted mostly by beach-going military personnel. Rest rooms, showers, snack bars, volleyball.

Gray's Beach
> *In front of the Halekulani Hotel.*
> A narrow stretch with good surfing. Rest rooms, surfboard rentals, snack bars, catamaran and canoe excursions.

Kahaloa and Ulukou beaches
> *In front of the Royal Hawaiian Hotel and Sheraton Moana Surfrider.*
> Strictly a tourist stretch (there's even a police station!). Rest rooms, showers, snack bar, surfing lessons, catamaran and canoe excursions.

Kuhio Beach Park
> *Between the Waikiki Beach Center and the seawall.*
> Good for surfing and bodysurfing, but the occasional deep spot makes it a bit too treacherous for kids and other inexperienced swimmers.

Queen's Surf
> *Across from the Honolulu Zoo.*

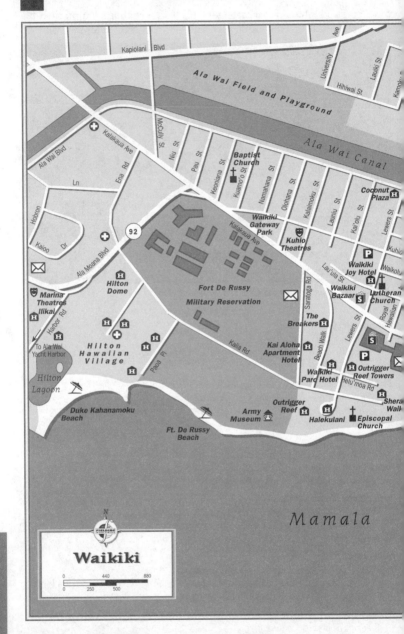

Kapiolani Blvd

Ala Wai Field and Playground

Ala Wai Canal

University
Hihiwai St
Lauiki St
Kamoku

Kalakaua Ave
McCully St
Niu St
Pau St
Keoniana St
Nahua St
Olohana St
Kalaimoku St
Launiu St
Kai'olu St
Lewers St

Ala Wai Blvd
Ena Rd
Ln
Nuamo'o St

Baptist Church

Coconut Plaza

Kalakaua Ave
Waikiki Gateway Park
Kuhio Theatres

Hobron
Kaioo Dr

92

Waikiki Bazaar
Waikiki Joy Hotel
Kuhio
Waikolu

Ala Moana Blvd
Saratoga Rd
Lau'ula Rd

Lutheran Church
Royal Hawaiian

Marina Theatres
Ilikai

Hilton Dome

Fort De Russy
Military Reservation

The Breakers

Harbor Rd

To Ala Wai Yacht Harbor

Hilton Hawaiian Village

Prava Pl

Kalia Rd

Beach Walk

Lewers St

Kai Aloha Apartment Hotel

Waikiki Parc Hotel

Outrigger Reef Towers
Helu'moa Rd

Hilton Lagoon

Duke Kahanamoku Beach

Ft. De Russy Beach

Army Museum

Outrigger Reef

Halekulani

Episcopal Church

Shera
Wall

Mamala

N

FIELDING

Waikiki

0   440   880
0   250   500

Laau St

Date

Lukepane Ave

Ekela Ave

Makaleka Ave

Palani Ave

Kamuela Ave

St

Iolani
High
School

Ala Wai

Golf Course

Clubhouse

a Wai Blvd

ha Dr

aukai St

Ave

Nohonani St

Waikiki
Market
Place

Nahua St

Walina St

Kanekapolei St

Ka'iulani Ave

Ala Wai Blvd

Tusitala St

eside

Waikiki
Trade Ctr.

Waikiki
Theatres

Kuhio
Mall

Cleghorn St

Kuhio

Ave

Ave

iki

International
Market Place

Kaiulani
Park

King's
Village

Ave

Ave

Assembly
of God

Wai Nani Wy

Ainakea Wy

Kaulana
Kai

Pualani Wy

Ka'iulani Ave

Kalakaua Ave

Koa

Uulu Ave

Prince Edward
Ave

Outrigger
Prince Kuhio

Community
Center

Kaneloa Rd

Hyatt
Regency

Outrigger
Waikiki

Sheraton
Moana
Surfrider

Aston Waikiki
Beachside Hotel

Liliuokalani

Kealohilani Ave

Hawaiian
Regent

Cartwright Rd

Makee Rd

alian

Waikiki Beach

Fr. Damien
Museum

St Augustine
Church

Ohua

Papaikalani

Lemon Rd

Ewa Hotel

P

Bay

Kuhio
Beach
Park

Kapahulu Ave

Honolulu
Zoo

Monsarrat Ave

P

Queen's Surf
Beach

To
Waikiki
Aquarium

Frequented by an odd mix of families, locals, and gay men who come to picnic, frolic, and watch the sun go down. Rest rooms, showers, picnic area.

San Souci

In front of Kapiolani Park.

Favored by experienced swimmers, training triathletes, canoeists, kayakers, kids, and near-naked sunbathers. Rest rooms, showers, picnic area, volleyball.

Ala Moana Beach Park

In Honolulu, northwest of Waikiki (in front of the Ala Moana Mall).

One of the island's most popular tourist beaches. Calm surf, jogging tracks, picnic and games areas, and plenty of oiled-up bodies set the scene. Rest rooms, showers, snack bars, lifeguards, tennis courts.

Diamond Head to Makapuu Point

Waialae Beach Park

Off Kahala Avenue (near the Kahala Hilton).

Draws windsurfers. Rest rooms, showers, picnic area.

Hanauma Bay

East of Hawaii Kai.

A marine preserve and a popular site for snorkeling and scuba-diving lessons. Rest rooms, showers, equipment rental, snack bar.

Sandy Beach

Two miles east of Hanauma Bay.

Brings the younger (somewhat rowdy) crowd who like to tempt fate by swimming in the treacherous surf. Rest rooms, showers.

Along Windward Oahu

Makapuu Beach Park

Across from Sea Life Park.

Suitable only for strong swimmers and lazy sunbathers. Rest rooms, showers.

Waimanalo Beach Park

South of Waimanalo town.

Has gentle surf but is quite obviously local turf. Rest rooms, showers, picnic area.

Bellows Field Beach

Near Waimanalo town.

An Air Force beach, available to others on weekends for good swimming and bodysurfing. Rest rooms, showers, picnic area, parking.

Kailua Beach Park

Near Kailua town.

A long, usually crowded stretch with ideal windsurfing conditions. Rest rooms, showers, picnic area, snack bar.

Kualoa Regional Park

North of Waiahole town, features superb bay and mountain views and grassy picnic areas. Rest rooms, showers, picnic and camping areas.

Waimea Bay attracts the world's best surfers with waves as high as 30 ft.

Around the Fabulous North Shore

Sunset Beach

South of Waialee (and the Turtle Bay Hilton).
A wide beach with wild winter surf and calm summer swimming. No facilities.

Ehukai Beach Park

About two miles southwest of Sunset Beach.
This beach is long and wide and features a great view of the fabled Banzai Pipeline. Rest rooms, showers.

Waimea Bay Beach Park

A few miles north of Haleiwa.
This is the world-famous beach that reels the world's top surfers into its humongous 25-foot waves—steer clear unless you're one of them or you've come in summer when the surf is calm.

Haleiwa Beach Park

North of Haleiwa town.
Another big-winter-surf, gentle-summer-waves spot. Rest rooms, showers, grassy areas.

On the Waianae Coast

Makaha Beach Park

Northwest of Makaha town.
Sought out by locals as well as winter surfers. Rest rooms, showers.

Yokohama Bay

North of Makaha.
Another beach favored mainly by locals. Rest rooms, showers.

Adventure Guide

Horseback riding on Oahu's North Shore

Want to do something a tad more active than shopping or tanning? Oahu has a variety of more action-packed activities to offer.

Trekkers will most likely start off at **Diamond Head**, where the trail will take you from the center of the crater up to the summit. The relatively new **Maunawili Demonstration Trail**, off Pali Highway (beyond Pali Lookout), leads through tropical forest along the windward edge of the Koolau Mountains. Also on the windward side, the **Hauula Loop Trail** winds through gorgeous plant life, ironwood forest, and Norfolk pine groves to a ridge-top with dynamite views. Various trails branch out from the top of **Tantalus** and **Round Top drives**, taking you to panoramic lookouts over the **Makiki Valley**. A favorite hike (during dry weather!) is into **Sacred Falls**, on the windward coast. Start off in the morning for the trek along Kaluanui Stream, into narrow canyon, a deep pool and the dramatic falls. For super-remote, isolated hiking on Oahu, go up to **Kaena Point**, at the western tip of the island. Casual hikers might want to try **Peacock Flat Trail** through the Mokuleia Forest Reserve, while serious trekkers go for the **Dupont Trail**, which leads up to Mount Kaala.

Camping is allowed at state, county and private campgrounds dotted around the island. State park sites include **Kahana Valley State Park**, **Keaiwa Heiau State Recreation Area**, **Malaekahana Bay State Recreation Area** and **Sand Island State Recreation Area**. Many of Oahu's beautiful beach parks are designated county sites. Campers should be forewarned that some (maybe even *many*) locals might not be particularly happy to see you spreading out on "their" land. If the situation feels uncomfortable at a camping area, you might consider bedding down elsewhere. Permits and reservations are necessary for state and county facilities.

For information on Oahu's hiking trails and designated campsites, contact the **Hawaii State Department of Land and Natural Resources** (*Division of State Parks, 1151 Punchbowl Street, Honolulu 96813,* ☎ *(808) 587-0300)*; or **City and County of Honolulu, Department of Parks and Recreation** (*650 South King Street, Honolulu 96813,* ☎ *(808) 523-4525)*. For additional info on trails and hiking conditions, contact the **State Division of Forestry and Wildlife** (*1151 Punchbowl, Room 35, Honolulu 96813,* ☎ *(808) 587-0166)*. To join an organized hike, try the **Sierra Club** (*1111 Bishop Street, Honolulu 96813,* ☎ *(808) 538-6616)*.

Oahu offers **diving and snorkeling** opportunities for all levels. **Kahuna Canyon**, near Mokuleia, features an amphitheater full of octopi, crabs, spiny lobsters, and unicorn fish. If wrecks are your thing, the **Waianae coast** shelters sunken ships. Green sea turtles are the main attraction at **Maunalua Bay**, near Diamond Head, while the North Shore's **Shark's Cove** offers summer diving into sunlit caverns. The underwater park at **Hanauma Bay**, east of Koko Head, is a top **snorkeling** spot with abundant tropical fish and sea turtles. Get advice and rent equipment from local dive shops, or sign up for an organized excursion. Waimea Valley's **Waimea River-to-Waimea Bay** is a favorite with **ocean kayakers**. Or sign up for a **sailing or parasailing** adventure (parasailors fly over the shores of **Ala Moana** and **Waikiki**). Oahu is paradise to **surfers** of every level—novices hit the gentle currents at **Waikiki**, while international pros hunt the perfect wave at the North Shore's **Waimea Bay** and **Banzai Pipeline**. Surfing lessons and rental boards are readily available. **Bodysurfers** frequent the waters of Kailua, Makapuu and Sandy beaches, while **windsurfers** and **sailboarders** pretty much stick to **Kailua Beach Park** (instructions and equipment are available).

OAHU

PEARL HARBOR

On December 7, 1941 the Japanese launched a surprise attack on the U.S. Pearl Harbor Naval Station. The offensive sunk or damaged nineteen ships, killing 2300 Americans and forced the U.S. into WWII. Pearl Harbor has since earned the distinction of being the only U.S. naval base to be honored as a national historic landmark.

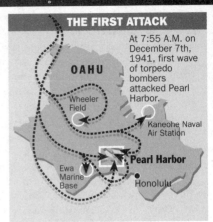

THE FIRST ATTACK

At 7:55 A.M. on December 7th, 1941, first wave of torpedo bombers attacked Pearl Harbor.

OAHU

Wheeler Field

Kaneohe Naval Air Station

Ewa Marine Base

Pearl Harbor

Honolulu

H1

U.S.S Utah Memorial

FORD ISLAND

PEARL HARBOR

The U.S.S. *Utah* memorial honors the fifty-eight crew members that died when their ship was struck by two torpedoes and sank. The ship can be seen from a viewing platform containing a flagpole and plaque dedicated to the ship's crew.

U.S. NAVAL RESERVATION

PEARL HARBOR ENTRANCE

U.S. NAVAL RESERVATION

U.S. NAVAL RESERVATION

The U.S.S. *Arizona* was sunk in the Pearl Harbor attack, entombing 1102 crew members in her hull. To honor the crew, the U.S.S. *Arizona* Memorial was built above the ship which lies, in tact, on the floor of the harbor.

One wall of the U.S.S. *Arizona* memorial contains 1178 engraved names of all the sailors who died aboard the ship.

90

EAST LOCH

Submarine Memorial Park

U.S.S Arizona Memorial Visitor Center

13A

13B

Aloha Stadium

Ferry

U.S.S Arizona Memorial

Halawa Gate

Salt Lake Blvd.

CAMP CATLIN NAVAL RES.

North Rd.

90

H1

Stack remains exposed

Makalapa Gate

15

The U.S.S. Arizona as it looked before the attack

Nimitz Gate

15A

15B

HONOLULU →

OAHU

What Else to See

View of Diamond Head and Waikiki hotels along the beach

Beaches, **sunsets** and **shops** rank as **Waikiki's** top attractions, along with people-watching, people-dodging and people-avoiding. Boat-lovers might be interested in the colorful craft anchored over at **Ala Wai Yacht Harbor**. The enormous **Hilton Hawaiian Village** is Hawaii's largest hotel with many restaurants, bars and shopping outlets. On Kaila Road, the **U.S. Army Museum of Hawaii**, housed inside a 1911 bunker, displays war memorabilia and exhibits. Art- and history-lovers should check out the huge murals in the **First Hawaiian Bank** as well as the Hawaiian-colonial architecture of the **Gump Building**, both on Kalakaua Avenue. The landmark **Halekulani Hotel** (on Kailia Road) and **Royal Hawaiian Hotel** (on Kalakaua Avenue) reflect images of old elegance in chaotic contemporary Waikiki. Pick up your Versace gown and Hermes scarf in the **Royal Hawaiian Shopping Center**, then ogle the handicrafts and souvenirs at the **International Market Place**. The four **wizard stones** in front of the bronze statue of surfing champ Duke Kahanamoku (next to the Sheraton Moana Surfrider Hotel) were supposedly bequeathed with healing power by four 16th-century Tahitian *kahuna* (priests). The small two-room

Damien Museum, on Ohua and Kalakaua avenues, pays tribute to the life of Father Joseph Damien of Belgium, who showed great compassion for lepers. **Kapiolani Park**, southwest of Diamond Head, is a 220-acre recreational area with the usual game and picnic fun, plus the site of the **Honolulu Zoo**, **Waikiki Aquarium**, **Waikiki Shell Amphitheater** and the finish line for December's world-famous **Honolulu Marathon**. At the end of Kalakaua Avenue, the 1927-built, 1990s-decrepit **Waikiki War Memorial Natatorium** is a decaying tribute to World War II's dead. When Kalakaua Avenue becomes Diamond Head Road, you have left Kapiolani Park and are on the road to **Diamond Head**.

In the hustle-bustle of **Honolulu**—Hawaii's commercial and legislative hub—you'll be immersed within both contemporary culture and the historic past. Explore the 300-acre **University of Hawaii** campus in Manoa Valley, almost as noteworthy for its eclectic mix of architectural styles as for its curriculum. Up Manoa Road, you can ooh and aah at hundreds of plants in the **Lyon Arboretum**, then take a break at nearby **Manoa Falls**. The **Punahou School**, founded in 1841, and alma mater of many important Hawaiians, sits on Punahou Street. Over at Kalakaua and Kapiolani avenues, the very big and very controversial **Hawaii Convention Center** is slated to open in 1997. Much of the state's best art is exhibited at **Honolulu Academy of Arts**, on Beretania Street. Shopping fiends will be satiated at **Ala Moana Shopping Center** (Hawaii's largest mall), **Ward Centre** or **Ward Warehouse**, all on Ala Moana Boulevard. Join local trendies for a meal on **Restaurant Row**, bounded by Ala Moana Boulevard and Punchbowl, Pohukaina and South streets. Up the road, the **News Building** cranks out Hawaii's two dailies—the *Honolulu Advertiser* and the *Honolulu Star-Bulletin.* The 1840s **Kawaiahao Church** (South King and Punchbowl streets) welcomes the public to its services; **King Lunalilo's Tomb** is near the church entrance and the bones of several other dignitaries are resting in the churchyard. Other South King Street sites include the 1821 **Mission Houses Museum** (Hawaii's first frame house), the 1929 **Honolulu City Hall**, the **King Kamehameha I Statue** and **Iolani Palace** (the nation's only royal palace).

Hawaii's governor and state legislators work out of the **State Capitol**, a wondrous piece of architecture bounded by South Beretania, Richards and Punchbowl streets. Statues of **Father Damien** and **Queen Liliuokalani** are nearby. Across from the State Capitol, **Washington Place** was the home of American John Dominis and his wife, the future Queen Liliuokalani. These days it's the governor's mansion. **St. Andrew's Cathedral**, founded by King Kamehameha IV, is situated on Queen Emma Square. Two "Big Five" headquarters are located at the 1929 **Alexander and Baldwin Building** (on Bishop Street) and the 1930 **C. Brewer Building** (on Fort Street). Learn all about Hawaii's seafaring days at the **Hawaii Maritime Center**, on Honolulu Harbor. A couple of piers away, **Aloha Tower Marketplace** draws locals and visitors to its restaurants and shops. Over on Maunakea Street, you can wander amid the flower-scented **lei workrooms** or the Asian food-scented **Maunakea Marketplace**. **Hotel Street**, between Bishop and River streets, is the city's famed red-light district (though attempts are being made to clean the place up).

Punchbowl Crater, Oahu, is a 115-acre memorial cemetery honoring those who died in wars from World War I through Desert Storm.

Punchbowl Crater (National Memorial Cemetery of the Pacific), off Tantalus Drive, welcomes visitors to its 115-acre cemetery commemorating those who died in wars from World War I through Desert Storm. Continuing up **Tantalus Drive** will take you to some great viewpoints and trailheads. Back in town, **The Contemporary Museum**, on Makiki Heights Drive, houses a selection of works by world-famous contemporary artists and sculptors (Tom Wesselmann, David Hockney, et al). On the other side of Tantalus Drive, you'll find the **Royal Mausoleum**—burial place for most of Hawaii's royal family. Take a tour of **Queen Emma's Summer Palace** (on the Pali Highway), the **Dole Pineapple Cannery** (on Iwilei Road) or the **Hilo Hattie Garment Factory** (on Nimitz Highway). Soak up everything Hawaiian in the extensive **Bishop Museum**, on Bernice Street.

The island's **southwest** area consists of heavily urbanized Pearl City and newly urbanized Kapolei. Sites to be seen are the famed **USS *Arizona* Memorial**, **USS *Bowfin* Submarine and Park**, **Moanalua Gardens** and **Pearlridge Center** (another shopping experience). In Kapolei, you won't miss the **Koolina Resort**. In sharp contrast, you won't find much along **West Oahu's Waianae Coast** other than some bays, beaches and very-native villages. (Be forewarned: this section of the island is reputedly not particularly hospitable to visitors, who should lock their vehicles and watch their backsides.) In **Oahu's Central District**, **Schofield Barracks** (headquarters of the U.S. Army's 25th Infantry Division) and **Dole Plantation** (pineapple heaven) are the noteworthy attractions.

You'll find various beaches, parks, and even a blowhole along the **southeast** section of Oahu. **Sea Life Park** features all types of sea critters and marine amusements including a Touch Pool and Whaling Museum. Continuing along the **windward coast**, you (and thousands of other sightseers) will come to **Nuuanu Pali Lookout**, a windy outlook on windward Oahu. Visit the tropical **Haiku Gardens** and **Byodo-in Temple**, in Kaneohe, and **Senator Fong's Plantation and Gardens**, in Kahuluu.

Heading up the **North Shore**, the **Polynesian Cultural Center** at Laie will introduce you to Pacific Island culture through a variety of performances and demonstrations. Unless you're Mormon, don't expect admission to the **Mormon Temple** (though you can visit the grounds). Two Arnold Palmer-designed golf courses are the main attraction at **Turtle Bay Hilton and Country Club** in Kahuku. Watch cliff-divers as they plunge over the 45-foot falls at **Waimea Falls Park**, then gasp and squeal as surfers hang ten on humongous winter waves at **Sunset** and **Waimea beaches**.

Aiea/Pearl City

Aiea

Children's Activities

Ice Palace   ★★

4510 Salt Lake Boulevard, in Stadium Mall, Aiea, ☎ (808) 487-9921.
Hours vary widely, call for schedule.
Hawaii's only ice-skating rink! Admission includes skates. Ask about the birthday package, where your tot and eight pals receive skate rentals, a large pizza, two pitchers of soda and table for two hours. The birthday celebrant even gets a specially wrapped gift. Pandemonium on weekends. General admission: $6.50.

City Celebrations

Hawaii State Fair   ★★

Aloha Stadium, 99-500 Salt Lake Boulevard, Aiea, ☎ (808) 488-3389.
Hours: 11 a.m.–midnight.
Late May. Celebrated its 50th year in 1996, this two-day event features rides, carnival games, food booths, exhibits and entertainment.

Hula Bowl Football All-Star Classic   ★★★

Aloha Stadium, Aiea, ☎ (808) 947-4141.
Held in-mid January. Sponsored by "Hooters" restaurant chain, this post-season college football all-star game spotlights the nation's top college athletes. This testosterone-heavy event celebrated its 50th anniversary in 1996. Parties, a championship golf tournament, boat parades and such go on before and after the big event.

NFL Pro Bowl ★★★

Aloha Stadium, Aiea, ☎ *(808) 486-9300.*

Held in early February. This annual all-star football game features the top stars from the National Football League.

Hiking

Aiea Loop Trail ★★★

Aiea Heights Drive, from Highway 78, Aiea.
Hours: 7 a.m.–6 p.m.
Closed: Wed., Thurs.

This 4.8-mile (round trip) loop trail is in Keaiwa Heiau State Park, north of Pearl Harbor. Keaiwa *Heiau* was an herbal healing center as well as a temple site for native Hawaiians some 300 years ago. Views of the harbor and the Koolau Mountains can be seen on this hike, along with the wreckage of a World War II cargo plane. A variety of native trees, including lehua, *ohia* and koa, grow heavily on the path, and in season, guavas are free for the picking. The park is a popular campsite. Rest rooms, shower, phone, drinking water available.

Central Oahu

Wahiawa

Museums and Exhibits

Tropic Lightning Museum ★★

Schofield Barracks, Wahiawa, 96857, ☎ *(808) 655-0438.*
Hours: 10 a.m.–4 p.m.
Closed: Mon., Sun.

Artifacts, photos, and archival material document the history of Schofield Barracks, and the 25th Infantry Division.

Tours

Dole Plantation ★★

64-1550 Kamehameha Highway, Wahiawa, 96786, ☎ *(808) 621-8408.*
Hours: 9 a.m.–6 p.m.

The pineapple industry is dying in Hawaii—so get here while you can. Among the attractions: fresh fruit, a variety garden, the "Story of Pineapple" exhibit, a goodies and gifts store, "Dole Whip" tastings. And yes, the Dole Plantation store is one of only two—count 'em, two—Dole stores in the world.

Honolulu

Downtown

City Celebrations

Chinese New Year/Narcissus Festival ★★★

Chinatown Cultural Plaza, Maunakea Street, downtown, ☎ *(808) 533-3181.*

Held in late January through the first week of February. Although you have to pay to get in to some of the events preceding Chinese New Year (the Narcissus Queen Pageant and Coronation Ball), there are loads of freebies. The exciting "Night in Chinatown" features lion and dragon dances, arts and crafts and food booths, and stage performances. Festivities begin with a parade that starts in the late afternoon in front of the State Capitol, followed by more of the same at the Chinatown Cultural Plaza.

First Night Honolulu ★★★
downtown Honolulu and Chinatown, downtown, ☎ *(808) 532-3131.*
Jan. 31. An alcohol-free block party (*ho'olaule'a*) featuring performing arts, cultural shows, games, parades, fireworks display and ethnic food booths. Family afternoon at the Honolulu City Hall (*Hale*) from 2:30–6 p.m.

Great Aloha Fun Run ★★★
Aloha Tower, downtown, ☎ *(808) 528-7388.*
Held in late February. One of the largest of its kind in the country, this charity 8.2-mile fun run begins at dawn at the Aloha Tower in downtown Honolulu and ends at the Aloha Stadium in the Aiea-Halawa Valley near Pearl Harbor. Entry fee.

Honolulu Marathon ★★★
Aloha Tower to Kapiolani Park, downtown, ☎ *(808) 734-7200.*
One of the largest marathons in the world, with more than 30,000 competitors. The 26.2-mile run begins at dawn from Aloha Tower in downtown Honolulu and ends at Kapiolani Park in Waikiki. Free to spectators.

King Kamehameha Celebration ★★★
Iolani Palace, King and Richards Streets, downtown, ☎ *(808) 586-0333.*
This is one of Hawaii's biggest state holidays (June 11) honoring Hawaii's greatest monarch, Kamehameha I. In Oahu, a statue decorating ceremony across from Iolani Palace and a floral parade from downtown Honolulu to Kapiolani Park are held prior to the date. But the main event is a hula competition in late June, with participants entering from as far away as Japan. Most events are free.

Taste of Honolulu ★★★★
Honolulu Hale (City Hall), 530 S. King Street, downtown, ☎ *(808) 536-1015.*
Two days in late June. At this tasty fest, you can accomplish in a weekend what would usually take a year to do—sample dishes from more than a dozen of Honolulu's best restaurants. Come with an empty tummy and a full wallet. Wine tastings, musical entertainment. Although admission is free, there's a tasting fee.

Fun For Free

Mayor's Aloha Friday Music Break ★★★
Tamarind Park, corner Bishop and King Streets, downtown, ☎ *(808) 527-5666.*
Hours: Noon
Closed: Mon., Tues., Wed., Thurs., Sat., Sun.
Celebrate "*Pau Hana*" (end of work)—well, almost—at this parkside noontime concert where the music—Hawaiian, jazz, soul, rock, country, whatevah—changes each week.

Royal Hawaiian Band Concerts ★★★
Iolani Palace, King Street, downtown, ☎ *(808) 922-5331.*
The famed band, the only full-time municipal band in the country (how do I get that gig?) presents an entertaining hour-long show of musical faves each Friday at 12:15 p.m. on the palace grounds and on Sundays at 2 p.m. at Kapiolani Park in Waikiki.

The Dole Pineapple Story   ★ ★

650 Iwilei Road in Dole Cannery Square, downtown, ☎ (808) 548-6601.
Hours: 9 a.m.–5 p.m.

Although the downtown cannery has ceased operations, the history of King Pineapple lives on by means of a multimedia presentation on nine screens shown every 30 minutes. There's also a museum of pineapple history, and a hands-on, arts/science/ cultural museum for children that has nothing to do with pineapples. The children's museum is open from 9 a.m.–1 p.m. Tuesday-Friday; Saturday-Sunday from 10 a.m.–4 p.m. Adults, $5; seniors, children, $3. Free samples, and free transportation from Waikiki and Ala Moana Center from 8 a.m.–4 p.m. Look for buses marked "Dole Cannery" and "Hilo Hattie."

Historical Sites

The lavishly decorated interior of Iolani Palace in downtown Honolulu includes a gilded throne room. Tours are given every 15 minutes Wed.-Sat.

Iolani Palace   ★ ★ ★ ★

King and Richards Streets, downtown, 96813, ☎ (808) 522-0832.
Hours: 9 a.m.–2:15 p.m.
Special hours: guided tours Wed.–Sat. Closed: Mon., Tues., Sun.

Surrounded by an elaborate Victorian iron fence in downtown Honolulu, this is the only government building in the United States that was once a royal palace. Iolani Palace was also the state Capitol until 1969. Built in 1882 by King Kalakaua after his voyage around the world, the palace is a polyglot of things that impressed him on the voyage. Among other features, it had electric lights before our own White House was wired up, telephone service, hot-and-cold running water and flush toilets. The building is a reflection of the Merrie Monarch, and restraint was not part of his personality. This is evidenced by its lavish interiors, done in the "American Florentine" style, including a gilded throne room. Following the king's untimely death in San Francisco in 1891, his sister Queen Liliuokalani ascended to the throne, only to be overthrown in a 1913 coup led by sugar magnate James Dole and others. She was held under house arrest in the palace and later tried for treason in the former throne room after a failed attempt by her supporters to restore her to power. It was during this time that she composed the melancholy paean "Aloha Oe" (Farewell to Thee). While waiting for the tour of the palace, the grounds are worthy of scrutiny. The barracks of the Royal Household Guards are located here, looking like a squat medieval castle and containing the ubiquitous gift shop. The domed pavilion and bandstand were built for the coronation of King Kalakaua. The governors of the state of Hawaii are still sworn into office here. The palace received a multimillion-dollar restoration in 1969, when the seat of government moved next door. Tours are given every 15 minutes from 9 a.m.–2:15 p.m. Reservations necessary. Children under five years not permitted. General admission: $8.

Kawaiahao Church ★★★

Punchbowl Street at King Street, downtown.

Oahu's oldest church was built to replace the original thatched structure built by the missionaries upon their arrival in 1820. Constructed of coral-block between 1837 and 1842 in the New England Congregationalist style, its clock was donated by Kamehameha III. The rear seats are still reserved for descendants of Hawaiian royalty and are marked by feather kahili standards and velvet kneeling pads. Outside the church you can see the tomb of King Lunalilo, who held the distinction of being Hawaii's only elected monarch. Although he reigned only a year before his death, he restored the right to vote and hold elective offices to commoners. As a final act, he chose to be buried here, with the people, instead of in the Royal Mausoleum in Nuuanu Valley. Sunday services at 10:30 a.m. are held in both English and Hawaiian.

Museums and Exhibits

Damien Museum ★★

130 Ohua Avenue, downtown, 96815, ☎ *(808) 923-2690.*
Hours: 9 a.m.–3 p.m.

This humble, small, two-room museum and archive commemorates Belgian priest Father Damien de Veuster, who devoted his life to the shunned victims of Hansen's disease (leprosy) in their permanent forced exile at Kalaupapa, Molokai. Displays include Damien's handwritten letters, photos of Kalaupapa and its residents. Visitors can watch an informative video about the life of the priest who died of the disease himself at the age of 49. Father Damien's proper title is now "Blessed" Damien. He was beatified by Pope John Paul in 1995 and is just one step from sainthood. Although his body is buried in Belgium, his hand has been returned to Kalaupapa, and is contained in a reliquary at the church he founded there.

Hawaii Maritime Center ★★★

Pier 7, Honolulu Harbor, downtown, 96813, ☎ *(808) 536-6373.*
Hours: 8:30 a.m.–5 p.m.

Near the Aloha Tower and situated at Pier 7 at Honolulu Harbor, this museum has an interesting potpourri of nautical displays, the best of which may be the whaling section. A new exhibit features a rare humpback whale skeleton, only one of two on display in the world. The 38-foot whale carcass was recovered, almost in its entirety, from the island of Kahoolawe. It took more than five years to put the 159 bones, including a 12-foot, 750-pound skull, back together. The museum also houses life-size dioramas that cover various settings, from a Matson liner state room to a dock-side tattoo parlor. There are two distinctive vessels docked outside the museum. One is the 266-foot, iron-hulled, square rigger *Falls of Clyde* (once owned by Matson Shipping Company), which was on the Hilo-to-San Francisco run, carrying passengers and sugar. When it's not cruising the Pacific, the *Hokulea*, a twin-hulled Hawaiian sailing canoe, is moored at the museum. Famous for its long-distance voyages to destinations as far as New Zealand using traditional methods of navigation, it just completed a successful round-trip journey to Tahiti. General admission: $7.50.

Honolulu Academy of Arts ★★★

900 S. Beretania Street, downtown, 96814, ☎ *(808) 532-8701.*

Hours: 10 a.m.–4:30 p.m.

Special hours: Sundays, 1–5 p.m.

If you're into Asian art, this museum is a must-see. Dedicated in 1927, the 33,000-piece collection includes priceless Japanese prints, furniture and Chinese bronze dishes from the 11th century B.C. Also notable are traditional and contemporary European (Pisarro, Van Gogh, Gauguin) and American (Maron's "Grand Canyon of the Yellowstone") masterpieces. There is also a small but select grouping of Hawaiian and Pacific artifacts. It is architecturally pleasing as well, with open courtyards, tiled fountains and an enclosed garden with a lily pond. The museum is also an cultural center. The Academy Theatre presents popularly priced classic films and concerts. Gift shop, library, café. General admission: $5.

Mission Houses Museum ★★★

553 S. King Street, downtown, 96813, ☎ *(808) 531-0481.*

Hours: 9 a.m.–4 p.m.

Closed: Mon., Sun.

Built between 1821 and 1841, this trio of New England-style, salt-box buildings formed the headquarters of the Sandwich Islands Mission. The oldest one was actually a prefabricated wooden dwelling brought around the Horn by the missionaries. It is the first frame house still standing in Hawaii. The Chamberlain House, built in 1831 of coral block, was named after the mission's accountant and quartermaster, Levi Chamberlain. It served as the store room and contains examples of the supplies necessary to support the missionary families as well as Chamberlain's office and pigeonhole desk where he no doubt kept an eagle eye on who took what. The Printing Office still houses the lead-type press that was used to print a Hawaiian Bible. The Mission Houses Museum offers the popular Christmas Candlelight Tours, and a "living history" tour with authentically costumed actors playing roles of 19th-century missionaries. Admission to the museum is free the fourth Saturday of each month. Historic walking tours; $7. Reservations required. General admission: $3–$5.

Music

Hawaii Opera Theatre

987 Waimanu Street, downtown, ☎ *(808) 596-7858.*

Hawaii's only state resident opera company presents three to four grand operas annually in the *Neal Blaisdell Theater, 777 Ward Avenue*. Performances are in the native language with an English translation. Call the hotline from 10 a.m.–5 p.m., Monday-Friday. General admission: $22 and up.

Parks and Gardens

Foster Botanical Gardens

50 N. Vineyard Boulevard, downtown, 96817, ☎ *(808) 522-7066.*
Hours: 9 a.m.–4 p.m.

The nation's largest collection of tropicals are spread out over 14 acres. Among the orchids and bromeliads are some peculiarly bizarre species: the fruit of the Coco de Mer palm weighs more than 50 pounds. That's some strange fruit. Tours on weekdays at 1 p.m. by reservation. A peaceful place to picnic. General admission: $5.

The Shows

Hawaii Theatre Center ★★★★

1130 Bethel Street, downtown, ☎ *(808) 528-0506.*

The 74-year-old downtown landmark reopened in May 1996 after a 10-year fundraising program, and a four-year, $24 million restoration. It was the high event of the social season. In its heyday, the Hawaii Theatre was the flagship theater of the state's largest movie company. It featured an 1800-seat auditorium, a mural by the famed Hawaii artist Lionel Walden and a five-ton Robert Morgan organ with 1128 pipes, even the first known theater "air conditioning" system. Employees would fan the air over big blocks of ice below the stage to cool off the delighted audience. As times and tastes changed, and the downtown area lost its cachet, a respectable program of silent films, vaudeville, plays and musicals were replaced by tawdry B movies. The building's interior and exterior fell victim to neglect as well, and the theater closed its doors in 1984. The "new" theater, which includes a state-of-the-art electronic sound system, wider seats and an enlarged orchestra pit, is now a multi-use facility booking everything from symphony orchestras to trade shows. One of the highlights of the three-day opening extravaganza was a musical concert—featuring a "new" Robert Morgan organ—salvaged from the unfortunately demolished Princess Theatre. General admission: Varies.

Honolulu Academy of Arts Academy Theatre

900 S. Beretania Street, downtown, ☎ *(808) 532-8700.*
Special hours: movies at 4 p.m. and 7:30 p.m., shows at 7:30 p.m.

Within Hawaii's oldest and largest art museum, the Academy Theatre features classic art-house movies for only $4, and music performances by eclectic acts. Recently featured were Quartetto Gelato, a hot classical/crossover Canadian band. General admission: $13–$15.

Honolulu Theatre for Youth

2846 Ualena Street, downtown, ☎ *(808) 839-9885.*

Entertaining and educational theater produced for tender, impressionable youth and their families. Recently on the boards was "And the People Spoke Music, Stories of the Marshall Islands," presenting the folklore of the Marshallese people through story, song and dance. Performances in various venues including the Richardson Theatre at Ft. Shafter. General admission: $9.

Kumu Kahua Theatre   ★★★

46 Merchant Street, downtown, ☎ *(808) 536-4441.*

A showcase for the diverse ethnic cultures that make up Hawaii, this eclectic group produces plays mostly written by, and for, local audiences. Themes include such topics as new immigrants dealing with the United States or the preservation of the traditional lifestyle while fighting off rich, greedy Haole/Japanese developers. Ticket prices are low, too. This is the place to feel the grime under the glitter. General admission: $9 and up.

Theme/Amusement Parks

The Outer Edge   ★★

Aloha Tower Marketplace, downtown, ☎ *(808) 528-5564.*
Hours: 10 a.m.–1 a.m.
Special hours: Fri., Sat. to 2 a.m.

We think 9000 square feet of virtual reality rides and games should keep the cyberkids occupied for hours, don't you? Located at Pier 10.

Tours

Chinatown Historical Walking Tour   ★★★★

Asia Mall, 1250 Maunakea Street, downtown, ☎ *(808) 521-3045.*
Hours: 10 a.m.–noon.
Special hours: Saturdays, 10 a.m. Closed: Sun.

Open-air markets, lei stands, herbal shops, a cleaned-up red-light district, historical sites (including the "new" Hawaii Theatre Center)—everything you can wiggle a wonton at are part of this exciting two-hour walking tour of Honolulu's revitalized Chinatown, which is one of the oldest in the United States. The Society also conducts an afternoon Temple Tour from 1–2 p.m. The price is $3. It covers Chinese temples, a Japanese Shrine, Chinatown Cultural Plaza and more. General admission: $5.

Honolulu Hale (State Capitol)   ★★

530 S. King Street, downtown, ☎ *(808) 547-7000.*
Hours: 8:30 a.m.–1:30 p.m.

An example of late '60s "theme architecture," the state Capitol symbolizes the triumph of form over function—its legislative chambers are cone-shaped to represent volcanoes, while the open-air rotunda has supporting columns meant to denote palm trees. Encircling the entire building is a reflecting pool symbolizing the Pacific Ocean. The elements thus described have been less than kind to the building itself. It was closed until just recently for extensive remodeling due to water and weather damage and asbestos removal. Tours are given daily at 8:30 a.m., 10:30 a.m., and 1:30 p.m.

Honolulu Time Walks ★★★★

2634 S. King Street, downtown, ☎ *(808) 951-8878.*
Hours: 7–11 p.m., Tues. only.

It's reported that ghosts (of the past, that is) have been sighted in downtown Honolulu. Raconteur Glenn Grant conducts "Haunted Honolulu" tours every Tuesday at 7 p.m.; and after a stroll with him you'll be spooked, too. Explore the suburbs of Manoa, Kahala and Makiki. The inventive Grant, who never runs out of topics, has more than 20 tours in his repertoire, many of them sounding like pulp fiction novels, such as "Scandalous Old Honolulu" and "Mystical Chinatown." The cost includes pub refreshment. General admission: $30.

Navatek I ★★★

2270 Kalakaua Avenue, Suite 708, downtown, 96818, ☎ *(808) 848-6360.*
Closed: Mon.

Until residents start complaining about invasion of privacy, *Navatek I's* two-hour Kahala Gold Coast Sunshine Tour lets you take a voyeuristic peek into the back yards of million-dollar homes that line the beach fronting the swank neighborhood. This cruise on a super-smooth, $6.5 million vessel with specially designed stabilizers is designed for people who turn green while watching "Flipper" reruns. The Kahala tour includes live Hawaiian entertainment, International (Tuesday-Thursday), or Hawaiian (Friday-Saturday) buffet lunch, two cocktails and tropical desserts. Daily except Monday from Pier 6 in Honolulu Harbor. Leaves at noon, returns at 2 p.m. Other cruises include the Premium Sunset Dinner Cruise (same route as above). The currently hot songstress Noelani Cypriano and her band, Hotline, are the onboard entertainment. Includes a gourmet five-course dinner, five complimentary drinks and a free gift. Leaves daily at 5:30 p.m. General admission: $27–$147.

Top Gun Tours ★★

P.O. Box 25204, downtown, 96825, ☎ *(808) 396-8112.*
Hours: 6:15 a.m.–1:45 p.m.

Also called Home of the Brave Military Base Tours. An experienced and knowledgeable guide dressed in an authentic World War II Army Air Corps uniform takes visitors to as many as five military bases/sites, including Pearl Harbor and the *Arizona* Memorial, all in one day. Routes and sites are subject to change without notice, depending on base operations. On a typical itinerary, you'll visit Hickam Air Force Base, Wheeler Army Airbase, Schofield Barracks, Punchbowl National Memorial and downtown Honolulu. Glenn Miller music and authentic broadcasts, FDR's fireside chats and his declaration of war, accompany narration on the tour bus. Lunch (not included in the tour price) is held at an officer's club. Vets and their families encouraged to share experiences. Women encouraged to wear their sensible pearls. White-glove inspection beforehand, and don't forget to wash behind your ears. General admission: $69.

Greater Honolulu

Beaches

Ala Moana Beach Park ★★★

1201 Ala Moana Boulevard, Greater Honolulu.

Just five minutes away from Waikiki, across the street from the Ala Moana Shopping Center, Ala Moana Beach Park is a favorite with local residents. Waters are clear, the sand is soft, and there are numerous picnic facilities on a large, grassy area. From some vantage points, you'll have million-dollar views of Diamond Head. Swimming is perfect in the sandy, shady lagoon protected by an offshore reef. Adjacent is Magic Island Beach, a failed resort turned into a park. Families with small children frequent the calm swimming cove. Lots of parking, but still gets crowded on weekends.

City Celebrations

Cherry Blossom Festival ★★

1525 Bernice Street, Greater Honolulu, ☎ *(808) 949-2255.*
Held in January-March. A celebration of Japanese contributions to Hawaii's cultural life. Many events are held at the Bishop Museum. Also other locations. General admission: Varies.

Hawaiian Song Festival ★★★

McCoy Pavilion, Ala Moana Park, Greater Honolulu, ☎ *(808) 266-7654.*
Mid March. Perpetuates Hawaiian music and culture with a song and competition contest.

Na Wahine O Hawaii ★★

McCoy Pavilion, Ala Moana Park, Greater Honolulu, ☎ *(808) 239-4336.*
Held in early July. For several years, the best *wahine* (women) in music and dance have performed their works at Ala Moana Park.

Punahou School Carnival ★★

1601 Punahou Street, Greater Honolulu, ☎ *(808) 944-5752.*
Held in early February. What? A school carnival in a guidebook? It's a great chance to rub elbows with local residents who show up in droves for old-fashioned, midway-style rides, food, a white elephant sale, games, and live and silent auctions.

Fun For Free

Concerts at Ala Moana Centerstage ★★★

1450 Ala Moana Boulevard, Greater Honolulu, ☎ *(808) 946-2811.*
Hours: 9:30 a.m.–9 p.m.
Special hours: Sundays, 10 a.m.–5 p.m.
A wide variety of free entertainment—drama, music, dance—are presented by top talent (Honolulu Theatre for Youth, the Royal Hawaiian Band, etc.) on an outdoor stage each week on a daily basis. Showtimes are noon, 2 p.m., 7 p.m., Monday-Saturday; Sundays, noon–2 p.m.

Historical Sites

Aloha Tower ★★★

Pier 9, Nimitz Highway, Greater Honolulu, ☎ *(808) 528-5700.*
Originally built in 1926, the Aloha Tower was the tallest building in Oahu. Emblazoned with the words "Aloha," the clock tower welcomed passenger liners when all tourists arrived by ship on "Boat Days." After a period of restoration, the Tower was reopened in 1994 as the centerpiece of the Aloha Tower Marketplace, a shopping area that dominates Pier 9 at the foot of Fort Street. There are spectacular views on

all four sides of the 10th-floor observation deck, reached via a tiny, slow elevator (stairs were closed upon last inspection). Claustrophobics beware. Recently, the fanfare of "Boat Days" has been attempted, if not exactly re-created. Every Friday, hula dancers with fresh leis bid farewell to the hokey *Windjammer* cruise boat as it departs Pier 9 at 7 p.m.

National Memorial Cemetery of the Pacific ★★★
2177 Puowaina Drive, Greater Honolulu, 96813, ☎ (808) 566-1430.
A sobering pilgrimage, the National Memorial Cemetery of the Pacific, situated in the Punchbowl Crater, is the final resting place of more than 30,000 U.S. Armed Services personnel (from World War II to Vietnam) and their families. Astronaut and native son Ellison S. Onizuka is also buried here. Known to the ancient Hawaiians as the "Hill of Sacrifice," the cemetery contains a monument with the names of all the youth lost in action in the Pacific carved in marble. A lookout surmounts the crater from which Diamond Head can be seen among the highrises in Honolulu. The American Legion conducts hour-long walking tours by appointment only. Call ☎ *(808) 946-6383* by 8:00 a.m. the day the tour is desired. Cost is $15. There's a road behind the memorial for those who can't make the stairs. Open Sept. 30-March 1, 8 a.m.–6:30 p.m.; March 2–Sept. 29, 7 a.m.–7 p.m.

Royal Mausoleum ★★★
2261 Nuuanu Avenue, Greater Honolulu, 96817.
Hours: 8 a.m.–4 p.m.
The most sacred burial ground in the islands, the Royal Mausoleum is the resting place for six of eight Hawaiian monarchs, including King Kalakaua and Queen Liliuokalani. King Kamehameha I is notably missing; he was the last of the Hawaiian kings to be buried in secret, which was the ancient way. Also on the three-acre site is a chapel built in 1922.

Museums and Exhibits

Bishop Museum and Planetarium ★★★★
1525 Bernice Street, Greater Honolulu, ☎ (808) 422-0561.
Hours: 9 a.m.–5 p.m.
Set on 10 acres, the Bishop Museum is perhaps the finest repository of Pacific and Hawaiian artifacts in the world. It was a gift to the people of Hawaii by Charles Bishop in memory of his wife Bernice Pauahi Bishop, a direct descendant of Hawaiian royalty. Mrs. Bishop, once betrothed to Prince Lot, inherited much of the core collection from her relatives. The central building is made of dressed volcanic stone, and is said to be the oldest structure of this type on the island. Its interior is highlighted by elaborate marble floors and fantastic koa woodwork, which seems to only get better with time. The core collection is in the multi-storied and balconied Hawaiian Hall. Here can be seen the original feathered cape worn by Kamehameha I when he completed the conquest of the islands, bowls adorned with human teeth, and perhaps most interesting of all, actual wooden gods worshiped by the ancient Hawaiians, carved in the Kona style. Very few of these have survived to this day, because they were all burned or destroyed when Hawaiian royalty converted to Christianity. In adjacent halls are other collections of Pacific island cultures, whaling

artifacts, a Science Center and Planetarium. In February 1990, the museum opened
its first major exhibit area in 90 years, the Castle Memorial Building, which houses
changing exhibitions. The first Sunday of the month is Family Sunday, a cultural
celebration with Hawaiian entertainment, food, displays and demonstrations. Free
admission for children ages five and under. General admission: $14.95.

The Bishop Museum set on 10 acres in Oahu is famous for its Hawaiian and
Pacific artifacts. The volcanic stone central building is the island's oldest.

Pacific Aerospace Museum   ★ ★

Honolulu International Airport, main lobby, Greater Honolulu, 96819, ☎ *(808) 839-*
0777.
Hours: 9 a.m.–6 p.m.
Special hours: Fridays, to 9 p.m., Saturdays to 10 p.m. Closed: Sun.
A good way to kill time at the airport, if the Honolulu traffic hasn't caused you to
almost miss your flight. Three theaters cover separate aspects of navigation and aviation, one of which recreates the attack of Pearl Harbor with holograms. An interesting display makes the analogy that the canoes that the ancient Polynesians
navigated to populate the Pacific islands were the spacecraft of our forefathers.
Don't miss the life-size replica of the *Challenger* flight deck. Many of the displays
are interactive and friendly. You'll leave with a better understanding of aviation history and the distinct feeling that Hawaii is the hub of aviation in the Pacific. General
admission: $3.

Queen Emma Summer Palace   ★ ★ ★

2913 Pali Highway, Greater Honolulu, 96817, ☎ *(808) 595-3167.*
Hours: 9 a.m.–4 p.m.
Built in 1948, the palace's architecture could be described as "Tropical Greek
Revival," in that it combines a broad lanai with Corinthian columns. Now a
museum, it was the summer home of King Kamehameha IV, Queen Emma and

their son, Prince Albert. Lauhala mats cover the floors. The museum houses a collection of royal heirlooms, perhaps the saddest of which is the koa cradle of the ill-starred Prince Albert, heir to the Hawaiian throne, who died at the age of four. Godson to England's Queen Victoria, he was named after her equally tragic consort. Queen Emma is still revered for her compassion for others. She built schools, hospitals and cared for smallpox victims in her own home. The queen outlived her husband as well as her son. When she died in 1885, the house remained vacant and fell into disrepair and was nearly torn down to make a baseball field. It was saved by local patrons and is now beautifully restored. Annual fund-raisers are held to maintain it. General admission: $4.

Wildlife Museum

1190 Dillingham Boulevard, Greater Honolulu, 96817, ☎ *(808) 848-0660.*
Hours: 8:30 a.m.–4:30 p.m.
More than 360 preserved wild animals from around the world, from collector W.T. Yoshimoto 42 countries. General admission: $6.95.

The Shows

A.K.A. ★★★

Manoa Valley Theatre and other venues, Greater Honolulu, ☎ *(808) 395-5972.*
Original skits, one-acts and short plays reflecting local issues are presented by this performing arts company. Catch them at the **Manoa Valley Theatre**, *2833 E. Manoa Road, Honolulu,* or **Ward's Rafters**, *3810 Maunaloa Avenue.* Donations of $10 are suggested. Loose schedule.

Aloha Tower Ice Theatre ★★

101 Ala Moana Boulevard, Greater Honolulu, ☎ *(808) 528-5700.*
This ice rink at the Aloha Tower Marketplace cost a cool million and features three performances with 34 of the world's top figure skaters. "Skate, Rattle, and Roll" and "Land of Ice" run 30 minutes, and are presented several times a day. Admission is $10.95. Evening hour long extravaganza is $24.95.

Kennedy Theatre ★★★

1770 East-West Road, Greater Honolulu, ☎ *(808) 956-2598.*
The University of Hawaii at Manoa's 600-seat theater presents a seasonal mix of classics, experimental theater, Grand Kabuki, Peking Opera, children's theater and, to a lesser extent, musicals. Avant garde adult offerings play late at night in the Earle Ernst Lab Theatre.

Manoa Valley Theatre ★★★

2833 E. Manoa Road, Greater Honolulu, 96822, ☎ *(808) 988-6131.*
Features the best contemporary works from Broadway and off-Broadway; the 1996-'97 season's lineup included *Tommy, Painting Churches, Prom Queens Unchained* (a campy environmental musical from those prom-laden '50s) and the Pulitzer prize-winner *Angels in America.* Popular. Admission varies.

The Brothers Cazimero–Hawaii from the Heart ★★★

1525 Bernice Street, Greater Honolulu, ☎ *(808) 847-MELE.*
Hours: 5–8:30 p.m.
Closed: Mon., Tues., Fri., Sat.

After 12 years as headliners at the Royal Hawaiian's Monarch Room, The legendary Brothers Cazimero (Roland and Robert) have begun a new engagement at Bishop Museum's Hawaiian Hall three nights a week. Hawaii from the Heart is a three-hour show that blends history, music and dance, culminating in a performance by the brothers. Other top island musicians usually make surprise appearances during the show. The ticket price includes a self-guided tour of three floors of exhibits at the Hawaiian Hall and a picnic supper on the museum lawn. The show itself begins at 7:30 p.m. General admission: $47.50.

Tours

Kapiolani Community College Walking Tours ★★★

4303 Diamond Head Road, Greater Honolulu, ☎ *(808) 734-9211.*
Special hours: call for schedule.

Kapiolani Community College sponsors fascinating two-hour walking tours of some of Honolulu's oldest neighborhoods. For example, participants might travel in time (figuratively, of course) to Kaimuki of the '40s and '50s with a couple who haven't lived anywhere else. On a walk through Makiki Valley, a storyteller describes landmarks and personalities of the valley's history. Itineraries change frequently, and most tours are given on weekends. Also recommended are the eclectic tours conducted by Willis Moore of the Hawaii Geographic Society. These might include a "Temple Walking Tour," in which Moore combines a Shinto shrine, St. Andrews Cathedral and other spiritual places in downtown Honolulu into one neat interdenominational package. Tours are $5 per person. For information, call *(808) 538-3952.* General admission: $5.

Makiki Heights

Children's Activities

Hawaii Nature Center ★★★

2131 Makiki Heights Drive, Makiki Heights, *(808) 955-0100.*
Hours: 8 a.m.–4:30 p.m.
Special hours: Sundays 1:30–4:30 p.m.

The Center sponsors terrific programs for kids that include everything from group hikes to fishing expeditions to the hands-on study of birds, bugs and other beasties. Everything is geared for an in-depth understanding of nature and the environment in a fun, non-boring, user-friendly way. Special programs for the physically challenged. Memberships available. General admission: $3–$5.

Hiking

Makiki Valley Loop Trail ★★★

Tantalus Drive, and Makiki Heights Drive, Makiki Heights.

These are three interconnecting trails (Makiki Valley Trail, Maunalaha and Kanealole) that begin at Tantalus Drive. The entire loop is about three miles long and begins at the Territorial Nursery, Hawaii's first native tree nursery. The Makiki Valley Trail itself affords views of Honolulu while you see and taste guava and mountain apples in season (summer usually).

Waikiki

Beaches

Waikiki Beach ★★★★

From the Ala Wai Canal to Kapahulu Avenue, Waikiki.

Yes, this is the world's most famous stretch of beach, and yes, you'll feel like the third sardine in a tin can while lying on the sand at the height of the day. If you're an early bird, take a peaceful morning stroll or run at 6 a.m. It's possible to walk the whole length from the Sheraton Waikiki at its core to Sans Souci Beach at the Diamond Head end. The population count seems to be highest at the center of the beach in front of the Sheraton Waikiki, or the Royal Hawaiian Hotel, less so at the outer fringes (the Hilton Hawaiian Village, or the New Otani Kaimana Beach). Swimmers share the waters with catamarans, inflatable rafts, outrigger canoes, inflatable floats and water-cycles with enormous wheels in neon colors, just in case you can't see them. Learn to surf here from the legendary beach boys (the real thing, not the flabby Wilson brothers). Try the rental stand in front of **Kuhio Beach Park**, *2453 Kalakaua Avenue*; look for the bronze statue of Duke Kahanamoku.

Children's Activities

Snooze at the Zoo ★★★★

Honolulu Zoo, next to Kapiolani Park, Waikiki, ☎ *(808) 971-7174.*
Special hours: 6 p.m.–9 a.m., Friday evening to Saturday morning.

Once or twice a month, kids and their parents can pack up their sleeping bags and spend the night at the Honolulu Zoo. The price of admission includes a light dinner, snacks (s'mores?), storytelling around a campfire, "after dark" tours of animal exhibits and breakfast the next morning. Limited to only 25 participants, so reserve in advance. Much better than a hotel room. But wait, there's more. Before, during and after a full moon, attend a "Zoo by Moonlight" behind-the-scenes tour of the nocturnal habits of zoo animals. Includes refreshments and a "hoary bat game." Usually held from 7–9 p.m. Adults, $6; ages 12 and under, $4. General admission: $27.

City Celebrations

Ala Wai Challenge ★★

Ala Wai Park, Waikiki, ☎ *(808) 923-1802.*
Hours: 9 a.m.–2 p.m.

Held in mid-January. Athletic fest for charity that centers around a quarter-mile outrigger canoe race up and down the Ala Wai Canal. Peripheral events include an ancient Hawaiian game competition.

Aloha Festivals ★★★

1201 Ala Moana Boulevard, Waikiki, ☎ *(808) 944-8857.*

This statewide cultural festival, the only one in the United States, celebrated its 50th anniversary in 1996. Held over a two-month period (September–October). Oahu celebrates with a floral parade from Ala Moana Park to Kapiolani Park, concerts at the Waikiki Shell and a Royal Ball. For general description, see "Molokai" chapter.

Great Hawaiian Rubber Duckie Race ★★★

Ala Wai Canal, Waikiki, ☎ *(808) 538-6789.*

Late March. To raise money for this "quacky" fund raiser for the United Cerebral Palsy Association, 20,000 people sponsor 20,000 rubber ducks and race them down the Ala Wai Canal. Free to spectators.

Hawaii International Sport Kite Championships ★★

Kapiolani Park, Waikiki, ☎ *(808) 922-5483.*
Early March. Sport kite-flyers from around the world compare air toys and perform high speed acrobatics in this annual event. Food booths and entertainment.

Honolulu International Bed Race ★★★

Kapiolani Park and various locations, Waikiki, ☎ *(808) 735-6092.*
Two days in late April. First it was rubber ducks on the Ala Wai Canal. Sheesh. These crazy Waikikians will do anything for charity—including racing beds in their 'jammies alongside Kapiolani Park. A must-see. Other events include electric-light parades, á la Disneyland, and a fireworks show.

Lei Day/Annual May Day Concert ★★★

Waikiki and various locations, Waikiki, ☎ *(808) 924-8934.*
Held on May 1. May Day is Lei Day in Hawaii, an islandwide celebration of the fragrant floral necklace of nostalgia and aloha. There are lei-making contests, pageants, music, arts and crafts, and a Lei Queen competition. The finale is the annual May Day Concert at the Waikiki Shell in Kapiolani Park. Featured are the legendary Brothers Cazimero, their friends and frequent surprise guests. Not to be missed. Call ☎ *(808) 545-4000* for ticket information.

Prince Lot Hula Festival ★★

Moanalua Gardens, Waikiki, ☎ *(808) 839-5334.*
Hours: 9:15 a.m.–4 p.m.
Held on July 20. Authentic ancient and modern hula as well as demonstrations and arts and crafts, honors Kamehameha V.

Saint Patrick's Day Parade ★★★

Fort de Russy Park, Waikiki, ☎ *(808) 377-1224.*
March 17, of course. There are loads of parades in Waikiki each year, but this tribute to Saint Pat is one of the biggest. Starts at Fort de Russy and finishes at Kapiolani Park's Waikiki Shell.

Fun For Free

Art Mart ★★

Montserrat Avenue, Waikiki.
Hours: 10 a.m.–4 p.m.
Closed: Mon., Wed., Thurs., Fri.
On weekends, the fence along the perimeter of the Honolulu Zoo becomes a colorful display of good, bad, mediocre and, in rare instances, superb works by local artists. They hope you will buy something.

Japanese Tea Ceremony ★★

245 Saratoga Road, in the Urasenke Foundation, Waikiki, ☎ *(808) 923-3059.*
Hours: 10 a.m.–noon.
Closed: Mon., Tues., Thurs., Sat., Sun.

The intricate rituals of the Chado—Japanese Tea Ceremony—are painstakingly explained, gesture by gesture, in this authentic teahouse maintained by a foundation with branches all over the world. The ceremony is free, but samples of green tea and accompanying delicacies are $2 per person. The foundation asks that guests wear long pants, socks (no holes, please—you'll upset the delicate balance) or hose.

Kodak Hula Show ★★★

Waikiki Shell in Kapiolani Park, Waikiki, ☎ *(808) 627-3300.*
Hours: 10–11:15 a.m.
Closed: Mon., Fri., Sat., Sun.
This beloved freebie has only been around since 1927 and still draws the crowds. Many of the endearing aunties dancing the hula have doing it since 1927. Even the most jaded among you will yell out "Aloha" with everyone else, guaranteed. Also worth going to is the Hilton Hawaiian Village's popular hula show accompanied by a fireworks display, which caps off the King's Jubilee, held every Friday, beginning at sunset; call ☎ *(808) 949-4321* for information. Mall wiggles at the Royal Hawaiian Shopping Center, Mondays, Wednesdays and Fridays from 6:30-8 p.m., *2201 Kalakaua Avenue,* ☎ *(808) 922-0588.*

Lucoral Museum ★★

2414 Kuhio Avenue, Waikiki, ☎ *(808) 922-1999.*
Hours: 9:30 a.m.–5:30 p.m.
Gemstones, rocks and minerals mingle with eccentric curiosities such as a dinosaur egg from China and a fish fossil from, of all places, Saudi Arabia. Jewelry-making classes, tours (reservations required) and a gift shop.

Royal Waikiki Historical Walk ★★

Hyatt Regency Waikiki ☎ *(808) 923-1234.*
Hours: 9 a.m.–10 p.m.
Gather at the Sharing Room, on the second floor behind the waterfall, where a professional storyteller leads one-hour walks on and near the grounds and beach where royalty lived and played. Hear about Princess Kaiulani and Ainahau, her nearby garden estate, her friend Robert Louis Stevenson, and Duke Kahanamoku. Reserve 24 hours in advance.

Hiking

Diamond Head Trail ★★★

Montserrat Avenue, Waikiki, ☎ *(808) 587-0300.*
Hours: 6 a.m.–6 p.m.
The climb to the top of this 760-foot-tall volcanic crater (don't worry, it's extinct) and symbol of Waikiki is only 0.7 miles long, but it takes an hour to go up and half an hour to come down. Really for intermediate hikers, it involves climbing two staircases, one with 76 steps, the other 99. Various other thrills and chills involve snaking your way through a dark 300-foot tunnel (part of an World War II military installation) and peering through long-unused gun embattlements. Upon reaching the summit, you'll be rewarded with a 360-degree view of Waikiki and Honolulu. There are also a number of observation points on the way. Wear a hat, a pair of reliable boots, but no slippers or sandals. Bring water—you'll need it. A flashlight for

the tunnel will prevent gouged knees and dinged-up foreheads. If you'd like a guided tour, The Clean Air Team offers fully narrated hikes every Saturday. No reservations necessary, meet at 9 a.m. at the front entrance of the Honolulu Zoo. Rest rooms, picnic tables, phones and drinking water available at the site.

Hanauma Bay to Toilet Bowl   ★★★

7455 Kalanianaole Highway, Waikiki.

This is a two-mile coastal hike past Hanauma Bay Beach Park. Toilet Bowl is a unique tide pool with a 10-foot-deep hole at its bottom. Wave action causes it to fill and flush, just like that handy porcelain thingy so necessary to our daily lives. Certain daredevils enjoy getting flushed in, but have to scramble out before it fills again. A rather slippery, dangerous activity, so if you're so inclined, don't do this alone. Or better yet, don't do it at all. On the other side of the bay, about 10 minutes away, is Witches' Brew, a cove with turbulent waters. Take a hint from the name and go for the view of Koko Crater and the green sand made of olivine crystals.

Judd Memorial Trail   ★★★

Nuuanu Pali Drive, Waikiki.

The highlight of this 1.5-mile hike is the Jackass-Ginger Pool, which is less than 15 minutes from the head of the trail. An easy family outing, it passes Nuuanu Stream (you might have to get your feet wet), a bamboo thicket, eucalyptus grove and Norfolk pines, which local residents use for Christmas trees. When it's wet enough, kids like to slide down several mud chutes on plastic sheets, aping Hawaiian *ali'i*, who used large ti leaves. Take Pali Highway to Nuuanu Pali Drive about half a mile to the Reservoir No. 2 spillway.

Historical Sites

View from Nuuanu Pali Lookout, Oahu

Pali Lookout ★★★★

Pali Highway, Waikiki.

Many tourists come here to see how many articles of clothing will be blown off their bodies by the high winds. A few do know it (and respect it) as a historical site. It was here where Kamehameha the Great defeated Oahu chief Kalanikupele in 1795, thereby unifying the islands under one ruler. A majority of the chief's men were forced off the precipice to their deaths. Not a pretty picture. A prettier one is the sight of the lush windward coast in the distance.

Museums and Exhibits

The Contemporary Museum ★★★

2411 Makiki Heights Drive, Waikiki, ☎ *(808) 526-1322.*
Hours: 10 a.m.–4 p.m.
Special hours: Sundays, noon-4 p.m. Closed: Mon.

Way up in Makiki Heights is Hawaii's only museum dedicated to modern art. Among the seven galleries of rotating exhibits is a permanent collection by David Hockney. Some say the gorgeous 1.5-acre gardens of this estate-turned-museum are better than the collections. There are more than 80 varieties of flowers and trees—magnolia, kukui, monkeypod, banyan, breadfruit and mango. Also a sculpted Asian garden, reflecting pool, and the Contemporary Café. Docent guided tours of the gardens by appointment only. Guided museum tours at 1:30 p.m. daily except Monday. Admission waived on the third Thursday of each month. General admission: $5.

U.S. Army Museum of Hawaii ★★

Corner of Kalia and Saratoga Roads, Waikiki, 96815, ☎ *(808) 438-2821.*
Hours: 10 a.m.–4:30 p.m.
Closed: Mon.

If you need a break from the Waikiki Beach heat, try the cool interior of the U.S. Army Museum. It's housed in Battery Randolph, at Fort deRussy, which occupies a prime piece of beachfront real estate. It probably survives only due to the fact that its massive construction makes it too difficult to remove. Built in 1909 and completed in 1914, it was one of several coastal artillery positions built for the defense of Oahu. Originally, it mounted a pair of 14-inch guns, which fired 2000-pound projectiles 18 miles away. The displays include a collection of military paraphernalia dating from ancient Hawaiian times to the present. Much attention is paid to the Army Corps of Engineers and their activities in Hawaii and the Pacific Region. It's easy to spot: just look for the concrete monolith with all of the armored vehicles (tanks, helicopters) out front. The gift shop has some cool "Rosie the Riveter"-type T-shirts for sale.

USS Bowfin Submarine Museum & Park ★★★

11 Arizona Memorial Drive, Waikiki, 96818, ☎ *(808) 423-1341.*
Hours: 8 a.m.–5 p.m.

Moored near the *USS Arizona* Memorial Visitor's Center is the *USS Bowfin*, an 1800-ton World War II diesel fleet submarine that sank 44 enemy ships during its career and received a Presidential Citation before the end of the war. A walk through its cramped exterior can leave one with the realization that it took a special type of person to inhabit such a small space with 80 other men on war patrol for months at a time. Perhaps one of the most terrifying displays is the Japanese Kaitan. This was the nautical equivalent of the Kamikaze, a suicide torpedo with one salient feature. It has a single seat for its human guidance system. The complex contains a museum, mini-theater, maritime gift shop, and sub displays surrounding an open-air pavilion. Children under four not allowed in the sub (for obvious reasons). General admission: $4–$8.

USS Bowfin *Submarine in Oahu is an 1800 ton World War II vessel that sank 44 enemy ships during its career. It now houses a fascinating museum.*

Music

AT&T Wildest Show in Town ★★★

Honolulu Zoo, Waikiki, *(808) 971-7171.*

Well, they say music soothes the savage beast...actually a very tame, serene event. This twilight concert series features top island musical entertainers. Picnicking is allowed, but don't feed the animals. Held every Wednesday from early June through August.

Parks and Gardens

Honolulu Zoo ★★★★

Kapiolani Park, Kalakaua Avenue, Waikiki, 96815, ☎ *(808) 971-7171.*
Hours: 9 a.m.–4:30 p.m.

Founded in 1914, the Honolulu Zoo has grown from a small animal shelter to a large zoological and botanical garden with more than 1500 animals. Here is where you will find the only snakes in Hawaii. Highlights are a simulated African savannah that encompasses 10 acres, some of the first Galapagos tortoises to be hatched in captivity, and a number of rare Hawaiian wildlife, including the state bird, the nene goose. The zoo also sponsors a number of exciting activities including a family sleep-over, "full-moon" walks, art shows and free twilight concerts. A great place. General admission: $6.

Lyon Arboretum ★★★

3860 Manoa Road, Waikiki, ☎ (808) 988-7378.
Hours: 9 a.m.–3 p.m.
A division of the University of Hawaii-Manoa, Lyon Arboretum is as noteworthy for its otherworldy aura as it is for its 196 acres of tropical plants. Located high up above the city, the gardens are often shrouded in mist. Reservations required for 90-minute guided tours offered on the first Friday and the third Wednesday of each month at 1 p.m., and the third Saturday at 10 a.m. Got that? The admission is actually a donation. General admission: $1.

Waikiki Aquarium ★★★★

2777 Kalakaua Avenue, Waikiki, 96815, ☎ (808) 923-9741.
Hours: 9 a.m.–5 p.m.
Located across from the tennis courts at Kapiolani Park. At 90 years old and change, the Waikiki Aquarium received a well-deserved $2.2 million renovation in 1994. Among the newest and noteworthy of the 64 exhibits is the Hawaiian Monk Seal Habitat, dedicated to the study and hopeful propagation of these slowly-disappearing (only 1500 are left) mammals. For people unable to snorkel Hanauma Bay, the Edge of the Reef Display or the Reef Machine may be the next best thing. It's an outdoor living coral reef ecosystem where visitors can make eye-to-eye contact and play touchy-feely with sea cucumbers, sea stars and other marine life. Current films are shown at the Sea Visions Theater. Continue to support the aquarium in its efforts by purchasing a memento in the Natural Selection Shop. General admission: $6.

The Shows

Aloha Showroom/Legends in Concert ★★★

2233 Kalakaua Avenue, Waikiki, ☎ (808) 971-1400.
Hours: 5–8:30 p.m.
Vegas' all-star superstar impersonator revue has landed in Waikiki, which is actually the Vegas of the Pacific. Features Broadway-caliber performers, who actually sing, not lip-synch, and a few of them, including "Little Richard" and "The Performer Formerly Known as Prince," look uncannily like the real thing. Two shows daily, dinner optional. Performer lineup varies. Watch for the free previews given daily in front of the Royal Hawaiian Shopping Center. Free tickets or at least "two-fers" are given out. General admission: $33–$135.

Diamond Head Theatre ★★★

520 Makapuu Avenue, Waikiki, 96816, ☎ (808) 734-0274.
A professional regional theater company, Diamond Head Theatre has been in existence for 82 years. It specializes, and does very well at, crowd-pleasing Broadway musicals made possible with talent and a 400-plus seat theater. General admission: $10 and up.

Hana Hou Supper Club/Don Ho ★★

2300 Kalakaua Avenue, Waikiki, ☎ (808) 922-4646.

OAHU

Closed: Mon.
At the Waikiki Beachcomber Hotel. The eternally youthful-looking Don Ho is a good sport. He says he hates "Tiny Bubbles" (so do we), but he performs it anyway for the bluehairs that love him. Don also provides a showcase for rising new talent. The price includes a candlelight dinner or cocktail seating. General admission: $32–$52.

Hawaii IMAX Theater   ★★★

325 Seaside Avenue, Waikiki, 96815, ☎ *(808) 923-IMAX.*
Hours: 11 a.m.–9 p.m.
Located next to the Waikiki Twin Theatres, in the heart of Waikiki, the IMAX theater is a great place to come in from the heat. The trademark five-story-plus high IMAX screen is 70 feet wide with six-channel digital stereo surround-sound. Watch the fascinating birth of a new volcanic island, Loihi, in the long-running feature "Hidden Hawaii," and "Ring of Fire," which is onscreen every 40 minutes. A second film, which changes every four months, is shown every other hour. Laser-light show after each presentation. General admission: $5–$7.50.

Honolulu Comedy Club   ★★

2045 Kalakaua Avenue, Waikiki, ☎ *(808) 922-5998.*
Hours: 8–9 p.m.
Special hours: Fri.–Sat., 10 p.m. Closed: Mon.
This standup comedy showcase features both locals and mainlanders. Two-drink minimum. In the Aston Waikiki Terrace Hotel. Reservations. General admission: $10–$12.

Polynesian Palace   ★★★★

227 Lewers Road, Waikiki, ☎ *(808) 923-7469.*
Closed: Mon., Sun.
The puckish Frank DeLima, known as Waikiki's Crown Prince of Comedy, and baby-faced Glen Medeiros, a Kauai native who had several Top 40 hits on the pop charts, are the "Pocho Knights," which is an affectionate island term for two wild and crazy Portuguese guys. The pair are the Martin and Lewis of Waikiki, with Medeiros playing straight man to the zany de Lima, in a series of musical-comedy routines that gently poke fun at Hawaii's diverse ethnic cultures. One show at 9:15 p.m., price includes one cocktail. When she's in town, Charo, the self-described "belle of coochie-coochie" and accomplished Spanish flamenco guitarist, performs at 7:15 p.m. Dinner seating at 6:15 p.m.; cocktail seating at 6:45 p.m. General admission: $19.50–$32.

Spectacular Polynesian Revue   ★★★

120 Kaiulani Avenue, Waikiki, ☎ *(808) 931-4660.*
Situated in the Sheraton Princess Kaiulani Hotel's Ainahau Showroom. Produced by Tahiti Productions, this long-running revue features tropical rhythms, fire-eating warriors, seductive maidens and dazzling costumes. Dancers come from Tahiti, Samoa, Fiji, New Zealand and Tokelau (wherever that is). It's almost as good as being in the South Pacific, without the $25 hamburgers. Two dinner and cocktail shows nightly. General admission: $51–$58.

The Magic of Polynesia ★★★★

2005 Kalia Road, in the Hilton Dome, Waikiki, ☎ *(808) 941-0924.*
One of Honolulu's top-paid performers, illusionist John Hirokawa has been compared to David Copperfield and Siegfried and Roy—not surprising, he has trained with them. One of his most mind-boggling tricks is the "Death Bed," where Hirokawa, chained from head to toe, lies seemingly helpless under 1500 pounds of steel and spikes. The rope suspending the spikes is set on fire—and Hirokawa has only 60 seconds to free himself. Does he? These nail-biting feats are lightened by a lavish Polynesian revue. Two dinner shows nightly at 6:30 and 8:45 p.m. General admission: $30–$56.50.

The Society of Seven ★★★★

Outrigger Main Showroom, 2335 Kalakaua Avenue, Waikiki, ☎ *(808) 922-6408.*
Lovingly called "SOS" by the legions of *kamaiianas* and visitors who flock to see them, year after year. Ensconced in this spot for the last 26 years, this truly talented group of musicians/comics/charmers specialize in elaborate Broadway numbers. Their late show currently features an elaborate theatrical production of *Beauty and the Beast*, peppered with comedy routines and spectacular costumes. Each one is an accomplished solo performer as well. Routines change frequently. Shows at 7:15 p.m. Wednesday–Saturday, and 9:15 p.m. Monday–Saturday. Higher admission includes a buffet dinner and one drink; lower includes one drink and a parking discount (!). General admission: $32–$55.

Tours

Atlantis Submarines ★★★

2005 Kalia Road, Hilton Hawaiian Village, Waikiki, ☎ *(808) 973-9811.*
Hours: 7 a.m.
Although Atlantis Submarine rides are available on the Big Island and Maui, only on Oahu will you find the *Atlantis XIV*, the latest in high-tech underwater exploration. The 100-foot-long, 160-ton sub submerges to a depth of 150 feet. Each of the 64 passengers gets one porthole. Recently, the company deliberately sank a ship, the 111-foot vessel *St. Pedro*, as part of a "reef enhancement project." This also means you get to go down and see all the curious marine life that have made the *St. Pedro* their new home. The descent to the site takes about 35–45 minutes, and is fully narrated. Souvenir guidebook included. Leaves from Port Hilton, beachfront at the Hilton Hawaiian Village. Other tours include the Atlantis Expedition $69, children $29; Atlantis Odyssey $79; children $39. General admission: $69–$148.

Round Top Road/Tantalus Drive ★★★

Starts at the end of Makiki Street, Waikiki.
The best overall view of Honolulu that's closest to the teeming city is from this vantage point. From the end of Makiki Street, the road makes a circle around Round Top Mountain—stop along the way for excellent views of Manoa Valley. The dense, dripping vegetation is punctuated by bursts of scarlet and fuschia, in the form of hibiscus and bougainvillea. At the apex is Puu Ualakaa State Wayside Park with a virtually unimpeded vista of half the island.

OAHU

USS Arizona *Memorial at Pearl Harbor is Hawaii's most visited monument.*

USS Arizona Memorial ★★★★

One Arizona Memorial Place, off Kamehameha Highway, Waikiki, ☎ *(808) 422-0561.*
Hours: 8 a.m.–3 p.m.
Special hours: closed Thanksgiving, Christmas, New Year's.
Dec. 7, 1941, marks a historical divide between a distant innocence and the world
of today. After almost six decades, the loss of the *USS Arizona* and its crew is perhaps the most salient memory of that day. Half of the 2300 fatalities of the Japanese
attack on Pearl Harbor died on this one ship in a matter of moments; 1100 of the
Arizona crew members remain entombed in her broken hull. The visitor center and
the museum contain a theater that shows an orientation film before a Navy launch
takes visitors to the off-shore memorial. The memorial is above, but does not touch,
the sunken hull. The "King," Elvis Presley, is given a lot of the credit for getting the
memorial built in 1962. He staged a benefit concert the year before, which raised
more than $60,000. The tour lasts 75 minutes. Next to the National Memorial
Cemetery of the Pacific (Punchbowl), this is the most visited monument in the
state, with more than 1.5 million visitors a year. Visits to the memorial are on a first-
come, first-served basis, and waits of up to three hours are not uncommon. Early
mornings are best, with the shortest lines. After noon, forget it.

Waikiki Trolley ★★

Royal Hawaiian Shopping Center, Waikiki, ☎ *(808) 596-2199.*
Hours: 8 a.m.–4:30 p.m.
A convenient, quickie way to see downtown Honolulu is via this old-fashioned trol-
ley that leaves every 15 minutes from the Royal Hawaiian Shopping Center. One-
or five-day passes available. The 20 stops along the route include the Bishop
Museum, the Hawaii Maritime Center and Chinatown. Get on and off at any point

OAHU

and re-board when you're good and ready. The Trolley can be hired for private events. General admission: $15–$25.

Leeward Oahu

Ewa

The Shows

Paradise Cove Luau ★★★

Ko Olina Resort, Ewa, ☎ *(808) 973-5828.*
Call for hours.

The food isn't the only star at this luau. Located in a private village on a 12-acre beachfront site, Paradise Cove likes to immerse visitors in island culture first. Before chowing down, watch and/or join in a lei-making or coconut-husking demonstration, play Maori stick games or Hawaiian bowling. Before the pig is removed from the underground *imu* oven, everyone gets to pull in a traditional *hukilau* fish net from the sea. Then guys with iron-cast hands remove the pig from the oven in an *imu* ceremony. OK, now it's time to "pig" out. Show afterwards climaxes with the exciting fire-knife dance. Price includes round-trip transportation from Waikiki. General admission: $27.50–$47.50.

Tours

Hawaiian Railway Society Tours ★★

Ewa Station, Ewa, ☎ *(808) 681-5461.*
Hours: 1–3 p.m.
Closed: Mon., Tues., Wed., Thurs., Fri., Sat.

Even if you're not a train buff, you will be after this charming excursion on a diesel locomotive once used by the Navy. The 90-minute route takes you through Barbers Point, an old sugar plantation, and Ko'Olina Resort. Afterwards, take a free look at an authentically restored 1900s-era parlor car that belonged to Benjamin E. Dillingham, founder of the Oahu Railway and Land Company. Queen Liliuokalani once graced the railway car with her regal presence. General admission: $5–$8.

Waianae

Beaches

Makaha Beach Park ★★★

84-369 Farrington Highway, Waianae.

Beautiful, uncrowded beach on Oahu's laid-back, very local westside, Makaha has perfect winter surf. Usually calm in summer months, folks must use caution while swimming at any time due to dangerous shore breaks. Snorkeling, scuba diving off shore. No parking, but there's a picnic area, rest rooms, phones and a lifeguard.

Waipahu

Tours

Hawaii's Plantation Village ★★★

97-695 Waipahu Street, Waipahu, 96797, ☎ *(808) 677-0110.*
Hours: 9 a.m.–3 p.m.

This is a fascinating museum of authentically furnished, re-created dwellings of eight ethnic groups that worked the sugar plantations of the early 19th century. Set in a three-acre garden, with labeled medicinal plants, there is also an original cook-house and a historical museum with photos, artifacts and documents. Guided tours every hour from 9 a.m.–3 p.m. The admission fee is actually a "donation." General admission: $3–$5.

North Shore

Haleiwa

Beaches

Ehukai Beach Park ★★★

59-337 Ke Nui Road, Haleiwa.

Across from Sunset Beach Elementary School in Haleiwa, Ehukai is more famously known as the Banzai Pipeline. This is a tube formed by monstrous waves breaking in a hollow fashion. Surfers disappear inside the tube, and hopefully emerge seconds later—surfing's ultimate maneuver. Calm and safe in summer, Banzai has wide stretches of sand for strolling or tanning. Lifeguard, rest room, showers, picnic areas.

Haleiwa Beach Park ★★★

62-449 Kamehameha Highway, Haleiwa.

Located just past rustic Haleiwa Town on the fabled north shore. Beginner surfing is good here, waves are gentle, swimming is calm in summer. Pros, look elsewhere. Scuba and snorkeling in a coral reef nearby. Also jet-ski and windsurfing lessons. Plenty of facilities: a small boat harbor, playing field, basketball courts, picnic tables, rest rooms.

Ke Iki Beach ★★★

Ke Iki Rd., off Kamehameha Highway, Haleiwa.

This "secret" North Shore beach has no official name; Ke Iki comes from the access road. Located a mile from Waimea Bay, it has a long, broad shore, often deserted. Swimming is not advisable due to the strong surf, so stroll, loaf or...use your imagination. No facilities, but you can use neighboring **Pupukea Beach Park**, *59-727 Kamehameha Highway*, with a parking lot, rest room and picnic area.

Sunset Beach ★★★

59-104 Kamehameha Highway, Haleiwa.

Aptly named for its spectacular sunsets, this is the site of the World Cup of Surfing. The rad surfers come out in the winter, but milder activities such as swimming and snorkeling are fine in summer, when things calm down a bit. Lifeguard, but no facilities.

Waimea Bay Beach Park ★★★

61-031 Kamehameha Highway, Haleiwa.

In winter, the world's largest ridable waves (30-footers) pound Waimea. Watch professional surfers do their thing. Glassy calm in summer, Waimea is beautiful all year. A great escape from Waikiki crowds, with its thick sand and wide beach. The ocean floor and reefs are clearly visible below the crystalline waters, which make it an excellent dive spot.

City Celebrations

Morey World Bodysurfing Championship   ★★

59-337 Ke Nui Road, Haleiwa, ☎ *(808) 396-2326.*
Held in January at Ekuhai Beach, home of the "Banzai Pipeline." Top bodyboarders compete for the best waves and try to outdo and outmaneuver each other for
fame, glory and money.

Triple Crown of Surfing   ★★★

Haleiwa, various locations, Haleiwa, ☎ *(808) 377-5850.*
November-December. An exciting series of events pits top professional surfers
against each other for a total of $215,000 in prize money.

Theme/Amusement Parks

Waimea Valley/Waimea Falls Park   ★★★

59-864 Kamehameha Highway, Haleiwa, 96712, ☎ *(808) 638-8511.*
Hours: 10 a.m.–5:30 p.m.

Waimea Falls Park is one of the only botanical gardens in the world that incorporates ancient archaeological sites and ridge-rides on an ATV (four-wheel-drive all-
terrain vehicle). Attractions are laid out fairly methodically throughout the bosky
1800-acre spread. Guests can follow a well-planned route on foot or by tram; a
detailed pictorial map is provided. Start perhaps by visiting a *Kauhale,* or Hawaiian
living site. You're encouraged to go back 300 years while a native Hawaiian guide
recreates activities common to daily life. Close by is the *Hale Iwi,* discovered by the
park's resident archaeologist in 1976. Translated to "house of bones," it contained
two burials and was believed to be the temple of an *ali'i.* Afterwards, watch a performance of the Waimea Valley Dancers, the park's hula *halau* (troupe). Guests will
probably be coaxed into trying a few moves themselves. Hawaiian games of skill are
also played, which will amuse the kids. In between, consider wandering about the
collection of more than 30 rare plant collections, some of them rated world-class.
The ones with red labels are endangered. One of the events nobody misses is the
cliff-diving show. Divers must plunge over the park's 45-foot waterfall, which feeds
into a shallow pool. The aforementioned ATV rides, plus mountain biking and kayaking, can be arranged at the Visitor Center. The park also has a snack bar and two
restaurants. The Proud Peacock is open until 9 p.m. General admission: $19.95.

Kaena Point

Hiking

Kaena Point Trail   ★★★

At the end of Route 930, Kaena Point.
This remote, wildly beautiful state park is the end of the road for both the north and
west shorelines. The four-mile trail is fairly strenuous, as well as hot and dusty, but
there are swimming holes along the way. You'll see coastal dunes, native plants, seabirds and perhaps a school of spinner dolphins or a Laysan albatross. The views of
the coast are spectacular. To get here, drive to the end of the paved road from
Route 930 on the North Shore or Route 93 on the West Shore. Follow the jeep trail
to Kaena Point.

Waialua

Pacific International Skydiving Center   ★★★

68760 Farrington Highway, Waialua, 96712, ☎ (808) 637-7472.
Hours: 8 a.m.–5 p.m.

Takes off from Dillingham Airfield in Mokuleia. Participants receive basic on-ground skydiving instruction followed by a tandem jump, where the student is attached to an experienced tandem master's harness, from exit until landing. Discounts for 10 or more foolhardy souls jumping at the same time. Tandem jumps are made from at least 8500 feet and go up as high as 13,000 feet. After you've survived this, you're ready for an accelerated free-fall course—you'll perform seven tandem dives until they feel you can go it alone, falling from 3000 to 4000 feet. Course price varies with the season. Gear rental and lift tickets are extra. Students must be at least 18 years of age and under 200 pounds. Also at the Airfield is Skydive Hawaii, ☎ *(808) 637-9700.* Tandem dives are $225. If you're staying in Waikiki or near there, you can arrange for a pickup. General admission: $175–$862.

Tours

Tsunami Aviation Hawaii   ★★★

68760 Farrington Highway, Dillingham Airfield, Waialua, 96791, ☎ (808) 944-3935.
Hours: 9 a.m.–4:30 pm

This is NOT your typical boring scenic ride. Potential daredevils can try loops, rolls, hammer heads, Cuban eights, and other "Top Gun" maneuvers in a state-of-the-art aerobatic sport biplane. The PITTS S2B, called the "Formula One" racer of planes, has won more acrobatic contests than any other aircraft. This adventure lasts about 15 minutes, and if you look up long enough to notice, you can see the entire North Shore panorama upside down. Flights depart every 20 minutes, first-come, first-flown, but reservations are accepted. Check in at the Tsunami Aviation hangar near the control tower. Also at Dillingham (or is it Daringham?) you can try the same antics as a co-pilot on a Stearman Bi-Plane. This is a fully restored 1941 vintage open cockpit, Stearman N2S built by Boeing as a primary pilot trainer for the military. Don a leather helmet and goggles for the full effect. Too wild for you? Just take a scenic tour of the North Shore (20 minutes) or a historic tour over Pearl Harbor, retracing a bombing route used by the Japanese on Dec. 7, 1941 (40 minutes). Flights daily, reservations recommended. Also popular is Mr. Bill's Original Glider Rides, a.k.a. the Honolulu Soaring Club, now in its 20th year of offering rides on bubble-topped, piloted one- to two-passenger glider rides, from 10:30 a.m.–5:30 p.m. Call ☎ *(808) 677-3404* for information.

Southeast Oahu

Hanauma Bay

Beaches

Hanauma Bay Nature Park   ★★★★

7455 Kalanianaole Highway, Hanauma Bay.
Hours: 7 a.m.–6 p.m.
Closed: Wed.

Located some 20 minutes from Waikiki, just past Hawaii Kai, Hanauma Bay is part of Koko Head Regional Park. This glorious marine reserve is a circular bay lined with a long, narrow, palm-fringed beach. Situated in the crater of an ancient volcano, it has absolutely fabulous snorkeling. Unfortunately, there are a number of serious problems here, including overcrowding and the overfeeding of fish, who were getting an unbalanced diet of peas and bread from eager visitors. In 1990, the park closed on Wednesday mornings, and it's now illegal for tour buses and vans to let people off without a permit. It's also the only beach park in Hawaii with an admission fee for nonresidents ages 13 and up, although this is waived for visitors who just want to stay in the parking lot and take pictures. Packets of approved fish food are available at the concession stand. Attendants now turn cars away if the park is full. These measures have cut the population explosion cleanly in half. There's still a heated controversy regarding the fees; the latest measure has been to cut the fee to $3 for nonresidents, and have residents pay $1. Get here early in the morning, and please don't step on the coral. General admission: $5.

Hawaii Kai

Hiking

Koko Crater Trail ★★★

Kealahou Street off Kalanianaole Highway, Hawaii Kai.
Hours: 9 a.m.–4 p.m.

Due to inadequate funding, the dryland botanical garden within Koko Crater has been allowed to deteriorate badly. Still, it's interesting to venture into the ancient volcanic tuff cone, peer at the cacti and then climb a rough trail to its 1200-foot summit. The trail, also unmaintained, is composed of old railroad ties long unused by the Army. The rotting wood is covered with overgrown vegetation, so watch your step. The lookout at the top affords super views of the Koolau Mountains, Diamond Head, the posh neighborhoods of Hawaii Kai and Kahala, and Koko Head.

Koko Head Trail ★★

Kalanianole Highway, at the Hanauma Bay entrance, Hawaii Kai.

Although this trail is not always open, it's short (one mile), fun for the family, and fairly easy. The short hike to the summit of Koko Head gives one a superb view over Hanauma Bay, Diamond Head, Hawaii Kai, the Koolau Mountains, and sometimes the island of Molokai, 200 miles across the channel.

Sandy Beach

Beaches

Sandy Beach ★★★

8801 Kalanianaole Highway, Sandy Beach.

Just around the bend from Hanauma Bay, and 30 minutes from Waikiki, Sandy Beach is the ultimate (advanced only) bodysurfing site on Oahu. Others can walk on the sand and savor the action from shore. The ocean here is a seductive temptress, beautiful but dangerous. Beware the strong undercurrents and large waves. Showers, phones, lifeguard, parking, rest rooms.

OAHU

Waialae

City Celebrations

United Airlines Hawaiian Open ★★★

Waialae Country Club, Waialae, ☎ *(808) 526-1232.*

Held for four days each year in mid-February. In a sea of avocado green and mai-tai
pink, top pro golfers swing and putt their hearts out for $12 million worth of prize
money. It's also a way for spectators to get into the exclusive, old-money Waialae
Country Club.

Upper Manoa Valley

Manoa Valley

Hiking

Manoa Falls Trail ★★★

End of Manoa Road, Manoa Valley, ☎ *(808) 587-0166.*

Less than a mile long, this trail is well-maintained and takes about 30 minutes each
way. The hike is deeply forested, and glimpses of the falls can be seen on various
points on the trail. Small, but steep and picturesque, Manoa Falls is a perfect picnic
spot, surrounded by lush, junglelike vegetation most of the year, especially after a
rain. The pools at the base, though, are too shallow for swimming. Although tempting, it's not advisable to hike above the falls. Take Manoa Road all the way to the
entrance of Lyon Arboretum, make a sharp left to a dirt road and parking area.
Note: The parking at the Arboretum is for patrons only.

Windward Oahu

Hauula

Hiking

Sacred Falls State Park ★★★

Off Kamehameha Highway, south of Hauula ☎ *(808) 587-0300.*

This one is a good workout. Recommended for surefooted hikers with some experience. An old cane road passes the slippery Kaluanui stream into a narrow valley
leading up to the waterfall. The falls, which drop some 80 feet, may be a bit of a dis-
appointment when you get to them. There's a swimming hole, but sharp rocks in
the water and ravenous mosquitoes (the official state insect) might make the experience less than blissful. If mountain apples are in season, they'll enhance your picnic
fixings. The area is subject to flash floods, even in sunny weather. If there are any
warning signs up, take them very seriously. The hike is about 4.5 miles round trip
and takes 1.5 hours to complete.

Kailua

Beaches

Kailua Beach Park ★★★★

Kalaheo Rd., in downtown Kailua, Kailua.

A two-mile stretch of white sand sloping gently outward to deeper water, Kailua
Beach is one of the country's most beautiful beaches. Also known as Oahu's windsurfing capital for its steady breezes; perfect for beginners. Schools nearby give les-

sons and rent equipment. Generally safe for swimming (no riptides), kayaking, walking and sunning are alternate activities. Located five miles past Waimanalo, and 50 minutes from Waikiki. There's a big parking lot, but it still gets full, especially on weekends. Rest rooms, showers.

Lanikai Beach ★★★★★

South of Kailua Beach Park, Kailua.

This beach, not far from Kailua Beach Park, is so spectacular that the Australian Tourist Board took a picture of it and tried to pass it off as one of theirs. The unbelievable turquoise water is shot with flashes of purple and the sand is absolutely pure and white. Lanikai is almost a private beach for the residents who have homes right on the water's edge. Many are just humble saltboxes built in the 1920s, but movie stars and moguls have built fancy ones since then. One problem is that the beach is eroding, and tumbling into people's swimming pools; you'll see sandbags, á la Malibu, in front of some of them. The reason it's relatively uncrowded is that access is off one road running along the beach. On the horizon are two offshore islands, both called Mokulua, and you can kayak or sail to them. No facilities or parking.

The Shows

The Lanikai Mortgage Players ★★

Between Kaiolena Drive and Aalapapa Drive, Kailua, *(808) 261-6469.*

This enterprising group performs for their health and to help maintain Lanikai Park—which is the group's main venue. Material is primarily old-fashioned melodramas, with wacky vaudeville routines and barbershop quartets thrown in. One recent show, *Say It Aint So, Joe, Or the Miracle of St. Fungo*, combined the themes of baseball, true love and corruption in the 1890s. General admission: $5.

Kaneohe

Beaches

Kualoa Regional Park ★★★

49-479 Kamehameha Highway, Kaneohe.

Only 35 minutes from Waikiki, Kualoa is the viewpoint for Chinaman's Hat island, named for the straw hats Chinese plantation workers wore in the late 19th and 20th centuries. More exciting is the Hawaiian name, Mokoli'i, who was a fierce dragon slain by Hi'iaka, Pele's younger sister. At low tide, you can wade to Chinaman's Hat/Mokoli'i. There's good snorkeling around the coral reef. Kite-flying is among the favored dry activities. Good camping, lifeguard, tons of parking, with lots of speed bumps, rest rooms, showers, picnic grounds.

Parks and Gardens

Byodo-In Temple ★★

47-200 Kahekili Highway, Kaneohe, 96744, *(808) 239-8811.*

Hours: 9 a.m.–4 p.m.

Situated in the Valley of the Temples Memorial Park (a cemetery) at the foot of the Koolau Mountains, this is a replica of a 900-year-old temple in Uji, Japan. Its bright-red exterior is a striking contrast to the chiseled and verdant cliffs that serve as a backdrop. Carp swim in the pool in front of it, and in the interior is a nine-foot-high gilded Buddha statue. Don't be bashful about ringing the three-ton bronze bell at the entrance—everyone else does it. Gift shop. General admission: $1–$2.

Senator Fong's Plantation and Gardens   ★★★

47-285 Pulama Road, Kaneohe, 96744, ☎ *(808) 239-6775.*
Hours: 10 a.m.–4 p.m.

After he retired from public life, Senator Hiram Fong opened his family's 725-acre plantation to the public. There are more than 100 different edible fruits and nuts grown in its orchards. Panoramic views of the windward coast can also be seen. Guided trams tour the property until 3 p.m. With 24 hour's notice, guests can engage in paintball games, hike, go mountain climbing or take Jeep rides into a rainforest. General admission: $5–$8.50.

The Shows

ASATAD Productions   ★★

45-720 Kea'ahala Road, Kaneohe, ☎ *(808) 247-6939.*

An acronym for "All Singing, All Talking, All Dancing Productions." Presents primarily adult works, including frequent gay themes. The company is based at the Little Theatre, Windward Community College. General admission: $12.

Laie

Beaches

Malaekahana Recreation Area   ★★★★

Kamehameha Highway, north of Laie, Laie.

Once a well-kept secret, this beautiful, sandy beach, protected by a coral reef, is becoming more popular, but it's fairly empty during the week. Local residents like to camp here on weekends. There are two islands across the reef from the beach, and it's possible to walk across to the closest one, Mokuauia (Goat Island), a bird refuge, at low tide. Wear reef walkers. Rest rooms, parking, picnic tables, camping.

Theme/Amusement Parks

Polynesian Cultural Center   ★★★★

55-370 Kamehameha Highway, Laie, 96762, ☎ *(808) 293-3333.*
Hours: 12:30–9 p.m.

One of Oahu's most popular attractions, the Polynesian Cultural Center takes at least one day to see. The core of the complex are seven authentically replicated islands that make up Polynesia and Melanesia. And the natives are more than friendly—all personnel, students from the nearby Brigham Young University, come from these islands and are trained to show you some aspect of their culture. For example, walk over to "Tonga," and a smiling woman will demonstrate how a piece of tapa cloth is made from bark. In "Samoa," a youth clambers up a coconut tree, husks and opens the fruit at warp speed. Visitors are meant to stroll and explore at their own pace. Within eight hours, you may have learned at least the rudiments of the Tahitian otea dance, or the basics of the Maori stick game *tititorea*. The center is constantly adding features and attractions—for example, a state-of-the-art IMAX theater, and a lavish new evening show. Better than any luau show you've ever seen, the "Horizons" extravaganza has more than 100 performers covering a four-tiered stage cut out of the side of a "volcano." Songs, dancing and other revelry follow. The finale is an astounding fire-knife show (the center hosts the annual Fire Knife Dance Championships). A $1.4 million shopping village, "The Treasures of Polynesia," opened in 1995. By the center's accounting, it has the world's largest selection of Polynesian handicrafts. Admission fees depend on ticket packages purchased; the lowest price is for admission only, the highest for admission, the luau, IMAX and the night show. General admission: $27–$92.

Waimanalo

Beaches

Makapuu Beach Park ★★★

41-095 Kalanianaole Highway, Waimanalo.
Known for advanced body/boogie-boarding. Waters are calm for reasonably safe swimming during the summer. Showers, phones, lifeguard, parking, picnicking, camping.

Waimanalo Beach Park ★★★

41-741 Kalanianole Highway, Waimanalo.
Long and wide, Waimanalo encompasses at least five beach parks, so there's plenty of room for everyone. It's great for learning how to bodysurf or boogie-board, because of the small, gentle waves. Great for picnicking. Located two miles past Sea Life Park. Picnic area, rest room, phones, lifeguard.

Theme/Amusement Parks

Sea Life Park ★★★

41-202 Kalanianaole Highway, Suite 7, Waimanalo, 96795, ☎ *(808) 259-7933.*
Hours: 9:30 a.m.–5 p.m.
Special hours: Fridays to 9:30 p.m.
Founded in 1964, Sea Life Park is both an amusement center and marine conservation/education enterprise. Animal shows are its main draw, but there are a number of breeding and treatment centers for endangered species. These programs are incorporated into a number of exhibits, including the Penguin Habitat and the Hawaiian monk seal care center. Sea Life Park has the world's only known "wholphin," named Kekaimalu, the result of a union between a false killer whale and an Atlantic bottlenose dolphin. Visitors can observe Kekaimalu being trained. One of the most popular attractions is the 300,000-gallon Hawaiian reef tank, with sharks and stingrays among the 4000 inhabitants. Children are drawn to the Touch Pool, where they can tickle a sea cucumber or stroke a spiny seastar. A bunch of comical sea lions are good for a few belly laughs, whether they're begging for herring (guests can buy fish to feed them) or performing a series of choreographed routines. Good fun for a good cause. General admission: $19.95.

Tours

Hideaway Tours ★★★

41-127 Nalu Street, Waimanalo, 96795, ☎ *(808) 259-9165.*
Hours: 7 a.m.–3:30 p.m.
Closed: Tues., Thurs., Sat., Sun.

OAHU

Spend a day in little-known Waimanalo with Darren Keawekaopuaokalani Akau on his Hana ("action") tour of Oahu. Akau, a former tour director, wanted to go on his own and show tourists the "real Hawaii." On a visit to a five-acre native Hawaiian family plantation, guests will make plumeria and ti-leaf leis, play Hawaiian games, and identify native plants. Also boogie-boarding and snorkeling at two separate beaches—if you've never done one or the other before, Akau, a certified lifeguard, will provide instruction. Instead of reciting from a manufactured script, Akau ad libs charming family stories and Hawaiian legends while pointing out unfamiliar landmarks along the way. Tour includes hotel pickup, lunch, use of boogie boards, picture postcards and a ti-leaf-wrapped gift. General admission: $70.

Sports

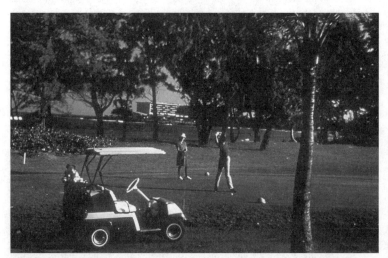

Hawaii's golf courses feature many scenic distractions.

More than 30 **golf courses** are sprinkled around Oahu, ranging from relatively inexpensive public courses to world-class (and big-priced) resort courses. The most sought-after public courses include par-72 **Hawaii Kai Golf Course**, par-72 **West Loch Municipal Golf Course**, par-72 **Pali Golf Course** and par-70 **Ala Wai Golf Course**. For exceptional resort courses, try the 18-hole, Arnold Palmer-designed **Links at Kuilima** or the George Fazio-designed, nine-hole course at the **Turtle Bay Hilton** and the two 18-hole courses at the **Sheraton Makaha Resort and Country Club**. The world's best golfers take to the links at Waialae Country Club (around the end of January) for the **Hawaiian Open Invitational Golf Tournament**. More than 150 county-run tennis courts are available to visitors, plus those at hotels, resorts, and country clubs. Free public courts in the Waikiki district are at **Ala Moana Park**, **Diamond Head Tennis Center** and **Kapiolani Tennis Courts**.

Oahu's waters draw fishers to the Waianae Coast where they try their luck with marlin, mahi-mahi, ahi and other game fish. Hop on board in Honolulu Harbor (Kewalo Basin) or Pokai Bay on the Waianae coast. Catch bass, Chinese catfish, sunfish and other **freshwater** species at **Nuuanu Reservoir** above Honolulu, or **Wahiawa Pubic Fishing Area** around Wahiawa town. **Horseback riders** can choose from a variety of trails at the 4000-acre **Kualoa Ranch** in Kaneohe, on the windward coast. Both guests and nonguests can rent horses at the **Sheraton Makaha Lio Stables** for rides into Makaha Valley, or the **Turtle Bay Hilton** for a trot around the resort's property (which includes a private beach).

Central Oahu
Wahiawa

Hawaii Country Club ★★★
1211 Kunia Road, Wahiawa, ☎ *(808) 621-5654.*
A semi-private club in the center of Dole Pineapple country. Course is 18 holes, par-72. Greens fees for U.S. citizens on weekdays, $10–$25; weekends, $35–$37. Foreign visitors; weekdays, $65; weekends, $69. Twilight for citizens and foreign visitors; weekdays, $7, with cart, $14; weekends, $9, with cart, $18. Pro shop, restaurant, driving range, putting green. General admission: $10–$65.

Honolulu
Downtown

Hans Hedemann Surf ★★★
350 Ward Avenue, Suite 106, downtown, ☎ *(808) 591-7778.*
Hours: 8 a.m.–6 p.m.
One- and two-hour private and group surf lessons are taught by Hedemann, a world pro-tour competitor for the past 17 years, and co-owner Tim Groh. Includes water safety, wave selection and location. All equipment and ground transportation provided. Also bodyboarding for $40 an hour, $60 two hours. Student discounts are offered. Location is arranged at time of booking. General admission: $50–$75.

Hawaii Bicycling League ★★★
P.O. Box 4403, downtown, 96812, ☎ *(808) 735-5756.*
Outside of Honolulu/Waikiki, coastal roads are relatively level, but traffic is frequent and heavy at times, especially along Kamehameha Highway on the windward coast past Kaneohe through the small hamlets of Laie, Kualoa and Kaawa. There have recently been a rash of accidents, with impatient drivers (a la Los Angeles) try-

ing to pass slow vehicles on the left, with sticky results. A few tough hills too, including the 1000-foot saddle between the Koolau and Waianae mountain ranges (windward and leeward). The Hawaii Bicyling League will provide you with buds and good tips. Its free weekend rides are open to all. The on- or off-road beginner rides meet on the first Sunday of each month. Riders must wear helmets and bring water bottles. A free newsletter is distributed in bicycle shops. Bicycle rentals are available from **Planet Surf**, *421 Nahua Street*, in Waikiki near the **Outrigger West Hotel**, ☎ *(808) 926-2060*; and on the North Shore, *59-051 Pupukea Road*, next to Foodland, ☎ *638-7167*, $12.50 a day, $30 for three days, $50 a week. Also recommended in the Waikiki area is **Blue Sky Rentals**, *1920 Ala Moana Boulevard*. Full range of bikes from $15–21 per day; also mopeds for $15 half-day, $20 full day, $85 a week.

Greater Honolulu

Ala Wai Golf Course   ★★★

404 Kapahulu Avenue, Greater Honolulu, ☎ *(808) 733-7387.*
Hours: 6 a.m.–6 p.m.
This 18-hole, par-70 course right in the heart of Waikiki is probably one of the most-played courses in the world. So it'll probably be a while before you get to scuff up the greens. Cart rental is $14. Half-price after 4 p.m. Large driving range, two putting greens, two pro shops, snack shop, lessons available. General admission: $40.

Atlantis Reef Divers   ★★★

1085 Ala Moana Boulevard, Room 102, Greater Honolulu, ☎ *(808) 973-9811.*
Dive Atlantis Reef from a 72-foot *Rainbow* catamaran, or from the *Explorer*, a 60-footer with a huge enclosed cabin, spacious dive deck and hot-water shower. Introductory scuba dives and two-tank guided tours for certified divers. Two-day dive packages take participants to the *Mahi*, a World War II minesweeper, wrecked off the Waianae Coast. New this year is Club Atlantis, a three-hour cruise off Waikiki at 12:45 p.m. Scuba, snorkel, boogie-board, play water basketball (using an innertube as a basket) or just lay in the sun. The rate includes a barbecue lunch. Massages are extra. $59 per person; $70 for cruise plus one tank dive for certified divers. Cruises leave from Port Hilton off the beach in front of the **Hilton Hawaiian Village**, *2005 Kalia Road*, in Waikiki. General admission: $75–$138.

Honolulu Lawn Bowling Club   ★★★

1201 Ala Moana Boulevard, Greater Honolulu, ☎ *(808) 545-2352.*
This perfectly civilized pursuit takes place at Ala Moana Park near McCoy Pavilion, four mornings a week at 9 a.m. The club offers lessons and memberships. Games are $3 a day, dues approximately $130 per year. General admission: $3.

Ilikai Hotel Sports Center   ★★★

1777 Ala Moana Boulevard, Greater Honolulu, ☎ *(808) 944-6300.*
Hours: 7 a.m.–10 p.m.
The Ilikai Nikko has one of the largest private tennis centers in Waikiki. There are five courts, including one lit for night play ($2 charge for the electricity). Registered

guests, of course, have priority. A pro is on hand for lessons. General admission: $5–$7.50.

Waikiki

Dan's Dive Shop ★★

660 Ala Moana Boulevard., Waikiki, ☎ *(808) 536-6181.*
An adventurous scuba dive explores the remains of the Navy's *Yard Oiler* 257 and other sunken wrecks. Tropical fish, eels in dark corners and crevices of coral-encrusted machinery. Photo ops abound.

Hawaii Kai Golf Course ★★★

8902 Kalanianaole Highway, Waikiki, ☎ *(808) 395-2358.*
Hours: 6 a.m.–6 p.m.
Public suburban course features two courses. The Championship course is a a par-72, 18-hole course. Greens fee weekdays is $85, weekends $95. The Executive Course is a par-54, 18-hole course. Greens fee weekdays is $37, weekends $42, cart $23.50. Driving range, pro shop, restaurant, putting green. General admission: $37–$85.

Paradise Snorkel Adventures ★★

270 Lewers Street, Waikiki, ☎ *(808) 923-7766.*
Hours: 7:30 a.m.–4 p.m.
Based in the heart of Waikiki, at the Holiday Isle Hotel, this rental and sales shop offers a public shuttle to Hanauma Bay for $9.95 that includes snorkel gear, round-trip transportation and fish food. The Sea Life Park and Hanauma Bay combo is $24.95. Snorkel gear alone is $6.75 for 24 hours, an optical mask, $6.50. Ask about three-day specials. General admission: $9.95–$24.95.

Tradewind Charters

1833 Kalakaua Avenue, Suite 612, Waikiki, 96815, ☎ *(808) 973-0311.*
Offers half-day sail and snorkeling excursions daily year-round. Guests can take turns at the helm if they choose, sailing down the Honolulu coastline and sipping cool ones while watching dolphins, flying fish and sea turtles. Cap it all off with snorkeling at Rainbow reef. All beverages and gear are provided. In season, a morning or afternoon four-hour whalewatching excursion is available on an uncrowded sailing yacht. Also private sailing lessons. You can charter one of the 32- or 72-foot sailing yachts for overnight and interisland cruises. Ask about weddings and burials at sea. General admission: $65.

Leeward Oahu

Kapolei

Ko Olina Golf Club ★★★★

92-1220 Aliinui Street, Kapolei, 96707, ☎ *(808) 676-5300.*
Hours: 6 a.m.–6 p.m.
Ted Robinson (when does this man sleep?) designed this 18-hole, 6867-yard, par-72 course that opened in February 1990. Rated one of America's top 75 resort courses by *Golf Digest*, Ko Olina was the site of the Hawaiian Ladies Open in 1994. The rolling course is laid out along a dry coastal plain, with thousands of rare trees,

OAHU

including coconut palm, banyan, monkeypod and firecracker plants. Robinson created eight water features (some may think they are hazards) on eight holes. The whole place is larger than life, with an enormous practice range, a fabulous clubhouse and a bar overlooking the tough 18th hole with its own lake and waterfall. A team of golf pros are at your service. Greens fees $65 after 2:30 p.m.; $35 after 4 p.m. General admission: $95–$145.

Waianae

Rainbow Diver II   ★★★

Pier 8, Waianae Boat Harbor, Waianae, ☎ (808) 625-7190.

Lee and Dinah Rodgers operate the only glass-bottom dive boat in Hawaii. It leaves from Waianae Boat Harbor on the leeward coast, far away from the madding crowds in Honolulu. This location makes it a lot easier to get to the to the *Mahi* shipwreck off Maili Point and Makaha Caverns, a popular site for experienced divers. The wreck is now the habitat of sea turtles, eels and colorful Hawaiian tropical fish. There are more than 20 other dive sites to choose from, including ones with intriguing names such as Jurassic Park, Land of Oz and Pray for Sex (!). Rainbow Divers offers PADI four-day certification and two-day advanced certification dives, and a "scuba discovery" one-tank dive with an instructor for $75 (not a certification). Also two-tank dives ($65–$75), three-tank sunset/night dives for $125 (48 hour advance reservations required). Snorkelers and ride-alongs allowed (gear included) for $25. Ask about snorkel cruises. The *Rainbow Diver II* has a sundeck and solar shower. Free soft drinks and snacks included. Waikiki hotel pickup and rentals available. General admission: $75–$125.

North Shore

Haleiwa

Raging Isle Sports   ★★★

66-250 Kamehameha Highway, Haleiwa, ☎ (808) 637-7700.

For exploring Haleiwa's new 3.5-mile beachside hike-and-bike trail, you'll need the right equipment. It's all available from this exclusive shop. Also rentals and repairs. Bikes also available from **Planet Surf**, *59-051 Pupukea Road*, next to Foodland, ☎ *(808) 638-7167*. Rentals are $12 for 24 hours, $30 for three days and $50 per week.

Surf & Sea Inc.   ★★★

62-595 Kamehameha Highway, Haleiwa, ☎ (808) 637-9887.
Hours: 9 a.m.–6 p.m.

Offers surf instruction for all levels. Teaches basic etiquette, wave-riding, safety and how to recognize currents. Surfboards are provided for beginning lessons. A two-hour, semi-private lesson is $58, with three persons per instructor. Also bodyboarding, windsurfing and scuba diving (certified and non-certified). General admission: $58.

Kahuku

Happy Trails Hawaii Ltd.   ★★★

Kahuku, past Waimea Valley, Kahuku, ☎ (808) 948-1235.

Hours: 8 a.m.–5 p.m.

Catering to newbies and first-timers, this out-of-the-way North Shore company specializes in small, intimate trail rides through a 380-acre private ranch above Waimea Valley. Rides meander through eucalyptus and ironwood groves, with panoramic views of the ocean and coast past Kaena Point. Owner Mark Becker says he wants to give guests a relaxed, truly "local" experience. Daily scheduled one- and one-and-a-half-hour rides begin with detailed instruction. Three times daily, at 8:30 a.m., 10:15 a.m. and 3:30 p.m. Special military and *kamaaina* rates. Reservations required, and some weight restrictions may apply. General admission: $35–$45.

Kahuku Golf Course ★★

P.O. Box 517, Kahuku, ☎ (808) 293-5842.
Hours: 7 a.m.–5 p.m.

Local residents enjoy walking, as well as playing on, this nine-hole municipal course. Pull carts $2, club rental, $10. No reservations, no pro shop, no clubhouse, no frills. First-come, first-served. General admission: $20.

Sunset Rides/Turtle Bay Hilton

57-091 Kamehameha Highway, Kahuku, 96731, ☎ (808) 293-8811.
Daily along the coast, 45-minute trail rides, rides for more experienced, $45, sunset rides $70 on weekends on Kuilima Point. General admission: $32–$45.

Turtle Bay Hilton & Country Club ★★★

57-091 Kamehameha Highway, Kahuku, 96731, ☎ (808) 293-8811.
Hours: 7 a.m.–5 p.m.

This secluded beachfront resort on 808 acres on Oahu's North Shore features two courses. The resort's newest course, The Links at Kuilima, is an 18-hole, par-72 course designed by Arnold Palmer, Ed Seay and Erik Larsen. It's designed like a British links course with tropical character. When it opened in 1992, it was hailed as one of top 10 in the world. Greens fee $125, guests $50, weekends $75. The older course, the Turtle Bay Country Club Course, is a par-36, nine regulation holes, with two sets of tees offering a full 18-hole challenge. $25 greens fee. General admission: $25–$125.

Turtle Bay Hilton–Nick Bolletieri Tennis Academy ★★★

57-091 Kamehameha Highway, Kahuku, 96731, ☎ (808) 203-8811.
Hours: 8–7 p.m.

The Turtle Bay Hilton offers 10 Plexipave courts, four of them lighted, on its 808-acre North Shore resort. A Tennis Center rents equipment and ball machines. Since 1991, the Nick Bolletieri Tennis Academy has maintained a campus on the resort, featuring intensive clinics and programs for all levels. Private lessons are $45 per hour; semi-private $22.50; group, $15. Prices below are for daily court rental. Expect somewhat windy conditions. General admission: $8–$12.

Waimea Valley

Waimea Valley Walks

Waimea Valley, ☎ (808) 638-8511.
Hours: 10 a.m.–5:30 p.m.

Fitness-walking program. Program leader Laura Stern leads participants in warm-up exercises, a 50-minute walk through valley and cool-down exercise. Fitness tips, tranquil refreshing atmosphere. First walk is free. Then's the kicker, the price is $40–$70.

Windward Oahu

Kaaawa

Kualoa Activity Club/Secret Island ★★★

49-560 Kamehameha Highway, Kaaawa, 96730, ☎ *(808) 237-8515.*
Call for hours.

Located on a 4000-acre ranch on Oahu's windward coast. One-hour trail rides every afternoon, and two-hour rides on weekends. If you're pressed for time, you can choose from a bevy of activities offered by the ranch from a helicopter tour, a historic trolley ride, target shooting, dune cycling, mountain-bike riding, also snorkeling and scuba (the ranch also owns a private islet) and more, all packed into an 8.5-hour day. This Deluxe Package costs $149. Included is pickup and return from Waikiki, an all-you-can-eat BBQ lunch, free access to the tennis court, a petting zoo and gardens. This is one of those places you expect Tattoo to come running out yelling, "Boss, boss, zee plen, zee plen." There are three other packages ranging in price from $69–$99 per person. Reservations required. General admission: $25–$35.

Kailua

Naish Hawaii ★★★

155-A Hamakua Drive, Kailua, ☎ *(808) 262-6068.*

What better place to learn windsurfing (also known as sailboarding) than on Oahu's prime windsurfing spot, Kailua Beach? Windsurfing champ Robbie Naish or one of his associates teaches three-hour introductory group lessons plus private lessons. All boards and sails are custom-made in the shop, so you can buy or rent gear here. Also repairs. They'll deliver everything to the beach for you. Beginners' equipment is $15 per hour, $30 for a full day; intermediate and advanced equipment is $25 for two hours. Also recommended is Kailua Sailboard Co., 130 Kailua Road, (808) 262-2555; all-day beach windsurfing package, from 9:30 a.m.–5 p.m. daily is $49. Also, all-day beach kayak tours for $35 per person and $59 per couple. Half- and full-day kayak and sailboard rentals available from $22–$36. Three-hour beginner lessons for $39 at 10:30 a.m. and 2 p.m. daily. Other packages include picnic lunch and transportation from Waikiki. General admission: $35–$55.

Kaneohe

Pali Golf Course ★★★

45-050 Kamehameha Highway, Kaneohe, ☎ *(808) 266-7612.*
Hours: 6:30 a.m.–6 p.m.

Highly popular 18-hole, par-72 municipal course. Use of cart adds $14 to the greens fee. Half-price after 4 p.m. Putting green, snack bar. General admission: $40.

Where to Stay

Hawaii Prince Hotel in Waikiki is designed so all rooms have ocean views.

The choices are many—condo bliss (or hell), nondescript high-rises, classic hotels, sprawling resorts, homey bed-and-breakfasts, beachy campsites, budget hostels, no-tell motels…with an equally wide range of price brackets and amenities. You'll find an enormous selection of accommodation options in and around Waikiki. In other areas of the island, however, your choices are somewhat (blissfully) limited. For historic and elegant ambiance, Waikiki's **Halekulani Hotel** (circa 1931) or **Royal Hawaiian Hotel** (circa 1927) are hard to beat. Other luxurious digs include the **Sheraton Moana Surfrider**, **Hilton Hawaiian Village** and **Hawaii Prince Hotel Waikiki** (all in Waikiki), the newly renovated **Kahala Mandarin Oriental Hotel** (Honolulu), **Ihilani Resort and Spa** (Waianae

OAHU

Coast) and **Turtle Bay Hilton** (on the North Shore). The **Outrigger** hotel group offers good value at its various properties. Peak travel months are January, February and August, and the best (and cheapest) rooms might be difficult to come by unless you've booked way ahead. Don't forget the ubiquitous package deals (ask your travel agent or scour newspaper travel sections) that include airfare, accommodations and rental cars in one (usually low) price. And, remember, rooms right *on* the beach are a lot more expensive than rooms a block or so away.

Honolulu

Greater Honolulu

Bed-and-Breakfasts

Manoa Valley Inn   **$99–$190**   ★★★★

2001 Vancouver Drive, Greater Honolulu, 96822, ☎ (800) 535-0085, (808) 947-6019, FAX (808) 946-6168.
Single: $99–$190. Double: $99–$190.
Staying at the Manoa Valley Inn is like going to visit your grandmother or a favorite aunt. There's a lot of mahogany furniture, crocheted table cloths, crystal and well-polished silver. The house itself is an inviting Edwardian bungalow with just the right amount of gingerbread. By Honolulu standards, its location is off the beaten path—in a residential neighborhood just a block from the University of Hawaii campus—but still convenient to downtown. Rooms are furnished with antiques; three share baths. For more privacy, you might want to book the Alexander Cottage (all accommodations are named after prominent missionary families) or the Guild one-bedroom suite. In any case, all have either four-poster or iron beds, fresh tropical flowers and lounge robes. Breakfast is served on the lanai as is an afternoon snack of fruit and cheese. Sunsets are gorgeous. Highly recommended, except for children under 12 or family pets. Smoking allowed on the lanai only. Amenities: balcony or patio. 8 rooms. Credit cards: A, DC, MC, V.

Hotels

Ala Moana Hotel   **$105–$185**   ★★★

410 Atkinson Drive, Greater Honolulu, 96814, ☎ (800) 367-6025, (808) 955-4811, FAX (808) 944-2974. Rated restaurant: Nicholas Nickolas
Single: $105–$185. Double: $105–$185.
The Ala Moana Hotel is big, but even with 1200 rooms, the staff here pays admirable attention to detail and the result is an elegant, smoothly running, international hotel with a large repeat clientele. Business travelers appreciate its close proximity to downtown and government centers. The Ala Moana Shopping Center, one of the largest in the Pacific, is located across the street (a sky bridge is provided for shopaholics), as is Ala Moana Park. The hotel has no fewer than six restaurants, including Tsukasa, which serves Japanese cuisine for breakfast, lunch and dinner, and the Royal Garden, which offers Chinese dishes in an elegant setting for lunch, dinner and a late-night snack. We normally find hotel supper clubs to be overpriced and not very good, but we do recommend that you make a nighttime visit to the Ala

Moana's Nicolas Nikolas penthouse restaurant. It's complete with soft lighting, well-prepared continental cuisine and a spectacular view of downtown Honolulu on one side, and Waikiki on the other. But nightlife doesn't have to stop there—continue celebrating afterwards with dancing at Rumours, currently on the Honolulu "hot spot" list. Accommodations are generally spacious and modern, but vary somewhat in amenities. All have mini-fridges, but not all have in-room safes. Lanais are available in the Waikiki Tower only. It might be worth it to book a room on one of the Concierge floors, where for a bit more dough, you'll get coffee service, a free morning paper, continental breakfast, a lounge, in-room steam and Jacuzzi, nightly turndown and a hair dryer in the bathroom. Amenities: Jacuzzi, balcony or patio, family plan, club floor, business services. 1200 rooms. Credit cards: A, DC, D, MC, V.

Executive Centre Hotel   **$125–$180**   ★★★

1088 Bishop Street, Greater Honolulu, 96813, ☎ (800) 949-EXEC, (808) 539-3000, FAX (808) 523-1088. Rated restaurant: Centre Court.
Single: $125–$180. Double: $125–$180.
As its name implies, the Executive Centre Hotel is one of the increasingly popular all-suite hotels catering to business travelers. The Executive Centre is close to state office buildings, courts, city government buildings, the Iolani Palace and the Aloha Tower Market Place. It's also conveniently located to the airport (the Pali Highway becomes Bishop Street, the hotel is on the right). Studio- and one-bedroom suites have either mountain or ocean views (a fabulous view of the harbor) and private whirlpool baths. One-bedroom suites contain full kitchens and a washer and dryer. Complimentary continental breakfast, free local calls (a terrific deal, believe us!) and a daily newspaper are included in the rate. All units have large desks, three telephones, private voice mail, and there's a 24-hour business center on the premises. The Centre Court restaurant is handy for private dining or business entertaining. It features island-style cuisine in an indoor-outdoor bistro setting and recently won Honolulu Magazine's "Hale Aina" award of merit for "Best Business Lunch." The hotel also offers an Executive Pass for frequent visitors. Discounts on parking, rooms and dining in the restaurant are part of the package. Amenities: business services. 114 rooms.

Hawaii Polo Inn   **$75–$145**   ★★

1696 Ala Moana Boulevard, Greater Honolulu, 96815, ☎ (800) 777-1700, (808) 949-0061.
Single: $75–$145. Double: $75–$145.
Located at the Yacht Club end of Waikiki, the reasonably priced Hawaii Polo Inn offers easy access to shopping at the Ala Moana Shopping Center and leisurely strolls at the Ala Moana Beach Park. Recently refurbished rooms and suites are furnished in beiges and blues and feature refrigerators, color TVs, coffee makers and daily maid service. Kitchenettes available in mini-suites and suites. Some suites have harbor views. Amenities: balcony or patio. 72 rooms. Credit cards: A, CB, DC, MC, V.

Hawaii Prince Hotel Waikiki   **$230–$360**   ★★★★

100 Holomoana Street, Greater Honolulu, 96815, ☎ (800) 321-OAHU, (808) 956-1111, FAX (808) 946-0811. Rated restaurant: Prince Court
Single: $230–$360. Double: $230–$360.

The Hawaii Prince Hotel Waikiki opened in April 1990, and it's ultrasleek. It's twin towers are designed so that all rooms have ocean views from their floor-to-ceiling glass windows overlooking the Ala Wai Yacht Harbor and Waikiki. The Hawaii Prince Waikiki is popular with golfers who really don't want to be out in the boonies. It has its own golf club and 27-hole mix-and-match course designed by Arnold Palmer and Ed Seay. The course covers 270 acres and has 10 lakes and 89 white-sand bunkers. Hotel guests receive preference when being assigned tee times, and shuttle service is available to and form the hotel. Guests have their choice of dining at any of the five locations in the hotel. The most formal is the Prince Court overlooking the yacht harbor. The food is described as Hawaiian bistro and is made from local produce. Hakone is open for lunch and dinner. It serves traditional Japanese cuisine. The Takanawa Sushi Bar is the most informal of the three and very popular with U.S. as well as Japanese guests. Amenities: tennis, exercise room, business services. 521 rooms.

Kahala Mandarin Oriental   **$260–$560**   ★ ★ ★ ★ ★

5000 Kahala Avenue, Greater Honolulu, 96816, ☎ (800) 367-2525, (808) 734-2211, FAX (808) 737-2478. Rated restaurant: Hoku's.

Single: $260–$560. Double: $260–$560.

Longtime visitors to Hawaii will be gratified to know that the Kahala Mandarin Oriental, which opened in March of 1996, is the much-loved Kahala Hilton with a face-lift and some much-needed ($75 million worth) renovations. Located 10 minutes from Waikiki, it seems today—as it did when it opened, to be on another island. Visitors used to wall-to-wall bodies will find themselves almost alone on the hotel's gorgeous 800-square-foot beach, with lots of grassy areas for those who don't want sand between their toes. On a recent late-afternoon visit, the lovely lobby, with its one-of-a-kind, multicolored, cut-glass chandeliers, was practically deserted. Perhaps guests were holed up in their newly redecorated rooms, designed to evoke the Hawaii of old, with Asian accents. The mahogany furnishings contrast handsomely with teak parquet floors, hand-loomed Tibetan area rugs, grass-cloth wall coverings, and local artwork. Some have four-poster beds. There's more mahogany in the sumptuous baths, including the vanity sink accented with traditional faucets and porcelain handles. There have been some startling changes as far as dining choices. The venerable old Maile Room has been reborn as a ballroom. In its place, the hotel has constructed a two-story facility adjacent to the lobby. The new signature restaurant is Hoku's, where every table in the multi-level room has an ocean view. Dishes, conceived by executive chef Oliver Alther (he worked with Michel Guerrard) include Indian naan bread and spicy kebabs, sushi and oysters from the open kitchen and sushi bar. The only thing unchanged about the Plumeria Café is its name. Now an open-air, casual eatery facing the sea, it features Hawaiian music along with casual meals served three times a day. The hotel hopes the built-in buffet area will make it Honolulu's premier weekend brunch location. Other new additions are a Keiki Club for the kids, a fully equipped business center and a fitness center replete with steam room, sauna and Jacuzzi. Oh, and regarding the famous bottle-nose dolphins that frolicked in the hotel's lagoon—housed at Sea Life Park while the hotel was closed—they are reportedly back, although we didn't see them. Amenities: health club, Jacuzzi, sauna, balcony or patio, business services. 370 rooms. Credit cards: A, DC, D, MC, V.

The New Otani Kaimana Beach Hotel $99–$240   ★ ★ ★

2863 Kalakaua Avenue, Greater Honolulu, 96815, ☎ *(800) 733-7949, (808) 923-1555, FAX (808) 922-9404. Rated restaurant: Hau Tree Lanai.*
Single: $99–$240. Double: $99–$240.
In our opinion, The New Otani Kaimana Beach Hotel is what a hotel in the tropics should be. The open-air lobby, renovated as part of a four-year, $10 overhaul which ended in 1989, features a cool marble floor and high ceilings. There's no need for clammy air conditioning. History and nostalgia buffs will be interested to find that Robert Louis Stevenson spent time here in the 1890s, when it was called the Sans Souci Hotel. In addition, the surrounding area was the site of a pitched four day battle during the Annexation Crisis. After annexation, the land was purchased by the McInerny family, retailing tycoons who built their residence where the hotel now stands. Elegant gatherings took place, and the comings and goings of prominent folk were often recorded in newspaper articles of the period. In these articles, the lanai and the hau tree that sheltered it are frequently mentioned. The same hau tree is now covered with fairy lights and lends its name to the hotel's landmark restaurant, the Hau Tree Lanai. The Kaimana Beach is located on Sans Souci Beach, another name for the section of Waikiki which is under Diamond Head. The hotel is surrounded by Kapiolani Park, and all rooms have excellent views either of the ocean or of the park and the city beyond (incredibly lovely at night). Rooms are comfortably sized and carry out the hotel's color scheme of pink, lavender, mauve, cream, and gray. Besides the normal tourist activities, guests or other visitors can purchase kites in the Kite Fantasy shop located on the premises—the park is a perfect place to fly them. The Diamond Head Climbers Hui (club) was founded here, and takes people up the 1.7-mile trail to the top of the old volcano. Public tennis courts and golf course nearby. Amenities: exercise room, balcony or patio. 125 rooms. Credit cards: A, MC, V.

Waikiki

Condos

Aston Waikiki Beach Tower $410–$610   ★ ★ ★ ★

2470 Kalakaua Avenue, Waikiki, 96815, ☎ *(800) 922-3368, (808) 926-6400, FAX (808) 926-7830.*
Single: $410–$610. Double: $410–$610.
These luxurious condominium apartments, located a short walk away from the beach, consist of one- and two-bedroom suites with gourmet kitchens, washer and dryer, wet bars and spacious wrap-around lanais overlooking all of Waikiki Beach. The tastefully decorated rooms, furnished in white, beige and gray, feature separate dining and living areas. There are only four suites per floor, assuring a feeling of exclusivity. The Aston Waikiki Beach Tower prides itself on personal pampering (especially at these prices), including in-room registration, turn-down service, valet parking and other niceties usually available only in the bigger resort hotels. If you're

really feeling flush, book the Penthouse or Presidential suite. On the property is a pool, paddle tennis court and meeting rooms. Children stay free. Amenities: Jacuzzi, sauna, balcony or patio, family plan. 139 rooms. Credit cards: A, DC, MC, V.

Ilima Hotel   **$82–$104**   ★★★

445 Nohonani Street, Waikiki, 96815, ☎ *(800) 367-5172, (808) 923-1877, FAX (808) 924-8371.*
Single: $82–$104. Double: $82–$104.

Only two blocks from Waikiki Beach, the Ilima is a condominium/hotel offering one of the best values for families on long stays. Accommodations range from studios (530 square feet) to 770-square-foot suites. Be warned, though, that the one- and two-bedroom suites are about the same size. The units we saw were done in an rather jarring juxtaposition of reds and terra cotta—definitely not your normal tropical color scheme. Nevertheless, all rooms, including studios, have lanais and kitchens with microwaves. The new Executive Suites contain king-size "waveless" waterbeds, or a regular mattress, whirlpool bath, entertainment center, extra large desk, extra phones and dataports. Extras include continental breakfast and newspapers. Note: The artwork in the lobby, possibly one of the largest collections of "Warrior and Beautiful Maiden" paintings in the world, may be worth a trip in itself. Judge for yourself. Amenities: exercise room, sauna, balcony or patio. 99 rooms. Credit cards: MC, V.

Hotels

Alana Waikiki   **$140–$180**   ★★★

1956 Ala Moana Boulevard, Waikiki, 96815, ☎ *(800) 367-6070, (808) 941-7275, FAX (808) 951-3114. Rated restaurant: Harlequin*
Single: $140–$180. Double: $140–$180.

Located at the entrance to Waikiki Beach on Ala Moana Boulevard, Alana Waikiki Hotel is for sophisticated travelers, not tourists, who desire something more than surf and sand. This boutique hotel is one of the only lodgings we know that has a complete business center with everything from fax machine rentals to translation services, plus a contemporary Museum Gallery AND a 30-piece collection of Picasso ceramics, all under one roof. Commissioned works by distinguished local artists are placed in each guest room. The so-called "luxury suites" are the most desirable accommodations, but all the rooms are spacious, furnished in taupe and mint shades, with plenty of Italian marble in the bathrooms. The Alana's two restaurants, Café Picasso and Harlequin, serve Pacific Rim and Mediterranean cuisine in spare but stylish surroundings. The Heliconia Bar is known for a combination of perfect martinis and piano music. The hotel has no beach, but there's a pool and the concierge can arrange for any watery desires you might harbor. Amenities: exercise room, balcony or patio, family plan, club floor, business services. 313 rooms. Credit cards: A, DC, D, MC, V.

Coconut Plaza Hotel   **$95–$150**   ★★★

450 Lewers Street, Waikiki, 96815, ☎ *(800) 882-9696, (808) 923-8828, FAX (808) 923-3473.*
Single: $95–$150. Double: $95–$150.

The Coconut Plaza is a good example of the growing number of boutique hotels that are becoming more popular in Honolulu and elsewhere. With 80 rooms, the hotel can offer many of the "touches" found in the mega-hotels and still maintain the personalized service that the larger hotels have lost. The Coconut Plaza is located three blocks from Waikiki and overlooks the Ala Wai Canal. Its main view from the lanais is the Koolau Mountains—not your usual Honolulu tourist view, but one that is nonetheless beautiful. The Coconut Plaza has undergone an extensive renovation and has emerged with an open-air, plantation-style decor. There's lots of whitewashed wicker, French doors in the lobby, and the obligatory potted palms to remind us we're in the tropics. The tastefully appointed guest rooms feature relatively subdued floral bedspreads and rattan furniture, including armoires. All but the standard rooms (with wet bar) have kitchen facilities with mini-fridge, microwave and a complete set of cooking utensils. An interesting touch is the use of honeycomb tile for flooring. We haven't seen this before, and we really like it. Together with dhurrie area rugs, it gives a very clean, cool look to the surroundings. Ten executive suites contain a parlor with a queen-size sofabed, adjacent to the bedroom. The new Club Room on the penthouse floor comes complete with a service kitchen, full bar, a living area seating 40 persons, state-of-the-art sound system, and a large-screen TV and VCR. It's ideal for parties, receptions and company functions. A complimentary continental breakfast is served daily in the lobby. Amenities: exercise room, club floor. 80 rooms. Credit cards: A, DC, D, MC, V.

Diamond Head Beach Hotel   **$170–$190**   ★ ★

2947 Kalakaua Avenue, Waikiki, 96815, ☎ *(800) 367-2317, (808) 922-3861, FAX (808) 924-1982.*
Single: $170–$190. Double: $170–$190.
The Diamond Head Beach Hotel is probably about as far from the crowds as it's possible to get in the Waikiki area. Situated at the end of Kalakaua Avenue near the base of Diamond Head, this tall and skinny 14-story building varies considerably in appointments. All but the hotel rooms have full kitchens, and the only ones with lanais are the one-bedroom apartments and suites. The standard and deluxe rooms have to make do with a balcony, but at least the latter have a glimpse of the ocean. All are nicely furnished in wicker and rattan. Although the property faces the ocean, there's no beach or pool. For travelers who don't want to be where the action is, this is a good choice. Included in the rate is a daily continental breakfast and watersports equipment. In-room safes and parking costs extra. Amenities: balcony or patio. 57 rooms. Credit cards: A, DC, D, MC, V.

Ewa Hotel   **$77–$100**   ★ ★

2555 Cartwright Road, Waikiki, 96815, ☎ *(800) 359-8630, (808) 922-1677, FAX (808) 923-8538.*
Single: $77–$100. Double: $77–$100.
The eight-story Ewa is located on the Kapiolani Park end of Waikiki, about a block from the beach. It's not far from the Ala Wai Golf Course or the lighted tennis courts in Kapiolani Park. The rather plain-vanilla rooms are furnished in rattan and have pastel walls and drapes. All but the standard rooms feature lanais and kitchenettes. There's a rooftop recreation deck where you can crane your neck to see the

ocean over the hotel's taller neighbors, but it's fine for sun-worshiping. Given its location, the Ewa offers comfort, a certain measure of style and good value. Amenities: balcony or patio. 90 rooms. Credit cards: A, DC, D, MC, V.

Halekulani $290–$470 ★★★★★

2199 Kalia Road, Waikiki, 96815, ☎ (800) 367-2343, (808) 923-2311, FAX (808) 926-8004. Rated restaurant: La Mer, Orchids
Single: $290–$470. Double: $290–$470.

The legendary Halekulani, in one guise or another, has been welcoming guests to Honolulu since 1907, when it was a residential hotel consisting of a house and five bungalows, situated on Waikiki Beach. In the late 1920s, the original house was torn down and replaced with a more fashionable plantation-style mansion. The mansion was in turn restored and became an integral part of the 1983 renovation. Today the Halekulani consists of five buildings ranging in height from two to 17 stories set among many of the original turn-of-the-century groves and plantings. It's also one of the world's greatest hotels, famed for understated luxury and exemplary services. A personal concierge takes new arrivals to their rooms to register. From then on, all guests are addressed by name. At evening turn-down, a sea-shell is left on the beds. Accommodations are tastefully laid out, with separate seating areas. Furnishings are in muted tones of beige and white with touches of gray and blue. Most have ocean views, and large lanais. Bathrooms feature a separate phone plus posh appointments and toiletries; terry-cloth robes are provided. Sybarites will appreciate the deep-soaking tubs. On a much more mundane level, we appreciated the adjustable reading lamps by the bed. Dining facilities at the Halekulani range from the informal House Without A Key (it takes its name from the Charlie Chan movie) to the ultra-sophisticated La Mer, which serves meals that are an engaging combination of Southern French technique and Island produce. Local seafood is a specialty. Orchids is the spot for breakfast or sunset viewing. There's a fully equipped fitness center with personal trainer available, and regular running sessions and aerobic classes are scheduled. The Beach Center arranges outrigger canoe rides, surfing lessons and more. But most people could spend a good deal of their vacation lounging by the oceanfront pool; its distinctive orchid centerpiece is constructed from over a million glass mosaic tiles imported from South Africa. Amenities: exercise room, balcony or patio, family plan, business services. 412 rooms. Credit cards: A, DC, D, MC, V.

Hawaiian Regent $150–$260 ★★★

2552 Kalakaua Avenue, Waikiki, 96815, ☎ (800) 367-5370, (808) 922-6611, FAX (808) 922-5222. Rated restaurant: Acqua
Single: $150–$260. Double: $150–$260.

The Hawaiian Regent takes up a whole block on Ohua Avenue between Kalakaua Avenue and Kuhio Avenue, which means there is plenty of space for shops and courtyards. It also means that Kalakaua Avenue runs between the Hawaiian Regent and Waikiki Beach, so guests will have to wait for the light to change before they hit the waves. The hotel is built in two towers—the Kalakaua Tower, which is closest to the beach, and the Kuhio Tower, which is taller and stands to the rear of the property. Note that some of the ocean view rooms in the Kuhio Tower have an ocean

OAHU

view but it's looking out over the roof of the Kalakaua Tower. Ask about location before you book your room. Rooms, all of which have lanais, color TVs with first-run movies, refrigerator and a safe, are generally good-sized and decorated in the hotel colors of gray, smoky blue, peach and cream. Chrome, black lacquer and smoked glass lend a high-tech touch to an otherwise tropical environment. Suites run $260–295. Within the hotel is Acqua, a highly regarded bistro on the third floor that overlooks Waikiki Beach and serves innovative Mediterranean-Pacific Rim cuisine; live salsa music is featured Thursday–Saturday. Amenities: tennis, balcony or patio, family plan. 1346 rooms. Credit cards: A, MC, V.

Hawaiian Waikiki Beach Hotel $110–$200 ★★★

2570 Kalakaua Avenue, Waikiki, 96815, ☎ *(800) 877-7666, (808) 922-2511, FAX (808) 923-3656. Rated restaurant: Captain's Table.*
Single: $110–$200. Double: $110–$200.
The Hawaiian Waikiki Beach Hotel is across the street from the beach, on the Diamond Head end of Waikiki. It's within minutes of the zoo, the Waikiki Aquarium and the Waikiki Shell. If a view or glimpse of the ocean is important to you, consider the hotel's Main Tower—it enjoys enough of a setback from its neighbors that almost all of the rooms have an ocean view. Be warned that very few rooms in the smaller, adjacent Mauka Tower have this advantage, but the prices are low by Waikiki standards. All units have voice-mail, safes, color TVs and pay movies; some have mini-fridges. The hotel sets an attractive Sunday brunch in the Captain's Table Restaurant (including omelettes made to order). Lounge with live entertainment in the evenings. Amenities: family plan, business services. 715 rooms. Credit cards: A, MC, V.

Hyatt Regency Waikiki $200–$345 ★★★★

2424 Kalakaua Avenue, Waikiki, 96815, ☎ *(800) 233-1234, (808) 923-1234, FAX (808) 923-7839. Rated restaurant: Ciao Mein*
Single: $200–$345. Double: $200–$345.
By now everyone knows that no hotel can claim to be a Hyatt unless it has a multi-story glassed-in atrium. The Hyatt Regency Waikiki is no exception. The building itself is two 40-story towers joined by a three-story atrium replete with foliage, waterfalls, ponds, lava rock and dendrobium orchids in season. Is it Hawaiian? We wouldn't presume to say, but it is impressive and there is no question that you are in a Hyatt. The hotel boasts that its rooms are oversized, and they don't exaggerate. The color scheme in the rooms, a restful combination of tones of dusty terra-cotta and natural wood, is a welcome relief from the inevitable beiges, tans and cremes found elsewhere. The upper floors of the Diamond Head Tower have been turned into the Regency Club, an area of superior service and extra attention for vacationers and business travelers. Guests in this section enjoy the services of a concierge during business hours, the use of a private lounge, complimentary breakfast with daily newspapers, daily cocktails from 5–7:30 p.m., and a sun deck with Jacuzzi, plus a 360-degree view of the city. Hint: if you can, locate a copy of the booklet called "101 Wonderful Things To On Oahu." In it are the recommendations of the Regency Club Concierges who tell you where to find antique Aloha shirts, who makes the best *malasadas* (Portuguese doughnuts), and how to locate a Chinese herbal pharmacy. In keeping with the current revival of interest in Hawaiian tradi-

tion and culture, the Hyatt Regency is taking pains to offer guests first-hand experience with authentic Hawaiian music, crafts, food and more. Visit Hyatt's Hawaii, a historical center, on the second floor. Quilts, tapa work, feather work and ancient artifacts are just a few of the exhibits. You may even hear Hawaiian spoken by hotel employees, who are encouraged to use the language as they go about their tasks. As you might expect in a hotel this size, guests have a number of options for dining. Ciao Mein, which despite its consciously cute name, is really a good restaurant offering diners the option of Italian or Chinese dinners served family style. The chefs have made a conscious effort to avoid heavy sauces and high fat. The Colony Seafood and Steak House is exactly what its name implies. Guests can select their fresh fish, chicken, beef or seafood from a refrigerated display case. It's then charcoal broiled to your taste. Mushashi offers sushi plus traditional and contemporary Japanese dishes. Amenities: Jacuzzi, balcony or patio, family plan, club floor. 1230 rooms. Credit cards: A, DC, D, MC, V.

Kai Aloha Apartment Hotel $65–$100   ★★

235 Saratoga Street, Waikiki, 96815, ☎ (808) 923-6723, FAX (808) 922-7592.
Single: $65–$100. Double: $65–$100.

The Kai Aloha Apartment Hotel is an old-fashioned, air-conditioned lodging for people who want to be within walking distance of Waikiki Beach (it's about a block away) and not pay exorbitant prices. It offers studios with private lanais and a itty-bitty kitchenette; a much better deal are the spacious one-bedroom apartments, with separate living areas, front and rear porches and full kitchens. These sleep up to five people. Rates include daily maid service, private phone, radio (but no TVs), iron and ironing board, and a coin-op laundry. Note: Saratoga Street is pretty noisy. Amenities: balcony or patio. 18 rooms. Credit cards: A, MC, V.

Kaulana Kai $99–$250   ★★

2425 Kuhio Avenue, Waikiki, 96815, ☎ (808) 922-7777, FAX (808) 922-9473.
Single: $99–$250. Double: $99–$250.

Conveniently located within walking distance of the beach and the Ala Wai Golf Course, the Kaulana Kai was once a rather run-down hotel that has been given a new lease on life. Recently renovated, it's now a boutique-style hotel, spruced up considerably with wood and marble accents. The spacious guest rooms, done up in dusty rose and beige tones, feature refrigerators and in-room safes. Some have kitchenettes or full kitchens. Complimentary breakfast and a shuttle to nearby attractions in Waikiki are among the amenities. There's a pool and a washer-dryer on several floors. All in all, a good value for families and couples on a budget. Amenities: Jacuzzi, sauna, balcony or patio. 69 rooms. Credit cards: A, DC, MC, V.

The Outrigger Waikiki $175–$305   ★★

2335 Kalakaua Avenue, Waikiki, ☎ (800) 688-7444. Rated restaurant: Duke's Canoe Club
Single: $175–$305. Double: $175–$305.

The Outrigger chain of hotels and resorts was founded by Roy Kelley, Jr. with the intention of bringing paradise within reach of the middle class. If your idea of paradise is being in the midst of the pack on Waikiki Beach, then the jumping, lively, Outrigger Waikiki (right on the beach) will be your ideal destination. Rooms are reasonably priced and reasonably sized. They have a few of the frills that the larger resorts have, but the emphasis is on value over luxury. What the Outrigger Waikiki does have is an outstanding entertainment offering in the Main Showroom where the Society of Seven presents a long-running spectacular that is a judicious and carefully extemporaneous combination of Broadway numbers, skits and audience participation. They've hit on a winning formula and it's been going on for years. Contemporary Hawaiian music is performed free each evening from 4–6 p.m. and from 10 p.m.–midnight at the hotel's legendary Duke's Canoe Club, a nostalgically decorated restaurant perched on the sand. Amenities: exercise room, Jacuzzi, balcony or patio, club floor, business services. 530 rooms.

Sheraton Moana Surfrider $230–$395   ★ ★ ★ ★

2365 Kalakaua Avenue, Waikiki, 96815, ☎ (800) 782-9488, (808) 922-3111, FAX (808) 923-0308. Rated restaurant: Ship's Tavern
Single: $230–$395. Double: $230–$395.

In the beginning there was the Moana. Built by the Matson Navigation Company, the Moana opened its doors on March 11, 1901, and has emerged relatively unscathed after the hotel closed for two years in 1987 for a $50 million, much-needed restoration. The only jarring note might be that the Moana was joined with the neighboring Surfrider, a "modern" tower that has architecturally little in common with the older facility. We would definitely recommend that you request the Historic Banyan Ocean rooms or even the City View rooms in the old building. The furnishings and paneling on each floor are made from a different wood: mahogany, oak, maple, cherry and Hawaiian koa. The now air-conditioned rooms are decorated in muted, subdued tones of gray and eggshell, with seafoam-green curtains and brass accents. The blue-wallpapered baths are small and rather dimly lit, but chic and pretty, with circular tubs, old-fashioned faucets and art deco light fixtures. Amenities include Hawaiian soaps and toiletries, and a hair dryer. All the modern conveniences are available including TVs, video-cassette players, refrigerators, mini-bars and safes hidden in wooden armoires. You can turn programs off and on by means of a "one-touch" bedside push-button system. One handy amenity is an illuminated slot for absent-minded guests to place their keycards in. The modern wings are well appointed but lack the charm of the original, but most have lanais and ocean views. The older wing has lanais on only two floors. As part of the restoration process, the management has designed a daily historical walk through the hotel that ends in the Historical Room. Memorabilia from the hotel's past is displayed in special cabinets in various of the public rooms. Among them are the christening dress of the first child born in the hotel (silent screen star Julia Moana Kuhn), newspaper clippings pertaining to the death (under ambiguous circumstances) at the hotel of Mrs. Leland Stanford, and an invitation to a dance given in the ballroom by the officers of the *USS Arizona* on Sept. 22, 1941. The tour leaves at 11 a.m. from the Concierge's Desk in the main lobby. It's free and highly recommended. Facilities include four restaurants; the atmospheric Banyan Court is a delightful and traditional place for a buffet breakfast, afternoon tea, cocktails or Sunday Brunch. Amenities: balcony or patio, business services. 791 rooms. Credit cards: A, DC, D, MC, V.

Sheraton Princess Kaiulani   **$155–$250**   ★★★

120 Kaiulani Avenue, Waikiki, 96815, ☎ *(800) 782-9488, (808) 922-5811, FAX (808) 923-9912. Rated restaurant: Momoyama*
Single: $155–$250. Double: $155–$250.

There really was a Princess Kaiulani. She was the daughter of King David Kalakaua's youngest sister and the heiress presumptive to the throne of Hawaii. While still a child, she became the friend of Robert Lewis Stevenson, who wrote a poem in her honor before she left for school in England. Later, at the age of 17, she journeyed to the mainland where she raised support for the cause of an independent Hawaii. Despite her efforts, and those of other members of her family, Hawaii was annexed by the United States in 1898. Kaiulani's dignity and efforts on her country's behalf won her the affection of all Hawaiians. When she died at the age of 23, she was universally mourned. Kaiulani's childhood home was the royal estate, Ainahau, where the Princess Kaiulani now stands. The Robert Lewis Stevenson Room in the hotel has a well-researched permanent exhibition of photographs and documents pertaining to the life of the young princess and is well worth a visit. That bit of history aside, the hotel, located in the heart of Waikiki, is a thoroughly modern behemoth, and popular with tour groups. The smallish rooms are hotel-bland, modern and characterless. Your best bet might be the Junior Suites in the Ainahau Wing. They have the best views and are furnished with a wet bar, ice maker and whirlpool tub. Among the public rooms are four restaurants, including a Minute Chef for burgers and pizzas, and a Japanese eatery, Momoyama, which is popular with local residents for lunch. The hottest attraction is the Spectacular Polynesian Revue, with dancers from Tahiti, Samoa, Fiji, New Zealand and Tokelau. The show is offered twice nightly in the Ainahau Lounge. Amenities: balcony or patio. 1149 rooms. Credit cards: A, DC, D, MC, V.

Sheraton Waikiki Hotel   **$210–$380**   ★★★

2455 Kalakaua Avenue, Waikiki, 96815, ☎ *(800) 782-9488, (808) 922-4422, FAX (808) 922-9567. Rated restaurant: The Hanohano Room*
Single: $210–$380. Double: $210–$380.

Humongous. Bustling. With 1852 rooms, that's the only way to describe the 25-year-old Sheraton Waikiki. It's aimed at travelers who want the resort experience without a huge price tag, and for the most part, it delivers. The Sheraton has a full program of activities that include fun runs, aerobics, a walking tour through Waikiki to point out the area's history, arts and crafts programs, and cooking demonstrations. Entertainment includes soloists in the Lobby Bar, jazz and the best views in town at the penthouse-level Hanohano Room (where it's great fun to ride to the top in a glass elevator), popular Hawaiian music pool-side, and dancing at the Esprit nightclub. There's also a program for kids ages five–12. What are the rooms like? Viewful. Because of the incredible beachfront location, about 70 percent of them have ocean views. They range from the run-of-the-mill (city view/cheapest) to ultra-luxurious (luxury-ocean/most expensive)—there's something for everyone here. Along with private lanais, all have color TVs and first-run movies, mini-bars and refrigerators, toiletries, coffee makers and in-room video check-out. As of this writing, expect some major changes at the Sheraton Waikiki—selected guest rooms and suites will be refurbished, corridors brightened and meeting rooms and ballrooms upgraded as part of a five-year master plan. Amenities: balcony or patio, family plan, business services. 1852 rooms. Credit cards: A, DC, D, MC, V.

The Aston Waikiki Beachside Hotel $175–$305 ★★★

2452 Kalakaua Avenue, Waikiki, 96815, ☎ *(800) 321-2558, (808) 931-2100.*
Single: $175–$305. Double: $175–$305.

The Aston Waikiki Beachside Hotel prides itself on attentive personal service and has many repeat visitors. It was magically converted from a Motel 6 in the 1960s into an intimate European boutique property where the owners wanted to convey the feeling of an elegant kamaaina home of the 1900s. The custom furnishings, art and antiques were personally selected by Aston chairman Andre Tatibouet and his wife, Jane, including a Coromandel screen, a Chinese altar table and table lamps converted from Japanese candlesticks. One of the most striking pieces is an intricately carved red and black Chinoiserie secretary in the lounge above the lobby, which guests can use. Rooms are extremely well-appointed and decorated with hand-painted tiles in dusty rose, beige and cream, with hand-painted Oriental screens on the walls. Custom-designed armoires hide mini-fridges, TVs and videotape players. Pink and white applique bedcovers are used instead of heavy bedspreads, which gives it a finished look, and the goosedown pillows were imported from England. Maids leave a shell in a silk pouch at turn-down time. Baths feature French-milled soaps, Italian travertine marble floors and showers, and black-and-gold-lacquered vanities (containing a safe) and fixtures. Yukata robes are furnished on request. Phones are equipped with voice mail. Upkeep is meticulous, except for some spotting on the carpets. To our minds, these elegant trappings make up a lot for the smaller-than-average-sized quarters, which resemble staterooms on luxury cruiseships. They are also amazingly quiet, even though the hotel is in the heart of the Waikiki Beach action. Oceanfront rooms have lanais and great views of Kuhio Beach Park. Others are windowless, some have windows that look onto brick walls. There is no restaurant, but an authentic English or Hawaiian (the only one in the state) tea is served in the courtyard by an Italian fountain daily, and continental breakfast is included in the rates. By the summer of 1996, the hotel was to be offering special three-course dinners to guests on request. Amenities: balcony or patio. 79 rooms. Credit cards: A, DC, D, MC, V.

The Breakers $88–$98 ★★

250 Beach Walk, Waikiki, 96816, ☎ *(800) 426-0494, (808) 923-3181, FAX (808) 923-7174.*
Single: $88–$95. Double: $91–$98.

An older hotel located half a block from Waikiki, the Breakers will appeal to those who want a little less-formal environment than the newer high-rises. Rooms are reasonably sized, and have electric kitchenettes and air conditioning. The decor is pretty standard "hotel Hawaiian," but pleasant nonetheless. Well-established plantings around the pool area give the hotel the feeling of permanence (stay away, developers!). The snack bar/lounge at poolside isn't fancy, but the drinks are very cold, and the burgers are some of the best in town. 49 rooms. Credit cards: A, MC, V.

The Ilikai–Hotel Nikko Waikiki $185–$280   ★★★

1777 Ala Moana Boulevard, Waikiki, 96815, ☎ (800) 645-5687, (808) 949-3811, FAX (808) 941-1523. Rated restaurant: Sarento's.
Single: $185–$280. Double: $185–$280.

The Ilikai's location near the yacht harbor combines the best of both worlds—it's just a few minutes away from Honolulu's business district and is also perched ever so closely to the edge of Waikiki. Situated in this spot since 1964, it was a familiar landmark to old-time visitors. Its cachet faded a bit with the advent of newer, more exciting hotels, but a $50 million renovation in 1991 put it back on track. The Ilikai has gained back some pizzaz as the home of Coconuts Nightclub, one of Waikiki's best venues for jazz. Intimate Sarento's, on the top of the "I," is great for romantic interludes. Most of the Ilikai's rooms have lanais and are exceptionally large; some of them almost 600 square feet. White walls and pastel carpeting make them seem even more spacious. More than 200 rooms also feature full kitchen facilities, great for families and long stays. As you get to the upper floors, if the view seems familiar, it probably means that you still watch "Hawaii Five-O" reruns on television. Remember the opening shot with Jack Lord as Steve McGarrett and McGarrett is standing with his back to the Honolulu skyline? It was shot from the Ilikai penthouse balcony and the view is just as spectacular now as it was then. Amenities: tennis, exercise room, business services. 800 rooms.

The Outrigger Prince Kuhio $135–$195   ★★★

2500 Kuhio Avenue, Waikiki, 96815, ☎ (800) 688-7444. Rated restaurant: Trellises.
Single: $135–$195. Double: $135–$195.

The Outrigger Prince Kuhio, the chain's most luxurious property, has recently undergone an extensive refurbishment that includes converting the 34th and 35th floors of the hotel into the Kuhio Club with concierge service, complimentary continental breakfast, evening hors d'oeuvres and a guest library. Business travelers to the Kuhio Club have access to laser-printing facilities (for use with laptops), and postal and handling fees are waived for club members while using the hotel business center. The hotel has also installed a Meridian Mail voice-messaging system that is among the most advanced in the world. Guests are able to record their own messages on the voice-mail system or take advantage of pre-recorded greetings in English, Japanese, Korean or German. Incoming messages are held in the guest's private mailbox until they are retrieved via remote touch-tone phones from anywhere on the island. Located a block from the beach, the Outrigger Prince Kuhio has ocean views on one side and views of the Koolau Mountains on the other. Most rooms have private lanais, marble baths and wet bars. Complimentary coffee is offered daily in the lobby. Amenities: balcony or patio, club floor, business services. 625 rooms. Credit cards: A, DC, D, MC, V.

The Outrigger Reef $145–$275   ★★

2169 Kalia Road, Waikiki, ☎ (800) 688-7444, (808) 922-2887. Rated restaurant: The Shore Bird Broiler.
Single: $145–$275. Double: $145–$275.

The Outrigger Reef, which opened its doors in 1955, was one of Roy Kelley's earlier undertakings on Waikiki. It has recently undergone a $50 million renovation, which included repainting all the guest rooms. They are now furnished in washed white wicker, pale-brown carpets and have floral print bedcovers. Most rooms have lanais, and at least a partial view of the ocean. If you forgot to bring something with you, you can buy a replacement locally in one of the 15 shops and boutiques located in the lobby. Amenities: business services. 885 rooms. Credit cards: A, DC, D, MC, V.

The Outrigger Reef Towers $95–$100   ★ ★

227 Lewers Street, Waikiki, 96815, ☎ *(800) 688-7444, (808) 923-9861.*
Single: $95–$100. Double: $95–$100.
The Outrigger Reef Towers has become something of a landmark in the Waikiki area simply because it's been there so long (by Honolulu standards). First opened in 1959, it was another of Roy Kelley's successful attempts to market Hawaii to the masses. By today's standards the rooms are a little on the small side. Most have balconies, but the heavy full-length drapes give the rooms a needlessly heavy look, yet are useful for keeping the light out in the morning after a rollicking night out on the town. Furniture is institutional rattan and the room we saw was done in tones of blue—blue carpets, blue drapes, blue floral print on the beds, blue lamps...all it lacked was Elvis singing "Blue Hawaii." The Reef Towers' Polynesian Palace night club offers nightly entertainment. The local singing/comedy team of Frank DeLima and Glenn Medeiros (a Hawaiian Martin and Lewis) are immensely popular with residents. When she's in town, Charo (the "belle of cootchie cootchie") offers a cross-cultural experience as she offers a program of Latin comedy, dance and Spanish flamenco guitar under the palms. 480 rooms. Credit cards: A, DC, D, MC, V.

The Royal Garden at Waikiki $120–$500   ★ ★ ★ ★

440 Olohana Street, Waikiki, 96815, ☎ *(800) 367-5666, (808) 943-0202, FAX (808) 946-8777. Rated restaurant: Cascada, Shizu.*
Single: $120–$500. Double: $120–$500.
Opened in 1993, the Royal Garden is a tower of luxury located about a half-block from the beach. The lobby is a cool expanse of marble and brass and crystal chandeliers. The focal point are the terraced gardens surrounding the two swimming pools. A waterfall splashes above the main pool. Fronting the waterfall is the hotel's signature restaurant, Cascada, where you dine on Mediterranean-French cuisine under a hand-painted ceiling. The guest accommodations range from standard rooms to royal suites, and feature lanais, sitting rooms, "closet space for kings," marble baths and wet bars. Some rooms have lovely mahogany four-poster beds with padded headboards and satin quilts. All have some kind of ocean view; the vista gets better and the prices higher on the uppermost floors. Continental breakfast is included in the rates. Amenities: exercise room, Jacuzzi, sauna, balcony or patio, club floor, business services. 230 rooms. Credit cards: A, CB, DC, D, MC, V.

The Royal Hawaiian Hotel $275–$505   ★ ★ ★ ★

2259 Kalakaua Avenue, Waikiki, 96815, ☎ *(800) 325-3535, (808) 923-7311, FAX (808) 924-7098. Rated restaurant: The Surf Room*
Single: $275–$505. Double: $275–$505.
The publicity releases for the Royal Hawaiian describe its distinctive pink color as "plumeria pink." Perhaps we have led a too-sheltered life, but we've never seen a plumeria that's this particular shade of pink. Mexican pastries and ice cream, yes.

Plumeria, no. In fact, the Royal Hawaiian's Moorish facade has always reminded us a little of an ice cream mold (why isn't it melting?) of the Alamo set down among the banyan trees and coconut palms. At any rate, The Royal Hawaiian is one of the hotels constructed by the Matson Navigation Company in the days when a Honolulu was seven days away from Los Angeles or San Francisco. Since it opened its doors in 1927, The Royal has been a focal point of life on Waikiki and is still going strong after recently undergoing a $10 million refurbishment and several additions. If you crave nostalgia, ask for a room in the original building, which retains its high ceilings, native wooden paneling and views out into the tropical gardens. Expect a riot of pink, including the ironing boards and terry bathrobes. For fun, take a ride in the "Bathers Elevator." The newer and more expensive Tower Oceanfront rooms are in a modern addition. They are completely luxurious, and feature lanais, but lack the charm of the older section. The beachfront Surf Room, the hotel's main dining room, has been a gathering place for world travelers and locals for years. Here, freshly baked pink cookies are a traditional after-dinner treat, and a mai tai from the Mai Tai Bar right on the beach is like none other. Amenities: balcony or patio, business services. 526 rooms. Credit cards: A, DC, D, MC, V.

The Waikiki Joy Hotel $150–$205   ★★★

320 Lewers Street, Waikiki, ☎ *(800) 922-7866, (808) 923-2300. Rated restaurant: Capuccinos*
Single: $150–$205. Double: $150–$205.

The former Sherry Waikiki, this intimate boutique hotel with an Italian marble accented open air lobby IS a joy, especially for music-lovers. On the property is an in-house karaoke studio, with 15 private rooms, where guests can choose from a music library of more than 4000 songs and warble to their heart's content. A bar (de riguer to loosen you up) and hors d'oeuvres are part of the package; great fun for private parties. Also, each guest room, nicely decorated with new berber carpets and light blue and pink color schemes, is equipped with entertainment centers with state-of-the-art JVC Bose sound systems, as well as an oval Jacuzzi and refrigerator. If you want a lanai, you'll have to book one of the suites, located in an adjacent tower next to the pool. The Executive Suites have the largest ones, as well as full kitchens that include a rice cooker. Club Suites have a microwave and wet bar. Located off the veranda, where a daily complimentary breakfast is served, is Capuccinos Café, a coffee bar with a limited menu of finger sandwiches and pastries. In the summer of 1996, the hotel was to venture boldly into cyberspace with the addition of computers and modems so guests can surf the Internet. Amenities: sauna. 94 rooms. Credit cards: A, DC, D, MC, V.

Waikiki Parc Hotel $160–$245   ★★★★

2233 Helumoa Road, Waikiki, 96815, ☎ *(800) 422-0450, (808) 921-7272, FAX (808) 923-1336. Rated restaurant: Kacho, The Parc Café*
Single: $160–$245. Double: $160–$245.

The Waikiki Parc Hotel appeals to those who are searching for "affordable luxury." It has a great location, about 100 yards from the beach, but is about half the price of the Halekulani, its sister hostelry across the street. The rooms, which could be termed a little snug for big *haoles* (most guests are Japanese), are decorated in a clean, spare style. Somehow there's enough room for a rattan loveseat, a glass top coffee table, a writing desk, plus a comfortable queen bed. Color schemes are beige, blond and white, with touches of blue. Ceramic tile floors have inlaid carpets. Attractive white-shuttered doors open onto pocket lanais. Along with the ocean views, you get to gaze onto the Halekulani's famed orchid-tiled pool. The use of lighting in rooms is clever, well-thought-out and practical, including soft night-lights under the bedside tables, and overhead reading lamps with dimmers. Amenities include a mini-fridge and well-stocked honor bar, flashlight, hair dryer, custom toiletries and an in-room safe ($3.50 per day). Bath towels are nice and thick. There's a pool and sundeck on the eighth floor and a sundry shop off the lobby. The Waikiki Parc has two restaurants—the Parc Café, a local favorite, which serves four kinds of buffets (great homemade potato chips), and Kacho, which features a sushi counter in addition to table seating for Japanese meals. Amenities: balcony or patio. 298 rooms. Credit cards: A, DC, D, MC, V.

Resorts

Hilton Hawaiian Village   **$155–$335**   ★ ★ ★ ★

2005 Kalia Road, Waikiki, 96815, ☎ *(800) HIL-TONS, (808) 949-4321. Rated restaurant: The Bali, The Golden Dragon.*

Single: $155–$335. Double: $155–$335.

The Hilton Hawaiian Village is for sociable types who absolutely don't want to get away from it all. The resort is the largest in Hawaii and has more than 2500 rooms. At any given time, there are probably 4000 guests registered, and there's something going on 24 hours a day. It consists of several high-rise towers, has its own shopping centers, a Thai temple, a Japanese *minka* (farm house), and a 50-foot replica of a Japanese pagoda. The builders constructed a beach by blasting and dredging the rocky shoreline and replacing it with 30,000 cubic yards of sand. The main swimming pool, the 10,000-square foot "superpool," is surrounded by waterfalls and lava rock, often super-busy with kids. The grounds are home to 25 species of birds, and the artificial lagoon and ponds are stocked with Japanese carp selected for their brilliant coloring. The resort's most luxurious accommodations, and well worth the expense, are in the Ali'i Tower, consisting of 348 rooms and suites. One of the advantages is that guests in the tower are whisked to their rooms for check-in by the concierge, therefore avoiding the long lines at the main registration desk. Decor and furnishings are designed to evoke the turn-of-the-century feel of an elegant residence. This aim just about succeeds. Rooms are lovely, decorated in peach and pale blue tones, with light wood and wicker furniture, pewter bedside lamps and tasteful watercolors. Also reasonably spacious, there's enough room for a loveseat and easy chair. The hotel's flagship restaurants are The Bali, which features Pacific Rim cuisine, and The Golden Dragon, which has been serving Cantonese dishes since the hotel opened. After-dark entertainment includes the group Olomana, playing contemporary Hawaiian music on Friday and Saturday nights in the Paradise Lounge, and Noly Pa'a in the Shell Bar from Tuesday through Sunday. For a real change of pace, take in magician John Hirokawa's magic show in the Hilton Dome Showroom, twice nightly. Amenities: exercise room, Jacuzzi, balcony or patio, family plan, club floor. 2542 rooms. Credit cards: A, DC, D, MC, V.

Leeward Oahu

Kapolei

Resorts

Ihilani Resort and Spa   **$275–$550**   ★★★★★

92-1001 Olani Street, Kapolei, 96707, ☎ *(800) 626-4446, (808) 679-0079, FAX (808) 679-0080. Rated restaurant: Azul*
Single: $275–$550. Double: $275–$550.

Twenty-five minutes away from the Honolulu Airport, the Ihilani is far removed from urban chaos. It forms part of the 640-acre Ko Olina Resort and enjoys a gorgeous artificial beach-lagoon teeming with marine life. About 85 percent of the rooms in the 15-story tower have ocean or lagoon views. The rooms are generously proportioned at 680 square feet or more, and have large lanais. Comfortable padded teak furniture reminiscent of those found on the *Queen Mary* are strategically placed there for guests to enjoy their view in comfort. James Bond's "Q" might have had a hand in designing the state-of-the-art bedside telephones that turn off lights, control the room temperature, even tell you the time in any country in the world. Much better than the "Clapper." One of the major attractions of the resort is its 18-hole Ko Olina Golf Course, designed by Ted Robinson and voted one of the top 75 courses in the United States by *Golf Digest*. Morning tee times are reserved for hotel guests. The other major attraction is the hotel's health and fitness spa. Great use is made of seawater (it's one of the two places in the country to offer authentic Thalasso treatments) and sea weed therapies. Men's and women's massage rooms are available. Herbal wraps using Hawaiian herbs are a house specialty. Diners have a number of choices at Ihilani. Azul, serving Mediterranean cuisine is the premier restaurant. The Naupaka Terrace presents "cross cultural" cuisine in a relaxed setting with views over the lagoon and pool area, while Ushio-tei is a traditional Japanese restaurant with a sushi bar and some tatami rooms. The children's program, The Keiki Beachcomber's Club, is run by enthusiastic people who love what they do. Amenities: tennis, health club, exercise room, Jacuzzi, sauna, balcony or patio, family plan, business services. 387 rooms. Credit cards: A, DC, D, MC, V.

North Shore

Haleiwa

Rentals

Ke Iki Hale   **$85–$145**   ★★★

Haleiwa, 96712, ☎ *(808) 638-8229.*
Single: $85–$145. Double: $85–$145.

K'e Iki Hale is for people who don't mind roughing it—a little. Alice Tracy's beach compound consists of tidy, thatched, one- and two-bedroom oceanside cottages on an acre-and-a-half on wild and secluded K'e Iki Beach, located between Shark's Cove (great for snorkeling) and Ehukai Beach (home of the Banzai Pipeline). Units have large picture windows, and kitchens and are stocked with towels and utensils.

Outdoor showers hang from coconut trees. Other attractions include the nearby Polynesian Cultural Center, Waimea Falls Park, numerous restaurants and the hammocks in the yard. Units available by the week. 12 rooms. Credit cards: MC, V.

Kahuku

Resorts

The Turtle Bay Hilton   **$200–$285**   ★ ★ ★

57-091 Kamehameha Highway, Kahuku, 96731, ☎ *(800) HIL-TONS, (808) 293-8811, FAX (808) 293-1286. Rated restaurant: The Cove*
Single: $200–$285. Double: $200–$285.

The Turtle Bay Hilton, built in 1972, is located on the end of Kuilima Point, which juts out over roiling waves on Oahu's fabled North Shore. Although parts of the property are run down, especially the section facing the sea, this setting—and the fact that it's the only resort on this coast—are the hotel's biggest draws. One of the resort's two beaches is a sandy crescent protected by an offshore reef. There are 27 holes of championship golf, including the Links at Kuilima, which was ranked fourth among *Golf Digest's* top 10 picks for best new courses. Other recreational pursuits range from a game on one of 10 Plexi pave tennis courts or a clinic at the Nick Bolletieri Tennis Academy, to daily trail rides from the resort's stables. Among the five restaurant/snack shops are The Cove, a fine-dining establishment featuring live Maine lobster accompanied by sunset views. We liked the all-you-can-eat pizza and pasta bar with evening entertainment in the Bay View Lounge. If "Loco Moco" is playing when you get there, don't miss them—this duo is fabulous. Service standards are high and unfailingly courteous, including a housekeeping staff that will cheerfully bring you an iron and ironing board after 10 p.m. All accommodations have ocean views, some with lanais. Although large and comfortable, and decorated in orange, peach, teal and green schemes, furnishings seem dated, even after a 1992 renovation. Closet space is surprisingly ample. Amenities include coffee makers ($3 per packet), cable TV with free HBO and pay-per-view movies. Amenities: tennis, horseback riding, exercise room, balcony or patio, family plan. 485 rooms. Credit cards: A, MC, V.

Windward Oahu

Kailua

Bed-and-Breakfasts

Papaya Paradise Bed and Breakfast   **$70**   ★ ★

395 Auwinala Road, Kailua, 96734, ☎ *(808) 261-0316.*
Single: $70. Double: $70.

Far from the madding crowd on Waikiki, Papaya Paradise Bed and Breakfast is 20 miles away on the windward side of the island, just a short walk from one of the country's best white-sand beaches, Kailua Beach Park. Your hosts are Jeannette and Bob Martz, who offer two units in their contemporary bungalow. Although small, both have private entrances and private baths, and are furnished in tropical rattan and wicker. Each has two beds, two lounge chairs, ceiling fans and air conditioning, phone and cable TV. Units open onto a poolside lanai, where papaya, of course, is served for breakfast along with pancakes, eggs and home fries. Bob, the chef, is a retired Naval officer, and specializes in something called SOS—ground beef and gravy on toast. There's also a Jacuzzi and well-tended tropical garden. Beach gear, including coolers, are provided. Guests are free to use the refrigerator and microwave, and a small library. Free parking. Children under six are accepted, and there is a cat on the premises. Amenities: sauna. 2 rooms. Credit cards: not accepted.

Rental

John Walker's Beach House   **$325**

572 Kailua Road, Suite 201, Kailua, 96734, ☎ (808) 261-7895.

Single: $325. Double: $325.

John Walker was an adventuresome Scot who came to Hawaii in the 1870s. He became a contractor, and among his buildings are the Bishop Museum and Honolulu *Hale* (City Hall). This white bungalow with a stone wall and screened-in porches was his weekend retreat, one of the first to be built fronting the pristine white sands of the otherwordly Lanikai Beach. It's furnished with a comfortable mix of period furniture and functional rattan. It has three bedrooms, two baths, a kitchen, sauna and cabana. There's also a two-bedroom, one-bath cottage (at additional cost). The two buildings share a courtyard, while the main house has its own picnic/patio area. Amenities: sauna, balcony or patio. 5 rooms. Credit cards: MC, V.

Kaneohe

Bed-and-Breakfasts

Ali'i Bluffs Windward Bed and Breakfast   **$55–$65**

46-251 Ikiiki Street, Kaneohe, 96744, ☎ (808) 235-1124.

Single: $55–$65. Double: $55–$65.

The Ali'i Bluffs Windward Bed and Breakfast enjoys a privileged location overlooking Kaneohe Bay. A private home with bedrooms to let, it's a bed-and-breakfast in the true sense of the word—in fact co-host Donald Munro learned the art of running one from his mother who had one in Scotland. The decor is an interesting combination of Victorian pieces juxtaposed with collectibles from various periods. The Victorian Room (with attached private bath) has a walk-in closet and a double bed. The Circus Room (with a private bath across the hall) has extra-long twin beds. There are hair dryers in each room. An "expanded" continental breakfast of fruit, home-baked banana bread, toast and coffee, and assorted juices is served at a time designated by the guest (a gracious gesture). Late-afternoon tea is served in the living room, and ice and glasses are placed there in the evening for guests to make their own nightcap. The house has a pool, and beach gear, coolers and road maps are provided for trips to Kailua Beach Park, one of the state's best beaches, which is only 15 minutes away. No pets, please, as Munro and his partner De, an artist and retired fashion designer, have two small Maltese terriers (who, by the way, get along great with all the guests). 2 rooms. Credit cards: not accepted.

Hanauma Bay, Oahu

Byodo-in Temple, Kaneohe

Waimea Bay surfer

Surfboards on Waikiki Beach

Where to Eat

You'll find everything your stomach will ever desire in Oahu, where hotels and resorts routinely recruit some of the world's finest chefs (the way to the tourists' dollars is through their...). As with accommodations, there's something for every pocketbook—from cheap and filling plate lunches for a beach side picnic to silver-service fine dining on gourmet cuisine by candlelight. Feast on creative Pacific Rim specialties, traditional Polynesian favorites, fresh-from-the-sea fish, Japanese saimin or American Spam, a spectacular array of ethnic specialties (especially Chinese and Japanese), fast food galore, or just-picked fruits, nuts and veggies. The dining scene is centered mostly around Waikiki and Honolulu, though you won't go hungry anywhere on the island. Try one or more of the excellent restaurants in Honolulu's **Restaurant Row** (on Ala Moana Boulevard) or **Aloha Tower Marketplace** and don't miss out on a meal at one of the branches of **Keo's Thai Restaurant** or at **Orchids** (in the Halekulani Hotel).

Aiea/Pearl City

Aiea

Bandito's Cantina $ ★★
  98-151 Pali Momi Street, Aiea, ☎ *(808) 488-8888.*
  Mexican cuisine. Specialties: Blackened chicken tacos, seafood enchiladas.
  Lunch: 11 a.m.–9:30 p.m., entrées $6–$10.
  Dinner: 11 a.m.–9:30 p.m., entrées $6–$10.
  A fine spot to dine while shopping at Pearlridge Center, Bandito's makes some attempts to get creative with a few southwestern and Baja-style selections scattered among the usual combo plates. Decor is bright and corny, with wahines dressed up like señoritas from south of the border. It's great. Credit cards: MC, V.

Honolulu

Downtown

A Little Bit of Saigon $$ ★★
  1160 Maunakea Street, downtown, ☎ *(808) 528-3663.*
  Asian cuisine. Specialties: Pho, coconut chicken, green papaya and shrimp salad.
  Lunch: 10 a.m.–10 p.m., entrées $6–$16.
  Dinner: 10 a.m.–10 p.m., entrées $6–$16.
  This otherwise plain little Chinatown eatery makes a stab at decent decor with the addition of paintings and plants. But most people bypass the wall trimmings in favor

of staring into a cavernous bowl of *pho*—fat-free beef in a signature broth. Accompanying this small masterpiece are fresh basil leaves, onions and an array of appropriate condiments that you add as you like—bean sprouts for crunch and jalapeno peppers for ouch. If it's too hot for soup, another specialty, green papaya and shrimp salad, is appropriately zingy with a happy blending of cool mint, lip-puckering limes, garlic and chiles. If just an appetizer will do, the spring rolls with crabmeat and shrimp are recommended. Credit cards: MC, V.

Big Island Steak House $$$ ★★

101 Ala Moana Boulevard, Suite 279, downtown, 96813, ☎ *(808) 537-4446.*
American cuisine. Specialties: Black and Blue ahi, steaks, prime rib, fresh local seafood, Mauna Kea brownie.
Lunch: 11 a.m.–2:30 p.m., entrées $7–$12.
Dinner: 6–9:30 p.m., entrées $13–$19.

Decked out in a luxe beach-hut style, with steamer trunks, hula dolls and a wooden canoe, all that's missing from the dining room of this '40s Waikiki-style restaurant at the Aloha Tower Marketplace is a sarong-clad Dorothy Lamour swaying and singing to a corny old song. Everything is high camp to the max, including the pupu and cocktail menus written on coconuts. To immerse yourself in the whole experience, order the Mauna Kea brownie for dessert—this clever concoction is covered with ice cream, raspberry lava sauce and browned meringue, and brought to the table erupting in flames. The kids'll love it. Oh, and there are sensuous views of Honolulu Harbor from the open-air lanai. Features: outside dining, own baking.

Buddhist Vegetarian Restaurant $ ★★★

100 North Beretania Street, Chinatown Cultural Plaza, downtown, ☎ *(808) 532-8218.*
Chinese cuisine. Specialties: Cantonese vegetarian entrées, dim sum.
Lunch: 10:30 a.m.–2 p.m., entrées $8.
Dinner: 5:30–10 p.m., entrées $9.

Exactly as its name implies, the Buddhist Vegetarian Restaurant serves zingy dishes in the Cantonese vein without a trace of meat, in simple, Zen-like surroundings. This eatery's repertoire is surprisingly huge and inventive—tofu and seaweed are fashioned to resemble a fish fillet; the Hawaiian staple, taro, is sculpted into a receptacle cupping perfectly cooked veggies. Dim sum is rolled around on carts, the choices awaiting your selection. Not a few have exotic (perhaps revolting) ingredients such as moss and tree fungus mixed in with more prosaic carrots, broccoli, mushrooms and pine nuts. But don't be fearful—they're delicious. Like many Chinese restaurants, it's best to come here with a group, but be aware that there are only 12 tables. Open 8 a.m.–2 p.m. and 5:30–10 p.m. on Saturdays and Sundays. Reservations recommended. Credit cards: A, MC, V.

Gordon Biersch $$$

101 Ala Moana Boulevard, in the Aloha Tower Marketplace, downtown, ☎ *(808) 599-4877.*
American cuisine. Specialties: House-brewed beers, fish, steak, lobster.
Lunch: 11:30 a.m.–2:30 p.m., entrées $13–$19.
Dinner: 2:30 p.m.–11:30 p.m., entrées $13–$19.

Gordon Biersch does double duty as a restaurant/hot spot with music and a full-fledged brewery. And it ain't Primo beer, either. Two burly varieties (Marzen and dark Dunkel) plus a mellow Export our German friends would admire are concocted within the million-dollar, industrial-size, stainless-steel vats right within the establishment. Chef Kelly Degala's garlic fries are a perfect accompaniment, along with a host of other *ono* pupus. Added to the list of steaks and fish are some daring nightly specials from the "contemporary Pacific Rim" school of cookery. Most tables have great views of the Honolulu Harbor, especially from the open-air lanai, if you look up from partying long enough to notice. Features: outside dining, own baking. Reservations recommended. Credit cards: A, CB, DC, MC, V.

Indigo   **$$$**   ★ ★ ★ ★
1121 Nuuanu Avenue, Suite 105, downtown, ☎ *(808) 521-2900.*
Asian cuisine. Specialties: Goat cheese wontons with four fruit sauce, fiery explosions to heaven shrimp, Madame Pele's Mousse.
Lunch: 11 a.m.–2 p.m., entrées $12–$25.
Dinner: 5–9:30 p.m., entrées $12–$25.
When it opened, Glenn Chu's creative Eurasian restaurant with a "streets of Singapore" ambiance was voted the Best New Restaurant by the upstart *Honolulu Weekly.* Creative appetizers are the specialty here, including goat-cheese won tons with four-fruit sauce, vegetarian spring rolls, grilled spice chicken with Indigo peanut sauce, or lobster pot-stickers, so don't be afraid to graze. A dessert master (he used to own a pastry shop called RoxSan Patisserie in Ward Centre), chef Chu's signature dish is a kid's science experiment of a sweet called Madame Pele's Chocolate Volcano with Haupia Mousse; it actually breathes smoke as it's brought proudly to your table. Not for the bashful. Features: own baking, non-smoking area. Reservations recommended. Credit cards: A, DC, D, MC, V.

Pacific Vegetarian Café   **$**   ★ ★
Aloha Tower Marketplace, downtown, ☎ *(808) 536-6767.*
cuisine. Specialties: Vegetarian dishes with an international flavor, salads, sandwiches, soups.
Lunch: 9 a.m.–6 p.m., entrées $4–$6.
Dinner: 5–9 p.m., entrées $4–$6.
The Pacific Vegetarian Café (formerly the loftily named The Higher Taste) offers an intriguing take out menu of luscious-sounding international vegetarian specialties, all priced under $6. Called World Food, you can pick from five kinds of plate lunches or dinners from five countries. Be transported to Morocco, for example, with a taste of pastillas, traditional "special occasion" pies baked with a tofu, almond and onion filling with a touch of honey. Accompaniments include tabouleh, hummus, salad greens and chips. Items on the salad menu come in half ($3.50) or whole ($5.50) sizes; you may choose from spinach and shiitake salad with balsamic honey dijon dressing and pine nuts, or taco salad with fat-free refried beans and spicy soya burger in lieu of ground meat, served in a tortilla shell and topped with two cheeses and sour cream. Sandwiches (falafels, gardenburger, soy "sloppy joes") and soups (Hawaiian style miso with tofu) are also alternatives. Those less-hungry can opt for a baked potato or Indian samosas (both $3.50) from a list of light(er) bites. The Café is located on the second floor of the Aloha Tower Marketplace, in the Makai Food Lanai. Reservations not accepted. Credit cards: A, D, MC, V.

OAHU

People's Café $ ★★

1300 Pali Highway, downtown, ☎ *(808) 536-5789.*

Specialties: Hawaiian plate lunch, kalua pig, pipikaula.

Lunch: 10:30 a.m.–7:30 p.m., entrées $5–$10.

Dinner: 4–7:30 p.m., entrées $5–$10. Closed: Sun.

In a setting that's older than Don Ho's Polynesian revue, eating at this authentic Hawaiian coffee shop is like attending a neighborhood luau. The *pipikaula* (a type of beef jerky) served here is the definitive version. You can order it á la carte, but it also comes with the Kalua Plate ($8.80), a generous serving of appropriately smoky shredded pork, lomilomi salmon, chicken long rice, white rice and poi. If you're the more adventurous type, sample the squid luau or oxtail stew. Reservations not accepted.

Greater Honolulu

3660 On The Rise $$$ ★★★★

3660 Waialae Avenue, Greater Honolulu, ☎ *(808) 737-1177.*

Asian cuisine. Specialties: Pan-seared rock shrimp and taro cake, topped with banana salsa, osso buco Asian style.

Dinner: 5:30–9 p.m., entrées $12–$28. Closed: Mon.

Recipient of several distinguished dining awards, this "cross-cultural" (mostly Asian and European) restaurant is also one of the best places on the island to dig your fork into a choice steak. A signature dish of this type is pan-seared New York steak Alaea, seasoned fearlessly in secret house spices, and topped with crisp onions. In order to belong to the Hawaii Regional Cuisine club, you must "create, create, create," and chef/co-owner Russell Siu, along with Jim Gillespie, do their part with monthly changing menus. Added recently to a list of old faves such as ti-leaf-wrapped seafood topped with lomi tomato sauce and ahi katsu are homemade smoked chicken sausage and spinach salad with honey mustard dressing. If customers beg often enough, previous specials return. Russell's wife, Lisa, is a fantastic pastry chef; witness the oft-requested angel-food cake, or warm chocolate soufflé cake with vanilla ice cream and mocha sauce, and Mile High Waialae pie, made with layers of vanilla and coffee ice cream, macadamia brittle and caramel and chocolate sauces—this woman needs to be locked up for our own good. The restaurant also hosts cooking classes every other month, as well as wine dinners. Note: the Sius also operate a gourmet (natch) plate lunch place, **Kakaako Kitchen**, *1216 Waimanu Street*, between Pensacola and Piikoi Streets, Honolulu, ☎ *(808) 596-7488.* It's open Monday-Friday from 6:30 a.m.–2 p.m. Freshly baked pastries and desserts are a highlight. Features: own baking, rated wine cellar. Reservations recommended.

Credit cards: A, CB, DC, MC, V.

A Pacific Café–Oahu $$$ ★★★★

1200 Ala Moana Boulevard, in Ward Centre, Greater Honolulu, ☎ *(808) 593-0035.*

cuisine. Specialties: Appetizer bar, Caesar salad over parmesan mozzarella pizza bread, Toasted Hawaiian.

Lunch: 11:30 a.m.–2 p.m., entrées $7–$26.

Dinner: 5:30–10 p.m., entrées $7–$26.

Located on the third floor of Ward Centre, Jean Marie Josselin's new A Pacific Café (the original is in Kauai, and the second branch is in Maui) has even jaded Honolulu gourmands all agog. Opened in April 1996, it features Hawaii's first ever pupu (appetizer) bar. Situated next to the main dining room, the bar has an inviting open kitchen, outfitted with a wood-burning oven and a sushi area. Here, grazers can sit at a granite counter and watch chefs create a variety of little bites right before their dazzled orbs. On weekends, it stays open until midnight—perfect for the after-the-ater crowd. However, everyone must venture into the main dining room eventually, where diners are made to feel like the little mermaid in her undersea world. Josselin's artist wife, Sophie, and architectural designer Robert Mechielsen (from Malibu, of course) were responsible for the design concept, even down to the eclectic lighting fixtures, which were inspired by "visions of seaweed, sea creatures and beach glass." Wow. No expense was spared, from the slate floors imported from China, and artwork by local Kauai and Oahu artists. Another first for the Oahu restaurant is that it is the only branch to offer lunch. Although both lunch and dinner menus change with the seasons, a signature lunch item is smoked salmon pizza with herb cream cheese and arugula salad; at dinner patrons might try porcini and fresh herb-crusted island opakapaka with fennel and dry tomato Israeli couscous and baby vegetables. The magnificent desserts are the creations of Josselin's protege, John Castello, a Kauai native who started as a line cook. The "Toasted Hawaiian" is a steamed white-chocolate cake layered with haupia, toasted macadamia nut mousse served with caramel sauce and Tahitian vanilla bean creme anglaise. Features: own baking, rated wine cellar. Reservations recommended. Credit cards: A, CB, DC, D, MC, V.

Alan Wong's $$$ ★★★★

1857 South King Street, McCully Center, 5th Floor, Greater Honolulu, ☎ (808) 949-2526.
International cuisine. Specialties: Kalua pig on wonton nachos with refried taro, avocado salsa and chili sour cream.
Dinner: 5–9 p.m., entrées $17–$30.

Alan Wong is the much-lauded and ultra-creative former chef of the acclaimed dining duo the CanoeHouse/Le Soleil at the Mauna Lani Bay Hotel and Bungalows on the Big Island's Kohala Coast. Apparently, Wong felt he needed some big city grime in his bones, so he moved in April of 1995 to his own place in Honolulu. Although Big Islanders and resort guests may be mourning Alan's flight, Honolulu's smart set is happily consuming his wacky, wonderful, Hawaii Regional Cuisine standards and nightly specials. Recent menu items have included "Da Bag," steamed clams with kalua pig, shiitake mushrooms and spinach in a foil bag, or "Poki Pines," crispy ahi poke balls on avocado sashimi with wasabi sauce. And these are just appetizers. His entree list encompasses a wide variety of fresh-fish dishes such as furikake salmon with ume chiso rice cream on linguine, or seared peppered yellowfin ahi with a crispy Asian slaw and soy vinaigrette. The hoof-and-horn set will appreciate some incredible combinations ranging from braised veal shank with "smashed" taro in poi sauce with crab and corn, grilled New York steak with roasted garlic au jus, or roasted pork tenderloin medallions with coconut ginger sweet potato puree, pineapple, water chestnut and macadamia nut relish. Guests have just as much fun with dessert; pastry chef Mark Okumura recently dreamed up something heavenly called crispy macadamia nut meringue with fresh strawberries and strawberry sauce. From time to time, Alan Wong shares his spotlight with special guest chefs in a series of wine-tasting dinners. Features: own baking. Reservations recommended. Credit cards: A, MC, V.

Auntie Pasto's $$ ★★

1099 South Beretania Street, Greater Honolulu, ☎ *(808) 523-8855.*
Italian cuisine. Specialties: Seafood pasta, eggplant parmesan, pasta carbonara, chicken marsala.
Lunch: 11 a.m.–6 p.m., entrées $7–$12.
Dinner: 5–10:30 p.m., entrées $7–$12.

There's always a line to get in, and the decibel levels are so high you'll want to cover your ears, but the superior quality and huge portions of Italian food (especially pasta with a variety of sea creatures) make whatever discomfort you feel worth the trouble. Terrific appetizers and salads with fresh ingredients; marinated vegetable antipasto and fresh baked crusty bread accompany all entrées. The service is remarkably efficient and friendly for all the guff the staff has to put up with. Open until 11 p.m. Fridays; Saturday, 4 p.m.–11 p.m.; Sundays, 4 p.m.–10:30 p.m. Reservations not accepted. Credit cards: MC, V.

Ba-Le Sandwich Shops $ ★★

333 Ward Avenue, Greater Honolulu, ☎ *(808) 533-2843.*
Asian cuisine. Specialties: Vietnamese sandwiches.
Breakfast: 8 a.m.–6 p.m., entrées $2–$4.
Lunch: 8 a.m.–6 p.m., entrées $2–$4. Closed: Sun.

Although other items are available at this tiny shop with two or three tables and a deli case, the tasty Vietnamese sandwiches are as far as most people get. Ham, turkey and chicken are available as fillings, but the most traditional are head cheese, pâté or steamed pork. But what spices up these otherwise ordinary meats are the accoutrements: crispy fresh French rolls, a marinade of vinegar, soy and garlic, pickled carrots and turnips, and sprigs of cilantro. Ba-Le must be doing something right—there are nine other branches throughout the island. Features: own baking. Reservations not accepted.

Cliquo $$$ ★★★★

Niu Valley Shopping Center, 5730 Kalanianaole Highway, Greater Honolulu, 96821, ☎ *(808) 377-8854.*
French cuisine. Specialties: Rack of lamb, filet of opakapaka with watercress and Maui onion compote.
Dinner: 6-9 p.m., entrées $15–$28.

A relatively new kid on the dining block, Cliquo, (a pet name for a wild poppy that chef Yves Menoret remembers fondly from his Breton childhood) is a shopping center bistro that debuted in May 1995. Menoret, formerly with Hilton Hawaiian Village's acclaimed Bali Restaurant, in partnership with Bruno Chemel, specializes in light, "organic" (*Morbleu!* Escoffier is turning in his grave) French cuisine. Even the terrific desserts are created in the same vein, with maple syrup substituting for sugar, and low-fat yogurt for cream whenever possible. Apparently, its efforts have won droves of converts, as the restaurant has been constantly crowded since the doors opened. Features: own baking, rated wine cellar. Reservations recommended. Credit cards: A, D, V.

Coffee Haven $ ★★

1026 Kapahulu Avenue, Greater Honolulu, ☎ (808) 732-2090.
American cuisine. Specialties: Coffees, Italian sodas, teas, sandwiches, pastries.
Breakfast: 7 a.m.–2 p.m., entrées $3–$5.
Lunch: 10 a.m.–6 p.m., entrées $3–$5.
Dinner: 5–10 p.m., entrées $3–$5.

Coffee Haven is a mellow place that offers Internet access along with live guitar music and light meals. When not on-line or munching, patrons can sprawl on a couch (provided for that purpose) in a room that's decorated in a thrift-shop mode. Although coffee is the beverage of choice, there's an entire array of liquid treats, including ultra-sweet Italian sodas, fruit essences flavored with cream and fizzed up with soda water, New-Age teas, including Envy, a mix of green tea with "notes of lemon, mint and desire." When the munchies hit, have a bagel with cream cheese-pesto spread, smoked ahi or veggie sandwiches, or one of the daily specials, which range from eggplant parmigiana to curry chicken with rice. Scones, carrot cake and cheesecake are baked in-house. Open until midnight on Friday–Saturday; Sundays, 8 a.m.–9 p.m. Features: outside dining, own baking, non-smoking area.

Crepe Fever/Mocha Java $ ★★★

1200 Ala Moana Boulevard, in Ward Centre, Greater Honolulu, ☎ (808) 591-9023.
French cuisine. Specialties: Omelettes, frittatas, crepes, vegetarian entrées, espresso, spe-cialty coffees.
Breakfast: 8 a.m.–2 p.m., entrées $6–$9.
Lunch: 10 a.m.–6 p.m., entrées $6–$9.
Dinner: 5–9 p.m., entrées $6–$9.

A sprightly café where filled things are a specialty (crepes, natch, plus frittatas). Crepe Fever serves many purposes; it's perfect for a coffee break or snack (try the espresso milkshake), a quick breakfast (or any meal) at the counter, or a languid chew and gaze at the passing scene in the pseudo posh, constantly under construc-tion Ward Centre (note the British spelling) from a seat at an outside table. Break-fasts are the thing here, though, served all day, including a number of meatless offerings, and they're good, too. A particular favorite is a melange of eggs, potatoes and vegetables served with an Indian *chapati* (unleavened bread). A host of vegetar-ian dinner specials are offered daily except Sunday (when the place closes at 4 p.m.) from 5 p.m.–9 p.m. Friday nights feature live "coffee house" music from 8 p.m.–10 p.m., and an open mike night on Saturdays at the same time. Features: outside din-ing, own baking. Reservations not accepted. Credit cards: MC, V.

Down to Earth Deli $ ★★

2525 South King Street, Greater Honolulu, ☎ (808) 947-7678.
cuisine. Specialties: Ethnic vegetarian entrées, salad bar.
Lunch: 10 a.m.–6 p.m., entrées $4–$7.
Dinner: 5–9 p.m., entrées $4–$7.

A well-respected health-food store, Down to Earth Deli offers cheap sustenance to a variety of neo-hippies, UH students, a few kooks here and there, and other alter-

native-lifestyle types. It's loved for its salad bar stocked with stellar veggies and produce, and homemade dressings, as well as made-to-order international vegetarian
entrées. Items change daily, but the Thai, Middle Eastern and Indian dishes are recommended. No meat, fish or poultry, but dairy products, including cheese, are
served. You can get things to go (priced by the pound), or eat in, cafeteria-style.
Seating is at a counter with fewer than 10 seats, or in a cozy loft. Lubricate your
meal with freshly blended, good-for-you vegetable juices or herbal teas. A variety of
bran or fruit-filled muffins, cakes and other sweets are available every day. Features:
own baking. Reservations not accepted.

Hanatei Bistro　　　　　　　　　　$$$　　　　　　　　★★★★

6650 Kalanianaole Highway, Greater Honolulu, ☎ *(808) 396-0777.*
*French-Asian cuisine. Specialties: Charred ahi coated with seven Japanese spices with
shoyu lilikoi sauce, bouillabaisse.*
Dinner: 6–9 p.m., entrées $15–$28.
On Jin Kim, a trained operatic soprano, is also the chef behind this fabulous Contemporary French-Asian restaurant designed like an indoor Japanese garden, replete
with bridges and running streams. You might want to start your meal with wild
mushrooms served au gratin with parmesan and fresh herbs, and proceed to bouillabaisse de Chef On Jin, her own interpretation of the classic dish, combining
salmon and opakapaka with lobster, clams and shrimp in a broth redolent of saffron,
lemongrass and plum tomatoes. Many entrées can be ordered in smaller portions.
On the last Sunday of each month, Kim entertains dinner guests by singing three
sets of popular arias. Features: own baking, Sunday brunch. Reservations required.
Credit cards: A, MC, V.

Hoku's　　　　　　　　　　　　　$$$　　　　　　　　★★★

5000 Kahala Avenue, Greater Honolulu, 96816, ☎ *(808) 739-8888. Associated hotel:
Kahala Mandarin Oriental.*
cuisine. Specialties: Sushi, oysters, fresh Hawaiian fish, chicken and lamb kebabs.
Lunch: 11:30 a.m.–2:30 p.m., entrées $18–$26.
Dinner: 5:30–10:30 p.m., entrées $18–$30.
After the Mandarin Oriental Group purchased and refurbished the Kahala Hilton,
one thing they noticed was the lack of a restaurant with a view. A two-story addition
was built to house Hoku's, the hotel's kicky new multi-level signature dining establishment, which has panoramic views of the Pacific, the beach and sunsets from
every table. Located just off the lobby, the Hoku's features Honolulu's most extensive oyster and sushi bar, with the freshest seasonal oysters flown in regularly from
all over the globe: Belon from France, rock oysters from Sydney as well as good ole'
boys from the Texas Gulf Coast. In addition, guests can feast on a number of eth-
nically diverse dishes such as ahi sashimi with wasabi pesto, spread on seaweed naan
bread made in the open kitchen's tandoor oven. One floor below is the open-air
Plumeria Beach Café, with all-day casual dining, and American and Japanese-
themed buffets at breakfast, lunch, dinner and Sunday brunch. Features: own baking, rated wine cellar. Reservations recommended. Credit cards: A, MC, V.

I Love Country Café　　　　　　　　$　　　　　　　　★★★

451 Piikoi Street, Greater Honolulu, ☎ *(808) 596-8108.*

American cuisine. Specialties: Plate lunches, vegetarian offerings, stir-fries, homemade carrot cake.
Breakfast: 6 a.m.–9 p.m., entrées $6–$8.
Lunch: 10:30 a.m.–6 p.m., entrées $6–$8.
Dinner: 5–9 p.m., entrées $6–$8.

You won't hear George Jones sobbing into his drink from a jukebox at this no-nonsense café situated in a mall near Ala Moana Center. I Love Country has nothing to do with country, except perhaps where the lone chef wishes he was after sweating over the stoves all day. It's not a place to linger; the place prides itself on preparing fresh food as quickly as possible. Vegetarian dishes are a specialty, including stir fries and brown rice, spinach-stuffed ravioli and Philly cheese steaks made with mushrooms (or sizzling steak) and served on crunchy French rolls with sauteed onions. Also available are plate lunches, sandwiches, salads and fruit smoothies. Features: own baking. Reservations not accepted.

India Bazaar Madras Café $ ★★

2320 South King Street, Greater Honolulu, ☎ (808) 949-4840.
Indian cuisine.
Lunch: 11 a.m.–6 p.m., entrées $7–$8.
Dinner: 5–9 p.m., entrées $7–$8.

Catering to a college crowd (it's near UH Manoa) this airy Indian cafeteria and grocery features at least six tasty curries per day. Hefty portions are dished out on metal trays with compartments for the entrées and condiments. A generous pile of steaming saffron rice is the focal point of everything; to it is added chicken masala, tandoori or a trio of vegetable curries. Side dishes are always a stellar part of this type of meal, and India Bazaar's selection doesn't disappoint—the *samosas* (fried turnovers with meat or vegetables), *chapati* (unleavened bread), cooling cucumber raita and spicy *dal* (lentils) are just fine.

Irifune $ ★★

563 Kapahulu Avenue, Greater Honolulu, ☎ (808) 737-1141.
Japanese cuisine. Specialties: Tempura, ahi spinach salad.
Lunch: 11:30 a.m.–1:30 p.m., entrées $7–$8.
Dinner: 5–9:30 p.m., entrées $7–$8. Closed: Mon.

An atmospheric neighborhood joint that looks like the home of someone's pack-rat uncle, Irifune features dirt-cheap complete meals that include soup, tofu, salad and rice for under $10. Usually crowded most evenings; come for lunch. Credit cards: MC, V.

Keawe Kafé $ ★★

327 Keawe Street, Greater Honolulu, ☎ (808) 531-5930.
cuisine. Specialties: Plate lunches.
Breakfast: 7 a.m.–2 p.m., entrées $4–$6.
Lunch: 10 a.m.–2 p.m., entrées $4–$6.

A bright spot in a dull area, the Keawe Kafé is a real find in an industrial section off of Ala Moana Boulevard. Not totally unknown, there's usually a crowd waiting along with you for the daily special: one or two kinds of internationally themed plate lunches. One day, there may be a Jamaican plate complete with jerk chicken, barbecued mahimahi AND shrimp. Another time it'll be Greek or Filipino, or...Plates are served with "two-scoop" rice, and a choice of salad; the macaroni is the traditional

OAHU

option, and it's appropriately eggy and mayonnaisy, the way a respectable mac salad should be. Sandwiches are hefty; there's also homemade soup and crispy french fries. On Fridays, the chef puts on his performing hat and entertains patrons with Hawaiian songs—a fine way to welcome the weekend. Open early for breakfast, the Kafé offers a full range of coffee drinks. Reservations not accepted.

Keo's at Kapahulu $$ ★★★

625 Kapahulu Avenue, Greater Honolulu, ☎ (808) 737-8240.
Thai cuisine. Specialties: Lemongrass soup, curries, satay, salad, spicy rolls.
Lunch: 11 a.m.–5 p.m., entrées $9–$12.
Dinner: 5-10 p.m., entrées $9–$12.

Keo Sananikone is not a shy man—he's a world-class name-dropper who loves to have his picture taken with visiting celebrities and he'll even provide a list of those who've eaten at his restaurant since its opening almost 20 years ago. But he must be credited for breaking the stereotype of a typical humble, storefront Thai eatery. His three Keo's restaurants (this one is the original) are silky pastel boudoirs filled with art, orchids and exotic greenery, all lit by soft track lighting or lanterns. Long before the advent of Hawaii Regional Cuisine, Keo introduced exciting items, including his signature "Evil Jungle Prince"—a cabbage salad with chicken and fresh basil, coconut milk and chilis. It's little wonder he's been written up and lauded repeatedly by every major publication in the world, as well as by *Honolulu Magazine* and *Honolulu Weekly*. All produce, herbs and flowers are grown on two farms he owns on the island. Other locations: *1486 S. King Street, ☎ (808) 947-9988*, and at Ward Centre at *1200 Ala Moana Boulevard, ☎ (808) 596-0020*. Features: rated wine cellar. Reservations recommended. Credit cards: A, DC, MC, V.

Kincaid's $$ ★★★

Ward Warehouse, Greater Honolulu, ☎ (808) 591-2005.
American cuisine. Specialties: Fresh island fish, prime rib, rack of lamb Hunan style, hot Dungeness crab appetizer.
Lunch: 11:15 a.m.–2 p.m., entrées $9–$20.
Dinner: 5–10 p.m., entrées $9–$20.

Lauded for its seafood, Kincaid's also has some delicious salads at lunch, including a classic pea straight out of a Midwest farmhouse (only the water chestnuts give it away) or shrimp on romaine lettuce tossed with Maytag blue cheese dressing. Getting back to the fish, try the macadamia nut stuffed prawns with mango-banana chutney—yum. And if that wasn't rich enough for you, don't leave without lapping up one of the desserts, such as burnt cream—rich vanilla custard with fresh eggs and whole cream, topped with a caramelized, crackling, sugar crust. Sunset menu served from 5-5:45 p.m. Features: own baking. Reservations recommended. Credit cards: A, CB, DC, MC, V.

L'Uraku $$$ ★★★

1341 Kapiolani Boulevard, Greater Honolulu, ☎ (808) 955-0552.
Seafood cuisine. Specialties: Sashimi, baked oysters with uni, steamed fresh clams.
Lunch: 11 a.m.–2:30 p.m., entrées $12–$25.
Dinner: 5:30–10:30 p.m., entrées $12–$25.

One of Honolulu's newest East-West restaurants, L'Uraku specializes in elegant, understated Euro-Japanese cuisine, with an emphasis on seafood. Chef Hiroshi Fukui's credentials are impeccable: he spent a number of years in Japan preparing the imperial court dinners known as kaiseki. L'Uraku is also one of the few places in town that's not a coffee shop that serves a late supper menu from 10:30 p.m.–2 a.m. It's a great place to slip into when you get a craving for sashimi or baked oysters with uni at 1 a.m. Features: late dining. Reservations recommended.

Old Waialae Road $ ★★

2820 South King Street, Greater Honolulu, ☎ *(808) 951-7779.*
Asian cuisine. Specialties: Korean plate lunches, kimchi.
Lunch: 11 a.m.–9 p.m., entrées $8–$10.
Formerly Ted's Kim Chee To Go, new owners have put in enough seating for 40 bodies at small tables, so you can eat in as well as take food out. Some Italian specialties have been added to the Korean menu, but the most popular items remain the garlicky barbecue Koreans do so well, plus man doo, stuffed, deep-fried dumplings. Steamed rice, mac salad and crunchy veggies accompany most orders, as well as a small portion (that's all you'll need, believe me) of an incendiary kim chee that gave the place its name. If you choose to eat here, you can BYOB. Features: outside dining.

Olive Tree $ ★★

4614 Kilauea Avenue, Greater Honolulu, ☎ *(808) 737-0303.*
Mediterranean cuisine. Specialties: Fish or lamb souvlaki, octopus or calamari salad, baklava.
Dinner: 5–10 p.m., entrées $6–$10.
Souvlaki, that marvelous Greek standby of chewy pita bread folded around meats roasted on a vertical spit, is reliably good at this counter-type operation in a Kahala neighborhood. The lamb and fish versions are especially choice, as is the chicken. Mostly takeout, but there are a few covered outside tables. Features: outside dining. Reservations not accepted.

Ono Hawaiian Foods $ ★★

726 Kapahulu Avenue, Greater Honolulu, ☎ *(808) 737-2275.*
Hawaiian cuisine. Specialties: Laulau, kalua pig, Hawaiian plate lunches.
Lunch: 11 a.m.–7:30 p.m., entrées $7–$9. Closed: Sun.
Many local residents agree that Ono prepares the best authentic Hawaiian food anywhere. Excellent beef stew, kalua pig and raw fish dishes (*poke*), but the laulau is the thing. Service is particularly warm and welcoming. It's mostly a takeout business, but there are about 10 tables inside if you want to people-watch. Also recommended is Aloha Poi Bowl, 2671 S. King Street, ☎ (808) 944-0798. Try the squid luau. Reservations not accepted.

Roy's $$$ ★★★★

6600 Kalanianaole Highway, Hawaii Kai Corporate Plaza, Greater Honolulu, 96825, ☎ *(808) 396-7697.*
Hawaiian Regional cuisine. Specialties: Wood-roasted Szechuan baby back ribs, rack of lamb with rosemary potatoes in kiwi butter sauce.
Lunch: entrées $15–$28.
Dinner: 5:30-9:30 p.m., entrées $15–$28.

Roy Yamaguchi, the founding father of Hawaii Regional Cuisine (and he's barely in his 40s!) opened this handsome space overlooking Maunalua Bay, beneath Koko Head, in Hawaii Kai in 1988. It's now the flagship operation of a mini-empire of Roy's Restaurants (including one in the Philippines). If we had bottomless wallets and good earplugs, we would eat at Roy's every night. It's hard to fault any of his appetizers (except that they disappear too quickly) or fresh-fish preparations. At least six kinds of different ones are available nightly, including onaga, mahi-mahi or ahi, usually seared in a dry cast-iron skillet at high heat, and tossed lightly with outrageous sauce combinations that never fail to work. Don't you dare pass up Roy's Chocolate Soufflé (created in his Maui restaurant and now available in Honolulu) or you'll never forgive yourself. Open 5:30–10:30 p.m. Fridays; Saturdays, 5–10:30 p.m.; Sundays, 5–9:30 p.m. Features: own baking. Reservations recommended. Credit cards: A, CB, DC, D, MC, V.

Sam Choy's Diamond Head $$$

449 Kapahulu Avenue, Greater Honolulu, ☎ *(808) 732-8645.*
Specialties: Sam Choy's original fried poke, seafood laulau, pulehu steak, Hawaiian-style bouillabaisse.
Dinner: 5:30–9:30 p.m., entrées $19–$30.

Open for just one year at his Oahu location on the top floor of a mini-mall in Kapahulu, Sam Choy's is a certified big hit, especially with local residents. We attempted to dine there on a weekday after 8 p.m. without reservations. We were told that immediate seating was available at the "chef's counter," but that a regular table wouldn't clear until 9:30 p.m. After some discussion, we decided to opt for the former, which turned out to be one of the best seats in the house. Places are comfortably spaced, and you get to lean your elbows on a gleaming granite counter while observing the well-orchestrated routines of the line chefs. Service is uniformly excellent, by a smiling staff. Unfortunately, we weren't exactly awed by the food. Portions are much too big (as are the prices), mostly glorified meat and potatoes fare, although the "award-winning" seafood laulau, fresh island fish, assorted seafood and fresh vegetables wrapped in ti-leaves and steamed lived up to its name. We enjoyed the pile of crisp fried onions on the teriyaki rib steak better than the meat—we've had better elsewhere. All dishes are accompanied by soup of the day, salad and choice of starch. We had no room for dessert, but what looked especially good was "Mom's" bread pudding with caramel and coconut sauces and Chef Mike's (Sam's executive chef) chocolate decadence cake. Open Friday–Sunday from 5 p.m.–10 p.m. Features: own baking. Reservations recommended. Credit cards: A, MC, V.

Tai Pan on the Boulevard $$$

1680 Kapiolani Boulevard, Greater Honolulu, 96814, ☎ *(808) 943-1888.*
Euro-French cuisine. Specialties: Live seafood wok fried with udon noodles and black-bean sauce, salmon tartare.
Dinner: 6–9 p.m., entrées $12–$25.

At Tai Pan on the Boulevard, one of Honolulu's newer restaurants, you can enjoy excellent Euro-French cuisine without the noise and fuss found in many other foodie havens. In a serene atmosphere, you might want to start with chef Ernest

Limcaco's signature salmon tartare, a beautifully presented dish of fresh salmon mixed with green onion, lemon juice, sesame oil and spices, topped with enoki mushrooms, black sesame seeds and red caviar. It's served with a pungent wasabi mayonnaise and toast triangles. Also recommended are the baked jumbo prawns stuffed with clam soufflé, bearnaise sauce and creamed orso, or a grilled seafood brochette with lobster, prawns and scallops. Features: own baking. Reservations recommended. Credit cards: A, D, MC, V.

The Chowder House   **$$**   ★★
1050 Ala Moana Boulevard, Greater Honolulu, ☎ (808) 591-8681.
Seafood cuisine. Specialties: Clam chowder, broiled ono, marinated seafood platter.
Lunch: 11 a.m.–6 p.m., entrées $6–$13.
Dinner: 5–9 p.m., entrées $6–$13. Closed: Sun.
Tasty, reasonably priced seafood is available at this understandably popular spot on the first level of the Ward Warehouse. The most expensive item on the menu is lobster tail for $12.95, and it's served with dinner salad, bread and a choice of rice or fries. And since this is a chowder house, try one of the three versions (white, red and seafood) in a sourdough bowl. Reservations not accepted. Credit cards: A, D, MC, V.

The Old Spaghetti Factory   **$**
1050 Ala Moana Boulevard, Greater Honolulu, ☎ (808) 591-2513.
Italian cuisine. Specialties: Spaghetti with browned butter and mizithra cheese, mud pie, Italian cream sodas.
Lunch: 11:30 a.m.–2 p.m., entrées $5–$9.
Dinner: 5–10 p.m., entrées $5–$9.
Located on the second floor of the Ward Warehouse, this is one of an international chain of spaghetterias decorated in a Roaring '20s motif, with plenty of brass and frosted glass. The most interesting entree is the spaghetti with mizithra cheese imported from Greece. A great place to take fussy kids. Open Fridays from 5–11 p.m.; Saturdays from 11:30 a.m.–11 p.m.; Sundays from 4–10 p.m. Features: own baking. Credit cards: A, DC, D, MC, V.

Waiola Store   **$**   ★★
2135 Waiola Street, Greater Honolulu, ☎ (808) 949-2269.
cuisine. Specialties: Shave ice.
Hours: 9 a.m.–7 p.m.
This neighborhood market touts itself as the "King of Shave Ice," and in Honolulu at least, not many people dispute this fact. There are more than 30 flavors of homemade syrup available daily, poured onto ice that's as soft and fine as newly fallen snow. They have icky things such as bubble gum for the kids, but adults gravitate towards the mango, lilikoi and *haupia* flavors. Try the li hing mui (preserved plum) if you really want to blend in.

Waikiki

Acqua   **$$**   ★★★
2552 Kalakaua Avenue, Waikiki, ☎ (808) 924-0123. Associated hotel: Hawaiian Regent Hotel.
Mediterranean cuisine. Specialties: Phyllo-wrapped swordfish baked with white and balsamic vinegars, lamb encrusted with herb mustard.

Dinner: 5:30–10 p.m., entrées $13–$17. Closed: Sun.

Acqua opened in June of 1995 on the third floor of the Hawaiian Regent Hotel, joining a remarkable array of nightspots and dining rooms available at this location. Chef Mariano Lalica prepares generously portioned, intriguing Hawaiian-Mediterranean dishes that include rock-shrimp risotto, bouillabaisse and garlic sesame ahi pasta. Lalica's cohort in the pastry department, Robin Baronick, is drawing plenty of bravos for innovative, rich desserts; try her fruit cobbler. Live salsa music is featured nightly from Thursday–Saturday. Open until 11 p.m. on Fridays and Saturdays. Features: own baking, late dining. Reservations recommended. Credit cards: A, D, MC, V.

Cascada   **$$$**   ★★★

440 Olohana Street, Waikiki, ☎ (808) 943-0202. Associated hotel: Royal Garden at Waikiki.
International cuisine. Specialties: Moroccan-style veal shank, salmon tartar, peach melba.
Lunch: 11 a.m.–2 p.m., entrées $18–$30.
Dinner: 6–10 p.m., entrées $18–$30.

Cascada is a fanciful dining experience in the heart of bustling Waikiki Beach. Named after an artificial waterfall that fronts the restaurant, the best seats in the house are on a marble terrace under a hand-painted ceiling. The kitchen, helmed by Nick Sayada, a gentleman of Assyrian-Russian heritage, turns out an intriguing mix of Cal-Asian pupus, pastas, Moroccan entrées and ancient French desserts (how long has it been since you've had peach melba?). Features: outside dining, own baking. Reservations recommended. Credit cards: A, MC, V.

Ciao Mein   **$$**   ★★★

2424 Kalakaua Avenue, Waikiki, ☎ (808) 923-2426. Associated hotel: Hyatt Regency Waikiki.
Chinese and Italian cuisine. Specialties: Spicy kung pao chicken, Szechuan eggplant, petti di pollo, tiramisu.
Dinner: 6–9:30 p.m., entrées $10–$20.

Ciao Mein, the Hyatt Regency Waikiki's innovative restaurant, serves both Chinese and Italian dishes in a stylish, sexy and fun environment. You'll know you're on to something different when handed a mint-scented menu (at first we thought it was the server's aftershave). Oversized, squarish flasks of water are immediately placed on the zany tables, whose decor features free-form circles and squares of rice paper in assorted colors pasted onto the glass tops. Breadsticks as long and curly as a witch's fingernails come next, along with addictive cheese-herb rolls. These are accompanied by assorted East-West dippers, garlic pesto and olive oil from Marco Polo land as well as Chinese red pepper chili sauce. It's customary to order "family style," with a series of plates placed on the table and shared by all diners. For folks confused by the choices at hand (there are many of us), the kitchen prepares a daily "cultures collide" combo on one platter. Black-clad servers, sans attitude, don't hesitate to offer suggestions. From the Chinese side, the award-winning wok-fried eggplant in spicy Szechuan sauce, served as an appetizer, is suitably smoky and meaty, and the whole steamed fish with soy ginger sauce is sublime and perfectly cooked. One recommendation off the Italian menu is petti di pollo—sauteed breast of chicken on provolone, garlic cheese and prosciutto *Deliciozo*! For dessert, there's a sinful tiramisu, or an assortment of ice creams—lychee, ginger, espresso, etc., dolloped onto an artfully enameled tray. Sunday brunch served from 10 a.m.–2 p.m. Features: own baking, Sunday brunch. Reservations recommended. Credit cards: MC, V.

Hau Tree Lanai   **$**

2863 Kalakaua Avenue, Waikiki, ☎ *(808) 921-7066. Associated hotel: New Otani Kaimana Beach Hotel.*
American cuisine. Specialties: Eggs Benedict, fresh fish, seafood, steaks.
This postcard-lovely spot, shaded by umbrellas and a leafy hau tree of indeterminate age, juts out onto Sans Souci Beach, on the Diamond Head side of Waikiki. It's somewhat farther away from the crowds than most seaside eateries. Particularly favored for breakfast (ooh, those Eggs Benedict), the Hau Tree, lit by tiki torches, is also gorgeous at sunset and in the evenings. Features: outside dining, Sunday brunch. Reservations recommended. Credit cards: A, CB, DC, MC, V.

La Mer   **$$$**   ★ ★ ★ ★ ★

2199 Kalia Road, Waikiki, 96815, ☎ *(808) 923-2311. Associated hotel: Halekulani.*
French cuisine. Specialties: Ahi tartare and caviar, roasted Big Island lobster with couscous, Hawaiian vintage chocolate surprise.
Dinner: 6–10 p.m., entrées $13–$120.
The ultra-sophisticated, and oh-so-French La Mer, located on the second floor of the hotel, serves sublime dishes that are an engaging combination of Provencal flavors and the freshest island produce. Local seafood is a specialty, and we enjoyed the charbroiled opakapaka (pink snapper) with ginger. Other entrées included roasted barbarie duck with Hayden mango (the huge ones that are about the size of a football) and beef with Pacific oysters. For dessert, try the excessive Hawaiian Vintage Chocolate Surprise, a chocolate crust filled with warm chocolate sauce, or the mousseline of champagne with rhubarb and fresh berries. The only false note was the mango "tatin" tart with licorice ice cream. The tart was superb, as was the ice cream, but NOT together. Features: outside dining, own baking, rated wine cellar, private dining rooms. Reservations required. Credit cards: MC, V.

Nick's Fishmarket   **$$$**   ★ ★ ★

2070 Kalakaua Avenue, Waikiki, ☎ *(808) 955-6333. Associated hotel: Waikiki Gateway Hotel.*
Seafood cuisine. Specialties: Lobster, fresh Hawaiian fish, Australian rack of lamb.
Dinner: 5:30–10 p.m., entrées $12–$35.
In a town loaded with great seafood, Nick's was named number one in this category by readers of *Honolulu Magazine* in 1996. Their decision must have been due, in part, to a humongous selection of lobster from around the globe. Diners have a choice of sweet Atlantic Tristan rock lobster tails, slipper lobster from Brazil, Florida Keys whole lobster, as well as lobsters flown in live from Maine. These choice crustaceans can be tackled solo or combined with fresh Hawaiian fish, which changes nightly depending on availability. Other specialties include giant calamari steak, Alaskan king crab legs, roast chicken and Australian rack of lamb. Italian chef Eugenio Martignago is a whiz with appetizers, and diners have the option of making whole meals out of them. Oysters Rockefeller and the now ubiquitous seared ahi

sashimi are some of the options. Salads are popular items, particularly Nick's Special Salad, bay shrimp with a secret spinach dressing. Raspberry cheesecake is what most people order for dessert. Nick's also has a thriving bar scene; the Café Lounge features dancing and live music nightly. The restaurant is open until 11 p.m. Fridays and Saturdays. Late-night menu offered weekdays until midnight, and until 1 a.m. on Friday and Saturday. Features: own baking, rated wine cellar, late dining. Reservations recommended. Credit cards: A, CB, DC, D, MC, V.

Orchids $$$ ★★★

2199 Kalia Road, Waikiki, ☎ (808) 923-2311. Associated hotel: Halekulani.
American cuisine.
Breakfast: 7:30–11 a.m., entrées $15.
Lunch: 11:30 a.m.–2 p.m., entrées $15–$30.
Dinner: 6–10 p.m., entrées $15–$30. Closed: Sun.

Although there are a number of viewful spots to take in Diamond Head and Waikiki Beach scenes, few would dispute that Orchids' vantage point is one of the loveliest, especially when the sun says "bye-bye." Naturally the covered patio is the choicest spot, where only a stretch of lawn and a fence separate it from the calm waters of Waikiki Beach. No other meals are served on Sunday except brunch from 9:30 a.m.–2:30 p.m. Features: outside dining, own baking, Sunday brunch, rated wine cellar. Reservations recommended. Credit cards: A, CB, DC, MC, V.

Sarento's–Top of the Ilikai $$$ ★★★

1777 Ala Moana Boulevard, Waikiki, ☎ (808) 955-5559. Associated hotel: Ilikai/Hotel Nikko Waikiki.
Italian cuisine. Specialties: Lamb chops Mediterranean, opakapaka Italiano.
Dinner: 5:30–10:30 p.m., entrées $15–$30.

A romantic aerie atop one of Waikiki's older hotels, Sarento's replaces the old Top of the "I" that operated up here for ages. The main draws are the intimate booths separated by decorative glass partitions that allow for a little (or a lot) of impromptu smooching between courses. The views of Diamond Head and the Waikiki skyline are spectacular; on a velvet night, the string of high-rises are lit up like gems. Cuisine is mostly high-rent Italian with Mediterranean touches; the juicy lamb chops are served with feta cheese, kalamata olives and sautéed onions. Features: outside dining, own baking. Reservations recommended. Credit cards: A, D, MC, V.

The Bali $$$ ★★★★

2005 Kalia Road, Waikiki, ☎ (808) 941-2254. Associated hotel: Hilton Hawaiian Village.
French cuisine. Specialties: Fresh lobster tartar, Kaiwi channel opakapaka, chocolate souffle, ginger creme brulee.
Breakfast: 7 a.m.–10 p.m., entrées $9–$16.
Lunch: 11 a.m.–2 p.m., entrées $10–$19.
Dinner: 6–10 p.m., entrées $25–$30. Closed: Sun.

Blend a gorgeous seaside setting with Alsatian chef Jean Luc Voegele's classic French cuisine spiced up with Asian influences (he served stints at the world-famous Le Crocodile restaurant in Strasbourg, France, and the Conrad Hilton in Hong Kong) and you've got a romantic winner. The restaurant serves three meals a day (breakfast and lunch Monday–Friday only), but dinner is the meal of choice. If you order from the á la carte menu, things can get up in the stratosphere, but the nightly four-course chef's menu for $39.50 per person is a perfect inflation-fighter. Included is a choice of four appetizers, soup or salad, four entrées and a bevy of desserts, washed down by Kona coffee, espresso or cappuccino. Features: outside dining, own baking, rated wine cellar. Reservations recommended. Credit cards: A, DC, MC, V.

The Jungle Restaurant $ ★★
311 Lewers Street, Waikiki, ☎ (808) 922-7808.
American cuisine.
Lunch: 11 a.m.–3 p.m., entrées $4–$9.
A neighborhood bar and dance emporium with a state-of-the-art sound system, Jungle Restaurant is for those who like their music loud. It also happens to serve good food. Named by a local newspaper as one of the best places in town to have dinner under $10, the menu includes "wild" green salads with homemade dressings, pastas, chicken Dijon and a spicy Jungle burger served with garlic fries. A different bread pudding is prepared every evening, as well as chocolate cheesecake Grand Marnier, Snickers pie and whiskey pudding (boy, does the chef have a sweet tooth!). There's not much in the way of decor save for a few green plants, and you'll eat your meal off sturdy nondescript dinnerware and wipe off with paper napkins. Decent wines are available by the glass. No lunch weekends. Features: own baking.

The Parc Café $$$ ★★★
2233 Helumoa Road, Waikiki, ☎ (808) 921-7272. Associated hotel: Waikiki Parc Hotel.
International cuisine. Specialties: Four kinds of buffets.
Breakfast: 7–10 a.m., entrées $11.
Lunch: 11:30 a.m.–2 p.m., entrées $15.
Dinner: 5:30–9:30 p.m., entrées $22.
Local residents love the unpretentious atmosphere that goes along with the gourmet buffets at this contemporary, light-filled restaurant in the Waikiki Parc Hotel. At lunch, you might expect to find a taco station, an international array of salads, a create-your-own-sandwich bar, roast-herbed chicken, at least three kinds of cakes and pies, plus a frozen yogurt bar with toppings. Chef Alfonso Betiong even provides freshly fried, homemade potato, taro and sweet-potato chips to further expand your waist. The whole idea started with a Sunday brunch, which was later extended to include breakfast, lunch and dinner. An all-seafood spread is featured at night. The $15.50 Hawaiian lunch buffet (Wednesdays only) is perfect for those who want to experience luau food without the high prices. No lunch Sunday or Monday. Features: own baking, Sunday brunch. Reservations recommended. Credit cards: A, CB, DC, D, MC, V.

The Tea Cozi $ ★★★
Waikiki, ☎ (808) 931-2100. Associated hotel: Aston Waikiki Beachside.
English cuisine. Specialties: Hawaiian and British Tea and pastries. Closed: Mon.
Hours: 2:30 and 4:30 p.m., Tues.–Sat.
It might be an odd notion to sit down to a "veddy British" tea in the heart of Waikiki Beach, but Hawaiian monarchs enjoyed this tradition for many years before the overthrow of the kingdom (the royals were brought up in the European style).

Queen Kapiolani served tea to guests almost daily from the Blue Room at Iolani Palace. Today, there are several locations in Honolulu where you can enjoy this delightful, and totally civilized, afternoon treat. One of them is the Aston Waikiki Beachside where, when the doors are closed against the steamy heat, persistent pests proffering promotional leaflets and a chorus of beating drums from Kuhio Beach Park across the street, you enter a quiet universe of Coromandel screens, an 18th century Chinese altar table, and antique or reproduction Chinoiserie furniture (including a striking red-and-black-lacquered secretary that guests can use to write letters). Tea is served in an adjoining courtyard, where nothing is heard but a gurgling Italian stone fountain. Recently, while two ladies at an adjoining table sipped tea in the traditional English style, we partook of the only Hawaiian tea offered in the state. For $13.50, we had a choice of macadamia nut or passion fruit tea; naturally curious, we had one pot of each. The taste? Well, one was fruity, the other nutty, of course, and surprisingly delicious. Accompaniments included delicate, barely there, lilikoi and haupia cakes, and tiny finger sandwiches of crab salad, cucumber, and tomato and fresh basil (our favorite). Hawaiian fruit was advertised, but was apparently unavailable that day, as we received a plate of long-stemmed strawberries. One advantage is opting for the English tea ($12) is the variety—more than a dozen types from Earl Grey and rosehip to decaf English breakfast are listed. Scones with Devonshire-style cream come with both versions; the Hawaiian *kine* gets lilikoi butter served with them; the English, strawberry preserves. In any case, the service is sweet and unobtrusive—after the teapots and a fancy-tiered stand with the goodies are presented at your table, you are left alone to enjoy a few hours of bliss. Tea hours are 3 p.m. on Sunday. Features: own baking. Reservations recommended.

Leeward Oahu

Kapolei

Azul   **$$$**   ★★★★

92-1001 Olani Street, Kapolei, 96707, ☎ (808) 679-0079. Associated hotel: Ihilani Resort and Spa.
Mediterranean cuisine. Specialties: Grilled marinated lamb chops with couscous and walnut garlic mayonnaise, chocolate mystique.
Dinner: 6–10 p.m., entrées $18–$30.
Azul, the Ihilani Resort & Spa's signature restaurant, is a cool, sophisticated haven of mellowed native woods, immense wall paintings and massive flower arrangements. Oval tables are laden with fine linens, china and crystal. Service, though warm, is formal and correct. In contrast, the cuisine served here, developed by the now-departed executive chef "Suki" Sugiura, is inspired by sunny Mediterranean climes. Choice meats, fresh Hawaiian fish and fresh breads are prepared in a wood-burning oven and grill (de riguer for the '90s restaurant). Chef Suki has been replaced by Mark Adair, late of the Westin Resort in Vail and the Oaks on the Plaza at the Double Tree Hotels in Pasadena, Phoenix and Aurora, CO. Chef dair, who trained with Paul Bocuse, combines European cooking techniques with Asian flavors and ingredients. He will undoubtedly develop new dishes, as well as keep a few

familiar favorites, taking full advantage of produce from nearby farms and local woods for smoking and curing. Features: outside dining, own baking, rated wine cellar, private dining rooms. Reservations required. Credit cards: MC, V.

Waianae

Masago's $ ★

85-915-A Farrington Highway, Waianae, ☎ (808) 696-7833.
Pacific Rim cuisine. Specialties: Hawaiian plate lunches, Japanese dishes. Closed: Mon.
Masago's is a rare find in a sea of fast-food joints on this stretch of highway—hidden away next to an auto parts store, it serves a companionable mix of Japanese and Hawaiian specialties, along with burgers and such. The pork eggplant is legendary. Features: outside dining. Reservations not accepted.

North Shore

Haleiwa

Flavormania $ ★★★

66-145 Kamehameha Highway, Haleiwa, ☎ (808) 637-9362.
American cuisine. Specialties: Ice cream.
Lunch: 10 a.m.–6 p.m., entrées $2–$5.
Dinner: 5–9 p.m., entrées $2–$5. Closed: Mon.
Despite the silly name, this is the place in Haleiwa, maybe the world, for homemade ice creams. Try the coconut macadamia, cherries in paradise or the "chocolate sin." Salads, sandwiches, hotdogs, smoothies are also on the menu. Open until 10 p.m. on weekends. Reservations not accepted.

Kua Aina Sandwich $ ★★★

Kamehameha Highway, Haleiwa, ☎ (808) 637-6067.
American cuisine. Specialties: Burgers, mahimahi burgers.
Lunch: 11 a.m.–6 p.m., entrées $3–$5.
Dinner: 4–8 p.m., entrées $3–$5.
Some of the most delicious burgers in the world (yes!) emanate from this no-non-sense sandwich shop on the main drag of Haleiwa town. What makes these thick, cooked-to-order beauties (in one-third and one-half pound sizes) so fine is their quality ingredients, fresh buns, juicy tomatoes, Manoa lettuce, hot grilled onions and a splash of Vermouth. All are cooked to order and come with your choice of cheese (including provolone) and bun. And the pastrami was even better. The hand-cut french fries are extra. Other nonburger items include tuna and avocado, BLTs, mahi-mahi and roast beef. The best place to eat your sandwich is on one of the benches outside, where you can watch the streetside activity. The violently air-conditioned dining area has several booths, stained-glass windows and circa 1900 photos of old Haleiwa. Features: outside dining, non-smoking area. Reservations not accepted.

L & L Drive Inn $ ★★

66-197 Kamehameha Highway, Haleiwa, 96712, ☎ (808) 637-4700.
American cuisine. Specialties: Plate lunches, grilled pork chop with brown gravy, hot and spicy blackened New York steak.
Lunch: 9:30 a.m.–6 p.m., entrées $3–$10.

Dinner: 5–9:30 p.m., entrées $3–$10.

Starting from just one small drive-through plate lunch place in 1976, partners Eddie Flores Jr. and Kwock Yum Kam expanded their business to include 24 additional locations, mostly in shopping malls. It's one of those great places that appears out of nowhere when you're tired and hungry. Local residents have recommended L&L as an economical place to eat for under $10. The Haleiwa branch, situated in the Haleiwa Shopping Center, serves up a mean and hearty BBQ mix plate of short ribs (actually just one), chicken and teriyaki steak, piled on top of two scoops of rice and accompanied by a rather bland macaroni salad. There are a few booths for eating in, but the place does a brisk takeout service. Although called a plate lunch, all items are served until closing. Other items included fried chicken, beef curry, loco moco...even prime rib for $6.15! For smaller appetites, L&L offers "mini-plates," with just one scoop of rice and salad, which run from $3.20–$4.20. Chinese food is also served. Reservations not accepted.

Matsumoto Shave Ice   **$**   ★ ★

66-087 Kamehameha Highway, Haleiwa, ☎ *(808) 637-4827.*
American cuisine. Specialties: Shave ice.
Breakfast: 8:30 a.m.–5:30 p.m., entrées $1–$2.
Lunch: 10 a.m.–5:30 p.m., entrées $1–$2.

Matsumoto's, a little general store in Haleiwa founded in 1951, is probably the only establishment of its ilk to make the glossy pages of *Gourmet Magazine*. Its especially fine-grained ice, set at the right notch on the machine (syrups are commercially made), is also served with azuki beans and ice cream. Among the 19 flavors are Rainbow (strawberry, lemon and pineapple) and the Hawaiian Special (Pineapple, banana and coconut). You can also buy souvenir T-shirts and gaze at the photos of local and international celebrities on the walls. Down the road, and less well-known, is **Aoki's**, *66-117 Kamehameha Avenue,* ☎ *(808) 637-4985*, which some fans say surpasses Matsumoto's. Unlike other establishments, Aoki's makes its own syrups, including the "Volcano," which is lilikoi and banana with a "splash" of strawberry. Cones and cups are less than $2. Open noon–5:30 p.m. Closed Monday–Tuesday.
Credit cards: A, CB, DC, D, MC, V.

Kahuku

Ahi's   **$**   ★ ★ ★

Main Camp Road, Kamehameha Highway, Kahuku, 96762, ☎ *(808) 293-5650.*
Seafood cuisine. Specialties: Shrimp from local shrimp farms, fresh fish, teriyaki steak.
Lunch: 11 a.m.–6 p.m., entrées $5–$10.
Dinner: 5–9 p.m., entrées $5–$10. Closed: Sun.

Named for native Hawaiian owner Ahi Logan, not the fish, Ahi's should actually be called "Shrimpy's." It's specialty is fresh shrimp that's aquacultured at the Kahuku Shrimp Farm next door. Shrimp is served cocktail, tempura and scampi-style. There's also a platter served all three ways. Dishes are served with lots of starch—bread with butter, macaroni salad AND rice or creamy mashed potatoes. Great place to stoke up before running the Honolulu Marathon. If the surroundings look stark, it may be because Ahi's was once an army barracks. Very down-home, it's a local favorite for lunch or dinner under $10. Also Chinese dishes, burgers. Features: outside dining.

Windward Oahu
Kailua

Buzz's Original Steakhouse $$$ ★★★

413 Kawailoa Street, Kailua, ☎ *(808) 261-4661.*
American cuisine. Specialties: Steaks, seafood.
Lunch: 11:30 a.m.–2:30 p.m., entrées $15–$20.
When you're ready to come out of the sun, buzz over to Buzz's, conveniently located across from Kailua Beach Park. In an unabashedly corny Polynesian atmosphere (thatched roof, tiki torches), Buzz's offers tall cool ones in bright colors, plus simply grilled steaks, burgers and fresh fish. The all-you-can-eat salad bar, loaded with fresh ingredients, is acclaimed. Features: outside dining. Reservations not accepted.

Kaneohe

Kin Wah Chop Suey $ ★★

45-588 Kamehameha Highway, Kaneohe, ☎ *(808) 247-4812.*
Chinese cuisine. Specialties: Char siu, seafood.
Lunch: 10 a.m.–9 p.m., entrées $4–$13.
Dinner: 10 a.m.–9 p.m., entrées $4–$13.
This busy, bustling place serves excellent Cantonese food, and is one of Kaneohe's favorite family eateries. It's one of the few restaurants where a delicacy such as birds' nest or shark's fin soup can be sampled without robbing Fort Knox. Also recommended are sizzling platters and char siu (barbecued pork). A group of three could easily have dinner for under $20. Reservations not accepted. Credit cards: MC, V.

Nightlife

Oahu makes up for all the other Hawaiian islands combined in the nightlife department, with Honolulu and Waikiki (no surprise) the center of the action. Internationally known bands and traditional entertainers, hula and disco dancing, rowdy bars and ramshackle saloons, luaus and sunset cruises, heavy metal and soft jazz, country-western and down-home blues, full-on Polynesian spectacles, theater, ballet and the symphony all provide diversion for your non-beach time. Bars shut down at 2 a.m., but places with special cabaret licenses are allowed to keep pouring the booze until 4 a.m. (so long as live music stays on). Try **Anna Bannana's** (Honolulu) for lots of fun and live music; **Banyan Veranda** (Sheraton Moana Surfrider), for Hawaiian entertainment; **Rumors** (Ala Moana Hotel) for disco; **Pecos River Café** (Aiea) for country and western performers; **Don Ho** (Waikiki Beachcomber Hotel) for Hawaiian nostalgia; **Nick's Fishmarket** (Waikiki Gateway Hotel) for upmarket meat market; and **Hotel Street** (Honolulu) for prostitution and sleaze.

Honolulu

Downtown

Bars

Sand Island R&B ★★

197 Sand Island Access Road, downtown, ☎ (808) 847-4274.
Hours: 11 a.m.–2 a.m.
Frequented by aging bikers. Blues and R&B is the music of choice. Cover when mainland bands perform.

The Pier Bar ★★★

Aloha Tower Marketplace, downtown, ☎ (808) 536-2166.
Hours: 9 p.m.–12:30 a.m.
Closed: Mon., Sun.
This is a laid-back, outdoor waterfront bar with live music that's a local fave. Styles vary from rock to jazz or Hawaiian performed by the likes of Simplicity, Pacific Street or Henry Kapono.

Clubs

Sloppy Joe's ★★

Aloha Tower Marketplace, downtown, ☎ (808) 528-0007.
Hours: Noon–1 a.m.
Closed: Mon., Tues., Sun.
Fashioned like its namesake Hemingway hangout in Key West, with pics of Papa all over the place, Sloppy Joe's features live music and dancing four nights a week along with chili, Jamaican chicken, burgers and, natch, sloppy joes Caribbean-style. Cover applies after 8 p.m. only. General admission: $4.

Nightlife

Gordon Biersch Brewery Restaurant ★★

Aloha Tower Marketplace, downtown, ☎ (808) 599-4877.
Hours: 7–11 p.m.
Hawaii's first brew pub (it's a national chain, though) with $1 million worth of brewing paraphernalia to look at while you're listening to the sounds of (what else) Strange Brew, a live "island style" and pop band Thursday-Saturday. Yell out your requests.

The Fast Zone ★★

1154 Fort Street Mall, downtown, ☎ (808) 536-1035.
Hours: 10:30 a.m.–midnight.
Special hours: Saturdays, Sundays 6 p.m.–2 a.m.
Deliberately un-stylish, this club specializes in live punk and reggae played by local bands and caters to a starving student clientele. Like a dorm room, there's not much in the way of decor. No dirty socks, though. General admission: Varies.

Greater Honolulu
Clubs

Anna Bannanas ★★

2440 S. Beretania Street, Greater Honolulu, ☎ *(808) 946-5190.*
Hours: 11:30 a.m.–2 a.m.
College students share brewskis with profs at this "venerable" club that's been popular for—gasp—27 years. Ultra-casual in a studied way. Loud music (reggae, blues, alternative) reigns upstairs; serious drinkers congregate in the downstairs bar. General admission: $4.

Coconuts Nightclub ★★

1777 Ala Moana Boulevard, Ilikai Hotel Nikko, Greater Honolulu, ☎ *(808) 949-3811.*
Hours: 9 p.m.–1 a.m.
Special hours: Mondays, 8:30–11:30 p.m. Closed: Sun.
Honolulu is "going coconuts" for the weekend island music jams by groups such as All That Jazz and Kapena. Monday is big-band jazz night; sizzling salsa on Wednesdays. Other evenings you'll just have to settle for pool, aiming at an electronic dart board, and live shower singing at the karaoke bar. Darn, isn't there anything to do around here? Cocktails and pupus served. No drink minimum, validated parking. General admission: $10.

Rumours ★★

410 Atkinson Drive, in the Ala Moana Hotel, Greater Honolulu, ☎ *(808) 955-4811.*
Hours: 5 p.m.–2 a.m.
Special hours: Thurs.–Sun. to 4 a.m. Closed: Mon.
Elegant, dressy,'70s-style hotel nightclub with smooch booths. Mostly local crowd, mainstream, Top 40 playlist. To give you an idea, something called "Big Chill Friday Dance Night" has been a fixture here for more than two years. It's nice to know some things never change. Also ballroom dancing (!) on Wednesday and Sunday. General admission: $5.

Studebaker's ★★

500 Ala Moana Boulevard, Greater Honolulu, ☎ *(808) 531-8444.*
Hours: 5 p.m.–2 a.m.
Named after the vintage auto outside, this diner/club features "American Graffiti"-style entertainment until 9 p.m., when the place flips over into a "contemporary" mode (and all night Saturday). Country line dancing on Monday. Open until 3 a.m. on Saturdays; Sundays, 6 p.m.–2 a.m. General admission: $2–$4.

Nightlife

Blue Zebra Café ★★

500 Ala Moana Boulevard, Greater Honolulu, ☎ *(808) 538-0409.*
Hours: 9 p.m.–4 a.m.
Special hours: Sat., Sun. from 10 p.m.
Not too many tourists make their way to this Restaurant Row dance club, where everything but Top 40 is played, either live or on disc. But that shouldn't stop you. Acid-jazz on Friday–Saturday. Higher cover for weekends. Sunday free for over 21, $5 for others. General admission: $3–$5.

Boomer's Live House ★★

1130 N. Nimitz Highway, Greater Honolulu, ☎ (808) 533-0334.
Hours: 5 p.m.–2 a.m.

A haven for folks in the 35–49-year-old age bracket who still like to listen to music. Hip hop, house, acid jazz lovers need not apply. A lot of up-and-coming local acts attempt to get discovered here on Monday and Tuesday nights. Also comedy/ magic on Wednesdays, Hawaiian on Thursdays,'50s and'60s dance music Friday-Saturday, and jazz on Sundays. General admission: $2–$5.

Waikiki

Bars

Hanohano Room ★★★

Sheraton Waikiki, 2255 Kalakaua Avenue, Waikiki, ☎ (808) 922-4422.

Hot jazz, complimentary appetizers, and a drop-dead, 360-degree view of Diamond Head and all of Waikiki 30 stories above the beach. What else could you want? Oh, The Hanohano Room has its own glass elevator you can ride up and down for free. Stardust, a jazz/contemporary trio, plays nightly at 8:30 p.m.

House Without A Key ★★★★

Halekulani Hotel, Waikiki, ☎ (808) 923-2311.
Hours: 6 a.m.–10 p.m.

This legendary beachfront restaurant/cocktail lounge is one of the last vestiges of old Hawaii. Perfect for sunset watching with a cold mai tai in hand, while a steel guitar plays in the background. Top-notch Hawaiian music and dancing under the stars. Also in the Halekulani is the Lewers Lounge, for late-evening fare and jazz nightly.

Irish Rose Saloon ★★

227 Lewers Street, Waikiki, ☎ (808) 924-7711.
Hours: 11 a.m.–4 a.m.

Open for 11 years, the Irish Rose Saloon will still be there when you read this. Family run, this neighborhood bar, to quote the Honolulu Weekly, "is about as Irish as a bowl of Lucky Charms," so don't expect "Molly Malone." What you'll find instead is loud, live, rock-and-roll music competing with sporting events on satellite TV. Dart board.

Joy Square ★★

Hilton Hawaiian Village, 2005 Kalia Road, Waikiki, ☎ (808) 944-2525.

This karaoke fun palace features 11 private karaoke rooms, food, a massive video arcade and a refreshment bar for the kids. People like to celebrate birthdays here.

Punani's Bar ★★

1315 Kalakaua Avenue, Waikiki, ☎ (808) 946-0000.
Hours: 4 p.m.–2 a.m.

Live Hawaiian music from 9:30 p.m. Local style, lively, popular. Karaoke, dartboards, full bar, "heavy pupus."

The Jungle ★★

311 Lewers Street, Waikiki, ☎ (808) 922-7808.
Hours: 11 a.m.–4:00 am

Special hours: weekends from 6 p.m.

By day, The Jungle is just a neighborhood tavern, with bare wood floors, and a fully stocked bar against one wall, softened somewhat with tropical greenery. After 10 p.m., it reverts to a dance club. Progressive, house, techno music is played, very loudly, from a notorious, state-of-the-art sound system. Features live music occasionally, plus '70s disco on Sundays.

Clubs

Duke's Canoe Club   ★★★

2335 Kalakaua Avenue, Suite 116, Waikiki, ☎ *(808) 922-2268.*
Hours: 7 a.m.–midnight.
This beautiful beachfront club/restaurant, decorated in retro '30s and '40s Waikiki Beach revival, is dedicated to the great Duke Kahanamoku. Live Hawaiian music weekends draws a local crowd.

Eurasia   ★★

2552 Kalakaua Avenue, Waikiki, ☎ *(808) 921-5335.*
Hours: 9 p.m.–4 a.m.
Special hours: sports bar, 2–9 p.m.
One of Waikiki's newest hot spots, located on the second floor of the humongous Hawaiian Regent Hotel. Sort of like a Top 40 station, it features nightly "contests." No cover before 10 on Friday and Saturday evenings.

Hula's Bar & Lei Stand   ★★

2103 Kuhio Avenue, Waikiki, ☎ *(808) 923-0669.*
Hours: 10 a.m.–2 a.m.
An established gay dance club, Hula's is democratic and open to everyone, except skinheads and homophobes. Al fresco environment, with music videos playing constantly.

Maharaja   ★★

2555 Kuhio Avenue, Waikiki, ☎ *(808) 922-3030.*
Hours: 9 p.m.–4 a.m.
This gilded danceteria, with headquarters in Tokyo, is probably what Imelda Marcos' private disco looked like in her former New York townhouse. It's overmarbled, overbrassed, overglassed and overcrowded. The lake-sized dance floor is one of the largest on Oahu. Flee if you hate "Boyz 2 Men." Delicious but expensive food is served. Dress code for men. In the Waikiki Trade Center. General admission: $5–$8.

North Shore

Kahuku

Nightlife

Old Plantation Restaurant   ★★

56-565 Kamehameha Highway, Kahuku, ☎ *(808) 293-7427.*
Hours: 11 a.m.–2 a.m.
Special hours: dancing from 10 p.m.
Dancing and sometimes live music is offered Fridays and Saturdays at this restaurant in the Kahuku Sugar Mill Complex.

Windward Oahu

Kailua

Clubs

Jaron's Restaurant Kailua   ★★

> *201A Hamakua Drive, Kailua,* ☎ *(808) 262-6768.*
> *Hours: 10 p.m.–1:30 a.m.*
>
> One of Kailua's few nightspots is this restaurant, which features live music on Fridays and Saturdays only. General admission: Varies.

Shopping

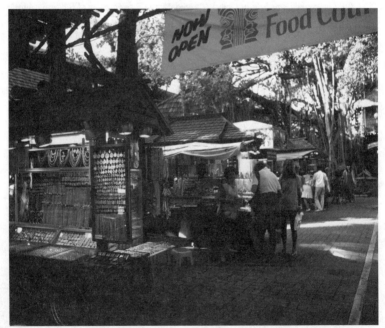

International Marketplace, Waikiki

Shopping in Oahu can easily be considered "sub-paradise" within the Big Paradise. You'll find malls and shopping centers throughout Honolulu, Waikiki, Pearl City and other major and minor population centers, plus scads and scads of small shops and boutiques tossed in along streets and shorelines, inside hotels and resorts. **Ala Moana Shopping Center**, in Honolulu, is Hawaii's largest and houses a Liberty House department store as well as branches of Louis Vuitton, Chanel and Gucci. Other Honolulu area shopping centers include **Ward Warehouse**, **Ward Centre** and **Aloha Tower Marketplace** (all on Ala Moana Boulevard). You'll no doubt notice the **ABC** stores around the Waikiki district—sundry shops that sell everything from sunscreen to potato chips.

Aiea/Pearl City

Aiea

Aloha Flea Market   ★★★

Aloha Stadium, Aiea, ☎ *(808) 486-1529.*
Hours: 6 a.m.–3 p.m.
Special hours: open most holidays. Closed: Mon., Tues., Thurs., Fri.
Held in the gargantuan parking lot of the Aloha Stadium, this tri-weekly flea market has clocked in some 30,000 visitors on busy weekends. Composed of two sections—new merchandise on one end and garage sale items on the other—locals and tourists alike can get excellent deals on gift items that are overpriced elsewhere (Read: Waikiki). Also toys, clothing, housewares, jewelry, books, fresh flowers and produce. If you've been to an event like this before, you know it's best to get here as early as possible. Haggling permitted. Examine before you buy, as all sales are final. Some merchants take cash only. General admission: 35 cents.

Kam Super Swap Meet   ★★★

98-850 Moanalua Road, Aiea, ☎ *(808) 483-5933.*
Hours: 5:30 a.m.–3 p.m.
Special hours: open most holidays. Closed: Mon., Tues., Thurs., Fri.
Across from Pearlridge Center in the parking lot of the Kam Drive-In Theaters. This is where local residents go for below-market priced fresh fish, produce and flowers (orchid plants for under $10). Many vendors have been renting stalls for years and have regular customers. Get there early, as most items are gone by noon.

Pearlridge Center   ★★

231 Pearlridge Center, Aiea, ☎ *(808) 488-0981.*
Hours: 10 a.m.–9 p.m.
Special hours: Sunday to 5 p.m.
The Ala Moana Center of the suburbs, Pearlridge Center is patronized by local residents and military families stationed near Pearl Harbor. A sprawling, two-part complex, it even has a monorail, á la Disneyland, to travel from one section to the other. It's almost as big as the Ala Moana Center, at 1.4 million square feet, and features the same anchor stores: Liberty House, J.C. Penney and Sears. There's also the requisite multi-screen movie complex and food court. For a tasty local treat, try the "Hurricane," an East-West mix of buttered popcorn and mochi crunch (Japanese rice crackers and seaweed) from the Cosmic Candy/Popcorn Planet in Phase II.

Honolulu

Downtown

Chinatown   ★★★★

Between River and Bethel Streets, downtown.

Honolulu's Chinatown reminds me of the Cole Porter song, "Come To The Super-
market In Old Peking." Cole wrote that you could buy everything from seaweed
soup to gizzard cakes to an egg that was "more or less decayed," even a "pill to kill
your mother-in-law." We're not attesting to the last item, but all other things on his
list can be procured in this historic nerve center that's one of the oldest of its kind
in the country. The place that most resembles Porter's musical concoction is the
Oahu Market, *145 N. King Street*, a landmark collection of stalls, shops, bargain
produce and Asian recipe ingredients. Local residents and chefs come for the fresh
papio and lomi lomi salmon, as well as Dungeness crab. Chinatown is the best place
to shop for Asian cooking ingredients. Come early for the best deals. Open 6 a.m.–
3 p.m., Monday-Saturday; until noon on Sundays. Call ☎ *(808) 841-6924*. Street
parking only. Other worthwhile stops include **Asia Mall** in the Chinatown Cultural
Plaza, *1250 Maunakea Street* ☎ *(808) 521-3045*, open 9 a.m.–9 p.m. daily. The
Chinatown Historical Society walking tours take off from here. The Mall is an
indoor flea market with a thrift shop, restaurants, jewelry and antique stores, even
acupressure and acupuncture specialists. Nearby is **Maunakea Market Place**, *1120
Maunakea Street* ☎ *(808) 524-3409*, with 70 stalls. Open daily 6 a.m.–6 p.m. All
along Maunakea Street are some heady shops where residents buy their special-
occasion flower leis. Some of them are: **Aloha Leis and Flowers**, *1145 Maunakea*,
☎ *(808) 599-7725*, open Monday-Sunday, 8:30 a.m.–9 p.m.; **Cindy's Lei and
Flower Shoppe**, *1034 Maunakea*, ☎ *(808) 536-6538*, open Monday-Saturday, 6
a.m.–9 p.m. Prices go as high as $20 depending on the exotic quality of the blooms.

Chinatown Historical Society Thrift Shop   ★★

1250 Maunakea Street, downtown, ☎ *(808) 521-3044.*
Hours: 9:30 a.m.–2 p.m.
Closed: Mon., Wed., Fri., Sat., Sun.

Shop for a good cause at this thrift shop that benefits the Chinatown Historical
Society. Also recommended: The Punahou Thrift Shop open Mondays, Wednesdays and Fridays from 9 a.m.–3 p.m. The campus is located at *1 Slade Drive*,
☎ *(808) 944-5848*. The also have a white elephant bazaar called **The Tank**, open
from April-December; for information ☎ *(808) 944-5752*. **The Owl's Nest Thrift**,
2445 Ka'ala Street, on the campus of the Mid-Pacific Institute, open Tuesdays,
Wednesdays, Fridays and Saturdays from 9 a.m.–1 p.m., ☎ *(808) 973-5122*. Proceeds benefit the Ronald McDonald House as well as the University. The University
of Hawaii's thrift shop, ☎ *(808) 956-7418*, open 10 a.m.–1 p.m. Tuesdays and
Wednesdays; Thursday, noon–3 p.m. One-hour validated parking.

Island Provision Company   ★★

900-A Maunakea Street, downtown, ☎ *(808) 531-5592.*
Hours: 10 a.m.–5:00 pm
Special hours: Saturdays, to 2 p.m.

This small, Chinatown-area shop fashions unique Hawaiian-style gift packages from woven lauhala or oversize coconut shells, which are then filled with island herbs, produce, sweets, coffee and condiments. Most are compact enough to take back home on the plane. Also good for hostess gifts.

Macadamia Classic ★★

2660 Waiwai Loop, downtown, ☎ (808) 836-8007.
Hours: 9 a.m.–4 p.m.

If you despise, or are allergic to, chocolate, these tasty morsels will satisfy your sweet tooth. Macadamia nuts are covered with fresh, preservative-free guava, passion fruit, coconut pineapple and something called Hawaiian espresso. Everything is color-coded, so you know what you're biting into.

Ramsay Galleries ★★★

1128 Smith Street, downtown, ☎ (808) 537-2787.

Ramsay ("Just Ramsay"), an award-winning architectural artist, features her own pen-and-ink drawings of historical buildings, plus the works of others each month in her Chinatown gallery.

Greater Honolulu

Ala Moana Center ★★★

1450 Ala Moana Boulevard, Greater Honolulu, ☎ (808) 946-2811.
Hours: 9:30 a.m.–9 p.m.
Special hours: Sunday, 10 a.m.–5 p.m.

At 1.5 million square feet, this open-air shoparama is touted as the state's largest, with an annual visitor count of 56 million. Many tourists head straight here right off the plane; some are reported missing in action. With 200 shops, it has surprisingly little kitsch, and a lot of class. The Center Court caters to Japanese tourists with such label-intensive procurers as Salvatore Ferragamo, Cartier, Dior, Fendi, Tiffany & Co., and so on. The mall is still anchored by midwestern stalwarts such as Sears (power-drill country), J.C. Penney, and Hawaii's own Liberty House. A, vast, tempting display of prepared foods, including sushi and French-style baked goods awaits at Shirokiya's, a branch of the Tokyo mid-market department store. Among the smaller shops and specialty stores, visit Crack Seed Center, featuring a dizzying array of mouth-puckering prepared plums and fruit sold by the pound. Free entertainment is a regular occurrence at the Center Stage on the Street Level. If you're faint from hunger, the Makai Market Food Court will make you faint with indecision; it resembles one of those new international buffets in some Las Vegas casinos. Relief can come from a walk across the center to Ala Moana Beach Park.

Aloha Tower Marketplace ★★★

101 Ala Moana Boulevard, Greater Honolulu, ☎ (808) 528-5700.
Hours: 9 a.m.–9 p.m.
Special hours: Fridays, Saturdays to 10 p.m.

With the historic Aloha Tower as its symbol and centerpiece, this atmospheric, 180,000 square foot waterfront complex opened in 1994 to help revitalize the Honolulu Harbor area. A second phase, which is expected to include a hotel, parking garage and office tower, will begin construction in 1999. Among the 120 shops is a retail outlet for the finely crafted koa (and other fine wood) furniture of Martin and MacArthur, Hawaii's premier cabinetmakers. A select collection of locally crafted vases, bowls, clothing and Aloha shirts (including the renowned Sig Zane line) and quilts are also represented. Of the seven restaurants and bars, many of them have waterfront views, and run the gamut from a branch of Seattle's Gordon Biersch Brewery to the Rodeo Cantina, which has the only tortilla-making machine in Hawaii, and six shelves containing more than 80 varieties of incendiary sauces. There's also an informal food court on the second level. Live entertainment daily and *Pau Hana* (end of work) concerts on Fridays.

Anne Namba Designs ★★★

2964 E. Manoa Road, Greater Honolulu, 96822, ☎ *(808) 988-9361.*
Hours: 10 a.m.–5:30 p.m.
Distinctive contemporary wear created from traditional and/or antique Japanese kimonos. Anne Namba's designs are a favorite of that noted fashion plate Hilary Clinton.

Changes ★★

2716 S. King Street, Greater Honolulu, ☎ *(808) 944-1039.*
Hours: 10 a.m.–6 p.m.
Special hours: Sat., until 5 p.m. Closed: Sun.
Stylish consigned clothing and accessories in good condition. If you want to unload some of your resort apparel, the owners will pay you cash up front. Also in the area is **Consigned Designs and Consign It For Kids!** *2885 S. King Street,* ☎ *(808) 942-2885*, which caters to working women and young families. Wedding gowns are a specialty item. Open Monday–Saturday, 10 a.m.–5:30 p.m.; Sundays, 11 a.m.–3 p.m.

Comme Ci Comme Ca ★★

3464 Waialae Avenue, Greater Honolulu, ☎ *(808) 734-8869.*
Hours: Noon–4 p.m.
Special hours: Sat., Sun., to 5 p.m. Closed: Mon., Tues.
A mix of collectibles and apparel in the mid- to upper-price range; also check out **Jan's Secret Closet**, *3427-A Waialae Avenue,* ☎ *(808) 739-1774*, for designer labels, mid-range prices. Open Monday-Friday, 10 a.m.–5:30 p.m.; Saturdays to 5 p.m.

Na Lima Mili Hulu No'eau ★★

762 Kapahulu Avenue, Greater Honolulu, ☎ *(808) 732-0865.*
Hours: 9 a.m.–9 p.m.
Special hours: Sat., to 5 p.m. Closed: Sun.
Auntie Mary Lou Kekuewa and her daughter Paulette run this store, which translates to "skilled hands touch the feathers." You'll find feather leis (head, neck, hat band), combs, instruction books and lauhala hats. Also offered are feather classes, two hours' minimum to get the basics.

Needlepoint, Etc. ★★★

1030 Kapahulu Avenue, Greater Honolulu, ☎ *(808) 737-3944.*
Hours: 10 a.m.–5 p.m.
Special hours: Sat., to 4 p.m. Closed: Sun.

If you're nuts for needlepoint, head on to this well-regarded shop that specializes in Hawaiian and Oriental needlepoint designs hand-painted on canvas. Instruction books and fabrics. Needlepoint, Etc. is located in Kilohana Square, a little warren of Oriental art galleries, restaurants, a coffee house, and other amusements worth looking into.

Nohea Gallery ★★★

Ward Warehouse, Greater Honolulu, ☎ (808) 596-0074.
Hours: 10 a.m.–9 p.m.
Special hours: Sat. to 6 p.m.; Sun. to 5 p.m.
On the ground floor of the Ward Warehouse. This well-regarded gallery and repository of local crafts carries woodblock prints by Dietrich Varez, pottery by Gail and Bunky Bakutis, plus stained glass, original paintings, jewelry and native wood bowls. More than 400 items are represented.

Nui Mono ★★★

2745 South King Street, Greater Honolulu, ☎ (808) 946-7407.
Hours: 9:30 a.m.–5:30 pm
The mother-and-daughter team of Elaine Costello and Lue Zimmerman creates hand-sewn, exotic and vividly colored custom clothing from antique kimonos and selected Japanese cottons. Also eyeglass cases, pillows, bags and toys.

R. Field Wine Company ★★★

1200 Ala Moana Boulevard, Greater Honolulu, ☎ (808) 596-9463.
Hours: 10 a.m.–9 p.m.
Special hours: Fri., Sat. to 10 p.m., Sun. to 5 p.m.
Along with fine wines, cigars from Brazil and Nicaragua, Petrossian caviar and boar meat, Richard Field is one of the few gourmet specialty shops to carry an extensive selection of foodstuffs from Hawaii's specialty growers. There are few places (unless you go to the source) that you can buy Kulana Organic Beef from Kahua Ranch on the Big Island, exotic tropical fruit trees and fresh herbs from Frankie's Nursery in Waimanalo, lettuce from Sun Bear Produce in Kona, coffee from Langenstein Farm, or Puna Goat cheese. And Field is the sole U.S. retailer for Kona-grown Hawaiian Vintage Chocolate. Much in demand by top chefs, HVC is the only organically farmed cocoa in the world. R. Field also sponsors a food festival every summer, with wine seminars, tastings, cooking demos and samplings. Gourmet foods are also on display. Free to the public.

Shop Pacifica ★★★

1525 Bernice Street, Greater Honolulu, ☎ (808) 847-3511.
Hours: 9 a.m.–5 p.m.
In the Bishop Museum. The best selection of Pacific handicrafts, located in a museum with the largest collection of Pacific artifacts in the world. Most notable for books, rare wood, jewelry, quilts and music.

The Pacific Handcrafters Guild ★★★

Ala Moana Park and other locations, Greater Honolulu, ☎ (808) 254-6788.
For really special gifts, residents turn to scores of craft fairs all over the island. The best resource is the Pacific Handcrafters Guild, the state's only juried membership organization for crafters. Almost 140 members display wares at four annual fairs in

May, July, October and December at Ala Moana Park and Thomas Square. The Island-Wide Handcrafters Christmas Fair is the state's largest, with 300 vendors. Usually Nov. 29–Dec. 1 at the Neal S. Blaisdell Exhibition Hall, *777 Ward Avenue*, Honolulu. For information, call ☎ *(808) 623-4050*.

Turnstyles   ★★★

P.O. Box 90663, Greater Honolulu, 96835, ☎ *(808) 674-0238.*
Modern-day craftsman Michael Lee is well-known for fashioning rare island woods such as koa, milo and kamani into beautiful calabashes. The entire process takes more than a year, including the final shaping and sealing—that's why prices can edge up to $600 per piece. More affordable are Lee's lathe-turned and hand-decorated pens for $25–$55 each.

Vue Hawaii, Inc.   ★★

1022 Kapahulu Avenue, Greater Honolulu, ☎ *(808) 735-8774.*
Hours: 10 a.m.–5 p.m.
Located in Kilohana Square. Distinctive island gifts, clothing, Hawaiian art and koa-wood items and bowls.

Ward Centre   ★★★

1200 Ala Moana Boulevard, Greater Honolulu, ☎ *(808) 591-8411.*
Hours: 10 a.m.–9 p.m.
Special hours: Sat., Sun. to 5 p.m.
Presently being expanded, this understated cluster of shops near the Ala Moana Center focuses more on glossy restaurants, cafés and a limited but noteworthy collection of gourmet and specialty food stores. Delectable bonbons can be had at The Honolulu Chocolate Company. Proprietor Richard Field of R. Field Wine Company proffers good advice along with escargot eggs, boar meat, Petrossian caviar, fine cigars, liquors and wines. Sample the Li Hing Wild Strawberries (a confection that's a cross between a gumdrop and crack seed) and the Banzai Mix at the Candy Company. On the third floor, Jean-Marie Josselin's newly opened A Pacific Café is the talk of the town, and there's also an indoor-outdoor branch of Keo's Thai Cuisine on the lower level. Slinky models glide blankly past the ladies who lunch at weekly fashion shows in selected eateries on Wednesdays.

Ward Warehouse   ★★★

1050 Ala Moana Boulevard, Greater Honolulu, ☎ *(808) 591-8411.*
Hours: 10 a.m.–9 p.m.
Special hours: Sat., Sun. to 5 p.m.
Facing Kewalo Basin and busy Ala Moana Boulevard, the two-story Ward Warehouse is low-slung and low-key; an altogether pleasant place to shop. It also has some of the nicest clothing boutiques in town, and a number of eclectic, tasteful craft stores and galleries. Among the former are Pomegranates in the Sun, for locally designed casual clothing and accessories, and Mamo Howell for muumuus with flair. Kincaid's, Orson's, the Chowder House and an outdoor food court are among the dining options if you get the munchies. Across the street is the Ward Farmers Market, *1020 Auahi Street,* ☎ *(808) 591-8411*, open Monday–Saturday, 7 a.m.–6 p.m.; Sundays to 1 p.m. Local food to go, as well as fresh fish, produce and tropical fruits from 13 vendors.

Antique Alley ★★★

2145 Kuhio Avenue, Waikiki, ☎ *(808) 924-3649.*
Features 35 vendors, including Hula Hands and Aloha Antiques, offering a unique selection of Hawaiian wares, including menu covers from the Matson liners *Lurline* and *Matsonia.* Given away as souvenirs, these romantic depictions of Hawaiian women, legends and lore are now all the rage among collectors of '30s and '40s Hawaiiana. Full sets in mint condition run about $450.

Body & Soul ★★★

131 Kaiulani Avenue, Waikiki, ☎ *(808) 926-2550.*
Hours: 9 a.m.–11 p.m.
Located in The King's Village Shopping Center. Probably the only shop in Hawaii to carry the NARS line of cosmetics created by make-up artist to the models (i.e. Cindy Crawford) Francois Nars. Also features the terminally hip and terminally expensive fashions of New Yorkers Betsey Johnson and Anna Sui and London's Todd Oldham, among others. You'll have to have Cindy's bod to wear them.

Ettore Bugatti Boutique ★★★

2174 Kalakaua Avenue, Waikiki, 96815, ☎ *(808) 949-4131.*
The Bugatti family designed automobiles, furniture, airplanes and trains. Now in Waikiki are two floors of quality merchandise inspired by these latter-day Leonardos. Among the clothing, silverware, handbags, luggage and watches is a Bugatti EB110, the fastest car in the world, and at $400,000, one of the most expensive. And it's not for sale. Attached to the store is a coffee house with indoor-outdoor seating.

International Market Place ★★

2330 Kalakaua Avenue, Waikiki, ☎ *(808) 923-9871.*
Hours: 9 a.m.–11 p.m.
Occupying the same spot since 1957, this open-air bizarre bazaar is a motley collection of what looks like 150 outdoor stalls selling gold neck chains. Reportedly there are plenty of T-shirts, watches, carved wooden tiki gods, coconuts you can mail home, and the like. The best thing about it is the 100-year-old Banyan tree that watches mutely over this den of thieves. Also psychic readings ("you are about to be parted from a large amount of cash"), pearl "diving" and on-the-spot charcoal drawings of your sweating visage. But it's worth seeing at least once. Daily entertainment and a decent ethnic food court.

Royal Hawaiian Shopping Center ★★★

2201 Kalakaua Avenue, Waikiki, ☎ *(808) 922-2299.*
Hours: 9 a.m.–10 p.m.
Special hours: Sundays to 9 p.m.
Sitting on six acres of land leased from the Bishop Estate, the Royal Hawaiian Shopping Center is billed as the "Rodeo Drive of Honolulu." This self-consciously upscale swankery with 150 shops is heavy into designer rags such as Hermes, Cartier, Sonia Rykiel, Ferragamo, Prada, Van Cleef and Arpels. It's for people who don't want to deal with the Ala Moana Shopping Center, which has the same kind of

label-intensive shops in its Center Court. Mostly Japanese clientele. The Royal Hawaiian Hotel is sadly dwarfed behind it, so you have to go through the center to get to it from Kalakaua Avenue. It has six Asian restaurants (one is a kiosk)—the best one and the priciest is Restaurant Suntory. The hot dog stand on the ground floor serves New England lobster rolls (!). The center offers a karaoke bar and a shooting club as between-shopping amusements. Also: hula lessons, ukulele lessons, lei-making, quilt-making and a Polynesian mini-show with dancers from the Polynesian Cultural Center.

The Little Hawaiian Craft Shop   ★★★

2233 Kalakaua Avenue, Waikiki, ☎ *(808) 926-2662.*
Hours: 9 a.m.–10 p.m.
Special hours: Sundays to 9 p.m.
An extensive collection of genuine Hawaiian-made collectibles from wood carvings to Niihau shells, needlepoint and cross-stitch kits, museum replicas. An oasis of simplicity in the overblown Royal Hawaiian Shopping Center.

The Military Shop of Hawaii   ★★

1833 Kalakaua Avenue, at Ala Wai Boulevard, Waikiki, ☎ *(808) 942-3414.*
Hours: 9 a.m.–6 p.m.
Collectors of military patches will go gaga at this shop that has the widest selection in town. Also insignia memorabilia, books, "survival candy," and apparel. Worth a stop to gaze at the "Great Wall of Patches."

Leeward Oahu
Waipahu

Waikele Center   ★★

94-790 Lumiaina Street, Waipahu, ☎ *(808) 676-5858.*
Hours: 9 a.m.–9 p.m.
Special hours: Sundays, 10 a.m.–5 p.m.
It had to happen—the outlet factory mall has landed in Hawaii. Located 15 miles from Honolulu, this open-air center debuted in 1995. Because of the "only available on the mainland" cachet, it's been a big hit with bargain hunting residents. Off-price designer clothing is the main draw, but you can also purchase luggage, china and kitchenware, furniture, crystal, chocolate and more, at what a lot of people think are good deals. Harassed moms can drop Dad and the kids off at the Discovery Zone, a family fun center. There's a food pavilion, restaurants and a trolley that shuttles bedazzled shoppers around the complex. Stores include: Off Fifth (Saks), DKNY, Anne Klein, Nine West, Fragrance Outlet, Guess, Levi's Outlet by Most, McInerny Designer Outlet, Mikasa, Tommy Hilfiger, Guess Kids and a Kmart (!).

North Shore
Haleiwa

Silver Moon Emporium   ★★★

66-037 Kamehameha Highway, Haleiwa, ☎ *(808) 637-7710.*
Hours: 10 a.m.–6 p.m.

Open for several years, this North Shore boutique in a tropical garden setting is owned by a professional model and make-up artist. The sexy and stylish merchandise includes one-of-a-kind designer clothing in silks and velvets, bustiers, retro-earrings, *pareus*, hats, jewelry boxes, umbrellas and candles.

Southeast Oahu
Kahala

Kahala Mall ★★

4211 Waialae Avenue, Kahala, ☎ *(808) 732-7736.*
Hours: 10 a.m.–9 p.m.
Special hours: Sun., to 5 p.m.
Just a few minutes away from the heart of Waikiki is this unpretentious mall catering to residents of the high-rent Kahala district. Tourists (or seasoned travelers) staying at the Kahala Mandarin Oriental make it over here, too. There are more than 90 shops, including a branch of Liberty House, an eight-screen movie multiplex, specialty boutiques, Hawaiiana gift stores, an espresso bar, even a New York-style deli (Bernard's) without New York-style attitude. The Following Sea ☎ (808) 734-4425, is a good source for one-of-a-kind handicrafts and gift items by Hawaiian artists.

Windward Oahu
Kailua

Elizabeth's Fancy ★★★

767-B Kailua Road, Kailua, 96734, ☎ *(808) 262-7513.*
Hours: 10 a.m.–4:00 pm
Closed: Mon., Sun.
Wall hangings, pillows, patterns, books, Christmas ornaments, whatever island quilter Elizabeth Root fancies—more than 300 of them are to be found within this tiny shop in Kailua. Most are inspired by her original designs. She carries a few selected items created by local artists and small manufacturers. You'll find a number of gift ideas priced under $20.

Tusitala Bookshop ★★★

116 Hekili Street, Kailua, 96734, ☎ *(808) 262-6343.*
Hours: 10 a.m.–9 p.m.
Special hours: Sundays to 6 p.m.
An excellent collection of rare and used books, with a definite focus on military history and Hawaiiana.

Kaneohe

Kauila Maxwell ★★★

46-056 Kamehameha Highway, Kaneohe, 96744, ☎ *(808) 235-8383.*
Hours: 9:30 a.m.–9 p.m.
Special hours: Sundays 10 a.m.–5 p.m.
A showcase for authentic Hawaiian gifts on the windward coast, Kauila Maxwell is located at Windward Mall. All merchandise, from bowls, jewelry, art objects, soaps and T-shirts must past muster from dedicated owner Susan Fernandez Kopper. All

items are tagged with explanations about their significance in Hawaiian culture. The store also carries its own line of T-shirts and stationery. Prices from $3–$5000.

Fielding's Fascinating Oahu Facts

A.k.a.	The Gathering Place
Main city	Honolulu
Flower	Llima
Color	Yellow
Area	594 square miles
Length	44 miles
Width	30 miles
Population	836,231
Highest point	Kaala Peak (4003 feet)

Honolulu Survival Guide

Getting There

Honolulu International Airport, about nine miles west of Waikiki, is one of the nation's busiest, serving about 1000 flights each day. The main terminal caters to international and domestic flights, while the interisland terminal serves the commuter and island-hopping trade. Both terminals provide plenty of facilities for travelers: information centers, car rental booths, gift and souvenir shops, newsstands, restaurants, snack bars, cocktail lounges, lockers, baggage claim areas and ticket counters. Domestic airlines are **American Airlines** (☎ *833-7600*), **American Trans Air** (☎ *833-0074*), **Canadian Airlines**, from Vancouver (☎ *839-2244*), **Continental Airlines** (☎ *523-0000*), **Delta Airlines** (☎ *833-8281*), **Hawaiian Airlines** (☎ *838-1555*), **Northwest Airlines**

(☎ *955-2255*), **Trans World Airlines** (☎ *800-221-2000*) and **United Airlines** (☎ *547-2211*). Interisland airlines are **Air Molokai** (☎ *521-0090*), **Aloha Airlines** (☎ *484-1111*), **Island Air** (☎ *484-2222*) and **Mahalo Air** (☎ *833-5555*). A large number of **foreign carriers** also serve Honolulu, though they are prohibited by law from transporting passengers from other U.S. cities.

Various **cruise ships** call into Honolulu throughout the year. Among the cruise lines that make Honolulu a regular stop are Cunard Line, P&O, Princess Cruises, Royal Cruises and Royal Viking. American Hawaii Cruises' SS *Independence* stops at Honolulu on its scheduled inter island excursions.

Getting Around

Taxis will be waiting outside baggage claim at the airport; a ride into Honolulu will run $20–25. Many island hotels and resorts will send their own airport shuttles (ask when booking your room), otherwise you can use **Trans-Hawaiian Services** (☎ *533-8765*); fare is about $8 into Waikiki. The public bus, known as **TheBus**, will take you from the airport to anywhere on the island for a piddly 85 cents, but no baggage is allowed.

You'll find plenty of **car rental agencies** at the airport and in Honolulu and Waikiki—with a number of small independents groveling alongside the big names. Rental agencies with airport counters and 24-hour service include **Alamo** (☎ *833-4585*), **Avis** (☎ *834-5536*), **Budget** (☎ *836-1700*), **Dollar** (☎ *831-2330*), **Hertz** (☎ *831-3500*) and **National** (☎ *831-3800*). Driving is easy on Oahu. One road (which changes names depending on where you are) hugs most of the coast, while another (which doesn't change names as often) slices through the interior. The main roads in Honolulu are King and Beretania streets; in Waikiki, the major ones are Kalakaua and Kuhio avenues. Rush-hour hell (the worst in Hawaii) is normally 6:30–8:30 a.m. and 3:30–5:30 p.m. on weekdays. Locals are unusually courteous drivers who will slow down and let you turn in front of them—don't honk unless it's an emergency and smile and wave your appreciation. Parking spots around Waikiki and central Honolulu are not particularly easy to find, though you should be able to nab a space in a public garage or shopping complex.

Baggage hassles aside, **TheBus** is quite some deal—85 cents (exact change necessary) is the fare to anywhere on the route, and the route goes all around the island, into the interior and to most of Oahu's towns and villages. On top of that, you can get one free transfer if you request it when boarding. Long-term visitors might want to spring for a monthly bus pass ($20). For information, call ☎ *848-5555*.

Taxis are not allowed to cruise and, for all legal purposes, must be booked ahead (they're often waiting at hotels). Fares are about $1.50 for the flagfall, $1.50 for each additional mile. Companies to try are **Aloha State Taxi**

(☎ 847-3566), **Charley's** *(☎ 531-1333)*, **SIDA of Hawaii, Inc.** *(☎ 836-0011)* and **TheCab** *(☎ 533-4999)*.

Aside from the super-developed areas, Oahu has excellent conditions for both **mopeds** and **bicycles**. For bicycle rentals, try the following Waikiki- or Honolulu-based companies: **Aloha Funway Rentals** *(2025 Kalakaua Avenue,* ☎ *946-2766)*, **The Bike Way** *(250 Ward Way,* ☎ *538-7433)*, **Blue Sky Rentals** *(1920 Ala Moana Boulevard,* ☎ *947-0100)* or **Fun and Sun Scooters** *(37 Olohana Street,* ☎ *946-2424)*. Motorcycles and mopeds are available from **Aloha Funway Rentals**, **Blue Sky Rentals**, **Fun and Sun Scooters** (above) or **Discount Moped Rentals** *(☎ 941-3623)*, **Island Scooters** *(☎ 924-9331)* and **Two Wheel Ventures** *(☎ 943-0223)*. You'll need a valid motorcycle license to rent scooters, and a driver's license for mopeds.

Limousine lovers can arrange for airport transportation and island tours with **Cloud Nine Limousine Service** *(☎ 524-7999)*, **Lowy Limousine Service** *(☎ 455-2444)*, **Rocy's Limousine** *(☎ 949-8001)* or **Your Royal Highness** *(☎ 941-4418)*.

Visitor Information

You'll find visitor information booths at Honolulu International Airport, or call into the Waikiki branch of the **Hawaii Visitors Bureau** *(2270 Kalakaua Avenue, 8th Floor, Honolulu 96815,* ☎ *(808) 923-1811)*.

MAUI

Big Beach (Makena) on a classic Maui day

It is common for Hawaii-bound visitors to completely bypass too-touristy Honolulu and head straight for almost-too-touristy Maui, the island running nearly neck-in-neck with Oahu as the Number One destination.

Known both as "The Valley Isle" and *"Maui no ka oi"* (or "Maui is best"), the island features plenty of beauty for its 91,361 residents and ever-increasing numbers of visitors—rainforest, jungle valleys, miles and miles of swimmable beaches and the world's largest dormant volcano. Couple the natural features with history, culture, posh resorts, exciting restaurants, and a growing plethora of man-made attractions and it's easy to see why the place is so popular. Maui, in fact, boasts more millionaires than many other resorts-of-the-rich-and-famous, including Palm Springs and the French Riviera.

Maui

OCEAN

Uaoa Bay

Waipio Bay

6 • Pauwela

• Haiku

365   360 • Huelo

Twin Falls

Kaupakulua

Puohokamoa Falls

Hui Noeau Visual Arts Center

• Makawao

Pukalani

• Olinda

377

• Pulehu

• Kula

Kula Botanical Gardens

378

Haleakala Visitors

Haleakala Crater

Puu Ulaula 10023'

Koolau

Forest

Reserve

Haleakala National Park

Seabird Sanctuary

Keanae

Waialua

Waialua Bay

• Nahiku

360

Hana Hwy

Hana Airport

Pukaulua Point

Helani Gardens

Hana Bay

Hana • Kauiki Head

Hana Maui Golf Course

31

Hamoa •

Petroglyphs

Puuiki

Koali •

Ohe'o Gulch (Seven Pools)

Kipahulu

Petroglyphs

Kaupo •

Kula Hwy 31

Natural Arch

Mamalu Bay

PACIFIC OCEAN

Kokomo Rd

156°20'

156°

This second-born island to Wakea and Papa was named for the much-revered, prankster demigod Maui who—according to legend—fished all the Hawaiian islands from the bottom of the sea, lifted the sky, and harnessed the sun from the top of Mount Haleakala ("House of the Sun"). Eventually, the Polynesian settlers turned Maui into a powerful land, ruled by kings and beset by raging wars.

Beginning in the late 1700s, *everyone* seemed to descend upon the island, making Lahaina the base of operations. Before the whites took over, however, an internal battle was waged. In the 1770s, Maui had two rulers, King Kalaniopuu of Hawaii had charge over the Hana District, while King Kahekili controlled the rest of Maui. In a grab to get Kahekili's piece of the action, Kalaniopuu—in 1776—made an unsuccessful invasion. Kahekili and his fierce warriors prevailed, only to lose out in 1790 to King Kamehameha the Great who built his palace at Lahaina around 1802. The town already had been seeing action—French Commander La Perouse and his expedition visited in 1786, Captain Vancouver and entourage followed in 1793. (Captain Cook never did make it. He sighted Maui in 1776 but couldn't find a good place to anchor, so he kept on moving.) In 1819 the whalers began stopping by, doing both their business and partying in Lahaina. Partying? In come the missionaries several years later to clean things up, convert the natives to Christianity, and put a stop to as much frivolity as possible. The whalers, of course, didn't take well to this intrusion but, after vehement and occasionally violent protests, sort of gave up the fight, if not their supposed vices. Within the next 40 years, Maui had celebrated its first Catholic Mass, written its first constitution, built its first royal palace and instigated its first steamship service. It was also during this period that Kamehameha III shifted Hawaii's capital from Lahaina to Honolulu. Sugar, however, made Maui all the sweeter.

In 1849, George Wilfong planted the first successful sugar plantation on the island, followed by the creation of James Campbell's sugar mill in 1861. But it was Claus Spreckels ("The King of Sugar") who really established Maui as a sugar capital. Spreckels managed to buy cheap land from the natives, win water rights by gambling with Kamehameha III, and build the Haiku Ditch to irrigate his crop. By the early 1900s, the island's center of activity shifted from Lahaina (which had long since lost its "capital" status to Honolulu) over to Paia, the designated plantation town. The island remained relatively quiet until the 1960s, when all of Hawaii became more tourist-friendly and Maui was "rediscovered."

Possibly Maui has been discovered a little too much. Though Old Lahaina and other historical sites continue to be preserved, developers have swooped in and thoughtlessly desecrated some parts of the island. Kihei, on the south shore, is a prime example—a once pristine area that has been turned into an ugly condo jungle.

Maui continues to flourish through agriculture such as sugar, pineapples, cattle, flowers and truck crops such as russet potatoes and sweet Maui onions—along with the illegal-but-abundant *pakalolo* (marijuana). Tourism, however, continues to be the island's primary economic stronghold with approximately 2.5 million visitors arriving annually—some of whom never leave.

Bird's-Eye View

Maui, the second-largest of the major Hawaiian islands (after the Big Island), is situated about 70 miles southeast of Oahu and measures a comparatively whopping 729 square miles (48 miles long and 26 miles wide). Created from two volcanoes connected by a low, sugarcane-planted, seven-mile wide isthmus, the island is basically divided into West Maui and East Maui, along with a few other defined regional areas. West Maui was formed by 5779-foot Puu Kukui (the oldest volcano) and is the smaller side—make that *much* smaller. Size obviously doesn't make a difference to visitors (the majority of which flock to this side) nor to residents (most of whom live there). The west (also dubbed "The Golf Coast") has the most stuff for the moneyed crowd and those who need civilization-away-from-civilization. Along with golf (and more golf), the west offers tropical forests, sugarcane fields and pineapple plantations, a long string of gorgeous beaches, a rugged east side, the newer resort community of Kapalua, the already famed Kaanapali resort area and the old whaling capital at Lahaina, center of tourist action and the local arts-and-crafts scene. From the town of Olowalu, on the Auau Channel, you can sight the islands of Kahoolawe, Lanai, Molokai and a glimpse of the Big Island. The isthmus—or Central Maui—contains Kahului (location of the principal airport) and the government seat of Wailuku, both highly populated commercial centers, and the small port area at Maalaea. East Maui, created by 10,023-foot Haleakala (the world's largest dormant volcano), is about four times larger than its sibling to the west and features an astounding array of terrain—farmland, mountains, jungle, desert, beaches and lava land. Most of the resorts are situated on the southwest area between Kihei (with the condo atrocities) and its antithesis, the comparatively well-designed town of Wailea. Whoop-it-up cowboy towns dot the countryside beyond, while wealthy celebrities and other VIPs reside in the hills around Kipahulu. The Hana Coast, on the eastern shore, is accessed by the infamous Hana Highway, a spectacular scenic drive that will take you across more than 50 bridges and around more than 600 curves. Upcountry Maui is composed of rural farms and ranches (sugarcane, pineapple, flowers), a winery and the majestic Haleakala, Maui's highest point.

Nature Guide

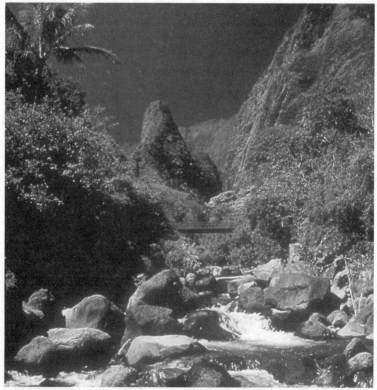

The famous Iao Needle at Iao Valley State Park, Maui is a 2250 ft. lava rock pinnacle covered with lush foliage.

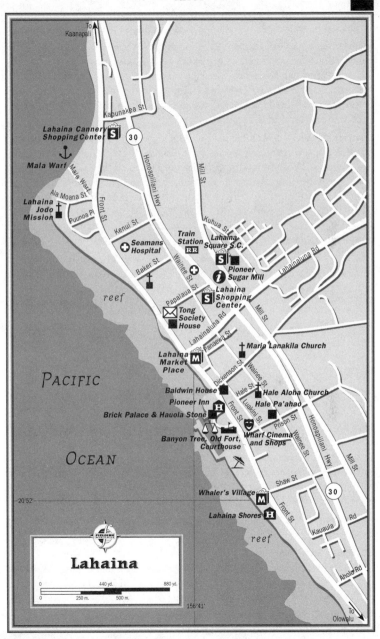

Lahaina

Dazzling flowers, trees and plant life are prolific throughout the island and easily seen in rainforests, reserves, parks, gardens and nurseries. Unfortunately, most of what you'll see is of the introduced variety—as on the other islands, Maui's indigenous flora is on the way out. Distinctive flowers include carnations (grown in the Kula area), *panini* (prickly pear cactus, found in the pasture land of Haleakala's windward slope), a rather magnificent assortment of protea (look on Haleakala's leeward slope) and the *ahinahina* (silversword, in and around the crater itself).

The *'i'iwi* and *amakihi* are two of Maui's most commonly found native birds. Among endangered species are the *akohe'kohe* (crested honeycreeper) and parrotbill, both found on the slopes of Haleakala around the 5000-foot mark; the dark-rumped petrel hangs out around the Haleakala Crater visitors center. Other indigenous birds include the white-tailed tropic bird, wedge-tailed shearwater, American plover and the nearly extinct *poouli*. The *alae ke'oke'o* (Hawaiian coot) and *ae'o* (Hawaiian stilt) are two of the island's more common waterbirds.

Many visitors come to Maui just to see the migration of the humpback whales. Come during the season—late November to early May—and find a vantage point just about anywhere along Maui's south coast.

Fielding's Beach Finder

With more than 150 miles of coastline—and about one-fifth of that harboring good beaches—you won't have a problem finding a spot to sun or swim. Maui, in fact, as more swimmable beaches than any of the other islands. Again, beware of strong currents and high surf—it's best to check with locals about conditions before plunging into the sea. Also, watch out for falling coconuts.

Beginning at the top of West Maui and moving down along the **southwest coast**:

D.T. Fleming State Park

A top spot for winter surfing and bodysurfing and year-round sunning and picnicking, though swimming is dangerous due to strong currents. Showers, rest rooms, parking, picnic facilities.

Kapalua Bay (The Beach Formerly Known as Fleming)

Just beyond the Napili Kai Beach Club.

A lovely palm-sheltered (usually crowded) bay with safe swimming and snorkeling. Showers and rest rooms.

Kaanapali Beach

This beach fronts a strip of condos and hotels but is otherwise a superb spot for summer swimming and year-round people-watching.

Black Rock

In front of the Sheraton Hotel.
Is tops for snorkeling. Showers, beach-equipment rentals.

Olowalu Beach

South of Lahaina.
A wonderful sandy area with good swimming and terrific snorkeling. No facilities.

Kamaole Beach Parks I, II and III

At the south end of Kihei.
Safe for swimming and snorkeling and are popular with locals. Rest rooms, showers, picnic facilities.

Ulua Beach

In Wailea.
Another popular (i.e., crowded) beach, good for swimming, snorkeling and body-surfing (in the right conditions). Rest rooms, showers.

Makena Beach

Southwest of Wailea.
A secluded "alternative" beach. The "Big Beach" area offers good snorkeling and swimming when the water is calm, while the "Little Beach" to the south is an unof-ficial nude beach. No facilities.

Over in **Central Maui** the beaches are fairly unremarkable.

Kanaha Beach Park

At Kahului Bay.
Has white sands, shady lawns, and is very popular with local families. Facilities include rest rooms, showers, picnic tables, and parking. (Take precautions against theft at this one.)

Hookipa Beach

Just east of Paia.
Draws the world's top windsurfers with its up-to-15-foot waves. Rest rooms, show-ers, picnic facilities and parking are all available.

The **Hana District** is rife with beautiful beaches. Two of the best are:

Waianapanapa State Park

Four miles north of Hana.
With fine snorkeling and swimming, as well as the legendary cave where the occa-sionally red tide-pool pays tribute to the demise of suspected-adulteress Popoalaea. Facilities include picnic facilities, rest rooms, showers, parking, and a hiking trail.

Kaihalulu Beach (also known as "Red Sand Beach")

Indeed has striking red sand and a beautiful cove for swimming and snorkeling. No facilities are on hand.

Adventure Guide

Maui's Hookipa Beach draws the world's top windsurfers with 15 ft. waves.

Maui offers scads of **hiking** possibilities, particularly in the mountainous, remote Upcountry district. Trekking within the **Haleakala National Park** is the not-to-be-missed hiking opportunity with 30 miles of trail leading through the crater. **Sliding Sands Trail** starts along the rim at about 9800 feet and drops to the crater floor, offering 10-miles' of cinder cone and lava flow closeups; **Kaupo Trail** leads through Kaupo Gap, past Kaupo Ranch, into Kaupo town; **Halemauu Trail** is a 10-mile hike from park headquarters to the crater floor, and links up with the Sliding Sands Trail. Scenery along the way includes lava flows, volcanic vents, cinder cones, red and black lava, and interesting vegetation. Stop at park headquarters for information, and be prepared for drastic changes in the weather—it can get very cold and nasty at 10,000 feet!

The **Polipoli State Park**, within the 21,000-acre Kula and Kahikinui Forest Reserve on the Haleakala slope, offers a variety of trails—from easy to rough—through magnificent forests of native *koa*, *mamane* and *ohia* trees as well as redwood, Monterey cypress, pine, eucalyptus and other introduced species. Many of the trails mix and mingle with each other, forming loops.

Along the coast, the three-mile **Hana-Waianapanapa Coastal Trail** is an easy trek past caves, blowholes, ancient *heiau* and clusters of *lauhala* trees. Or, retrace ancient history on the **King's Highway Coastal Trail**, down at the island's southernmost point, for views, stone ruins and remnants of Maui's last volcanic eruption in 1790.

Low energy? Just about anyone can do the cushy half-mile paved trail in **Iao Valley**, offering views of the Iao Needle.

For more **hiking information**, contact the **Hawaii State Department of Land and Natural Resources** *(State Parks Division, P.O. Box 1049, Wailuku 96793,* ☎ *(808) 243-5354)*, the **State Division of Forestry and Wildlife** *(52 South High Street, Wailuku 96793,* ☎ *(808) 243-5352)*, or **Haleakala National Park** *(P.O. Box 369, Makawao 96768,* ☎ *(808) 572-9306)*. Some of Maui's best **walking tours** are organized by **Hike Maui** *(P.O. Box 330969, Kahului 96733,* ☎ *(808) 879-5270)*.

Camping is prevalent on Maui, with an excellent range of campsites and cabins available near most of the scenic areas and along the beaches. A variety of campsites are up for grabs at **Haleakala National Park**. You can set up on the south rim, along the coastal road, near park headquarters, or even at the bottom of the crater. Permits and maximum-stay regulations vary. For more information, contact Haleakala National Park at the address above. Overnight camping is allowed at both **Polipoli Springs State Recreation Area** and **Waianapanapa State Park**. Permits and reservations are necessary. Contact the **Maui Division of State Parks** *(54 South High Street, Wailuku 96793,* ☎ *(808) 243-5354)*. For information and permits to camp at Maui's **beach parks**, get in touch with the **Department of Parks and Recreation** *(Recreation Division, 1580 Kaahumanu Avenue, Wailuku 96793,* ☎ *(808) 243-7389)*.

Just about any of your favorite **watersports** can be indulged in Maui's glorious waters with its plethora of coral reefs and bathing-bath temperatures. The usual rules apply—check with locals before plunging into the sea, and watch for strong currents and high waves. One of the best—and most popular—spots for **scuba and snuba diving** is at the 160-foot-wide **Molokini Crater**, an underwater park with plenty of marine activity. Next most popular dive site is the world-famous **Cathedrals**, off the south coast of Lanai, which are a church-like network of coral-latticed caves. Experienced divers only should attempt the area around the **Seven Sacred Pools** and areas along the back of West Maui. Other beaches that draw **snorkelers** and **divers** include **Waianapanapa State Park** near Hana, **Baldwin Beach Park** in Paia, **Ulua** and **Wailea** beaches in Wailea, **Kamaole Parks I, II** and **III** in Kihei, **Olowalu Beach**, **Black Rock** in Kaanapali and the **Marine Conservation District** at Honolua Bay.

The "windsurfing capital of the world" is located at **Hookipa Beach**, east of Paia, and lures top international **windsurfers** to the March and April championship events. Other windsurf-friendly areas are **Kealia Beach** in Kihei and **Kanaha Beach Park** in Kahului. The **Kihei Coast** is a favorite for **ocean kayaking**, while **boaters** like to set sail for **Lanai** or **Molokai**. Thrill seekers can sign up for **water-skiing**, **parasailing** or **jet skiing**.

Board surfers can ride the waves at **Honolua Bay**, **Maalaea**, **Hookipa**, **Lahaina Harbor**, **Napili Bay**, **Baldwin Park** and **Lower Paia Park**, while **bodysurfers** catch them at **Mokuleia Beach** ("Slaughterhouse" to locals), **Makena**, **Wailea**, **Ulua**, **Napili Bay** and **Baldwin Park**.

A large number of local operators rent equipment and offer organized excursions for almost all the watersports.

What Else to See

Many varieties of exotic flowers and plants are found in The Iao Valley in Wailuku, Maui. Hiking trails and a park surround the famous Iao Needle.

Central Maui basically consists of the commercial/industrial/business town of **Kahului** (where you'll probably arrive at the airport) and the county seat of **Wailuku**. Most visitors don't even bother to stop at either place, preferring instead to ensconce themselves at one of the resorts. **Kaahumanu Center**, on Kaahumanu Avenue in Kahului, is the one-stop mall and cineplex fix. You can view Hawaiian crafts and artifacts at the **Bailey House**, on Main Street, then bone up on sugarcane history at **Alexander & Baldwin Sugar Museum**, on Hansen Road. **Highway 320** will take you into **Kepaniwai Park and Heritage Gardens** and, at the end of the road, **Iao Valley State Park** with its 2250-foot high stone **Iao Needle**. Adventurous sorts might want to head west along the very narrow **Highway 340** that runs from Wailuku to Honokohau.

West Maui is the side of the island where most of the tourists go. Poised at the top of the Honopiilani Highway is the protected **Marine Life Conservation District**, consisting of **Honolua** and **Mokuleia bays**, underwater reserves filled with tropical fish. Head down to **Kapalua Bay Hotel** or **Ritz-Carlton Kapalua** to bask in elegance (or a round on one of the three courses at **Kapalua Golf Club**), or skip the dress-up act and scoot over to **Kapalua Beach** for a picnic and safe swim. Try not to be disgusted at the glut of condos as you pass through the communities of **Napili**, **Kahana** and **Honokowai**. For a special meal, stop in Kahana at **Roy's Kahana Bar & Grill** or **Roy's Nicolina**. On a budget or a diet? Then hit town on Monday or Thursday for island-fresh produce at the **Farmer's Market**. At **Kaanapali Beach Resort**, you can visit a handful of big hotels (the Westin Maui and Hyatt Regency Maui—both built by dream-big developer Chris Hemmeter—are the most distinctive and/or costly). Cruise over to **Whalers Village** and browse the exclusive shops (how about a diamond something from **Tiffany's**?).

The old capital and rowdy one-time whaler's town of **Lahaina** is, these days, the centerpoint for Maui visitors who flock to the clubs, restaurants, shops and galleries, most of which are on or around **Front Street**. The whole town was designated a National Historic Landmark in 1962. The old **Seamen's Hospital**, on Front Street, has been restored but is not open to the public. See the 12-foot-high Buddha at **Jodo Mission**, next to Mala Wharf. James Campbell's **Pioneer Sugar Mill** stands on Lahainaluna Road, and just north the old **Sugarcane Train** operates out of Lahaina Station. View implements and artifacts relating to the Chinese immigrant laborers at **Wo Hing Temple**, on Front Street. **The Hawaii Experience Dome Theater**, on Front Street, presents hourly shows that include a closer-than-you'll-ever-want-to-get volcanic eruption. Imagine the hanky-panky that went on inside the 1860s **Lahaina Inn** on Lahainaluna Street (David Paul's **Lahaina Grill**, inside the once-decadent bar, is one of the trendiest restaurants in town). At the northeast end of Lahainaluna Road, the restored 1830s **Hale Pai (House of Printing)** stands as a reminder of the Protestant missionary presence. The 50-foot-plus **Banyan Tree**, on Front Street, was planted in 1873 (when it was just eight feet tall) and is the largest banyan in Hawaii. Nearby, **505 Front Street** has been decked out to look like a New England whaling town—within are shops, restaurants and boutiques. The old **Lahaina Courthouse**, built in 1857 and reconstructed in 1925, now houses the **Lahaina Arts Society** and a couple of galleries. The turn-of-the-century **Pioneer Inn** is a good place to stop for a drink or burger while soaking up local atmosphere. Just across from the Pioneer Inn, the Brig *Carthaginian II* is the world's only true-to-the-original restored brig. Watch the action, or engage in reminisces of bygone whaling days, at **Lahaina Harbor**. The **Baldwin Home**, on Front Street, is the one-time home of missionary Dwight Baldwin and Lahaina's oldest standing building. In 1852, convicts got to build their very own prison, called **Hale Paahao** ("the stuck-in-irons house"), at Prison and Wainee streets. Also on Wainee Street, **Wainee Churchyard** shelters the bones of missionaries and royalty including Queen Keopuolani, King Kamehameha I's wife. **Wailoa Church**, next door, was originally built by Hawaiian chiefs in 1832 though the structure you'll be looking at was erected in 1953.

Continuing **south from Lahaina**, you'll arrive at the seaside community of **Olowalu**, notable both for the 1790 Olowalu Massacre and the present-day **Chez Paul Restaurant**. **Olowalu Beach** is a tourist and snorkeler's favorite. Heading inland from Maalaea Harbor, along the Honopiilani Highway, **Maui Tropical Plantation** will knock you out with its 112-acres of Hawaiian flowers, fruits, nuts, sugarcane and other agricultural delights. A string of atrocious condos, sunny beaches and ritzy resorts line the route **from Kihei to Makena**.

The biggest attraction of rural **Upcountry Maui** has got to be 27,284-acre **Haleakala National Park** and the enormous crater. Other Upcountry sights to see include **Tedeschi Vineyards**, the nine-mile scenic **Olinda Drive** and the cowboy-turned-artsy-town of Makawao.

Highlight of the **Hana Coast** is definitely the view-, twist- and plant-a-thon **Hana Highway** between Kahului Airport and Hana. Enroute are plenty of nature walks, beaches, waterfalls, caves and scenic lookouts. Stop off at **Keanae Arboretum** to view wonderful displays of plant life, and investigate the caves, coves, pools and beaches of **Waianapanapa State Park**. In Hana, check out the changing exhibits at **Hana Cultural Center**, do a safe swim at **Hana Beach Park**, hang with the locals at **Hasegawa General Store** and explore the **Seven Sacred Pools** (which are many more than seven, and not particularly sacred—at least not to the Hawaiians!).

Central Maui

Kahului

Kaahumanu Center

> *275 Kaahumanu Avenue, Kahului,* ☎ *(808) 877-3369.*
> *Hours: 9 a.m.–5:30 p.m.*
> *Special hours: to 9 p.m. Thurs., Fri.; 10 a.m.–4 p.m. Sun.*

Only five minutes from Kahului Airport, it features more than 60 stores and restaurants. Favorite for residents with Sears, Liberty House, J.C. Penney and the Japanese counterpart, Shirokiya. Frequent free activities and entertainment.

Beaches

Kanaha Beach Park ★★
Amala Place, near Kahului Airport, Kahului.
A popular windsurfing spot near the airport with picture-perfect white sand; the only drawback being the loud planes flying overhead. Fine for swimming, with barbecue pits, picnic tables, showers and phones.

City Celebrations

Art Maui ★★★
340 Kahului Beach Road, Kahului.
Hours: 11 a.m.–5 p.m.
Closed: Mon.
One of Hawaii's most prestigious juried art shows, held in March at the Kazuma International Gallery, at the Maui Arts and Cultural Center. Showcases a variety of art representing Maui County. Painting, drawing, prints, photography, fiber arts, collages and sculpture must all have been created within the past two years. Artists interact with attendees.

Hiking

Hike Maui ★★★★
P.O. Box 330969, Kahului, 96733, ☎ *(808) 879-5270.*
Ken Schmidt is the granddaddy of hiking guides, and he's spawned many imitators. Schmidt, a naturalist who lived in the wilderness for three years, leads guided natural history excursions and hikes to rainforests, waterfalls and the Haleakala Crater. Make reservations way in advance as these hikes are VERY popular. Half and full day itineraries include lunch, waterproof day packs, rain ponchos, first-aid gear, water bottles. Maximum group size is six to eight people. Children, $35–$55. General admission: $60–$90.

Kanaha Pond Waterfowl Refuge ★★★★
Haleakala Highway 36, Kahului, 96732, ☎ *(808) 243-5352.*
Just east from Kahului Airport, heading towards Paia, is this nesting site for migratory waterfowl and native birds, including Hawaiian heron, coot and stilt. Sketch, photograph or just observe these fine-feathered friends while walking on one of two circular trails, each a mile long. Permits required.

Museums and Exhibits

Paper Airplane Museum ★★
Maui Mall, 70 East Kaahumanu Avenue, Kahului, ☎ *(808) 877-8916.*
Hours: 9 a.m.–5 p.m.
Situated next to the House of Pancakes in Maui Mall, the Paper Airplane Museum is reputed to be the only facility of its kind in world. More than 2000 aircraft models and kits can be found, from postage-stamp size to one with a wing span of six feet. All are made from at least 95 percent paper. Numerous items made from Hawaiian juice cans. Regular construction demos scheduled.

MAUI

The Shows

Maui Arts & Cultural Center   ★★★★

Maui Central Park, Kahului, ☎ (808) 242-2787.
Hours: 10 a.m.–5 p.m.

Private citizens raised $11.3 million to help build this two-year-old, visually friendly, yet technically sophisticated community arts and theater center. The 12-acre complex features the 1200-seat Castle Theater (James Taylor and Carlos Santana performed here recently) and the more intimate, 300-seat McCoy Studio Theater. Both the Maui Community Theater (Maui OnStage) and Maui Academy of Performing Arts call the Center home. Also on the grounds are an outdoor amphitheater, and *a pa hula*, or earthen platform, used exclusively for ancient Hawaiian chants. The 4100-square-foot Kazuma Gallery houses a valuable collection of arts and crafts commissioned especially for the center. An annual Spring event is Art Maui, one of Hawaii's most prestigious juried shows. Good news for visitors who won't be on the island long enough to attend a performance: the center offers free 90-minute tours of most of the facilities every Tuesday at 11 a.m. Reservations are required.

Tours

Alex Air   ★★★

P.O. Box 330626, Kahului, 96733, ☎ (808) 871-0792.

The founder of this family-owned company helped develop the Hughes 300 helicopter, and today the AlexAir fleet includes 11 helicopters and 14 airplanes. Ten kinds of helicopter tours are offered, on four-passenger Hughes 500'copters. Window seats are guaranteed. Flights longer than 30 minutes include a free video, "choreographed" to Alpine stereo music. AlexAir rarely cancels flights; heavy rain means more waterfall activity and light tradewinds. Reservations three to five days in advance. Ask for repeat-visitor and *kamaaina* rates. General admission: $69–$240.

Best of Maui Cassette Tours   ★★

Route 380 (Dairy Road), Kahului, ☎ (808) 871-1555.

Whether on the way to Hana or the Haleakala Crater, you'll most likely pass this roadside stand with a bright yellow awning. It's not selling maps to stars' homes, although there are enough of them living here. Instead, for $20 you can purchase an audiocassette tour of either site; the detailed explanations will point you in the right direction. The company will even provide you with a tape player—just don't take your hands off the wheel while changing sides. The complete package includes a flower/bird ID card, guide books, coupons, huge full-color map, "I Survived Hana Highway" certificate and a videotape, "Visions of Maui." General admission: $20.

Biplane Barnstormers   ★★★

Kahului Airport, Kahului, ☎ (808) 878-2860.

Wayne Wagner, who's been flying folks around for more than 30 years, offers five sightseeing tours for one or two passengers, or a thrilling aerobatic ride for one in an authentic reproduction of a 1935 WACO open-cockpit biplane. Wagner communicates with his passengers via intercom (kinda hard to yell up there). For an authentic experience, wear a leather helmet, goggles, silk scarf and pretend you're the Red Baron. General admission: $48 and up.

Blue Hawaiian Helicopters ★★★

Kahului Airport Hangar 105, Kahului, 96732, ☎ *(808) 871-8844.*

There are no helicopter companies in Molokai, so if you want to fly over the spectacular Kalaupapa Peninsula (see Tours and Historical Sites) you might want to try Blue Hawaiian's Molokai-West Maui air tour, a 65-minute flight that takes you over the isolated former leper colony separated from the rest of the island by the world's highest sea cliffs. Blue Hawaiian's new ASTAR helicopters are reportedly stable, spacious and fairly quiet (plus they provide special Bose headsets that cancel all cabin noise), offering 180-degree views for all passengers. This company, in business for 12 years, employs ex-military aviators with at least 11,000 logged hours and 20 years' experience each. Many readers (and locals) recommend Blue Hawaiian as providing the best service (it rarely cancels flights, which can be a hassle for passengers with tight itineraries and high expectations). The company offers six other tours, including a Sunset Spectacular. This aerial tour of Hana/Haleakala ends with a landing at a selected vantage point on Maui to view the sunset, while refreshments are served. A videotape of your experience (including sighs, screams and narration) is included. Twenty-four-hour cancellation notice required. From Lahaina, take Highway 30 to 380 to 36; turn right to 37, turn left, continue one quarter mile to stop sign; second right after stop, second building on left. General admission: $130–$220.

First Class Yacht Charters ★★

107 Kahului Heliport, Kahului, 96732, ☎ *(808) 667-7733.*

Along with whale-watching and sunset sails, this company offers a unique experience: a 1.5-hour competition sail adventure for $35. This journey simulates an America's Cup style race, with two trained crews on equally matched 65-foot yachts challenging each other to finish first. You get to watch while on board and take in incredible views. No sailing experience necessary, but prepare to get wet. In a special two-fer deal with Sunshine Helicopters, if you book a ride with the latter, you get the competition sail free. Trips depart from either Lahaina Harbor or Kaanapali Beach. General admission: $25–$65.

Hawaiian Helicopters ★★★

Hangar 106, Kahului Airport, Kahului, 96732, ☎ *(808) 877-3900.*

Hawaiian Helicopters features a fleet of ASTAR touring helicopters with 180-degree unobstructed viewing from every seat. If you can afford it, take a deluxe air-ground tour; after flying over Haleakala crater and selected valleys and waterfalls, you touch down in Hana, where a champagne picnic is set out for you in Waianapanapa State Park. Reservations required. Call toll-free, ☎ *(800) 346-2403* on the mainland; in Hawaii, call ☎ *(800) 994-9099.* General admission: $89–$285.

Maui Downhill Bicycle Safaris ★★★

199 Dairy Road, Kahului, 96732, ☎ *(808) 871-2155.*
Hours: 24 hours

Former VP Dan Quayle and his flock chose to bike down Haleakala Volcano with this outfit, which provides "safari" bikes with heavy-duty brakes, helmets, windbreakers and gloves. It starts at the 10,023-foot summit of the volcano. You can choose from among six rides, which range from 22 to 38 miles; longer ones include continental breakfast at the Kula Lodge and lunch. It's a lot of fun, although you look kinda funny dressed in a space suit following other funny-looking people down the mountain. It's something the whole family can enjoy, with only 400 yards of pedaling involved. Includes two guides, escort van. The cheapest ride doesn't include round-trip transportation. General admission: $48–$115.

Sunshine Helicopters   ★★★

107 Kahului Heliport, Kahului, 96732, ☎ (808) 871-0722.

When this company refers to its Black Beauties, it doesn't mean drugs or horses. Rather, it's talking about a fleet of ASTAR helicopters, offering 180-degree views and a "sky cam" four-camera video system. The outgoing pilots have more than 30 years of flying experience and excellent safety records, with more than 10,000 flight hours each. Tours include the West Maui Deluxe tour, a complete circle tour that includes an extinct volcano, Pu'u Kukui, and Honokohau, the island's tallest waterfall, at over 1100 feet. The most popular tour flies over Hana and Haleakala, at $129 per person. Private charters available, with custom picnic baskets, for $20 per person. Ask about horseback riding and cabin rentals. Minimum 30 minutes. Free video of flight included. General admission: $99–$1020.

Makawao

Hiking

Nature Conservancy Hikes Maui   ★★★

P.O. Box 1716, Makawao, 96768, ☎ (808) 572-7849.

Conservancy guides lead monthly hikes to Waikamoi and Kapunakea preserves every month. Kapunakea, in the West Maui mountains, protects many types of rare Hawaiian plants, animals and natural communities. Hikes are along a historical trail on the lower edge of Honokawai Valley. Not for people with a fear of heights (or hikes!). Space is very limited. Waikamoi, on the slopes of Haleakala, protects a high-elevation rainforest, and alpine shrub land, home of rare native birds and plants that exist nowhere else on Earth. The National Park Service also conducts hikes here on Monday and Thursday mornings at 9 a.m. Call ☎ (808) 572-9306 for details. Work parties clear the preserves from invasive weeds; these are scheduled every third Saturday of the month. Reserve for all hikes way in advance. The $25 donation helps to defray costs, nonmembers receive a one-year membership including all benefits. General admission: $25.

Museums and Exhibits

Hui Noeau Visual Arts Center   ★★★★

2841 Baldwin Avenue, Makawao, 96768, ☎ (808) 572-6560.
Hours: 9 a.m.–4 p.m.
Closed: Mon.

Meaning "Club of Skills," this is Maui's first art league formed by missionary descendant Ethel Baldwin and her circle of friends. The group grew to become a prestigious visual arts organization bringing the world's leading artists to Maui for exhibits, classes, lectures and workshops. Hui Noeau is now housed in the gracious old Baldwin estate, Kaluani, and hosts important island shows in its gallery. The small gift shop is a treasure trove of some of the best island-made arts, crafts, clothing and jewelry. Offers more than 400 art programs each year, most of them hands-on studio classes. If you're here at Christmas, don't miss the annual holiday crafts fair featuring handmade items made on Maui.

Tours

Open Eye Tours ★★★

P.O. Box 324, Makawao, 96768, ☎ *(808) 572-3483.*
Custom-designed, half-day (up to five hours) and full-day (up to 10 hours) tours by photographer Barry Fried, a man of many talents, who's led Elder Hostel tours, been a volunteer educator with the Hawaii Nature center, and is a PADI certified scuba instructor. Active types can tour rainforests, craters or wildlife reserves. Or if you're not particularly outdoorsy, he'll take you to an exotic garden, a cultural center, an artist's studio, or show you where the best local eateries are. Caters mostly to solos and couples; three or more, add $55 per person. Includes chauffeuring, snacks and beverages; gourmet meals on request. Tours available on all islands. General admission: $100–$225.

Paia

Beaches

Baldwin County Park ★

Hana Highway 36, towards Paia, Paia, ☎ *(808) 243-7230.*
A rather noisy (it's just 100 feet from the highway) county park with a wide swath of beach that's popular with locals. Not quite the ultimate destination, but it's there. Tent sites available in a fenced area somewhat away from the beach, for 15-20 people, limit three days. There's drinking water and restroom facilities. Children's admission, 50 cents for under 18. General admission: $3.

Hookipa Beach ★★

Hana Highway, east of Paia, Paia.
If your bod hasn't seen the sun lately, approach this beach with extreme trepidation. This turf is dominated by bronzed, buffed godlets who are top-class (or wannabe) windsurfers from around the globe (mostly Europe), plus a few weatherbeaten fisher-folk who couldn't care less. Hookipa is the boardsailing capital of the world, and site of two major world-class competitions, awarding purses of up to $180,000. The small beach is rock-strewn, and the swimming? Well, forget it. Picnic area, phone, showers.

Tours

Cruiser Bob's Original Downhill Bike Tour ★★★

99 Hana Highway, Paia, 96770, ☎ *(808) 579-8444.*
Cruiser Bob started it all: now there's Snorkel Bob, Windsurf Bob, you name it, but there's only one Bob Kiger, originator of the 38-mile downhill bicycle coast from Haleakala Crater to his exclusive base lodge in a Chevron station in Paia. Three

tours, but the most popular is the Sunrise Tour with a hotel pickup at (yeow!) 2 a.m. Service is excellent. Meals, equipment, shuttle included. General admission: $49–$120.

Pu'unene

Museums and Exhibits

Alexander and Baldwin Sugar Museum ★★★

3957 Hansen Road, Pu'unene, 96784, ☎ *(808) 871-8058.*
Hours: 9:30 a.m.–4:30 p.m.
Special hours: daily from mid-June to Aug. 31. Closed: Sun.

While no longer king of Maui agriculture, sugar is at least a princeling (and it still rots your teeth). Not far away from this converted factory superintendent's home-turned-museum is the actual mill itself, still chugging away. One of two mills operated by Alexander and Baldwin on Maui (the other is in Paia), it processes some of the 36,000 acres of sugarcane grown on the island by the 125-year-old company. In each of the award-winning museum's six rooms, the exhibits, documents and photographs focus on the humble plantation worker rather than trumpet the achievements of the bosses. Among the rare treasures is the only known labor contract in the world written in Hawaiian, and a working model of a Cuban cane crusher assembled by an American prisoner of war in the Philippines. $1.50 for children six to 17; free for children five and under. Gift shop. General admission: $3.

The Shows

Maui Academy of the Performing Arts ★★

P.O. Box 518, Pu'unene, 96784, ☎ *(808) 244-8760.*

This performing troupe and acting academy's theater season runs from July through May. For an enriching experience, sign up for one of the weekly classes, held at the Maui Arts and Cultural Center (see listing).

Waikapu

Parks and Gardens

Maui Tropical Plantation ★★

Honopiilani Highway, Waikapu, ☎ *(808) 244-7643.*
Hours: 9 a.m.–5 p.m.

Six miles from the Kahului Airport, this 150-acre plantation and agricultural extravaganza is campy but fun. All kinds of produce, including flowers, veggies, nuts, sugarcane, bananas and pineapples, are on display for your perusal and/or purchase. There's always something to catch your eye; in one corner someone is stringing a lei, husking a coconut or cutting up pineapple. A film on the sugar industry is constantly on view in the Pavilion. Of course, there's a 45-minute tram tour to take it all in (optional, $8 per person). The kids can have their picture taken with "Joe" the Hawaiian horse (who wears a flower lei around his neck). Hungry? The restaurant is open for lunch and dinner, and there's an all-you-can-eat Hawaiian Country Barbecue on Tuesday, Wednesday and Thursday nights from 4:30 to 7:30 p.m. The fare is mediocre, but plentiful, and includes grilled sirloin, country chicken, "plantation" chili and fixin's. Entertainment provided by a four-piece cowboy band. The whole schmeer will run you $48.95; Children, five–12, $19.95; Toddlers free.

Wailuku

Hiking

Iao Valley ★★★★

West Main Street to end, park in lot, Wailuku, 96793, ☎ (808) 243-5354.
The famous Iao Needle is a 2250-foot lava-rock pinnacle covered with lush foliage that points a velvet finger at the sky. A lovely park is built around it, where visitors can stroll, viewing many varieties of exotic flowers and trees or climb the path to a sheltered lookout. The trail begins at the parking lot, and climbs 500 feet to the valley overlook. You can also take a side trail up to Iao stream, but the rocks near the stream are pretty slippery. Trails also go deep into the valley, but are dangerous to travel due to flooding. Along the road to the valley is Kepaniwai Park (see "Parks and Gardens"), where gardens and replicas of ethnic dwellings can be seen. Parking, picnic facilities, rest rooms. Hawaii Nature Center Maui offers guided hikes of Iao Valley; call ☎ *(808) 244-6500.*

Waihee Ridge Trail ★★

Camp Maluhia Kahekili Highway, Wailuku, 96793, ☎ (808) 243-5352.
This tough trail climbs 2.5 miles to a peak overlooking Wailuku, with lush jungle views of cliffs, gorges and a wet native scrub forest. Wear long pants, rain gear and hiking boots—no sneakers. Pick up a free plant photo guide and maps from the Department of Land and Natural Resources weekdays at *54 S. High St., Room 101, Wailuku,* ☎ *(808) 243-5352.*

Museums and Exhibits

Bailey House Museum ★★★

2375-A Main Street, Wailuku, 96793, ☎ (808) 244-3326.
Hours: 10 a.m.–4 p.m.
Once the home of missionary Edward Bailey, this restored 1833 building is run by the Maui Historical Society. Docents provide fascinating running commentary while showing off an excellent collection of Hawaiian artifacts, including rare examples of *kapa*, or bark cloth, clothing and period furniture. Of particular interest is a collection of landscape paintings done by Bailey himself. General admission: $3.

Parks and Gardens

Kepaniwai Cultural Park ★★

Iao Valley Road, Wailuku, 96793, ☎ (808) 243-7389.
Hours: 7 a.m.–7 p.m.
At this pleasant park located on the bank of Iao Stream, you can see representative dwellings, gardens and sculptures of most of the diverse ethnic mix of peoples that live in Hawaii. You'll also see living examples in the families that picnic and barbecue in the park. There's also a public swimming pool.

Maui Zoological and Botanical Gardens ★★

Kanaloa Avenue, Wailuku, 96793, ☎ (808) 243-7337.
Hours: 9 a.m.–4 p.m.

Not worth going out of your way for, but it's a nice place to stroll and take the kids; best of all it's free. If you missed seeing a *nene* goose in Haleakala National Park, here's your chance. The botanical section features more than 150 species of native Hawaiian plants.

The Shows

Maui OnStage

68 North Market Street, Wailuku, 96793, ☎ (808) 244-8680.

Also known as the Maui Community Theater, this company is housed in two venues: the $28 million Maui Art and Cultural Center, and the historic old Iao Theater. While the group has no specific season, at least eight major productions and two experimental plays are staged each year. Call for schedule and prices.

Tours

Maui Molokai Sea Cruises   ★★★

831 Eha Street, Wailuku, 96793, ☎ (808) 242-8777.
Hours: 7:15 a.m.–11:15 a.m.

Year-round snorkeling adventures to Molokini Crater on the *M.V. Prince Kuhio*, the largest cruise vessel in Maui waters. The vessel seats 250, but takes only 150 passengers. The typical crew includes a NAUI certified snorkel instructor. Both the upper-viewing deck and air-conditioned lower deck have full service bars. A 12-foot bowsprit extends out over the water for a thrilling ride. Includes everything but towels. Also private charters, theme parties for groups and sunset dinner sails. Pickup from selected hotels. General admission: $75.

East Maui

Hana

Beaches

Hamoa Beach

Left on coast road, three miles south of Hotel Hana Maui, Hana.

This crescent-shaped, 100-foot wide beach has sand that looks like someone forgot to put the top on the pepper shaker. It has an idyllic, lush setting, inspiring James Michener to call it "the only beach I have ever seen that looks like the South Pacific—and it's in the North Pacific." (Or something like that). Used by the Hotel Hana Maui's guests, but it's public. Facilities include rest rooms, shower, snack bar, benches, lounges and lifeguard.

Red Sand Beach (Kaihalulu)

Hana.

This beach, whose Hawaiian name means "roaring sea," is reached by a trail that starts at the Hana Community Center and wraps around the coast of Kauiki Hill. The path is well-trod but narrow, steep and perilous. Beware. Its red sands were formed by hot cinder fallout from an exploding volcano. When you reach it, you'll be surrounded by red cinder walls and natural rock jettys. Great for sun, snorkel, locals, hippies and tourists. Used for nude sunbathing. Some of the roughest swimming on the island. No facilities. Park on street by softball diamond next to hotel.

Waianapanapa State Park   ★★★★

Three miles north of Hanna ☎ *(808) 243-5354.*

Three miles from Hana town, this ruggedly beautiful beach park has it all. Activities include hiking on footpaths trod by Hawaiian kings, swimming in lava-tube caves, or setting out a beach mat on a black sand beach (swimming is unsafe). The choice of camping facilities include 12 cabins and tent sites with ocean views. The cabins house six people each, and are equipped with linens, cooking facilities and utensils. Cost is $5 per person for six people, and $10 for a single camper (less for children under 11). Maximum stay is five nights. Reservations taken a year in advance, and they are extremely hard to get. For information, write to the Division of Parks, 54 South High Street, Wailuku, HI 96793. General admission: $5–$10.

City Celebrations

Haku Mele O Hana   ★★★

Hotel Hana-Maui's Plantation House, Hana.
Hours: 9 a.m.–5 p.m.

One of Maui's most important cultural events celebrates authentic Hawaiian song and chant compositions. Original works by top *halaus* (schools) are performed in the fall, usually on the last Saturday in September, after an intensive three-day work-shop held in the spring. Hana's own award-winning *halau*, Na Mamoali'i O Ka'uiki, participates every year.

Maui Food Festivals   ★★★★

Hana and various locations, Hana.

If you timed it right, you could spend a year eating fairly cheaply and extremely well from booths at Maui's various food and wine festivals, where top island chefs (also some of the best in the state) perform culinary wizardry before your eyes. Pretend it's spring (around the last weekend of March) and we're in Hana for the East Maui Taro Festival. Here's your chance to sample taro pancakes, taro tempura or poi balls. When you look up from your plate, there's a farmer's market, poi pounding demos, and Hawaiian games to look forward to. For more info, call ☎ *(808) 248-8972*. In April, the question on everyone's lips is "Are you going to the Ulupalakua Thing?" That's local talk for the Maui County Ag Trade Show, held at the Ulu Ranch and Tedeschi Winery. The focus is on up-country produce, but the food booths feature munchies from just about everywhere. Amateur chefs can participate in a Fresh Fruit contest. Information, ☎ *(808) 875-0457*. Every weekend in July the Kapalua Bay Hotel and Villa sponsors the Kapalua Wine and Food Symposium. Functions include seminars, demos, discussions and (pant, pant) tastings. It culminates in a Chefs' Seafood Festival, where 10 of Hawaii's premier chefs prepare an oceanside gourmet banquet. For information, call ☎ *(808) 669-0244*. The Maui Onion Festival, held in August at the Whalers Village Shopping Village in Kaanapali, honors the island's famous sweet onion grown in up-country Kula. Watch cooking demos or enter an onion recipe cook-off. You'll have an opportunity to nosh at a farmer's market and from a food court offering plenty of Maui onion concoctions. For information, call ☎ *(808) 661-4567*. Top chefs from more than 30 restaurants try to outdo each other in September when A Taste of Lahaina takes place. There's continuous entertainment, and beer and wine flows like rain. Make arrangements to attend the gala dinner under the stars that kicks off this two-day grande bouffe. Admission is free; guests purchase scrip for tasting at food booths. For information, call ☎ *(808) 667-9175*. Had enough? I have, I'm stuffed.

Historical Sites

Fagan Memorial ★★

On a hilltop across from the Hotel Hana-Maui, Hana.

The people of Hana erected this 30-foot-high lava rock cross on a hilltop in 1960 after the death of Paul Fagan, founder of Hana Ranch and the Hotel Hana-Maui. The views of the Hana coast from the top of the memorial are absolutely tops!

Museums and Exhibits

Hana Cultural Center ★★

Box 27, Hana, 96713, ☎ (808) 248-8622.
Hours: 10 a.m.–4 p.m.

Although small, this museum is packed with rarities, including a 100-year-old fishing net made of woven vines, turtle shell fishhooks, koa canoe paddles, poi boards, baskets, turtleshells and quilts, as well as photo and bottle collections. These will keep you occupied for hours. It's free, but donations are more than welcome; the museum exists to preserve Hana's history.

Tours

Hana Highway ★★★★★

Hana Highway (360), Hana.

Just remember while you're stuck behind some bozo going 10 miles an hour down this road: Getting there is half the fun. With this mind-set, the 51-mile route (from the Kahului Airport), involving 617 curves and 56 one-lane bridges, won't be so aggravating. Don't think of the Hana Highway as a means to an end, like you're on a morning commute to a job you hate anyway. Besides, you've traded that neck-choking tie for an Aloha shirt, that power suit for a sundress. Relax. Let Selma and Chet from Kansas go by, get off the road, and take in the sights, slowly. Highlights include Twin Falls, just past the two-mile marker, with a great swimming hole; Kaumahina State Wayside Park, at sea level, where you can explore tide pools; and Keanae Arboretum (at mile marker 16), with six acres of native trees, bamboo and indigenous Hawaiian crops. The twisty, curvy highway straightens out just before Hana, but before you explore the town proper, you can take the coast route past the Hana Airport to Waianapanapa State Park, with its incredible black-sand beach. Back in town, enjoy the waterfront and beach area, have lunch at Tutu's, a beach shack serving good mahi burgers and haupia (coconut pudding) ice cream. Don't pass up the Hasegawa General Store, where you can pick up an official "I Survived the Hana Road" T-shirt. After a few hours here you can return the way you came or continue past Kipahulu and the Pools of Oheo, on the eastern side of Haleakala National Park. Ask a ranger about road conditions along this end; if it isn't washed out, continue the back way out of Hana. After four miles of potholes and dirt, the road eventually becomes paved again. The desert-like terrain is nothing like the road you just came on, but it'll get you back to Kahului. Following are the main precautions for the Hana Highway: call for a weather report. This road is no fun in a squall. Travel on a weekend. There will be fewer delivery trucks, commuters and less road work. Tank up before you go. There are no gas stations between Kahului and Hana. Allow at least three hours travel time each way, and an additional hour if you're traveling to Kipahulu.

Keanae
Parks and Gardens

Keanae Arboretum   ★★★

On Hana Highway, between Huelo and Keanae, Keanae.

This hike is for hardy beginners, but the whole family will enjoy it. The complete hike is 2.3 miles, with a 200-foot elevation. You'll see a variety of native and introduced plants and trees, many of which are identified. Paths are wide and well-kept, and when the stream has enough water in it, you can soak your feet or swim. Bring good walking shoes and bug repellent, and don't drink from the streams.

Kipahulu
Hiking

Waimoku Falls   ★★★★

Highway 31 between Hana and Kipahulu 96713, ☎ *(808) 248-7367.*

Situated in the East Maui section of Haleakala National Park, the trail to the falls is two miles long, past a gate that's 100 yards south of the Pools of Oheo. The well-maintained trail includes wonderful views of the upper falls. You'll pass through a beautiful bamboo forest. Fun for the whole family, with swimming holes aplenty. Plenty of parking, picnic tables, camping and rest rooms.

Historical Sites

Lindbergh's Grave   ★★★

Piilani Highway, 10 miles south of Hana Town, Kipahulu.

The great aviator, who lived in Hana for the last years of his life, is buried under a block of Vermont granite in the graveyard of Palapala Hoomau Congregational Church. Somewhat out of the way, the church is reached via a rutted, gravel drive off the Piilani Hwy about a quarter-mile past Oheo Gulch. Sometimes a sign is nailed up to a tree about 100 feet from the church driveway, but it's best to ask a local for directions.

Parks and Gardens

Pools of Oheo   ★★★★

Piilani Highway, south of Hana, near Kipahulu 96713, ☎ *(808) 248-7375. Hours: 9 a.m.–5 p.m.*

This is the new Hawaiian name for the long-controversial Seven Sacred Pools, a gulch and stream that flows through some 22 pools in Kipahulu, which is part of Haleakala National Park, reached on a potholed road past Hana. Since the mid-1970s, when Hawaiian became an official language, efforts have been made to change the name, which was started by an activity director at the Hotel Hana-Maui way back in the unenlightened '40s, to attract tourism in the area. This delightful spot is for everyone who has always dreamed of bathing under a waterfall. At the

Pools of Oheo, not one, but several waterfalls spill into tiered pools leading to the sea where you can swim. Rangers conduct nature walks and proffer advice on nearby hiking trails that you can do yourself.

Tours

Ohe'o Stables

Kipahulu Ranch, Star Route 1, Box 151A, Kipahulu, 96713, ☎ (808) 667-2222.

This refreshing horseback ride is unusual in that it is the only one that traverses the Kipahulu section of Haleakala Park, which is one mile past the Pools of Oheo. The three-hour mountain ride takes in panoramic views of Waimoku falls and five to seven smaller ones. Weight limit is 250 pounds, "no exceptions." Rides leave promptly at 11:30 a.m. and 2:30 p.m. Remember that it's three hours from West Maui and Kihei to Kipahulu; leave at 7 a.m. for the early ride. Don't forget your bathing suit for a swim after the ride. Includes snacks. General admission: $95.

Northwest Maui

Kahakuloa

Kianna Kai

Kahakuloa, ☎ (808) 575-9165.

The only deep-sea fishing charter to operate off the scenic North shore. Couples sightseeing with angling. Shares a cut of the catch. Charter aboard 21-foot Alii Kai, caters to small groups. Captain is "ono King" Chris Ingrisano. Call for rates.

South Maui

Kihei

Beaches

Kamaole Beach Parks

Along South Kihei Road, Kihei.

These are three consecutive, top-flight beach parks located across the street from Dolphin Plaza and Rainbow Shopping Mall, on South Kihei Road. Depending on weather conditions, all are great for swimming, snorkeling, kayak launching, sailing, whale-watching and boogie-boarding. Parking is plentiful and close, with spacious picnic areas for family gatherings. Arguably, the best of the trio is Kamaole III, with the finest sand. At its end is Peace Park, with only a few trees, lots of grass and a fairly gentle slope. You'll see a lot of kite-flying activity in the afternoon, due to trade-wind activity. Facilities include a lifeguard, BBQ grills, phone and showers. One drawback is the high wind factor, especially in the afternoon, which creates fast currents and blowing sand. Watch for the red-flag alert.

Hiking

Kealia Pond National Wildlife Refuge

On both sides of Route 31 between Routes 30 and 350, Kihei.
Hours: Mon.–Fri., 7:30 a.m.–4 p.m.

This protected, 691-acre federal refuge and sanctuary for 30 or more species of birds can be toured via an easy, two-mile hike (each way) that's just a short drive from Kihei. Because the route follows the coast and beach, you can walk the shoreline and even swim in the surf if you wish. Along with birds such as the ae'o, a black-necked stilt, or the black-crowned night heron, there are frequent sightings of the hawksbill turtle between July and December. These rare creatures, with long, narrow beaks, often get as big as 200 pounds. The females come here to nest—unfortunately crossing a busy highway to do so. Recently officials have posted roadside warning signs to alert motorists. Kealia is also a good vantage point for whale sightings in November–April. Plans call for 4400 foot boardwalk along south side of refuge. Begin the hike at the turnout at the three-mile marker on the ocean side of Route 31. Plenty of parking. Information, refuge office at *101 N. Kihei Road.*

Outfitters Maui ★★★
2439 South Kihei Road, Kihei, ☎ (808) 875-4848.
Hiking tours brought to you by Michael and Melissa McCoy, owners of South Pacific Kayaks. "Maui Hiking Adventures: Streams and Waterfalls," $55, three to four hours, both morning and afternoon tours available. You'll see native birds and learn about flora and fauna. Includes snacks and backpack. Bring hiking shoes, hat, visor. Easy. "Hidden Treasures," six to seven hours, $85. Takes you to a less accessible area, including waterfalls, deep valleys and crystal-clear pools. Easy to moderate. Includes lunch, beverage and backpack. Bring bottled water. "The Bamboo Forest Tour," in the Hana/Kipahulu area, traverses swimming holes, Waimoku Falls and a singing bamboo forest. Easy to moderate, nine to 11 hours, includes lunch, $115. Also Haleakala or La Perouse Bay snorkel treks. Exact areas vary. Reservations required. On mainland call ☎ *(800) 776-2326.* General admission: $55–$115.

Tours

Ocean Activities Center ★★★
1847 South Kihei Road, Kihei, 96753, ☎ (808) 879-4485.
The first company to offer group snorkeling trips to Molokini islet, one of Maui's finest snorkeling spots, and thanks to other imitators, now the most crowded. Offices are located in resorts and hotels all over the island. Books a variety of activity packages, from sunset dinner cruises to deep-sea sport-fishing charters to whale-watching. There are two excellent Molokini snorkel cruises, including a deluxe package with a continental breakfast and deli lunch, mai tais, gear, instruction and shuttle transportation. Leaves 7:15 a.m. and returns 12:15 p.m. from Maalaea harbor slip 58. The plain-vanilla Molokini snorkel cruise is only $39.95, children $20, with continental breakfast, light deli lunch and beverages. Ask about the Lanai Snorkel Cruise. General admission: $25–$635.

Pacific Whale Foundation ★★★
101 North Kihei Road, Kihei, 96753, ☎ (808) 879-8811.
Every day from December-May, this nonprofit scientific research foundation offers 10 humpback whale-watching cruises out of Lahaina and Maalaea Harbors. Trips are guided by knowledgeable marine naturalists, most of them involved with whale research. Both of the whale-watching vessels, the *Manute'a*, a 50-foot sailing catamaran, and *Whale II*, a 50-foot sailing yacht, or the *Whale One*, a 53-foot motor vessel, offer a combination of sunny observation decks and protected, shady cabins.

Scientific hydrophones enable you to hear the whales' songs. All profits support the Foundation's efforts to save the whales. Other "Eco-Adventure" tours include a Molokini/Turtle Arches Picnic Snorkel, Lanai Wild Dolphin and Snorkeling Adventure, and a Taste of Maui Dinner Cruise. Ask about a new internship program to study dolphins off the coast of Lanai in the summer of 1997. General admission: $19 and up.

Pride Charters, Inc.

208 Kenolio Road, Kihei, 96753, ☎ (808) 874-8835.

Ride the *Pride*, a 65-foot maxi catamaran, specifically built for Molokini Excursions. The high-powered engines allow for the longest time in the water, and two snorkel sites are included, in addition to Molokini. The Morning Molokini Snorkel includes breakfast, a barbecue lunch, snorkel equipment, boogie boards and optical masks. Scuba, snuba and underwater camera rentals available for an extra fee. Leaves from Maalaea Harbor public loading dock daily from 7:30 a.m.–1:30.pm. Ages 13–18, $60; five–12, $40; four and under, free. Also afternoon sunset/snorkel, afternoon whale-watch cruise, and sunset cocktail cruise (Wednesdays only). General admission: $30–$70.

La Perouse Bay

Hiking

King's Highway Coastal Trail ★★

Past Makena Beach and Ahihi-Keanau Reserve, La Perouse Bay.

This 11-mile round-trip trail, actually used by kings on their interisland route to collect taxes, is well marked, but hot, and marked by rough, sharp lava, and you can easily lose your footing. Sound lovely so far? The trail is important for its historical value, as it leads past the site of an ancient Hawaiian village decimated in a 1700s lava flow. You can still see the original house foundations. The trail passes the shoreline in places and the views of La Perouse Bay are entrancing. Bring lots of water and watch out for sunstroke and dehydration. No facilities. Contact Maui Hiking Safaris for a guided tour (see "Tours").

Maalaea Bay

Tours

Navatek II

Maalaea Harbor, Maalaea Bay, ☎ (808) 661-8787.
Hours: 8:45 a.m.–2:45 p.m.

Navatek II has revolutionized ocean travel in Hawaii with its patented motion-control technology developed by Lockheed. Even sensitive passengers can forget about seasickness. This luxurious vessel features a spacious tanning deck with lounge chairs, air-conditioned main cabin and amphitheater seating. The company's main offering is the "Lanai Voyage of Discovery," where guests are taken to a secluded bay off the Lanai coast to snorkel. Includes a gourmet waffle-bar breakfast, barbecue lunch, full-service bar and a marine life naturalist providing expert narration on the history and legends of Lanai. You don't even need snorkel gear; even prescription masks are provided. Optional: snuba, therapeutic massage, video services. Children's admission: $64. Other cruises include the Sunset Odyssey Dining Experience, a two-hour dinner cruise with entertainment and full bar leaves the harbor at 5:30 every day except Wednesdays, Fridays and Sundays. Cost per person is $85; children $45. Also a whale-watch cruise (January–April) for $55; children, $35. General admission: $127.

Makena

Beaches

La Perouse Beach ★★★

End of Makena Alanui Road, Makena.

Beautiful area to snorkel, swim, scuba-dive, kayak and surf, but only for experienced folks. Not much of a beach, it's remote, winds are bad in the afternoon, with large shore breaks, and no lifeguards, but the area is significant historically. French explorer Admiral Jean Francois Galaup, Comte de La Perouse (!), anchored his two frigates in the bay in 1786, in a spot where a 14th-century Hawaiian village used to be located. He's believed to be the first *haole* to set foot on Maui. You can still see the remains of the village, decimated by a 1790 lava flow. To get here, take Makena Alanui Road past the Maui Prince Hotel, continue on past Ahihi Bay, keep going past Ahihi Bay for a few miles. When the road becomes four-wheel-drive only, you're there. Parking by the ocean. No facilities.

Maluaka Beach ★★★★

In front of the Maui Prince Hotel, Makena.

A beautiful white-sand beach next to the Keawalai Church and fronting the Maui Prince Hotel in Makena, south of Kihei. You can swim to a turtle reef about 100 yards off the south end. Good for swimming and boogie-boarding. Phone and showers.

Oneloa Beach ★★★

Beyond the Maui Prince Hotel at Makena Resort, Makena, 96753.

Also called Makena or Big Beach, for its miles and miles of soft, golden, unbelievable sand. Waters are always clear, clean and of varying turquoise hues. But swimming can be treacherous, as waves crash right onto the beach and can be very dangerous. In winter, humpbacks frolic in the channel fronting the beach. Some snorkelers have experienced hearing the whales' songs while under water. No facilities, and it gets pretty hot due to lack of shady trees. Directions: Take Highway 31 or Piilani Highway to Wailea Resort. Follow Wailea Alanui to Makena Alanui past the Maui Prince, turn right on a dirt road that runs down to a parking lot at the beach.

Puu Olai Beach ★★★

Past the Maui Prince Hotel, Makena.

One mile south past the Maui Prince Hotel, you can't help but notice a 360-foot-high, red-cinder cone overlooking the ocean. This is Puuolai, one of Haleakala's craters under which is a large cave, said to be the sacred dwelling place of Mano, the ancestral shark deity. At the north end of the cinder cone is a trail leading up a cliff and over to a gorgeous beach that's an unofficial "bathing suits optional" stretch.

It's patrolled occasionally, so beware. Snorkeling, bodysurfing are all great. No facilities.

Sacred Beach

Makena.

Sunbathe and snorkel or do something unmentionable at this romantic, off-the-beaten track beach where weddings often take place. Directions: Go on Wailea Alanui Drive about eight miles south of the Kea Lani Hotel and turn into the beach parking lot marked Paipu Beach. Walk north over a sand dune and you'll come out on a very secluded beach.

Tours

Makena Stables ★★★

7299 South Makena Road, Makena, 96753, ☎ (808) 879-0244.

Hours: 7 a.m.–6 p.m.

Located a mile from the Maui Prince Hotel, Makena Stables offers three-hour morning and sunset guided-rides that include refreshments served on a hill overlooking the lava flows and the islands of Molokini and Kahoolawe. On clear days, the snowcapped peaks of Mauna Kea Volcano on the Big Island can be seen through the clouds. A six-hour ride takes visitors to the heart of Ulupalakua Ranch and to Tedeschi Vineyards. Picnic lunch included. Some familiarity with horses recommended. Trail is dusty, wild and sometimes desolate. Windy at dusk. Weight limitation is 250 pounds; age limit 12 years. General admission: $105–$145.

Off the Maui Coast

Molokini Islet ★★★★

Three miles offshore from Makena, Off the Maui Coast.

Molokini isn't a new-fangled kind of string bikini. Rather, it's a funny-looking, crescent-shaped, uninhabited land mass that sits between Maui and Kahoolawe, and rises 156 feet above sea level. The reason it looks that way is that its northern rim has eroded away with time, forming a protected cove ideal for diving and snorkeling. In fact, its incredible popularity has caused the state to enact new rules, including the prohibition of fish feeding. Despite arguments that feeding fish draws the critters to the site, adding excitement and color to scuba and snorkeling trips, the state remains adamant, countering that feeding draws sharks and eels to the area as well. A marine life conservation district since 1977, Molokini draws innumerable dive and commercial tour boats daily.

Wailea

Beaches

Wailea Beaches ★★★★

Kihei Road in front of the Wailea Resorts, Wailea, 96753, ☎ (808) 879-4461.

Five gorgeous white-sand beaches indent the shores of this posh, master-planned community on 1500 acres. Wailea, Ulua, Polo, Mokapu and Keawapuku beaches are considered some of the finest, with excellent swimming, snorkeling, scuba and sunbathing conditions year round. Each winter, humpback whales are often breaching just offshore. One great free activity is the Wailea beach walk, a public path overlooking all the beaches and ocean in front of the big resorts. The path is one mile long and runs from the Kea Lani Hotel at the south end to Stouffer's hotel at the north. This is also a popular jogging trail.

City Celebrations

Celebration of Whales ★★★

3900 Wailea Alanui Drive, Wailea, ☎ (808) 874-2221.

You won't find any "nuke the whales" bumper stickers on Maui; along with two whale museums, there are countless commercial cruises taking visitors on whale-watch expeditions during the humpback whales' annual migration from Alaska to Maui to breed, give birth and nurse their young. Not only are whales big business, people here sincerely love them. This annual, four-day festival, held at the Four Seasons Wailea Hotel around the last week of January, features video screenings, art exhibits, educational workshops and naturalist-narrated whale-watching tours. Cost varies according to activity.

Upcountry

Haleakala National Park

Many visitors are awed by the 1000 ft. Cinder Cones in Haleakala Crater.

Parks and Gardens

Haleakala National Park   ★★★★★

P.O. Box 369, Makawao, Haleakala National Park, 96768, ☎ *(808) 572-9306.*

Hours: 7:30 a.m.–4 p.m.

The "House of the Sun," a mammoth, dormant 10,023-foot volcano, offers great hiking and camping, and is inarguably the best place to watch the sun wake up in the morning from several vantage points. Just before the entrance to the park is Hosmer Grove, a perfect picnic, camping and hiking area surrounded by eucalyptus, cedar, juniper and spruce trees. It's a mostly level half-mile walk, loaded with birds. Bring binocs. On Mondays and Thursdays at 9 a.m., there's a three-hour, ranger-led hike into a rainforest that begins at the Grove. The first viewpoint, at 8800 feet, is Leleiwi Overlook, which is not for people afraid of their own shadow. In late afternoon, on cloudy days, you might see your image reflected in the mist. Kalahaku Overlook, at 9325 feet, showcases a garden of silverswords-unique plants found only in Hawaii. A 10-mile drive from headquarters takes you to the House of the Sun Visitors Center, with its interesting geological exhibits, and to Pu'u 'Ula'ula Overlook, at the crater summit, where panoramic views of Maui and other islands may be seen on clear days. From the visitor center there are several trails that allow you to explore the crater. While traversing Sliding Sands Trail (yes, it's slippery and S-T-E-E-P; watch those knees) you're sure to feel intimidated by the 1000-foot cinder cones you'll pass on the way to the crater floor. This trail meets midway with Halemauu Trail, a semi-tough route that's five miles each way from the crater floor to the rim. The Kaupo Trail descends 6100 feet out of the crater after only 8.5 miles, with weather changing from wet to broiling in less time. It winds up in the isolated, southeastern coast town of Kaupo; recommended for overnight trips; all trails are recommended for experienced hikers only. If you want to camp, there are also three remote cabins in the crater that are reached by hiking between four and 10 miles on two trails. The cabins are equipped with 12 bunk beds, a wood-burning stove, cooking utensils, toilets and a limited amount of drinking water and firewood (for which there is an additional fee). Fees are $5 a night for adults and $2.50 a night for children under 12, with an additional $2.50 per person for firewood. Minimum of $15 a night total, excluding firewood, and a key and cleaning deposit is required. Because of high demand, reservations are made on a lottery basis on the first day of the month two months prior to your proposed stay. For example, if you wish to stay in cabins in March, reservation must be in by Dec. 31 in order to make the lottery date of Jan. 1. Winners are notified by mail; three-night maximum, only two nights may be spent in any one cabin. There are also 15–20 free tentsites available every day on a first-come, first-served basis. Check in at park headquarters from 7:30 a.m.–5 p.m. A schedule of daily talks and guided hikes is posted on the bulletin board. Call ☎ *(808) 572-7749* for information on daily weather conditions, tours and programs. Dress in layers when you visit the park; it gets cold up there. General admission: $5.

Kula

Hiking

Polipoli Springs State Park ★★★

Waipoli Road, Kula, 96790, ☎ *(808) 243-5354.*
Camping, hiking, picnicking opportunities are available at this damp, 10-acre park
in upcountry Maui at 6200 feet. Although warm enough during the day, the park is
always cold at night and often drops to below freezing in winter. With more than
51 inches of rain falling here annually, mildew is a factor. Pitch your tent among
pine and cypress trees; there's space for about 20 campers. Parking, barbecues, but
only one toilet, no showers. Bring your own water, as the what's available is not
potable. There's a separate campsite behind a locked gate with a lone cabin that
requires a four-wheel drive vehicle to reach. Cabin sleeps 10, same fees as other site.
Maximum stay is five nights. Reservations taken a year in advance. For information,
write to Division of State Parks, 54 South High Street, Wailuku, HI 96743. General
admission: $5–$10.

Parks and Gardens

Enchanting Floral Gardens of Kula ★★★

RR1, Box 696-B, on Highway 37, Kula, 96790, ☎ *(808) 878-2531.*
Hours: 9 a.m.–5 p.m.
Although it's located halfway up to Haleakala Volcano, this showcase of upcountry
bounty is only 20 minutes from the Kahului Airport. Rare white pineapples, blue
and red jade vines and more proteas than you thought existed are featured among
the more than 700 species of flowers and 30 varieties of fruit trees. Local families
like to come up here to picnic, and weddings are often held in one of the gazebos,
which are available for rent. Survey the surrounding scene from two 10 feet high
viewing towers. Self guided tour. General admission: $4.

Kula Botanical Garden ★★★

Kekaulike Avenue, Route 377, Kula, 96790, ☎ *(808) 878-1715.*
Hours: 9 a.m.–4 p.m.
Not just a prime picnic spot, this six-acre garden boasts more than 1700 tropical
plants; it takes at least two hours to appreciate it all. Everything can be seen on a
garden walk, and there are paved walkways with wheelchair access. Protea, introduced in the 1960s from its native South Africa, flourishes here. The Educational
Garden, featuring plants indigenous to Hawaii, including the increasingly rare sandalwood tree, is a learning experience. Don't forget your camera. Gift shop. General
admission: $4.

Tours

Aloha Bicycle Tours ★★★

P.O. Box 455, Kula, 96790, ☎ *(808) 249-1564.*
Hours: 9 a.m.–4 p.m.
If riding down Haleakala Volcano in a regimented, straight line while wearing a
moon suit doesn't appeal to you, try one of these bicycle tours. Marc Friezner, a
two-time Haleakala Hill Climb and Hawaii State Bicycling champion with 16 years'
experience, conducts small, relaxed bike rides in the Volcano and Kula area.

Friezner and his wife Karen offer both downhill and "rolling hill" rides. The Volcano Bike Adventure Tour, which takes about seven hours, combines a ride down 21 switchbacks through Haleakala Ranch with sightseeing tours of the Sunrise Protea Farm, Silver Cloud Ranch, and wine tasting at Tedeschi Winery. Riders may go at their own pace, and nonriders can follow along in the tour van. Snacks and refreshments provided. Includes new 21-speed mountain bikes and safety gear. Some kind of mountain biking experience required. Gnarlier, off-road suspension tours for more-experienced riders are available; tour routes depend on ability of riders. Limited to four persons. For both rides, participants must be at least 4-foot-10; no pregnant women or those with heart conditions allowed. Rides leave from Harold Rice Park in Kula. General admission: $89–$99.

Looking toward West Maui from Ulupalakua upcountry

Crater Bound ★★★

P.O. Box 265, Kula, 96790, ☎ (808) 878-1743.

Owner Craig Moore and his staff offer hikes, mule rides (just started in April of 1996) and overnight camping trips into Haleakala crater, Oheo in Kipahulu or combinations of both. For example, guests travel from Haleakala summit to Paliku Campground for two nights. After a hike to Kaupo Gap, they're driven to Kipahulu for camping near waterfalls and pools. Guides and wranglers are state-certified tour guides that are trained through the park service. General admission: $80–$500.

Pony Express Tours ★★★

Crater Road (Highway 378), Kula, 96790, ☎ (808) 667-2200.

This company offers one of the few horseback rides in the world that venture into a dormant volcano crater. Rides are also available on the largest working cattle ranch in Maui. The most intensive adventure lasts all day, covers 12 miles and goes all the way to the crater floor. It's advised for those who "feel at ease on the saddle." A short, one-hour ride on the Haleakala ranch, with stops at Haleakala National Park, Tedeschi Winery and protea farms, is also available. Deli or picnic-style lunches are included in the longer rides. Guides are experienced wranglers with a broad knowledge of plant life, geology and crater legends. Riders must be at least 10 years of age, under 65, in good health for elevation levels (up to 10,000 feet), and weigh under 235 pounds. Advance reservations highly recommended. Write to: P.O. Box 535, Kula, Maui, Hawaii 96790. General admission: $35–$150.

Ulupalakua Ranch

Fun For Free

Tedeschi Winery Tasting Room   ★★

Ulupalakua Ranch, Ulupalakua Ranch, ☎ *(808) 878-6058.*
Hours: 9 a.m.–5 p.m.
Special hours: tours between 9:30 a.m.–2:30 p.m.

You might not like the pineapple wine, called Maui Blanc, that's grown on this 22-acre, upcountry winery, but you'll certainly love the ambience of the tasting room, a weathered old brick building that served as a jailhouse for the 20,000-acre Ulupalakua Ranch. There are several other interesting products to sample, including Plantation Red, the first red table wine developed by the winery, and Maui Brut champagne, which made its debut at the inaugural banquet of President Reagan. In addition, you can see how the wine is processed and bottled during a half-hour tour of the winery and the manicured grounds; daily between 9:30 a.m. and 2:30 p.m. Just before arriving at the vineyard, stop in at the Ulupalakua Ranch Country Store—it's the one with the wooden cowboys on the porch, carved by the ranch's resident sculptor. The winery, the only commercial vineyard on Maui, is a collaboration between California vintner Emilio Tedeschi and ranch owner Pardee Erdman. The winery is located about 10 miles past the junction of Highways 377 and 37, up the slopes of Haleakala volcano.

West Maui

Kaanapali Beach

Beaches

Kaanapali Beach   ★★★

Kaanapali Resort, Honopiilani Highway, Kaanapali Beach, 96761.
Built in the 1960s and '70s by the Amfac Corporation (one of Hawaii's "Big Five"), the resort is nestled at the foot of rolling canefields. Many of Maui's most elegant hotels sprawl along three miles of golden beach. Some of the best snorkeling on Maui can be had in the turquoise ocean around Black Rock, where the Sheraton Maui (being renovated at press time) is situated. Colorful reef fish are tame and even ask for tips. A stroll along the beach from the Hyatt Regency past the Maui Marriott and the Westin Maui brings you to Whalers Village, a collection of fancy shops and restaurants. In general, the ocean here, while bathtub warm, is better for sunbathing than swimming, due to frequent shore breaks. A red flag warning system is there in lieu of lifeguards.

An aerial view of Kaanapali Beach, Maui

Museums and Exhibits

Hale Kohala Whale Museum

2435 Kaanapali Parkway, Kaanapali Beach, 96761, ☎ (808) 661-9918.

Hours: 9:30 a.m.–10 p.m.

One of two whaling museums in the Whalers Village. This one is 3500 square feet. Devoted to evolution of humpback whale, the museum features see-and-touch displays, computer terminals where visitors may punch up whale facts, a theater showing videos on such topics as the humpback's migratory patterns and impressive whale models, including a 16-foot model of a baby humpback skeleton. Gift shop with everything from crystal whale figurines to the latest ecology books.

Whalers Village Museum of the Pacific ★★

Whalers Village Shopping Center, Building G, Kaanapali Beach, On the third floor, ☎ (808) 661-5992.

Hours: 9:30 a.m.–10 p.m.

This engaging museum on the third floor of Whaler's Village that will delight the kids as well as Mom and Dad, features a half-hour film presentation about Hawaii's whaling era, more than 100 whaling implements, a six-foot model of a whaling ship, scrimshaw, harpoons, sailors' journals, tools and historic photographs. Also in Whaler's Village is the Hale Kohala Whale Museum and Pavilion at the entrance (how can you miss it?). The museum zeroes in on the evolution and migratory patterns of the humpback whale, Maui's most-welcome winter visitor. Humpy factoids are accessed on computer terminals, and kids aren't snarled at for touching the life-size marine models–especially a 16-foot humpback calf and its favorite food, the squid (here in 3-D).

Music

Na Mele O Maui ★★

2525 Kaanapali Parkway, Kaanapali Beach, ☎ (808) 661-3271.
The Kaanapali Beach Resort hosts a celebration of Hawaiian music each December. Events include hula performances, a *keiki* song contest, and arts and crafts exhibits.

The Shows

Auntie Aloha's Breakfast Luau ★★★

Kaanapali Beach Hotel Plantation Room, Kaanapali Beach, ☎ (808) 661-0011.
Hours: 8:15–10 a.m.
This fun-luau is presided over by Auntie Aloha, a big lady with an infectious smile who proclaims, "You can suck 'em up, cuz in Hawaii mo' big, mo' better, mo' beautiful." The only one of its kind in Hawaii, this breakfast luau features mai tais along with your Special Ks. Also live music, dancing, tips on Maui and a side-splittin' slide show called "Auntie's Comedy Activities Review." All-you-can-eat breakfast of taro pancakes, sweet-bread French toast, coconut and passion fruit syrups, Portuguese sausage, fruits, and homemade breads. The most inexpensive luau in town, in Maui's most Hawaiian resort. General admission: $13.95.

Tours

Westin Maui Botanical Tours ★★★

2365 Kaanapali Parkway, Kaanapali Beach, 96761, ☎ (808) 667-2525.
Hours: 10:30–11:30 a.m., Fri. only.
Botanical tours of the hotel grounds by David Simons, Maui native and horticulturist. The vast collection includes flora of most of the HOT spots of the world, including Southeast Asia, the American Tropics, Barbados, Madagascar, Brazil and Polynesia. You'll see seven species of palms, three varieties of ferns, including a tree fern unique to Hawaii, used for making leis, and a 40-foot-tall Singapore plumeria.

Westin Maui Wildlife Tour ★★★

2365 Kaanapali Parkway, Kaanapali Beach, 96761, ☎ (808) 667-2525.
Hours: 10–11 a.m.
Closed: Tue., Thurs., Fri., Sat.
The 12-acre water wonderland of the Westin Maui is home to loads of colorful birds that squawk and talk, including Kolohe, a rose-breasted cockatoo that sings and hops on people's hands. You'll see most of them in this fascinating avian tour that meanders all over the property. Most intriguing is the collection of swans—among them a pair of European mutes—the jealous male can be seen protecting his mate from humans.

Kahului

City Celebrations

Maui Marathon ★★

P.O. Box 330099, Kahului, 96733, ☎ (808) 871-6441.
Hawaii's oldest point-to-point marathon celebrated its 25th anniversary in March 1995. The race starts at Maui Mall in Kahului and ends at Whaler's Village in Kaanapali. The usual limit is 1000 runners, and proceeds support Maui charities.

For entry information, send a self-addressed, stamped envelope to the address above.

Kapalua

Beaches

D.T. Fleming State Park ★★★

1 Ritz Carlton Drive, follow shoreline access sign, Kapalua.

Naturally landscaped by sand dunes and ironwood trees, Fleming Beach fronts the Ritz-Carlton Kapalua resort. Wide enough for long, romantic strolls, with good waves for surfing and bodysurfing. Not so great for swimming, though, as nasty winter riptides can make you feel like laundry in a spin cycle.

Kapalua Bay ★★★★

Lower Honoapiilani Road, Kapalua.

A spectacular white-sand beach with great coral and lots of fish that's perfect for snorkeling, with fabulous views of Molokai and Lanai. It's protected from wind and waves by an ancient lava flow that extends well out into the ocean at the north end of the beach. Facilities include: rest rooms, showers, a landscaped path to the beach, lifeguard. Directions: Drive south from the Kapalua Bay Hotel (1 Bay Drive) to the first shoreline access sign, turn right toward the ocean to a public lot. If parking lot is full, go back to the main road and turn right, park on the road across the street from the Napili Kai Beach Club and walk down to the beach via the shoreline-access through the tunnel.

Fun For Free

Celebration of the Arts ★★★

One Ritz-Carlton Drive, Kapalua, 96761, ☎ (808) 669-6200.

More than 40 Hawaiian island artists and hula *halaus* (hula schools) offer lessons and demonstrations of the traditional and contemporary arts of Hawaii each year during the Easter weekend on the grounds of the Ritz-Carlton, Kapalua. The only "hands-on" workshop in Maui, participants can attend free workshops on hula and chant, lei-making, lauhala-weaving, basket-weaving and other crafts. Art supplies and instructions are also complimentary. Admission is charged for a Hawaiian food celebration and concert. Top performers in the past have included Henry Kapono and Keali'i Reichel.

Music

Maui Chamber Music Festival ★★★★

Sacred Hearts Church, Kapalua, ☎ (808) 243-2284.

Early June. Once known as the Kapalua Music Festival, this two-day gala features the creme de lá creme of classical performers from around the globe. Evening performances at 7:30; also a matinee at 3 p.m.

Lahaina

Beaches

Wahikuli Beach ★★

Highway 30, beyond Lahaina, Lahaina.

Wahikuli Beach is popular for those seeking a more serene scene than its neighbor, glitzy Kaanapali Beach. Scuba divers favor its safe waters to teach beginners. Picnic tables, showers, toilets, parking. Across from the police station.

Much of Lahaina, Maui has been designated a National Historic Landmark. Most of the island's major art galleries are located along the main street.

City Celebrations

Aloha Festivals   ★★★★

Under the Banyan Tree, Lahaina, ☎ *(808) 944-8857.*
For a general description, see Aloha Festivals, "Molokai" chapter. Visitors and residents get together under the famous old Banyan Tree (the largest in the state) to share ethnic food and festivities, including music, dance, arts and crafts.

Fun For Free

Aloha Friday Arts and Crafts Fair   ★★★

Lahaina Center, Lahaina, ☎ *(808) 667-9216.*
Hours: 3–8 p.m., Fri. only.
Local artisans and "aunties" sell wares; also a Polynesian review with an authentic drum dance, as well as Tahitian and Hawaiian hula.

Friday Night is Art Night   ★★★

Front Street, Lahaina, ☎ *(808) 667-9175.*
Hours: 7–10 p.m., Fri. only.
With dozens of galleries packed easel-to-easel on this rejuvenated downtown Lahaina street, it's hard to separate the art from the drek. But every Friday evening, merchants compete in a friendly way for your attention, providing demonstrations and gallery shows, complimentary wine and hors d'oeuvres, while roving musicians of various abilities play lively tunes. Many artists are on hand to sign autographs and go one-on-one with visitors. In June, there's a block party and juried art show. The Mardi Gras-like atmosphere is heightened on Halloween, when Front Street is closed off to car traffic. The action culminates in a wild costume contest.

Hula Shows ★★

1221 Honoapiilani Highway, in the Lahaina Cannery, Lahaina, *(808) 661-5304.*

The Lahaina Cannery shopping center presents a *keiki* (children's) hula show every Sunday at 1 p.m., and on the first Thursday of each month at 7 p.m., ancient songs and dances are interpreted by members of the hula *halau* (school) Ho'oulu o Ka'ula. Other free shows are featured at the Whalers Village in Kaanapali, *(808) 661-4567* every Wednesday and Sunday at 1 p.m. A complete open-air Polynesian revue plus a fashion show (of grass skirts?) is offered at the Wailea Shopping Village, *(808) 879-4474* Tuesdays at 1 p.m.

Historical Sites

Hale Pa'ahao ★★

Prison Road, Lahaina.

Hale Pa'ahao, which means "stuck in irons house," was the first prison in Lahaina, built somewhat reluctantly by convicts out of coral stone in the 1850s. Difficult prisoners, held here for such nefarious acts as working on the Sabbath or dangerous horse-riding, were restrained the old-fashioned way—by wall shackles or ye olde ball and chain.

The Brick Palace and Old Fort Ruins ★★

Wharf Street, Lahaina.

Sharing the same lot as the Banyan Tree are the ruins of a palace commissioned by Kamehameha I and built by two ex-convicts from Australia. It was the first Western building in the islands. Next to the excavated foundations are the remnants of a fort built of coral blocks brought in from the reef in the 1930s to guard missionaries from angry whalers mad at them for introducing stringent moral rules and spoiling their fun. The original fort covered one acre and was approximately 20 feet high. In the same area closer to the Banyan Tree is the Old Courthouse, built of stones from Hale Piula, an unfinished two-story palace originally built for Kamehameha III.

The Masters' Reading Room ★★

On the corner of Front and Dickenson Streets, Lahaina.

Arguably the oldest building in Maui, this coral block and field-stone building was restored in 1970. Originally a missionary store house, it later became an officers club for whaling captains. Today, it serves as headquarters for the Lahaina Restoration Foundation.

The Pioneer Inn ★★★

Hotel and Wharf Streets, Lahaina.

Once the only hotel in West Maui until the late 1950s, the Pioneer Inn's facade dates from 1901, as do the comical house rules still posted in the public rooms, including, "If you wet or burn you bed, you going out." New guest accommodations and shops were added in 1965, carefully built to match the original. Renovated again in 1995, the once-funky rooms have been updated quite handsomely. A prime tourist attraction, especially for its colorful, rowdy bar. Across the street is the equally famous Banyan Tree, which is more than 60 feet high, casting shade on two-thirds of an acre, great on a hot Lahaina day, the original "Lahaina Cooler." The tree was planted in April 1873, to mark the 50th anniversary of the beginning of Protestant missionary work in Lahaina.

The Seamen's Cemetery   ★★

Waine'e Street, Lahaina.
Herman Melville's cousin was buried here, and so was one of his shipmates. Over the years, marked graves of sailors have gradually disappeared, until now only one or two are identifiable.

Waiola Church and Cemetery   ★★★

Wainee Street, near Shaw Street, Lahaina.
Originally called Waine'e, this was the first stone church in the islands (1828–1832), built by natives for the Protestant mission. Sundays were a lively scene, with 3000 Hawaiians packed together on the floor, ringed by calabash spittoons for tobacco chewing chiefs and ships' masters. Native royalists burned it in 1894 to protest the annexation of Hawaii by the United States Rebuilt several times after another fire (due to unknown reasons) and a whirlwind blew it down, it was rebuilt to its present state in 1951 and renamed Waiola, or "Water of Life." Behind it is the cemetery where great and obscure chiefs and commoners, seamen, missionaries and children (mortality was very high) were buried. Tombs were marked with glass-framed pictures. Among the dead are Queen Ke'opuolani, the first royal Christian convert and the wife of Kamehameha I.

Museums and Exhibits

Carthaginian and Old Pioneer Inn at Lahaina Harbor, Maui

Baldwin Home Museum   ★★★

Front and Dickenson Streets, Lahaina, 96767, ☎ *(808) 661-3262.*
Hours: 10 a.m.–4:15 p.m.
In the early 1960s, the Lahaina Restoration Foundation lovingly restored the 150-year-old clapboard and coral stone residence and office of Revered Dwight Baldwin,

a Protestant medical missionary. Old furniture and antique buffs will most likely covet the 1860 piano, koa bed and kapa quilts in the various rooms. Other items interest include the first toilet used on Maui and a collection of medical instruments. Narrated tour. $2 for seniors, free for all children if accompanied by parent. General admission: $3.

Brig Carthaginian II

Lahaina Harbor, Lahaina, 96761, ☎ (808) 661-3262.
Hours: 10 a.m.–4 p.m.

A floating maritime museum berthed in Lahaina Harbor, this 93-foot, two-masted replica of a 19th-century sailing ship features an entertaining video on (you guessed it) whales. Kids get in free. General admission: $3.

Lahaina Whaling Museum

865 Front Street, Lahaina, ☎ (808) 661-4775.
Hours: 9:30 a.m.–9 p.m.

This free museum, located in the Crazy Shirts' outlet in Lahaina, has a small but unique collection of rare 19th-century whaling artifacts. Crazy Shirts' tycoon Rick Ralston acquired his treasures both on Hawaii and on numerous scouting trips to New England seaports over a 33-year period. The collection of scrimshaw, carved by lonely sailors for loved ones at home, is outstanding. Try to forget that these are carved from genuine whales' teeth and bone, and just enjoy them for the artistic value. You'll see ivory clothespins, jewelry and even a swift, an expanding whalebone and ivory marvel used to wind yarn for knitting. Also interesting is a huge ship's figure from the *Carthaginian*, a replica of a 19th-century, square-rigged bark, used in the movie "Hawaii."

Lahainaluna School/Hale Pai

At the end of Lahainaluna Road, Lahaina, 96761, ☎ (808) 667-7040.
Hours: 10 a.m.–4 p.m.

Lahainaluna, the oldest U.S. school west of the Rockies, accepted its first students in 1831. Now a public high school, it has more than 700 students, about 120 of whom are boarders from remote areas of the state. The only building that survives from the old days is Hale Pai, which was made into a small museum, and houses the island's first printing press; the first Hawaiian newspaper was printed here. The dormitories are open to the public during David Malo Day (April 20), when the school honors its most prestigious student. Malo was the author of "Hawaiian Antiquities," an early history of the Sandwich Islands. Special events include a traditional feast of Hawaiian delicacies prepared by students, and a sunset pageant featuring the school's chorus and dancers.

Wo Hing Temple Museum ★★

858 Front Street, Lahaina, 96761, ☎ (808) 661-3262.
Hours: 10 a.m.–4 p.m.

Among the photos and displays of Chinese culture and their contributions to the Hawaiian economy is a Taoist shrine affiliated with the Chee Kung Tong, a Chinese fraternal society with branches all over the world. Those interested in the history of cinema will be pleasantly surprised to find regularly scheduled showings of Thomas

Edison's 1898 and 1906 films of old Hawaii in an adjacent building. Donation requested.

Parks and Gardens

Jodo Mission and Buddha ★★★
Near Mala Wharf, Lahaina.
The 3.5-ton statue of Buddha at the oceanfront Jodo Mission Park near Mala wharf was erected to mark the 100th anniversary of the arrival of the first Japanese plantation laborers in 1868. The grounds and building of the mission are open to the public.

The Shows

The Hawaii Experience Domed Theater ★★★
824 Front Street, Lahaina, 96761, ☎ *(808) 661-8314.*
Hours: 10 a.m.–10 p.m.
If you didn't get up in time to greet the sunrise at Haleakala National Park, you can experience it vicariously at this giant domed theater with surround sound. The current feature, shown on a 180-degree, wrap-around screen, is "Hawaii, Islands of the Gods," a cinematic voyage around the islands. Shows every hour on the hour. General admission: $6.95.

Tours

Atlantis Submarines ★★★
Leaves from Pioneer Inn on Front Street, Lahaina, 96761, ☎ *(808) 667-6604.*
Hours: 8 a.m.–3 p.m.
This well-known company gives travelers a voyage to the bottom of the sea (well, not quite) on a comfortable, battery-powered, 80-ton, 48-passenger sub. You won't get the bends or ear infections; in fact you won't even get wet. There are three one- and two-hour narrated rides available. The most expensive is the Odyssey Adventure, a dive to 120 feet, with transportation from major hotels included. Whale-watch cruise in season. The moderately priced ($79) Expedition Adventure takes place during nonpeak hours, and seating is limited. The cheapest is the Discovery Adventure, a late-afternoon, 30-minute dive. Children, $39 on all rides. Ask about special "fly-dive" packages with Sunshine Helicopters. General admission: $69–$89.

Ironwood Ranch ★★★
5095 Napili Hau Drive, Lahaina, 96761, ☎ *(808) 669-4991.*
Friendly ranch hands take everyone from beginners to advanced riders on several horseback riding excursions; the lowest priced is through a pineapple plantation. A sunset ride is $100; picnic ride through a rainforest is $135. Also private rides. General admission: $75–$135.

Kawika's Aina Tour Company ★★★
505 Front Street, Suite 231, Lahaina, 96761, ☎ *(808) 667-2204.*
Hours: 7 a.m.–2 p.m.
Special hours: sunset tours available.
Specializes in tours to Kahakuloa, an isolated valley on Maui's seldom-visited northwest shore about 28 miles from Lahaina, and home to fewer than 75 residents, most

of them of Hawaiian ancestry. Van tours are led by local guide Kawika (David) Paui-lihau, on a recently paved, but narrow, potholed and twisty road. You'll pass dense jungle with coconut palms, mangoes and breadfruits. The valley has deserted beaches for snorkeling, but the main draw are some of the people you'll meet, who still live off the land and fish for food. Although homes have electricity, most prefer to use lanterns for lighting and gas generators for washing machines and fridges. You'll get a kick out of the gong Pauilihau strikes to announce his arrival in the valley. There's one roadside vendor, so it's advisable that you bring a picnic. Other tours available: Sunrise and Sunset to Haleakala ($80 per person) and all-day trips to Hana ($100 per person) General admission: $80–$100.

Lahaina-Kaanapali & Pacific Railroad ★★★

Honoapiilani Highway, P.O. Box 816, Lahaina, 96767, ☎ *(808) 661-0089.*
Hours: 8:55 a.m.–6 p.m.
This fun, 1890s-era, steam-powered locomotive shuttles tourists between Kaanapali and Lahaina, where the parking situation can be horrendous. Also called the "Sugar Cane" Train, it puffs merrily through a real sugar plantation, while a conductor prattles on (and sometimes sings) knowingly about King Sugar's history and its impact in the islands. Ask about two-for-one deals with the Hawaii Experience Domed Theater and Nautilus Maui. General admission: $8–$12.

Luckey Strike Charters ★★

P.O. Box 1502, Lahaina, 96767, ☎ *(808) 661-4606.*
OK, stop with the cigarette jokes, already. These nice folks have nothing to do with the Philip Morris product. It's a sport-fishing charter company run by Tad and Cindy Luckey, who have 20 years' experience leading customers to marlin, mahi-mahi, tuna, wahoo, shark and other big fish. You and your party can have the *Lucky Strike II,* a 50 foot. Delta equipped with state-of-the-art electronics and computerized downriggers all to yourself, for half-, three-quarter- or full-day trips. Maximum six passengers on private charters. Share boat trips can be arranged. In addition, a smaller sportfishing boat, the 31-foot. Uniflite Sport Fisher, *Kanoa,* is available for charter (maximum six passengers). No license required. All equipment, bait and ice provided; bring your own lunch, beverages, and sun protection. Boats leave from Slips 50 and 51 at Lahaina Small Boat Harbor. General admission: $75–$800.

Maui Hiking Safaris ★★

P.O. Box 11198, Lahaina, 96761, ☎ *(808) 573-1716.*
Randy Warner operates this hiking tour service to waterfalls, bamboo forests and ancient lava flows. Morning or afternoon, half–or full-day tours range from five to nine hours in length, including driving time. Limited to six people, with a minimum of two. Randy provides narration on Hawaiian history, botany and volcanology. Gear supplied; provide your own food. Not for beginners or whiners—Randy prefers competent, experienced hikers on his trips, and no smoking is allowed. Reserve 24 hours in advance. Meets in Kahului in the commuter lot on Dairy Road and Puunene Avenue. General admission: $49–$79.

Nautilus Semi-Submersibles ★★★

From Slip 10 in Lahaina Harbor, Lahaina, 96761, ☎ *(808) 667-2133.*

Although these vessels resemble subs, the 58-foot boats don't submerge, which makes a trip a lot less expensive than submarine tours. While the vessel itself stays on the surface, the spacious viewing cabin is under the waterline. Passengers can also choose to ride topside part of the way. After direct boarding from Lahaina Harbor, the boat sets out for a shallow coral reef outside of Lahaina. This is when divers leap overboard and bring sea urchins, octopus and other marine creatures right to windows before releasing them. While this is happening, outboard cameras video the action around the vessel so no one misses a thing. Carries up to 34 passengers. Children $15.95; under five free. Trips daily at 9 and 10:15 a.m.; noon, and 1:15 and 2:45 p.m. General admission: $29.95.

The Maui Princess   ★★★

Lahaina Harbor, Pier 3, Lahaina, ☎ (808) 661-8397.

For general description, see The Maui Princess, "Molokai" chapter. General admission: $50.

Whale Mist Charters   ★★

840 Wainee Street, Suite 224, Lahaina, 96761, ☎ (808) 667-2833.

This whale-watching trip leaves four times daily from Lahaina harbor's Slip 6, located next to the Pioneer Inn and Banyan Tree. Children under 12, $25. Also Sunset Sail. Check-in is 15 minutes before departure. There is a 24-hour cancellation notice. Shaded lounge area, rest room, beverages, snacks. If you don't see a whale, you get another trip free. General admission: $29–$35.

Windjammer Cruises   ★★

658 Front Street, Lahaina, 96761, ☎ (808) 667-2179.
Hours: 5:30 p.m.–7:30 p.m.

Popular, touristy, sunset dinner cruise aboard the 70-foot, three-masted schooner, *Spirit of Windjammer*. The two-hour trip includes an open bar (Yipee!) with unlimited libations. Load up on the buffet style dinner of prime rib, fresh Alaskan salmon, sides, and dessert. Stake out a place on the viewing deck, which, while large, fills up fast with as many as 91 bodies. A two-hour, whale-watching cruise is a good deal for $36.95 (mid-December to mid-April). Boats leave daily from Slip 1, Lahaina Harbor. General admission: $37.

Zip-Purr Charters   ★★★

P.O. Box 12256, Lahaina, 96761, ☎ (808) 667-2299.

Capt. Mike "Turk" Turkington and Julie (sounds like "The Love Boat") operate this 47-foot sailing cat with a large covered cabin. Mike, a former firefighter and professional surfer born on Oahu, designed the boat himself. From January-April they offer a six-hour, Lanai Snorkel Sail/Whale-Watch expedition. The trip stops at two pristine snorkel spots, including Turtle Reef. Limited to 35–37 passengers. Ask about a two-hour Sunset Cocktail Sail/Whale Watch. Tours leave from the Hula Grill restaurant in Whalers Village, Kaanapali Beach. A 24-hour cancellation notice is required. General admission: $44.50 –$79.95.

Sports

Hiking Haleakala Crater, Maui

Maui is practically synonymous with **golf** and **tennis**. Golfers will find clubs and courses at the ritzy resort areas of Wailea and Kaanapali. Big names include Kapalua Golf Club, Makena Golf Course, Maui Country Club, Pukalani Country Club, Royal Kaanapali, Sandalwood Country Club, Silversword Golf Course, Waiehu Municipal Golf Course, Waikapa Valley Country Club, and Wailea Golf Club. Or come for one of the **tournaments**: Asahi Beer Kyosan Golf Tournament at the Wailea Golf Club (February), Kaanapali Classic Senior PGA Golf Tournament at the Royal Kaanapali (October), Isuzu Kapalua International Golf Championship at Kapalua Golf Club (November) and the Kirin Cup World Championship of Golf (December).

You'll find **tennis courts** all over the island—some are attached to resorts and hotels, some are private clubs, others are free public courts. For more information on public courts, contact **Maui County Department of Parks and Recreation** *(200 South High Street, Wailuku 96793,* ☎ *(808) 243-7232)*. The big tennis event is the Kapalua Open, held on Labor Day weekend.

Anglers can sign up with a charter at Lahaina or Maalaea harbors to try your luck with Maui's various game fish such as marlin, mahi-mahi and tuna. Maui is a fantastic place for **horseback riding**, with stables and trails around the island offering excursions into virtually every type of terrain, from tropical forests and remote beaches to pineapple fields and the Haleakala Crater. **Cyclists** thrill to the ride down Haleakala, while **joggers** can't wait to run up the volcano during the annual (August) 36-mile **Haleakala Run to the Sun**. The **Maui Marathon** (March) is another top running event.

Central Maui

Kahului

Club Lanai ★★★

355 Hukilike Street, Kahului, 96732, ☎ *(808) 871-1144.*

For description, see Club Lanai under Lanai chapter. General admission: $89.

Hawaiian Island Windsurfing ★★★★

415 Dairy Road, Kahului, 96732, ☎ *(808) 871-4981.*

Hours: 8:30 a.m.–6:30 p.m.

This retail store and rental facility is also known as Windsurfing West, one of the best windsurfing schools on the island. It will rent you everything you need, even a car-roof rack. Other full-service outfits include Hawaiian Sailboarding Techniques, *444 Hana Hwy, Kahului, 96732,* ☎ *(808) 871-5423,* open Mon.–Sat., 9 a.m.–5 p.m., $60 for 2.5-hour classes, private 1.5-hour lessons, $67.50, owned by top champion Alan Cadiz. Hunt Hawaii, *P.O. Box 989, Paia, 96779,* ☎ *(808) 575-2300,* offers rentals, lessons and accessories. Open 9 a.m.–6 p.m., complete rental rigs $35 day, private two-hour lessons, $75; includes equipment. Maui Windsurf Co. and Maui Magic Windsurfing Schools, *520 Keolani Place, Kahului, 96732,* ☎ *(808) 877-4696.* 8:30 a.m.–5:30 p.m. Rentals $46 day, $250 week, three-hour course $59.

Makawao

Hiking Paradise ★★

P.O. Box 1582, Makawao, 96768, ☎ *(808) 573-0464.*

Custom half- or full-day rainforest, waterfall or mountain hiking trips. Ponchos, backpacks, snacks (for half-day trips) and lunch (full-day only) provided. Advance booking required; 10 percent discount for those reserving two weeks in advance. From the mainland, call ☎ *(808) 227-7741.* General admission: $45–$85.

Makawao Rodeo ★★

Oskie Rice Arena, Olinda Avenue, Makawao, ☎ *(808) 572-9928.*

No cardboard cowpokes here, no sir. This is the real thing, with barrel racing, calf roping, bull riding and more, all part of the annual Makawao rodeo. It's a skill test for all qualified contenders from throughout the state, including little 'uns. Held over the Fourth of July Weekend, it's kicked off by a colorful parade.

Waiehu

Waiehu Golf Course   ★★

Waiehu, Northwest of Wailuku, Waiehu, 96793, ☎ *(808) 243-7400.*
Hours: 7 a.m.–5 p.m.

On the old Hawaii north shore, with a very tranquil setting, this par-71, 6330-yard course is the cheapest of three municipal golf courses. Lower price is for weekday play. General admission: $33–$38.

Waikapu

Grand Waikapu Country Club   ★★★★

2500 Honoapiilani Highway, Waikapu, 96793, ☎ *(808) 244-7888.*
Hours: 7:30 a.m.–6 p.m.

We don't mean to be disrespectful, but this golf club, designed by Frank Lloyd Wright, looks like a Taos pueblo as conceived by George Lucas. Within is a restaurant with a 180-degree view of Maui and Haleakala. Associated with the Grand Wailea Resort, the Club's literature boasts how this $140 million course is "the most expensive in the U.S." and that it's the only course in Hawaii that uses "two million gallons of water per day." The hilltop setting is 1000 feet above sea level, and every hole has panoramic views. Takes only a limited number of players per day, so that every golfer can enjoy a round. Caddy service. Spa Grande facilities included in the greens fee, $30 for non-players. Regular fee is, again, "the most expensive in the U.S." General admission: $200.

South Maui

Kihei

Ed Robinson's Diving Adventures   ★★★

P.O. Box 616, Kihei, 96753, ☎ *(808) 879-3584.*
Hours: 8 a.m.–4 p.m.

This highly recommended company, which caters to certified divers only, is operated by Ed Robinson, a widely published underwater photographer and dive master. Professional, experienced divers come to Maui expressly to dive with Ed. Robinson knows where all the out-of-the way sites are, and customizes each dive trip depending on the skill level and interest of the participants. Ask about the three-day "Ultimate Dive Package," where divers choose among trips to Lanai, Molokini and Maui's south shore, as well as a two-tank Sunset/Night dive and a progressive three-tank adventure trip. A 10-percent discount is offered with this package. Trips leave from Kihei Boat Ramp, usually at 6:45 a.m. Photography courses available. Ride-alongs and snorkelers, $80. General admission: $90–$140.

Kelii's Kayak Tours   ★★★

Kihei, 96753, ☎ *(808) 874-7652.*

Experienced local guides take small groups on ocean-kayaking and snorkeling trips to inaccessible, out-of-the-way shoreline areas and coves. You'll probably have an encounter or two with green sea turtles, or see whales and dolphins in season. Tours include: Maui's South Shore-Makena, Ahihi Bay, LaPerouse; 2.5 hours, two departures daily 7:30–11 a.m. from Makena Landing. This is a leisurely paddle in gentle ocean conditions. $55 per person, includes snorkel equipment and light refreshments. Also caters to corporate, and company groups. General admission: $55–$85.

Maui Dive Shop ★★★

Azeka Place II Shopping Center, Kihei, 96753, ☎ (808) 879-3388.
A PADI five-star instructor development center, with 10 locations in shopping centers throughout the island. Teaches classes from beginner to instructor level, with two complete classroom facilities at the above location, and one in the Kahana Gateway Shopping Center. Various daily dive-adventures include a one-tank Molokini back-wall dive with a vertical drop of 300 feet for $69.95. Dive trips are taken on a 32-foot, 12-passenger dive boat, the *Ala Kai*, or a six-passenger, 25-foot Boston Whaler, *MDS Express*. Included are snacks, drinks and all equipment. Also snorkeling trips to Molokini, specializing in small groups of no more than 16 people. Private charters available. General admission: $69.95 and up.

Silversword Golf Course ★★

1345 Piilani Highway, at Lipoa, Kihei, ☎ (808) 874-0777.
Hours: 7 a.m.–6 p.m.
Although it offers ocean views from every hole, players may be defeated by the wind gusts at this 18-hole, par-71, 6404-yard public course located above Kihei at the Maui Research and Technology Park. General admission: $69.

South Pacific Kayaks ★★★

2439 South Kihei Road, Kihei, ☎ (808) 875-4848.
Longtime Hawaii residents Michael and Melissa McCoy offer paddling and snorkeling tours along remote coastlines for all ages and levels of experience. Scuba-quality, silicone snorkel gear provided. The company also rents kayaks; singles (from $15) and doubles (from $35). Includes car-top carrier, paddles and life vests. Reservations required. From mainland call ☎ *(800) 776-2326.* General admission: $55–$85.

Makena

Makena Resort Golf Courses ★★★

5415 Makena Alanui Drive, Makena, 96753, ☎ (808) 879-3344.
Hours: 6 a.m.–7 p.m.
These two 18-hole golf courses, designed by Robert Trent Jones, Jr., are located in the Makena Resort in front of the Maui Prince Hotel in a rustic, oceanfront setting south of Wailea. The North Course, a 6567-yard, par-72 course, features breathtaking views of Haleakala Crater and natural obstacles that add to the challenge. The 6629-yard, par-72 South Course features natural rolling fairways, undulating greens and captivating ocean and mountain views. The signature 16th hole runs parallel to the ocean and is rarely described as easy. Special afternoon and evening rates are $70. Pro shop, and a restaurant on the 19th hole that serves the best saimin on Maui. A new golf school opened in July 1995. Includes a room/golf package with five nights at the hotel, three days of instruction, including 10 hours of private lessons, with a pro playing along for nine holes, unlimited golf and practice balls, and high-tech video analysis. General admission: $110.

Maui Prince Hotel Tennis Club ★★★

5415 Makena Alanui Road, Makena, 96753, ☎ (808) 879-8777.
Hours: 7 a.m.–9 p.m.

The Maui Prince Hotel Tennis Club, a complete facility, features six plexi-paved courts, two lit for night play. Apparel shop with logo-inscribed racquets, shoes and accessories. Lessons available. General admission: $14–$18.

Wailea

Wailea Golf Club ★★★★

100 Wailea Golf Club Drive, Wailea, 96753, ☎ (808) 875-5111.

Composed of three award-winning courses, Blue, Gold and Emerald. Gold, designed by Robert Trent Jones, Jr., is Wailea's claim to golfing fame. Natural hazards include ancient lava rock walls built by early Hawaiians that were left in place and incorporated into the course. Players also have to contend with the breathtaking scenery, which makes it hard to keep your mind on the ball. Facilities include a clubhouse, complete pro shop and the SeaWatch restaurant with a spectacular view. The Blue course, meandering through the resort amidst million-dollar homes, is the Club's grande dame, designed by Arthur Jack Snyder. It's a course for everyone, with wide fairways for the high handicapper. Facilities: clubhouse and fairway restaurant. New in 1995, Wailea Emerald has a tropical look. Also designed by Robert Trent Jones, Jr., it has great views of Mount Haleakala, the ocean and lush gardens. Has a double green shared by the 10th and 17th holes. Separate chipping and putting areas, practice bunker, driving range with three built-in target greens surrounded by traps. Lessons, $40 for a half-hour. General admission: $55–$130.

Wailea Tennis Club ★★★★

131 Wailea Ike Place, Wailea, 96753, ☎ (808) 879-1958.
Hours: 7 a.m.–9 p.m.
Special hours: grass courts 10 a.m.–6 p.m.

Called "Wimbledon West," this club caters to Wailea resort guests and features 11 Plexipave courts, three of them lit for night play. It's the only club in Hawaii with three grass courts available to the public. Daily tennis clinics. Court rental, $10 day guests and owners, $15 nonguests. Grass court rental, $20 day for guests and owners, $25 nonguests. General admission: $10–$25.

Upcountry

Kula

Chris' Adventures ★★★

P.O. Box 869, Kula, 96790, ☎ (800) 224-5344.
Hours: 8 a.m.–6 p.m.

Chris and his associates offer on- and off-road cycling adventures for small groups every day, morning or afternoon. The varied itinerary includes a "Haleakala Wine Trek," in which participants bike down Haleakala Volcano to the Tedeschi Winery and beyond; this trek is recommended for riders of all abilities. Also hike/bike adventures and "Inn-to-Inn" vacations, which are three- to eight-day biking and/or hiking trips for all levels, with options for the more advanced (or masochistic) participants. Includes all meals, transportation, equipment, lodging, and extras;

price ranges from $200–$275 per day. Call Chris' Adventures tour planner for details, dates and trip itineraries. General admission: $110–$275.

Pukalani

Pukalani Country Club ★★

360 Pukalani Street, Pukalani, 96768, ☎ *(808) 572-1314.*
Hours: 7 a.m.–4 p.m.
It's just a short cruise up Haleakala Highway to this 160-acre club with a par-72 championship course designed by Bob Baldock. Lovely upcountry setting with cool climate and panoramic views. The driving range is open until 9:30 p.m. The clouds ringing Haleakala often break here, creating a hole, hence the name "pukalani." Offers a good restaurant serving Hawaiian plate lunches. General admission: $33–$62.

Ulupalakua Ranch

Papaka Sporting Clays ★★

Ulupalakua Ranch, Ulupalakua Ranch, ☎ *(808) 879-5649.*
Hours: 8:30 a.m.–4:30 p.m.
Learn the fine art of clay target shooting, a veddy British sport that has recently come to Maui. Papaka Sporting Clays is situated in an old cinder cone on the 20,000-acre Ulupalakua Ranch. Participants shoot at colored clay targets representing different game birds (and one wabbit!). There are 35 scenarios you can choose from, to suit all levels of expertise, from greenhorn to James Bond. The most difficult is a klutz's nightmare, where a computer picks several targets that whiz through the air at different speeds and positions, and you have to shoot them all at the same time. The price includes use of either a semi-automatic Browning, Remington 8 or Beretta shotgun, a padded vest and other protective gear, 75 targets, 75 shells and shooting instruction. Guests are picked up and returned from the Maui Prince in Makena and other hotels at the Wailea resort. Corporate and *kamaaina* rates available. Two daily sessions; morning 8:30 to 11:30 a.m., afternoon, 1 to 4:30 p.m. Reservations required. Age limit: 11 years. Information: 1325 South Kihei Road, Suite 212, Kihei, HI 96753. General admission: $95.

West Maui

Kaanapali Beach

Kaanapali North and South Courses ★★★★

Kaanapali Resort, Kaanapali Beach, 96761, ☎ *(808) 661-3691.*
Hours: 6:30 a.m.–4:30 p.m.
These championship courses serve the Kaanapali Resort area. Kaanapali North, an 18-hole, par-72, 6305-yard course, was laid out by Robert Trent Jones, Sr. The 18th hole demands a shot over water and is said to be one of the toughest holes in the islands. The South Course, an 18-hole, par-72, 6250-yard course, was a piece-of-cake, executive layout until Arthur Jack Snyder put in a water hazard. Good for all levels. Higher price for non-resort guests. Pro shop. General admission: $90–$110.

MAUI

Kapalua

Kapalua Resort Golf Courses ★★★★

Kapalua Resort, 300 Kapalua Drive, Kapalua, 96761, ☎ (808) 669-8044.
Hours: 6 a.m.–7 p.m.

The Kapalua Golf Club is known as one of the finest in the world with three championship courses. The Bay Course, opened in 1975, was designed by Arnold Palmer and Francis Duane and incorporates magnificent ocean panoramas, lush tropical terrain and the beaches of Kapalua. The signature hole extends onto an ocean-framed black-lava peninsula. The Village course, designed by Palmer with Ed Seay, rises into the West Maui mountains, and travels through eucalyptus and Cook pine trees, past a lake and alongside ridges plummeting hundreds of feet into deep green valleys. It's complex enough for seasoned pros and enjoyable for beginning golfers. The newest course is the Plantation course, designed by Bill Coore and Ben Crenshaw, set on 240 acres of dramatic natural terrain, and is home to the Lincoln-Mercury Kapalua International. It's the most challenging of the three. Offers lessons at $40 per hour, rentals, a one-day golf school for $225, video golf lessons, and daily clinics at $20 per day. General admission: $115–$125.

Kapalua Tennis Garden and Village Tennis Center ★★★★

100 Kapalua Drive, Kapalua, 96761, ☎ (808) 665-0112.
Hours: 7 a.m.–6 p.m.

One of the finest clubs in the country, this is actually two facilities, The Tennis Garden and the Village Tennis Center. Each feature 10 Plexipave courts for day and night play. Also full-service pro shops, snack bars, lounge areas. Home of Wilson Kapalua Open. Private lessons, rentals, tennis program, matchmaking (!). Lower fee for resort guests. Children under 18 free when playing with parents. General admission: $10–$15.

Lahaina

Absolute Sportfishing ★★

P.O. Box 10511, Lahaina, 96761, ☎ (808) 661-2591.

Four types of trips to choose from on the *Absolute*, a Bertram 31-foot, 440-horsepower sportfishing charter boat. Full- or half-day, morning or afternoon sportfishing and bottom fishing. Arrive on Kaanapali Beach 15 minutes prior to departure. All equipment and ice provided. Either private charter or split private–two groups of one or two persons, each group paying half the cost. Four-passenger limit preferred. General admission: $225–$675.

Dive Maui ★★★

900 Front Street, Lahaina, 96761, ☎ (808) 667-2080.

Offers state-of-the-art training and professionally guided scuba and snorkeling tours. Dive Maui personnel have instructed rescue teams and tourist operations in the South Seas on underwater safety. Get certified while on Maui with a three-day PADI certification class; $139 includes gear, books, card fees, six ocean dives and more. If you've already got a card you may be ready for an advanced open-water course or perhaps move up to dive master. If you just want to dip a fin in the water, try the introductory scuba class for $34.95. Closely guided, it's an easy way to discover the wonders of scuba and perhaps see a green sea turtle up close. Guided tours include Molokini fish preserve, the Lanai Cathedrals, night dives at Black Rock Marine Preserve, rafting and whale-watching. General admission: $34.95–$400.

Extended Horizons ★★

Box 10785, Lahaina, 96761, ☎ *(808) 667-0611.*
Hours: 8 a.m.–8 p.m.

Dive Lanai on *Extended Horizons II*, a 36-foot, custom aluminum dive boat. Limited to small groups, including 13 divers, the captain, and a dive crew of two, with six divers maximum per guide, all of whom are professional naturalists. All dive gear provided. There are 60 dive sites available, with average depths of 60–70 feet, and divers' requests are taken into consideration. The crossing to Lanai takes as little as 30 minutes. Refreshments provided. Ask about night dives, a PADI introductory course, and open-water referrals. Departure from Mala Wharf, Lahaina. Reservations required. General admission: $65–$99.

H20 Tropical Tours ★★

Mala Wharf, behind the Lahaina Cannery Mall, Lahaina, ☎ *(808) 665-0488.*
Hours: 7 a.m.–7 p.m.

Captain your own boat—in this instance, a Projet, made by Zodiac, which is a 14-foot, rigid-hull inflatable boat with a jet propelled engine, and a top speed of 37 miles per hour. It has a driver's seat that you straddle like a motorcycle with a steering wheel for maneuverability. No outboard prop is attached to the boat. It holds up to six passengers, but the company recommends no more than four adults per boat. The craft contains life jackets, a ship-to-shore radio (but are they listening?) and dry bags for storage, and can be operated anywhere within the Maui, Lanai and Molokai triangular area. Lowest rate is for one hour of rental. Highest price is for a full eight-hour day. Half-day rate is $295. Early birds leaving by 7 a.m. get a 25 percent discount off the half-day rate. Cooler rental $5; includes ice. Reserve two days in advance. For more information write P.O. Box 252, Maui, Hawaii 96761. General admission: $95–$560.

Hawaii Ocean Rafting ★★

P.O. Box 381, Lahaina, 96761, ☎ *(808) 667-2191.*

Hawaii Ocean Rafting offers a variety of snorkeling trips to Lanai aboard a hard-back inflatable raft (otherwise known as a Zodiac). It will take you to three prime snorkel sites in virgin territory, where you'll likely see dolphins cavort (no guarantee, though). There's whale-watching in season. Fare includes continental breakfast, snacks, deluxe deli lunch (on full-day excursions only) or beach barbecue, full open bar, all snorkeling gear and instruction. Participants also get two hours of sunbathing time. Trips are limited to groups of eight to 12 people. The raft is about 50 percent canopy-covered. Wear a swimsuit, and don't forget sunscreen, a hat, towel and light coverup. Kodak underwater cameras available. Getting there is half the fun, believe us. Boats leave from Lahaina Harbor loading dock, departure times vary depending on trip length (two-hour, full-day, half-day and three-quarter-day trips available.) Reservations required. General admission: $29–$129.

Lahaina Divers ★★

143 Dickenson Street, Lahaina, 96761, ☎ *(808) 667-7496.*
Hours: 8 a.m.–8 p.m.

Lahaina Divers, Maui's first PADI five-star dive center and instructor development center, conducts at least one beginning diver certification course each week. SSI, NAUI and IDEA referral students may complete open-water training requirements in two afternoons, beginning any day of the week. If you've already got your card, go on one of the center's two- or three-tank dives or night dives from the *Endeavor* or the *Reliant,* two fast and comfortable dive boats. Looky-loos welcome. General admission: $55–$115.

Lahaina Divers Turtle Charter ★★★

143 Dickenson Street, Lahaina, 96761, ☎ *(808) 998-DIVE.*
Hours: 8 a.m.–8 p.m.

A new offering from Lahaina Divers, Maui's first five-star PADI dive center and instructor training center, is the "Turtle Reef Dive Charter," a snorkel/dive/seminar combo. Prior to your trip, instructors give you the skinny about the rare Hawaiian green sea turtle, one of the company's favorite "dive buddies." The four-hour expedition leaves from Lahaina Harbor daily at 12:30 p.m. Higher price is for certified and introductory divers; lower price for snorkelers. General admission: $55–$79.

Maui Surfing School ★★

Lahaina Harbor behind Kam III School, Lahaina, ☎ *(808) 875-0625.*

Andrea Thomas guarantees that you'll learn to surf in one lesson or you'll get your money back. Her method was developed for beginners, cowards and non-swimmers. Two-hour group lessons, or private sessions. Custom "surfaris" for competent surfers who want insider tips on different breaks. Equipment provided. Call for rates. For more information, write P.O. Box 424, Puunene, HI 96784. On the mainland, call ☎ (800) 851-0543.

Nancy Emerson School of Surfing ★★

Lahaina, ☎ *(808) 244-7873.*

Nancy, a former surfing champion, claims along with rival Andrea Thomas that she created the method of teaching people to surf in one lesson. We don't want to start a fight between the two, so you decide. Emerson developed her technique in 1973, and has operated schools for beginners since 1980. All instructors are personally trained by Nancy. Two-hour group or private lessons. See Nancy's golden retriever "Apache" surf from 12:20–1:30 p.m. every Friday in Lahaina. Bring your camera and the kids. Call for rates and times.

Ocean Riders ★★

P.O. Box 967, Lahaina, Maui, 96767, Lahaina, Departs from Mala Wharf in Maui, ☎ *(808) 661-3586.*

Snorkel Molokai's mysterious North Shore via one of this company's high-speed inflatable Zodiac rafts. Trips are full-day adventures, and the captain selects a different itinerary daily, based on ocean and wind conditions. Included are high-quality snorkel equipment and instruction, a continental breakfast, mid-morning fruit platter, snacks and buffet lunch. Ocean Riders carries all "kids" ages six to 75. Private charters available. Leaves Mala Wharf at 7 a.m. and returns between 2 and 4 p.m. Ask about trips to Lanai plus whale-watching expeditions. General admission: $130.

Offshore Adventures ★★★

900 Front Street, Lahaina, 96761, ☎ *(808) 667-2080.*
A division of Dive Maui, Offshore Adventures takes small groups to a calm cove on the backside of Lanai on three-quarter- and half-day snorkeling tours. Includes continental breakfast, buffet lunch and high-quality gear. General admission: $39 – $120.

Trilogy Excursions ★★★★

P.O. Box 1119, Lahaina, 96767, ☎ *(808) 661-4743.*
Hours: 6:30 a.m.–1 a.m.
Starting from a single 50-foot Trimaran in 1973, the Coon family gradually expanded to a fleet of four vessels, becoming the oldest and most popular sailing company in Maui. Today, it is the only charter-operator licensed to use Lanai's Manele Bay and features the most memorable sailing/scuba/snorkeling excursions to the "Private Island." All trips leave from Maui's Maalaea Harbor at 6:30 a.m., returning at 1 p.m.; or visitors can now opt for an overnighter at either Manele Bay Hotel or Lodge at Koele ($285.58, fare based on double occupancy, extra person, $191.00; children ages nine–15, $126.33; eight years and under, $83.87, includes tax and state harbor fees). Trips include "Discover Lanai" with introductory scuba and certified scuba dives, snorkeling (lessons and gear included), and a narrated island tour, guided by a Lanai resident. Tour price includes an eye-opening continental breakfast of "Mom's" famous fresh-baked cinnamon rolls, and an all-you-can-eat BBQ lunch (plus fresh fruit, juice, sodas and snacks served all day). Cost is $158.18. Ask about the "Weekend Sea-fari," which combines a photo/road rally and four-wheel-drive exploring, plus all the other activities outlined above. General admission: $158.18.

UFO Parasail ★★

P.O. Box 10536, Lahaina, 96761, ☎ *(808) 661-7836.*
Hours: 8 a.m.–4 p.m.
After a shuttle takes participants out to sea, they are lifted hydraulically on and off a premium winch boat for safe, dry landings. Standard rides go up 400 feet for seven minutes; deluxe rides are double that for 10 minutes. Maximum six flyers per trip, total ride is approximately one hour. No age requirement, but flyers must weigh at least 100 pounds to fly alone; tandem flights available at double the single price. Weight limit 325 pounds, or at the discretion of the captain. Observers allowed for $15.93 per person. Leaves from Kaanapali Beach. Season is May 16 through Dec. 14. General admission: $34.50–$50.96.

Where to Stay

Next to Oahu, Maui has the most rooms for visitors in its hotels, resorts, B&Bs and condos—plenty of condos. Unfortunately, this island also averages out as the most expensive of the Hawaiian islands in terms of accommodation. Price, obviously, is determined by where you decide to stay and, in most cases, the time of year you visit. The low season generally runs from after Easter to before Christmas, and rooms can be discounted 25 percent or more during this period. On **West Maui**, where most of the tourists stay, you can choose from more than 80 hotels and condo units. The major resorts are the **Kaanapali Beach Resort** and the **Kapalua Bay Resort**, both crammed with high-class condo complexes and hotels such as the Westin Maui, Marriott and Hyatt Regency. There are a few condos and some funkier hotels in Lahaina, and more condos around **Maalaea Bay**. On **East Maui**, you can't miss the hideous sea of condos (popular with vacationing families) at **Kihei**, while down the coast **Wailea** offers more luxury hotels and tasteful condos. A variety of accommodations, from rustic to flash, can be found in **Hana**. And don't overlook **Kahului**, in **Central Maui**, for convenience and value.

Central Maui

Haiku

Bed-and-Breakfasts

Halfway to Hana House   **$50–$65**   ★★

100 Waipio Road, Haiku, 96708, ☎ (808) 572-1176, FAX (808) 572-3609.
Single: $50–$55. Double: $55–$65.

Halfway to Hana House is a cozy studio unit in a private home set in the country 30 minutes from Kahului airport. Colorful tropical plants and flowers, fruit trees and herb gardens surround the property. Only a short walk to freshwater pools and waterfalls, horseback riding and country trails for hiking, the B&B is a good point of departure for both Hana town and Haleakala volcano. The host, Gail Pickholz, is a longtime resident (more than 25 years) and outdoor enthusiast, and she'll be happy to be a personal resource guide to secret places away from the tourist trail. She often takes guests on snorkeling and kayak jaunts. The light and airy accommodation has its own entrance and bath, a double bed, mini-kitchen and outdoor covered patio with an ocean view. Rattan furnishings are offset by exotic floral arrangements and original, locally produced art. Nice gestures include chocolate macadamia nuts by your pillow (yum). Amenities: balcony or patio. 1 room. Credit cards: not accepted.

Pilialoha Bed and Breakfast Cottage   **$95**   ★ ★ ★

2512 Kaupakalua Road, Haiku, 96708, ☎ *(808) 572-1440, FAX (808) 572-4612.*
Single: $95. Double: $95.

Guests rave about the genuine sense of Aloha they receive during their stay at this aptly monikered property, which means "friendship" in Hawaiian. The hostess, Machiko Heide, an artist, is as sweet as her name, and the little B&B cottage on her two-acre spread is decorated with lots of personal touches, including hand-painted bed pillows and artful arrangements of anthuriums and other exotic blooms. Evidence of her green thumb is everywhere, including 100 bug-free rose bushes, all labeled for your edification. The two-bedroom cottage has one room with a queen bed and another with a twin. The living room has a queen-size sofa bed, and extra futons are kept in the closet. Up to six people can be accommodated, but it is more comfortable for two. It also has a fully equipped kitchen, living room with cable TV and phone, washer/dryer and iron. The Heide's will also loan you beach gear. Fresh fruit, homemade bread, pastry or muffins and beverages are supplied daily; all you have to do is dish them up. The upcountry location is convenient to several interesting areas, including the cowboy-rodeo town of Makawao, the summit of Haleakala National Park, and Maui's windsurfing capital, Hookipa. There's a minimum two-night stay. 1 room. Credit cards: not accepted.

Cottages

Maui Dream Cottages/ Halelea   **$490**   ★ ★ ★

265 West Kuiaha Road, Haiku, 96708, ☎ *(808) 575-9079, FAX (808) 575-9477.*
Single: $490. Double: $490.

The two stand-alone cottages that compose Maui Dream Cottages are on a two-acre estate on a hilltop on the north shore of Maui, 12 miles from the Kahului Airport. These very private retreats are fenced in, and there is 1.5 acres of open lawn for relaxing or for active kids to play on. Hammocks are stretched between palm trees. You could live on the huge variety of fruit that drops off the trees on the estate—these include coconuts, bananas, avocados, papayas, mangoes, even passion fruit—the list goes on and on. The closest beach for swimming is five minutes from the house, and management recommends that the surrounding pineapple fields (Haiku used to be an old plantation town) are great for long runs or just walking. The handsomely furnished and roomy cottages are fully equipped with designer kitchens with microwave, washer-dryer, phone, TV and VCR. It sleeps from two to five people comfortably. Also available for rent by the same owners is a private residence, *Halelea* (House of Joy), which is on the point of Tavares Bay on 10,000 square feet of land near Paia and Hookipa Beach Park. For $385 per night, you get 3650 square feet of antique and art-filled living space with three bedrooms, four baths and a self-contained pool house/cottage with kitchen and bath. Designed by one artist, furnishings and features are custom-made, including outside decks constructed of imported Indonesian coconut wood. The living-room floor, although made of hardwood, resembles Japanese tatami matting. The main bath is a replica of an old Japanese bath house, with a Jacuzzi offering ocean views. Reservations should be made early, for obvious reasons, as many people book a year in advance for all these dream properties. Amenities: Jacuzzi, sauna, balcony or patio, family plan. 2 rooms.

Kahului

Hotels

Maui Seaside Hotel   **$60–$100**   ★

100 Kaahumanu Avenue, Kahului, 96732, ☎ *(800) 367-7000, (808) 877-3311, FAX (808) 922-0052. Rated restaurant: Vi's*
Single: $60–$100. Double: $60–$100.
An informal, Hawaiian family-owned oceanfront hotel on Kahului Bay, the Maui Seaside is three miles from Kahului Airport. Each room (none have ocean views) features two double beds, ceiling fan as well as air conditioning, refrigerator and color TV. Some have kitchenettes, rather pricey for $100 per night. Vi's, the on-site restaurant, offers a mid-priced, varied menu of local and international dishes. There's a garden and pool area.The hotel caters to seniors and others looking for a comfortable, homey bargain. Amenities: exercise room. 190 rooms. Credit cards: A, MC, V.

The Maui Palms Hotel   **$55–$75**   ★

Kaahumanu Avenue, Kahului, 96732, ☎ *(800) 367-5004, (808) 877-0071, FAX (808) 871-5797. Rated restaurant: East West Dining Room*
Single: $55–$75. Double: $55–$75.
A budget hotel on five acres, the Maui Palms is a low-slung, two-story building of no particular architectural merit, fronting the beach on Kahului Bay. The rather garishly decorated rooms, with lipstick-red bedspreads, have small louvered windows with patterned drapes that look like one of Rush Limbaugh's ties. Amusements include a pool, and the East West Dining Room, offering a nightly steam-table spread called the Imperial Japanese Buffet. A shuttle van is available for airport pickup and return. A decent choice for those who have business in Kahului or are on their way to somewhere else. 103 rooms. Credit cards: MC, V.

East Maui

Hana

Heavenly Hana Inn   **$175–$175**   ★★

4155 Hana Highway, Hana, 96713, Five minutes from Hana Airport, ☎ *(808) 248-8442, FAX (808) 248-8442.*
Single: $175. Double: $175.
This Japanese-style inn, although miles away from anything, is a delight for lovers of Asian art. Two stone lions, symbols of luck and well-being, greet guests at the front gate. The central lobby and lounge feature Tonsu-type furniture and brand-new eucalyptus wood flooring, installed shortly after new owners bought the property from longtime proprietor Alfreda Wurst. Guests sleep on queen-size platform futons, and new bathrooms have vanities and deep-soaking tubs big enough for two. One unfortunate change is the removal of the kitchenettes; no meals except a

Ulupalakua country, Maui

Haleakala, Maui

Road to Hana, Maui

Carthaginian and Old Pioneer Inn, Lahaina Harbor

Cinder cones, Haleakala crater

MAUI

continental breakfast are served, and there are no restaurants in the immediate vicinity. 3 rooms. Credit cards: not accepted.

Condos

Hana Kai-Maui Resort Condominiums **$110–$165** ★★

1533 Uakea Road, Hana, 96713, ☎ (800) 346-2772, (808) 248-8426, FAX (808) 248-7482.

Single: $110–$165. Double: $110–$165.

Nestled in a sheltered cove facing the black-sand Papolana Beach, the Hana-Kai Maui Resort Condominiums consists of a pair of two-story structures housing 18 simple, but fairly spacious and neatly kept, studio and one-bedroom units. All have oceanfront views and lanais with a molded plastic table and chairs. Complete kitchens (sans dishwashers) are thoughtfully provided, as Hana's grocery stores are shuttered by 6:30 p.m. and there are only a sprinkling of eateries in the area. There are no TVs or radios; the only music you hear is your significant other whispering in your ear and the sound of the surf beating against the waves outside your quarters. The management touts its "exquisite spring-fed pool," but before you jump in, remember it is there for aesthetic reasons only. Barbecue facilities. Daily maid service. Amenities: balcony or patio, family plan. 18 rooms. Credit cards: A, MC, V.

House Rentals

Blair's Original Hana Plantation Houses **$70–$150** ★★★

P.O. Box 249, Hana, 96713, ☎ (800) 228-HANA, (808) 248-7686, FAX (808) 248-8240.

Single: $70–$150. Double: $70–$150.

For more than 10 years, Blair Shurtleff has been offering "alternative" (and very affordable) accommodations for travelers looking for the real Hana experience. His unique collection of rentals includes the Garden House, three miles from the town of Hana. The tropical-style dwelling offers two units, including a downstairs studio with a private entrance, suitable for two persons, renting for only $70 a night. It has a queen-size bed with combination bath, plus a full kitchen and cable TV. Available for $10 more is Lani Makaalae Studio, which has a whirlpool tub/shower on an outdoor deck under plumeria trees. One of Blair's most upscale properties (for $150 per night) is the solar-powered Waikoloa Beach Cottage, situated on a half-acre lot just steps from a black-sand beach. Sleeping up to five guests (there's also a separate Japanese sleeping room for two), the cottage is decked out in exotic woods and has large picture windows overlooking Hana Bay. All houses feature fully equipped kitchen facilities, barbecue grills and beach access. Blair and his associates are all longtime residents and will help arrange such head-clearing activities as yoga/stretch classes, massages and more. Amenities: Jacuzzi, balcony or patio. 12 rooms. Credit cards: A, MC, V.

Rentals

Ekena **$135–$275** ★★★

P.O. Box 728, Hana, 96713, ☎ (800) 262-9912, (808) 248-7047.

Single: $135–$275. Double: $135–$275.

Two apartments are available in this spacious, two-story hillside home above Hana. Its prime attraction is wrap-around decks affording awesome 360-degree views of the ocean, the Hana coast and the surrounding hills. The lower-level (and lower-priced) unit features 1700 square feet of living space, and includes one or two bedrooms, two baths, a fully equipped kitchen, dining room, TV and VCR, and washer/dryer. The 2000-square-foot, skylit, second-story apartment offers the same amenities and facilities. The hostess has a green thumb; her tropical blooms are everywhere in evidence. Amenities: balcony or patio. 2 rooms. Credit cards: not accepted.

Resorts

Hotel Hana–Maui   **$395–$795**   ★★★★

At Hana Ranch, off Highway 31, Hana, 96713, ☎ (800) 325-3535, (808) 248-8211, FAX (808) 248 -7202. Rated restaurant: Hana Ranch Restaurant
Single: $395–$795. Double: $395–$795.

For close to 50 years, the Hotel Hana Maui has been drawing a legion of repeat visitors despite several changes of ownership. The 66-acre property, located on what was once a cattle ranch, hasn't really changed much, despite a top-to-bottom renovation by the Rosewood Corporation of Dallas in the mid-'80s. Although it has been a member of ITT Sheraton's Luxury Collection (sounds like a haute couture line) of fine hotels since 1989, the resort is still staffed by a family of locals whom many veteran guests know by their first names. Sometimes the phone lines at the reception desk are quirky, and the food in the restaurant is less than stellar, but these are just minor wrinkles in an otherwise streamlined operation. Accommodations are in 97 rooms and suites housed in a series of single-story, plantation-cottage style buildings. All are decorated in a blissfully tasteful manner, including huge beds covered with painstakingly stitched Hawaiian quilts, with mountains of pillows propped against a bamboo headboard. Hardwood floors gleam, and artful flower arrangements are everywhere, even in the hand-tiled baths, which feature deep-soaking tubs overlooking private gardens. Latticed lanais offer sea views. Amenities include wet bars, refrigerators with ice-makers, and Kona coffee beans with a grinder. You'll also find a brolly for sudden rain squalls, but no TVs, radios, telephones or clocks are anywhere in evidence. One could live very happily and permanently in one of the top-of-the-line Sea Ranch Cottages (reached by shuttle). Each has an outdoor spa and deck, and are considerably larger than other dwellings. If you can be lured out of your lodgings, partake in some of the outdoor activities, which are a big thing at the resort, including horseback riding, picnics and barbecues on nearby Hamoa Beach. On-site sports facilities include two tennis courts, two pools and a jokey three-hole practice "golf course" with tees marked by coconuts. Amenities: tennis, horseback riding, health club, Jacuzzi, balcony or patio, family plan. 97 rooms. Credit cards: A, MC, V.

Huelo Point

Bed-and-Breakfasts

Huelo Point Bed and Breakfast   **$95–$105**   ★★★

P.O. Box 1195, Huelo Point, ☎ (808) 572-1850.

Single: $95. Double: $105.

This has got to be the most unusual B&B accommodation in Maui—a secluded, glass-walled gazebo, perched atop a 300-foot cliff, directly overlooking Waipio Bay, where whales spawn. The property, located on a flower farm, includes amenities such as a hot tub, outdoor shower, rock-lined pool and, of course, the view. From here, you can explore hiking trails to private waterfalls. The hosts, Guy and Doug, live on the property in a palatial home, which they also rent out for $2000 a week (that's the day rate some resorts charge for a suite). Friendly and helpful, they have suggestions for all the fun things you can do in the area. Despite the back-of-beyond location, it's only a few minutes' drive to Paia, where restaurants, shops and beaches abound. Also, you're half way to Hana. Amenities: Jacuzzi, balcony or patio. 1 rooms. Credit cards: not accepted.

South Maui

Kihei

Bed-and-Breakfasts

Aloha Pualani   **$39–$99**   ★★

15 Wailana Place, Kihei, 96753, ☎ *(800) 782-5264, (808) 874-9265, FAX (808) 874-9127.*

Aloha Pualani, situated 100 feet from Maalaea Bay beach, is a bed-and-breakfast/condominium combo offered by hosts Keith and Marina Dinsmoor. The Dinsmoors maintain five two-story units surrounding a heated pool and tropically landscaped (you were expecting firs and pine trees?) courtyard. All are one-bedroom suites with 1.5 baths and a living/dining area. Amenities include fully equipped kitchens, washer and dryer, color cable TV, phone and ceiling fan. Best of all is an oceanfront lanai upstairs. A continental breakfast is served for $5 a day. Keith and Marina live on the property and are always on hand to cater (within reason) to the needs of their guests. Double occupancy rates start at $39 per day (plus tax) for a one-month stay off season; there's a three-night minimum year-round. Amenities: balcony or patio. 5 rooms. Credit cards: MC, V.

Ann and Bob Babson's Vacation Rentals   **$70–$105**   ★★★

3371 Keha Drive, Kihei, 96753, In Maui Meadows, just above Wailea, ☎ *(800) 824-6409, (808) 874-1166, FAX (808) 879-7906.*
Single: $70–$105. Double: $70–$105.

For more than four years, Ann and Bob Babson, an enthusiastic couple transplanted from Northern California, have run a bed-and-breakfast operation from their contemporary wooden home in Maui Meadows, a residential suburb above Wailea. The house, on a half-acre of land, is landscaped with tropical fruit trees and flowers, including avocado, papaya, plumeria and red ginger. Many guests enjoy just sprawling in the double hammock and taking it all in, even though Kihei beaches are a mere five-minute drive away. The bed-and-breakfast units, on the second floor of the house, include the one-bedroom, one-bath Bougainvillea Suite. It's furnished in white-washed rattan, with a queen bed and small refrigerator. It offers both ocean and mountain views. The 450-square foot Molokini Suite, decorated in a tasteful but spare Oriental style, also has a small fridge, a king-size bed with a skylight above it, and a rocking chair. The large bathroom has double sinks and a whirlpool tub/shower combination. On the ground floor is the Hibiscus Hideaway, a one-bedroom, one-bath apartment. It has a private entrance and its own garden. Adjacent to the main house is the Sunset Cottage, with two bedrooms (it sleeps six, with a sofa bed in the living room) and two baths. Special touches include a cathedral ceiling and covered lanai off the living room where you can see whales doing their thing in season. The Cottage and the Hideaway have kitchen facilities. Guests who opt for breakfast are provided with an "all you can eat" repast of juice, coffee, fruit, homemade granola, muffins and scones. Sometimes a hot, freshly prepared item such as quiche, pancakes, french toast or coconut waffles is on the menu. Unfortunately for slugabeds, the Babsons serve breakfast fairly promptly at 7:30 a.m., as the couple feel most guests like to get up and go. Also, Ann and Bob are vegetarians, so don't expect any meat dishes. All units have cable TVs and telephones. A laundry basket is provided in the rooms, and the Babsons will do your laundry for a nominal fee. Beach chairs and towels are also provided. The Babsons delight in their guests discovering bed-and-breakfast living for the first time, whether they're honeymooners or seniors. If you don't have an itinerary planned for Maui, when you ask for their brochure, Ann and Bob will send you several pages of things to do and places to eat on the island. It seems the Babsons have indeed found the vocation of their dreams. They also run an interisland reservation service, and are happy to match people with other hosts in Maui when they're full. Notice to animal-lovers: no pets are allowed, as Ann and Bob have two frisky indoor cats (they also have two outdoor cats and a pair of birds). Amenities: balcony or patio. 4 rooms. Credit cards: MC, V.

Eva Villa $90–$95   ★ ★ ★

815 Kumulani Drive, Kihei, 96753, ☎ (808) 874-6407, FAX (808) 874 -6407.
Single: $90–$95. Double: $90–$95.

Eva Villa is located at the top of residential Maui Meadows, just above Wailea, on the dry side of the island. This striking, modern, white-concrete-and-glass, two-story home has wraparound terraces plus a rooftop deck, where the sunset views are spectacular. On a clear day, you can see the neighbor islands of Lanai, Molokini and Kahoolawe. Your live-in hosts are Rick and Dale Pounds, who reside on the second level; the entire first floor is rented out to guests. The Studio, which is approximately 600 square feet, overlooks the pool and Jacuzzi. The spacious room contains a queen-size bed, plus a sleeper-sofa and a private bath. A full kitchen has a counter-bar and eating area. The Apartment, a little bigger at 680 square feet, has two bedrooms equipped with a queen-size bed and two twin beds, and a private bath. The living room also has a pull-out sofa bed. A kitchenette includes a microwave, two-burner hot plate and refrigerator. Both units have private entrances and cable TV. The Pounds also offer a one-bedroom cottage with a queen-size bed and private bath located away from the property, with a full kitchen, laundry facilities and cable TV. The living room has a sofa bed. It boasts its own wraparound lanai with barbecue grill and a laundry room. All guests are welcome to use the beautiful pool and spa, barbecue facilities and outside tables and chairs. There are also well-cared-for grounds to stroll around in, with tropical fruit trees and flowers and a lily pond teeming with koi. Rick and Dale stock all kitchens with fresh island fruit, juices, breads and condiments for guests to prepare at their leisure. The house is only minutes away from Kihei, Wailea and Makena beaches, six championship golf courses, resort hotels and shopping areas with two large grocery stores. Amenities: Jacuzzi, balcony or patio. 3 rooms. Credit cards: not accepted.

Condos

Hale Hui Kai   **$95–$160**   ★★

2994 South Kihei Road, Kihei, 96753, On Keawakupu Beach, ☎ *(808) 879-1219, FAX (808) 879 -0600.*
Single: $95–$160. Double: $95–$160.
A mile-long beach extends from the front door of the Hale Hui Kai (meaning "House by the Sea") to the Wailea resort area. You can literally fall out of your room to the sand from one of the two-bedroom, two-bath apartments at this fairly tasteful property, a series of wood-shingle buildings, some with Polynesian peaked roofs. Units are spacious and individually appointed, with wall-to-wall carpeting and twin or queen-size beds. All-electric kitchens (isn't it nice someone else is footing the bill?) contain a dishwasher and refrigerator. There's a laundry room. Besides that great beach, there's a small pool. Adjacent to the property is Carelli's, one of Maui's best Italian restaurants. Instead of going on a whale-watching cruise, you can save money by staying here and watching the great humpbacks cavorting just outside your front door. Amenities: balcony or patio, family plan. 40 rooms. Credit cards: not accepted.

Hale Kamaole   **$89–$129**   ★★

2737 South Kihei Road, Kihei, 96753, ☎ *(800) 367-2970, (808) 879-1221.*
Single: $89–$129. Double: $89–$129.
Hale Kamaole is a low-rise condo complex with beach access from a two-lane road across from the property. Spacious lawns, with palm trees, hibiscus, plumeria and other tropical plants, give it a garden-like setting. All of the individually owned and decorated one- or two-bedroom units contain fully equipped kitchens, cable TVs and telephones. Most have queen or king beds and a sofa bed in the living room, but some one-bedroom apartments only have twin beds. A few upper-level, two-bedroom units possess lofts. All have lanais, except for ground-floor accommodations, which have to make do with a parcel of concrete with some tables and chairs. On-site facilities include two swimming pools with barbecue grills, and a tennis court. There's no maid service (laundromat on premises), but isn't it better than having someone knocking at your door at 8 a.m. when you're trying to sleep? Amenities: balcony or patio, family plan. 187 rooms. Credit cards: MC, V.

Kamaole Beach Royale Resort   **$95–$120**   ★★★

2385 South Kihei Road, Kihei, 96753, ☎ *(800) 421-3661, (808) 879-3131, FAX (808) 879 -9163.*
Single: $95–$120. Double: $95–$120.
Situated across from Kamaole Beach Park I, this unremarkable-looking, six-story stucco building with aqua accents features rather attractive one-, two- or three-bedroom apartments. Furnishings are the requisite wood and rattan, but the pieces here are of good quality, and some include swivel rockers with ottomans in the separate

MAUI

living areas. Some bedrooms have wicker chests at the foot of the beds for storage. All have private lanais, some with views of neighboring islands; all have vistas of Haleakala. Amenities include ceiling fans, color cable TV and telephones. Full kitchens with dishwashers and washer/dryers are provided. If you'd like a break from the beach, you can sunbathe by the pool or up on the roof garden. Those who can't leave the office behind have a conference room for conducting power meetings. Five-day minimum stay required. Amenities: balcony or patio. Credit cards: not accepted.

Kamaole Sands $95–$275   ★★★
2695 South Kihei Road, Kihei, 96753, ☎ (800) 367-5004, (808) 874-8700, FAX (808) 879 -3273.
Single: $95–$275. Double: $95–$275.
A fairly large complex of staggered mid-rise white concrete buildings, the Kamaole Sands nevertheless offers nicely landscaped gardens and rock pools with fountains as a cooling touch. But no one spends much time on the grass, as this property sits across from one of Maui's most famous beach parks, Kamaole III. Accommodations, with separate living, dining and sleeping areas, are much larger than you'd expect, and well-kept, with light rattan and wood furniture. All studios and one-, two- or three-bedroom units have private lanais, color cable TVs and fully equipped kitchen facilities. Ceiling fans compensate for the lack of air conditioning. There's a pool, including a wading pool for tots, two whirlpool spas, four tennis courts, a sundeck and barbecues. If you tire of cooking en suite, the complex's Sandbar restaurant is a welcome change. Amenities: tennis, Jacuzzi, balcony or patio. 440 rooms. Credit cards: A, MC, V.

Kihei Kai Oceanfront Condominiums $90–$105   ★★
61 North Kihei Road, Kihei, 96753, On Maalaea Bay, ☎ (800) 735-2357, (808) 879-2357.
Single: $90–$105. Double: $90–$105.
This beige-and-brown, wood-and-concrete, two-story building has a nice location on Maalaea Bay and a protected cove with gentle surf ideal for families with children. Lounge chairs and round tables with stone benches dot the lawn facing the beach, where cookouts are a daily happening. Plain-but-comfortable, air-conditioned, one-bedroom units have private lanais; oceanfront views from some of them are gorgeous. Others have pool or garden views and a peek at the sea over the trees. Amenities include kitchens with microwaves, ceiling fans, cable TVs and phones. A tiled pool is surrounded by tropical flowering plants. Laundry facilities on the premises. Amenities: balcony or patio. 24 rooms. Credit cards: not accepted.

Mana Kai Maui $105–$205   ★★
2960 South Kihei Road, Kihei, 96753, ☎ (800) 367-5004, (808) 879-1561, FAX (808) 874 -5042. Rated restaurant: Five Palms Beach Grill
Single: $105–$205. Double: $105–$205.
This eight-story property is conveniently located on an excellent white-sand beach on a quiet stretch of South Kihei that's perfect for swimming. Although billed as a condo resort, the Mana Kai Maui also offers poorly situated hotel rooms with twin beds as well as spacious one- and two-bedroom suites decorated in easy-on-the-eye

taupes and beiges, twin or king beds with quasi-Hawaiian quilts, and light, tropical, woven-rattan furniture. Private lanais are wide enough for a table and chairs. Fully equipped kitchens have plenty of storage space and contain a counter with bar-stool seating. All have color TVs. The two-bedroom units can sleep up to six people; these are ideal for families. Facilities include an open-air restaurant and lobby lounge and a pool. Included in the rates are a rental car; breakfast is supplied for hotel guests only. Amenities: balcony or patio. 67 rooms. Credit cards: A, MC, V.

Maui Isana Resort $120–$160 ★★

515 S. Kihei Road, Kihei, 96753, ☎ *(800) 633-3833, (808) 879-7800, FAX (808) 874 -5321. Rated restaurant: Isana Restaurant*
Single: $120–$160. Double: $120–$160.

The Maui Isana, with a location just a short walk from the beach, will appeal to lovers of Japanese food as well as windsurfers and divers. This small complex of white, concrete buildings with pink-tile roofs has its own dive/sport shop with instructors on hand, and a restaurant specializing in Teppanyaki-style cooking. It also has a sushi bar. The one- and two-bedroom apartments have separate living areas, with lanais separated by louvered glass windows and sliding doors. Framed Japanese prints grace the walls. You have a choice of a queen or two twin beds. All suites have attractive spic-and-span kitchens with blue-tiled floors, plus a washer and dryer, color TVs and radios. A free-form pool and jacuzzi is situated in the center of the complex. There's also a cocktail lounge upstairs, called the Mermaid Bar. An in-house activity desk will book tours for you upon request. Amenities: Jacuzzi, balcony or patio. 50 rooms. Credit cards: A, MC, V.

Punahoa Condominiums $93–$135 ★★

2142 Iliili Road, Kihei, 96753, Near Kalama Park, ☎ *(800) 564-4380, (808) 879-2720.*
Single: $93–$135. Double: $93–$135.

Small and intimate, all of the 15 apartments in this three-story property face the ocean. You have your choice of studios, or one- or two-bedroom units, all with living rooms with sofa beds, large lanais (some corner units have two), fully equipped kitchens (including full sets of dinnerware), color cable TVs and phones. The beach, while not directly in front of the Punahoa, is only 50 feet away, so you won't miss the lack of a pool, unless you don't like saltwater. Beach towels are provided in rooms. There's not much else to do here, but if you use the place as a base to explore the Kihei area, you'll be happy with the prices; in low season, a studio for two runs as low as $66 a night! Management will gladly assist you with car-rental deals. Minimum stay is five nights. Amenities: balcony or patio, family plan. 15 rooms. Credit cards: not accepted.

Hotels

Maui Oceanfront Hotel $90–$160 ★

2980 South Kihei Road, Kihei, 96753, ☎ *(800) 367-5004, (808) 879-7744, FAX (808) 874 -0145.*
Single: $90. Double: $160.

A simple, low-rise hotel that management likes to call "quaint," the Maui Oceanfront is only yards from a terrific stretch of beach. Only a few rooms have sea views. All are air-conditioned, with double or twin beds, and tiled baths with shower. The

MAUI

white-rattan furniture includes a writing desk. Amenities include color cable TV and a refrigerator. A one-bedroom family unit sleeps four. Continental breakfast, included in the rates, consists of coffee and doughnuts. Carelli's, one of Maui's best Italian restaurants, is adjacent to the property. Amenities: Jacuzzi. 87 rooms. Credit cards: A, MC, V.

Rentals

Aikane Ohana Vacation Rentals   **$75–$95**   ★★

558 Kaleo Place, Kihei, 96753, ☎ (808) 879-5454.
Single: $75–$95. Double: $75–$95.

Aikane Ohana is Richard and Janna Hoehn's private home located one mile from Kihei beaches in a gated residential area. The more expensive of the two units available is a 725-square-foot, two-bedroom apartment with a full kitchen, and a living room with cable TV. The private bath has a shower only, but nice touches include marble countertops, koa-wood cabinets and full-size closets. One-bedroom contains a king-size bed, the other a queen. Both have tiled floors, marble countertops, koa-wood cabinets, lots of closet space with full-length mirrors, and private baths with shower only. Each room has a skylight and ceiling fan, and incredible city, ocean and neighbor-island views. In addition, it has a 400-square-foot lanai equipped with a patio table and chairs, plus loungers. For $75 per night, you can rent a studio apartment with a private bath, located off the swimming pool and spa area. Although considerably smaller than the apartment, it's comfortably and completely furnished with a king-size bed, two night stands, a dresser, table with four chairs, rocking chair and color TV and stereo. It has an ironing board and iron. The kitchen has a full-size refrigerator, microwave, toaster oven and even a blender and wok. Each apartment has its own private entrance. Extras for both units include use of the pool and spa, beach gear, and free local calls. Laundry facilities cost extra. No breakfast or food is provided, but there are grocery stores nearby. No smoking permitted anywhere on the premises, including the lanai and pool area. The Hoehns offer a 10 percent discount for weekly stays, and 20 percent discounts for monthly stays. Amenities: Jacuzzi, balcony or patio. 2 rooms. Credit cards: not accepted.

Kathy Scheper's Maui Accommodations   **$49–$80**

1587 North Alaniu Place, Kihei, 96753, ☎ (800) 645-3753, (808) 879-8744, FAX (808) 879 -9100.
Single: $49–$80. Double: $49–$80.

Kathy Scheper offers several alternatives for your Maui beach vacation. All accommodations are just steps away from world-class strands in the Kihei area. A terrific deal is a custom-designed cottage for $80 per night (only $65 from May 1 through Dec. 14) that Kathy says is perfect for honeymooners, although it sleeps four (how about a double wedding?). The cottage is air-conditioned and features color cable TV, stereo, fully equipped kitchen, washer and dryer and complete bedding. Also available are beach mats and coolers. Enjoy the warm evenings on a private patio with an umbrella table set and Webber barbecue grill. This cottage has private covered parking just outside the front door. Also on offer is a studio apartment for a single traveler or a couple on a budget ($49 per night, $39 on the dates above). It has a private patio with an outdoor shower as well as a half-bath. Cooking facilities include a small refrigerator and microwave. All bedding and towels are provided, and it has color cable TV and a radio. Kathy also offers an apartment that sleeps four in the Kai Nani Beach Condominiums, which is just across the street from Kamaole II beach park. It has a large master bedroom and private lanai, color cable TV, stereo, full kitchen with utensils; bedding, beach gear and even golf clubs and tennis rackets are supplied. The condo has a huge pool on the premises and a laundry room. It rents for $80 per night in high season (December 15–April 30), and $65 per night from May 1 through December 14. Ask about monthly rates. There is a two-week minimum stay over the Christmas holidays. Amenities: balcony or patio. 3 rooms. Credit cards: not accepted.

Ma'alaea Village

Condos

Makani A Kai   **$95–$175**

280 Hauoli Street, Ma'alaea Village, 96793, Near Ma'alaea Harbor, a few miles away from Kihei, ☎ *(800) 367-6084, (808) 244-7012, FAX (808) 242-7476.*

Single: $95–$175. Double: $95–$175.

This handsome low-rise condominium development in a tropical garden setting is one of the nicest of seven such properties situated side-by-side near the Maalaea Boat Harbor. The Makani A Kai sits on the quietest stretch of a lovely five-mile beach that is often neglected by tourists. The beach is home to some rare Hawaiian bird species. All of the one-, two- or three-bedroom units, set around a courtyard, have some views of the sea, but the most desirable oceanfront properties are often booked solid, especially in high season. Decor, depending on the owner, varies, but most eschew the all too typical bright floral prints for muted beige fabrics with light patterns, shoji screens and other Orientalia. Nearest to the Makani a Kai is the Hono Kai, with a half-moon-shaped pool right at the ocean's edge. Some of the one-bedroom units (with limited ocean view) go for the reasonable price of $75 a night in low season. Two- and three-bedroom apartments are also available. There are laundry rooms on every floor, which is good for families with kids. Only two-bedroom apartments are available at the Kanai A Nalu, next door to the Hono Kai. They run from $145 to $175 a night; $100 to $125 in low season. The cheerfully decorated units (some might say gaudy) feature white-wood furniture with pink-and-green check upholstery, offset with clean grayish-blue carpeting. Its palm-tree-lined courtyard features a waterfall, barbecues and a freshwater pool. Common to all these sister properties are completely furnished kitchens with microwaves and dishwashers, color TVs, lanais and direct dial phones. The harbor location is convenient to whale-watching, snorkeling, fishing or sunset dinner cruises, as well as restaurants, a deli and store, and even a fresh fish market. The hustle and bustle of Kihei is only 20 minutes away. Minimum stay is five nights. Amenities: balcony or patio. 24 rooms. Credit cards: MC, V.

MAUI

Makena

Bed-and-Breakfasts

Vi & Boogie's Makena Landing Studios   **$95**   ★★★

*5100 Makena Road, Makena, 96753, Two miles from Wailea resorts, 18 miles from
Kahului Airport, ☎ (808) 879-6286.*
Single: $95. Double: $95.

Readers rave about this oceanfront B&B that draws tons of repeat visitors. About a
mile from Makena's famous Big Beach, Makena Landing Studios is situated in an
enviable location with its expansive front lawn and concrete deck facing a lava-rock
coastline. Close to the Wailea resorts, it's also an excellent vantage point for spotting humpback whales in season. But the main reason for visiting is the warm welcome from owners Vi and Boogie Lu'uwai, a native Hawaiian couple who rent out
two studio apartments with private entrances on opposite ends of the second floor
of their comfortable cedar-wood home. Built on land that has been in their family
for more than 100 years, the couple, not surprisingly, are intimately familiar with
the area and culture. They're also great cooks as well, providing a homemade gourmet breakfast each morning, plus snacks (three-night minimum stay required). The
comfy studios have a queen-size bed, combination baths (including bathroom supplies), sparkling white kitchens with refrigerator, microwave, coffee maker and utensils, color TVs and private telephone, and oceanfront lanais. For all this bounty, is it
so surprising that Vi and Boogie need prospective guests to reserve at least four
months in advance? Amenities: balcony or patio. 2 rooms. Credit cards: not accepted.

Condos

Makena Surf   **$320–$525**   ★★★

*5100 Makena Alanui Road, Makena, 96753, ☎ (800) 367-5246, (808) 879-1959, FAX
(808) 874 -3554.*
Single: $320–$525. Double: $350–$525.

The Makena Surf enjoys a gorgeous and very private location on a lava-rock promontory above Paipu Beach on Maui's southwest coast. Guests seeking isolation and
proximity to deserted beaches waiting to be explored will love this property, but if
you have a rental car, it's just a short haul to the Wailea resorts and their attendant
golf, tennis and shopping glitz. The elegant and individually appointed and air-conditioned one-, two- and three-bedroom apartments all have at least a partial ocean
view. Luxury accoutrements include ceiling fans, a wet bar, whirlpool tubs, in-room
safes, fully-equipped kitchens with microwave, washer and dryer, and private lanai.
Two pools and two whirlpool spas are provided, as the beach is better for snorkeling
and strolling than swimming. Other sports facilities include a putting green, four
tennis courts (two lit for night play) and free tennis clinics. Special golf rates are
available at Makena Resort. Three-night minimum stay. Amenities: tennis, Jacuzzi,
balcony or patio, family plan. 100 rooms. Credit cards: A, MC, V.

Maui Prince Makena Resort has one of Hawaii's best beaches.

Resorts

Maui Prince Hotel   **$220–$830**   ★ ★ ★ ★ ★

5400 Makena Alanui Road, Makena, 96753, ☎ (800) 321-MAUI, (808) 874-1111,
FAX (808) 879 -8530. Rated restaurant: Prince Court
Single: $220–$830. Double: $220–$830.

The Maui Prince Hotel, in the Makena resort, three miles from Wailea, is designed
in a V-shape so that all of its guest rooms and suites have ocean views from their private lanais. Facing one of Maui's best, and surprisingly uncrowded, beaches, the
hotel enjoys a tranquil sense of isolation. Subtly yet elegantly decorated, the hotel
eschews the bells and whistles of its flashier competitors. The pearl-painted and tiled
lobby and public areas include a 30,000 square-foot courtyard, where a koi pond,
Japanese footbridge and rock garden invite contemplation. This quietude is only
momentarily interrupted by the soothing sounds of a nearby waterfall, or the
refined strains of piped-in classical music. Accommodations are spacious and ame-
nity filled, including complimentary cookies, nuts, caramel corn, sodas and other
snacks. Ice is replenished daily. Slippers as well as robes are provided. Combination
baths have phones and vanities. Entertainment consists of color TV and in-room
movies as well as VCRs, plus that ocean view from a private lanai. There's 24-hour
room service from one of five excellent restaurants, including the award-winning
Prince Court. The former executive chef, the well-regarded Roger Dikon, was
replaced by his sous chef, Greg Gaspar, in late 1995. Often a guest chef at many
local food and wine festivals, Gaspar, a specialist in Pacific Rim cuisine, unveiled a
new menu in January 1996. Among his innovative offerings are five pepper spice
onaga on kula corn custard, with mescalun greens and mango vinaigrette. Kaiseki
dinners and sushi are both stellar in the traditionally decorated Hakone restaurant.
Lighter meals are available ál fresco at Café Kiowai. Besides splendid and

uncrowded golf (36 holes) and tennis facilities (six courts), there are two oval pools (no waterslides), a catamaran to take guests to Molokini atoll, and a full-service ocean-activity center. The Prince Kids Club keeps youngsters (guests and non-guests) occupied. Complimentary shuttle to the neighboring Wailea resorts. Amenities: tennis, horseback riding, balcony or patio, family plan. 310 rooms. Credit cards: A, DC, MC, V.

Wailea

Condos

Maui Polo Beach Club   **$270–$380**   ★★★

3750 Wailea Alanui Drive, Wailea, 96753, ☎ *(800) 367-5246, (808) 879-1595, FAX (808) 874 -3554.*

Single: $270–$380. Double: $270–$380.

The exterior of this staggered, white eight-story condominium looks rather like a county hospital on the beach, but the designer interiors of the one- or two-bedroom apartments are handsomely furnished with overstuffed chaise lounges and couches in muted tones of white, beige and taupe. All the better to set off the gorgeous ocean views from the wide lanais, which are roomy enough to contain another chaise lounge, this time in white wicker, as well as a table and chairs. All bedrooms have marble baths, and some have walk-in closets. Full kitchens and washer and dryer in all units. The complex is named after Polo Beach (no turf club in sight, however), a sheltered cove once named Dead Horse Beach; the new name is somewhat more palatable. There's excellent snorkeling nearby, and swimming is good in summer, but the Polo Beach Club also provides guests with an oceanfront pool and spa. Other facilities include a barbecue area; special golf rates available at Makena Resort. Daily concierge and maid service. Three-night minimum. Amenities: balcony or patio, family plan. 71 rooms. Credit cards: A, MC, V.

The Palms at Wailea   **$165–$225**   ★★★

3200 Wailea Alanui Drive, Wailea, ☎ *(800) 688-7444, (808) 879-5800, FAX (808) 874 -3723.*

Single: $165–$225. Double: $165–$225.

The Palms at Wailea, a sparsely landscaped cluster of white two-story buildings with archways and red-tile roofs, look like they belong on the Costa del Sol instead of Hawaii. The air-conditioned, one- and two-bedroom "villas" contain elegantly furnished ocean- or garden-view suites, each with a spacious lanai. In-room amenities include ceiling fans, color TVs with videotape players, and full kitchens. On the premises are shops, a pool and whirlpool, and laundry facilities. Nearby are championship golf and tennis facilities, and Wailea beach is just a short stroll away. Amenities: sauna, balcony or patio. Credit cards: A, MC, V.

Wailea Ekahi Village   **$139–$319**   ★★★

3750 Wailea Alanui Drive, Wailea, 96753, ☎ *(800) 367-5246, (808) 879-1595, FAX (808) 874 -3554.*

Single: $139–$319. Double: $139–$319.

Destination Resorts' Wailea Ekahi Village, a 34-acre property on handsome, half-mile-long Keawakupu Beach, is one of the lowest-priced condominiums in this swanky area, but that doesn't translate as low-quality. The studios and one- and two-bedroom apartments are situated on a terraced hillside, and all units come with a private lanai, fully equipped kitchens with microwaves and washer and dryer. Some units are air-conditioned. Facilities include your choice of four pools, with one facing the ocean, two paddle tennis courts and shuffleboard (do people really play shuffleboard anymore?). Special golf rates available at the neighboring Makena and Wailea resorts. Daily concierge and maid service. Three-night minimum stay. Amenities: balcony or patio. 55 rooms. Credit cards: A, MC, V.

Wailea Ekolu Village   **$159–$229**   ★★★

3750 Wailea Alanui Drive, Wailea, 96753, ☎ (800) 367-5246, (808) 879-1595, FAX (808) 874 -3554.
Single: $159–$229. Double: $159–$229.
A pretty bargain especially for golfers, the 18-acre Wailea Ekolu Village offers reasonably priced one- and two-bedroom condominium apartments situated within sight of Wailea's world-class Blue course. Naturally the ocean-view units will cost you a bit more, but all accommodations feature private lanais, kitchens with microwave and washer/dryer. If a ceiling fan does not suffice, make sure to request an air-conditioned unit. The complex's landscape architect combined manicured grounds with a slightly garden-of-Edenish look, especially around one of the two pools, which also features a recreation pavilion. The other pool, close to one of the parking lots, is more exposed to ol' Sol's rays. Golf widows (and widowers) can spend some quality time here. Amenities: balcony or patio. 26 rooms. Credit cards: A, MC, V.

Wailea Elua Village   **$335–$540**   ★★★

3750 Wailea Alanui Drive, Wailea, 96753, ☎ (800) 367-5246, (808) 879-1595, FAX (808) 874 -3554.
Single: $335–$540. Double: $335–$540.
A luxurious, private and gated 24-acre condominium complex, Wailea Elua Village is located just steps away from intimate Ulua Beach, which is frequented by film stars on holiday. Some of the spacious, high-ceilinged one-, two- and three-bedroom condominiums have wraparound lanais with barbecue grills, perfect for private entertaining. All are centrally air-conditioned and equipped with full-size kitchens with all the amenities, as well as a washer and dryer. If you tire of the beach, (beach chairs and cooler provided) which is one of the best swimming, snorkeling and bodysurfing stretches in Wailea, there are two freshwater pools. Other facilities include a paddle tennis court, putting green and beachfront pavilion with gas barbecue grill. Special golf rates are available at the neighboring Wailea and Makena resorts. You can also swing the old racket at one of the 14 professional courts (three grass) at the Wailea Tennis Club, called "Wimbledon of the West," which is adjacent to the Wailea Elua's sister property, the Grand Champions Resort. A beachfront walkway provides easy access to world-class restaurants and shopping. The hotel's concierge is on hand to arrange other amusements. There's a three-night minimum stay. Amenities: Jacuzzi, balcony or patio. 61 rooms. Credit cards: A, MC, V.

Wailea Grand Champions   **$169–$229**   ★★★

3750 Wailea Alanui Drive, Wailea, 96753, ☎ (800) 367-5246, (808) 879-1595, FAX (808) 874 -3554.

Single: $169–$229. Double: $169–$229.

These classy, spacious condominium apartments on 11 rather crowded acres are sandwiched between the Wailea Tennis Club and Wailea Blue Golf course, so they're ideal for aspiring champions in either sport. The buff-colored two- and three-story buildings contain one- and two-bedroom apartments with either a garden view or partial ocean view from private lanais. Full of light from wide windows, the units have separate living areas with plush carpeting and rattan furniture (including swivel chairs), enhanced by potted plants. All are air-conditioned, and feature fully equipped kitchens with microwave, and a washer/dryer. Daily maid service. Facilities include two pools, two spas and barbecue areas. Special golf rates available at Wailea and Makena Resorts. Ask about tennis packages. Amenities: Jacuzzi, balcony or patio, family plan. 27 rooms. Credit cards: A, MC, V.

Resorts

Aston Wailea Resort   **$245–$1350**   ★★★★

3700 Wailea Alanui Drive, Wailea, 96753, ☎ *(800) 321-2558, (808) 879-1922. Rated restaurant: Hula Moons.*

Single: $245–$1350. Double: $245–$1350.

Formerly the Maui Inter-Continental, this 20-year veteran of the Wailea resort scene passed into Aston's capable hands early in 1996. Although already well-entrenched in its lovely 22-acre oceanfront spot, Aston aims to continue to preserve the property's tradition of being the most "Hawaiian" resort on this platinum coast. The chain is banking on a little help from the convention and banqueting trade (there are 29 meeting rooms with more than 45,000 square feet of space and a conference pavilion) to keep the revenue flow steady. Individual travelers needn't be dismayed, as there are more than enough facilities to go around, including the beach, three freshwater swimming pools and a spa, two restaurants (the whimsically named Hula Moons is an award-winner), a lounge, and championship tennis and golf nearby. Guest rooms and suites are spread out among seven rosy-roofed, low-slung buildings and a seven-story tower. Generously oversized, even a standard room measures at least 436 square feet. Each has a separate dressing and bath area. Soothingly decorated in peach and gray tones, with sturdy rattan and blond-wood furnishings, including a chaise lounge; many have king-size beds. There are 46 suites with five floor plans. Mini-suites have a separate bedroom and living room, while the top-of-the line Ali'i Suite features two bedrooms, two baths, a living room and dining room. Although not loaded with amenities, both suites and rooms include private lanais, mini-fridges and color TVs with in-room movies. The Aston Wailea has no health spa, but massage and body care service are available on an on-call basis. Recommended for jet-lagged guests is a combination of Swedish, Oriental and Shiatsu techniques, at $70 an hour. A children's program, called Club Gecko, gives parents a break Thursday–Saturday. The resort puts on an award-winning traditional luau every Tuesday, Thursday and Friday from 5–8 p.m. While under the auspices of the Inter-Continental, the resort implemented a $7 daily fee to cover various charges, including telephone calls and newspaper delivery; check to see if this charge is still in effect at time of booking. Amenities: Jacuzzi, balcony or patio, business services. 516 rooms. Credit cards: A, DC, MC, V.

Four Seasons Resort Maui at Wailea $295–$5000   ★ ★ ★ ★ ★

3900 Wailea Alanui Drive, Wailea, 96753, ☎ (800) 334-6284, (808) 874-8000, FAX (800) 874 -6449. Rated restaurant: Seasons.
Single: $295–$5000. Double: $295–$5000.

This elegant beachfront property, which opened in 1990, was the prestigious Four Seasons chain's first foray in the islands, and it's designed with architectural sensitivity, blending serenely within its environment. Several subtly colored buildings with pale-blue roofs, no higher than eight stories each, are oriented around the water, with stunning views from the public areas and guest rooms. A high-ceilinged, open-air lobby invites lingering (or malingering) with comfortable seating areas and thousands of dollars' worth of artistically arranged flowers. Adjoining the lobby is an elegant bar-lounge overlooking the Pacific on one side, and the West Maui mountains on the other. Entertainment consists of a lone acoustic guitar plucked each evening from 8 p.m.; the bar is open until midnight. Another lovely room is the Library Lounge, supplied with the latest magazines, books and newspapers to look over while sipping morning coffee. Handy to the health club, guests can even borrow gym clothes here. A more prosaic choice is the Games Room, where the kids can be parked to play video games, shoot pool or pick out tunes from the jukebox. Food is served here as well, but it's a no-smoking, no-alcohol zone. There are three additional restaurants, all facing the sea. Seasons, a special-occasion type of place, showcases American regional cuisine. The chef is George Mavrothalassitis (whew!), known as Chef Mavro, who trained in the top kitchens of France. A lot more relaxing is the Pacific Grill, where loading up on the hearty breakfast buffet is encouraged. The Grill gets gussied up at night, serving East-West specialties prepared in an exhibition kitchen. Lunch, dinner, pupus and cocktails are on hand at Seaside, an oceanside, outdoor dining spot. Hawaiian entertainment from sunset on. Service has always been a hallmark of the Four Seasons; sometimes it's carried to an extreme here. Attendants spritz guests with Evian water at the cabana-dotted beach or by the pool(s). Chilled towels and ice water are replenished to prevent heat-stroke. Children are well looked after; the Kids for All Seasons programs includes year-round supervised activities for youngsters ages five to 12. Each of the rooms and suites are at least 600 square feet, with 85 percent boasting ocean views. All have private lanais, some have two. Soothing decor schemes include soft-cushioned rattan and wicker furnishings in peach and blue pastels, ceiling fans, wood shutters and teak armoires. Striated marble baths include an eight-foot counter with double vanities, soaking tub and separate shower. The activities desk can arrange everything from sport fishing to horseback adventures. Golf and additional tennis nearby. Amenities: tennis, health club, exercise room, Jacuzzi, sauna, balcony or patio, family plan, club floor, business services. 380 rooms. Credit cards: A, DC, MC, V.

Grand Wailea Resort Hotel and Spa $380–$3000   ★ ★ ★ ★

3850 Wailea Alanui Drive, Wailea, 96753, ☎ (800) 888-6100, (808) 875-1234, FAX (808) 874 -5143. Rated restaurant: Kincha, Grand Dining Room Maui.
Single: $380–$3000. Double: $380–$3000.

The Grand Wailea, an oceanfront spa resort completed at a cost of $600 million in 1991, is the most expensive hotel ever built in Hawaii. Management justifies this fact by stating that the developer's concept was to design a hotel that would revive the "wonderful dream of the early 1900s in Hawaii." 1900s Hawaii by way of Las Vegas, 1996, is more like it. The 42-acre oceanfront property (where even the employees get lost) is designed around a garden atrium with a marvelous excess of fountains, waterfalls, pools and interconnecting waterways. You might opt for a chamber in the 100-room Napua Tower, with a 700-square-foot club room that starts at $580 a night. Prices go up to $1400 for a one-bedroom suite; the 5500-square-foot Grand Suite, where the hotel's billionaire owner usually resides when he's in town, is only a mere $10,000 a night. Actually a self-contained hotel within the resort, the Napua Tower features two lounges, where a complimentary continental breakfast, afternoon tea and evening cocktails are served. But even if you can only afford a lower-echelon Terrace room ($380 per night), it will be at least 650 square feet, and all guest wings are positioned to face the ocean in some capacity. All are spectacular, with separate living, dining and sleeping areas, louvered wooden windows, tile or polished wooden floors, Oriental carpets and custom furnishings that include antique sculpture and porcelain pieces, inlaid-wood desks and pencil-post two-poster beds. Huge tiled baths have plenty of counter space, sunken tubs and separate shower areas. Amenities common to all include three phones, "interactive" TVs, mini-bar, coffee maker and lanais. There are eight restaurants and 12 lounges, 14 tennis courts, six landscaped gardens (one for each wing) and probably the most talked-about body of water on the islands, the Wailea Canyon Activity Pool. Sort of a Disneyland ride in miniature, the 2000-foot-long pool has valleys, water slides, waterfalls, caves, a rope swing, white water rapids, grottos, a Jacuzzi and sauna. Amenities: tennis, health club, exercise room, Jacuzzi, sauna, balcony or patio, family plan, club floor, business services. 767 rooms. Credit cards: A, CB, DC, MC, V.

Kea Lani Hotel Suites & Villas $265–$1195 ★★★★★

4100 Wailea Alanui, Wailea, 96753, 25 minutes from Kahului Airport, ☎ (800) 882-4100, (808) 875-4100, FAX (808) 875-1200. Rated restaurant: Kea Lani Restaurant Single: $265–$1195. Double: $265–$1195.

If you saw the movie 10, the sight of this pristine, blazingly white pleasure palace on Wailea's Polo Beach might bring a flash of recognition. Indeed, the 413-room, 22-acre property and its attendant 37 oceanfront villas was designed to resemble Las Hadas, the legendary resort in Manzanillo, Mexico, where Dudley Moore lusted after a corn-rowed Bo Derek. The central feature of the resort, besides the sense of deja vu it engenders, are two huge, free-form, lagoon-style swimming pools connected by a 140-foot waterslide; one has a swim-up bar. Tented cabanas protect virgin skin from the sun's rays. The resort's beach activities center offers snorkel sets, boogie boards, floats and more for rent ($5 an hour for an umbrella!). Whale-watching, deep-sea fishing and other water-related activities can be arranged here. Beach butlers proffer cold towels, juices, snacks and sightseeing tips. Dates are optional. When you feel the need to crash, you'll have a lot of elbow room to do it in; accommodations are either in one-bedroom suites of at least 840 square feet of living space, or the dreamy split-level villas with one, two or three bedrooms. Suites, some with ocean views, all have separate living areas with sofa beds and two private, double lanais. Amenities are legion; how about an entertainment center with a 21-inch TV and VCR plus a CD/laser-disc setup? There's an additional 19-inch TV in the bedroom, and laser discs and videos are available in the lobby. Add to that list a two-line phone with modem hook-up, wall safe, wet bar and refrigerator, microwave and coffee maker. If you opt for a villa that sleeps up to eight adults (many affordable packages available, including use of a luxury car or mini-van), you'll get the same amenities as above, plus a private plunge pool and sun-deck, two marble bathrooms, gourmet kitchen with all the trimmings and a washer-dryer. A Villa manager will take your order for groceries prior to check-in and have everything stocked for you when you arrive. Dining options include the Kea Lani Restaurant, offering Executive Chef Steve Amaral's Pacific cuisine in an open-air setting; Caffe Ciao, an upscale bakery-deli, and Polo Beach Grille and Bar, with a casual menu. Amenities: exercise room, Jacuzzi, balcony or patio, family plan, business services. 413 rooms. Credit cards: A, MC, V.

Stouffer Renaissance Wailea Beach Resort $275–$485   ★ ★ ★ ★

3550 Wailea Alanui Drive, Wailea, 96753, 17 miles from the Kahului Airport, ☎ (800) 468-3571, (808) 879-4900, FAX (808) 874 -5370. Rated restaurant: Raffles

The Stouffer Renaissance Wailea Resort is a trio of six-story buildings set in a lushly overgrown and extensive tropical garden fronting semi-private, golden-grained Mokapu Beach, which is excellent for bathing and snorkeling, and rarely used by anyone other than hotel guests. The 15.5-acre property also offers access to an impressive array of sporting activities, including the nearby Wailea Golf Club and its three top-rated, 18-hole golf courses, Blue, Gold and Emerald. The Wailea Blue Course, designed by Arthur Jack Snyder, has been rated by *Golf Digest* as one of the state's top five. Amenities include three phones, two with fax-modem capabilities, cable TV and VCRs in armoires, mini-bar and in-room safe. All have sitting areas with a loveseat and chaise lounge, and deluxe bath treats include double vanities, hair dryer, lighted makeup mirror and his-and-her *hapi* (short Japanese robes) coats. Some suites have Jacuzzi tubs. The most desirable accommodations are in the Mokapu Beach Club, consisting of 26 beachfront rooms in three wings. In addition to the amenities offered in the regular rooms and suites, these choice spots also feature terry robes and a complimentary continental breakfast served on the private lanais. Beach Club guests also have a Club Manager at their beck and call, and receive VIP check-in, personal room escort, use of a private pool and private beach cabana. Wow! But if you can't get a berth here, be gladdened by the fact that the resort is designed in a unique T-shape, which affords all guests a variety of choice views. A plethora of dining and entertainment, all within arm's reach, are available at four restaurants and a lounge. Raffles, on the third floor, is the resort's signature restaurant, showcasing fresh island products and featuring Pacific Rim cuisine, with an emphasis on seafood. Amenities: tennis, health club, exercise room, Jacuzzi, balcony or patio, family plan, business services. 347 rooms. Credit cards: A, DC, MC, V.

Upcountry

Kula

Bloom Cottage   **$95**   ★★★

229 Kula Highway, Kula, 96790, ☎ (800) 262-9912, (808) 878-1425.
Single: $95. Double: $95.

Surrounded by an herb and flower garde, this cute-as-a-button, white country cottage with green shutters on a one-acre property is a terrific deal. For $95, you get
the whole two-bedroom dwelling for yourself, and owners Herb and Lynne Horner
have filled it with lots of comfy things, including books and magazines (Lynne is an
editor of the *Maui News*), videos for the VCR and a sewing basket in case you pop
a button. The living room has a beamed ceiling, floral curtains, a big, wide, rattan
couch with comfy pillows to sprawl out on, and a FIREPLACE! In the bedroom,
the bamboo four-poster bed is topped with a handmade quilt, and room decor
includes Victorian prints and a heritage koa rocking chair. Fresh, seasonal herbs
scent the air. See you there! No children under 10 years or pets. Amenities: balcony
or patio. 1 room. Credit cards: not accepted.

Puluke's Farm   **$75**   ★★

203 Wahelani Road, Kula, 96790, ☎ (808) 878-3263, FAX (808) 878 -3263.
Single: $75. Double: $75.

The entrance to Haleakala Volcano Park is 10 minutes from the door of this B&B.
Your accommodation is a studio with a queen-size bed on the second floor of a private home with a wrap-around deck overlooking the West Maui mountains on one
side and an open valley with a patchwork quilt of farmer's fields on the other. The
newly decorated unit has a private entrance (your hosts, the Lepolstats, live on the
property), and is equipped with its own kitchen, full bath and laundry facility.
There's a color TV and VCR to keep you amused. The refrigerator is stocked with
muffins, rolls or croissants, as well as fresh fruit, juice, milk and coffee so you can
prepare your own breakfast. Because you're on a 3500 foot elevation, the temperature at night often drops to the low 50s (it rises rapidly to 75 degrees once the sun
rises, though) so bring some warm clothes, which you'll need if you're going to visit
the volcano. Puluke's Farm is a place where you won't need an alarm clock, as roosters crow at dawn to roust you out of bed. Daily rates drop to $50 if you book the
studio for three nights or more. There's no maid service. Amenities: balcony or
patio. 1 rooms. Credit cards: not accepted.

Inns

Kula Lodge and Restaurant   **$100–$150**   ★★

On Highway 377, on the way to Haleakala Volcano Park, Kula, 96790, ☎ (800) 233-
1535, (808) 878-1535, FAX (808) 878 -2518. Rated restaurant: Kula Lodge Restaurant
Single: $100–$150. Double: $100–$150.

Stellar views of the West Maui mountains plus a good restaurant are the main draws
to this popular upcountry retreat, which has five rustic but comfortable cabins,
some with fireplaces, available for your lounging pleasure. Reservations should be
made at least three months in advance, and if a fireplace is important to you, make
sure you reserve Chalets No. 1 or 2. The aforementioned chalets have queen-size

beds, a private porch and stairs leading to a loft with twin beds; these are the nicest and priciest. Next in line are Nos. 3 and 4, which are fun for kids and adults masquerading as kids, as they have a ladder leading to a sleeping loft with a set of futon beds. It also has queen beds and a private porch. The fifth Chalet has only one story, plus a queen-size bed and private porch. None of the chalets have TV or phones. The front desk will take messages, and there is fax service as well as public phones on the premises.The Kula Lodge Restaurant is one of the last dining places on the way to the summit of Haleakala. As you would expect, early morning sunrise breakfast (it's open from 6:30 a.m. to 9 p.m. daily) and sunset supper times are the most desirable, so get there early. Amenities: balcony or patio. 5 rooms. Credit cards: MC, V.

Ranches

Silver Cloud Upcountry Guest Ranch   **$75–$135**   ★★★

Old Thompson Road, Kula, 96790, 35 minutes from Kahului Airport, ☎ (808) 878-6101, FAX (808) 878 -2132.

Single: $75–$135. Double: $75–$135.

Silver Cloud Ranch, in the Ulupalalua area of upcountry Maui, was originally part of Thompson Ranch, which was founded in 1902. The nine-acre property, with 11 rooms and suites located in the former plantation house and a cowboy bunkhouse plus a self-contained cottage, is a fine alternative vacation choice for those who think the beach areas are too crowded. All accommodations have been recently renovated. The guest rooms in the Plantation Home have private baths; many with their own entrances. The spacious, second-floor King Kamehameha and Queen Emma suites command breathtaking panoramic views. The Paniolo (cowboy) Bunkhouse apartments feature roomy studios with kitchenettes, large bathrooms and lanais providing views of the ocean or the mountain. The Haleakala Suite, with both ocean and mountain views, is a special part of the Paniolo Bunkhouse, with a separate living and bedroom area, fireplace, full kitchen and lanai. The romantic and private Lanai Cottage, surrounded by its own flower gardens, has a private porch where you can great the sun or bid it adieu daily. Warmed indoors by a wood-burning stove, it has a king-size bed, complete kitchen and a big red bathtub (there's no shower) that you can fill up with bubble bath. Everyone gets breakfast, which is served in a garden sunroom adjacent to the kitchen in the Plantation Home; you're also welcome to use the kitchen to prepare lunch or dinner. None of the accommodations has phones, but messages are posted on a bulletin board, and there's a common telephone in the living room. Fax service is available. In keeping with the ranch ambience (it's no longer a working ranch) Silver Cloud has a lot of furry and four-footed friends, including three horses, a pot-bellied pig named Rupert, Daisy the cow, hens that lay eggs and some very friendly cats. You might be tempted to take them into your room, but the hosts advise against this, since fellow guests may have allergies. The owners, Mike and Sara Gerry, live in the caretaker's cottage next to the Plantation Home and are almost always on hand if you need them or have any questions. Maid service is provided after the fourth day of your visit. Amenities: balcony or patio. 12 rooms. Credit cards: not accepted.

West Maui

Honokawai

Condos

Nohonani   **$108–$134**   ★★

3723 Lower Honoapiilani Road, Honokawai, 96761, South of Kahana, two miles from Kaanapali, ☎ (800) 822-RENT, (808) 669-8208, FAX (808) 669 -2388.
Single: $108–$134. Double: $108–$134.

All of the individually owned apartments in this small, low-slung, attractively landscaped condominium complex were thoughtfully designed so that all the rooms, including the bedrooms, face the ocean and a sandy beach. Guests also have seaside seats by the nicely sized pool that's surrounded by an ample amount of loungers to share, plus picnic tables, and barbecues for outdoor entertaining. If more breathing space is needed, a public park and playground for the kiddies is nearby. A grocery story is a block away, making it a snap to stock up the fully equipped kitchens in the one- and two-bedroom units. There are washer-dryers in each of the two-bedroom apartments, which sleep up to six people. A laundry room is on the premises as well. Amenities common to all accommodations include color TV and telephones. Maid service upon check-out, but additional service can be arranged. The proximity to a great beach, relatively low prices and a caring management make the Nohonani a terrific value. Three-day minimum stay. Amenities: balcony or patio. 28 rooms.
Credit cards: MC, V.

Papakea Oceanfront Resort   **$119–$204**   ★★

3543 Lower Honoapiilani Highway, Honokawai, 96761, Between Kapalua and Kaanapali Beach, ☎ (800) 367-7052, (808) 669-4848, FAX (808) 661-4683.
Single: $119–$204. Double: $119–$204.

A low-key, low-rise condominium on 13 well-tended acres, the Papakea Oceanfront Resort offers two pools and a sauna to make up for its lack of a good swimming beach. But the sparkling sands of Kapalua and Kaanapali are close by, so if you're the type who doesn't need to step directly into the ocean from your room, this property may suffice. The setting is quite lovely, though, with three of its 11 red-roofed buildings situated almost directly on the seawall. An activities desk is on hand to assure that guests don't get bored, and there are weekly happenings planned, including island orientations, "swimmercize classes," putting tournaments (on two 18-hole putting greens), tennis clinics and round robins (three lighted tennis courts). Individually furnished apartments range from studios with sofa beds and baths with shower only to two-bedroom suites with deluxe combination baths and king or double beds. All have fully equipped kitchens, spacious private lanais, washer/dryer, ceiling fans (no air conditioning) and color TV. Daily maid service is provided, which is ideal for families with kids. Amenities: tennis, Jacuzzi, balcony or patio. 364 rooms. Credit cards: MC, V.

Kaanapali

Aston Kaanapali Shores   **$150–$650**   ★★★

3445 Honoapiilani Highway, Kaanapali, ☎ (800) 922-7866.
Single: $150–$650. Double: $150–$650.

Aston's most complete resort on a strategic stretch of Kaanapali Beach, this nine-story property offers a wide range of units for couples and families, as well as a year-round camp program for children. Air-conditioned accommodations include lanai-less hotel rooms with refrigerators only, and studio, one- and two-bedroom condominium apartments with gourmet kitchens, washer-dryers and private lanais. The most desirable (and priciest) guest chamber is the oceanfront Aloha Suite, which runs $500 per night. Most units have wide windows and are furnished in sandy tones and feature sturdy rattan furniture. Amenities include color TVs and in-room safes. There's daily maid service. Free tennis, putting green, video game room, beauty salon, gift/apparel shop, restaurant, guest activities desk. Amenities: tennis, health club, Jacuzzi, sauna, balcony or patio, family plan, business services. 430 rooms. Credit cards: MC, V.

Maui Kaanapali Villas $145–$255 ★★★

45 Kai Ala Drive, Kaanapali, ☎ *(800) 922-7866, (808) 667-7791.*
Single: $145–$255. Double: $145–$255.
This bright, attractive Aston property on an 11-acre oceanfront estate is surrounded by pools and gardens. Featured are hotel rooms and condo units. All rooms are air-conditioned and feature refrigerators, while spacious studios and one-bedroom condo suites have complete kitchens. Amenities include three pools, a restaurant, shuffleboard and shuttle to nearby golf. Note: Since all condo units are individually owned, the number of available units at any one time varies. Amenities: Jacuzzi, balcony or patio, family plan. 200 rooms. Credit cards: A, DC, MC, V.

Resorts

Embassy Suites Resort $240–$2401 ★★★★

104 Kaanapali Shores Place, Kaanapali, 96761, ☎ *(800) 462-6284, (808) 661-2000,*
FAX (808) 667-5821. Rated restaurant: North Beach Grille.
Single: $240–$1200. Double: $2401.
This trio of flamingo-pink towers, located on north Kaanapali Beach, was the first to offer the all-suites concept to Hawaii when it opened in 1988. It's proved to be a wild success, especially with families looking for the space associated with condo living plus the added amenities and services of pricier resorts. The one- and two-bedroom suites, at 820 and 1100 square feet, respectively, are nearly twice the size of most first-class hotel rooms. Decor standards (as well as prices) are much higher than comparable Embassy Suites on the mainland. A nice grouping of pale salmon and silver-striped easy chairs and a love seat in the separate living area face a blond-wood encased entertainment center containing a 35-inch color TV that's wired for HBO and cable, along with a VCR, and stereo system with AM/FM and dual cassette player. A mini-kitchen is equipped with a microwave, refrigerator with ice maker, wet bar and coffee maker, with Kona coffee replaced daily. The big, wallpapered baths are unexpectedly luxurious, with tiled floors, two marble vanities, a deep-soaking tub and separate shower. Details include custom mirrors, floor lamps, potted plants and ceiling fans. Lanais can be accessed from either the living area or bedroom. Included in all this largesse is a complimentary breakfast buffet of fruit, pastries, cereals and juices, as well as cooked-to-order omelettes. Cocktail hour at

the Moonbeams Bar is also a daily happening. Unlike most Embassy Suites hotels, where the morning repast is all that's offered, lunch and dinner—as well as snacks and to-go items—are available from three venues. The offerings at the white-napkin North Beach Grille, with an oceanfront vista, run the gamut from seafood to pasta, and what the resort calls "Maui's finest salad bar." At poolside is the Ohana Grill (no "e") where homemade pizza can be eaten in bathing attire. Adjacent to the lobby is the Deli Planet, where sandwich makings or picnic baskets can be prepared for meals on the run. What do to for fun on-site? Shoot into the one-acre pool via a water slide, rent snorkeling equipment, take a windsurfing lesson, or luxuriate in the spa. There's a seven-day, year-round "Beach Buddies" program for kids (ages 4–10). Amenities: exercise room, Jacuzzi, balcony or patio, family plan, business services. 413 rooms. Credit cards: A, CB, DC, D, MC, V.

Hyatt Regency Maui $245–$900 ★★★★★

200 Nohea Kai Drive, Kaanapali, 96761, ☎ *(800) 233-1234, (808) 661-1234, FAX (808) 667-4498. Rated restaurant: Swan Court.*
Single: $245–$900. Double: $245–$900.

The Hyatt Regency Maui, conceived by developer Christopher Hemmeter, was first in a series of increasingly spectacular "mega-resorts" that have popped up in profusion all over the islands. Three connecting towers overlook fantastic gardens, including the vast swimming pool with its network of waterfalls, a grotto, 130-foot water slide, rope swing and swim-up cocktail bar. A tourist attraction in and of itself, the resort also has its own wildlife park, a collection of Asian and Pacific Art valued at more than $2 million, teak-paneled and Chinese-carpeted elevators, and a special, rooftop, deep-space telescope, called "Big Blue." Guests and the general public are treated to a guided tour of the Hawaiian skies three nights a week in a popular show presented by the Hyatt's resident "Director of Astronomy." Much of the 16-year-old property has been undergoing an $11 million renovation; guest rooms, meeting facilities, the health club and poolside restaurant are being upgraded. Guest rooms feature mahogany and rattan furniture, in-room refrigerators, remote-control TVs, private lanais, separate sitting areas, and king or double beds. More than three-quarters of the rooms have at least a partial ocean view. The resort offers a bountiful array of services, including "Camp Hyatt," a children's program, watersports, game room, library, six hard-surface tennis courts, access to championship golf courses, bike rental and shops. There are a number of excellent, but pricey, restaurants and lounges, including the Lahaina Provision Company, featuring a Chocoholic Bar, and the Swan Court, winner of a Travel Holiday award and named one of the Top 10 Most Romantic Restaurants in the world by "Lifestyles of the Rich and Famous." Amenities: tennis, health club, exercise room, Jacuzzi, sauna, balcony or patio, club floor, business services. 815 rooms. Credit cards: A, DC, MC, V.

Sheraton Maui

2605 Kaanapali Parkway, Kaanapali, 96761, ☎ *(800) 334-8484, (808) 661-0031.*
The Sheraton Maui recently reopened after a top-to-bottom, $150 million redevelopment. Originally opened in 1963, it was the first hotel on the Kaanapali Coast, immediately receiving awards for a design that incorporated its stunning natural

environment. On the natural lava headland called Black Rock (a prime snorkeling spot), it faces a wide, white sandy beach, surrounded by waterways and tropical landscaping. The 23-acre resort features 510 rooms, including 30 extra large quarters especially suitable for families. All are appointed with tropical furnishings, Hawaiian artwork and deluxe amenities. An elevated lobby in the center of the hotel provides panoramic views of Black Rock, the Pacific and the islands of Molokai and Lanai. The lower level features casual, open-air restaurants. Oceanfront rooms and suites are located somewhat apart from the rest of the hotel in a separate wing on the crest of Black Rock. Other facilities include an exercise room, fresh-water swimming lagoon, three tennis courts and a pro shop, and a slew of water-related activities. Amenities: tennis, exercise room, Jacuzzi, balcony or patio, business services. 510 rooms.

The Westin Maui   **$245–$2750**   ★★★★★

2365 Kaanapali Parkway, Kaanapali, 96761, Three miles west of Lahaina, ☎ *(800) 228-3000, (808) 667-2525, FAX (808) 661-5764. Rated restaurant: Sound of the Falls. Single: $245–$2750. Double: $245–$2750.*

The Westin Maui is a pale pink, S-shaped resort set upon a fine stretch of Kaanapali Beach. In keeping with the rosy theme, a flock of imported Chilean flamingos are an integral part of the resort's ever-growing collection of exotic wildlife. Two guest towers and public rooms are surrounded by an extensive series of water gardens and lagoons and a vast pool area that's really an aquatic playground, with two water-slides, waterfalls and a swim-up Jacuzzi hidden in a grotto. Sound familiar? It was conceived by Christopher Hemmeter, who developed the nearby Hyatt Regency. The small but nice rooms feature rattan furnishings, contemporary art, TVs with movies, mini-bars, coffee makers, refrigerators, and lanais. The poshest quarters are in the Royal Beach Club, sort of a penthouse within a luxury hotel, perfect for executives who feel guilty about leaving their offices. Extra amenities include a conference table and telescopes for whale-watching and star-gazing. One of the Westin's signature restaurants, the romantic Sound of the Falls, has been incorporated into The Villa, serving Pacific Rim cuisine and fresh island seafood. Unique to the Westin (and Hawaii) is the Japanese Guest Services Department, providing separate check-in and translation services. Honeymooners will be gratified to know that the resort also has an on-site Director of Romance, the only one in the state. Guests and nonguests alike are invited to tour the 12-acre property's wildlife, botanical and art collections; call the concierge for information. Additional services include a children's program and camp, ocean activities center, watersports, massage services, hiking and historical tours, and shuttle to off-site tennis and golf. Amenities: health club, Jacuzzi, sauna, balcony or patio, family plan, club floor, business services. 761 rooms. Credit cards: A, CB, DC, MC, V.

Kaanapali Beach

Condos

Kaanapali Alii   **$245–$650**   ★★★

50 Nohea Kai Drive, Kaanapali Beach, 96761, ☎ *(800) 642-6284, (808) 667-1666, FAX (808) 661-1025.*

MAUI

Single: $245–$650. Double: $245–$650.

This quartet of 11-story buildings with a central courtyard facing the sea is one of Maui's most luxurious condominium options. The only resort on the gilded Kaanapali coast to win AAA's Four-Diamond award, the Kaanapali Alii features one- and two-bedroom, split-level oceanfront units that are at least 1500 square feet each. Tricked out with luxurious amenities, they are all centrally air-conditioned, and contain two tiled combination baths with a whirlpool tub in the master bath, separate living and dining areas, private lanais, fully equipped kitchens, washer/dryer, two color TVs and in-room safes. Picture windows take in startling views of neighbor islands. The roomy lanais, with bougainvillea climbing around the railings, are big enough to contain several wicker loungers and a small dining table and chairs. Decor is quietly tasteful (except for fuschia-colored lamp bases in some units). Some of the larger apartments have sunken sitting areas in the bedrooms. Services include complimentary newspapers, room service, daily maid service, grocery delivery, charging privileges at nearby resorts (including the Westin and the Marriott) and a concierge. All sports activities are complimentary; a tennis pro is on hand for lessons. There's also a children's wading pool and beach-activities center. Amenities: tennis, exercise room, Jacuzzi, sauna, balcony or patio, family plan. 264 rooms. Credit cards: A, MC, V.

Maui Eldorado   **$110–$280**   ★ ★ ★

2661 Kekaa Drive, Kaanapali Beach, 96761, ☎ (800) 367-5004, (808) 661-0021, FAX (808) 667-7039.
Single: $110–$280. Double: $110–$280.

Situated on 10 attractive acres on a hillside overlooking the sea and an 18-hole golf course, this two-story, wood-shingled condominium spoils its guests with a private beach club right on an excellent sandy beach, where scuba diving lessons are regularly given. Otherwise, there's not much else on-site, except for a trio of swimming pools. Whalers Village shopping center can be reached on foot, but it's much more than a "stroll away," although management claims otherwise. You can buy a few sundries in the convenience store in the lobby. Lodgings are in hotel rooms with kitchenettes, individually owned and decorated studios, and one- or two-bedroom suites with full kitchen facilities and washer-dryers. Most have two combination baths per unit. All are air-conditioned, and have private, spacious lanais. There's daily maid service. Amenities: balcony or patio. 121 rooms. Credit cards: MC, V.

The Whaler   **$170–$555**   ★ ★ ★

2481 Kaanapali Parkway, Kaanapali Beach, 96761, ☎ (800) 367-7052, (808) 661-4861, FAX (808) 367-7052.
Single: $170–$555. Double: $170–$555.

Right next door to the shopping wonders of Whalers Village and across the street from the Royal Kaanapali Golf Course, the Whaler is a beachfront condominium where you won't have to go far to amuse yourself. But if neither of the above activities turns your crank, you can take a dip in the pool or luxuriate in the spa that separates the complex's two 12-story buildings. Other diversions include an exercise room and sauna, five tennis courts with a pro shop and, of course, there's the beach, which is divine for swimming. A beach-activities center is adjacent for renting gear or arranging a scuba, snorkeling or sailing expedition. Accommodations consist of studios, one- and two-bedroom apartments, and a presidential suite. Some have full or partial ocean views, others garden vistas, but all are spacious enough (largest ones can sleep six) and designer standards are high, with a remarkable lack of the usual floral print fabrics. Baths are marble, but the lovely, wrap-around, blue-tiled lanais are marred somewhat by tacky, albeit rust-proof, molded plastic tables and chairs in some units. The Whaler offers guests plenty of conveniences, including 24-hour desk and switchboard, wake-up calls, daily maid service, concierge, coin-laundry, dry cleaning, mini-mart and lots of free underground parking. If you must stay in a high-rise, the Whaler is a good choice. Amenities: tennis, Jacuzzi, sauna, balcony or patio, family plan. 360 rooms. Credit cards: A, CB, DC, MC, V.

Hotels

Kaanapali Beach Hotel   **$145–$535**   ★★★

2525 Kaanapali Parkway, Kaanapali Beach, 96761, *(800) 262-8450, (808) 661-0011, FAX (808) 667-5978. Rated restaurant: Tiki Terrace.*

Single: $145–$535. Double: $145–$535.

In case you're wondering, part of Old Hawaii does exist on Kaanapali Beach's gold coast, in the form of this U-shaped, old-fashioned and nicely time-weathered resort hotel, where employees are asked to attend regular classes (on company time, no less) on Hawaiian culture and values. In turn, staff members share with guests what they've learned, in the form of ti-leaf skirt-making, lauhala weaving, and even pineapple-cutting instruction. One of the hotel's loveliest traditions is the Friday night Spirit of Aloha, at which employees from different departments sing traditional songs, dance the hula and present hand-fashioned crafts. Delighted by complimentary coffee parties and other sincere gestures, some returnees couldn't even dream of staying anywhere else. Accommodations, spread over four guest wings, are decidedly unflashy, but generally satisfying. Some have two queen beds or one king bed, and marble combination baths (except in the older Molokai Wing). Better rooms and suites have hand-painted armoires, wicker armchairs and writing desks. Some have ocean or partial ocean views; lower-priced units have vistas of the courtyard or garden, but all have private lanais. Amenities include refrigerators, in-room safes, coffee makers and color TVs with movies. All are air-conditioned, but there are ceiling fans to whirl the breezes around on cooler days. Besides a whale-shaped pool, the hotel has a beach-activities center and offers free scuba lessons. Boogie boards and other gear can be rented here as well. Whalers Village and other shopping centers are close by, but there are a couple of on-site stores for souvenirs and such. Among the hotel's three eateries is the affordably priced Mixed Plate (formerly the Koffee Shop), which offers all-you-can-eat buffets three times a day. The Tiki Terrace is open daily for breakfast and dinner and features Hawaiian specialties, plus a Sunday Champagne brunch. Snacks and drinks by the pool can be had at the Tiki Grill and Tiki Bar, respectively. If you're still hungry for more, Auntie Aloha's raucous breakfast luau is a regular happening. Amenities: balcony or patio, family plan, business services. 431 rooms.

MAUI

Resorts

Maui Marriott   **$240–$400**   ★★★★

100 Nohea Kai Drive, Kaanapali Beach, 96761, Off Highway 30 from Lahaina, ☎ (800) 228-9290, (808) 667-1200, FAX (808) 667-2047. Rated restaurant: Nikko.

Single: $240–$400. Double: $240–$400.

Unsurprising, reliable and comfortable, the 720-room Maui Marriott resort is composed of two multi-windowed, white, mid-rise buildings situated around an open-air courtyard planted generously with lush foliage and tropical flowers. One of its big draws is its location. The resort sits on a choice stretch of sugary white sand smack dab (or darn close to) the center of Kaanapali Beach. Almost all the oversized rooms and suites are positioned to face the sea. Nicely turned out in pinkish beige tones with touches of light gray and green, accommodations have queen-size sofa beds as well as king or two twin beds, glass-topped tables and carved, easy-on-the back, blond-wood chairs. Armoires discreetly mask TVs. Baths are marble, and there's a mini-bar and private lanai with at least one lounge chair. There are plenty of dining and entertainment options, including Banana Moon, Maui's only video disco (a dubious achievement award should be given for that). The Lobby Bar offers karaoke, comedy nights and large screen-TV. Another lounge, the Makai Bar, overlooking the beach, offers Hawaiian music, "Hungry Hour" specials and sunset libations. Of the four dining rooms, the toniest is Nikko Steakhouse, offering Japanese Teppanyaki cookery as well as sushi and yakitori dishes. It's only open for dinner, as is Lokelani, the resort's seafood restaurant. All meals are served at the Moana Terrace, which has a buffet breakfast daily. Kau Kau is an informal outdoor grill and bar by the pool. Besides eating, drinking and sunning on the beach, guests can play tennis on five courts and take lessons from the resident pro. A beach recreation center rents out snorkeling equipment, hobie cats, surf skis and boogie boards. Lava rock waterfalls splash through two free-form, interconnecting swimming pools, and there are a twin pair of whirlpool spas. Children have their own pool and *keiki* program in the summer. Off-site activities include 36 holes of championship golf at the adjacent Royal Kaanapali Golf Course. Souvenirs, gifts and forgotten items can be picked up at 18 retail shops on the premises. One warning: the ocean directly in front of the hotel may be lovely, but isn't great for swimming, due to riptides, powerful shorebreaks and other nasty things. Amenities: tennis, exercise room, Jacuzzi, balcony or patio, family plan, business services. 720 rooms. Credit cards: A, CB, MC, V.

Kahana

Condos

Kahana Sunset   **$150–$235**   ★★★

4909 L. Honoapiilani Highway, Kahana, 96761, ☎ (800) 669-1488, (808) 669-8011, FAX (808) 669-9170.

Single: $150–$235. Double: $150–$235.

These are fairly luxurious condos situated on tropical gardens planted with hundreds of exotic plants, flowers and shrubs. It fronts a hidden, reef-protected bay and a safe, sandy beach. On offer are one-bedroom, one-bath apartments, and two-bedroom, two-bath townhouses with ocean and garden views, as well as split-level "executive" oceanfront townhouses with two bedrooms and 2.5 baths. All have private lanais, but the townhouses have lanais on both levels. Amenities common to all include ceiling fans, color cable TV, fully equipped kitchens with microwaves, refrigerators with ice-makers, and a washer and dryer. There's a garden-side pool and barbecue pits on the property, but not much else; sightseeing and entertainment are within a short driving distance away. Amenities: balcony or patio. 79 rooms. Credit cards: MC, V.

Kahana Village $180–$280   ★★★

4531 Honoapiilani Road, Kahana, 96761, ☎ (800) 824-3065, (808) 669-5111, FAX (808) 669-0974.

Single: $180–$280. Double: $180–$280.

These low-rise, two-story, wooden condominium apartments, facing a quiet cove and reef-protected white sand beach, offer a lot of amenities for your vacation dollar. Lots of space, for one thing. All ground-level apartments are 1700 square feet, with two or three bedrooms and two full baths with a sunken tub in the master bath, plus a study and wet bar. The second-floor units are a bit smaller, at 1200 square feet, but they all have at least two bedrooms and two full baths; the second bedroom is a loft. Consider these if you like a lot of sunshine, since they feature skylights and open-beam ceilings. Furnishings are classy, with chic, designer rattan furniture upholstered in mostly solid color fabrics. Color TVs and VCRs are ensconced in rattan etageres. Fine touches include ginger jar lamps, magazine racks and healthy potted plants. Large private lanais with loungers offer partial or prime ocean views. Kitchens are outfitted with a Jenn-Aire range, dishwasher and microwave. Other amenities include a washer-dryer and telephone. Most apartments can accommodate up to six persons. Designers didn't stint on the facilities outside the rooms, either. The 40-foot oval pool features an oversize deck, and there's a beachside pavilion and private entertainment center with a jacuzzi and barbecue. The property is positioned somewhat away from the rest of Kahana, but is a short drive from championship golf and tennis, and the shopping and restaurant opportunities in Kaanapali and Lahaina. There's a five-day minimum stay. Amenities: Jacuzzi, balcony or patio, family plan. 42 rooms. Credit cards: not accepted.

Mahina Surf $110–$130   ★★★

4057 Lower Honoapiilani Road, Kahana, 96761, ☎ (800) 367-6086, (808) 669-6068.

Single: $110–$130. Double: $110–$130.

The Mahina Surf is situated on a two-acre spread facing a handsomely designed lawn and a big, oceanfront pool with barbecue facilities. The condominium apartments are ideal for families and include one-bedroom units that sleep from two to four people, and two-bedroom, 1.5 or two-bath units that accommodate up to six comfortably. Features available throughout the complex include separate living areas, full-size, all-electric kitchens with all the appliances needed for a carefree vacation (unless you're the chef). All have phones and color TVs and VCRs. There's a three-night minimum stay, and extra persons, including children, are charged $8 per night. Amenities: balcony or patio. 56 rooms. Credit cards: MC, V.

Noelani $87–$170 ★★★

4095-L Honoapiilani Road, Kahana, 96761, ☎ *(800) 367-6030, (808) 669-8374, FAX (808) 669-7904.*
Single: $87–$170. Double: $87–$170.

Adjacent to a perfect sandy cove with a small beach for sunning and snorkeling, all of the 50 privately owned oceanfront condos at Noelani have private lanais. Studios and spacious one-, two- and three-bedroom units are comfortably furnished in light pastels and wood and rattan furnishings. All have complete kitchens; studios have microwaves and access to laundry facilities, while the larger apartments feature a washer and dryer, and dishwashers. Amenities include ceiling fans, color cable TV and VCRs. Linen and guest supplies are provided, and a maid comes in to clean midweek. Recreational facilities include two partially hand-tiled seaside pools with barbecues, where new guests are treated to continental breakfast and an island "orientation." Ask about special car-rental packages and off-season rates. Extra person charge is $7.50 per day. Amenities: balcony or patio. 50 rooms. Credit cards: A, MC, V.

Polynesian Shores $85–$160 ★★★

3975 Lower Honoapiilani Road, Kahana, 96761, ☎ *(800) 433-MAUI, (808) 669-6065, FAX (808) 669-0909.*
Single: $85–$160. Double: $85–$160.

A fun, partylike atmosphere permeates from this airy, pleasantly designed, two-acre property consisting of several staggered, two-story wooden buildings separated from each other by a heated pool and a well-tended lawn. Besides the lovely, but rocky oceanfront location (a sandy beach is nearby), the focal point is a wide redwood deck at the water's edge supplied with barbecues and tables and chairs. Lit by tiki torches in the evening, this is where management passes out appetizers (pupus) so all guests may partake and meet one another. These affairs happen in winter, when humpback whales put on a show directly in view of the revelers. The pleasantly furnished, one-, two- and three bedroom units (some with lofts, cathedral ceilings and three baths) are reached by neatly landscaped pathways. All feature wide, wrap-around lanais with excellent views. They are fully furnished and have complete kitchens, including microwave, dishwasher, toaster, blender and coffee maker, as well as all utensils. Cable TV and direct-dial phones in all units. A coin-operated laundry is on the premises. Contact the management for preferred car-rental rates. Three-night minimum stay. Amenities: balcony or patio, family plan. 52 rooms. Credit cards: D, MC, V.

The Sands of Kahana $175–$260 ★★★

4299 Lower Honoapiilani Highway, Kahana, 96761, ☎ *(800) 367-7052.*

Active types will enjoy a myriad of on-site amusements and activities at this attractive complex fronting Kahana Beach. Separating the four nine-story buildings housing the one-, two- and three-bedroom apartments is a geometrically shaped pool and open-air restaurant and cocktail lounge with entertainment, good for sunset suppers. Next to the pool is a beach volleyball setup. Three tennis courts are lit for night play, and you can practice golf strokes on a putting green. A concierge is on hand to arrange off-site fun and games. Individually owned apartments (this is also a popular time share, or "vacation interval" resort) are generously sized, and decorating schemes differ wildly. Some are tasteful and subdued, maybe a little dull, others shout "Aloha!" with brocade-patterned wallpaper, and bright pink fabrics clashing with robin's egg blue lamps. Generally, floor plans include open living and dining areas, private lanais and big kitchens with two pantries, double-door refrigerators, microwaves and coffee makers. All have washer/dryers and cable TV with HBO. Daily maid service. Amenities: tennis, balcony or patio. 155 rooms. Credit cards: A, CB, DC, MC, V.

Kapalua

Resorts

Kapalua Bay Hotel & Villas $200–$1260 ★ ★ ★ ★

One Bay Drive, Kapalua, 96761, 10 miles north of Lahaina, ☎ *(800) 367-8000, (808) 669-5656, FAX (808) 669-4694. Rated restaurant: The Bay Club.*
Single: $200–$1260. Double: $200–$1260.

The Kapalua Bay Hotel and Villas was built in 1978 and extensively renovated in 1995 to the tune of $6 million. The 1800-acre property's somewhat-isolated location, on a private pineapple plantation fronted by one of Hawaii's (and possibly the world's) most beautiful beaches, draws seasoned travelers who welcome the quiet, understated elegance of the hotel's design, a series of low-rise structures surrounded by beautifully landscaped tropical grounds, The ivy-draped, open-air lobby is particularly pleasant, with views of the ocean and a profusion of orchids. Service seems to be a strong point, with new arrivals greeted like VIPs by smiling staff members offering leis (the floral kind), perfumed towels and glasses of guava juice. The subtlety in decor is carried on to the 194 oversized (more than 500 square feet) rooms and suites with ocean or garden views. While sleeping quarters are comfortable enough, the marble baths are spectacular, supplied with thoughtful features such as his-and-her vanities, robes, hair dryers, make-up mirrors and a selection of skin products. Each chamber has a color TV with video player and current hit movies provided at no charge, a mini-bar and refrigerator, in-room safe, and private lanais with mesh furniture for leisurely outdoor meals. Clustered nicely on a hillside, the resort's 100 one- and two-bedroom villas offer even more space and a modicum of independent living, with fully equipped kitchens and washer/dryers, in addition to the same features offered in the hotel rooms. Villa guests enjoy the services, restaurants and leisure facilities of the hotel, but also have their own pools. Grocery delivery is available. Always a golfer's retreat, the resort offers three championship 18-hole courses. Two, the oceanview Bay Course and the Village Course, which rises into the scenic Maui Mountains, were designed by Arnold Palmer. The Plantation Course, the newest of the trio, was designed by Ben Crenshaw and Bill Coore. Tennis enthusiasts aren't neglected, either, with a choice of 20 Plexipave courts lit for night play. Lazier types can sun or swim on one of three white-sand beaches, snorkel, scuba-dive and attack the waves on a boogie board; a beach-activities center rents gear and arranges watersports and lessons. Two pools provide freshwater relief. There are stables nearby for horseback riding. A children's program, Kamp Kapalua, is offered to youngsters ages five–12. For $25 per child ($45 for two), a whole week's worth of supervised fun is planned (Monday–Friday only), including

Hawaiian games, a nature walk, snorkeling, exotic fruit-tasting and more. Other features: shopping adjacent to hotel, beauty salon, resort and airport shuttle, baby-sitting. Amenities: tennis, exercise room, balcony or patio, family plan, business services. 294 rooms. Credit cards: A, MC, V.

The Ritz-Carlton Kapalua $285–$2800 ★ ★ ★ ★

One Ritz-Carlton Drive, Kapalua, 96761, ☎ *(800) 241-3333, (808) 669-6200, FAX (808) 665-0026. Rated restaurant: Anuenue Room.*

Single: $285–$2800. Double: $285–$2800.

The Ritz-Carlton, Kapalua is one of the newer additions (1992) to the Kapalua luxury resort scene, designed in the traditional Hawaiian style of the late 19th century. Located on a spectacular 37-acre hillside property sloping down to a lovely white-sand beach, the resort, consisting of two six-story wings, features oversized guest rooms with private lanais; 80 percent overlook the sea. The 58 extra-spacious suites are the most desirable accommodations, but common amenities include marble bathrooms with separate tub and stall shower, double vanities, make-up mirror, hairdryer, phone, plush terry his-and-her bathrobes, fully stocked honor bar and refrigerator, color TV and in-room safe. Appointments are sedate, including king-size beds with bamboo headboards and tasteful, but dull, art. Sliding shuttered doors let in balmy breezes. Extra services and a sense of privacy can be yours in the deluxe Ritz Carlton Club, on the top three floors of the Napili wing. A specially cut key opens the elevator to this exclusive enclave with a private lounge staffed by a concierge. Guests can repair here several times a day for complimentary continental breakfast, afternoon tea, evening hors d'oeuvres and after-dinner chocolates. Cocktails and beverages are served continuously. The Ritz-Carlton gladly welcomes and caters to large groups, with a 143-seat amphitheater (the only one in a Maui hotel), two ballrooms, and two boardrooms with fireplaces. The Kapalua Golf Club, surrounding the hotel, offers 54 championship holes. Rates include complimentary use of the on-site health facility. Some activities, such as power walking and aqua aerobics, are free; others, including yoga classes, massage therapy (one hour of Swedish, Lomi-Lomi or Shiatsu is about $80), aromatherapy and reflexology, require an extra charge. One of the area's best dining rooms, the Anuenue Room (formerly The Grill) is on resort property, serving light island cuisine, with herbs grown in the Ritz-Carlton garden. It has piano entertainment nightly. There are five other eateries and lounges, including the Beach House and Bar, for casual snacks, lunches and cocktails. If you are thinking of getting hitched on Maui, be aware that the resort employs its own "Honeymoon Coordinator." She can work with potential newly-weds as long as two months in advance of arrival. Additional amenities and facilities include: Artists in Residence Program, "Ritz Kids" children's program daily except Sunday, 24-hour room service, nightly turn-down, valet service, complimentary airport shuttle, car rental, baby-sitting, shops, beauty salon. Amenities: tennis, health club, exercise room, Jacuzzi, sauna, balcony or patio, family plan, club floor, business services. 550 rooms. Credit cards: A, CB, DC, MC, V.

Lahaina

Bed-and-Breakfasts

Blue Horizons $75–$95 ★★★

3894 Mahinahina Street, Lahaina, 96761, ☎ (800) 669-1948, (808) 669-1965, FAX (808) 661-1896.

Single: $75–$95. Double: $75–$95.

Jim and Beverly Spence, originally from Atlanta, welcome guests from all over the world to their two-story custom home located between Kahana Beach and Honokawai Beach Park. Convenient to Kaanapali and Kapalua resort areas, this B&B offers five affordable rooms and suites, all with private baths. The Lanai Room, actually a studio, is priced at $85 a night, and is the largest of the three rooms. It has two twin beds that convert to a king, and a kitchenette with a stove and small refrigerator. The Orchid and Ginger Rooms, each with a queen-size bed, contain a refrigerator. On the first floor are two apartment/suites that open to a redwood deck with an ocean view. Like the Lanai Room, these units have a stove and small fridge, but contain private living areas with a sofa bed. All accommodations are air-conditioned, with color TVs. The Spences provide a large breakfast spread every day except Sunday, and everyone is welcome to use their gourmet kitchen, which is fully equipped with a dishwasher, microwave and coffee maker. When not out seeing the sights, guests can barbecue, swim in the tiled pool, or lounge in the spacious, high-ceilinged living room with a VCR and video-tape library. For beach forays, (just a short stroll away) the Spences loan out beach gear. They can also assist with activity advice and car-rental discount packages. Additional amenities include a washer and dryer and iron and ironing board. There's an extra charge of $15 for more than two people per room. Amenities: balcony or patio. 5 rooms. Credit cards: A, MC, V.

Garden Gate Bed and Breakfast $55–$99 ★★

67 Kaniau Road, Lahaina, 96761, ☎ (808) 661-8800, FAX (808) 667-7999.

Single: $55–$99. Double: $55–$99.

Two blocks from the beach and a few minutes from Lahaina Town, this serene B&B on a quarter-acre consists of a 475-square-foot Garden Studio, suitable for up to four people with a queen-size bed, queen sleeper-sofa, sitting room with TV, telephone and private combination bath. A wide private deck overlooks the ocean. A cheaper alternative is the rather small Molokai Room, in the main house, which can squeeze in two people; it also has a private bath. If you stay in the studio, which has its own kitchen, you'll find it stocked with local fruits, cereals, Kona coffee and other breakfast fixin's for you to dish up when you please. Your hosts, Ron and Welmoet Glover, deliver fresh-baked French pastries, muffins or a loaf of bread to your door daily. Molokai Room guests receive the same menu, but are served at table. Facilities include a "soft-tub" spa in the garden. The Glovers are more than willing to recommend fun stuff to do in Maui. There's a three-night minimum stay. Smoking allowed outdoors only. Amenities: Jacuzzi, balcony or patio. 2 rooms. Credit cards: not accepted.

Old Lahaina House   **$50–$95**   ★★

PO Box 10355, Lahaina, 96761, ☎ (800) 847-0761, (808) 667-4663, FAX (808) 667-5615.

Single: $50–$95. Double: $50–$95.

If you like reasonably-priced B&B living, Old Lahaina House could be the perfect place to stay on Maui. Only two blocks away from the hubbub of Lahaina Town, it's in a quiet, peaceful neighborhood, just across the street from a viewful beach popular with local surfers. Enthusiastic hosts Sherry and John Barbier offer several lodging options. Two of the most expensive rooms have king-size beds and private baths, plus refrigerators and microwaves, one has a lanai. In the mid-range ($60 per night) are two rooms with a shared bath, and two twin beds each. The lowest priced accommodation shares a bath with the hosts and has a full-sized bed. All are air-conditioned, and feature TVs and phones. Breakfast consists of fresh pastries from a French bakery, fruit, juice, hot beverages and locally made jams and jellies. Lots of socializing goes on in and around the pool area, where guests can splash around with the assorted water toys provided. Amenities: balcony or patio. 5 rooms. Credit cards: A, MC, V.

The Guesthouse   **$55–$89**   ★★★

1620 Ainakea Road, Lahaina, 96761, ☎ (800) 621-8942, (808) 661-8085, FAX (808) 661-1896.

Single: $55–$85. Double: $59–$89.

More than half the guests at this delightful B&B are repeat visitors, and some never leave, including a local tour operator, who booked a room and is still there after two years. The owner, dive master Tanna Swanson Branum, got into the business after she came to Maui on a two-week vacation nine years ago and decided this was where she wanted to be. Visitors have gotten married on the grounds; one even borrowed Tanna's wedding dress. The Guesthouse is situated in a one-mile stretch of residential homes between Lahaina and Kaanapali Beach. Branum calls four of her five guest rooms "honeymoon suites," and they certainly are romantic. All are individually and eclectically decorated, and feature either a hot tub on a private wooden deck or an indoor, oversize, tiled Jacuzzi tub for two surrounded by potted plants. One especially lovely room has a huge rattan four-poster bed, parquet floor and a stained glass mural of dolphins cavorting. All suites have a queen-size bed, (three have an additional twin bed) color TV with remote control, refrigerator, phone and private lanai. Bargain-hunters can opt for a room that shares a bath with the hosts. It has most of the amenities the suites have, except for the spa and lanai. Guests are allowed free rein in the quiet living room, which has floor-to-ceiling windows overlooking an attractive pool. The family room is gathering place for video-watching. There's a kitchen for preparing snacks as well as barbecue facilities. Picnic and beach supplies are provided in the laundry room. Breakfast includes Hawaiian coffee, home-baked bread, tropical fruits and juices in addition to a hot repast of French toast or banana pancakes. When they aren't busy attending to guests, your hosts also operate a tour company and can offer special car-rental rates and discounts on island activities. Not suitable for children under 12. Amenities: Jacuzzi, balcony or patio. 5 rooms. Credit cards: A, D, MC, V.

Condos

Honokeana Cove Resort Condominiums **$105–$175** ★★

5255 Lower Honoapiilani Road, Lahaina, 96761, Eight miles north of Lahaina, one mile north of Kapalua Resort, ☎ (800) 237-4948, (808) 669-6441, FAX (808) 669-8777. Single: $105–$175. Double: $105–$175.

Snorkeling fans will delight in the private cove teeming with tropical fish and sea turtles right in front of this peaceful condominium property. Personable and small, Honokeana Cove offers 38 units contained in a series of naturally weathered brown-shingled buildings, some with ocean views. Management stresses that staying here is like being a guest in someone's second home, instead of "an impersonal hotel room," and in each individually decorated one-, two- and three-bedroom unit (some with loft) you'll find a blender and microwave in the kitchen, a VCR and cable TV. Families (or couples who like their space) will probably appreciate a town-house apartment with three baths. Besides the snorkeling cove, the only other on-site diversion is the pool where, if you're feeling friendly, you can join up with other guests at the weekly pupu (appetizer) parties. If a crescent-shaped, sandy beach is your thing, Napili Bay is only a five-minute walk away. The Kapalua Resort's tennis facilities and three championship golf courses are less than a mile north of the property. There's a three-night minimum. Amenities: balcony or patio. 38 rooms. Credit cards: MC, V.

Lahaina Shores Beach Resort **$120–$225** ★★

475 Front Street, Lahaina, 96761, 10 minutes from Kapalua West Maui Airport, ☎ (800) 628-6699, (808) 667-1666, FAX (808) 661-1025. Single: $120–$225. Double: $120–$225.

Lahaina Shores, a quasi-plantation-style mansion that's been converted into a seven-story hotel, is also the only lodging that's right on the historic whaling town's only beach. Its Front Street address is convenient to a growing list of terrific restaurants; your rate includes room charge privileges at selected eateries. In many small ways, management here provides a number of services that prove to be a boon for a guest seeking solid value and convenience. Although not considered a B&B, guests are treated to a welcoming continental breakfast, free of charge, on the morning after arrival, which also includes an orientation meeting with the activities staff. (The hotel also has a full-time concierge.) Poolside lunch service is on order from a nearby restaurant. Accommodations are perfectly acceptable, if not exceptional, whether you're in a studio, a one-bedroom apartment or an ocean-front penthouse. Most of the centrally air-conditioned, 199 rooms are spacious and light-filled, with cream-colored walls and un-gaudy tropical furnishings. All have full kitchens with microwave and coffee makers, some with a built-in counter and cushioned bar-stool seating. Other amenities include remote-control color TVs with VCRs and a private lanai. There's daily maid service as well as a laundry room. Dry cleaning is also available. Facilities include a pretty pool, which is rather small and crowded, and a whirl-pool spa. For families with children or long term guests, there may be no better value than this lodging, especially in Lahaina. Amenities: Jacuzzi, balcony or patio, family plan. 199 rooms. Credit cards: A, DC, D, MC, V.

Puunoa Beach Estates   **$580–$800**   ★★★

45 Kai Pali Place, Lahaina, 96761, One mile from the center of Lahaina, ☎ *(800) 642-MAUI, (808) 667-1400, FAX (808) 667-5631.*
Single: $580–$800. Double: $580–$800.

Talk about an exclusive retreat—Puunoa Beach Estates offers just 10 super-luxurious two- and three-bedroom condo apartments directly facing a sandy, and fairly calm, beach only a mile away from Lahaina. All of the snazzily appointed units are at least 1700 square feet. As you enter through an etched-glass doorway, you'll find someone has left a basket of fresh fruit for your enjoyment, as well as a complimentary package of groceries in the refrigerator. All the homes are individually appointed (probably by a selected interior designer), but one of the most stunning details, among many, are the sloped-wood ceilings. Some units have separate lofts. Before doing anything else, you might want to soak your jet-lagged bones in the Roman Jacuzzi tub that's big enough for two (there's also a separate shower). But wait, there's still more—every apartment contains a wet bar, fully-equipped kitchen, dining room, living room and private oceanfront lanai with a couple of bentwood chaise lounges. Amenities include two color TVs, video player, stereo, in-room safe, toiletries, terry robes, hair dryer, iron and ironing board and washer-dryer. A newspaper is delivered to your door daily, a maid will clean up after you, a concierge will attempt to do your bidding, and you have use of a full-size car—unfortunately no chauffeur is provided. Amenities: tennis, Jacuzzi, sauna, balcony or patio. 10 rooms.
Credit cards: A, MC, V.

Hotels

Pioneer Inn   **$90–$225**   ★★

658 Wharf Street, Lahaina, 96761, Behind the Lahaina Small Boat Harbor, ☎ *(800) 457-5457, (808) 661-3636, FAX (808) 667-5708. Rated restaurant: Snug Harbor*
Single: $90–$225. Double: $90–$225.

The once-dowdy (and cheap) guest rooms of this plantation-era historic hotel, built in 1901, were extensively renovated in January 1995, although the rowdy atmosphere in the famous ol' Bar and Grill hasn't changed a whit. After all, the place has a reputation to protect, with a location looking out to Lahaina Harbor. Keep in mind that if you stay here, you'll have to put up with looky-loos wandering the public areas of the establishment, which is a tourist attraction in itself. The aforementioned Bar and Grill, for example, trimmed with gleaming dark woods, and a mural of leaping dolphins over the bar, features a plethora of nubile maidens on canvas, and there's still a possibility that a brawl may erupt now and then. But we wouldn't want to discourage the management's efforts to gentrify the place—it does have a pretty dining room, called Snug Harbor, with a reasonably elegant and romantic setting overlooking the ocean and harbor. Surrounded by bougainvillea, the courtyard is also a nice place to sip a drink and set a spell, under wide umbrellas. Guest rooms and suites are now air-conditioned, and all feature private baths (you used to have to share a bath) and lanais. Deluxe rooms and suites have wet bars and refrigerators. All feature one queen bed; suites have an additional Murphy bed. There are souvenir and gift shops, but not much else in the way of facilities, since all the action in the harbor and in town is just a step away from your front door. Amenities: balcony or patio. 50 rooms. Credit cards: A, MC, V.

Inns

Aloha Tony's   **$45–$54**   ★ ★

13 Kauaula Road, Lahaina, 96761, ☎ (880) 57A-LOHA, (808) 661-8040, FAX (808) 661-8045.
Single: $45. Double: $54.

Aloha Tony, an electrician and would-be writer who says he needs to improve his spelling abilities first, maintains three popularly priced guest rooms in his modest home. The house is across from a neighborhood beach with access to a New England-style shopping center. All rooms are smallish but cheerfully furnished with bright, folksy bedspreads, rag rugs, ceiling fans, rockers or easy chairs. The homey decor in Room #2 includes a desk, a modest collection of books (there's a substantial library in the living room) and plants. None has a private bath. A nice touch are the coolers in each room, and beach mats doled out on an honor system. No breakfast is available, but Tony "surrenders" one shelf in his fridge for guest use, and all have "incidental" (as Tony puts it) kitchen privileges. No lighting up inside the house, but a porch is just outside where guests are welcome to "smoke away." Laundry facilities available. Free parking. There's a three-night minimum. Amenities: balcony or patio. 3 rooms. Credit cards: MC, V.

Lahaina Inn   **$89–$129**   ★ ★ ★

127 Lahainaluna Road, Lahaina, 96761, ☎ (800) 669-3444, (808) 661-0577, FAX (808) 667-9480. Rated restaurant: David Paul's Lahaina Grill
Single: $89. Double: $129.

It's hard to believe that the Lahaina Inn, a pristine example of quiet Victorian splendor, was a beat-up old dive until 1989. That's when Crazy Shirts, Inc. owner Rick Ralston (whose hobby is architectural restoration) took it in hand, installing 1800s-era antique locksets that actually function—wow, that's dedication! Most guests feel transported into another world once behind the doors of the two-story, cream-colored wooden structure, located right smack in the middle of bustling Lahaina Town. After checking in, you ascend a carved wooden staircase to one of the 12 individually decorated guest rooms on the second floor. You may want to spend a few moments checking out the varied treasures, including antique, leaded-glass lamps, armoires, rare Oriental carpets, and lightly striped or floral-patterned wallpaper. The full-size beds are either dark, carved wooden affairs with giant-size headboards or a more feminine white iron. Many bed coverings are hand-crocheted lace. Amenities in each room include a private balcony supplied with a wicker rocker, and cotton yukata robes. A continental breakfast, consisting of orange juice, warm croissants and freshly brewed Kona coffee is supplied on a sideboard outside the rooms each morning. All rooms are cooled by ceiling fans and air conditioning (partly due to street noise from partygoers outside) and have modern, tiled private baths and telephones. There are no TVs, but classical music is piped in. No children under 15 years accepted. Smoking on lanais only. At street level, where an old salt carved in wood stands guard, is the acclaimed David Paul's Lahaina Grill, which has constantly been rated as the best Maui Restaurant. Amenities: balcony or patio. 12 rooms. Credit cards: A, D, MC, V.

The Plantation Inn　　　　　　　$119–$219　　　　　　★★★

174 Lahainaluna Road, Lahaina, 96761, ☎ *(800) 433-6815, (808) 667-9225, FAX (808) 667-9293. Rated restaurant: Gerard's Restaurant*

Single: $119–$219. Double: $119–$219.

One of the two buildings that compose The Plantation Inn does recall the look of the old South—down New Orleans-way. The two-story property, with lacy verandas, surrounding a courtyard and hand-tiled pool, appears to have been transported from the Vieux Carre. Most of the guest rooms are contained in the annex behind this lovely structure, but no matter where you're lodged, you'll be impressed with the attention to detail: all quarters have hardwood floors, brass or canopy beds, brass fixtures, Craftsman-like wood detailing and ceiling fans (central air conditioning is provided). One room, with an Oriental theme, has an immense, carved Chinese canopy bed that'll make you feel like Empress Tzu Hsi. Some have exquisitely detailed, stained-glass windows above French doors. All have private tiled baths (some with Jacuzzi tubs) and access to a breezy veranda. Amenities include remote-control TVs, VCRs and refrigerators; some suites have kitchenettes. Note that the pool (with an attached spa) is 12 feet deep, and meant for aspiring divers. The first floor of the inn is given over to Gerard's Restaurant, a highly rated establishment serving French cuisine embellished with Hawaiian produce. Just down the street is one of Maui's best restaurants, David Paul's Lahaina Grill (in the Lahaina Inn) so you can have a moveable feast. Amenities: Jacuzzi, balcony or patio. 19 rooms. Credit cards: A, MC, V.

Napili

Condos

Napili Sunset　　　　　　　　$85–$249　　　　　　★★

46 Hui Drive, Napili, 96761, ☎ *(800) 447-9229, (808) 669-8083, FAX (808) 669-2730.*

Single: $85–$249. Double: $85–$249.

Location, location, location—that's what makes this otherwise unprepossessing (but reasonably priced) condominium a good value—a sugary stretch of beautiful Napili Beach lies just behind the property. The more desirable one- and two-bedroom beachfront apartments are furnished in pale pink, beige and white fabrics, with art work to match. Lanais are large enough to contain a table and chairs; it's a lovely place for a sunset supper or sunrise breakfast. The lower-priced garden-view studios are in a separate building away from the beach, but all units boast fully equipped kitchens with microwaves, ceiling fans (no air conditioning) and cable TVs. There's daily maid service. Facilities include a pool, library and barbecue pits. For other recreational activities, Kapalua Resort's tennis, golf, dining and shops are only a short walk away. There's a minimum three-night stay. Amenities: balcony or patio, family plan. 42 rooms. Credit cards: MC, V.

MAUI

Napili Surf Beach Resort   **$79–$175**   ★★★

50 Napili Place, Napili, 96761, 10 miles from Lahaina, ☎ (800) 541-0638, (808) 669-8002, FAX (808) 669-8004.
Single: $79–$175. Double: $79–$175.

The old adage "you can't judge a book by its cover" certainly applies to this beach-front low-rise. Although the four two-story white-cinder-block buildings won't win any design prizes, the grounds are lush and lovely, planted with tropical flowers and the requisite swaying palm trees, and the white-sand beach in front of the property is a stunner. It's great for swimming or sunning, and a snorkeling reef is nearby. Also, the prices are pocketbook friendly; even the studios contain fully equipped kitchens (grocery stores are nearby) with dishwashers and microwaves and roomy lanais. Cooled by ceiling fans and ocean breezes, all units feature the requisite light-rattan furniture, capiz-shell lamps, and floral quilts on the queen, twin and sofa beds. Ocean views are better in the one-bedroom apartments than they are in the studios. Limited guest facilities include two pools (the two garden-view wings have a pool all to themselves), barbecue pits and shuffleboard courts. Laundry room. Five-night minimum stay. Amenities: balcony or patio, family plan. 54 rooms. Credit cards: not accepted.

Hotels

The Mauian   **$110–$140**   ★

5441 Lower Honoapiilani Road, Napili, 96761, ☎ (800) 367-5034, (808) 669-6205, FAX (808) 669-0129.
Single: $110–$140. Double: $110–$140.

A beachfront hotel for traditionalists who eschew the bright lights and glitz of Kaanapali and Wailea resorts, the Mauian has been drawing the same clientele for more than 30 years. Beautiful and underrated, half-mile wide Napili Bay is just outside the low-rise property's front door, although a pool with a pretty garden is provided. The hotel touts proudly that it has "no TV or phones in the rooms," which are otherwise equipped with all-electric kitchens with microwaves and utensils, and lanais with ocean views. Guest rooms are actually studios, which are nicely and tropically furnished with wicker and rattan, cooled by ceiling fans and sea breezes. Ideal for families, it has two twin beds as well as a queen-size bed. No charge for children under 12. Facilities include an Ohana (family) room where guests missing media stimulation can repair to the only TV and VCR on the grounds. Shuffle-board courts, laundry room. Two public phones, one courtesy phone. Once a week, the affable manager, Joy Baccetti, hosts a sunset "Aloha" party as well as fresh-baked island treats; coffee is provided every morning. Amenities: balcony or patio, family plan. 44 rooms. Credit cards: MC, V.

Napili Bay

Resorts

Napili Kai Beach Club   **$150–$520**   ★★★

5900 Honoapiilani Road, Napili Bay, 96761, Nine miles north of Lahaina, ☎ (800) 367-5030, (808) 669-6271, FAX (808) 669-0086. Rated restaurant: Sea House
Single: $150–$510. Double: $160–$520.

Encompassing a respectable 10 acres on a dreamy stretch of beach, the Napili Kai Beach Club is a monument to unpretentiousness. For more than 30 years, this resort has hosted a number of repeat visitors who wouldn't dream of staying anywhere else, although fancier facilities are available in more fashionable areas, for about the same price. The difference is the genuine Aloha spirit, including the Friday night Polynesian show featuring local *keikis* (kids) who study Hawaiian dance, history, language and legends through the resort's Napili Kai Foundation. Staying here can be an endless round of fun, if you're the sociable type—there are weekly coffee and tea parties, putting parties (on the 18-hole putting green, with 50-cent cocktails) and Wednesday Mai Tai parties. A boon for families is an array of free children's activities (ages six–12) held on Easter and Christmas and from June 15 through August 31. Those who like to be left alone can snorkel quietly in Napili Bay (snorkeling equipment provided free) or stroll along the beach. Freshwater fans have a choice of four pools to swim in. Quiet time can also be spent on your own private lanai, all with ocean views. Of the 162 accommodations, the second-level suites are especially nice, with beamed ceilings, ceiling fans, plenty of seating areas, shoji screens and soothing, tasteful furnishings. Some have deluxe, tiled kitchenettes with microwaves and dishwashers. All have color TVs. Not every room has air conditioning, so keep this in mind when making a reservation. You can have your three squares a day in the well-regarded Sea House restaurant; imbibe some liquid refreshment in the Whale Watchers bar or Down Under lounge, or conquer the munchies with a snack in the Beach Pagoda. Daily afternoon tea in lobby. Facilities include two 18-hole putting greens (golf privileges nearby), shuffleboard courts, barbecue pits. Tennis court adjacent to hotel (court fee, $10 per day, hotel provides complimentary tennis rackets). Free use of beach gear and equipment. A minimum of seven nights is required for stays over the Christmas holidays (December 20–January 1). Amenities: Jacuzzi, balcony or patio, family plan. 162 rooms. Credit cards: MC, V.

Where to Eat

No one will go hungry on Maui, no matter what they like to eat. Sophisticated tastes are appeased at any number of gourmet restaurants—most of which are attached to a hotel or resort—where Pacific Rim, Hawaiian Regional, and Nouvelle Hawaiian cuisines are served in style. Best bets for the fancy set include **Seasons** (The Four Seasons, Wailea), **Raffles** (Stouffer's Wailea Resort), **The Grill** (Ritz-Carlton Kapalua), **The Grand Dining Room** (Grand Wailea Resort), **Prince Court** (Maui Prince Hotel, Makena), **Swan**

Court (Hyatt Regency Maui, Kaanapali Beach Resort), **Gerard's** (Plantation Inn) and **Bay Club** (Kapalua Bay Resort). You'll also find a large number of trendy restaurants dotted around Maui. Just some of the noteworthy are **David Paul's Lahaina Grill** (Lahaina), **Chez Paul** (four miles south of Lahaina), **Avalon Restaurant and Bar** (Lahaina), **Longhi's** (Lahaina) and **Haliimaile General Store** (near Pukalani). Call well in advance for reservations at the fine-dining restaurants (men should be prepared to don jacket and tie at some). You can pick and choose from a veritable slew of "ordinary" local spots and mom-and-pop establishments, where you can feast relatively inexpensively on everything from sandwiches and fresh fish to ethnic cuisine (Asian, Mexican, Italian, etc.). Vegetarians and health-fooders will be well taken care of at a number of natural food shops and delis. And don't pass up the **fresh produce** at **fruit stands** and **farmer's markets**. Lastly, you absolutely *must* do a luau night while on Maui. The evening includes a stuff-your-face feast, open bar, and Hawaiian entertainment for a cost of $40–50. Two of the most authentic presentations are at **Stouffer's Wailea Beach Resort** and **Old Lahaina Luau**.

Central Maui

Haliimaile

Haliimaile General Store   **$$$**

900 Haliimaile Road, Haliimaile, ☎ *(808) 572-2666.*
Asian cuisine. Specialties: Szechuan barbecued salmon, Peking duck salad, pina colada cheesecake, chocolate macadamia fudge pie.
Lunch: 11 a.m.–2:30 p.m., entrées $10–$17.
Dinner: 5:30–9:30 p.m., entrées $25–$40.
The Haliimaile General Store is situated in a tin-roofed, salmon-hued, false-front building that's reached via a cane road in an off-the-beaten path location just a few miles from Kahului. This very IN restaurant features eclectic Asian-inspired entrées created by caterer and chef Beverly Gannon. Gussied up (but not too much) to re-create the ambience of the plantation store it once was, it's a lot of fun for the eye as well as the palate. Along one wall is a deli-bakery case, on the other, a tall shelf full of colorful Italian crockery. Ingredients are simple, but of the best quality, and enhanced by tricky and flavorful seasonings that Beverly has conjured. Diners rave about succulent paniolo pork ribs served with mashed potatoes or Szechuan barbecued salmon, among other things. Also recommended for a bountiful Sunday brunch served from 10 a.m.–2:30 p.m. Features: own baking, rated wine cellar, non-smoking area, private dining rooms. Reservations recommended.

Kahului

Lucy's Cyber Restaurant   **$**   ★★

161 Alamaha Street, Kahului, ☎ *(808) 871-1135.*
American cuisine. Specialties: Espresso, pupus, sandwiches, plate specials, computer classes, Net-surfing.
Breakfast: 8 a.m.–2 p.m., entrées $6–$11.
Lunch: 10 a.m.–4 p.m., entrées $6–$11.
Dinner: 4 p.m.–2 a.m., entrées $6–$11.

Also called the Katchi-Katchi Espresso Bar, for reasons unknown, Lucy's, located in the old Lopaka Bar and Grill, offers computers for classes and Internet surfing, along with low-tech amusements such as a dart board, pool table and jukebox. If you can tear yourself away from your monitor, cups of a robust, special Spanish coffee, overstuffed sandwiches, plate specials and pupus are available on a small but diverse menu. An ethnic-vegetarian buffet is offered twice a week on Sunday and Monday at 6 p.m. for $15. Lucy welcomes your e-mail; contact her at lucyspl@maui.net. Features: late dining.

Marco's Grill and Deli $$ ★★
444 Hana Highway, Suite M, Kahului, 96732, ☎ (808) 877-4446.
Italian cuisine. Specialties: Chocolate cinnamon French toast, omelettes, pastas, pizza.
Breakfast: 7 a.m.–2 p.m., entrées $5–$9.
Lunch: 11 a.m.–5 p.m., entrées $7–$11.
Dinner: 5–10 p.m., entrées $9–$20.

The DeFanis family, who hail from New Jersey, of all places, have set up shop in a fairly new restaurant strategically located on the route to and from the Kahului Airport. Marco, the patriarch, is a hands-on guy who cooks everything to order himself, as well as baking the bread, grinding the sausage and roasting the coffee. Ideal for an early breakfast before (or after) flights, patrons can choose from a number of interesting omelettes served with oven-roasted potatoes. You can have a classic cheese omelette, or go for broke with shiitake mushroom or roasted pepper and provolone. An unusual and delightful eye-opening special is chocolate cinnamon French toast. A big menu of hot and cold sandwiches, salads, appetizers, pizza, pastas and generally Italian specialties are on order for lunch or dinner; try the seafood rustica, a hollowed-out crusty bread filled with mahi-mahi, clams, scallops, shrimp and crab meat in a light cream sauce. Marco's is open from 7:30 a.m. on Saturdays and Sundays. Features: own baking, Sunday brunch, wine and beer only. Credit cards: MC, V.

The Class Act $$ ★★
310 Kaahumanu Avenue at Maui Community College, Kahului, ☎ (808) 242-1210.
International cuisine. Specialties: Four-course $10 lunches.
Lunch: 11 a.m.–12:30 p.m., entrées $10. Closed: Mon., Tue., Thur., Sat., Sun.

Four-course luncheon menus that feature a different region or culture are prepared and presented by culinary students at Maui Community College twice a week for only $10. Understandably, you should reserve up to two weeks in advance, on Wednesdays and Fridays between 8:30 and 10:30 a.m. Recent feasts have included "A Taste of Greece" featuring Greek (what else?) salad, pureed yellow split pea soup with roast lamb, chicken skewers with hot lavish, and baklava. For those watching their weight or cholesterol levels, one "heart-healthy" alternative per day is offered. This one rates a "10" for effort. Features: own baking. Reservations required.

Makawao

Casanova Italian Deli $$$ ★★★
1188 Makawao Avenue, Makawao, ☎ (808) 572-0220.
Italian cuisine. Specialties: Wood-fired pizza, fresh pasta, island fish.
Lunch: 11:30 a.m.–2:30 p.m., entrées $9–$23.

Dinner: 5:30–9:30 p.m., entrées $9–$23. Closed: Sun.

The management at this upcountry Italian deli and restaurant wants you to eat here because "Dining in Rome is too far away." We don't think we've had a pizza in Rome (or in Italy) that was as good as the wood-fired diskies they serve up here. The casanovas in question are the owners, four stylish guys from the mother country (one is from Rome) who like to wear their shirts with the buttons open way down. One or more of them might be in evidence, lending a romantic atmosphere to go along with the equally yummy antipasti, pasta, fresh fish and desserts, including the omnipresent tiramisu. Pizza served until 11 p.m. The adjoining deli is open daily from 8 a.m.–6:30 p.m. There's dancing nightly on Maui's "biggest dance floor," and the bar is open until 1 a.m. Features: own baking. Reservations recommended. Credit cards: MC, V.

Crossroads Café   **$$**   ★★★

3682 Baldwin Avenue, Makawao,.
American cuisine. Specialties: Ethnic vegetarian dinners, coffee drinks, desserts.
Breakfast: 8 a.m.–2 p.m., entrées $5–$9.
Lunch: 11 a.m.–5 p.m., entrées $6–$12.
Dinner: 5–8 p.m., entrées $8–$12.

Heaven for vegans and skeptics alike, this cozy, no-booze, no-red-meat, no-foolin' cowtown café does draw the granola and sprouts crowd—but also features excellent vegetarian dinners with different themes every evening. Surprise chefs often don the apron here and whip up heavenly things that even die-hard carnivores will appreciate. Live music performances on Saturday nights. Open from 9 a.m.–5 p.m. on Sundays. Features: own baking, non-smoking area. Reservations not accepted.

Paia

Mama's Fish House   **$$$**   ★★★

799 Poho Place, Paia, 96779, ☎ (808) 579-8488.
Seafood cuisine. Specialties: Raw fish salad.
Lunch: 11 a.m.–4 p.m., entrées $17–$20.
Dinner: 4–9:30 p.m., entrées $20–$30.

Located in a grove of coconut palms between Paia and Hookipa Beach, Mama's is a perfect dining destination for those driving to Hana. Situated in a pretty, breezy, converted beach house with sliding windows, and a low, wood-slatted ceiling, Mama's was the first fresh-fish house in Hawaii when it opened in 1973. Fishermen deliver their catch right to the door. Inside, walls are decorated with old photos, tables are covered with tapa cloths. Fish is served all manner of ways, pan-fried with Maui onion and chili, sautéed with bananas, tropical fruit and coconuts, or raw, as in the fresh marinated poki salad, served with taro chips. Also terrific is ahi sashimi with spicy wasabi and soy sauce dip. There are a few chicken and steak dishes, as well as sandwiches and salads. One drawback is that, despite the low-key setting, Mama's is very expensive, although portions are generous. Features: outside dining, private dining rooms. Reservations required. Credit cards: A, CB, DC, D, MC, V.

Picnics   **$**   ★★

30 Baldwin Avenue, Paia, 96779, ☎ (808) 579-8021.
American cuisine. Specialties: Spinach Nut Burger.

Breakfast: 7-11 a.m., entrées $5.
Lunch: 11 a.m.–7 p.m., entrées $5–$7.

When it first opened 16 years ago, this local hangout made the most of its position as the last stop for food and gas on the road to Hana. The clever marketing ploy was to specialize in selling picnic lunches to go, called the "Holo Holo Pikinike." Hence, its name. Picnics still continues the moveable feast tradition, replete with a cooler loaded with ice and a "Road to Hana" cassette tape (deposit required), beverages, salads and fresh cookies or muffins, depending on how many are in your party. Provided free of charge is a guide to Hana. Although not included in the packed lunch deal, don't miss Picnics' original-recipe spinach nut burger. Even veggie haters will love this savory concoction of chopped nuts, sesame seeds and secret spices, mixed with Popeye's delight, all topped with cheddar cheese on a fresh baked roll. Add crisp bacon and Swiss cheese, and it becomes the Windsurfer, which is the restaurant's most popular item. Other offerings are Hawaiian pancakes with tropical fruit mixed into the batter, fish tacos, fresh salads made with Haiku greens, frozen yogurt, low-fat shakes, sundaes and coffee drinks. Features: own baking. Reservations not accepted.

The Vegan $ ★★

115 Baldwin Avenue, Paia, ☎ (808).
Vegetarian cuisine. Specialties: Pad thai, lemon-broiled tempeh.
Lunch: 11 a.m.–3 p.m., entrées $6–$9.
Dinner: 4 p.m.–8:30 p.m., entrées $6–$9. Closed: Mon.

Even non-vegetarians may like the ingenious way with green stuff and meat substitutes this small, time-worn eatery puts out. Their treatment of Thai dishes, including curried vegetables, and that old stalwart, pad thai noodles, are particularly notable. Variations on Indian, Mexican and Italian themes are also available. Servings are generous, the prices low, and everything is prepared to go. Features: nonsmoking area. Credit cards: MC, V.

Wunderbar Restaurant $$ ★★★

89 Hana Highway, Paia, ☎ (808) 579-8808.
International cuisine. Specialties: Breakfast dishes, salads, sandwiches on flatbread, fresh seafood.
Breakfast: 7:30-11:30 a.m., entrées $4–$10.
Lunch: 11:30 a.m.–2:30 p.m., entrées $4–$10.
Dinner: 5–10 p.m., entrées $8–$19.

Wunderbar has an Austrian chef, and there are a few German and Swiss items on the huge menu, but this is not strictly an Old World restaurant. In fact, the eclectic menu traverses the globe, with sashimi, Greek salad and eggs with "two-scoop rice" making regular appearances. Popular with Paia sailboarders and surfer dudes and dudettes, Wunderbar is open for early breakfast, so they can carbo-load before hitting the waves. Pancakes range from one to three stacks of blueberry, coconut banana and even chocolate varieties, all served with homemade peach butter. There are also three preparations of eggs benedict, called "bennies," either regular kine, veggie or a spicy Cajun fish version. All sandwiches, even burgers, are served on fresh flatbread. One salad offering, Grilled North Shore ono and Maui avocado on Kula greens with lemon butter vinaigrette, won first place in the Taste of Lahaina food fest. The dinner menu gets somewhat fancier and quite a bit pricier; try a Swiss specialty, Zuri Gschnetzlets, which is sliced veal with creamy mushroom sauce. Cocktails and pupus are served from 11:30 a.m.–5 p.m. Children's menu available. Features: outside dining, own baking. Reservations recommended. Credit cards: A, DC, MC, V.

Pukalani

Pukalani Country Club $ ★★

360 Pukalani Street, Pukalani, 96768, ☎ (808) 572-1325.
American cuisine. Specialties: Hawaiian plate lunches, breakfasts, sandwiches.
Breakfast: 8 a.m.–2 p.m., entrées $5–$12.
Lunch: 8 a.m.–2 p.m., entrées $5–$12.
Dinner: 5–9 p.m., entrées $5–$12.

Located in a lovely upcountry setting, this restaurant in the Pukalani Country Club is perfecto for après golf. Extremely popular at lunch, with locals and tourists jamming together for attention. Authentic Hawaiian plate lunches are served with poi or rice, chili pepper, fresh Maui onions and haupia. Good ole American breakfasts and sandwiches are also available, as well as drinks and pupus at "Happy Hangover Time" and dinners. Features: outside dining. Reservations not accepted. Credit cards: A, MC, V.

Wailuku

Maui Bake Shop and Deli $ ★★

2092 Vineyard Street, Wailuku, ☎ (808) 242-0064.
European cuisine. Specialties: European-style pastries.
Breakfast: 6 a.m.–6:30 p.m., entrées $1–$12. Closed: Sun.

Radiating an olde-world European ambience, this excellent bakery provides yummy breads and pastries as well as sandwiches and quiches perfect for a light and cheap breakfast or lunch. Try a veggie quiche or a piping-hot stuffed pizza bread. Whole pies and tortes are available for takeout. Saturday hours: 7 a.m.–5 p.m. Features: own baking. Reservations not accepted.

Maui Boy $ ★★

2102 Vineyard Street, Wailuku, ☎ (808) 244-7243.
Polynesian cuisine. Specialties: Teriyaki, roast pork plate.
Breakfast: 7–11 a.m., entrées $4–$9.

Sometimes the mayor and other notables show up at this humble but clean and oh-so-good local watering hole that's famous for its teriyaki chicken plate lunches. Accompanied by two scoops of rice and potato/mac salad, it'll fill you up for only $6.95. Equally mouthwatering is the roast pork and Hawaiian plates with poi, laulau, lomi-lomi salmon and kalua pig for just a dollar or so more. Also worth knowing about for hearty breakfasts of French toast made with Portuguese sweet bread, omelettes or pancakes. Reservations not accepted. Credit cards: MC, V.

Sam Sato's $ ★★

1750 Wilipaloop, Wailuku, ☎ (808) 244-7124.
Japanese cuisine. Specialties: Manju, saimin.
Breakfast: 8 a.m.–2 p.m., entrées $4–$7.
Lunch: 11 a.m.–2 p.m., entrées $4–$7. Closed: Sun.

Sam Sato's, a Maui institution founded in 1932, recently relocated to an industrial park in Wailuku called the Millyard, is famous for sweet pastry buns of Japanese origin, called manju. Traditionally filled with a mashed red paste made from azuki beans (an acquired taste), local versions feature everything from pineapple (natch) to coconuts and even white-bread apple. Sam's specialty is a prized white lima bean concoction originally made by his mother, Mite. Even if you don't like manju, buy a couple of boxes (they're only about 50 cents each) to give as gifts to island friends, who love them. Sato's also makes a mean bowl of saimin, as well as tasty, low-priced plate lunches. Features: own baking, non-smoking area. Reservations not accepted.

East Maui

Hana

Café at Hana Gardenland $ ★★★

Hana Highway and Kalo Road, Hana, ☎ (808) 248-7340.
American cuisine. Specialties: Hanamole and chips, steamed eggs and salsa.
Breakfast: 9 a.m.–11 a.m., entrées $3–$9.
Lunch: 11 a.m.–5 p.m., entrées $3–$9.

Located at the end of the drive along the Hana coast, this refreshing café, nestled inside the Hana Gardenland nursery, offers a small but comprehensive menu of healthful dishes for breakfast and lunch only. Aside from being one of the few places in tiny Hana to get a meal outside of the Hotel Hana-Maui, this eatery's claim to fame is the 1993 visit of First Lady Hillary Rodham Clinton. Apparently eating light, Mrs. Clinton ordered the steamed eggs and salsa served with Maui Crunch toast; and so too can you. Also recommended by satisfied diners is the ahi tuna salad sandwich, or "hanamole" (guacamole Hana-style) served with taro chips. No alcohol. Features: outside dining, non-smoking area. Reservations not accepted. Credit cards: A, MC, V.

South Maui

Kihei

A Pacific Café $$$ ★★★★

Azeka Place II, South Kihei Road, Kihei, ☎ (808) 879-0069.
Pacific Rim cuisine. Specialties: Wok-charred mahi-mahi with a garlic sesame crust and lime-ginger sauce.
Dinner: 5:30–10:30 p.m., entrées $12–$23.

Cookbook author and celebrity chef Jean-Marie Josselin has arrived in Maui in a big way. Flush with his successes on Kauai, he has taken over a big chunk of Azeka Place 2, the Kihei mini-mall. The restaurant encompasses an outre trio of dining rooms with seating for 200 patrons. Special features include a wood-burning grill and even a Tandoori oven. His Gallo-Asian cooking is served up on plates artistically hand-painted by his wife, Sophie. The resident chef is George Gomes, who has worked side by side with Josselin on Kauai for over a year. From starters to desserts, one can dine on flavors that span the globe. A signature appetizer is Tiger Eye Sushi Tempura with Chinese mustard sauce. For a soup course, choices include such diverse items as red Thai coconut curry soup with Hawaiian fish and calamari, to southwestern tortilla soup with tomato onion salsa and smoked tomato aioli. A version of

Caesar salad features blackened ahi. Throughout the menu, you'll find pastas and risottos as well as crisp roasted "peking-style" duck with Asian greens, garlic mashed potatoes (a current food fad) and kumquat sauce. And for dessert? How about a "terrine" of white-chocolate cake, steamed with a lilikoi mousse and glazed with a white-chocolate ganache and chili (yes!) flake lilikoi sauce? If you'd like to try these wonders at home, pick up a copy of Jean-Marie's book, *Taste of Hawaii*, which is for sale at the restaurant. If he's there, Jean-Marie will sign it for you personally. Features: own baking, rated wine cellar. Reservations required. Credit cards: A, MC, V.

Alexander's $$ ★ ★
1913 South Kihei Road, Kihei, Across from the whale at Kalama Park, ☎ *(808) 874-0788.*
American cuisine. Specialties: Fish and chips, chicken, ribs.
Lunch: 11 a.m.–4 p.m., entrées $5–$17.
Dinner: 4 p.m.–9 p.m., entrées $5–$17.
Alexander's motto (since 1990) has been "Great Food Fast at Great Prices." At Alexander's you have a choice of fish for the tempura-batter dipped fish and chips, including mahi-mahi, ono and ahi. This treatment is available for an assortment of shellfish; if you're watching calories, anything (except clams and calamari) can be served broiled. Ribs, chicken and fish can be ordered by the piece or in various combinations. American-style pupus (onion rings, buffalo wings, etc.) and sandwiches are also available. It's mostly takeout, but there's a covered lanai outside if you want to eat in. Features: outside dining. Reservations not accepted.

Azeka's Ribs $
1280 South Kihei Road, Kihei,.
Best known for legendary cook-your-own ribs. Bill Azeka, the owner of the shopping center, celebrated his 46th business anniversary in March 1996.

Carelli's on the Beach $$$ ★ ★ ★
2980 South Kihei Road, Kihei, ☎ *(808) 875-0001.*
Italian cuisine. Specialties: Zuppa di Frutta di Mare, Carelli's famous pizza, Tiramisu.
Dinner: 5:30–10 p.m., entrées $12–$30.
By no means is Carelli's a self-effacing establishment. The management blatantly lists the number of celebrity guests who dine here regularly, from paesano Sly Stallone to Robert Shapiro (!). Executive chef Lallo Scalera toured the world cooking for his ex-employers, Michael and Janet Jackson. Hardly renowned for their gourmet tendencies, this would hardly be a recommendation except for the fact that normal Joes and Janes alike love the place. Among the plethora of virtues are an enviable location right on the edge of Keawakapu Beach, professional service, incredible sunset views, wonderful homemade pastas and seafood dishes, and some of the best Mai Tais on the island. Other features include a wood-burning pizza oven (try the house special, homemade Italian sausage with roasted red peppers, sauteed maui onions and provolone cheese). Cocktails and a "mangia" menu are served until 11 p.m. Features: outside dining, own baking, private dining rooms. Reservations required. Credit cards: A, MC, V.

Five Palms Beach Grill $$$ ★ ★
2960 South Kihei Road, Kihei, ☎ *(808) 879-2607. Associated hotel: Mana-Kai Maui.*

American cuisine.
Lunch: 11 a.m.–3 p.m., entrées $7–$12.
Dinner: 5–9 p.m., entrées $15–$21.

You can't get much closer to the beach than in this open-air, oceanfront restaurant in a Kihei condo complex. Sigh over the sunsets or cheer whale antics while dining on a serviceable menu of burgers, fish tacos, salads, pizzas and prime rib or ribs for lunch and dinner. Four to six specials are prepared each day as well. If you want to save some money, sit in the bar, where inexpensive sandwiches are available. There's also poolside service. Breakfast is available on weekends only, from 8 a.m.–2 p.m.; on Saturdays and Sundays, the restaurant stays open until 10 p.m. for dinner. Features: outside dining, Sunday brunch, private dining rooms. Reservations recommended. Credit cards: MC, V.

Kihei Prime Rib House $$$ ★★

2511 Kihei Road, Kihei, ☎ (808) 879-1954.
American cuisine. Specialties: Prime rib, salad, cheese, bread, and fruit bar.
Dinner: 5–10 p.m., entrées $20–$25.

One drawback to this meat-and-seafood eatery with a broad ocean view is that many other bargain-searching travelers have heard about it. Like you, they've come to stuff themselves at the all-you-can-eat salad bar, which also includes bread, cheese and fresh island fruit, all for $11.95. Between 5 and 6 p.m., prime rib, fresh fish and chicken dishes are available for the same price, in addition to the salad bar. Just imagine the chaos that ensues. Still, the room is pretty, with tasteful artwork on the walls, and sunsets are equally scrumptious. A new feature is live musical entertainment from 9 p.m. to midnight, and a late-night pupu menu to accompany the tunes. If you've already eaten, partake of a glass of wine or coffee and dessert, including blueberry lemon jazz "surprise," carrot cake, cheesecake, key lime, mud or pecan pie; all for $4.50. Reservations recommended. Credit cards: CB, DC, MC, V.

La Pastaria $$ ★★

41 East Lipoa, Suite 4A, Lipoa Shopping Center, Kihei, ☎ (808) 879-9001.
Italian cuisine. Specialties: Gourmet herb-dough pizza, fresh pasta.
Dinner: 5–10 p.m., entrées $9–$18.

Nothing fancy here, but everything is freshly made, including pastas and sauces, pizzas, calzones, salads and a changing list of desserts prepared nightly by an in-house pastry chef. Diners have their choice of 12-inch traditional or gourmet pizzas; try the grilled eggplant made with red bell peppers, sun-dried tomatoes, feta, mozzarella and pesto. Also children's menu, specialty coffees and smoothies. A favorite with the Kihei condo crowd and local residents. Features: own baking. Reservations recommended. Credit cards: DC, D, MC, V.

Stella Blues Café $$ ★★

1215 South Kihei Road, in Long's Center, Kihei, ☎ (808) 874-3779.
American cuisine. Specialties: Breakfasts, deli items, coffee drinks, vegetarian specialties.
Breakfast: 8–11 a.m., entrées $5–$7.
Lunch: 11 a.m.–5 p.m., entrées $5–$8.
Dinner: 5–9 p.m., entrées $12–$17.

Stella Blues is a cheerful, neighborly café in a shopping center setting with indoor-outdoor seating. An outdoor patio is planted with flower boxes. Inside is a high-ceilinged room with plastic chairs, floral cloths under glass-topped tables, and a deli case in one corner. All dishes are prepared using fresh ingredients from Kula growers. On the breakfast and lunch menu, you'll find scrambled tofu and tempeh burgers as well as pastrami or corned beef on rye. A little on the politically correct side, the place announces that it serves "dolphin-safe" albacore. At dinner there are meatless pastas, steaks, chicken, ribs and Alaskan crab cakes. Desserts change daily. Flavored espresso drinks are served until closing. Good, live local entertainment Wednesday through Saturday. Features: outside dining, own baking, Sunday brunch. Reservations recommended. Credit cards: MC, V.

Maalaea Bay

Buzz's Wharf $$$ ★★★

Honoapiilani Highway, Maalaea Bay, Turn right at Maalaea sign, look for blue roof,
☎ *(808) 244-5426.*
American cuisine. Specialties: Prawns Tahitian, surf-and-turf combos, 16-ounce Porterhouse on a sizzling platter, fresh fish.
Lunch: 11 a.m.–5 p.m., entrées $12–$20.
Dinner: 5–10 p.m., entrées $12–$20.

A local favorite, this old-Hawaiian style restaurant overlooks Ma'alaea Harbor, where the sunset views are picture-postcard perfect. From your table, you can watch fishermen deliver the catch-of-the-day to the front door. Menu items are uniformly excellent, and wonderful in their simplicity. Juicy New York steaks are served with lobster, crab, prawns or shrimp. Depending on what the chef thinks is good that day, fresh fish ranges from mahi-mahi to spearfish. Shellfish offerings include fresh Pacific pan-fried oysters, shrimp tempura and Maui-grown rainbow trout. Buzz's even has a bowl of Saimin humbly thrown in with an array of appetizers. Sharp serving staff. Features: outside dining. Reservations recommended. Credit cards: A, MC, V.

Maalaea Waterfront Restaurant $$$ ★★★

50 Haouli Street, Maalaea Bay, ☎ *(808) 244-9028.*
American cuisine. Specialties: Baked prawns Wellington, Colorado roasted lamb rack.
Dinner: 5–9:30 p.m., entrées $15–$25.

Located in the Maalaea yacht basin, this oceanfront restaurant is definitely a family affair. Chef Ron Smith mans the burners, while he depends on his mom and two brothers to manage the front room. They must be doing a wonderful job; the restaurant was duly knighted by the *Maui News* for two years standing as having the "best service" in town. Chef Ron keeps up the quality control by personally selecting the fresh catch as it halts by his front door. At least five kinds of fish, prepared nine ways from Sunday (whew!) are on the nightly menu, including grilled ahi, yellowfin tuna paired with Hawaiian Amaebi shrimp in the shell, and "two scoop" jasmine rice, sauteed scallions and shiitake mushrooms sauced with shrimp, and ginger-coconut milk. Also unusual (to Hawaii) is the live Maine lobster chowder. In a more traditional vein, Caesar salad is prepared at tableside. Creator Cesar Cardini would have approved. Features: outside dining, own baking, Sunday brunch, rated wine cellar. Reservations recommended. Credit cards: A, MC, V.

Makena

Hakone $$$ ★★★★

5400 Makena Alanui Drive, Makena, 96733, ☎ *(808) 874-1111. Associated hotel: Maui Prince Hotel.*

Japanese cuisine. Specialties: Sushi bar, sukiyaki, kaiseki dinners.

Dinner: 6–9:30 p.m., entrées $25–$35.

Masterful chefs were imported from Japan to prepare excellent sushi and kaiseki dinners in an understatedly elegant room in the Maui Prince Hotel. Service is particularly thoughtful and gracious. There are two other branches statewide, but this is probably the best one. Features: own baking, private dining rooms. Reservations recommended. Credit cards: A, CB, DC, MC, V.

The Prince Court $$$ ★★★★

5400 Makena Alanui Drive, Makena, ☎ *(808) 875-5888. Associated hotel: Maui Prince Hotel.*

Pacific Rim cuisine.

Dinner: 6–8:30 p.m., entrées $22–$34.

The Prince Court, the Maui Prince's signature restaurant, is elegant enough for a family of royals, but still welcoming to lesser mortals with its tradition of polished, unobtrusive service. Greg Gaspar, who served as sous chef under the gifted and now-departed Roger Dikon, has created a new menu of Pacific Rim dishes. Starters include carpaccio of opakapaka and ahi with osetra caviar or smoked duck salad. Continue your feast with kiawe roasted Thai free range chicken or seared peppered salmon sashimi. A dessert that will remain long in your memory and on your waistline is the chocolate caramel brittle flan. If you or your wallet can't make it for dinner, there's always the Brodbigdanian Sunday brunch (from 9:30 a.m.–1 p.m.), a Friday night seafood buffet and Saturday prime rib buffet, as well as a soup and salad bar. Who says this royal roost isn't democratic? Features: own baking, Sunday brunch, rated wine cellar, private dining rooms. Reservations recommended. Credit cards: A, CB, DC, D, MC, V.

Wailea

Bistro Molokini $$$ ★★★

3850 Wailea Alanui Drive, Wailea, 96753, ☎ *(808) 875.1234. Associated hotel: Grand Wailea Resort.*

Italian cuisine. Specialties: Pizzas, sandwiches, salads.

Dinner: 6–9 p.m., entrées $16–$30.

An open-air café with an Italian twist overlooks both the formal pool of the Grand Wailea Resort and the Pacific Ocean. Not a bad spot for pizzas, sandwiches and "Italian home cooking" emanating from an exhibition kitchen and wood-burning oven. Also open for pupus and specialty cocktails. Features: outside dining, own baking. Reservations required. Credit cards: A, MC, V.

Café Kula $$ ★★★

3850 Wailea Alanui Drive, Wailea, 96753, ☎ *(808) 875-1234. Associated hotel: Grand Wailea Resort.*

cuisine. Specialties: Ahi tuna sandwich with grilled pineapple, Kula tomatoes and Maui onions.

Breakfast: 6:30 a.m.–3 p.m., entrées $7–$12.
Lunch: 10 a.m.–3 p.m., entrées $7–$12.

An open-air terrace restaurant with counter-style service at the Grand Wailea Resort, Café Kula specializes in "Spa Nouvelle" cuisine. Guaranteed to remove the rubber tires around your waist acquired from the resort's famed luau. Fresh produce is delivered daily from Maui farmers. The menu is heavy on Kula tomatoes and Maui onions, fresh herbs, black beans and seafood, and light on fats and salt. Offered to guests are weekly cooking classes to apply these guilt-free techniques to the home stove. Features: outside dining, own baking. Credit cards: A, MC, V.

Caffe Ciao I and II $ ★★★

4100 Wailea Alanui Drive, Wailea, 96753, ☎ *(808) 875-4100. Associated hotel: Kea Lani Hotel.*
Italian cuisine. Specialties: White Truffle Pizza, grilled chicken breast with arugula.
Breakfast: 6:30 a.m.–1 p.m., entrées $5–$8.
Lunch: 10 a.m.–8 p.m., entrées $5–$8.
Dinner: 5–8 p.m., entrées $5–$8.

A stylish Italian bakery, gift shop, deli-and-café combination in the Kea Lani Hotel, Caffe Ciao I and II offers mid-priced breakfast, lunch and dinner opportunities for guests and nonguests. Eat inside or out, or purchase some take-home, made-from-scratch breads, breakfast pastries, house-cured meats and pastas. You can stock your hotel room or condo with a signature line of condiments by executive chef Steve Amaral. The indoor dining area is reminiscent of a café on the Via Veneto, with Roman columns, marble tables and a checkerboard floor. In the evening, dining al fresco is enhanced by hundreds of tiny lights twinkling in the surrounding trees. Among the specialties of the house are wood-fired pizzas and a number of pasta dishes. Features: outside dining, own baking. Credit cards: A, DC, MC, V.

Hana Gion $$$ ★★★

3550 Wailea Alanui Drive, Wailea, 96753, ☎ *(808) 879-4900. Associated hotel: Stouffer Renaissance Resort.*
Japanese cuisine.
Dinner: 6–10 p.m., entrées $17–$35. Closed: Thur.

The Stouffer Renaissance Resort's newest restaurant is a cozy, quiet, 64-seat restaurant featuring contemporary Japanese decor. This is the place to sample authentic regional cuisine from Kyoto. The attached sushi bar is also well thought of by visitors and residents alike. Features: own baking, private dining rooms. Reservations recommended. Credit cards: A, MC, V.

Humuhumunukunukuapua'a $ ★★★

3850 Wailea Alanui Drive, Wailea, 96753, ☎ *(808) 875-1234. Associated hotel: Grand Wailea Resort.*
Seafood cuisine.

Named after the unpronounceable (to us Haoles) state fish, "Humu" is a cluster of South Seas-style thatched roof huts on a tropical fish-filled, one-acre lagoon in the Grand Wailea Resort. The handcrafted restaurant, with fanciful railings made of *ohia* wood, serves Pacific Rim cuisine with an emphasis on (natch) seafood. The adjoining cocktail lounge boasts Maui's largest aquarium, and an unbeatable sunset

MAUI

view. Features: outside dining, own baking. Reservations required. Credit cards: A, MC, V.

Joe's Bar & Grill $$$ ★★★

131 Wailea Ike Place, Wailea, In the Wailea Tennis Club, ☎ *(808) 875-7767.*
cuisine. Specialties: Quesadilla with smoked salmon, goat cheese, and corn-and-avocado salsa, crab dip and pancetta.
Lunch: 11 a.m.–2 p.m., entrées $10–$20.
Dinner: 6–10 p.m., entrées $15–$25.
Joe and Beverly Gannon of the oh-so-hot Hailiimaile General Store have set up new digs, this time in the tony Wailea resort area. Recently opened for lunch, this is a place where you'll likely see a celebrity or two nibbling after a few tennis games (David "Baywatch" Hasselhoff has a home nearby). The restaurant, which features lighting design by Joe himself, offers a great view of the Wailea coast and its own superstars, the humpback whales (sounds like a rock band). You'll probably feel like a whale after feasting on one of Beverly's fabulous pies—such as apple walnut with cinnamon ice cream, black-bottom banana cream, or pina colada. Features: own baking. Reservations recommended. Credit cards: A, MC, V.

Kea Lani Restaurant $$$ ★★★★

4100 Wailea Alanui Drive, Wailea, ☎ *(808) 875-4100. Associated hotel: Kea Lani Hotel.*
International cuisine. Specialties: Chicken-coconut soup with kaffir lime leaf and kha ginger, petite filet mignon with venison sausage.
Dinner: 5:30–10 p.m., entrées $24–$30.

Overlooking the ocean, the Kea Lani Hotel's dressy, southern Mediterranean-style restaurant is open to the breezes. It offers gourmet dining and similar service, and indoor and outdoor tables are designed to face the setting sun. Very romantic. In good weather (which is most of the time), request a seat on the patio. The combination of light breezes, tiki torch lighting, and moonlight is intoxicating. Executive chef Steve Amaral's creates new menus monthly, featuring dewy-fresh produce grown on his organic garden on the grounds of the resort. He has more than 150 varieties of herbs, rare fruits and vegetables, including 18 kinds of mint and 30 types of hot peppers to choose from! He also pickles and bottles his own condiments, including a spicy mango barbecue sauce. Some potent libations could start the evening off with a bang, including the "Lava Flow"—a blend of light rum, pineapple juice, coconut, banana and strawberries. Several vegetarian selections are available each evening. Try the chef's four-course tasting menu for $49. Service is polished and extremely knowledgeable. Features: outside dining, own baking. Reservations required. Credit cards: MC, V.

Kincha $$$ ★★★★

3850 Wailea Alanui Drive, Wailea, 96753, ☎ *(808) 875-1234. Associated hotel: Grand Wailea Resort.*
Japanese cuisine. Specialties: 14-course kaiseki dinners, filet of salmon en papillote.
Dinner: 6–9 p.m., entrées $25–$35.
Descend one flight below the main lobby of the Grand Wailea Resort to this tranquil re-creation of a Japanese ryokan that features rocks blasted out of Mt. Fuji. You may never see a restaurant outside of Japan like this again, due to both "economic

and technological reasons." Indeed. Aside from elaborate 14-course kaiseki dinners that range from $40 to $300 per person, a new Continental menu has been added. For "only" $34 or so, you can taste grilled Angus tenderloin and shrimp provencal with duchess potatoes, or a delectable sauteed snapper on wild mushroom bordelaise with roasted pinenut and rice croquettes. There's also a sushi and tempura bar. As of this writing, the Grand Wailea's signature restaurant, The Grand Dining Room, is no longer open. Features: own baking, private dining rooms. Reservations required. Credit cards: A, MC, V.

Pacific Grill $ ★ ★ ★ ★

3900 Wailea Alanui Drive, Wailea, 96753, ☎ (808) 874-8000. Associated hotel: Four Seasons Resort Wailea.
Asian cuisine.

Go for the bountiful breakfast or salad-laden lunch buffets if you can't afford dinner. But you may miss out on the wonderful pan-Asian cuisine served in front of you at the Oriental exhibition kitchen. Seaside views, especially from a patio seat, are as delicious as the food. Features: outside dining, own baking, Sunday brunch, rated wine cellar. Reservations recommended. Credit cards: A, CB, DC, D, MC, V.

Raffles $$$ ★ ★ ★

3550 Wailea Alanui Drive, Wailea, 96753, ☎ (808) 879-4900. Associated hotel: Stouffer Renaissance Wailea.
cuisine. Specialties: Roast Lanai Venison with twin potatoes, poha berry and red currant sauce.
Dinner: 6:30–10 p.m., entrées $15–$21. Closed: Sun.

This elegant, marble-trimmed, third-floor dining room is the Stouffer Renaissance Wailea Beach Resort's signature restaurant. Fresh island seafood and venison from Lanai are among the offerings on the Pacific Rim menu. To start off a memorable meal, try the salad of North Pacific shellfish with papaya lime coconut dressing. Executive Chef Hector Morales offers a chef's special each evening. Cocktails until 11 p.m. Jazz entertainment Friday-Saturday from 7 p.m–10 p.m. Features: own baking, private dining rooms. Reservations recommended. Credit cards: A, MC, V.

Sea Watch Restaurant $$$ ★ ★ ★ ★

100 Wailea Golf Club Drive, Wailea, 96753, ☎ (808) 875-8080.
Pacific Rim cuisine. Specialties: Molokai French Toast, fresh fish several ways.
Breakfast: 8 a.m.–3 p.m., entrées $5–$9.
Lunch: 8 a.m.–3 p.m., entrées $5–$9.
Dinner: 3–10 p.m., entrées $9–$24.

Probably the most viewful restaurant in Maui, the Sea Watch is actually the clubhouse restaurant for the Wailea Golf Course. For those who been exposed to many dreadful, rubbery meals in golf clubs over the years, this indoor-outdoor eatery is a fabulous exception. Specializing in Pacific Rim cuisine, the Sea Watch also serves local-style breakfasts until 3 p.m. Eggs and things are accompanied by "two-scoop" rice. You can also have ono French toast made with Kanemitsu Bakery bread from Molokai. If you eschew breakfast, how about a fish sandwich? No ordinary fish filet here—you get whatever's fresh that day, served with ginger-scallion mayonnaise. At dinner, just try to get past the scrumptious appetizers such as Chinese five-spice crab cakes, smoked salmon Napoleon, layered with Maui onions, endive salad and dill creme Fraiche, or pot-stickers filled with scallops and shrimp, stir-fried shiitake mushrooms, tobiko caviar and orange sesame butter sauce. Chef Michael Baker is masterful with seafood, but there are also lamb, beef and chicken dishes. Just a sampling of the dessert cheesecakes: lilikoi with macadamia nut crust, or vanilla bean with crunchy almond crust. Features: outside dining, own baking. Reservations recommended. Credit cards: A, CB, DC, D, MC, V.

Seaside   **$$$**   ★★★

3900 Wailea Alanui Drive, Wailea, 96753, ☎ *(808) 874-8000. Associated hotel: Four Seasons Resort Wailea.*
cuisine. Specialties: Striped nairagi (marlin) with ginger-green onion sauce.
Lunch: 11:30 a.m.–3 p.m., entrées $7–$16.
Dinner: 6–9 p.m., entrées $21–$25.

The Four Seasons Resort recently invested $1 million to transform the poolside Cabana Café into Maui's only "full beachfront" restaurant. Among the new additions is a rotisserie, where island chickens are roasted whole and served with olive oil, rosemary and caper mashed potatoes. New executive chef George Mavrothallasitis is all excited about the unusual varieties of fish brought to his kitchen by Maui fishermen. Chef Mavro, one of the founders of Hawaiian Regional Cuisine, believes in handling the seafood as little as possible, "using fresh herbs and seasonings to bring out the true flavors." Sample the tombo, or fresh albacore tuna, served with a light sauce of capers, black olives and oregano tomatoes. For dessert, we recommend apple tart with rhubarb ice cream or chilled cheesecake souffle with lilikoi sauce. An excellent array of sandwiches (even a $9 jumbo hot dog), salads, vegetarian dishes and frozen yogurt are available at lunch. An extensive pupu menu is available from 3 p.m.–6 p.m. Features: outside dining, own baking, rated wine cellar. Reservations recommended. Credit cards: A, CB, DC, MC, V.

Seasons   **$$$**   ★★★★

3900 Wailea Alanui Drive, Wailea, 96753, ☎ *(808) 874-8000. Associated hotel: Four Seasons Resort Maui.*
Gourmet American cuisine.
Dinner: 6–9:30 p.m., entrées $17–$35.

Service, ambience and views are all sublime at this, The Four Seasons' main dining room. The regionally influenced menu showcases contemporary U.S. cuisine. What was already a good thing can only reach the stars since renowned chef George "Mavro" Mavrothalassitis took over the resort's kitchens. Dancing every evening until 10:30 p.m.. Features: outside dining, own baking. Jacket requested. Reservations recommended. Credit cards: A, MC, V.

Upcountry

Keokea

Grandma's Coffee House   **$**   ★★

End of Highway 37 on the way to Tedeschi Vineyard, Keokea, ☎ *(808) 878-2140.*
American cuisine. Specialties: Coffees, pastries, sandwiches.
Breakfast: 7 a.m.–2 p.m., entrées $3–$7.
Lunch: 11 a.m.–5 p.m., entrées $3–$7.

A cute, family-operated coffee house in a little hamlet near Haleakala Volcano gets a big thumb's up from many visitors and locals. Besides the coffee drinks (cappuccino, caffe latte), Grandma's has yummy soups, sandwiches and fresh-baked desserts. Also food to go. Features: own baking. Reservations not accepted.

West Maui

Kaanapali

Hula Grill $$$ ★★★★

2435 Kaanapali Parkway, in Whalers Village, Kaanapali, 96761, ☎ *(808) 661-3894.*
Seafood cuisine. Specialties: Wok charred Ahi, homemade ice cream sandwich.
Lunch: 11 a.m.–5 p.m., entrées $10–$13.
Dinner: 5–9:30 p.m., prix fixe $12–$23.

Peter Merriman, a founding member and current president of the Hawaii Regional Cuisine chef's society, offers some of the best fish on Maui in a lovely beach house setting off Kaanapali Beach. On summer evenings, just before the sun sets, there's no better place for dining than in the outdoor Barefoot Bar, (open from 11 a.m.– 11 p.m.) which is right on the sand. A number of appetizers, sandwiches, salads and pizzas from a kiawe wood-fired oven are served here. Seafood is showcased throughout the large menu; a typical starter is a dim sum of scallop mousse and chunks of lobster, folded in a gyoza wrapper, then poached and sautéed, and served with guava plum sauce. Fish-haters will gravitate toward the small but hearty selections of steak, chicken and pork chops. Merriman swears that he offers absolutely "the best" prime New York steak, served with herb butter, roasted tomato and Maui onion rings. For lunch, choices include small and "bigger" salads, sandwiches and pizza from the kiawe wood-fired oven; these go as low as $6.95 for a pineapple and jalapeno pizza with mozzarella and provolone. Save the best for last: the homemade ice cream sandwich, which consists of ice cream between two brownies covered with raspberry sauce. See if you can stand up afterwards. Sometimes free desserts are offered to repeat visitors. Features: outside dining, own baking, private dining rooms. Reservations recommended. Credit cards: MC, V.

Kaanapali Beach

Cook's at the Beach $ ★★★

2365 Kaanapali Parkway, Kaanapali Beach, ☎ *(808). Associated hotel: The Westin Maui.*
American cuisine.

Accented by a free Polynesian revue each evening (except Sunday), this casual, poolside restaurant features an all-you-can-eat prime rib buffet (from 6 p.m.–9 p.m.) for $22.95. A salad bar plus a choice of fish, chicken and other dishes are included. Japanese specialties and a "health conscious" menu are alternative choices. Features: outside dining, own baking, late dining. Credit cards: A, MC, V.

Lahaina Provision Company $$$ ★★★

200 Nohea Kai Drive, Kaanapali Beach, 96761, ☎ *(808) 661-1234. Associated hotel: Hyatt Regency Maui.*
Seafood cuisine.
Lunch: 11:30 a.m.–2 p.m., entrées $12–$25.
Dinner: 6–11 p.m., entrées $12–$25.

The "provisions" in this super-nosher's delight is the Chocoholic Bar in the evening and the tropical seafood spread and salad bar at lunch. Add to that an alfresco, garden setting overlooking two of the Hyatt's fantasy pools PLUS the blue Pacific. Are we in heaven yet? Sandwiches and grilled steaks are also featured. Attire is casual, but flip-flops are the minimum footwear. Features: outside dining, own baking, non-smoking area. Reservations recommended. Credit cards: A, MC, V.

Leilani's on the Beach $ ★★★

2435 Kaanapali Parkway, Kaanapali Beach, 96761, ☎ (808) 661-4495.
American cuisine. Specialties: Fresh fish, steak.
Dinner: 5–10 p.m., entrées $6–$10.

In Whaler's Village, Leilani's has its own kiawe-wood-fired ovens where ribs, chicken and fish are smoked daily. The seafood menu contains the freshest catch of the day, sizzled in lava rock broilers along with meats and fowl. Views are splendid. The service staff treats everyone like family. Light meals are served downstairs from 11:30 a.m. Features: outside dining, late dining. Reservations recommended. Credit cards: A, MC, V.

Mixed Plate $ ★★

2525 Kaanapali Parkway, Kaanapali Beach, ☎ (808) 661-0011. Associated hotel: Kaanapali Beach Hotel.
American cuisine. Specialties: International buffets.
Breakfast: 6 a.m.–2 p.m., entrées $8–$10.
Lunch: 10 a.m.–9 p.m., entrées $8–$10.
Dinner: 5–9 p.m., entrées $8–$10.

Located in the former Koffee Shop at the Kaanapali Beach Hotel, Mixed Plate is one of the better dining bargains on Maui. For only $7.95, which includes a salad bar, beverages and dessert, you get to choose from a buffet of international specialties that change depending on the day of the week. For example, Tuesday is Japanese Day, with tempura, chicken katsu and stir-fry dishes on the menu. If you want to try Hawaiian food without going to an expensive luau, show up on Aloha Friday, when you'll get to taste poi and laulau. On weekends, a combo of all cultures can be sampled. In the evenings, between 4–7 p.m., early bird specials include prime rib AND a dinner buffet for only $9.95. Reservations not accepted. Credit cards: MC, V.

Nikko $$$ ★★★

100 Nohea Kai Drive, Kaanapali Beach, ☎ (808) 667-1200. Associated hotel: Maui Marriott.
Japanese cuisine. Specialties: Teppanyaki dinners, sushi, sashimi.
Dinner: 6–9:30 p.m., entrées $22–$40.

This cheery, Japanese restaurant in the Benihana-style, features the usual knife-wielding dervishes posing as chefs. One of Maui's oldest ethnic restaurants, Nikko now features sushi, sashimi and teriyaki combos in addition to its teppanyaki menu. All dinners come with miso or tori soup, Nikko salad, a shrimp or scallop appetizer, steamed rice and teppanyaki veggies, and green tea. Among the desserts, if green tea ice cream doesn't suffice, one can choose from chocolate macadamia nut pie, fresh fruit in plum wine or chocolate sushi—this trompe l'oeil sweet consists of cooked rice and white chocolate rolled into a sushi shape, and topped with a "fish" of fresh fruit, served with mango sauce. Banzai! Features: own baking. Reservations recommended. Credit cards: A, CB, DC, D, MC, V.

Swan Court $$$ ★★★★
200 Nohea Kai Drive, Kaanapali Beach, 96761, ☎ *(808) 661-1234. Associated hotel: Hyatt Regency Maui.*
International cuisine.
Breakfast: 6:30-11:30 a.m., entrées $14–$35.
Dinner: 6–10 p.m., entrées $14–$35.
Japanese gardens, waterfalls and, yes, swans gliding gracefully past your table are the highlights of one of Hawaii's (maybe the world's) most romantic restaurants. The Pacific Rim-Southwestern cuisine is excellent as well, though it needn't have to be. If you can't afford dinner, at least try it for the breakfast buffet or Sunday brunch. Evening attire (e.g. jacket and tie) is suggested, but not required. Piano music until 11 p.m. Features: outside dining, own baking, Sunday brunch. Reservations required. Credit cards: A, MC, V.

The Villa Restaurant $$$ ★★★★
2365 Kaanapali Parkway, Kaanapali Beach, 96761, ☎ *(808) 667-2525. Associated hotel: The Westin Maui.*
Seafood cuisine.
Dinner: 6–9 p.m., entrées $17–$35.
A visually stunning restaurant in a visually stunning resort, the Villa is a waterland of lagoons where pink flamingos play. The tropical libations are just as colorful. A special place for a dream date. Oh, and the food? It's Pacific Bistro cuisine and fresh, top-notch island seafood. Wear your fanciest duds. The Sound of the Falls, the resort's former premier restaurant, is now open only for Champagne Sunday brunch from 10:30 a.m.–2 p.m. Features: outside dining, own baking, Sunday brunch, rated wine cellar. Reservations recommended. Credit cards: A, MC, V.

Kahana

Erik's Seafood Grotto $$ ★★★
4242 Lower Honoapiilani Highway, Kahana, ☎ *(808) 661-3123.*
Seafood cuisine. Specialties: Cioppino, ahi salad, burgers, steamed clams.
Lunch: 11:30 a.m.–2 p.m., entrées $8–$15.
Dinner: 5–10 p.m., entrées $8–$15.
Open for lunch and dinner every day, Erik's has been catering to area diners and lucky Kahana Villa condo dwellers for nearly 15 years. The seafood-heavy menu hasn't changed much since the days of the late owner, Erik Jakobsen, who formulated many of the original dishes, including clam steamers and coco pie. There's an attached oyster bar where you can stay put or start your meal with steamed clams, a sashimi platter, oysters "a la Erik" or barbecue shrimp. The main restaurant menu features bouillabaisse or Italian cioppino served atop a steamy mound of fettuccine. Lighter eaters will enjoy the seared ahi salad with wasabi dressing. Meat-eating friends won't be disappointed in the hefty burgers served on French rolls, filet mignon or rack of lamb. Erik's is open for early-bird specials from 5–6 p.m. Another branch has opened in Kihei, at the Kamaole Shopping Center. Reservations recommended. Credit cards: A, MC, V.

MAUI

Roy's Kahana Bar and Grill $$$ ★★★

4405 Honoapiilani Highway, in the Kahana Gateway Center, Kahana, ☎ *(808) 669-5000.*
International cuisine. Specialties: Dark chocolate soufflé, Roy's grilled Szechuan baby back ribs, smoked and peppered duck.
Dinner: 5:30–9 p.m., entrées $15–$27.

With the opening of Roy's Kahana Bar and Grill (on the second floor of the Kahana Gateway Center), superstar chef Roy Yamaguchi declared he was "returning home" to Maui, where he visited his grandparents as a child. Obviously, hungry Mauians enthusiastically welcomed him back; shortly after opening, Roy's was declared Maui's "overall best" restaurant. Like its big brother in eastern Honolulu, the high-ceilinged, 140-seat restaurant wraps around a copper-enclosed open-view kitchen. Decor includes handmade koa wood tables and a changing exhibit of local art. A huge menu includes innovative starters, salads, "imu-baked" pizzas, meats, game and pastas. On the dessert tray one may find such belt-busters as "peachy apple" cobbler, pineapple cheesecake and a fabulous dark-chocolate soufflé. Most people love Roy's, but there are a few grumbles about the gushy wait staff (better than getting the cold shoulder) and overpriced wines. Features: own baking, rated wine cellar, non-smoking area. Reservations recommended. Credit cards: MC, V.

Roy's Nicolina Restaurant $$$ ★★★

4405 Honoapulani Highway, in the Kahana Gateway Center, Kahana, Just north of the Kapalua Airport, ☎ *(808) 669-5000.*
Pacific Rim cuisine. Specialties: Original Dark Chocolate Souffle, individual baked imu pizzas.
Dinner: 5:30–9 p.m., entrées $15–$27.

Opened by Roy Yamaguchi, the godfather of Pacific Rim (he calls it "Euro-Asian") cuisine, Roy's Nicolina is the twin sister to, and sits side-by-side with, Roy's Kahana Bar and Grill. Both of these shopping-center locations share the same seasonally fixed menus, and high-energy atmosphere, but each offers its own nightly specials. Recently, executive chef Jacqueline Lau, who created the individual "imu-baked" flatbread pizzas, a special feature, departed for Roy's new place on the Big Island, Roy's Waikoloa Bar and Grill. Lau told me that the pizzas will remain on the menu. Some of the innovative toppings include Kula tomato, basil and brie with caramelized onions, and spinach and seafood marinated in tequila with black beans, cheddar and chunky guacamole sauce. Don't leave without visiting what the restaurant calls "Pastry Land." The devilish original dark chocolate soufflé (20-minutes' preparation time) with a liquid chocolate center is killer-good. Features: own baking, rated wine cellar, non-smoking area, private dining rooms. Reservations required. Credit cards: A, MC, V.

Kapalua

Jameson's Grill and Bar $$$

200 Kapalua Drive, Kapalua, ☎ *(808) 669-5653.*
American cuisine. Specialties: Steaks, seafood.
Lunch: 11 a.m.–3 p.m., entrées $5–$13.
Dinner: 5–10 p.m., entrées $18–$24.

MAUI

Too new to review at press time, the former Kapalua Grill and Bar, which overlooks the 18th hole of the Kapalua golf course, is now Jameson's Grill and Bar, an off-shoot of the classic Jameson's by the Sea on Oahu's North Shore and in Kailua-Kona. An outdoor patio has been added. New management will keep some of the old menu standbys, including J.J.'s baked artichokes, great burgers, Australian rack of lamb with garlic, Dijon mustard and madeira sauce, shrimp and scallop Linguine and fresh fish, but will add the most popular Jameson's dishes, such as Black Angus meats and poached opakapaka in white wine with garlic hollandaise. Stay tuned. Features: outside dining. Reservations recommended. Credit cards: A, D, MC, V.

Sansei the Sushi Bar $ ★★★

115 Bay Drive, in the Market Shops, Kapalua, ☎ *(808) 669-6286.*
Asian cuisine. Specialties: Sushi, Asian-style grazing menu.
Dinner: 5:30 p.m.–2 a.m., entrées $5–$13.

Sansei the Sushi Bar, which opened in the old Market Café location at the Kapalua Shops, brings some light-hearted (and low-priced) fun to this rather tony, staid resort area. Not strictly a sushi bar (raw-fish haters, come back!), Sansei offers a number of traditional Japanese as well as Euro-Pacific dishes served family style, to share at table. Among the yummy items are shrimp and pork pot-stickers, fried Maryland soft-shell crab, seared ahi over Kula greens, and crispy Long Island duck with homemade apricot chutney and Szechuan peppercorn salt. It's also one of the few places in the area that stays open way past the witching hour (sushi served until 1 a.m.). We hope this grazer's paradise will thrive. Features: late dining. Reservations recommended.

The Anuenue Room $$$ ★★★★

One Ritz-Carlton Drive, Kapalua, 96761, ☎ *(808) 669-6200. Associated hotel: The Ritz-Carlton Kapalua.*
French-Hawaiian. Specialties: oven roasted onaga, grilled Kona lobster, paniolo glazed lamb rack.
Dinner: 6:30–9:30 p.m., entrées $17–$35. Closed: Mon., Sun.

Responding to grumbles that the old name of this restaurant, The Grill, didn't live up to its lovely setting, management changed it to the Anuenue Room, which means "rainbow." The menu, table settings and decor were updated as well. The new menu is Hawaiian by way of Provence, directed by executive chef Patrick Callarec and overseen by chef Craig Cannole. A changing exhibit of island art enhances the gorgeous room with a landscaped patio and three sliding glass walls that offer views of Oneloa Bay, Molokai and the third hole of the Bay course. Try the chef's signature menu of three courses plus an "amuse bouche" and a glass of wine for $49 per person. Features: outside dining, own baking, rated wine cellar. Reservations required. Credit cards: A, MC, V.

The Bay Club $$$ ★★★

1 Bay Drive, Kapalua, ☎ *(808) 669-8008. Associated hotel: Kapalua Bay Hotel & Villas.*
Seafood cuisine. Specialties: Salads tossed table-side, chef's catch of the day.
Lunch: 11:30 a.m.–2 p.m., entrées $14–$25.
Dinner: 6–9:30 p.m., entrées $14–$25.

Established in 1977, this beautiful, award-winning seafood restaurant sits above Kapalua Bay, which was voted the United States' best beach. Both lunch and dinner in the newly renovated dining room or terrace offer a spectacular view of Molokai and Lanai. Lunch features salads tossed at table-side, including regular or seafood Cobb, with bay shrimp, scallops, smoked salmon, diced avocado and more with an herb dressing, or Caesar, served as is, or with grilled chicken or shrimp. You can also order from a tempting sandwich menu. Come nightfall, whatever fresh fish the chef has prepared is recommended. One recent offering included kiawe-smoked grilled swordfish, portobello mushrooms and Maui onions, served with shoestring "Yukon Gold" potatoes, covered with a light sauce of Calvados cream. There's also a small menu of meat and poultry dishes. Service is excellent. Features: outside dining, own baking, rated wine cellar. Reservations required. Credit cards: A, MC, V.

The Terrace   **$**   ★★★★
One Ritz-Carlton Drive, Kapalua, 96761, ☎ *(808) 669-6200. Associated hotel: Ritz-Carlton Kapalua.*
Asian cuisine. Specialties: Grilled shutome in a lemon grass essence, Peking duck with island honey and spices.
Specialty buffets (Chinese/Oriental, Italian and seafood) are offered three times a week, plus chef Wyatt Lo's Pacific Rim delicacies are featured at this panoramic restaurant encircled by glass doors that open to a patio. Sunday brunch is served from 10:30 a.m.–2:30 p.m. Features: outside dining, own baking, Sunday brunch. Reservations recommended. Credit cards: A, MC, V.

Lahaina

Avalon Restaurant   **$$$**   ★★★★
844 Front Street, Lahaina, 96761, .
Pacific Rim cuisine. Specialties: Chili-seared salmon tiki-style, Avalon summer rolls with Asian pasta, Caramel Miranda.
Lunch: 11:30 a.m.–2 p.m., entrées $9–$30.
Dinner: 3 p.m.–midnight, entrées $9–$30.

A relative old-timer on the Maui "Hawaii Regional Cuisine" scene, Avalon is the creation of husky, ponytailed Mark Ellman and his sister Gerry. A former Hollywood caterer to the stars, Mark opened his theatrical Lahaina restaurant in 1988. Quite a few slumming celebrities show up from time to time to nosh at this noisy eatery facing a courtyard, where tables are a little close together, and the service is sometimes pretentious. But Ellman's healthy cuisine is consistently good, and no more over-the-top than some of his competitors in the Pacific Rim arena. Most feature local produce from nearby farms. Prices are also reasonable for a trendy operation. A nice-size salad such as classic Chinese chicken, with haiku baby greens, crispy rice noodles, and macadamia nuts tossed in ginger sesame vinaigrette, or a vegetarian gado-gado salad with tofu and coconut peanut sauce, will only set you back $11–12. There is a mini-menu of sandwiches, including a cheeseburger (!) with taro chips. Go all out and order the house signature dish, chili-seared salmon, tiki style, which is a layered salad of mashed potatoes, eggplant, salmon, greens, island and tomato salsa with plum vinaigrette. Angus steak, Australian rack of lamb and fresh fish of the day are also good choices. Patrons rave about the fresh-fruit mai tais.

Well-chosen wine list; also wine by the glass. Features: outside dining, own baking, rated wine cellar, non-smoking area, late dining. Reservations recommended. Credit cards: A, MC, V.

Cheeseburger in Paradise $ ★★

811 Front Street, Lahaina, ☎ *(808) 661-4855.*
American cuisine. Specialties: Burgers, Philly Cheesesteak.
Lunch: 11 a.m.–11 p.m., entrées $6–$12.
Dinner: 11 a.m.–11 p.m., entrées $6–$12.

Arguably the best known burger place in Maui, Cheeseburger in Paradise is correctly named, if only for the breathtaking location. Almost everyone gets an ocean-front seat, so maybe it doesn't matter that the cheeseburgers, although large, are tasteless. But that's about the only problem. There are many other items to choose from, including great onion rings and potent tropical drinks. Recently added to the menu are some enticing chicken sandwiches, a Philly Chicken and Swiss, consisting of grilled chicken breast with a jumble of peppers, onions and Swiss and Cheddar cheese on top. A Cajun-style chicken sandwich comes from an original New Orleans recipe. For vegetarians, there are tofu and veggie burgers as well as baked, stuffed potatoes. One reader wrote to say that he thought that the owners were "really cool." Well, why not? They're in paradise, after all. Features: outside dining, late dining. Reservations not accepted. Credit cards: A, MC, V.

David Paul's Lahaina Grill $$$ ★★★★

127 Lahainaluna Road, Lahaina, 96761, ☎ *(808) 667-5117. Associated hotel: Lahaina Inn.*
International cuisine. Specialties: Tequila shrimp and firecracker rice, kalua duck.
Dinner: 6–11:30 p.m., entrées $16–$27.

Loaded with awards and accolades, this friendly and noisy Pacific Rim-Italian-Mexican-what-have-you (chef David Paul Johnson calls it "New American") restaurant is located in the sedate Lahaina Inn. The voluminous menu of tantalizing delights changes with the seasons, but returning diners (and they are faithful) can always expect such signature dishes as tequila shrimp with firecracker rice and fried maki sushi. The former wickedly combines rice, vanilla beans, chili oil, tequila, brown sugar and other spices with five fat tiger prawns. In the latter, prawns and a julienne of vegetables are wrapped in seaweed and quickly deep-fried. You get the picture. Desserts are made fresh daily; try the sample platter. David Paul's opens at 5 p.m. for complimentary cheese and more than 20 wines (there is a 1200-bottle collection) available by the glass. Entertainment on Friday and Saturday from 8:30 p.m.– 11 p.m. Features: own baking, rated wine cellar, non-smoking area, late dining, private dining rooms. Reservations required. Credit cards: A, MC, V.

Gerard's $$$ ★★★★

174 Lahainaluna Road, Lahaina, ☎ *(808) 661-8939. Associated hotel: Plantation Inn.*
French cuisine. Specialties: Shiitake and oyster mushrooms in puff pastry, lamb rack grilled with persillade crust.
Dinner: 6–9 p.m., entrées $24–$35.

A gracious little gem of a restaurant comfortably ensconced in a stylish inn that recalls New Orleans' French Quarter. Gerard's features Euro-Pacific cuisine backed by chef Gerard Reversade's classic French culinary techniques. Dining is especially lovely on the covered veranda or in a garden patio. The whole restaurant, including the dining room, has the feel of an old plantation, with white-wicker chairs and tables covered by tutti-frutti pink cloths. The seasonally changing menu is enhanced by a well-chosen wine list and a palate-cleansing sorbet served between courses. Don't miss anything prepared with wild mushrooms, including the signature dish of shiitake and oyster 'shrooms in puff pastry. Features: outside dining, own baking, rated wine cellar. Reservations required. Credit cards: A, MC, V.

Kimo's Restaurant $$$ ★★★

845 Front Street, Lahaina, ☎ (808) 661-4811.
American cuisine. Specialties: Prime rib, fresh fish, Original Hula Pie.
Lunch: 11 a.m.– 3 p.m., entrées $6–$10.
Dinner: 5:30–10:30 p.m., entrées $11–$20.
Well-established on the Maui restaurant scene, Kimo's occupies two floors in a building facing the water. The open-air, oceanfront lanai is a popular party spot, with its romantic sunset views. Lunch is mainly hearty sandwiches and salads; at dinner, a crowd of carnivores overwhelms the place for a monster portions of prime rib, which goes fast. There's also a substantial fresh fish menu. Another signature specialty is the Original Hula Pie, which the management swears is what "sailors swam to shore for." Kimo's isn't cheap, but all dinners come with Caesar salad, a basket of freshly baked carrot muffins, sour herb rolls and steamed rice. Children's menu and vegetarian specialties available. Features: outside dining, Sunday brunch, private dining rooms. Reservations recommended. Credit cards: MC, V.

Longhi's $$$ ★★★

888 Front Street, Lahaina, ☎ (808) 667-2288.
Italian cuisine. Specialties: Lobster cakes with red pepper sauce, prawns amaretto, spaghetti putana, steaks.
Breakfast: 7:30 a.m.–2 p.m., entrées $14–$25.
Lunch: 11 a.m.–10 p.m., entrées $14–$25.
Dinner: 5–10 p.m., entrées $14–$25.
Longhi's, specializing in seafood and Italian specialties, and a Maui landmark for almost 20 years, may be resting too comfortably on its cushy collection of laurels and awards. Many readers have found it uneven and disappointing, food-and-service-wise. Some are uncomfortable with the lack of a menu; servers come over to tables and recite the night's offerings. Still, that's the way it's always been done, and possibly the way it will remain. The place has its very loyal following, so owner-chef Bob Longhi shouldn't have much to worry about. Among the seafood dishes, a fine choice are the delectable prawns Amaretto, if they're on the menu. Desserts are all house-made and include airy soufflés. Longhi's is also open for breakfast; try the home-baked cinnamon rolls, washed down with excellent coffee. Features: outside dining, own baking, private dining rooms. Reservations recommended. Credit cards: A, D, MC, V.

Moose McGillycuddy's $$ ★★

844 Front Street, Lahaina, 96761, ☎ (808) 667-7758.
American cuisine. Specialties: Breakfast, burgers, fish and chips, fajitas, fish tacos.

Breakfast: 7:30-11 a.m., entrées $4–$9.
Lunch: 11 a.m.–4 p.m., entrées $8–$11.
Dinner: 4–10 p.m., entrées $8–$11.

The Moose isn't subtle—not with such tongue in cheek (we think) menu items as the Lassie Omelette, containing Kal Kan, liver snaps and bone chips that "must be eaten outside in a bowl." But it's a great place to party, and the people food is some of the most reasonable in Maui (two other locations on Oahu). Aside from the poochie special, there are 21 types of omelettes, all made with at least four eggs, ono (delicious) pupus, burgers, sandwiches and "Specialties of the Moose," which include fish and chips, fajitas and fish tacos. For dessert? Chocolate Moose—what else? The bar scene starts with happy hour daily from 3-6 p.m., when drinks are only a buck each. Reservations not accepted. Credit cards: MC, V.

Old Lahaina Café and Luau $$$ ★★★

505 Front Street, Lahaina, ☎ *(808) 667-1998.*
Polynesian cuisine. Specialties: Kalua pig, mahi-mahi, haupia.
Dinner: 5:30–8:30 p.m., entrées $60. Closed: Sun.

This renowned, authentic Hawaiian feast and entertainment extravaganza is even popular with local residents. Held on beachfront property that was once a royal estate, the Old Lahaina Luau features pretty good food, with kiawe-wood grilled steaks along with the expected kalua pig (roasted in an underground imu). Sit on the ground on woven mats and gaze out to sea while dancers arrive, seemingly out of nowhere, the old-fashioned way, in torchlit canoes. Beverages extra. Features: outside dining. Reservations required. Credit cards: A, MC, V.

Pacific'o $$$ ★★★

505 Front Street, Lahaina, ☎ *(808) 667-4341.*
Seafood cuisine. Specialties: Prawns and basil won tons, Ahi parfait, Banana "Imu Style" fish.
Lunch: 11 a.m.–3 p.m., entrées $8–$24.
Dinner: 5:30–10:30 p.m., entrées $8–$24.

Tucked away behind the New England-style 505 Front Street shopping center, Pacific'o offers cold mai tais and jazz on the beach four nights a week plus chef James McDonald's award-winning contemporary Pacific cuisine. The lunch and dinner menu features daily creations of soup, pasta and specials, with a strong emphasis on fresh fish. Chef McDonald's shrimp won tons served with both spicy sweet-and-sour sauce and Hawaiian mango salsa, placed first in the Taste of Lahaina contest in 1993; he won again the next year for his ahi parfait, which is cured fish mousse wrapped in a thin slice of ahi sashimi with watercress salad and passion-fruit dressing. Also terrific is fish of the day "imu" style, enclosed in a banana leaf with lemon grass pesto and vanilla bean sauce, and grilled. Meat-eaters will also be pleased with Peking duck, Kiawe-grilled New York steak, and assorted lamb and chicken dishes. Features: outside dining. Reservations required. Credit cards: A, MC, V.

Paniolo Coffee Company $

Lahaina Center, Lahaina, ☎ *(808) 661-8788.*
American cuisine. Specialties: Coffee drinks, snacks, sandwiches.
New espresso bar also has shave ice and blended frozen yogurt.

MAUI

Planet Hollywood   **$$**   ★★

744 Front Street, in the Pioneer Mill Building, Lahaina, ☎ (808) 667-7877.
American cuisine. Specialties: Smoked St. Louis Ribs.
Lunch: 11 a.m.–midnight, entrées $7–$20.
Dinner: 11 a.m.–midnight, entrées $7–$20.

Planet Hollywood is a showcase of TV and movie memorabilia, as opposed to rival
Hard Rock Café, which owes its soul to rock and roll. Oh, and food is served, too,
including investor Arnold Schwarzenneger's mother's apple strudel. Aside from
nachos, gourmet pizzas, salads, grilled meats, malts and rich desserts, the Planet
makes a concession to Hawaii by offering blackened ahi. Distractions include the
cyborg from *Terminator 2*, Mel Gibson's motorcycle from *Lethal Weapon III*, the
"Alien" creature and, if you can find it, Jack Lord's (book em Dan-o) police badge
from "Hawaii 5-O." Also featured is a souvenir area where everything from PH
backpacks to boxer shorts is available for purchase. Features: late dining, private din-
ing rooms. Reservations recommended. Credit cards: A, MC, V.

Napili

Koho's Grill and Bar   **$$**   ★★

5095 Napilihau Street, Napili, ☎ (808) 669-5299.
American cuisine.
Lunch: 11 a.m.–5 p.m., entrées $5–$9.
Dinner: 5–10 p.m., entrées $9–$15.

Relaxed and casual, Koho's offers two shopping center locations, one in Napili and
the other in Kahului, at 275 Kaahumanu Avenue. Both are combination sports bar/
restaurants with a family atmosphere; the Napili eatery also has a new game room
where patrons can throw darts and play pool. Pupus, plate lunches (with two-scoop
rice), Mexican dishes, sandwiches, old-fashioned milk shakes and burgers are served
all day. After 5 p.m., a fancier steak, chicken and seafood menu is offered, served
with soup or salad. Gooey, rich desserts are on the order of something called a
Kilauea Snowball, which is vanilla ice cream rolled in graham cracker crumbs, deep-
fried and served in a cinnamon tortilla with honey and walnuts. Can't you just feel
your waistline expanding? The Kahului location is open for breakfast daily from 7
a.m. Reservations not accepted. Credit cards: MC, V.

Maui Tacos   **$**   ★★

5095 Napilihau Street, Napili, ☎ (808) 665-0222.
Mexican cuisine. Specialties: Mexican fast food, soft-shell tacos.
Lunch: 11 a.m.–9 p.m., entrées $3–$7.
Dinner: 11 a.m.–9 p.m., entrées $3–$7.

Maui Tacos grew from one Napili location to four; all are located in high-trafficked
shopping malls. Brilliant. For under $7, (most average $2 or $3), you can feast on
a variety of enchiladas, tostadas, quesadillas, nachos, burritos and oh, yes, Maui
tacos. What's a Maui taco? It's a double soft-shell tortilla served with a base of
whole black or pinto beans. Fillings include chicken, steak (only Montana "natural
pride" beef is featured), fish or veggies. You can also have a single-shell taco, as well
as an old-fashioned "hard taco," the kind that bursts into pieces after one bite. Also

available are guacamole and chips, "surf" burritos named after Maui beaches, and a taco salad. All dishes are served à la carte. Reservations not accepted.

Olowalu

Chez Paul $$$ ★ ★ ★

Olowalu Village Road, Olowalu, Four miles south of Lahaina, ☎ *(808) 661-3843. French cuisine.*

Dinner: 6:30 and 9:30 p.m., entrées $22–$30.

Although it looks a little like a dive, this quiet, classic French restaurant in out-of-the-way Olowalu (Olowhere?) is considered one of the best on the island. The owner-chef is Lucien Charbonnier (love that name), and a single item on the menu, Waterzooi de Homard au Champagne, shows off his Belgian origins. Here is one of the few places left in Maui where you can order *escargots*, served like they do in the mother country, in their shells, with garlic butter. Only two seatings per night are available, so make sure you reserve. Features: rated wine cellar, private dining rooms. Reservations required. Credit cards: A, DC, MC, V.

Nightlife

You'll find more to do in the evenings on Maui than you would, say, on Kauai or the Big Island, but not nearly as much as over in Waikiki. Lahaina is the center of night life for the youthful set, with venues that include the **Hard Rock Café**, **Planet Hollywood** and **Moose McGillycuddy's**. Try **Blackie's Bar** (also in Lahaina) for hot jazz. Big names such as Mose Allison and Willie Nelson play at **Casanova Italian Restaurant**, in Makawao. Kaanapali has more to do for a broader range of ages, with much of the activity focused at the various hotels and resorts. One of the island's hottest **discos** is in the **Inu Inu Lounge** at Wailea's Maui Inter-Continental Hotel. For giggles, hit the Monday night **Comedy Club** at Maui Marriott (Kaanapali Beach Resort). The old **Pioneer Hotel** in Lahaina is a good drinkin' bar. **Maui Arts and Cultural Center**, in Kahului, is the venue for large concerts and other live entertainment. The **Maui Community Theatre**, **Baldwin Theatre Guild** and **Maui Youth Theatre** stage plays throughout the year, and various musical presentations are scheduled by the **Maui Symphony Orchestra** and **Maui Philharmonic Society**. During the summer, the **Kapalua Music Festival** brings fine musical groups to the island. Art lovers should visit Lahaina's galleries on **Art Night** (Friday evenings, 7–9 p.m.) when artists are on hand, along with drinks and snacks. Film buffs should plan to come in late November and early December when the **Inter-**

national Film Festival is on—most of the larger towns have local cinemas as well. Other entertainment consists of **Polynesian revues**, **luaus** and **sunset cruises**.

South Maui

Kihei

La Pastaria ★★

41 East Lipoa Street, Kihei, ☎ *(808) 879-9001.*
Jazz piano entertainment nightly except Fridays, when the mood changes to hip-hop and funk; Saturdays it's mellow time again with folk guitar.

Makena

Molokini Lounge ★★

5400 Makena Alanui Drive, Makena, 96753, ☎ *(808) 874-1111.*
Hours: 5–10:30 p.m.
Relaxing, comfortable lounge at the Maui Prince Hotel. Low-key music Hawaiian style daily. Entertainment alternates between a solo guitarist and a mellow duo.

Wailea

Aston Wailea Resort Luau

3700 Wailea Alanui Drive, Wailea, 96753, ☎ *(808) 879-1922.*
Hours: 5–8 p.m.
This oceanfront luau at Wailea's oldest resort (formerly the Maui Intercontinental-Wailea) is a recipient of the Hawaii Visitors Bureau's prestigious Kahili Award for perpetuating the "essence of Hawaii." Preceding a hula show and a performance by a world-champion fire-knife dancer, there's an *imu* (underground oven) and torch-lighting ceremony. Tariff includes an open bar with tropical libations. General admission: $26–$52.

Tsunami

3850 Wailea Alanui, Wailea, ☎ *(808) 875-1234.*
Hours: 9 p.m.–2 a.m.
Tsunami (means tidal wave) is the hottest and most expensive club in the most expensive resort in Hawaii, the Grand Wailea. It boasts laser lights, video monitors and a hydraulic dance floor. Stylish decor with an electrified ceiling, casting a pink-ish glow over everyone. Karaoke on Sundays and Mondays, free admission. Cover charge on Fridays and Saturdays when the club stays open until 4 a.m. General admission: $10.

West Maui

Kaanapali Beach

Clubs

The Comedy Club

100 Nohea Kai Drive, Kaanapali Beach, 96761, ☎ *(808) 667-1200.*
Hours: 8:30–11:30 p.m., Mon. only.

Local comics hit the boards and try to get you to laugh every Monday at the Lobby Bar of the Maui Marriott Resort; sometimes they succeed. The action moves to the Sports Page in Kihei on Tuesday at 8 p.m.

Nightlife

Makai Bar ★★

100 Nohea Kai Avenue, Kaanapali Beach, 96761, ☎ *(808) 667-1200.*
Hours: 4:30 p.m.–midnight.
This popular local watering hole, nestled darkly within the Maui Marriott Resort, has a reputation for having the best pupus in town. Oh, and there's live music nightly.

Maui Marriott Luau ★★★

100 Nohea Kai Drive, Kaanapali Beach, 96761, ☎ *(808) 661-5828.*
Hours: 5–8 p.m.
One of the better hotel luaus, the Maui Marriott's feast offers preshow entertainment, including lei-making, coconut cutting, ti leaf skirt-weaving and hula lessons. Copious all-you-can-eat buffet includes an open bar. A highlight is the fire dance performed by a Samoan chief. General admission: $48.

Tour of the Stars ★★★

200 Nohea Kai Drive, Kaanapali Beach, 96761, ☎ *(808) 661-1234.*
Hours: 8–10 p.m.
Nightly astronomy show atop the Hyatt Regency Maui, where guests can gaze through binoculars and a special, deep-space telescope (called "Big Blue") for a personal guided tour of the Hawaiian skies. Before the show, the hotel's "Director of Astronomy" gives everyone an orientation of what they're about to see. Pretty neat. Shows three times a night, seating limited to 10 people per show. Private viewings available. Reservations required. General admission: $12.

Lahaina

Clubs

Blue Tropix ★★★

Lahaina Center, Lahaina, ☎ *(808) 667-5309.*
Hours: 6 p.m.–2 a.m.
Closed: Mon., Thur., Fri., Sat., Sun.
This eclectic dance club and restaurant on the wharf in Lahaina features recorded music with a DJ Tuesday through Saturday and live reggae every Monday. Gender bender reviews on Sundays. Who knows what will happen? General admission: $5.

Nightlife

Pacific'o ★★★

505 Front Street, Lahaina, 9, ☎ *(808) 667-4341.*
Hours: 9 p.m.–midnight.
Closed: Mon., Tue., Wed., Sun.
Local publications have deemed the live jazz on the beach at Pacific'o restaurant the best on the island. The food ain't half bad either. The location is somewhat hidden away behind the New England-style 505 Front Street shopping center.

Shopping

Malls and **shopping centers** are poised in the larger towns such as Lahaina, Kahului, Wailuku, and Kihei, and feature icons such as **Woolworth's**, **Sears** and **Longs Drug Store**. Front Street, in Lahaina, is the tourist mecca of arts-and-crafts galleries, schlock souvenir shops, unique boutiques and one-of-a-kind specialty stores. **Wailea Shopping Village**, near Wailea Resort, houses a variety of upmarket shops and boutiques. **Whalers Village**, in Kaanapali, is home to about 65 exclusive outlets, including the Maui branches of **Louis Vuitton** and **Tiffany's**. In addition, all of the large hotels and resorts have their own shopping arcades. Although Lahaina boasts a large number of sleek **art galleries**, Paia—on the other side of the island—is the center for less-commercial local works. **Aloha** and **resort wear** can be purchased everywhere from Sears and Liberty House to small specialty shops. Pick up native **Hawaiian crafts** at **Lahaina General Store** (Lahaina), **Lahaina Scrimshaw** (Lahaina), **John of Maui & Sons** (Haiku, in Upcountry Maui), **Maui Crafts Guild** (Paia), **Lahaina Printsellers Ltd.** (six island locations) and elsewhere around the island. Take some Hawaiian taste home with you by purchasing already-passed-agricultural-inspection fruits, coconuts, macadamia nuts, Maui potato chips and other goodies—**Take Home Maui** (Lahaina) and **Paradise Fruit** (Kihei) are two reliable companies.

Central Maui

Kahului

Kahului Swap Meet ★★★

Puunene Road, Kahului.
Hours: 6:30 a.m.–noon, Sat. only.
An almost-free activity, this lively swap meet next to the Post Office in Kahului is where locals come to buy and sell everything you can think of, including clothing and jewelry. Way below normal retail, no overhead. General admission: $50 cents.

Makawao

Maui Hands ★★

3620 Baldwin Avenue, Makawao, *(808) 877-0368.*
Made on Maui arts and crafts by 150 local artisans. Wares range from fine art and prints to basketry, ceramics, woodwork and handcrafted jewelry. Another location in Kahului at the Kaahumanu Center, 275 Kaahumanu Avenue, Kahului, (808) 877-3369.

Paia

Katie's Place Gifts and Collectibles ★★

Corner of Hana Highway and Baldwin Avenue, Paia, 96779, ☎ *(808) 579-8660.*
Linen, lace, antique hula girls and Hawaiiana themed items are on offer here as well
as Maui Polo Club shirts. From August through October, stop by Maui Polo Club
outdoor field, where first chukker is at 1:30 pm.

Maui Crafts Guild ★★★

43 Hana Highway, Paia, 96779, ☎ *(808) 579-9697.*
Hours: 9 a.m.–6 p.m.
A co-op of about 30 island artists operates out of a restored old sugar plantation
store in Paia. The pottery, jewelry, baskets and other crafts are some of the best
you'll find on Maui.

Wailuku

Bailey House Museum Gift Shop ★★★

2374-A Main Street, Wailuku, 96793, ☎ *(808) 244-3326.*
Hours: 10 a.m.–4 p.m.
Tired of gaudy T-shirts and velvet paintings of whales that glow in the dark? For
some truly distinctive souvenirs of your trip, the Bailey House Museum's gift shop
offers the largest selection of books on Hawaiian history and culture, plus koa jewelry and lauhala baskets you won't see anywhere else.

Wailuku Antique Row ★★★

North Market Street, Wailuku, 96793.
This is a quiet business district that's virtually tourist-free. Locals come here to dig
up vintage treasures in stores sandwiched between banks and pawn shops. Some of
the better stores include Ali'i Antiques, at #158, for Hawaiiana as well as quality
Asian, European and early American antiques (☎ (808) 244-8012). Traders of the
Lost Art, at #159, specializes in ritual carvings, masks and musical instruments from
New Guinea. Also paintings, furniture, jewelry and clothing. Open 1 p.m.–6 p.m.
(☎ (808) 242-7753) Memory Lane, at #130, is the place to come for rare Aloha
shirts (☎ (808) 244-4196). Jovian Gallery, at #7, is not your father's gift shop!
Distinctive cards, one of a kind T-shirts and clothing, jewelry. Also a local artists'
showcase. You'll leave with something. Open Mon.–Sat. 10 a.m.–6 p.m. (☎ (808)
244-3660).

East Maui

Hana

Hana Coast Gallery ★★

Hotel Hana-Maui, Hana, 96713, ☎ *(808) 248-8636.*
Hours: 9 a.m.–5 p.m.
Special hours: 9 a.m.–9 p.m.; Wednesday-Saturday.
This 2500-square-foot gallery showcases the work of more than 50 of Hawaii's
(many from Hana) finest artists. There's quantity here as well as quality; bronze
sculptures, featherwork, oil paintings and lauhala jewelry.

Hasegawa General Store ★★★

On Hana Road, opposite the Chevron station, Hana, 96713, ☎ *(808) 248-8231.*
Hours: 8 a.m.–5:30 p.m.
Special hours: 9 a.m.–3:30 p.m. Sun.

Completely rebuilt after a fire, the Hasegawa General Store features the town's only automated teller machine, which was a big deal when it was installed two years ago in the old location just a stone's throw away. As much a historic landmark as it is a shopping resource, the store has been owned and operated by the same family since its founding in 1910 by the current owner's grandfather and granduncle. "As you walk through the doorway what a great surprise, there's a wonderful variety of merchandise," so goes the song written by Paul Weston about the store, which is crammed with a maze of merchandise everywhere you look. You can even buy three cassette versions of the Hasegawa General Store song, books, sarongs (one of Maui's largest selections) and most important, an oft-imitated, original custom-printed T-shirt proclaiming "I survived the Hana Highway." Celebrity sightings are common; Kris Kristofferson, Carol Burnett and Jim Nabors are among the notables with homes nearby.

Hina Malailena

Next to Wananalua Church, Hana.

A 10,000-square-foot shopping complex, named after Hana's guardian star, is scheduled to open in November 1996. Designed to look like an ancient Hawaiian village with buildings set on terraces, tropical landscaping and retaining walls made of lava rock, the center will be the biggest deal in Hana history. At press time, the only shopping available is in the historic Hasegawa General Store, or within the Hotel Hana Maui. The proposed shopping mall will have 16 to 18 shops and food outlets, as well as a bazaar area with space for entertainment, exhibits and demonstrations. Is Hana ready for this? Check for status.

Northwest Maui

Kahakuloa

Kaukini Ranch Gallery and Gift Shop ★★

On Route 340, east of Kahakuloa, ☎ *(808) 244-3371.*
Hours: 10 a.m.–5 p.m.

A pleasant route on a previously unpaved road near the secluded Hawaiian valley of Kakahuloa leads you to a gallery-shop owned and operated by the affable Karen Lei Noland. The gallery, which is situated in a ranch house owned by Noland's family since 1943, is a showcase of jewelry, ceramics and paintings by more than 40 Maui artisans and artists, including Noland herself. Drop in and "talk story" with Karen, who can answer your queries about the untrammeled north shore of west Maui. It's about an hour away from Lahaina.

South Maui

Kihei

Kihei Farmers Market ★★

61 South Kihei Road, Kihei.

Hours: 1:30–5 p.m., Tues. and Fri. only.

A farmer's market with an oceanfront setting, offering fresh produce as well as T-shirts, jewelry and more.

Upcountry

Kula

Curtis Wilson Cost Gallery ★★★

Haleakala Highway, Route 377, Kula, 96790, ☎ *(808) 878-6085.*
Hours: 8:30 a.m.–4:30 p.m.

Located in the Kula Lodge, on the highway to Haleakala National Park, this gallery features the work of Maui's foremost traditionalist painter, Curtis Wilson Cost. Although his originals are expensive, Cost's reflective, peaceful, detailed landscapes of upcountry life and its denizens are available in limited-edition prints, serigraphs, laser prints, T-shirts, sweatshirts and notecards at very reasonable prices.

Sunrise Market and Protea Farm ★★

Highway 378 off Keakulike Avenue, Kula, ☎ *(808) 876-0200.*

A refreshing stop on the way to the summit of Haleakala Crater. This market and flower farm features colorful protea growing in a walk-through garden. The fresh varieties last for weeks, and through the farm's unique process, dry beautifully, retaining their amazing colors. Purchase and ship home fresh flowers, dry wreaths, baskets and dolls.

Upcountry Harvest ★★

P.O. Box 480, adjacent to the Kula Lodge, Kula, 96790, ☎ *(808) 575-6470.*

Under new ownership, the former Kula Protea Gift Shop offers a wide range of protea flowers, both fresh and dried. These unusual flowering plants, from an ancient strain, are named after the Greek god Proteus, who, myths say, could assume many forms. About 50 varieties have been introduced to the slopes of Haleakala, where they flourish in the rich volcanic soil, warm cloudy days and cool nights. At Upcountry Harvest, owner Neil Waldo takes dried protea and forms these unworldly blooms into wreaths, flower arrangements and even hula dancers. Prints by some of Maui's leading artists, jewelry, ceramics, baskets, books and a variety of interesting items are for sale.

West Maui

Kaanapali Beach

Ka Honu Gift Gallery ★★

2435 Kaanapali Parkway, in Whaler's Village, Kaanapali Beach, 96761, ☎ *(808) 661-0173.*
Hours: 9 a.m.–10 p.m.

This well-established (28 years), family-owned gift shop specializes in handmade island products, wood items, unique koa-wood music boxes that play Hawaiian tunes, traditional quilts and pillow kits, soaps, perfumes and Maui potpourri. It's also Christmas here all year with a perennial collection of more than 3000 locally made ornaments, including a cute Santa in a grass skirt carrying a surfboard.

Whalers Village ★★★

Kaanapali Resort, Kaanapali Beach, ☎ *(808) 661-4567.*

Hours: 9:30 a.m.–10 p.m.

Recently expanded and renovated to the tune of $3 million, this shopping center features more than 70 shops and restaurants, and due to its location, many of them are on the posh side. Just added to the Chanel, Coach, Tiffany and Co., Louis Vuitton and Hunting World flock are Maui branches of the European leather lords Salvatore Ferragamo and Gucci. About 14,000 square feet of floor space has been added to accommodate new stores; ousting Chico's Cantina, one of Maui's most popular Mexican restaurants. Also six existing stores, including a branch of Maui Divers and Elephant Walk, have been given face-lifts, whether they were needed or not. Whalers Village is also home to the Whale Center of Pacific's two free museums.

Kapalua

Honolua Store ★★★

502 Office Street, Kapalua, 96761, ☎ *(808) 669-6128.*

Hours: 6 a.m.–8 p.m.

In 1983, after 65 years of business, and the retirement of Mr. Hew, the 72-year-old manager, this old pineapple plantation store was in danger of being shut down. But the owners of the Kapalua Resort kept it going, fixed it up (a lot) but kept the homey front porch. It sells everything from fresh fish to logo shirts as well as golf-related items. Condo owners and hotel guests stop in for vintage wines and gourmet takeout. You can also buy inexpensive (nothing over $6) breakfasts, sandwiches and plate lunches; when construction workers were building up the resort, the kitchen served up 489 lunches in a single day. Outside seating.

Lahaina

Hunt Gallery ★★

143 Lahainaluna Road, Lahaina, 96761, ☎ *(800) 538-3247.*

Hours: 10 a.m.–10 p.m.

This year-old gallery, located about a half-block from Front Street, features changing exhibits, original oils, acrylics, bronze sculptures, woodcarvings, ceramics and soapstone works by island artists.

Lahaina Arts Society ★★

649 Wharf Street, Lahaina, 96768, ☎ *(808) 661-0111.*

Hours: 10 a.m.–5 p.m.

Special hours: Saturday-Sunday, 10 a.m.–4:30 p.m.

This gallery operated by a consortium of Maui artists brings a plethora of generally fine art to the people. Housed in the historic old courthouse at the east end of Front and Wharf streets, you can also watch artists at work (and perhaps buy something) under the Banyan Tree on weekends and holidays.

Lahaina Printsellers ★★★

1221 Honoapiilani Highway, in the Lahaina Cannery, Lahaina, 96761, ☎ *(808) 667-7843.*

A well-known purveyor of antique maps and old prints, Lahaina Printsellers also offers hand-painted reproductions of the currently in-vogue menu covers made popular by Eugene Savage on the Matson liners *Lurline* and *Matsonia* in the 1930s. Every Monday, Wednesday and Friday, at 2 p.m., artist Stephen Strickland gives free demonstrations of antique engraving and printing.

Lahaina Scrimshaw   ★★

845 Front Street, Lahaina, ☎ *(808) 661-8820.*

Did you know that more scrimshaw (carved designs on whale bone, teeth and ivory) is found and purchased on Maui than anywhere in the world? Now you do. Find a complete selection of the real thing at this shop, including genuine whales' teeth, men's and women's jewelry, and framed original pieces. Also in Whaler's Village.

Fielding's Fascinating Maui Facts

A.k.a.	**The Valley Isle**
Main city	**Wailuku**
Flower	**Lokelani**
Color	**Pink**
Area	**729 square miles**
Length	**48 miles**
Width	**26 miles**
Population	**91,361**
Highest point	**Haleakala (10,023 feet)**

Maui Survival Guide

Getting There

Most Maui-bound flights stop first at Honolulu International Airport, though United, Delta and Hawaiian Air run direct flights to Maui from the mainland. Kahului Airport, two miles east of central Kahului, is the island's principal airport (servicing approximately 100 flights per day) and offers a full range of airport facilities. Airlines are **Aloha** (☎ *(808) 244-9071)*, **American** (☎ *(808) 244-5522)*, **Delta** (☎ *(808) 871-0882)*, **Hawaiian** (☎ *(808) 871-6132)*, **Island Air** (☎ *(808) 877-5555)* and **Mahalo Air** (☎ *(808) 877-7444)*.

About 50 flights per day operate out of **Kapalua-West Maui Airport**, situated between Kaanapali and Kapalua resort areas, and the best airport for West Maui visitors. Airlines served include **Air Molokai** (☎ *(808) 877-0026)* and **Island Air** (☎ *(808) 877-5755)*.

Very small **Hana Airport**, just east of Hana, is a remote airstrip serving visitors to Hana.

Two **ferry services** operate out of Maui: **Expeditions** (☎ *(808) 661-3756)* runs between Lahaina and Lanai five times daily ($50 round-trip); The **Maui Princess** (☎ *(808) 661-8397)* travels once-daily between Lahaina and Molokai ($50 round-trip).

Getting Around

Maui has no public transport and, unless you plan to stay put in one hotel or resort, a rental car is the best way to travel around the island. If you fly into Kahului Airport, you can take **Trans-Hawaiian Shuttle** (☎ *(808) 877-7308)* to Kaanapali resort and other West Maui areas. **Akina Tours** (☎ *(808) 879-2828)* shuttles between the airport and Kihei, Wailea and South Maui. For taxi service, contact **Yellow Cab of Maui** (☎ *(808) 877-7000)* or **A-1 Taxi** (☎ *(808) 667-5675)*. Fares are high: $30 to Wailea, $50 to Kaanapali, $65 to Kapalua. Car rental agencies are **Alamo** (☎ *(808) 871-6235)*, **Avis** (☎ *(808) 871-7575)*, **Budget** (☎ *(808) 871-8811)*, **Dollar** (☎ *(808) 877-2731)*, **Hertz** (☎ *(808) 877-5167)*, **National** (☎ *(808) 871-8851)* and **Thrifty** (☎ *(808) 871-7596)*.

A **free trolley** shuttles between **Kapalua-West Maui Airport** and Kaanapali hotels. **Taxis** should be waiting outside the baggage claim area. Fares are $7 to

Kapalua, $12 to Kaanapali and $60 to Wailea. Courtesy phones inside the terminal summon car-rental companies.

The Hotel Hana Maui shuttles its guests to and from isolated **Hana Airport**. There are no taxis and no buses. **Dollar Rent-a-Car** *(☎ (808) 248-8237)* and **Word of Mouth Rent a Used Car** *(☎ (808) 877-2436)*—a local company—are the two car-rental options in town.

Before renting a car, determine if you will need a **four-wheel-drive** vehicle. Many car-rental firms won't cover your off-the-beaten-path or upcountry excursions. Some of the standard companies, such as Hertz, carry four-wheel-drive vehicles, or try **Maui Rent A Jeep** *(☎ (808) 877-6626)*. Expect to pay a lot more than you would for a conventional car.

Roads in Maui are good, parking is easy. Several major byways traverse the island. The Mokulele Highway (Highway 350) will get you from the Kahu-lui Airport down to Ihei, Wailea and Makena on East Maui. The Honoapi-ilani Highway (Highway 30) runs from Wailuku down to Maalaea and along the coastal towns of Olowalu, Lahaina, Kaanapali, Kahana and Kapalua. For travel between Kahului and Haleakala, take the Haleakala Highway (Highway 37). And, of course, the most talked-about road on Maui is the **Hana Highway** (Highway 36) between Kahului and Hana—a 56-mile super-scenic route with more than 50 bridges and 600 twists and turns.

Taxis on Maui are metered and *not* cheap. They're suitable really only for short trips between hotels and shops or restaurants. Call ahead for service. Some of the 20 or so companies are **Yellow Cab of Maui** *(☎ (808) 877-7000, Kahului Airport)*, **West Maui Taxi** *(☎ (808) 667-2605, Lahaina)*, **Resorts and Kaanapali Taxi** *(☎ (808) 661-5285)*, **Alii Cabs** *(☎ (808) 661-3688, Lahaina)*, **Kahului Taxi Service** *(☎ (808) 877-5681)*, **Kihei Taxi** *(☎ (808) 879-3000)* and **Wailea Taxi** *(☎ (808) 874-5000)*.

Mopeds and bicycles are great for most Maui travel, though some of the big-ger hills can be difficult to negotiate, and heavy traffic and narrow shoulders can wreak havoc for cyclists. Rent mopeds (about $50 per day, $150 per week) from **Fun Rentals of Maui** *(☎ (808) 661-3053, Lahaina)*, **A&B Moped Rental** *(☎ (808) 669-0027, Honokowai)* or **Go Go Bikes** *(☎ (808) 661-3063, Kaanapali)*. Bicycles can run $10-25 per day, or $45–85 per week (racing bikes are highest). For rentals, contact **Fun Rentals** *(☎ (808) 661-3053, La-haina)*, **South Maui Bicycles** *(☎ 874-0068, Kihei)*, **Maui Mountain Bike Adven-tures** *(☎ (808) 669-1169, Honokowai)* or **Kukui Activity Center** *(☎ (808) 875-1151, Kihei)*.

And, on the other end of the transportation spectrum, how about a chauf-feured **limousine**? Call **Arthur's Limousine Service** *(☎ (808) 871-5555, Kahu-lui)*.

Visitor Information

Get local information from the **Maui Visitors Bureau** *(1727 Will Pa Loop, Wailuku 96793,* ☎ *(808) 244-3530)* or the **Maui Chamber of Commerce** *(26 Puunene Avenue, Kahului 96732,* ☎ *(808) 871-7711)*. You'll also find **information kiosks** located at Kahului Airport.

KAUAI

Horseback riding along scenic trails is a great way to see Waimea.

This island was known to the ancient Hawaiians as *Kauai-a-mamo-ka-la-ni-po,* which translates to "the fountainhead of many waters from on high and bubbling up from below" (a phrase that doesn't exactly roll off the tongue). A lot of modern-day Hawaiians from the other islands refer to Kauai—not flatteringly-as a place for "the newly wed or nearly dead." Well, of *course* a place called "The Garden Isle" is going to attract a fair percentage of romantics and retirees, but it also lures Eden-seekers, New Agers and Hollywood film crews who have long used this plot of paradise as a movie set. And it certainly lured Madame *Pele,* the volcano goddess herself, who made the island her first home. Kauai is, geologically, the oldest of the Hawaiian islands and the first to be populated (current tally is 50,947).

435

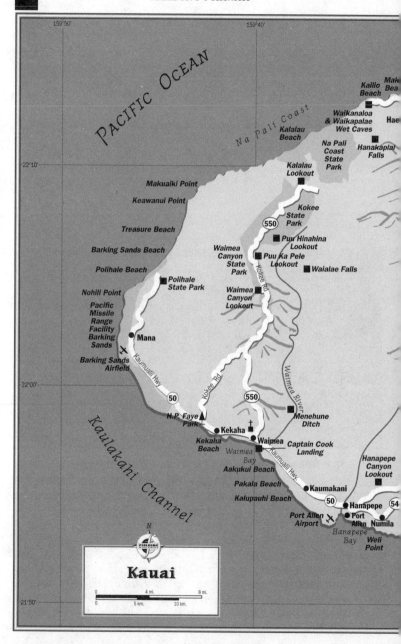

KAUAI

PACIFIC OCEAN

Na Pali Coast

Kailio Beach

Mak Bea

Waikanaloa & Waikapalae Wet Caves

Hae

Kalalau Beach

Na Pali Coast State Park

Hanakapial Falls

Kalalau Lookout

Makuaiki Point

Keawanui Point

Kokee State Park

550

Treasure Beach

Puu Hinahina Lookout

Barking Sands Beach

Waimea Canyon State Park

Puu Ka Pele Lookout

Waialae Falls

Polihale Beach

Polihale State Park

Waimea Canyon Lookout

Kokee Rd

Nohili Point

Pacific Missile Range Facility Barking Sands

Mana

Kaumualii Hwy

Barking Sands Airfield

Kokee Rd

Waimea River

50

550

Menehune Ditch

H.P. Faye Park

Kekaha

Waimea

Captain Cook Landing

Kekaha Beach

Waimea Bay

Kaumualii Hwy

Hanapepe Canyon Lookout

Aakukui Beach

Pakala Beach

Kaumakani

Kalupauhi Beach

50

Hanapepe

54

Port Allen Airport

Port Allen

Numila

Kaulakahi Channel

Hanapepe Bay

Weli Point

N

FIELDING

Kauai

0   4 mi.   8 mi.

0   5 km.   10 km.

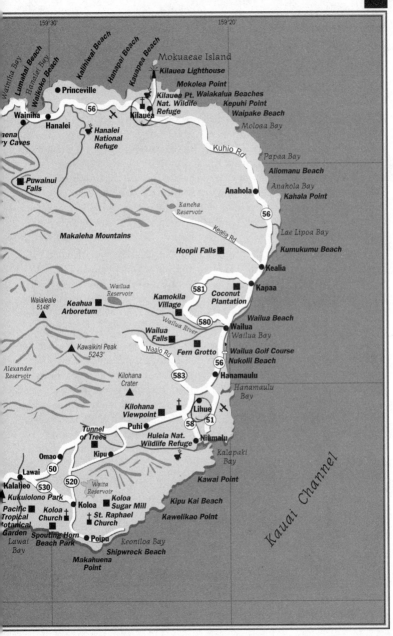

159°30' 159°20'

Wainiha Bay
Lumahai Beach
Hanalei Bay
Waikoko Beach
Kalihiwai Beach
Hanapai Beach
Kauapea Beach
Mokuaeae Island
Kilauea Lighthouse
Mokolea Point
Princeville
Kilauea Pt. Waiakalua Beaches
Nat. Wildfire
Kilauea   Refuge
Kepuhi Point
Waipake Beach
Wainiha
Hanalei
Moloaa Bay
Hanalei
National
Refuge
aena
ry Caves
Kuhio Rd
Papaa Bay
Aliomanu Beach
Puwainui
Falls
Anakola Bay
Anahola
Kahala Point
Kaneha
Reservoir
56
Makaleha Mountains
Kealia Rd
Lae Lipoa Bay
Hoopii Falls
Kumukumu Beach
Kealia
Wailua
Reservoir
Kapaa
Waialeale
5148'
Keahua
Arboretum
Kamokila
Village
581
Coconut
Plantation
580
Wailua Beach
Wailua
Wailua River
Wailua Bay
Kawaikini Peak
5243'
Wailua
Falls
Maalo Rd
Fern Grotto
Wailua Golf Course
56
Nukolii Beach
Alexander
Reservoir
Kilohana
Crater
583
Hanamaulu
Hanamaulu
Bay
Kilohana
Viewpoint
Lihue
Puhi
58
51
Tunnel
of Trees
Huleia Nat.
Wildlife Refuge
Niumalu
Kipu
Kalapaki
Bay
Omao
Kawai Point
Lawai
50
Kipu Kai Beach
Kalaheo
530
520
Waita
Reservoir
Kukuiolono Park
Koloa
Koloa
Sugar Mill
Kipu Kai Beach
Pacific
Tropical
Koloa
Church
St. Raphael
Church
Kawelikao Point
otanical
Garden
Spouting Horn
Beach Park
Poipu
Lawai
Bay
Keoniloa Bay
Shipwreck Beach
Makahuena
Point

Kawai Point

Kawai Channel

KAUAI

Kauai's first known settlers, the pre-Polynesian *Menehune*, were apparently anything but romantic or retiring. They were reputedly short (two- to three-feet all), muscle-bound South Pacific elflike creatures (possibly remnants from Lemuria, the legendary lost continent) who possessed amazing engineering skills—which they practiced only between dusk and dawn—and harbored supernatural powers. Their mysterious disappearance is still a subject bandied about from classrooms to cocktail parties.

Captain James Cook's arrival and departure is no mystery. In 1778, Cook cruised into Waimea Bay on the south shore—the first Hawaiian island he stopped at—and it didn't take long before the whole cruel world knew about the islands. When Kamehameha the Great went on his "unifying" spree, Kauai was the last holdout—the island farthest from all the others and, therefore, saved from the ravages of warfare. When the island was turned over to the king, it was through negotiation with King Kaumualii of Kauai, *not* the result of bloody battles. *And*, eventually, Kaumualii ended up throwing Nihau into the deal.

The 1800s brought all kinds of goings-on: a Prussian smooth-talker convinced Kaumualii to build a Russian fort overlooking Waimea Bay (its remains still remain); the missionaries arrived—Protestants *and* Roman Catholics; the first sugar was planted on the island at Koloa in 1835, followed by the islands' first successful sugar refinery; and leprosy made its unwelcome appearance.

Kauai came out of World War II relatively unscathed, taking a minimal hit at Nawiliwili Harbor, but not much else. Agriculture continued to thrive, sweetened not only by sugar production but by successful tries with beef, papaya, sugar, taro, macadamia nuts, coconuts, fruit and other crops. Life went on peacefully until the 1960s, when developers set their sights on the island, first constructing a hotel in Wailua, then spreading out to Poipu, Princeville and other areas. The economy continued to be fueled by agriculture, the military machine and especially by the influx of tourists (no matter what their reason for visiting).

In 1992 came Hurricane Iniki. Goodbye tourism. Iniki demolition-derbied into the island, causing extraordinary damage and devastation, scaring the tourists off to *anywhere else*, leaving locals to clean up the considerable mess. The islanders rallied to the cause, banding together to put their Garden Isle back in shape, the outcome being a re-energized destination and big plans for the future. Before Iniki hit there had been a strong anti-development movement on the island. Afterwards, however, many residents realized they badly needed those tourist dollars coming in and tried to be more amenable. The fairly-agreeable-to-all solution has been to favor low-rise developments, clustered in pockets (rather than spread abysmally from one side of the island), and to steer visitors toward ecotourism and local culture.

Though Kauai hasn't yet recovered fully from Iniki's onslaught (some hotels are still closed, various buildings remain boarded up), the island has bounced back to its lush, green, exquisitely beautiful, Garden-Isle condition—good enough to please all you romantics and retirees.

Bird's-Eye View

Round-shaped Kauai, the fourth-largest and northernmost of the major Hawaiian islands, lies about 100 miles northwest of Oahu and has the distinction of being the only island without a view of any other land. Sitting at the center are Mount Kawaikiki (5243 feet), the island's highest spot, and Mount Waialeale (5148 feet), the "wettest spot on earth" with an average rainfall of about 470 inches per year! Geologically the oldest of the Hawaiian islands, 549-square-mile Kauai (35 miles long and 25 miles wide) is also geologically the most stunning tribute to Mother Nature, Madame *Pele* or *whomever*, a land of magical beauty at almost every turn. Most of the Kauai's mushy, wet and steep interior is inaccessible and there is no road encircling this island, either. Located on the sunny south coast is Lihue, the principal town and main airport location; the Poipu resort area; popular white-sand beaches; a barrage of sugar plantation towns; Waimea, Captain Cook's landing place, and spectacular, rainbow-hued Waimea Canyon (also known as the "Grand Canyon of the Pacific"). Above the canyon, is cool (sometimes cold) Kokee State Park. The 14-mile-long Na Pali Coast, on the western slopes of Waimea Canyon, is a rugged, dramatic area of 4000-foot-high sea cliffs that tower above wild surf—with no way to get to it except by boat, helicopter or some very narrow (and arduous) trails. Above Lihue, along the east coast (or coconut coast), are Wailua town and its Wailua River (Hawaii's only navigable river) and Wailua River State Park (with the Fern Grotto and Wailua Falls, two faves on the tourist circuit), more glorious beaches, the Coco Palms Resort, Kapaa and other sleepy towns, and Anahola Beach Park—a top choice on the swimming and camping circuit. Up on the north coast, in the Hanalei district, are Kilauea Point (the northernmost place of all the major Hawaiian islands), a frenzy of exquisite beaches, taro fields, semicircular Hanalei Bay and the chic (i.e., quiet and expensive) Princeville resort area. Ahead are the wet and dry caves, the village of Haena and Haena State Park, and beaches that double as movie sets.

Nature Guide

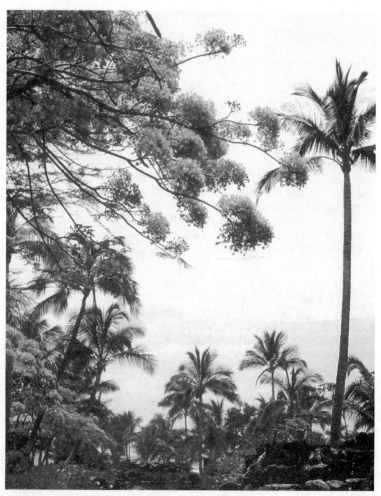

Lush Kauai lives up to its "Garden Isle" nickname.

The Garden Isle (also called "Garden of Eden") lives up to every expectation of bloom and birdie. Plant life and feathered friends thrive in the lush greenery, and even many endangered species still dwell on Kauai, particularly inland areas around Alakai Swamp and Mount Waialeale. Unfortunately, in the indigenous flora and fauna must compete for space with—like the other islands—the many species that have been introduced over the past couple of centuries.

Search the upper forests for the nearly extinct *nukupu'u*, the *i'iwi* and the *pueo* (Hawaiian owl). The Alakai Swamp shelters species such as the *o'u* and Hawaiian creeper, while the indigenous elepaio can be found around Kokee. Waterbirds include the *alae ula* (Hawaiian gallinule), *alae ke'oke'o* (Hawaiian coot), *ae'o* (Hawaiian stilt), *moli* (Laysan albatross), *ua'u kani* (wedge-tailed shearwater), great frigate bird, white-tailed tropic bird and red-footed booby. House finches, the golden plover, the cattle egret, the western meadowlark, the common mynah, and the northern cardinal are among the common introduced species.

Introduced fauna includes black-tailed deer, feral pigs and goats, ring-necked pheasants, doves, quails and that highly destructive mongoose.

Fielding's Beach Finder

Kauai's fabulous, drop-dead beaches were made more so by the demon Hurricane Iniki, which swooped in, cleaned them up and plumped them full of fresh white sand. This is the dream island for beach lovers—beaches to surf, swim, snorkel, comb and hide away at. The stuff movies are made of, or—in this case—*at*. Scenes from *The Thorn Birds*, *Jurassic Park* and *The South Pacific* were all filmed on Kauai sands.

The sunny south shore beaches are best in winter for swimming, surfing, bodysurfing and snorkeling, as summer months can see high surf. The opposite applies on the north shore (where the movies were made) when winter months pull wild surf conditions and hazardous swimming. In summer, however, the north shore becomes a favorite swimming spot. Eastern shore beaches are best left alone, particularly in winter when rip currents and rough surf roll in. Before you hit the water, ask locals or contact the **State Department of Land and Natural Resources** (☎ *(808) 241-3446*) or the **County Department of Parks and Recreation** (☎ *(808) 241-6670*).

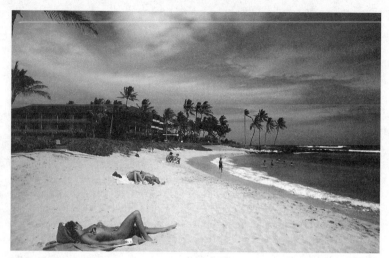

Poipu Beach is the favorite of the resort crowd.

Kalapaki Beach

Located near Lihue.

One of Kauai's best with a sheltered bay, gentle waves and a good place to learn or brush up on surfing, boogie boarding or windsurfing. Lifeguards, rest rooms and showers are on hand.

Hanamaulu Bay

A little farther up the coast, this is a less crowded option.

Around Wailua

Lydgate Beach Park

A good pick for families who want to beachcomb, picnic, snorkel and swim (if it's not too windy). Facilities include rest rooms, showers and a playground.

Kapaa Beach and Waipouli Beach

Near Kapaa.

These are beaches are on either side of town.

Donkey Beach

Offers a bit more seclusion at the end of sugarcane road, with white sands, good surfing, dangerous swimming in winter months and no facilities.

Anahola Beach Park

For safe swimming and snorkeling, try this beach at the south edge of Anahola Bay. Rest rooms, showers and camping with permit are available.

On the South Shore

Poipu Beach Park

The favorite of the resort crowd with white sands, shady palms, and good surfing, swimming, and snorkeling. Showers, rest rooms, lifeguards, nearby deli, and (usually) lots of people.

Brennecke's Beach

Off Ho'owili Road.

This was—pre-Iniki—one of Hawaii's best bodysurfing sites. With its sandbar blown to smithereens, its still good for strong bodysurfers, particularly in summer months. No facilities.

Salt Pond Beach Park

In Hanapepe.

Another family favorite for safe swimming, windsurfing and picnicking. Rest rooms and showers.

Kekaha Beach Park

West of Kekaha.

Offers more good swimming, surfing, snorkeling and—horrors!—*dune buggying* (watch out where you lay your body down!). No facilities.

Polihale Beach

Through the sugarcane fields at the end of a dirt road.

Affords great views of the massive Na Pali cliffs but the rip currents are usually too strong for anything else. Again, watch out for those dune buggies! No facilities.

Along the North Shore

Kalihiwai Beach

North of town.

Usually a good swimming and bodysurfing venue. No facilities.

Anini Beach

On the Hanalei side of Kalihiwai Bridge.

A perfect spot for beginning windsurfers, swimmers and snorkelers. Rest rooms, showers, picnic area.

Hanalei Beach Park

North of Hanalei

A choice spot for Na Pali coast views, experienced surfers and anyone who would like to just laze their life away. Rest rooms, showers.

Lumahai Beach

West of Hanalei.

This is where Mitzi Gaynor, in the movie "South Pacific," washed some man out of her hair—though she could've saved some time by throwing him into the treacherous rip currents (swimming in summer months, *only*). No facilities.

Haena State Park

Just beyond Haena.

Offers prime surfing in winter and swimming in summer. Rest rooms, showers; Tunnels Beach, near Haena at the end of a dirt road, is a good bet for swimming and snorkeling. No facilities.

Ke'e Beach

Where the road comes to an end.

This beach marks the head of the Kalalau Trail and is popular for summer swimming and snorkeling and winter oohing and aahing. Rest rooms, showers.

Adventure Guide

Kauai's drop-dead gorgeousness and profusion of natural features make it a winner for adventure both on land and in the sea.

Treks, particularly into the remote wilderness, should be at the top of the list for any avid hiker. Kauai's most famous *de rigeur* excursion is the rather strenuous **Kalalau Trail**, an 11-mile (one way) trek leading from near **Ke'e Beach** to **Kalalau Beach**, on the **Na Pali Coast**. On the way to this spectacular beach, you'll pass the lushest of lush—rainforest, deep valleys, steep cliffs, clear streams, choruses of birds, a botanical garden's worth of flora and heart-stopping views upon views.

Fern Grotto is a popular tourist excursion.

You'll be able to choose from a wide variety (about 45 miles) of trails in **Kokee State Park** above **Waimea Canyon**. Take the 100-yard **Cliff Trail** for a fantastic ogle at the multi-colored canyon, or continue along the 1.5-mile **Canyon Trail** past waterfalls and forests, to an even *more* impressive lookout. Experienced hikers might want to take the 2.5-mile **Kukui Trail** down to the canyon floor and then along the three-mile **Koale Canyon Trail** that traverses the Koale Canyon's southern reaches. The 3.5-mile **Kawaikoi Stream Trail** will take you along a trout stream, old cedar and redwood groves, and plenty of stunning scenery. Another strenuous hike is the 3.5-mile **Alakai Swamp Trail** into Hawaii's largest swamp that will reward you with a close-up look at indigenous bird and plant life, as well as a lot of bog, rain and mud. Check in with **park headquarters** before attempting *any* hikes.

Obtain information of trail conditions as well as free maps from the **Department of Land and Natural Resources** *(State Parks Division, 3060 Eiwa Street, Lihue, HI 96766, ☎ (808) 241-3444)*.

Campers can choose from free areas on **State Division of Forestry** trails, those under the auspices of **county and state parks** (which include Kokee State Park, Polihale State Park and several beach parks) or one of the "unofficial" sites tucked along hideaway beaches. Keep in mind that those official sites require campers to have tents, as well as permits. Get information and permits for state parks from the **Department of Land and Natural Resources** (above), or for county parks, contact the **Division of Parks and Recreation** *(4193 Hardy Street, Lihue, HI 96766, ☎ (808) 241-6670)*.

Check the calendar before **diving and snorkeling**. If it's winter, you'll probably be limited to the more docile south shore but, come summer, don't miss the premier waters of the north shore. Off Poipu, **Sheraton Caverns** afford divers archways and lava tubes to explore (watch for turtles and bright Hawaiian lobsters). Northwest of Hanalei Bay, **Oceanarium's** cove is filled with archways, ridges and pinnacles teeming with brilliantly colored tropical fish and coral. **Cannon's Reef**, also on the north shore, is another good spot with lava tubes, passing turtle parades, and plate coral to be discover. **Snorkelers** should try the waters at **Poipu Beach Park**, **Salt Pond Beach Park**, **Haena State Park**, **Ke'e Beach**, **Anini Beach**, **Pakala Beach** and **Kekaha Beach**. **Windsurfers** lean toward **Anini Beach** and **Kalapaki Beach**, while **sailboarders** favor **Anini Beach** and **Haena State Park** as well as **Poipu Beach Park**. **Ocean kayakers** paddle the **Huleia River** (leading into the wildlife sanctuary) or around **Hanalei Bay** (or brave the Na Pali Coast). **Boating** is popular (and often the only way) for exploring **Wailua State Park**, **Menehune Fish Pond**, the **Fern Grotto** (good for water-skiing), **Hanalei** and **Huleia National Wildlife Refuges**, and a variety of other no-other-way-accessible areas. Organized excursions are available for of the above water adventures (see "Sports" below).

Surfers should talk to locals and heed all warnings—the sea can be danger-ous and demonic during those winter months, particularly on the north shore (with, of course, the best surfing). Top spots include **Tunnels**, **Donkey Beach**, **Anahola Beach**, **Pakala Beach** and the east end of **Hanalei Bay**. For surf conditions, call **KUAI Surfline** (☎ *(808) 335-3611*).

What Else to See

Natural attractions are the big sightseeing lure on Kauai—canyons, swamp land, steep cliffs, verdant valleys, rainbows, prisms, grottoes and such. If you're looking for tropical glitz, stick to Honolulu and Waikiki.

Around **Lihue**, you can explore the "downtown" section of this old planta-tion town and island commercial- and government center. **Kauai Museum** presents displays relating to the island's history, culture, and geology. Plea-sure craft and U.S. Navy vessels call in at **Nawiliwili**, over in the harbor, while sunners and swimmers drop in to nearby **Kalapaki Beach**. View an 1860s homestead at **Grove Farm**, settled by George Wilcox, a descendant of intrepid New England missionaries. Heading southwest from Lihue, you'll come to the **Menehune Fish Pond**, along the Huleia River—an engineering feat created by those leprechaun-esque *Menehune* dwellers. Close by is **Kilohana Estate**, a sugar-plantation-turned-visitor attraction, with carriage rides, tours, arts-and-crafts galleries, and various shops.

Along the **south shore**, Kauai's first sugar mill—circa 1835—sits at **Koloa** along with a variety of other restored 19th-century structures. Check out thousands of varieties of plants (including those growing in an authentic Ha-waiian garden) at **Kiahuna Plantation Resort and Gardens**. Next is the condo-land resort community at **Poipu** along with **Poipu Beach Park** and a few other noteworthy beaches. Watch water shoot from an ancient lava tube at **Spout-ing Horn Park**. Slightly inland, the **National Tropical Botanical Garden** protects almost 200 acres filled with plant life. **Kukuiolono Park**, above Kalaheo, af-fords great views of the area. Historic **Hanapepe Valley and Canyon Lookout** allow you to glimpse bits of days past, while the town of **Hanapepe** lets you see a setting from "The Thorn Birds" miniseries. The ancient Hawaiians har-vested their special "Hanapepe" salt at the ponds near **Salt Pond Beach Park**, where swimming and fishing are more the activities of today. You'll be de-parting from **Burns Field**, near the ponds, if you've signed on for a helicopter tour of **Niihau**—just a 12-minute flight away.

Aerial view of Hanalei Bay

West of Hanapepe, the remnants of **Fort Elizabeth** (or Russian Fort), built in 1817, immortalize the antics of German doctor Georg Anton Schaeffer. The **Menehune Ditch**, across Waimea River bridge, is a reminder of the intriguing engineering skills of those busy little elves. At **Waimea**, you're standing in the steps of Captain Cook, who made this his first Hawaiian landing site back in 1778. The missionaries followed in the early 1800s and constructed **Waimea Christian Hawaiian and Foreign Church**. Finally you've reached **Waimea Canyon**, the 10-mile-wide "Grand Canyon of the Pacific," rife with multicolored walls and sun and shadow play—and a *must* on the Kauai pilgrimage list. A few miles from the canyon lookout, **Kokee State Park** offers 4345 acres of nature-filled everything, with 45 miles of hiking trails covering the area. Catch a fantastic view (come early before it mists up) from 4000-foot-high **Kalalau Valley Lookout**. Ride the dirt road through sugarcane fields to reach remote **Polihale State Park**, an isolated beach that kisses the Na Pali Coast.

On the **eastern shore**, north of Lihue, **Wailua Falls** are twin waterfalls used as backdrop for the now-defunct "Fantasy Island" opening shots. You'll be able to spot *heiau* (ancient temple) ruins around the town of **Wailua** on the Wailua River. Family oriented **Lydgate Beach Park** is a good place to take a break for swimming and picnicking. Catch a cruise (with Hawaiian singalongs) from **Wailua Marina** for a jaunt into the very touristed **Fern Grotto**. See another plunging cascade at **Opaekaa Falls** then blast your brain into reality at Kapaa, Kauai's largest town. Up to the north, **Anahola Beach Park** is another popular swimming and picnicking area.

Along the more remote **northern coast**, first stop is the old plantation town of **Kilauea**, and nearby **Kilauea Point National Wildlife Refuge** (home to endangered birds, including the *nene*, Hawaii's state bird) and **Kilauea Lighthouse**. Ogle more glorious views at **Kalihiwai Valley Overlook**, then hit the sands or protected waters at **Anini Beach**. Next is **Princeville Resort** with its high-end hotel, condos, restaurants and golf courses. **Hanalei Valley Overlook**, across from the shopping center, lets you peek into taro fields and wildlife refuge from high above. Cross the one-lane, circa-1912 bridge into **Hanalei**, where you can visit the 1830s **Waioli Mission** and get a feel of the missionary lifestyle. Re-live your favorite *South Pacific* movie moments at **Hanalei Bay**, **Lumahai Beach** and **Haena State Beach Park** (but beware the strong currents). Near Haena, you'll no doubt want to explore the **Maniniholo Dry Cave** and **Waikapalae and Waikanaloa Wet Caves**. **Kee Beach** marks the end of the road as well as the beginning of the famous 11-mile **Kalalau Trail**. Visit the stone ruins of **Lahiau's Hula *Helau***, former dance floor of Laka, goddess of the hula. Continuing along Kalalau Trail, venture two miles to **Hanakapiai Beach**, or go the whole hog into the remotest-of-remote **Na Pali Coast State Park**.

East Shore

Kapaa

Beaches

Donkey Beach ★★★

Highway 56, just past the 11-mile marker, Kapaa.

This secluded, "swimsuit optional" white-sand beach is accessible only by foot, a casual 20-minute walk through sugarcane fields on a dirt road or by mountain bike (eight minutes). A local hangout, one used to be able to drive to it when the road was maintained by the Lihue Plantation Company, which still owns the land but no longer cultivates sugarcane. They've closed the road, even rolled boulders in front of the entry and put up "No Trespassing" signs everywhere, so come at your own risk. A popular gay beach in the '70s (it used to be a hippie beach), Donkey Beach is dangerous for swimming due to shore breaks and other hazards, but surfers and sunbathers love it.

Kealia Beach ★★★

Highway 56, north of the 10-mile marker, Kapaa.
Located between Kapaa Beach Park and Donkey Beach on Highway 56, this 150-foot-wide, half-mile-long beach is excellent for surfing, boogie boarding (on the north end), bodysurfing and frolicking in the sand. Very large sandbar.

Museums and Exhibits

Kauai Historical Society

4-241 Kuhio Highway, Kapaa, 96746, ☎ (808) 822-3373.
Hours: 10 a.m.–3:30 p.m.
Special hours: by appointment only. Closed: Sat., Sun.
Books, photos, archival material relates to Kauai. Learn how tourism and growth affects the island.

The Shows

Kauai Coconut Beach Resort Luau ★★★

Coconut Plantation, Kapaa, 96746, ☎ (808) 822-3455.
Hours: 6:30–10 p.m.
Closed: Mon., Wed., Fri.
The Hawaii Visitors Bureau award the coveted Kahili award to the Kauai Coconut Beach Resort for excellence in luauing. The festivities actually begin in the morning with the *imu* ceremony (guests are invited to watch). Here is where the pig, or *pua'a*, is prepared and buried in an underground oven, covered with banana and ti leaves to provide moisture and the delectable smoked *kalua* flavor. The pig is left to cook for the remainder of the day. The next time you'll see the porker is in the evening sometime after 6:30 p.m., when it's removed from the *imu* after a torch-lighting ceremony. The luau feast, besides the pig, includes cocktails and drinks, poi, sweet potato, lomilomi salmon, beef teriyaki, mahi-mahi and a variety of salads. The dessert spread features coconut cake and fresh fruit as well as haupia. Top-of-the-line, authentic entertainment follows, choreographed by Kumu Hula Kawaikapuokalani Hewitt, a renowned hula teacher, so you know you won't get schlock. General admission: $45.

Smith's Tropical Paradise Luau ★★★

174 Wailua Road, Kapaa, ☎ (808) 822-4111.
Hours: 6–9 p.m.
Closed: Tues., Thurs., Sat., Sun.
A little commercial (they all are), Smith's version is pleasant nonetheless, and reasonably priced for what you get. Walk through a 30-acre botanical garden, watch the *imu* ceremony, quaff cocktails and fruit juices, and pick through the buffet. The show is held at an open-air lagoon theater called a *halau*. The stage seems to float

on a lagoon, with a volcanic backdrop, and as the "volcano" erupts, Madame Pele rises out of the inferno. Included are dances from Hawaii, Tahiti, New Zealand and our favorite, the Samoan fire dance (How do they do it? Why do they do it?). General admission: $47.

Tours

Smith's Tropical Paradise

174 Wailua Road, Kapaa, 96746, ☎ *(808) 822-4654.*
Hours: 8:30 a.m.–4 p.m.
Smith's provides a combo thrill of walking through, or taking a tram through, a pleasant 30-acre garden and lagoons with a nightly luau and Polynesian show Monday, Wednesday and Friday at 6:30 p.m. (see listing). It's also a departure point for Wailua River cruises to the Fern Grotto (9 a.m.–3:30 p.m.) Times and prices below are for the gardens only. General admission: $5–$8.

Lihue

Beaches

Kalapaki Beach

In front of the Kauai Marriott Resort, Lihue.
A half-moon shaped, white-sand beach, Kalapaki Bay Beach, surrounded by Nawiliwili Harbor, is not the place to come for solitude or peace and quiet. Still, it's a perfect place for a swim, as any rogue wave action is tempered by a jetty. A favorite family beach. Lifeguard, free parking.

Children's Activities

Wally World

4359 Kalepa Street, Lihue, 96766, ☎ *(808) 246-8660.*
Hours: 3–6 p.m.
Closed: Tues.
Wally World, a Lihue "family fun" center, is notable for having the only bumper boat (similar to bumper cars) facility in Hawaii. Appropriately called "Splash and Bash," participants try to bump each other off, all in the spirit of fun, in aquatic bumper boats, around a 5500-foot pond. The understandably sturdy vessels are outfitted with modified Honda outboard motors. The eight-minute ride costs $3 per driver and $1 per passenger. Height requirement is 44 inches. Open until 9 p.m. Friday; Saturday, 10 a.m.–9 p.m.; Sunday, 10 a.m.–6 p.m. General admission: $3.

City Celebrations

Aloha Festivals

Rice Street, Lihue, ☎ *(808) 955-8411.*
This statewide, two-month-long fall festival honors the *makahiki*, the ancient Hawaiian time of music, dance and feasting, when war was not permitted. But there's also a not-so-hidden agenda: the festivals are meant to attract visitors to the islands after the summer rush. In 1996, the Aloha Festivals celebrated its 50th year. Each island takes a week off to party. A big parade, block parties, luaus, children's events, hula competitions and brass-band concerts are just some of the fun events.

May Day Hula Contest, Princeville, Kauai

Museums and Exhibits

Kauai Museum   ★★★

4428 Rice Street, Lihue, 96766, ☎ (808) 245-6931.
Hours: 9 a.m.–4:30 p.m.
Special hours: to 1 p.m. Saturdays. Closed: Sun.

More than 30 years old, this is the largest historical museum in the outer islands. Collections are housed in two adjacent structures: The Wilcox Building, the city's former public library, was built in the 1920s. It contains offices, the Museum Shop and five galleries used for temporary exhibits. Depending on your visit, you might see some fascinating photographic displays of historical photographs from the sugar plantation days, or Japanese woodblocks, ceramics, lacquerware and textiles, or perhaps some rare Hawaiian quilts. The Museum Shop is a destination by itself, and can be visited on its own (admission is therefore waived). One of the best on the islands, it's a repository of Hawaiian books, quilts, woodwork, Niihau shell leis, maps and more. Next door, the Rice Building contains a permanent collection, called "The History of Kauai." It manages to cover the geologic formation of the island, its changing cultures—from the ancient Hawaiians who lived off the land, to the history of sugar—all on two floors. A valuable community resource, Kauai Museum conducts classes in lauhala-weaving or quilt-making, hosts an annual summer crafts fair and sponsors activities for kids. Children under six free, six–17, $1. General admission: $5.

The Shows

Kauai Community College Performing Arts Center   ★★★

P.O. Box 343, Lihue, ☎ (808) 245-3408.

The Kauai Community Players and the Kauai Concert Society have a new home in this 550-seat theater. The $12 million center was severely damaged by Hurricane Iniki in 1992, shortly before its opening. It was rebuilt and opened three years later.

Tours

Air Kauai Helicopter Tours ★★★

3651 Ahukini Road, Lihue, 96766, ☎ *(808) 246-4666.*

Chuck DiPiazza, the owner-pilot, is the only guy that gets to fly the company's six-passenger ASTAR jet helicopter (why not—it's his ship!). Only one flight a day is offered. Called an executive tour, the hour-long adventure is as comfortable as it is exhilarating. The air-conditioned helicopter is equipped with a BOSE noise-cancelling headphone system, so you can hear the onboard narration clearly. All seats are forward-facing. Chuck has a perfect safety record, and readers who've flown with him say the ride is definitely worth it. General admission: $159.

Fly Kauai/Kumulani Air ★★★

Leaves from the Commuter Terminal, Lihue Airport, Lihue, ☎ *(808) 246-9123.*

Those who don't dig helicopters but would like to see Kauai's inaccessible wonders via an aerial tour can opt for a comfy ride in a sleek, deluxe, twin-engine Cessna 402 (up to nine passengers) or 206 (up to five passengers). There are no middle seats! Prices start as low as $49 for a 45-minute complete island tour, a "Jurassic special" that covers various sites seen in the movie of the same name, and a Three Island Tour flyby over Kauai, Niihau and Lehua Island (north of Niihau). General admission: $49 and up.

Grove Farm Homestead ★★★

Highway 58, one mile southeast of Lihue 96766, ☎ *(808) 245-3202.*
Special hours: tours 10 a.m. and 1 p.m.; Mon., Wed., Thurs. Closed: Tues., Fri., Sat., Sun.

Founded in 1864, Grove Farm, the old homestead of George Wilcox, scion of Kauai's wealthiest sugar-growing family, is now an 80-acre living history museum. Wilcox, the son of missionaries, applied his Yale degree to revolutionizing agriculture. He was the first to use irrigation in the cultivation of sugar, and transported cane to the mill by means of railcars (until he came along, oxen did the laborious, tedious work). George's last descendant, his niece Miss Mabel, willed upon her death in 1978 that the homestead would be opened to the public as a "living" museum. In 1980, the first visitors saw the home the way she left it, including beautiful but well-used furniture, the kind no one has the time to make anymore. The homestead and its grounds are a window to a tranquil past (at least from the owners' perspective), when Big Sugar was the center of the island's economy. Tours by reservation only; reserve at least two weeks in advance. Closed federal holidays and Jack Hall Day (Jan. 2). General admission: $5.

Kauai Lagoons Wildlife Tours ★★

South Seas Tour, 3901 Mokulele Loop, Lihue, 96766, ☎ *(808) 245-2222.*
Hours: 10 a.m.–4 p.m.

An outfit called South Seas Tours has assembled exotic animals from around the world, such as kangaroos, wallabies, monkeys, flamingos, llamas, gazelles and rare birds, which live on seven islands spread out on a mile-long waterway. The 45-minute boat tours on brass and wood Venetian mahogany launches run on the hour. South Seas Tours also offers outrigger canoe rides through the Lagoons. General admission: $14.

Kauai Mountain Tours ★★★
P.O. Box 3069, Lihue, 96766, ☎ (808) 821-0010.
The only concessionaire to take travelers exploring the back roads and interior depths of Na Pali Kona Forest Reserve and Waimea Canyon, Kauai Mountain Tours utilizes comfy, air-conditioned four-wheel-drive vans with seating for no more than 11 passengers. The seven-hour tour includes a continental breakfast and deli-style lunch. Not much walking required, but have broken-in shoes, a jacket, camera and binocs. Reserve at least a day in advance. General admission: $84.

Safari Helicopters ★★★
3225 Akahi Street, Lihue, ☎ (808) 246-0136.
Although many companies throughout the state are now flying the plush ASTAR helicopters, Safari's owner/pilot Preston Myers claims to have been the first to operate this "Cadillac of sightseeing helicopters" in Kauai. Myers, an interesting guy who flew "secret" missions over Laos and was even shot down over the "Golden Triangle," has an unblemished safety record (more than 30 years of flying experience and almost 10 on Kauai). Also unique to Safari Helicopters is the "SafariCam" video/sound system that records each tour by means of a trio of onboard video cameras. Safari offers three tours: the Deluxe Waterfall Safari, the Deluxe Island Safari and the Circle Island Safari. Routes vary according to weather conditions. Tours depart daily from Lihue Airport. Advance reservations are required; there's a 24-hour cancellation policy. General admission: $139–$179.

Puhi

Tours

Kilohana Plantation ★★★
Highway 50, Puhi, ☎ (808) 245-5608.
Hours: 9:30 a.m.–9:30 p.m.
Special hours: to 5 p.m. Sun.
Once the centerpiece of a 27,000-acre sugar tract, Kilohana (which translates as "not to be surpassed") is the name of both the grand estate and manor house belonging to grower Gaylord Parke Wilcox and his family. Built in 1935, the 15,000-square-foot Tudor-style house was the most expensive (if not the showiest) home ever built in Kauai. Painstakingly restored from vintage photographs, the main house and attendant structures have been given over to retail shops, art galleries and a restaurant named after the old patriarch. Visitors can wander for free (and freely) through 35 acres of tropical gardens, the former sugar workers' camp and farm. Herbs and vegetables from the garden are used in the restaurant. If you'd like to see the place in style, take a 20-minute ride in a fancy, 100-year-old carriage drawn by Clydesdale horses $7 for adults and $4 for children. Available Monday-Saturday from 11 a.m.–6:30 p.m.; Sundays to 5 p.m. Did you know that it takes a ton of water to produce a pound of sugar? You'll learn this and more on hour-long

tours of the sugarcane fields in a horse-drawn wagon available Tuesdays, Thursdays and Saturdays at 11 a.m. and 2 p.m. Other highlights include sugarcane tastings and inside tips about harvesting and processing techniques. Price is $21 for adults; $10 for children under 12 years. Reservations required, ☎ *(808) 246-9529.*

Wailua

Beaches

Lydgate Beach Park

Highway 56 to Leho Drive, Wailua.

An ideal family beach, Lydgate Beach Park features a huge enclosed stone seawater pool excellent for swimming year-round. What this means is that the open ocean beyond should be avoided for its strong currents and heavy surf. Don't scoff—many lives have been lost due to drownings. The beach itself is wide and sandy. Playground, changing rooms, rest rooms, showers, picnic facilities. Also in this area are the remains of the Hikina A Ka La *Heiau*—a circle of boulders surrounding a grassy, empty field. North of the *heiau* is a metal marker commemorating the site of *Hauola*, a City of Refuge.

Hiking

Nounou (Sleeping Giant) Trail ★★★

Kuhio Highway to Haleilio Road, Wailua.

After doing this hike, your kids can claim they had a picnic on a giant's chest! On the way you can tell them the story about the friendly (but always hungry) giant who befriended the *Menehunes*, Kauai's original "little people." In exchange for as much poi as he could eat, he hung around to protect his friends from their enemies. One day, full of food as usual, he lay down to nap and was out cold during a surprise attack by unfriendliest. The *Menehunes* tried to rouse him by throwing stones at him; he inadvertently swallowed one and choked to death. The poor guy didn't even know what hit him (yuk, yuk). The climb to this famous landmark is about 1.75 miles through a native Hawaiian forest and takes two hours round trip to complete. It helps to be in fairly good shape to do this hike, as it can get slippery. Ocean, mountain and river views, strawberry guavas to pick and eat reward the intrepid.

Historical Sites

Holoholo Ku Heiau

Highway 580, Wailua.

Located just past the shuttered Coco Palms Resort, this is believed to be the oldest *heiau* on Kauai. Dedicated to Ku, the ancient god of battle, the site is marked by a sacrificial stone on the southwest corner, where prisoners of war were offered up to appease him. Farther up Highway 580, at the top of the hill overlooking the Wailua River, is Poliahu *Heiau*, where the highest alii in the area lived and worshiped. Stones from the river were laboriously hand carried to the site, which was believed to have contained six separate structures in its heyday, from private spiritual communication towers to more mundane (but necessary) dining halls and storage rooms. A walk east off a dirt road leads to a path to a bellstone used to announce royal births at the Holoholoku *Heiau*.

Tours

Waialeale Boat Tour/ Fern Grotto Cruises   ★★

Up the Wailua River, Wailua, ☎ *(808) 822-4908.*

Hours: 9 a.m.–3 p.m.

Waialeale Boat Tours is one of two companies that offer trips up the Wailua River, to the legendary Fern Grotto, the site of many marriage ceremonies (the other company is Smith's Motorboat Company). The slightly clunky, oversize, flat-bottom riverboats leave daily from the Wailua River Marina on the south shore of the river. The ride to the Grotto is a pleasant, relaxing 40-minute trip. Guides point out sights along the way, including their namesake mountain. You'll probably be told that films like Elvis' *Blue Hawaii* and *Islands in the Stream* (from a Hemingway story) were filmed on this route. At the Grotto, guests take an easy, five-minute walk on a paved walkway to the mouth of the cave, dripping naturally with ferns. The natural acoustics enhance the obligatory performance of the "Hawaiian Wedding Song" and other ditties. Guides also relate ancient Hawaiian historical facts and legends through music and hula, plus an informative lecture about the plants and history of the area. Tours are 1.5 hours long and leave daily at 9, 9:30, 10, 10:30 and 11:30 a.m., and at 12:30, 1:30 and 3 p.m. The company also offers kayak rentals. General admission: $15.

North Shore

Anini

Beaches

Anini Beach County Park   ★★★★

Anini Beach Road, Anini.

A shallow lagoon surrounded by a protected, exposed reef allows for year-round swimming, which makes Anini unique on Kauai. Also a prime windsurfing spot, especially for beginners, who find the calm, steady breezes keep both them and their sails afloat. Campsites, BBQ pits, showers and pavilions. From April through early September, catch a polo game every Sunday at 3 p.m. at the Kauai Polo Field, just beyond the park toward the mountains. For more information on this "sport of kings," call ☎ *(808) 826-6177.*

Hanalei

Beaches

Hanalei Bay   ★★★★

Highway 56 to Weke Road, Hanalei.

A two-mile sandy crescent just behind the town of Hanalei, this gorgeous bay encompasses Waioli Beach Park, Hanalei Pavilion Beach Park and Black Pot Beach Park. All are excellent for swimming (exercise caution in winter), surfing, bodyboarding and sailing. Facilities include picnic tables, showers, rest rooms and parking. Lifeguard on duty.

Bali Hai at Hanalei Bay lives up to its reputation.

Ke'e Beach   ★★★★

From Hanalei, take Kuhio Highway to its end, Hanalei.

A primo snorkeling beach at the end of the road that leads to the Na Pali Coast State Park. There's more fish to be found here than anywhere on the north shore. The sandy-bottomed lagoon is surrounded by a coral reef that protects snorkelers from the ornery ocean. Fabulous for swimming in the summer; exercise caution in winter (and at all times). Rest rooms, shower, parking lot, lifeguard.

Lumahai Beach   ★★★★

A few miles past Hanalei Bay, Hanalei.

Gather your love some puka and other delicate shells for a necklace on this fabulous white-sand North Shore stretch. Aside from strolling and picture-taking, this is about the only safe activity on the beach where Mitzi Gaynor "washed that man right out of her hair" in *South Pacific*. Dangerous for swimming at all times, especially so in winter. Mighty waves break directly on the shore here, and there's no lifeguard to bail you out. To get there from Kuhio Highway, pull over at the west end of the point just beyond Hanalei Bay and walk down the trail through the lauhala trees to the east end of the beach.

Museums and Exhibits

Waioli Mission House Museum   ★★★

Highway 56, Hanalei, 96766, ☎ *(808) 245-3202.*
Hours: 9 a.m.–3 p.m.
Closed: Mon., Wed., Fri., Sun.

One of Kauai's first American-style houses, the Waioli Mission House was built in 1837 as the residence of the Rev. William P. Alexander. Before that, Alexander and his wife, Mary Ann, had tried valiantly to fit in with their Hawaiian flock by living in

Waimea Canyon, Kauai

Horseback riding, Kauai

Wailua Falls, Kauai

Hanea Beach, Kauai

a grass hut for two years. Later, other missionaries lived in the house, including Abner and Lucy Wilcox, who taught out of here for two decades. Their descendants eventually became the dominant landholders on the island. The Mission House was turned into a museum in 1952, and is on the list of the National Register of Historic Places. Also part of the original mission compound is the Waioli Social Hall, just in front of the house. This is the original mission church, built in 1841, and one of the best examples of Hawaiian architecture.

Parks and Gardens

Limahuli Garden ★ ★ ★ ★

Off Kuhio Highway, past Haena Beach Park, Hanalei, 96714, ☎ *(808) 826-1053.*
Hours: 9 a.m.–2 p.m.
Closed: Mon., Sat.

This magical, well-organized garden at the base of ancient cliffs was donated to the National Botanical Garden in 1994 by private owners. Part of a 900-acre forest reserve, Limahuli nurtures more than 300 varieties of endangered Hawaiian plants, some thought to be extinct, within its 17 acres. Highlights include the virginal Limahuli Stream, ancient taro patches and a 300-foot overlook to the ocean. For $10 you can wander on your own for two hours through a well-marked half-mile long loop trail, helped along by a pamphlet and identification markers. Guided tours are $15. Reserve in advance, as the gardens are limited to a dozen visitors per day. General admission: $10–$15.

Tours

Captain Zodiac ★ ★ ★

Box 456 (in Ching Young Village), Hanalei, 96714, ☎ *(808) 826-9371.*

In the 1970s, Clancy Greff (alias "Captain Zodiac") started taking groups of people along the Na Pali Coast on a sturdy, 23-foot inflatable Zodiac boat. Schools of imitators have spawned since then and have even improved on this idea (power catamarans that can maneuver into sea caves, etc.), but the Cap is still da "original." Offered are three- to four-hour morning and afternoon excursions along the fabled North Shore coast, venturing into sea caves, with a stop for snorkeling (weather conditions permitting). The most popular trip is the five-hour expedition, which adds on a visit to Nualolo Kai, site of an ancient Hawaiian fishing village, an excellent snorkeling spot. In season, whale-watching (December–April) and sunrise and sunset cruises (May–September) are available. Backpackers tackling the Kalalau Trail can take advantage of the Captain's drop-off and pick-up service (from Kalalau Beach) offered once a day in summer. General admission: $65–$115.

Na Pali Eco Adventures ★ ★ ★

Departs from Hanalei Bay, Hanalei, ☎ *(808) 826-6804.*

In our opinion, the best way to cruise the Na Pali Coast is in an inflatable Zodiac vessel, but for those with bad backs or who dislike a lot of bouncing around, Capt. Steve Cole's power catamaran might be the thing for you. The cat is designed to travel in and out of sea caves, and is also swift, allowing more time for exploring the area. All seats are forward-facing and have comfortable back rests. The politically correct tours are conducted by crews who are trained naturalists and environmentalists. Choose from a two-hour sightseeing adventure/dolphin-watching cruise (beverages provided), or a four-hour "Ultimate Snorkel Adventure," with instruction and snorkeling equipment, snacks and beverages included. Both leave at 7:15 a.m. and 12:15 p.m., seven days a week. Also recommended is Catamaran Kahanu, (808) 826-4596, open 6:30 a.m.–8 p.m. daily. Two tours are available, including a four-hour morning snorkel/whale watch (includes gear and snacks) or a 2.5-hour whale watch/sightseeing charter. Can't decide between a Zodiac or a power catamaran? Hanalei Sea Tours, ☎ (808) 826-PALI offers you a choice of both. You might have to break up family members, but it keeps the fur from flying. The three-, four- and five-hour tours include snorkeling gear, lunch and cold drinks, and cost from $55 to $110. Departures are from Hanalei daily; whale-watching via Zodiac from Nawiliwili Harbor from December to April. General admission: $65–$110.

Kalihiwai

Beaches

Kalihiwai Beach ★★★★

Off Kalihiwai Road west of Kilauea, Kalihiwai.

Although Kauai has a bevy of gorgeous strands, this bay beach with golden sand is a wow. There are no facilities, and it's usually uncrowded, used by local residents. Kalihiwai is like a warm bathtub in summer, perfect for sissy swimmers. A different story in winter, when surfers, bodysurfers, boogie-boarders and such take over the place. Rinse off the salt in a clear stream conveniently located at the end of the bay. Note: there are two Kalihiwai Roads off of Kuhio Highway; take the first one, or you'll have to ford the stream. Also off Kalihiwai Road (turn right off the first dirt road, you'll see a number of cars parked in a dirt lot) is not-so-secret Secret Beach, reached via a steep path that takes about 15 minutes (or five if you're a goat). One of Kauai's best "clothing alternative" beaches, and no wonder–secluded and lush, the surroundings are distinctly Garden of Eden-like. Miles of golden sand for strolling, swimming in summer only, snorkeling, surfing. No facilities.

Kilauea

Museums and Exhibits

Kilauea Point National Wildlife Refuge ★★★

One mile north of Kilauea 96764, ☎ (808) 828-1413.
Hours: 10 a.m.–4 p.m.
Special hours: call to make sure they're open. Closed: Sat., Sun.

A seabird and mammal refuge maintained by the U.S. Fish and Wildlife Service, the focal point is the historic lighthouse, built in 1913. This venerable structure guided commercial ships between Hawaii and the Orient for 62 years. Standing 52 feet high, the lighthouse's original oil lamp and Fresnel lens created a 250,000-candlepower beam that guided ships to shore from as far as 21 nautical miles away. It was replaced by an automatic version in 1976. The cliffs and hillsides off the point are home to the largest colony of seabirds in the main Hawaiian islands. Common sightings include increasingly rare redfooted boobies, nene geese, wedge-tailed shearwaters and, occasionally, a Laysan albatross. From December to May, visitors can be entertained by migrating humpback whales and perhaps a school of playful spinner dolphins playing court jester. General admission: $2.

Tours

Guava Kai Plantation ★★

Kuhio Highway, Kilauea, ☎ *(808) 828-1925.*
Hours: 9 a.m.–5 p.m.

If you've got the blahs, nothing's better for you than Vitamin C-packed guava (higher than oranges, even), a delectable yellow fruit with a pink interior and tons of seeds. At the 480-acre Guava Kai Plantation, where sugarcane once flourished, these babies are processed into juice (free samples), made into jams and jellies, and more. Plant tours given in summer only (off-season you can take a short nature walk that's pleasant but nothing special). Gift shop.

Na Pali Coast

Hiking

Kalalau Trail ★★★★

Haena State Park, Na Pali Coast, ☎ *(808) 241-3444.*

If you've hiked this trail, you've seen the "real" Kauai. The difficult, 22-mile (round trip) hike over five valleys will reward you with unparalleled views of the Na Pali Coast, magnificent waterfalls, and ancient Hawaiian ruins. Some folks settle for the abbreviated but still-strenuous hike from Ke'e Beach two miles to Hanakapiai Valley. Hanakapiai Beach has oceanfront campsites, a fresh-water stream and caves to explore. Swimming is pretty dangerous year-round. Those going the whole hog can spend the night here and go on four more miles to Hanakoa Valley the next day; then it's five more miles to Kalalau Valley at the end of the trail. Must-sees along the up-and-down trek include a viewful but wet foray to spectacular Hanakapiai Falls, with a natural pool, but beware of flash floods in inclement weather, and debris and fallen trees at all times. Before the trail ends at Kalalau Valley, there are three smaller valleys to traverse, such as Waiahuakua Valley, where ancient terraces farmed by Hawaiians now provide well-needed shelter. Note: Recommended for surefooted (it helps to have hooves), experienced backpackers in good to excellent shape, but everyone must be prepared for muddy, slippery conditions throughout the entire trail; sturdy boots with good tread are a necessity, as are plenty of sunscreen, insect repellent, backpacking equipment, a waterproof tent and drinking water—or boil water for five minutes. Permits are required for Hanakapiai, Hanakoa and Kalalau Valleys and are available from the Division of State Parks.

Princeville

Beaches

Hideaway's Beach ★★★

Trail starts right before the Princeville Hotel, Princeville.

You must be a surefooted hiker to get to this hidden gem (probably the reason it remains hidden), which is reached by a steep trail that tends to get washed out during winter rains. The beach also has an irritating habit of disappearing during this time. In the summer, Hideaways is perfect for all sorts of activities, including swimming and sunbathing; there's a protected lagoon for some excellent snorkeling. Facilities? Nah.

City Celebrations

Prince Albert Music Festival ★★★

Princeville Hotel, Princeville, ☎ *(808) 826-2286.*

Held in late May. Now in its second year, the two-day Prince Albert Music Festival is dedicated to the memory of Prince Albert, the only child of King Kamehameha IV and Queen Emma. The tragic prince died at age four in 1862. Featured are performances by classical musicians from around the world, masters of slack-key guitar and a statewide hula competition for boys. General admission: $20–$40.

South Shore

Koloa

City Celebrations

Koloa Plantation Days ★★★

Old Koloa Town, Koloa, ☎ *(808) 332-9201.*

Mid-July through August 4. This week-long celebration honors the birth of sugar plantations in Hawaii, with a parade, entertainment, crafts, games, sports tournaments, cooking demonstrations and a luau.

Tours

Capt. Andy's Sailing Adventures ★★★

Box 1291, Koloa, 96756, ☎ *(808) 822-7833.*

Cruise aboard the *Spirit of Kauai,* a posh, modern, custom-designed sailing catamaran with teak-trimmed modern cabins and freshwater showers. Leaving from Port Allen in Hanapepe (on Highway 541) or from Kukuiula Harbor by Spouting Horn, Capt. Andy's company was one of the first to conduct tours of the Na Pali Coast. Half-day winter whale-watching/snorkeling with state-of-the-art hydrophonic sound system to hear the whales' songs; Na Pali cruises in summer. Includes snorkeling equipment, instruction, buffet lunch (salads, sandwich makings, fruit, beverages). Also sunset sail with snacks and cocktails. Readers think he has a great crew. General admission: $40–$65.

Poipu

Beaches

Brennecke's Beach ★★★

One hundred yards east of Poipu Beach, Poipu.

Rocks have replaced the beach and underwater sandbars washed out first by Hurricane Iwa and then by Iniki (sand is supposed to be trucked in someday). These sandbars caused a perfect break that could handle waves up to 10 feet. Still attracts bodyboarders and bodysurfers (who have to contend with agro surfers) at all times of the year.

Mahaulepu Beach ★★★

Three miles from the end of Poipu Road, Poipu.
Hours: 7:30 a.m.–6:30 p.m.

To get to this remote, uncrowded, two-mile-long, white-sand beach, you'll have to drive through a rough cane road three miles east of Poipu Beach on Poipu Road. Turn right after the road "T's," pass the first turnoff leading to a gravel quarry, and pull up to the McBryde Sugar Plantation Guard Booth, where you sign a waiver. Actually three beaches in one (Kawailoa Bay, Haula Beach and Gillin's Beach), Mahaulepu was once an ancient Hawaiian fishing village. In 1796, King Kamehameha landed here to capture the island from Chief Kaumalii (he failed, but got his revenge later). Kawailoa is the first beach you come to; just south of Kawailoa past a lava field is Haula Beach and the Aweoweo sand dunes. North of Kawailoa is Gillin's Beach (so called for a supervisor of the Grove Farm Company, owner of the land, who built a home here). About 200 yards past a stream is a natural amphitheater. No facilities anywhere except for an unpaved parking lot.

Poipu Beach Park ★★★

Hoona Road, Poipu, 96756, ☎ *(808) 742-6722.*
Poipu Beach Park offers crystal-clear waters, near-shore snorkeling, safe swimming, wading and surfing. Families and the faint of heart love the natural kiddie wading pool. The palm tree-shaded lawn at the park is great for picnics or just relaxing. Surfing spots are slightly off-shore, where a reef provides perfect waves for beginner, intermediate and advanced surfers. Facilities include bathrooms, showers, picnic tables and pavilions. Brennecke's Beach Broiler operates a convenience store across the street. For contrast, take a walk along the shore (you'll have to clamber over some rocks) to beaches fronting the Stouffer Waiohai and Poipu Beach Hotel and the Kiahuna Plantation (the Stouffer and Poipu Beach have been left as they were after Hurricane Iniki battered the area).

Shipwreck Beach (Keoneloa) ★★★

On Poipu Road, in front of the Hyatt Regency Kauai, Poipu.
Fronting the Hyatt Regency Kauai, the beach is wide, broad and beautiful, but the ocean here is generally unsafe for swimming most of the year. It's best left for advanced surfers and windsurfers. Excellent for sunbathing and strolling; covered walkway if you'd prefer not to get sand between your toes. Particularly romantic in the evening on a clear night after a few drinks and jazz music at the Hyatt's Stevenson's Library.

Parks and Gardens

Moir Gardens ★★★

Kiahuna Plantation, 2253 Poipu Road, Poipu, 96756, ☎ *(808) 742-6411.*
Hours: 24 hours
Surrounding the former home of the Koloa Sugar Plantation Company's last manager, Moir Gardens encompasses 35 acres of lagoons, lily ponds, a world-famous cactus garden (yes, in Kauai), flowers and fruit trees.

Spouting Horn Beach Park ★★★

Highway, 520 to Lawai Road, Poipu.
This attraction is so popular that it has a parking lot for tour buses. There are also souvenir stands selling mostly shell jewelry. Below a fenced-off area, Spouting Horn is actually a lava tube formed by steam expansion as the lava hit the ocean eons ago.

The tidal surge moves air in there like a piston, which makes a really scary dragon-like roar. When a wave of sufficient force pushes water instead of air into it, it shoots a geyser skyward sometimes as high as 60 feet at high tide. We hate to admit it, but we come here all the time.

Tours

Lawai and Allerton Gardens ★★★

Tours leave from Spouting Horn Park, Poipu, 96765, *(808) 332-7631.*
Hours: 9 a.m.–2 p.m.

After a lengthy post-hurricane cleanup, these world-class, back-to-back botanical and scientific gardens reopened in 1995. Allerton, the first stop on the fully narrated tour, is a 100-acre, former oceanfront estate garden that belonged first to Queen Emma, wife of King Kamehameha IV in the 1800s, and later to Robert Allerton, who landscaped it with his son over a period of 20 years. Together, they built an amazing assemblage of lawns, pools, gazebos, statues and a mermaid fountain. Lawai Garden, which some visitors have called "too technical," boasts the largest collection of native Hawaiian plants in the world on its 186 acres. Note for movie buffs: the gigantic Moreton Bay fig trees were used as a dinosaur-laying ground in *Jurassic Park*. Tours of Allerton are given in antique communal taxicabs called sampans, while Lawai is traversed on foot. Despite the high price tag, these tours (both are included in the rate) are always booked solid, so reserve well in advance. The 2.5-hour tours are given five times a day. General admission: $25.

Outfitters Kauai

Poipu Plaza, 2827 A Poipu Road, Poipu, 96756, *(808) 742-9667.*

This Poipu Beach-based company will take you on guided kayaking, bicycling and snorkeling trips, or combinations of both. Popular areas include Poipu Beach (of course), the Wailua River, the Na Pali Coast and Waimea Canyon. Half- and full-day rentals and good advice are offered for those who wish to explore on their own.

West Shore

Hanapepe

Beaches

Salt Pond Beach Park ★★★

Off Highway 50 at the west end of Hanapepe, Hanapepe.

Probably the driest beach on the island (it rarely rains here), Salt Pond also has the most sublime water, making it popular with families with small children. Hawaiian families cultivate salt pans nearby (they've been doing it for generations). Other activities include shelling, snorkeling and tide pool exploring. Also surfing and windsurfing on an outside reef. Facilities for camping and picnicking, showers, rest rooms. Lifeguard on duty.

Tours

Bali Hai Helicopter Tours, Inc. ★★★

Highway 50, next to Lappert's Ice Cream, Hanapepe, *(808) 335-3166.*
Hours: 7 a.m.–7 p.m.

Bali Hai Helicopter Tours has an exclusive permit to operate out of the Port Allen Airport in Hanapepe, which is close to all the major scenic areas on Kauai. Not only that, owner/pilot James Lee has flown more than 20,000 helicopter hours and maintains a 14-year accident-free record. His fleet of Bell 206B Jet-Ranger helicopters was chosen for its safety and superior visibility (four passengers have forward-facing seats). Also highly recommended are Jack Harter Helicopters, ☎ (808) 245-3774, based out of the Lihue Airport. It's probably the first company to have offered helicopter tours of Kauai. Harter and his team of knowledgeable pilots also favor Bell Jet Ranger 'copters. Ask to fly with Jack or Mark; some Harter junkies have taken either the 60- or 90-minute tours as many as four times. Hint: the best seat in the Bell Jet Ranger is up front with the pilot; the worst is the middle one in the back. General admission: $59 and up.

Kalaheo

Parks and Gardens

Olu Pua Botanical Gardens and Plantation ★★★

At the intersection of Highway 50 and Highway 540, Kalaheo, 96741, ☎ (808) 332-8182.
Hours: 9:30 a.m.–2:30 p.m.
Perhaps overshadowed a bit by Kilohana Plantation, Olu Pua Gardens shares a similar history. This 12-acre estate surrounds the home of the former plantation manager of Alexander and Baldwin's Kauai Pineapple Company. Designed by the great C.W. Dickey in 1900s, it was the site of many balls, fetes and galas. The estate has been turned into a botanical garden lush with orchids, heliconia, flowering hibiscus, ginger and more. Six guided tours, which include a visit to the old homestead, are given daily, 9:30 a.m.–2:30 p.m. General admission: $10.

Kekaha

Beaches

Polihale Beach ★★★★

Highway 50 past Kekaha, Kekaha.
This huge (15 miles), isolated, endlessly windy (but certainly not unknown) beach marks the west end of the Na Pali Coast. An unworldly place, with sand dunes and immense sawtooth cliffs that tower over you, Polihale is near an area the ancient Hawaiians believed was the departure point for Po, the underworld of the dead (Brrrr!). More than 16 miles long, there's so much sand here they should truck it over to Brennecke's Beach. Sometimes the wind is so fierce, flying grains feel like ant bites on exposed skin. But there are nice covered pavilions to picnic in, and it's one of the best areas for sunset watching. Never go in the water, even in summer (when we were there last, the only person we saw in the ocean was a lone windsurfer, obviously an expert). Facilities include campsites (camping may be temporarily discontinued, check), showers and rest rooms. No lifeguard on duty. To get here, take Highway 50 past Kekaha and the Pacific Missile Range Facility; bear right at Mana. Follow signs inland to dirt roads running north in the sugar cane fields. Head north five miles to the end of the road. Park in the state lot and walk to the beach.

Kokee State Park

Hiking

Alakai Swamp ★★★

Kokee Road, Kokee State Park, 96796, ☎ *(808) 335-5871.*

Kauai's rainforest, the largest wetland area in the state, is a birdlovers heaven, and a mud haters hell. Come to photograph rare avian creatures, including the nearly extinct Hawaiian *iiwi* bird, which can only be found on Hawaii. Natural wonders include almost 30 waterfalls. A boardwalk has been erected recently on the seven-mile-long trail (round trip) to protect hikers from the mid-thigh mud—but you will get dirty, so be prepared. It's about a five-hour trek. Off Camp 10 Road (Mohiki Road) in Kokee State Park, a four-wheel-drive road, or park in the Puu O Kila Lookout lot, and walk to the trail head.

Awaawapuhi Trail ★★★

Route 550, Kokee State Park, Kokee State Park, 96796, ☎ *(808) 335-5871.*

Although it's a seven-mile round trip, this 3.5-mile trail through a pristine forest reserve may be worth the trouble. The apex is a dizzying promontory at the 2500-foot elevation that overlooks the inaccessible Na Pali Coast. These are views people pay big bucks to see from a helicopter. There's also a welcome picnic spot at the end of the trail, and the way back via the Nualolo Trail is a piece of cake. Be sure to pick up a plant guide from the Division of Forestry and Wildlife, although many species are marked. The trail-head begins just before the 17-mile marker on Highway 550; look for a telephone pole numbered "4/2P/152."

Halemanu Kokee Trail ★★★

Off Halemanu Road, Kokee State Park, Kokee State Park.

Another pleasant family-type outing, this is a 1.2-mile hike and self-guided nature trail through the Halemanu forest and its native species of trees, flowers and plants, including the pesty but beloved banana poka and blackberry. Bring binoculars and a field guide to identify Hawaiian birds such as *iiwi, apapane* and *elepaio.*

Museums and Exhibits

Kokee Natural History Museum and Gift Shop ★★

Kokee State Park, Kokee State Park, 96752, ☎ *(808) 335-9975.*
Hours: 10 a.m.–4 p.m.

Adjacent to Kokee Lodge, the Kokee Museum is an interesting stop while exploring Kokee State Park and Waimea Canyon. The small building contains natural history and cultural exhibits, where you'll learn some interesting factoids about Pacific weather systems. A compilation of heart-stopping footage taken by local residents (a don't-miss) during Hurricane Iniki can be viewed on video as well as a more light-hearted assemblage on Hawaiian birds. The museum gift shop offers a surprisingly comprehensive selection of koa wood bowls, tapa cloth-inspired ornaments, prints of rare birds, slack key guitar instruction books, cassettes, cookbooks, jewelry and kappa quilt pillow covers. Donations gratefully accepted. Adjacent to Kokee Lodge. Guided hikes are given in summer for a nominal fee.

Makaweli

Tours

Niihau Helicopters ★★★★

P.O. Box 370, Makaweli, 96769, ☎ (808) 335-3500.

The most expensive beach excursion in Hawaii and perhaps the world is a no-frills visit to two golden shores on the "forbidden" island of Niihau, sans barbecue lunches, glib guides or even bottled water. For $250 per person, you get a blissful three hours on Keamano Beach (with superb snorkeling, swimming and whale-watching) and Keanahaki Beach (lousy swimming, but great for beachcombing, especially for Niihau shells). Bring all supplies, including water, and a small wad to buy a Niihau shell necklace from locals ($100 and up). The only way to get here is by helicopter, which takes off from Burns Field on Lele Road in Kauai; Burns Field is off Highway 50 in West Kauai, between Hanapepe and Waimea. Reservations required. General admission: $250.

Waimea

Hiking

Iliau Nature Loop/Kukui Trail ★★★

Waimea Canyon State Park, Waimea.

Accessible via the Kukui Trail, which is on the western edge of the canyon. Named for the *iliau* plant, which is related to the silversword, this easy, quarter-mile loop trail is fun for the whole family, and there's plenty to see for such a short walk. A fair number of other native plants are all identified for your edification. This trail is also a terrific vantage point into the canyon. You can also venture 2000 feet into the heart of the canyon from here, a short but tough 2.5-mile hike. Some choose to spend the night at Wiliwili Camp at the end of the trail. Just remember, if you make this a day trip, it's a long (three hours) uphill trek from the bottom.

Waialae Canyon Trail ★★★

Waimea Canyon State Park, Waimea.

Accessible via the Kukui Trail, following the east rim of Waimea Canyon, this rugged, steep, 1.5-mile trail will reward you with a refreshing swim and picnic at Waipoo Falls, a 3200 foot waterfall, amid rare birds and native plants. You'll need a full day, especially if you venture six miles beyond the Falls to Canyon and Kumuwela Trails, which returns to Highway 550 via the Halemanu–Kokee trail.

Historical Sites

Russian Fort/Fort Elizabeth ★★

Highway 50, just southwest of Waimea River Bridge, Waimea.

A Russian fort in Kauai? All that remains today is a foliage-covered, eight-sided wall that once stood 12 feet high and 300 feet wide. It housed a magazine, armory, barracks, officers quarters and a sandalwood trading house. At one time, the Russians and the Hawaiians had a sandalwood trading operation going (until the supply ran out). The project was started in 1816 by Anton Schaeffer, a German physician-diplomat-charlatan, who involved Kauai's King Kaumualii in a revolt against King Kamehameha. Fort Elizabeth is only one of four forts built in Kauai. One, Fort

Alexander, was built on Puu Poa Point, where the Princeville Hotel now stands. After Kaumualii wisely backed down, Schaeffer was thrown out, and the Hawaiians finished the fort in 1817, ultimately using it for ceremonial purposes. It was declared a national historic monument in 1966, but plans to build a historic park in 1970 when the state acquired it have not happened.

Waimea Canyon State Park covers 1866 acres.

Parks and Gardens

Waimea Canyon   ★★★★

Route 550 (Kokee Road) or Waimea Canyon Road, Waimea.

This 25-square-mile chasm in the earth is part of the 1866-acre Waimea Canyon State Park. Mark Twain deemed it the "Grand Canyon of the Pacific," and on clear days, many would agree with the old curmudgeon. The park is a playland of camping, hiking, great scenery, even fishing. The curvy 20-mile road to the canyon traverses forests of koa, silver oak, eucalyptus and the lehua tree groves sacred to Pele. From the Waimea Canyon lookout point at 3400 feet, you can see into a 10-mile, 3657-foot gorge, an artist's palette of purples, greens and blues. The canyon changes hues depending on time of day. The late afternoon is best, especially when the sun isn't obscured by clouds–the dramatic wall-of-fire effect is caused by the sun's rays blasting on exposed orange volcanic walls. Don't forget a jacket; it gets cool up here.

Tours

Liko Kauai Cruises   ★★★

P.O. Box 18, Waimea, 96796, ☎ (808) 338-0333.

The captains and crews of this company are all raconteurs familiar with Hawaiian legends, history and lore—well-trained by the native Hawaiian owners. Test out their knowledge while exploring sea caves, waterfalls, uninhabited valleys and other wonders on a Na Pali Cliffs Adventure tour on a 38-foot cabin cruiser, the *Na Pali Kai* (takes up to 32 persons, but limited to 24) or the *Kihele Kai*, a 27-foot, six-passenger power catamaran. Also whale-watch cruises in season. Both boats have padded seating, shaded twin viewing decks, freshwater shower and rest room. Includes snorkeling and equipment, deli lunch and game fishing. Cruises leave daily from Kikiaola Harbor in Waimea at 8:30 a.m. and return at 1 p.m. The two-hour whale-watch cruises leave at 2 p.m. Both vessels are available for charter. Free for children under three. General admission: $50–$85.

Sports

Kauai has long beckoned **golfers** to its links faster than Bloody Mary was able to pawn off her "Younger Than Springtime" flesh. The primo fix are the holes of **Princeville Resort's Makai Course** (par 36) and **Prince Course** (par 72), both awesome and challenging and designed by the illustrious Robert Trent Jones, Jr. **Kaiahuna Golf Club**, next to Poipu Beach Resort, offers another Jones creation at its par-70 course. Junior also had his hand at the drawing board for the newer par-72 **Poipu Bay Resort Golf Course**. At **Kauai Lagoons Re-**

sort, you can select either the par-72 Lagoons course or the Kiele course (designed by Jack Nicklaus). The par-72 **Wailua Municipal Golf Course**, next to the Wailua River is an excellent—and inexpensive—public course.

If **tennis** is your game, you'll find 20 lighted public courts and numerous private facilities at hotels and resorts. Resorts that allow public access include **Hanalei Bay Resort**, **Holiday Inn Kauai Beach**, **Poipu Kai Resort**, **Kiahuna Beach and Tennis Resort**, and **Princeville Resort and Complex**. Public courts are located in **Hanapepe**, **Kekaha**, **Kalahea**, **Kapaa**, **Koloa**, **Lihue**, **Wailua** and **Waimea**. For a complete list of county tennis courts, contact the **Kauai County Parks and Recreation Department** *(4193 Hardy, Lihue 96766, ☎ (808) 241-6670)*.

Fish are plentiful off shore and in stream. A number of charter companies take anglers **deep-sea fishing**, particularly in the area around **Niihau** and along the **north coast**. **Freshwater streams** near Kokee and Waimea Canyon are well-stocked with bass and trout. For information, contact the **Department of Land and Natural Resources** *(Division of Aquatic Resources, P.O. Box 1671, Lihue 96744, ☎ (808) 241-3400)*. For fishing licenses (not necessary for recreational ocean angling), contact the **Department of Land and Natural Resources** *(Division of Aquatic Resources, 1151 Punchbowl Street, Honolulu 96815, ☎ (808) 587-0077)*.

Explore Kauai's beaches, valleys and vistas by **horseback** on various escorted rides, or arrange a private ride through one of the stables.

East Shore
Kapaa

Bubbles Below Dive Charters   ★★★

6251 Hauaala Road, Kapaa, 96746, ☎ (808) 822-3483.

Ken and Linda Bell were the first to take divers on regularly scheduled trips to Niihau. Offered once a week in the summer, these three tank dives are for experienced divers with a spirit of adventure (you may have to share the water with sharks). Another extraordinary summer dive is a two-tank, six-hour trip to Mana Crack, a sunken barrier reef with a drop-off range of 50–90 feet. At most times of the year, four-hour morning and afternoon dives in the waters around Kauai are available, as is a 2.5-hour night dive. Equipment, snacks, drinks and a dive computer are included. Underwater still and video photography available on advance notice for $50. Ride-alongs and snorkelers allowed for $50 per person. The number of divers per trip are usually limited to six or 10 people. General admission: $70–$200.

Snuba Tours of Kauai   ★★

5795 Lauloa Place, Kapaa, 96746, ☎ (808) 823-8912.
Hours: 8 a.m.–8 p.m.

Sort of a cross between scuba and snorkeling, snuba enables you to go deeper into Kauai's undersea environment without heavy scuba tanks. This company will provide instruction and equipment. General admission: $49 and up.

Gent-Lee Fishing Charters ★★★

P.O. Box 1691, Lihue, 96766, ☎ (808) 245-7504.

Special hours: departures at 7 a.m. and 1 p.m.

Deep-sea fishing for marlin, ahi (yellowfin tuna), mahi-mahi, ono, barracuda and aku on a fully-equipped (three to five fighting chairs), 36-foot Radoncraft Sportfisher. Rates are based on four- and six-hour share charters for four–six people, and four-, six- and eight-hour exclusive charters for up to 16 people. Half price for spectators. Includes tackle, ice and nonalcoholic beverages. Gent-Lee retains the right to the fish, but everyone gets a share, and the crew will even filet the catch. Services available for the physically challenged, but not advisable for pregnant women. 24-hour cancellation policy. Leaves daily from Nawiliwili Harbor. Ask about overnight fishing excursions to Niihau. Also recommended is **Sport Fishing Kauai**, *P.O. Box 1195, Koloa, 96756, ☎ (808) 742-7013* or *☎ (808) 639-0013*, or **Anini Fishing Charters**, *Anini Beach, ☎ (808) 828-1285*, open daily from 6 a.m.–10 p.m. How about some freshwater fishing? Hook some small and large mouth bass, but remember, you'll have to toss the critters back. **Cast and Catch**, *☎ (808) 332-9707*, will show you where these guys are bitin' (usually in reservoirs along sugarcane roads). You must have a freshwater fishing license, available from the Kokee Lodge. Guides have at least 10 years experience. The 17-foot aluminum boats are fully equipped, and all rods, tackle, live bait and beverages are supplied. Full-day and half-day charters available. Airport and hotel pickup can be arranged. General admission: $90–$1900.

Kauai Athletic Club ★★

4370 Kukui Grove Street, Lihue, ☎ (808) 245-5381.

Hours: 6 a.m.–10 p.m.

Special hours: Sat., 8 a.m.–6 p.m.; Sun., 9 a.m.–4 p.m.

A reasonably priced way to assuage guilt after too much luau food, Kauai Athletic Club offers a weight room, aerobics classes (more than 30 a week), cardio room, racquetball, handball, an outdoor pool and jacuzzi—all for a $12 day use fee. There's even a "Fitness after Sixty" program. Just stay away from the Burger King and Taco Bell that are just across the street. General admission: $12.

Kauai Lagoons Resort Golf Club ★★★

Kalapaki Beach, P.O. Box 3330, Lihue, 96766, ☎ (808) 241-6000.

Hours: 7:30 a.m.–2 p.m.

Located at the Kauai Marriott near the airport, the Kauai Lagoons Golf Course consists of the Kiele and Lagoons Courses, both 18-holers designed by Jack Nicklaus. The former, overlooking Kalapaki Beach and Nawiliwili Harbor, is ranked third-best in the state, and was the site of the 1991 PGA Grand Slam of Golf. This course is a must for experienced golfers—the 13th hole tees off over a bay, so it's pretty unforgiving. The Lagoons course is kinder and gentler, and is suitable for golfers of all levels. Reward yourself later with an excellent buffet lunch at the club's Terrace Restaurant, (808) 241-6080; price is $12. General admission: $100–$145.

Wailua Municipal Golf Course ★★

3-5351 Kuhio Highway, Lihue, 96766, ☎ (808) 241-6666.

Hours: 7 a.m.–5 p.m.

Rated in the top 75 of all municipal courses in the country, Wailua Muni was the first course constructed on Kauai in 1937, initially built as a nine-holer. It's certainly one of the prettiest, with three oceanside holes and plenty of lush landscaping. Good for beginners as well as those who like a challenge. Probably the best value for your dollar, and lots of locals play here, so reservations are a must—up to a week in advance. Greens fees are $20 on weekends; carts $14. Driving range, pro shop, putting green. General admission: $18–$20.

Puhi

Paradise River Rentals ★★

Kilohana Plantation, Highway 50, Puhi, ☎ (808) 245-9580.

Hours: 8:30 a.m.–6 p.m.

Navigate up to six rivers on your own in a one- or two-person kayak, a collapsible Porta-Bote, or power boat (Jeep Wrangler included). The self-guided tours include a "can't get lost" map, cooler, picnic tarp and waterproof bags. Guided river and ocean trips are also available. Another location in Kapaa, on Kuhio Highway, opposite Kojima's ☎ (808) 822-1112. General admission: $50–$120.

Wailua

Esprit de Corps Riding Academy

Olohena Road, Wailua, ☎ (808) 822-4688.

Hours: 7 a.m.–7:30 p.m.

Guided-trail tours ranging from three hours to an all-day adventure. No more than four guests per tour. The only company on the island that lets you trot and canter your horse. For riders with some experience, although beginners are welcome. Unspoiled areas, waterfalls, edible plants and flowers. Also offers stock seat or western riding and hunt seat (jumping) for advanced riders. A philanthropic concern, EDC turns over some profits to the academy's apprenticeship program for underprivileged and physically challenged local children. Weight restrictions apply. Reservations required. Hint: bring a bag of carrot sticks or apple chunks for your horse.

Kauai Water Ski and Surf Co. ★★★

4-356 Kuhio Highway, Wailua, ☎ (808) 822-3574.

Hours: 9 a.m.–7 p.m.

Water ski the Wailua River (the only fresh-water skiing area in the whole state), where conditions are ideal about 95 percent of the year. Kauai Water Ski, located in the Kinipopo Shopping Village, will provide a MasterCraft ski boat with a personal driver, equipment (including Wakeboards and Kneeboards), as well as instruction. Passengers can hitch a ride for free. Kayaks, surfboards, body boards, fins and snorkel sets for rent. Also recommended is Ski Enthusiast, ☎ (808) 822-2796, open 8 a.m.–10 p.m. Expert instruction from beginner to advanced. General admission: $25–$80.

North Shore
Hanalei

Bluewater Sailing Company ★★

P.O. Box 1318, Hanalei, 96714, ☎ (808) 822-0525.
Half-day, four-hour sailing trips from Hanalei Bay (May-September) and Port Allen Harbor in Hanapepe (April–October), aboard a 42-foot Pearson ketch-rigged yacht, the *Lady Leanne II*. Summer trips of the Na Pali Coast involve a snorkel stop at a remote cove; gear included. A two-hour sunset sail also is offered. Exclusive charters available. General admission: $45–$75.

Kayak Kauai Outfitters ★★★

P.O. Box 508, Hanalei, 96714, ☎ (808) 826-9844.
Hours: 8 a.m.–5:30 p.m.
Located one mile past the Hanalei Bridge, Kayak Kauai Outfitters specializes in guided river and ocean kayak tours—some safe and relaxing, and others quite rigorous. Good for first-timers in reasonable shape (and confident in the water!) is the three-hour guided tour of the Hanalei River and National Wildlife Refuge, which includes snorkeling. This tour leaves twice daily from the above address at 9:15 a.m. and 1:15 p.m. any day of the year. Rates include choice of a single or double kayak, snorkel gear, water resistant bags and refreshments. Also in the same category is the five-hour Wailua River and Waterfall Adventure (some hiking involved). More rad types will enjoy the Na Pali Sea Kayak Voyage along the Na Pali Coast, where participants explore a volcanic sea cave. This is quite a workout, and involves about five to six hours of intermittent paddling—just in case, the company's van picks you up at the other end! Ask about natural history hiking tours and bicycle beach cruises. Also rentals (hiking, camping gear, outrigger canoes and river boats). General admission: $55–$130.

Kayak Kauai Outfitters Bicycle Beach Cruise ★★★

P.O. Box 508, Hanalei, 96714, ☎ (808) 826-9844.
Hours: 8 a.m.–5:30 p.m.
Two guided bicycle tours offer two perspectives of the island. The Hanalei Cruise takes in Waioli Mission and Church, taro fields and lovely island homes before winding up in Hanalei Bay for a refreshing swim. The Kapaa Cruise involves pedaling along a level bikeway along the beach and reef; perhaps you'll spy a spouting humpback whale (in season), green sea turtles and spinner dolphins. This cruise also includes a swim in either a saltwater pool or freshwater stream, and/or a reef hike. Both are three hours in length, and include bicycle, helmet and refreshments. Great for all family members. Two cruises per day in the morning and afternoon. General admission: $45.

Princeville Ranch Stables ★★★

On Kuhio Highway, just east of the Princeville resort, Hanalei, 96714, ☎ (808) 826-6777.
Formerly known as Pooku Stables, this well-established company, operating out of a working cattle ranch, offers popular trail rides, including one to a secluded waterfall for a refreshing swim. For $104.40 per person (maximum of six), the four-hour

ride involves a short, steep 10-minute hike, sans horse. This tour is often booked solid, so it might help to call ahead before leaving home. For $57.30 per person, take the 1.5-hour "Hawaiian Country Ride" across the ranch, where you'll see panoramic views of the Hanalei Mountains, the taro fields of Hanalei Valley, Hanalei Bay and the Pacific Ocean. New in 1996 is the Cattle Drive Ride. After learning a few principles about working cattle, participants get to round up a herd at sunrise and drive them across ranchlands to their final resting arena. This adventure is offered on Wednesdays only, at 7:30 a.m. for $125 per person, limit four. No riding experience necessary. Private rides of two or three hours are also available. Long pants and covered shoes recommended. Weight restrictions apply. Riders must check in a half-hour before departure. Reservations required. General admission: $58–$166.

Windsurf Kauai ★★★

P.O. Box 323, Hanalei, 96714, ☎ *(808) 828-6838.*
Special hours: call for appointment.

Anini Beach is the best place to learn to windsurf, according to the experts, who claim that anyone can learn, regardless of age (yeah, right), as long as you pay attention to instructions. Ideal conditions include a shallow, reef-protected lagoon and a steady, gentle breeze. All you have to do is bring your suit and lots of sunscreen–Windsurf Kauai will supply the rest. Also recommended is Anini Beach Windsurfing, *Box 1602, Hanalei, 96714,* ☎ *(808) 826-9463.* Also equipment rentals and sales. General admission: $75.

Princeville

Princeville Health Club and Spa ★★★

5-3900 Kuhio Highway, Princeville, 96722, ☎ *(808) 826-5030.*
Hours: 7 a.m.–8 p.m.
Special hours: Sat. from 8 a.m., Sun. to 6 p.m.

Work out, flake out or have someone labor over you for the day ($12 day-use!), week ($40) or month ($90). These temporary memberships include admission, private locker, unlimited exercise classes, weight room, lap pool, whirlpool, dry sauna and steam room. Spa treatments and towels extra, of course. Aerobicize or do a routine on a Lifecycle or Stairmaster (that is, if the views of Bali Hai from the floor-to-ceiling windows don't distract you). Several massage therapies, from Swedish to deep tissue to aromatherapy to Hawaiian lomi lomi are available. Pamper your pores with a facial using the Aveda natural-skin care line and a vaporizer, or wrap that bod in seaweed or Hawaiian sea salt. Prices for massage or facial and body treatments per hour are reasonable and include the use of the steam, sauna, jacuzzi and locker rooms. General admission: $12–$90.

Princeville Resort Golf Courses ★★★★

P.O. Box 3040, Princeville, 96722, ☎ *(808) 826-5000.*
Hours: 7:30 a.m.–2 p.m.

A golfer's nirvana, the Princeville Resort's courses include the 18-hole Prince Course, designed by Robert Trent Jones, Jr., which has been ranked numero uno in the state by Golf Digest. The Makai Course, also designed by Jones, is divided into three nine-hole segments; you can choose to face the ocean, lakes or woods, or combine the three. It was the home of the Women's Kemper Open for five years. Both the Prince and Makai courses have fantastic views—the Prince meanders through 390 acres of rolling terrain, interspersed with junglelike foliage, waterfalls, streams and ravines. Even the jaded Jones, after designing more than 160 courses in 33 countries over a 27-year career, was moved to say: "In all the world, I never expect to find a more spectacularly beautiful place to build a golf course than Princeville, overlooking Hanalei Bay." Wow. If you opt to play the Makai Course's 27 holes all at once, you'll need to repair to the adjoining Princeville Health Club and Spa for a "Golfer's Massage," a half-hour treatment concentrating specifically on the neck, back, legs, and feet. You'll need it. General admission: $85–$150.

Princeville Tennis Club   ★★★

P.O. Box 3040, Princeville, 96722, ☎ *(808) 826-3620.*
Hours: 8 a.m.–6 p.m.
Centrally located next to the Princeville Resorts' Makai Clubhouse, this is one of the best choices on the island for tennis. There are six courts available (lower price is for resort guests), professional instruction by appointment ($25 for a half-hour private lesson, $40 for an hour, $10 for group clinics), programs and tournaments. Memberships are available by the week, month, quarter or year. Full-service pro shop ($5 racquet rental, $15 ball machine rental). General admission: $10–$13.

South Shore

Koloa

CJM Country Stables   ★★★

1731 Kelaukia Street, Koloa, 96736, ☎ *(808) 742-6096.*
Offering three coast and mountain trail rides from its headquarters in the Poipu area, CJM, an acronym for "come join me," is run by Jim Miranda, a real Hawaiian paniolo (cowboy). While moseying along the bluffs overlooking Mahaulepu Beach, Miranda relates colorful stories about the area and Kauai ranching in general. The early morning ride from 8:30–11:30 a.m. includes a breakfast picnic. Groups are purposely kept small (so they can keep track of you), with only eight riders or so per outing. General admission: $40–$65.

Poipu Bay Resort Golf Course   ★★★

2250 Ainako Street, Koloa, 96756, ☎ *(808) 742-8711.*
Hours: 8 a.m.–5 p.m.
Situated next to the Hyatt Regency Kauai on Kauai's south shore, the Poipu Bay Resort Golf Course is a 210-acre, 18-hole, par-72 Scottish-links-style course designed by Robert Trent Jones, Jr. Nicknamed the "Pebble Beach of the Pacific," this newish, 6845-yard-long course played host to the PGA Grand Slam of Golf shortly after it opened in 1994. Among the hazards are stunning ocean views, 86 bunkers, several lakes and trade winds. Oh, and parts of the course stop just shy of intimidating sea cliffs. Fees include a cart; second round, $75. Facilities include a pro shop, clubhouse/restaurant, driving range, putting and chipping green, practice sand bunkers and locker/shower rooms. A few minutes west, the Kiahuna Golf Club, 2545 Kiahuna Plantation Drive, ☎ *(808) 742-9595,* also designed by Jones,

is a par-70, 18-hole course with 27 well-preserved archaeological sites. Look out for the 14th hole. Great fun for experienced golfers on a budget: it's $45 per round, including cart. Facilities include a driving range, pro shop, snack bar and putting green. General admission: $85–$135.

Poipu

Sea Sport Divers ★★★

2827 Poipu Road, Poipu, ☎ *(808) 742-9303.*
Hours: 8 a.m.–5 p.m.

Located in the Poipu area, Sea Sport Divers is Kauai's only full-service PADI and NAUI Scuba Training facility. It offers half-day, two-tank boat excursions to some of Kauai's best cave dives. One is Sheraton Caverns, just offshore from the Sheraton Kauai. These underwater grottos range from 35 to 60 feet in depth. The so-called General Store is a 65- to 80-foot deep reef with a wide variety of marine life (eels, turtles, sharks, manta rays) and a submerged 19th-century steamship to explore. For those just getting started, Sea Sport Divers will help you get certified, with free pool lessons and introductory dives (no experience necessary). Ask about private charters to Niihau, the "Forbidden Isle," with 130-foot deep reef walls and night dives. Top-quality equipment, rentals and repairs are available 24 hours a day. Also recommended is Fathom Five Adventures (love the name), *3450 Poipu Road, Koloa,* ☎ *(808) 742-6991,* also a five-star outfit offering certification courses and two-tank dives. It's open Monday-Saturday from 7:30 a.m.–6 p.m.; Sundays until 4:30 p.m. If you're staying on the eastern shore, there are several companies in the Kapaa area, including Aquatic Adventures, *4-1380 Kuhio Highway, 96746,* ☎ *(808) 822-1434,* a service-oriented PADI five-star dive center, and Dive Kauai Scuba Center, *976 Kuhio Highway, #C,* ☎ *(808) 822-0452.* Both offer certification and specialty dives, including wreck dives to the *Luckenbach* (no, you won't see Waylon and Willie and the boys—that's in Texas), a German freighter that sank 40 years ago. Small groups are preferred for individualized instruction. The latter has its own custom- built dive boat. General admission: $65–$350.

Poipu Beach

Margo Oberg's Surfing School ★★

Kiahuna Plantation Resort, Poipu Beach, ☎ *(808) 742-6411.*

Lessons by a seven-time world champion. Special beginner classes. Prices below are per person, per hour. For a complete line of surfing equipment and clothing, sales and rentals, try Progressive Expressions, ☎ *(808) 742-6041.* General admission: $40.

The Anara Spa ★★★

Hyatt Regency Kauai, Poipu Beach, ☎ *(808) 742-1234.*

This 25,000-square-foot spa features outdoor lava-rock showers and colorful flowers. Within the facility are 10 indoor/outdoor treatment rooms, a 25-yard heated lap pool in an open courtyard, a Turkish steam bath and Finnish saunas. La'ao Ma Anara, or day at the Spa, offers a complete Hawaiian-flavored spa treatment—after a 10-minute steam bath, you'll be coated with red clay found at the base of Waiale-ale (native healers find it to be extremely medicinal) mixed with sea salt. Afterwards have a lomi-lomi massage and seaweed facial, followed by lunch at Kupono Café, and a complimentary hand-painted *pareo* for your pains. Not bad. General admission: $20–$130.

Kalaheo
Sports/Recreation

Kukuiolono Golf Course ★★

Kukuiolono Park, Kalaheo, 96741, ☎ *(808) 335-9940.*
Hours: 6:30 a.m.–4:30 p.m.
This nine-hole course is cheap at $5 a round. No reservations taken; first-come, first-served basis only. Facilities include a golf club/restaurant, driving range, pro shop, putting green. General admission: $5.

Makaweli

Niihau Safaris ★★

Box 370, Makaweli, HI 96769, Makaweli, 96769, ☎ *(808) 335-3500.*
The Robinson family of Niihau is (very) slowly opening the island to outsiders, including avid (and wealthy) hunters who can pay $1400 per person per day to go on wild boar (there are about 8000 on the island) and ram-stalking trips. You can hunt all by yourself or bring a party of seven (maximum). Choose your weapons— bow and arrow, shotgun or rifle. Arrival is by helicopter, a 20-minute flight over the Kaulahiki Channel. Reservations required; for information, see Keamano Beach listing. General admission: $1400.

Waimea

Na Pali Explorer I

9633 Kaumalii Highway, Waimea, 96796, ☎ *(808) 335-9909.*
Leaves from Kikiaola Harbor between Kekaha and Waimea. Unforgettable rafting trek along Kauai's pristine coastline on the *Explorer I*, the latest in Zodiac technology. A hard-hull Hurricane Zodiac is a custom-designed craft, twin volvo engines, deep V fiberglass hull for speed, maneuverability and shallow draft can glide to more remote coastal areas than most other vessels. Na Pali Coast Day Trek, beach landing at Nualolo Kai sea caves, depending on the weather. Narrated hike of ancient Hawaiian fishing village, snorkeling, continental breakfast and catered picnic lunch.

Where to Stay

The brighter side of Hurricane Iniki's rampage is that many of Kauai's accommodations that were previously in need of remodeling or refurbishment were forced into action. You'll find a lot of choices on the island, from bud-

Fielding WORLDWIDE **HAWAII**

KAUAI B&B's

Kauai, the "Garden Island," is lush with tropical forests. Sparsely populated, relative to the bigger Islands, Kauai's secluded B&B's are for people who want to avoid the crowds.

KAUAI
OAHU
MAUI
HAWAII

KAUAI

Haena Point
Princeville
Kilauea Lighthouse
Na Pali Coast
560
Kepuhi Point
Hanalei
Kilauea
56
Makaha Point
Kalalau Lookout
Anahola
Kuaehu Point
KOKE'E STATE PARK
Mt. Waialeale
Opaekaa Falls
581
Kapaa
550
Waimea Canyon
580
Wailua
Mana
Wailua Falls
583
50
Lihue
Lihue Airport
Kekaha
Waimea
0   5
miles
50
Capt. Cook Monument
Port Allen
530
Koloa
Lawai
Puolo Point
Poipu
Makahuena Point

KALAHEO PLANTATION

This 1926 plantation style house sits on Kalaheo Plantation. The three accommodations offer king size beds, living rooms and kitchens. The B&B is located at 4579 Puuwai Rd. PO Box 872 Kalaheo, Hawaii 96741. 888 - 488-9538.

HALE 'AHA "HOUSE OF GATHERING"

This bed and breakfast offers ocean views and is built on a Princeville Golf Course fairway. In addition to a presidential and honeymoon suite, there are four rooms available, each with a private deck. This B&B is located at 3875 Kamehameha Rd. P.O.Box 3370 Princeville, Kauai, Hawaii 96722. 800 826-6733

HISTORIC B&B

Once a Buddhist mission, this B&B is now a cultural landmark. Located in the Hanalei Valley, centrally located on Mainstreet. P.O. Box 1662 Hanalei, Hawaii 96714 808 - 826-4622.

ALOHA COUNTRY B&B

Breathtaking mountain and waterfall views surround this B&B. This B&B has two large luxury suites, and offers tennis courts, hiking trails and swimming holes. 505 Kamalu Rd. Kapaa, Kauai 96746. 808 - 822-0166.

HALE KUA GUESTS

There are two cottages to choose from, each has two bedrooms, queen size beds and kitchens. This B&B is located at 4896 E. Kua Rd. P.O. Box 649, Lawai, Kauai, Hawaii 96765. 800 -332-8570 get rooms to swanky resorts with B&Bs, condos and campsites well-represented. If you have deep pockets, like to be surrounded by other well-heeled guests, and want access to a couple of top golf courses, **Princeville Resort**, on the north shore, will probably satiate you. Visitors who like to be close to Kauai's ancestral heritage and ancient culture usually opt for east-coast accommodations—such as the famous **Coco Palms Resort**—so as to be close to the sacred **Wailua River**. The majority of visitors head straight for the south shore and **Poipu Beach** where the sun in plentiful, the surf is calm year-round, and there's is an abundance of condos, as well as hotels. For more economical hotels, motels and apartment hotels, **Lihue** or **Kapaa** are the best places to bed down.

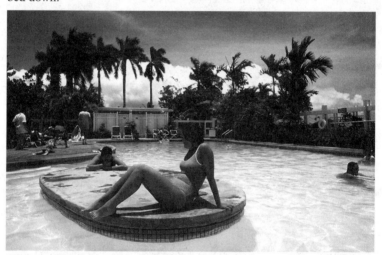

Kiahuna Plantation pool

East Shore

Hanamaulu

The Outrigger Kauai Beach Hotel **$125–$750** ★ ★ ★

4331 Kauai Beach Drive, Hanamaulu, 96746, ☎ *(800) 688-7444, (808) 245-1955, FAX (808) 246-9085. Rated restaurant: Jacaranda Terrace*
Single: $125–$750. Double: $125–$750.

Known and loved by residents for an authentic Hawaiian atmosphere, this is a 25-acre, oceanfront luxury resort built around an attractively landscaped central pool area, with an island in the center, surrounded by swaying palm trees. Of the three interconnecting pools, one is reserved for children. The airy lobby is a popular meeting spot. But fewer than half of the rooms have ocean views. The rest are described as pool/lagoon or mountain views. While most people come to Hawaii for the ocean view, perhaps you can develop a passion for the mountains when you can save $45 per day by looking at them instead of the ocean. Rooms are all comfortable and done in typical tropical pastel colors and have sliding doors that lead out onto lanais. Entertainment is a mixed bag. Robbie and Puamohala Kaholokula (Robbie is the hotel's sales manager) perform on a regular basis in the Mele Lounge. On Thursday, Gilligan's, the hotel's night club, turns into a comedy lounge with performers from the Mainland circuit. On Sundays, the Jasmine Ballroom is the location of the Legacies show, which is a musical tour of Kauai and the other Hawaiian islands. Most of its cast is local and performs the ancient chants and *na mele* (songs) with grace and enthusiasm. Doors open at 6:15 p.m. for a mai tai punch hour. At this time, local craftspeople are on hand to display their products. The Hale Kipa Terrace offers a well-regarded weekly seafood buffet. Amenities: tennis, health club, Jacuzzi, balcony or patio, family plan, business services. 350 rooms.

Kapaa

Bed-and-Breakfasts

Alohilani Bed & Breakfast   **$85–$95**   ★★★

1470 Wanaao Road, Kapaa, 96746, ☎ (800) 533-9316, (808) 823-0128.
Single: $85–$95. Double: $85–$95.
The Alohilani ("Bright Sky") Bed and Breakfast Inn has an upcountry location above Kapaa Town, approximately 20 minutes from the airport. Accommodations consist of three units, all with cable TV, microwaves, and private baths.The most interesting is the Malulani Guest Cottage, which is detached from the main house and is filled with antiques, dolls and other reminders of the island's past. The deck that surrounds the cottage on all sides affords views of the ocean, mountains and valley. Breakfast is served on the deck or in the gazebo in the garden. You can expect Hawaiian coffee, fresh juices, tropical fruits, breads and muffins and homemade jams and jellies. Amenities: balcony or patio. 3 rooms. Credit cards: not accepted.

Hale 'O Wailele   **$120–$175**   ★★★★

7084-A Kahuna Road, Kapaa, 96746, ☎ (800) 77K-AUAI, (808) 822-7911, FAX (808) 823-8883.
Single: $120–$175. Double: $120–$175.
Nestled at the base of the Makaleha Forest Reserve, Hale 'O Wailele (House of Leaping Waterfalls) is a modern plantation home turned B&B that's part of an eight-acre native Hawaiian family estate and tropical flower farm. The three suites within the Hale all feature Hawaiian collectibles and art, imported hardwood floors and Persian rugs, Italian marble baths, refrigerators, private sunning decks and Jacuzzis. Large color TVs have built-in VCRs. The largest of the three suites, the Canoe, affords views of the namesake waterfalls while you lie in bed, resting on imported Egyptian cotton sheets. The suite also has a separate dining area. Due to the increased popularity of Hale o Wailele, the estate trustees opened up another house, Waonahele, or "House at the Edge of the Forest," with three additional suites that range in price from $120–$140. The most intriguing, from a romantic point of view, is The Candlenut Suite. Perched on the highest point of the estate, the suite has an unobstructed view of the Pacific Ocean, and at night you can see the glittering lights of Kapaa town. The rate includes a Hawaiian-style breakfast buffet. Activities on the estate include flower lei making, barbecuing in the coconut grove,

working out in the gym, or swimming in the new lava-rock-terraced waterfall swimming pool. The latter is a popular backdrop for weddings; the estate caters to Hawaiian-style nuptials, complete with luau receptions. If you must leave the estate, you'll be provided with hiking and beach gear free of charge; snorkeling gear, golf carts, and mountain bikes are available for a nominal fee. Gracious host Ohelo Kaopio has been known to accompany guests on kayaking trips and other adventures, and will provide you with directions and maps to numerous nearby beaches, some of them "swimsuit optional." Amenities: exercise room, Jacuzzi, balcony or patio. 6 rooms. Credit cards: MC, V.

Kakalina's Bed & Breakfast $70–$75   ★★★

6781 Kawaihai Road, Kapaa, 96746, ☎ (808) 822-2328.
Single: $70–$75. Double: $70–$75.

Kakalina's Bed & Breakfast is located on a working tropical flower farm. Guests are welcome to visit the gardens and enjoy the variety of exotic flora they contain. (Note: hostess Kathy Offley operates a gift service, Kauai Exotix, that will ship flowers and/or other tropical goodies back to the Mainland.) The B&B is located 10 miles from the airport, and offers easy access to either mountain or beach activities. Of the two units, the semicircular Hale Akahi suite is the most intriguing—it's the handiwork of host Bob Offley, who's a master carpenter. Both have private entrances and private baths, color TVs and VCRs, coffee makers, microwaves, refrigerators and laundry facilities. Naturally, tropical plants and flowers are used extensively inside the house. Breakfast is usually fresh juice, fresh fruit, pastries and Kauai (not Kona) coffee. 2 rooms. Credit cards: not accepted.

Wailua Country Vacation Rentals $50–$80   ★★

505 Kamalu Road, Kapaa, 96746, ☎ (808) 822-0166, FAX (808) 822-2708.
Single: $50–$80. Double: $50–$80.

With its two-acre front yard, the Wailua Country B&B Rentals property at Kapaa well deserves the adjective "spacious." Located behind Sleeping Giant Mountain, the 5000-square-foot main residence has been recently remodeled, but retains the pre-Iniki arched Spanish facade which looks out onto numerous tropical fruit trees and a rushing brook that cuts thorough the lawn. Hawaiian and European antiques have been used to furnish the units and give them an exceptionally homelike feel. The beautiful oak floors are scattered with Persian and Oriental rugs. The rental units are located on the second floor. One suite has a large bath with Jacuzzi. Neither has kitchen facilities, but a breakfast of fresh-baked bread, homemade jam, fresh fruits, coffee and tea is included in the rates. On the same property, but away from the main house, are three new cottages, with neat white paint and pink-tile roofs. Interiors have a feminine touch, with lacy curtains, plenty of white wicker and wooden furniture. We especially like the two-bedroom cottage with its French doors opening out onto its private lawn with a strategically placed hammock under exotic fruit trees. (If you lie very still, you'll see an astounding number of tropical birds using the bird bath or sipping nectar from the native flowers that grow with uninhibited exuberance in the shadow of Sleeping Giant Mountain). The cottages have either kitchenettes or full kitchens. Cottage guests add an extra $5 for breakfast. All units have color TVs and ceiling fans. Washer and dryer available for a fee. Amenities: Jacuzzi, balcony or patio. 6 rooms. Credit cards: not accepted.

Condos

Lae Nani   **$175–$295**   ★★★

410 Papaloa Road, Kapaa, 96746, ☎ (800) 367-7052, (808) 822-4938.
Single: $175–$295. Double: $175–$295.

Situated on seven manicured acres across a pretty but rocky beach, Lae Nani means "beautiful point of land," and this attractive condominium complex is situated on a site chosen as a place of worship by ancient Hawaiians. The ruins of the Kukui *Heiau*, where fires were lit at night to guide voyagers home, sit on the promontory along the beach, next to the property's manmade, lava-rock saltwater pool. First built in 1978, the Lae Nani was rebuilt twice, once in 1990 and again in 1993 after being struck by both Hurricane Ewa and Hurricane Iniki. The compound is well-maintained and unprepossessing from the outside, but the individually owned and decorated units are surprisingly spacious and elegant inside. A third-floor corner unit, #536, is particularly handsome and has a sweeping view of the ocean and the city lights at night from the large lanai. This two-bedroom, two-bath apartment is furnished in an Asian-Tropical motif, in dramatic hues of purple, beige and pale green. A trio of high-quality rattan sofa chairs with huge pillows as backrests are arranged companionably around a glass-topped coffee table. A particularly striking piece is an armoire (with color TV, VCR, cassette player, even a tape collection) with bamboo tusks as handles. The master bedroom has a king-size bed and the second bedroom has two twins. Baths are outfitted with toiletries, and hair dryers are furnished on request. Closet space is more than ample. Kitchens in all units are well-equipped with a microwave, stove, refrigerator with ice-maker, dishwasher and loads of utensils, even down to an ice cream scoop. There's daily housekeeping service (they don't do dishes, though), and a coin-operated laundry (units don't have washer/dryers). Activities include a barbecue by the pool, or a pleasant walk on the beach along the neighboring hotels. The Lae Nani is also conveniently next door to the Coconut Marketplace, which is open late for a bite or two or a round of window-shopping. Amenities: Jacuzzi, balcony or patio, family plan. Credit cards: A, DC, D, MC, V.

Plantation Hale   **$88–$100**   ★★

484 Kuhio Highway, Kapaa, 96746, ☎ (800) 775-4253, (808) 822-4941, FAX (808) 822-5599.
Single: $88–$100. Double: $88–$100.

Newly redecorated one-bedroom units (called suites) have been furnished in white wicker with tropical pastel accents. All have dining and sitting areas, and kitchenettes with refrigerators, but no dishwashers. Other additions include a spa and pool deck. Guests can walk to kitschy Coconut Plantation with its varied selection of touristy shops, run-of-the-mill restaurants and movie theaters. If that doesn't suit your needs, nearby Kapaa has unique boutiques, ethnic eateries (even a world class one, The Pacific Café) a farmer's market, art galleries and much more to assuage feelings of boredom. Amenities: Jacuzzi, balcony or patio. 151 rooms. Credit cards: A, CB, DC, D, MC, V.

Hotels

Aston Kauai Beachboy Hotel $115–$185   ★★

4-484 Kuhio Highway, Kapaa, ☎ *(800) 922-7866, (808) -.*
Single: $115–$185. Double: $115–$185.

The Aston Kauai Beachboy is designated as a beachfront hotel, but unfortunately the beach it fronts isn't too great for bathing. It has two swimming pools, including a wader for the kids, plus shuffleboard and volleyball. The Beachboy also has the added attraction (or detraction) of its location in the Coconut Marketplace. Because it's an older (but well-maintained) property, the plantings around it are well-established and especially attractive. Rooms have been recently redone in bright, contemporary pastels. Amenities: tennis, balcony or patio, family plan, business services. 243 rooms. Credit cards: A, DC, D, MC, V.

Hotel Coral Reef $49–$89   ★★

1516 Kuhio Highway, Kapaa, 96746, ☎ *(808) 822-4481.*
Single: $49–$89. Double: $49–$89.

A haven for the budget traveler, the Coral Reef is situated in a coconut grove 50 feet from a sandy beach. The main building offers cheaper and less-desirable accommodations with no view of the ocean. The Oceanfront Building has well-proportioned rooms with ocean views, louvered windows and private lanais. The units have been recently redecorated and the color scheme tends to run to tones of dusty rose and blue. Actually, it blends very well with the blue ocean outside and the effect is quite pleasing. No phones in rooms, but there's a pay phone in the lobby, as well as complimentary coffee service. Amenities: balcony or patio.

Kauai Coconut Beach Resort $95–$170   ★★★

P.O. Box 830, Kapaa, 96746, ☎ *(800) 22A-LOHA, (808) 822-3455, FAX (808) 822-1830. Rated restaurant: The Flying Lobster*
Single: $95–$170. Double: $95–$170.

As its name implies, the Kauai Coconut Beach Resort sits gracefully within a 10-acre coconut grove along Waipouli Beach. All guest rooms were completely redecorated in January 1995 in a Hawaiian plantation-style, featuring hand-carved custom furnishings, louvered wooden shutters, wood carvings and rich teal carpeting. Each has a refrigerator and a coffee maker with free coffee (increasingly rare these days). The room rate includes a complimentary breakfast buffet and complimentary cocktails and pupus. Along with an award-winning Friday-evening luau, there's a nightly torch-lighting ceremony and a Hawaiian immersion program ranging from storytelling to crafts demonstrations. Restaurants include the Flying Lobster, which serves up this choice crustacean at a reasonable price, and throws in a salad bar and lobster bisque to boot. Cocktails and entertainment at Cook's Landing Lodge. Shopping opportunities nearby at Coconut Plantation and Kapaa Town. Amenities: tennis, Jacuzzi, balcony or patio, family plan. 311 rooms. Credit cards: A, CB, DC, D, MC, V.

Lihue

Condos

Aston Kauai Beach Villas   **$170–$295**   ★★★

4330 Kauai Beach Drive, Lihue, 96766, ☎ *(800) 922-7866, (808) 245-7711.*
Single: $170–$295. Double: $170–$295.

These nicely priced luxury condominiums fronting a white-sand beach are surrounded by coconut palms, lush gardens and a reflecting lagoon (with swans!). The spacious one- and two-bedroom units are fairly self-sufficient, with complete kitchens and washer/dryers. One distinct advantage the property has, though, is that it shares the facilities of the neighboring Outrigger Kauai Beach Hotel. Signing privileges are available at any of the Outrigger's restaurants, which comes in handy when cookin' ain't dandy. The Wailua Golf Course is next door. Amenities: tennis, balcony or patio, family plan. 150 rooms. Credit cards: A, MC, V.

Colony Banyan Harbor Resort   **$80–$140**   ★★

3411 Wilcox Road, Lihue, 96766, ☎ *(800) 777-1700, (808) 245-7333, FAX (808) 246-4776.*
Single: $80–$140. Double: $80–$140.

The Colony Banyan Harbor Resort occupies a privileged position overlooking Kalapaki Bay and the Kiele Golf Course, and is a reasonably priced alternative to the more-opulent Kauai Marriott. When guests aren't going to the beach or shopping, activity centers around a curved pool with a wide deck, or the tennis courts. Tropically decorated one- and two-bedroom suites feature fully equipped kitchens with a variety of utensils, full-size refrigerators and coffee makers with a welcome packet of Kona (why not Kauai?) coffee. All have washer/dryers. Daily housekeeping is provided. Unlike many condominiums, the Banyan Harbor offers personal service from a concierge staff who will cheerfully help you spend your time if you aren't content to just sit and soak up the atmosphere. Amenities: tennis, balcony or patio, family plan. 148 rooms. Credit cards: A, DC, D, MC, V.

Resorts

Kauai Marriott Resort and Beach Club   **$225–$1800**   ★★★★

Kalapaki Beach, Lihue, 96766, ☎ *(808) 245-5050. Rated restaurant: Kukui's*
Single: $225–$1800. Double: $225–$1800.

The Kauai Marriott took up the slack when the pretentious Westin was turned into kindling after Hurricane Iniki devastated the island in 1992. Although part of the new resort is a time-share operation, it boasts an enviable location on gorgeous Kalapaki Beach, near Lihue. The pool, in particular, is spectacular and meanders over 26,000 square feet and is replete with bridges and fantastic animals spouting water. The gardens are meticulously cared for by an attentive staff and deserve more attention than they get from most guests. Because of the proximity to the beach, extensive watersports are available, from swimming to kayaking to fishing. There's horseback riding and hiking nearby, and it's adjacent to a 36-hole golf course. There are six restaurants, including the '40s Waikiki-themed Duke's Canoe Club, and two cocktail lounges. Accommodations feature mini-bars, free cable TV and in-room movies; some have ocean views. Decor is a little of the stodgy side, though, with dark carpeting and dark drapes with valences, which could make guests feel a little claustrophobic. But we guess that's what the great outdoors are for. Amenities: health club, exercise room, Jacuzzi, sauna, balcony or patio, family plan, business services. 355 rooms. Credit cards: A, CB, DC, D, MC, V.

Wailua

Kauai Resort Hotel   **$69–$159**   ★★

3-5920 Kuhio Highway, Wailua, 96746, ☎ *(800) 367-5004, (808) 245-3931, FAX (808) 822-7339. Rated restaurant: The Pacific Room*
Single: $69–$159. Double: $69–$159.

The Kauai Resort Hotel has a nice location on family-oriented Lydgate Beach Park, with protected, manmade, lava-rock pools perfect for swimming and snorkeling. It's just 10 minutes from Lihue Airport. The spacious units, which management boasts are the largest on Kauai, consist of hotel rooms with microwaves, studios with full kitchens, and one-bedroom cottages with kitchenettes. All have air conditioning, color cable TV and in-room refrigerators. Most can accommodate up to five people. Interior decor is bright and cheery, with dark-green carpets, floral-print bedspreads, rattan furniture and Pegge Hopper prints on the walls. The Pacific Dining Room is open for breakfast, lunch and dinner, while the Pikake Terrace is a cocktail lounge that serves snacks. The hotel lobby is the scene of frequent Hawaiian entertainment. There's a free hula show on Thursdays from 5–5:30 p.m. from June–November, hula demonstrations Mondays, Tuesdays and Wednesdays at 4:30 p.m., and an arts and crafts sale Monday–Thursday from 4–6 p.m. Ask about the free rental car packages. Amenities: tennis, Jacuzzi, family plan, business services. 197 rooms. Credit cards: A, DC, D, MC, V.

North Shore

Anahola

Bed-and-Breakfasts

Mahina Kai   **$95–$115**   ★★

Box 699, Anahola, 96703, ☎ *(800) 337-1134, (808) 822-9451.*
Single: $95–$115. Double: $95–$115.

Mahina Kai is the guest wing of a distinctive Asian-Pacific country home. We would add that the emphasis is overwhelmingly on the Asian, with wide, sloping, blue-tile roofs, water gardens and shoji screens. Several of the rooms have sliding panels that open onto private lanais and gardens filled with exotic tropical plants. Mahina Kai is a popular setting for corporate meetings. There is a 1000-square-foot meeting room available in the garden Tea House and four private meeting-rooms available in the main house. Continental breakfast is available for occupants of the bedrooms; the apartment has its own kitchen. Extras include bicycles, snorkeling and beach gear. Amenities: Jacuzzi, business services. 4 rooms.

Hanalei

Historic B&B   **$55–$65**   ★★

P.O. Box 1662, Hanalei, 96714, ☎ *(808) 826-4622.*
Single: $55. Double: $65.

The eclectic traveler will insist on spending at least one night at the Historic B&B when visiting Hanalei. Right in the center of town across the street from the Wishing Well Shave Ice truck, it was constructed in 1901 as a place of worship for the Japanese Buddhist workers on the local plantations. It served as a focal point for the Japanese community for more than 80 years. When a new temple was constructed in the early 1980s, the older building fell into disrepair and was due to be razed. However, local businesspeople, realizing that this was a true piece of the history of Kauai, raised sufficient funds to move it across the island to Hanalei. Today it has been meticulously restored and is listed on the National and State Historic Registries of Buildings. Co-owner Jeff Shepherd is an artist and professional chef. His artwork is displayed on the walls and he is responsible for the gourmet breakfasts that appear every morning in the breakfast room. Sample: Belgian waffles topped with sliced mangoes and toasted coconut with a side order of sunrise papayas and hot Kona coffee. The spotless property has polished hardwood floors, and some of the rooms have bamboo-canopied beds with beautiful cross-stitched quilts and gauzy mosquito netting. There is a $3 charge for using the washer/dryer. No small children or pets. 3 rooms. Credit cards: not accepted.

River Estate Bed & Breakfast   **$115**   ★ ★ ★

P.O. Box 169, Hanalei, 96714, ☎ *(808) 826-6411.*
Single: $115. Double: $115.

The River Estate consists of two beautifully furnished separate houses, the Tree House and the Guest House, fronting the Wainiha River, on one property. The Guest House is the smaller of the two and offers a high degree of privacy. It's very popular with honeymooners. The Tree House is larger and sleeps up to eight people. It takes its name from the fact that it's built on 13-foot pilings (building codes require this because of the proximity to the ocean and tidal waves). Kids love this, and sitting on the lanai 13 feet up really does give the feeling of being in a tree house. Owner Mark Barbanell takes great pride in the gardens surrounding the units and it shows in the well-tended lawns and flower beds. Many guests just like to sit in the yard and enjoy the view as well as the sound of the river that cuts through the property. All bedrooms have king-size beds, ceiling fans and private baths. Each house has a fully equipped custom kitchen and large covered deck, cable TV and phone. There's a washer/dryer for guest use. Optional continental breakfast. Amenities: balcony or patio. 2 rooms. Credit cards: MC, V.

Condos

Hanalei Colony Resort   **$110–$205**   ★ ★ ★

P.O. Box 206, Hanalei, 96714, ☎ *(800) 628-3004, (808) 826-6235, FAX (808) 826-9893.*
Single: $110–$205. Double: $110–$205.

Hanalei Colony Resort bills itself as the "last" resort before the road ends at Na Pali. It should actually say the "only" resort, as the only accommodations in the immediate area are a few vacation home rentals. However, nothing will ever be able to detract from the resort's unequaled location on the beach on Kauai's North Shore. The resort takes full advantage of a narrow strip of land between the beach and the volcanic cliffs behind it. The corner beach front units are especially popular because of their 180-degree view of the ocean. A mai tai on one of these lanais is a real experience. All of the breezy, light-filled units have two bedrooms, separate living and dining areas and kitchens. They are almost identically furnished with comfortable rattan furniture. Note: there are no TVs, stereos or dishwashers. This is one place you really can get away from it all. Amenities: Jacuzzi, balcony or patio, family plan. 52 rooms. Credit cards: A, DC, D, MC, V.

Hotels

Hanalei Bay Resort/Embassy Suites $135–$1000   ★★★

P.O. Box 220, Hanalei, 96714, ☎ *(800) 367-5004, (808) 591-2235, FAX (808) 596-0158. Rated restaurant: Bali Hai Restaurant*
Single: $135–$1000. Double: $135–$1000.

The Hanalei Bay Resort and Embassy Suites Kauai are billed as "two great vacation experiences at one fantastic location." The former is one of the world's top resorts, a classic romantic getaway built in 1972. Many local residents think it has the same view of the fabled bay and the cliffs of "Bali Hai" as the tony Princeville Hotel, but at half the price. Recently, Castle Resorts and Hotels bought it and the adjoining Embassy Suites, married the two facilities and celebrated with a $10 million renovation. The newish Embassy Suites features 75 one-, two- and three-bedroom oversized suites (at least 1091 square feet) with fully equipped kitchens and the complimentary cooked-to-order breakfast and afternoon cocktails typical of the chain. The Hanalei Bay contains 140 spacious rooms with a refrigerator and coffee maker, and studios with kitchenettes. Upper-floor units have lofts. The Bali Hai Restaurant has incredible sunset views, Pacific Rim cuisine and the best jazz on the island Sundays in the adjoining Happy Talk Lounge. Amenities: tennis, Jacuzzi, balcony or patio, family plan. 215 rooms. Credit cards: A, CB, DC, D, MC, V.

Kilauea

Bed-and-Breakfasts

Hale Ho'o Maha $55–$80   ★★★

P.O. Box 422, Kilauea, 96754, ☎ *(800) 851-0291, (808) 828-1341.*
Single: $55–$80. Double: $55–$80.

Hale Ho'o Maha (House of Rest) is a split-level home on five acres of landscaped grounds. Among other things, it has great beach access (the fantastic Kalihiwai Bay is a 10-minute stroll down the road, and Secret Beach is a 15-minute hike from the front door). The four guest rooms are named after tropical fruits. One of them, the Pineapple Room, features a seven-foot circular bed with a custom-quilted, pineapple-motif bedspread. All have color cable TV, phones and ceiling fans. Two have private baths. The hosts, Toby and Kirby (one's a he, the other a she) Searles love the great outdoors; Toby will even take you scuba diving. If you want to explore the other side of the island, ask them about their cabin in Kokee State Park. 4 rooms. Credit cards: MC, V.

Makai Farms $75   ★★

P.O. Box 93, Kilauea, 96754, ☎ *(808) 828-1874.*
Single: $75. Double: $75.

Accommodations at Makai Farms consist of a private, detached apartment away from the main residence on a family-owned farm devoted to the cultivation of orchids. From the upstairs bedroom there are gorgeous mountain and ocean views. It has a king-size bed and sleeper sofa. Downstairs is a kitchen (light meals and snacks only, please) and bathroom with shower. There's another shower outside for washing off sandy feet. Breakfast fixings are provided, including farm-fresh fruit and hen-laid eggs. Makai Farms is in a great location just outside Kilauea, midway between the golf courses of Princeville and only minutes from the fabled beaches on the Na Pali coast. Children welcome. Two-night minimum preferred. Amenities: family plan. 1 room. Credit cards: not accepted.

Princeville

Hale 'Aha   **$90–$210**   ★★★

3875 Kamehameha Road, Princeville, 96722, ☎ *(800) 826-6733, (808) 826-6733.*
Single: $90–$210. Double: $90–$210.
Hale'Aha overlooks the sixth green of the Princeville's Makai Golf course on one side and the ocean on the other. The three-story house is furnished in tropical pastels with touches of rattan and native wood. The most interesting accommodation offered is the 1000-square-foot Penthouse Suite, which occupies the entire top floor. It has a drop-dead view of the golf course, the ocean and the mountains, all of which are visible from the private balcony. The vaulted ceilings give a feeling of extra space, and ceiling fans keep the air moving. Bountiful continental breakfasts include fresh fruit smoothies and Kona coffee. Ruth and Herb Bockelman, the hosts, are some of the warmest people around (although no children are permitted) and like to call their establishment "a friendly alternative to a fine hotel." We agree. Amenities: balcony or patio. 4 rooms. Credit cards: MC, V.

Condos

Sealodge at Princeville   **$80**   ★★

P.O. Box 3400, Princeville, 96722, ☎ *(808) 826-7168.*
Single: $80. Double: $80.
Also known as "Hardy's Happy Hula Hut," this comfortable one-bedroom condominium offers spectacular ocean views for a reasonable price in a million-dollar location. It's situated at Sealodge at Princeville, a cedar-shake complex on a bluff overlooking the ocean, totally rebuilt after the hurricane. This ground-floor unit is comfortably furnished in white-washed rattan and has picture windows on all sides. The "Hut" is fully equipped with a washer/dryer, coffee maker, toaster, microwave, TV and VCR, cassette player, dishwasher, refrigerator and stove. The secluded beach is reached via a steep path (marked "use at own risk"), but other great North Shore strands are only five minutes away. Lazier types can use the pool, which is right next door. Two-night minimum. Amenities: balcony or patio. 1 room. Credit cards: not accepted.

The Cliffs at Princeville   **$85–$250**   ★★

P.O. Box 1005, Princeville, 96714, ☎ *(808) -.*
Single: $85–$250. Double: $85–$250.

Adjacent to the famed 45-hole Princeville Golf complex designed by Robert Trent Jones, Jr., the sprawling Cliffs at Princeville provides good value for golfers who can't afford the Princeville Hotel. Accommodations are either one-bedroom, a one-bedroom with loft, or four-bedroom units. Each features a fully equipped kitchen, two full baths, maid service, wet bar, color TV, guest sofabed and two private lanais with ocean or mountain views. Some have VCRs and extra TVs. Amenities: tennis, Jacuzzi, sauna, balcony or patio, family plan. Credit cards: A, DC, D, MC, V.

Resorts

Princeville Hotel   **$290–$465**   ★ ★ ★ ★ ★

5520 Kahaku Road, Princeville, 96722, ☎ *(800) 826-4400, (808) 826-9644, FAX (808) 826-1166. Rated restaurant: La Cascata, Café Hanalei*
Single: $290–$465. Double: $290–$465.

Whatever one thinks of the Princeville Hotel and its Versailles-size lobby, with acres of obsidian and green marble, gilt-topped columns, richly embroidered Renaissance tapestries and Greek sea-god statues, nobody disputes the fact that the hotel sits on one of the most stunning pieces of real estate on Kauai. The trio of buildings that makes up the property terrace down a ridge, directly fronting Hanalei Bay and the mysterious, sawtooth cliffs better known in Hollywoodland as "Bali Hai." Views of the sunset from the floor-to-ceiling windows of the The Living Room, the hotel's modestly named lounge, are legendary. Yet this stunning vantage point has come with a painful price. If it can be believed, the opulence you see today is relatively new—the hotel, like most of the structures on the island, was devastated by Hurricane Iniki in 1992. A failed sprinkler system caused extensive flooding, and the entire 10th floor collapsed. After a $35 million repair job, the hotel re-opened in October 1993, and within two months was booked to capacity. Besides the glorious setting, people continue to come for the world-class golf, excellent food and the warmth of the staff (for all its trappings, the atmosphere is completely unpretentious). Guest rooms are all nicely sized and amenity-filled, and decorated in beige or green color schemes. Try to book a Prince Junior suite, on floors 8–11; these have especially gorgeous views, which extend to the sumptuous marble baths with spa tubs and gold fixtures. One unique feature to all rooms is the "magic" window in the bathroom that becomes opaque at will by electronic means (why you'd not want to look at THAT view is a mystery). Among the hotel's entertainments is an in-house movie theater, where you can watch *South Pacific* until you gag (first-run pictures are also shown, for variety). To immerse yourself in the real thing, take a lauhala weaving class or watch a poi-pounding demonstration. When hunger strikes, there's room service, the beach bar or afternoon tea and snacks in the aforementioned Living Room, which also features first-class Hawaiian entertainment. There are two top-rated restaurants, La Cascata, offering Mediterranean-Italian food, and the indoor-outdoor Café Hanalei, known for its lavish Friday seafood buffet. Pu'u Poa, the hotel's stretch of beach, dotted with yellow striped covered loungers, has lovely golden sand that's raked daily. There's also a large pool with a swim-up bar, three Roman-style Jacuzzis and a wading pool for the kids. All manner of watersports, from kayaking to scuba diving, can be arranged. Amenities: tennis, health club, exercise room, Jacuzzi, sauna, balcony or patio, family plan, business services. 252 rooms. Credit cards: A, DC, D, MC, V.

South Shore

Koloa

Bed-and-Breakfasts

Island Home **$65–$75** ★★

1707 Kelaukia Street, Koloa, 96765, ☎ (808) 742-2839.
Single: $65–$75. Double: $65–$75.

A stay at Island Home ensures that the beach is never far away. A walking path near the B&B extends from Shipwreck Beach to Brennecke's Beach. You'll also get plenty of privacy at a good price. The two units in the large residence have their own entrances, tasteful interior decor, private baths, TVs and VCRs, a microwave and refrigerator. Laundry facilities are available. Breakfasts consist of tropical fruits, beverages and homemade breads. Coolers, beach mats and towels are provided. Hosts Mike and Gail Beeson will be happy to recommend activities on the island. 2 rooms. Credit cards: not accepted.

Resorts

Hyatt Regency Kauai **$280–$1800** ★★★★★

1571 Poipu Road, Koloa, 96756, ☎ (800) 233-1234, (808) 742-1234, FAX (808) 742-1557. Rated restaurant: Dondero's, Ilima Terrace
Single: $280–$1800. Double: $280–$1800.

Having opened in 1990, the Hyatt Regency Kauai is a relative newcomer among the resorts on Kauai. Its facilities are interesting in that their builders have deliberately eschewed the modern high-tech school of architecture and were determined to re-create traditional plantation-style dwellings of the '20s and '30s. Have they succeeded in achieving instant age? Yes. The building that houses the main entrance and lobby is impressive. Situated above an artificial lagoon and with sturdy pillars supporting a green-tiled, hipped roof, the building is firmly anchored to its surroundings. Reminiscent of an Oriental temple, the hotel is mysterious and invites exploration. The interior of the Hyatt Regency Kauai is everything we had been led to expect. The lavish use of native woods gives a sense of stability and harks back to earlier, less-harried times. Equally evocative of another era are the cast-bronze lighting fixtures and gates used throughout the public areas. Some are authentic pieces, salvaged from demolished buildings, and others are reproductions, but we challenge you to determine which is which. We can only applaud the builder's decision to minimize the use of air conditioning in favor of wide verandas, high ceilings and sliding doors that encourage a natural flow of air. As a result, there is no need for artificial cooling in the public areas. Guests rooms are exceptionally large with separate sitting areas and large lanais. Furniture is either rattan or more substantial wooden pieces designed to complement the '20s and '30s style. There are six restaurants in the hotel, including the Ilima Terrace, which serves breakfast, lunch and dinner, and Dondero's, offering Italian regional cuisine in a stylish setting featuring lots of marble and intricate tile work. Our favorite, though, is the Tidepools. Guests can begin the evening with pupus and tropical drinks in the lounge, and then move on to the ál fresco dining rooms (elegant thatched huts) situated among the artificial lagoons. Candlelight, tradewinds, palm trees... speaking of lagoons, the Hyatt Regency has more than 10 acres of them, all linked by streams, waterfalls and waterslides, one of which is a stomach-lurching 140 feet tall. Guests can swim, float or otherwise propel themselves from lagoon to lagoon past a carefully composed tropical landscape that includes the artfully placed wreckage of an interisland schooner. In certain circles, golf on the par-72, 6956-yard course designed by Robert Trent Jones, Jr. is the main reason to come to Hawaii. It will be the location for the 1997 Grand Slam of Golf Tournament. Others can proceed to the Anara Spa, where the preferred treatment is Hawaiian lomi-lomi massage, in which a mixture of red clay from the base of Mount Waialeale and sea salt is applied to the entire body, after which one is wrapped in ti leaves. It's possible to spend your whole vacation without leaving the Hyatt's grounds—there's that much to do. Amenities: tennis, health club, Jacuzzi, sauna, balcony or patio, family plan, club floor, business services. 600 rooms. Credit cards: A, DC, D, MC, V.

Lawai

Bed-and-Breakfasts

Marjorie's Kauai Inn   **$45–$70**   ★★★

P.O. Box 866, Lawai, 96765, ☎ *(800) 717-8838, (808) 332-8838.*
Single: $45–$70. Double: $45–$70.

Marjorie's rooms are perched overlooking the spectacular Lawai Valley. From private lanais, guests can look down on the tree tops or across at the mountains on the other side of the valley. The Valley View and Tradewind rooms have been constructed recently. Both have queen-size beds, private baths and a mini-kitchen with microwave and coffeemaker, plus laundry facilities. The Puka is aimed at the single traveler on a budget. It has its own private entrance, too, and a comfortable futon serves as seating as well as the bed. All rooms have cable TV and phones. Nearby activities for Marjorie's guests include ocean kayaking and sugarcane-road bike riding. But don't try to keep up with her—at age 47, she rode a bike across the North American continent, alone. Amenities: Jacuzzi, balcony or patio. 3 rooms. Credit cards: not accepted.

Condos

Hale Kua   **$75**   ★★

P.O. Box 649, Lawai, 96765, ☎ *(800) 440-4353, (808) 332-8570.*
Single: $75. Double: $75.

At Hale Kua, you have your choice of a guest cottage or condo, both located in the little town of Lawai. The property is surrounded by lush gardens with a hammock for afternoon reading and there's a hiking trail right out the back door. Our preference is for the guest cottage, which has sweeping views over the Lawai Valley down towards the ocean. Both units, though, are nicely decorated in tropical pastels and feature a separate bedroom with a queen-size bed, full bath, kitchen, queen sleeper in the living room, cable TV and VCR, telephone and washer/dryer. Barbecue grills are available for guests' use, along with coolers and other beach gear. Continental breakfast is an additional $5 per person. Hale Kua is close to Poipu-area beaches and a comfortable drive away from the Waimea Canyon. 2 rooms. Credit cards: not accepted.

Poipu

Bed-and-Breakfasts

Gloria's Spouting Horn Bed & Breakfast $150   ★★★

4464 Lawai Beach Road, Poipu, 96756, ☎ (808) 742-6995.
Single: $150. Double: $150.
Gloria's Bed & Breakfast was a fixture on the Kauai scene before Hurricane Iniki quite literally blew it out to sea. Fortunately, owners Gloria and Bob Merkle rebuilt their establishment, and the result is what may be the pluperfect bed-and-breakfast establishment in Hawaii, or anywhere, for that matter. This time around, all rooms are oceanfront rooms, and none are more than 30 feet from the waves. In the yard there's a lava-rock shower under a mango tree to wash off the saltwater off before you go inside. Each room is furnished individually with antiques. Probably the most famous room is the Puana Aloha, with a sensual canopy of intertwined willow branches. All have private Japanese-style soaking tubs. Guests get off to a good start each morning with a Hawaiian breakfast served on the lanai (or you can serve yourself and take your breakfast back to your room on a tray). Homemade pastries are served with fresh juice. Gloria uses her best English china and linens for this. She will be happy to share her recipes with guests, but they must promise to send her a recipe from the mainland (or wherever) when they get back. Gloria's is also a favorite venue for weddings and groups; up to 25 can be accommodated. Host Bob Merkle is also an ordained minister and will perform the ceremony. No children under 14, no pets. Amenities: balcony or patio, business services. 5 rooms. Credit cards: not accepted.

Condos

Colony Poipu Kai $160–$220   ★★

1941 Poipu Road, Poipu, 96756, ☎ (800) 777-1700, (808) 742-6464, FAX (808) 742-7865. Rated restaurant: The House of Seafood
Single: $160–$220. Double: $160–$220.
The Colony Poipu Kai is BIG—set on 110 acres, the grounds offer guests the use of six swimming pools, nine tennis courts (with resident pro), two nearby beaches, and an activity center if you run out of ideas. Overlooking the tennis courts is an excellent restaurant, the House of Seafood. Units of up to three bedrooms are situated in a series of three-story buildings; many are directly on the ocean. All are furnished with fully equipped kitchens, and the choicest ones feature cathedral ceilings, sleeping lofts, washer/dryers and microwaves. Daily maid service is provided. Amenities: tennis, balcony or patio. Credit cards: MC, V.

Poipu Kapili $160–$310   ★★★

2221 Kapili Road, Poipu, 96756, ☎ (800) 443-7714, (808) 742-6449, FAX (808) 742-9162.
Single: $160–$310. Double: $160–$310.
The Poipu Kapili will more than satisfy travelers with discriminating tastes. Set on five acres, these plantation-style buildings with bright-green hipped-roofs are newly

rebuilt after the hurricane. All of the apartments are unusually spacious—the one-bedroom units are at least 1150 square feet, and the two-bedroom apartments are 1820 square feet and have three bathrooms. Most are two-story townhouses, and you'll never hear a peep from the neighbors. One could spend a few days getting orientated to the different rooms and views. Decor depends on the individual owner, but all feature beautiful, louvered, mahogany sliding doors and high ceilings with revolving fans. All have separate living areas, gourmet kitchens and tons of closet space. Some are outfitted with oversized, woven, dark-stained rattan lounge chairs with pillowy cushions, sofas and loveseats, organized in comfortable group-ings around a sophisticated entertainment center with a 25-inch television, VCR, CD and tape player. Some owners have thoughtfully provided current paperbacks, books and magazines for guests to take to the beach. Artwork by local painters and craftsmen decorate the walls and shelves. There are extra TVs in the bedrooms; the master bedroom has a second VCR. Beds are extremely comfortable, with bamboo headboards and patchwork quilts and pillows. The master suite faces the beach, which is across the street. This beach is rocky, but surfers like it for the great breaks. Sandy Poipu Beach Park is just a short walk away. Two story units have patios on the ground floor and balconies (no lanais) on the second floor. Some thoughtful touches help make a visit here memorable: A fresh herb garden is available for guests to liven up their meals, bananas from an employee's yard are sometimes left on doorsteps, and there's a weekly poolside continental breakfast. There are videos ($3 per day) and paperbacks to check out in the office, but you'll have to rent them before closing time at 5 p.m. Amenities: tennis, balcony or patio. 60 rooms. Credit cards: MC, V.

Sunset Kahili   **$85–$125**   ★★

1663 Pe'e Road, Poipu, 96756, ☎ (808) 742-7434, FAX (808) 742-6058.
Single: $85–$125. Double: $85–$125.

The Sunset Kahili, on a bluff overlooking the ocean, has 35 units in a five-story building. Although the exterior looks like a county hospital, the individually deco-rated apartments are nicely furnished by individual owners and therefore reflect 35, distinct personalities. Shoji screens separate living and sleeping areas. All have mod-ern kitchens with all the trimmings, including an ice-making fridge, washer/dryer and dishwasher. If you decide to stay here, get a room on the third, fourth or and fifth floors. They have views of the ocean and Poipu Beach. The first- and second-story units have a view of the ocean and gardens only. Nevertheless, all units have spectacular sunset views, and the spray rising from Spouting Horn is usually visible from the lanais. Brennecke's Beach, the bodysurfers' mecca, is within walking dis-tance, as is Poipu Beach, with its snorkeling, surfing and swimming. Guests can also walk to nearby restaurants, shopping, tennis and golf. Amenities: balcony or patio, family plan. 36 rooms. Credit cards: MC, V.

Whaler's Cove   **$225–$375**   ★★★

2640 Puuholo Road, Poipu, 96756, ☎ (800) 367-7052, (808) -.
Single: $225–$375. Double: $225–$375.

Whaler's Cove makes the most of its beachfront location and the buildings are laid out to the natural curve of the ocean. Unfortunately there's no sandy beach, but there is the sound of the waves and the wind blowing thorough the coconut palms. The reception areas and all of the individually owned units feature thousands of dollars' worth of koa wood. Each apartment has two bedrooms and two baths, a dining area, gourmet kitchens and washer/dryer, and some have Jacuzzi tubs in the master baths. Decor varies from apartment to apartment, but they are all uniformly luxe. Some are furnished with Asian antiques, whitewashed wicker and wood, and extra-high platform beds topped with plump cushions. Facilities include a video library. An enthusiastic staff provides concierge service. Amenities: balcony or patio. 39 rooms.

Inns

Poipu Plantation $85–$110   ★ ★ ★

1792 Pe'e Road, Poipu, 96756, ☎ (800) 733-1632, (808) 742-6757.
Single: $85–$110. Double: $85–$110.
Although this property, which is within walking distance to Poipu's best beaches, bills itself as a B&B, it really isn't. If any breakfast is served, you've got to make it yourself in the fully equipped kitchen provided in the unit. Affordable, secluded and quiet, the seven units have one or two bedrooms. Wicker furniture and flowered chintz cushions combine nicely with hardwood floors for a feeling of tropical sophistication. Shoji screens separate the living room from the bedrooms. All have ceiling fans and air conditioning (unusual for these parts). Services include coin-op washer/dryers and an outdoor barbecue/spa area. Amenities: Jacuzzi, balcony or patio. 7 rooms. Credit cards: MC, V.

Resorts

Sheraton Kauai Beach Resort

2440 Hoonani Road, Poipu, 96756, ☎ (800) 325-3535, (808) 742-1661, FAX (808) 742-9777. Rated restaurant: Outrigger Room
After being leveled by Hurricane Iniki, the Sheraton Kauai Beach Resort is scheduled to reopen in November 1997. About 90 percent of its rooms will have ocean views. Guests will be able to enjoy oceanfront dining in the Outrigger Room, and there will be live entertainment nightly in the Drum Lounge. Other features will include a freshwater pool, three tennis courts and access to five major golf courses. 510 rooms.

Poipu Beach

Bed-and-Breakfasts

Poipu Bed & Breakfast Inn $110–$140   ★ ★ ★

2720 Hoonani Road, Poipu Beach, 96756, ☎ (800) 827-6478, (808) 742-1146, FAX (808) 742-6843.
Single: $110–$140. Double: $110–$140.
The Poipu Bed & Breakfast Inn is an imaginative and successful re-creation of Old Hawaii as it should have been. The main building is a 1933 plantation house, renovated and brought up to 1990s specifications. It's close enough to the beach that you can hear the waves pound outside. Guests enter the Great Room through orig-

inal French doors. They are greeted by white wicker furniture, country pine, an abundance of tropical flowers and the inn's signature antique carousel horses. Guest rooms are individually decorated with local art and tropical print fabrics. Native woods have been used lavishly on floors, ceilings and the sliding doors, and louvered windows that let in the trade winds. Bathrooms are state-of-the-art and most have whirlpool tubs. All rooms have color TVs and VCRs, and there's a video library, but no in-room phones. Guests are welcome to have afternoon tea in the Great Room, and a continental breakfast is served a few doors down the street at the Ocean Front Inn, a sister establishment. 4 rooms. Credit cards: MC, V.

The Ocean Front Inn   **$125–$175**   ★ ★ ★

Hoonani Street, Poipu Beach, 96756, ☎ *(800) 827-6478, (808) 742-1146, FAX (808) 742-6843.*
Single: $125–$175. Double: $125–$175.

The Ocean Front Inn offers a variety of luxurious rooms, each with its own personality. The Dolphin Cove Suite and the Coral Cove Suite both have whirlpool tubs-for-two and private ocean-view lanais. They are a favorite with honeymooners. The remaining three rooms are just as luxuriously furnished, but face the gardens. Families traveling together are fond of renting the Orchid and Palm Rooms and converting them into a suite. All of the rooms are tastefully decorated in pastel tones, with wicker and antique pine accent pieces. Amenities: Jacuzzi, balcony or patio. 5 rooms. Credit cards: MC, V.

Condos

Kiahuna Plantation   **$155–$450**   ★ ★ ★

2253 Poipu Road, Poipu Beach, 96756, ☎ *(800) 688-7444, (808) 742-6411, FAX (808) 742-7233. Rated restaurant: The Plantation Gardens*
Single: $155–$450. Double: $155–$450.

After sustaining considerable hurricane damage, the Kiahuna Plantation reopened in October 1995, to the delight of many repeat visitors. It's a delightful property, consisting of a number of trim, low-slung white buildings spread out on a coconut grove, facing its own stretch of golden-sand beach. The former home of a sugar plantation manager (aren't they all?), it was recently placed under the aegis of Outrigger Hotels and Resorts, which hasn't changed anything; in fact, all of Outrigger's packages and programs now apply to the Kiahuna Plantation. The individually owned units are spacious one- and two-bedroom apartments with louvered shutters and classy wood and rattan furnishings. Each has a living and dining area, fully equipped kitchen, color TV and videotape player, and ceiling fans. Naturally, the ocean-view units are the most desirable. Unusual for a condominium, the Kiahuna Plantation also offers a myriad of entertainment options. A "*Keiki Klub*" takes kids (ages five–12) in hand for a round of daily activities, from storytelling to Hawaiian games. There's a beach-activities center, concierge, gas barbecues and picnic tables. Across the street is the resort's own five-star tennis facility (free to guests), pro shop and swimming pool. Two 18-hole championship golf courses, The Kiahuna Golf Club and Poipu Bay Resort Course, are located nearby, as is shopping and dining in Poipu Shopping Village and Koloa Town. An added attraction on the property is Moir Gardens, featuring a world-class cactus garden. Daily maid service, laundry, beach towels. Amenities: tennis, balcony or patio, family plan. 330 rooms. Credit cards: A, CB, DC, D, MC, V.

Resorts

Embassy Vacation Resort–Poipu Point   **$260–$1000**   ★★★

1613 Pe'e Road, Poipu Beach, ☎ (800) -, (808) 742-1888.
Single: $260–$1000. Double: $260–$1000.

The Embassy Vacation Resort at Poipu Point, which opened in 1995, is located on the opposite end of a scenic beachwalk from the luxurious Hyatt Regency Kauai. The property, which is partly a time-share resort and condominium, makes no attempt to ape its older neighbor. It has a casual, friendly, party-hearty atmosphere, with free mai tais and pupus by the pool every afternoon, champagne punch and continental breakfasts with shell leis for the ladies, and an "island orientation," which is actually a non-too-subtle way to get you to purchase a unit for two weeks a year. But nobody pushes you to go—there's always the conveniently located video in your room, which will attempt to do the same thing in the comfort of your suite. The resort makes up for the lack of a good beach with a way-cool swimming pool with real sand and lots of deck chairs (sandy beaches are close by). And the pool is open 24 hours a day for moonlight dips. All of the 217 accommodations are one-, two- or three-bedroom suites with washer-dryers and complete kitchens. The kitchens are strangely placed right in the middle of the room, but they are great, modern, gourmet utilities, with granite counter-tops, double sinks, a toaster, coffee maker (a packet costs $1.50), dishwasher and even a trash compactor. Refrigerators come with cold (actually cool) water dispensers. There's also a wet bar. The living/dining area is more traditional, with green- and white-striped drapes, bamboo and wicker tables, a comfortable sofa and tasteful watercolors on the walls. The bathrooms are the suite's best feature, with lovely custom-tile floors, a big soaking tub, separate shower and a double sink in snazzy red marble. Bedrooms have blond-wood furnishings, a two-poster bed and an armoire concealing a TV (there's a bigger one in the living room). The room is cooled by a ceiling fan (quiet) as well as an air-conditioner (noisy). There's also tons of closet space, especially in the two-bedroom suites. The large, double lanais are a boon, especially in a deluxe, oceanfront unit. But you can't help but notice the unfortunate rust stains that have been allowed to eat into the concrete deck, ceiling and walls (come on folks, you're barely two years old!). This oversight is permissible in a budget motel, but when your room rate nudges into the $500-a-night range, there's just no excuse. Amenities: exercise room, Jacuzzi, balcony or patio, family plan. 217 rooms. Credit cards: A, MC, V.

West Shore

Waimea

Camping Grounds

Kokee Lodge Cabins   **$35–$45**   ★★

P.O. Box 819, Waimea, 96796, ☎ (808) 335-6061.
Single: $35–$45. Double: $35–$45.

The Kokee Lodge Cabins are in bucolic, 4345-acre Kokee State Park, which is more than 3000 feet above sea level. These rustic, mail-order-kit-style, cedar-log dwellings sleep up to seven persons. Some have just one large room, others have up to two bedrooms, with a queen-size bed in the living/kitchen/and dining area. The kitchen has a working stove and refrigerator and a number of utensils. Another nice touch are the bathrooms with hot showers. Towels and bedding are supplied, but at these prices, there's no cleanup service. Because of the altitude, it tends to get cold at night, so an efficient Franklin stove is provided, and Presto logs are sold, plus there's plenty of wood to be found (but don't cut down any trees!). The Kokee Lodge within the park serves breakfast and lunch, but closes at 3:30 p.m. It's advisable to bring a supply of food and water, and perhaps your own portable barbecue grill, as none are available. 12 rooms. Credit cards: not accepted.

Resorts

Waimea Plantation Cottages   **$180–$470**

9400 Kaumualii Highway, Waimea, 96796, ☎ (800) -, (808) 338-1625, FAX (808) 338-1625.

Single: $180–$470. Double: $180–$470.

Located on a spiritual plane somewhere between the ethnic chic of the Kona Village on the Big Island and the retro opulence of the Princeville Hotel, the Waimea Plantation Cottages offer the kind of Hawaiian vacation that gets written about in the J. Peterman Company catalog—a vacation in the seductive Hawaii between the wars, when ceiling fans were high-tech and people traveled by interisland steamer. The Waimea Plantation Cottages are exactly what they say they are—plantation cottages that at one time housed employees of the Kekaha Sugar Company and Waimea Sugar Mill. Most were built in the '20s and '30s, but one of them dates back to the 1880s. The cottages are randomly placed in a grove of 765 coconut palms that were planted in the early years of this century. The cottages have been painstakingly restored down (up?) to their corrugated iron roofs and now contain many period furnishings of mahogany, wicker and native koa. Floors are painted wood or hardwood and covered with woven grass mats. Numerous windows covered with café curtains let in air and light. A few concessions have been made to progress and the kitchens and bathrooms (with tubs big enough for two) are completely modern. We were saddened to hear that the Grove Dining Room, the resort's only restaurant, has closed. We'll miss the Portuguese bean soup and the reasonable prices. There really isn't much to do here and that is the great part of the appeal. The black-sand beach is great for walking, but the water is muddy and the surf is usually too rough for swimming. There's a pool and a clay tennis court, which was reputedly a gift from the plantation's founder, H.P. Faye, to his wife around 1910. Horseshoe and croquet sets are available from the main office. Drinks are usually prepared by guests who enjoy them while seated in Adirondack chairs on their lanais. Waimea Plantation Cottages are usually booked well in advance. Amenities: tennis, balcony or patio. 48 rooms. Credit cards: MC, V.

Where to Eat

Your stomach will be happy on Kauai. Freshly caught fish and freshly picked produce lead off many menus, along with traditional Hawaiian flavors and an impressive assortment of ethnic cuisines. You can dine ritzy, cheap or in between, often with a picture-postcard ocean view tossed in to the deal. Lihue, in particular, has a wonderful selection of budget eateries and, yes, you'll find an all-too-ample supply of fast-food chains sprinkled about. For picnics and snacks, take advantage of local food vendors, produce stands and farmer's markets. Dress is casual at all but the swankiest restaurants.

East Shore

Hanamaulu

Hanamaulu Restaurant & Tea Hou   **$$$**

3-4291 Kuhio Highway, Hanamaulu, ☎ *(808) 245-2511.*
Asian cuisine.
Lunch: 9 a.m.–1 p.m., entrées $10–$20.
Dinner: 4:30–9 p.m., entrées $5–$30. Closed: Mon.
The Hanamaulu Restaurant offers a hefty menu of Japanese and Chinese specialties at skinny prices in a variety of settings—an ordinary dining room, a delightful tea house (advance reservations required) or, if you like to banter with the chef or rub elbows with fellow patrons, the sushi bar or teppanyaki counter. The ginger-fried chicken, tempura items and sushi handrolls are all recommended. Features: private dining rooms. Reservations recommended. Credit cards: MC, V.

Kapaa

A Pacific Café   **$$$**   ★★★★

Kauai Village, Kuhio Highway, Kapaa, ☎ *(808) 822-0013.*
Pacific Rim cuisine. Specialties: Appetizers, fresh seafood, dessert.
Dinner: 5:30–10 p.m., entrées $22–$24.
The original. The first of Jean Marie Josselin's acclaimed Pacific Rim restaurants sits hidden away in an obscure shopping center location near a Safeway (we missed it on our first walk-through). Tantalizing things await within, though. The sleek interior is designed in a sleek '40s Hawaiian-Japanese motif, with a changing exhibit of original art and a viewing kitchen for show-off chefs. This inventive cuisine features fresh quality ingredients, including greens, veggies and herbs grown on the restaurant's own certified farm. All dinners (menus change nightly) are accompanied by an assortment of foccacia breads and muffins, but don't neglect to order one of the appetizers ($6.95–9.75 each) called "first tastes." These are sometimes better than

the entrées. A signature dish is deep-fried tiger-eye sushi with wasabi beurre blanc. Also beautiful to look at (and eat) are the poached scallops ravioli with tobiko caviar and lime ginger sauce, and the green papaya spring roll with sweet-sour sauce. The trouble with these dainties is that after two bites, pouf! they're gone. Soups and salads are priced the same as appetizers. Some examples are Thai coconut curry basil soup with fresh island fish and shrimp, and a spicy seared ahi salad with Kauai romaine and Caesar dressing. Many entrées are prepared on a wood-burning grill, served with seasonal veggies and rice. They're presented like gift packages on hand-thrown, oversize ceramic dishes in dizzying designs. The individual chops in the Hunan lamb rack are split and tied with green onion sprigs. Stunning. Desserts are mini-sculptures with kooky names ("Toasted Hawaiian" and "Heat of Passion") that are almost too pretty to eat, but you do. Features: own baking, rated wine cellar. Reservations required. Credit cards: A, CB, DC, D, MC.

Aloha Diner $ ★★

971-F Kuhio Highway, Kapaa, ☎ *(808) 822-3851.*
Hawaiian cuisine. Specialties: Hawaiian plate lunches, kalua pig, laulau, pipikaula.
Lunch: 10:30 a.m.–3 p.m., entrées $6–$11.
Dinner: 5:30–9 p.m., entrées $6–$11. Closed: Mon., Sun.
This restaurant's name gives you a clue to what's inside: local-style food in a down-to-earth environment. Set in a small, unobtrusive shopping center, the Aloha Diner offers plate lunch combos of kalua pig or laulau with lomi salmon with a choice of rice or poi; dinners are similar but with more choices and at a higher price. Everything is available à la carte. Friends recommend the *pipikaula*—homemade, dried sirloin fried in oil, similar to beef jerky.

Hana-Ya $$

1394 Kuhio Highway, Kapaa, ☎ *(808) 822-3878.*
Japanese cuisine. Specialties: Sushi, tempura, tempura udon.
Lunch: 11:30 a.m.–2 p.m., entrées $5–$17.
Dinner: 5:30–9:30 p.m., entrées $5–$17.
What, a sushi bar with no sake? Yes, it's true, Hana-Ya has no liquor license, but you're welcome to BYOB. The surroundings are utilitarian, with few tables and a small sushi bar, but the food is great, especially the tempura udon (saimin with a couple of Godzilla-sized tempura shrimp on top), and the spicy hamachi and salmon skin rolls.

Mema Thai-Chinese Cuisine $$

Wailua Shopping Plaza, Kapaa, ☎ *(808) 823-0899.*
Specialties: Crispy shrimp rolls, lemon grass soup, sweet basil seafood, vegetarian dishes.
Lunch: 11 a.m.–2 p.m., entrées $7–$15.
Dinner: 5–9:30 p.m., entrées $7–$15.
Behind a Sizzler in a Kapaa shopping center, this long-time ethnic fave is elegantly decked out with fine linens, glassware, artwork and orchid sprays. Billed as half a Chinese restaurant, Mema's features that old standby, cashew chicken, in a mild melange of roasted nuts, garlic and onions, stir-fried together. Vegetarians will be pleased with a huge list of choices from spring rolls to sticky rice. The various concoctions ranging from fresh basil with mixed vegetables, red chili with coconut

milk, and red, green, yellow and house curries can be mixed with any meat, chicken or seafood (even calamari and scallops with some orders) you desire. No lunch served on weekends. Owner Me Choy's siblings own The King and I, not far away at 901 Kuhio Highway, in the Waipouli Plaza, ☎ *(808) 822-1642.* A bit plainer in appearance, there's sometimes a friendly rivalry as to which is better. Specialties include beef, pork or chicken sautéed in a fresh basil sauce (the grow their own herbs here) with chili, garlic, mushrooms and oyster sauce. The King and I is open for dinner only, from 4:30–9:30 p.m. daily; until 10 p.m. Fridays and Saturdays. Credit cards: A, CB, DC, D, MC, V.

Papaya's Garden Café   **$**   ★★★
Kauai Village, Kapaa, ☎ (808) 742-9122.
American cuisine. Specialties: Baked goods, espresso, vegetarian entrées and burgers.
Breakfast: 9 a.m.–8 p.m., entrées $2–$10.
Lunch: 11 a.m.–8 p.m., entrées $2–$10.
Dinner: 5–8 p.m., entrées $2–$10. Closed: Sun.
A health-food store/café/deli/espresso bar situated in a tropical garden setting, Papaya's radiates a fine sense of well-being. Bakery goods include chocolate tofu pie and tahini maple cookies. This is serious stuff. If you're hungry for more than sweets, the kitchen issues out garden and tempeh burgers, grilled fish, chicken teriyaki, avocado sandwiches, Thai curries, stuffed baked potatoes, homemade soups and more. To-go specials are popular, and are priced by the pound. One day they may have spanakopita, shepherd's pie or marinated baked tofu. There's counter seating plus a few outside tables. Features: outside dining, own baking. Reservations not accepted. Credit cards: MC, V.

The Bull Shed   **$$**   ★★★
796 Kuhio Highway, Kapaa, ☎ (808) 822-3791.
American cuisine. Specialties: Prime rib, pork baby back ribs, garlic tenderloin, Australian lamb rack, salad bar.
Dinner: 5:30–10 p.m., entrées $11–$19.
This old favorite, opened in 1973, is a bit hard to find for first-timers (just look for McDonalds across the street). Decimated by Hurricane Iniki, the surroundings and the food have improved since it was rebuilt. The ocean view and beachside location are unchanged, though still great. Long waits are guaranteed for BIG portions of the trademark dish, prime rib, garlic tenderloin (a pungent filet steeped in fresh garlic and herb marinade and broiled) ribs, chicken and seafood. The rack of lamb is a full rack. One problem is that it can get a little stuffy, even with a non-smoking section. Wallet-friendly prices. Entrées include a trip to the salad bar. Children's menu, cocktails from 4:30 p.m. Reservations for six or more only. Features: outside dining. Credit cards: A, CB, DC, D, MC, V.

Lihue

Barbecue Inn   **$$**   ★★
2982 Kress Street, Lihue, ☎ (808) 245-2921.
American cuisine. Specialties: Japanese dishes, prime rib, sandwiches on homemade bread.
Lunch: 10:30 a.m.–1:30 p.m., entrées $4–$7.

Dinner: 5–8:30 p.m., entrées $7–$15. Closed: Sun.

Comfortably air-conditioned, the venerable Barbecue Inn is favored by local residents and politicos. The small room is decked out with vinyl booths and a bar with a TV set constantly buzzing with sports events. Many newcomers walk in and ask, where's the barbecue? Nowhere, really; menu items are simple, unfancy things residents like (teriyaki chicken, pork chops, tempura, steak, prime rib), but are made with the finest ingredients. All sandwiches are prepared on thick-sliced, home-baked bread. Loaves are available for takeout. Produce is locally grown, and only fresh fruit is served. One friend is fond of the miso soup—it reminds him of the kind his mom makes. For under $7 you can get a complete meal, accompanied by soup, beverage, that great fresh bread and dessert. At dinner, add a salad and a veggie. Tuna sandwiches are made with fresh ahi. Dinner hours are 4:30–8:45 p.m. on Fridays and Saturdays. Features: own baking. Reservations not accepted.

Café Portofino $$ ★★★

3501 Rice Street, Pacific Ocean Plaza, Lihue, ☎ *(808) 245-2121.*
Italian cuisine. Specialties: Rabbit in wine sauce, veal shanks, calves liver, sweetbreads in cream sauce.
Lunch: 11 a.m.–2 p.m., entrées $10–$19.
Dinner: 5–10 p.m., entrées $10–$19.

Homemade pastas, sauces, breads, sorbets and gelati are made daily in this classy, polished, authentic Italian café with a lanai offering a glimpse of lovely Kalapaki Bay. Stylish owner Guiseppe Avocadi, a native of the Italian Riviera (blue eyes, gleaming teeth and open-neck silk shirts) presides over the festivities. Residents like it for business lunches and special occasions. Local rabbit is featured in one of the signature dishes, coniglio in a white wine, black olive and herb sauce. Also fresh daily fish, osso bucco in an orange sauce, several veal preparations and bistecca di vitellone—sounds mo' bettah than New York strip steak, doesn't it? Live music (usually) jazz plays Thursday–Saturday. No lunch on weekends. Features: outside dining, own baking, private dining rooms. Reservations recommended. Credit cards: A, CB, DC, D, MC, V.

Duke's Canoe Club $$

On Kalapaki Beach, Lihue, ☎ *(808) 246-9599. Associated hotel: Kauai Marriott Resort. American cuisine. Specialties: Fresh daily fish, tossed Caesar salad, prime rib, Koloa pork ribs, Kimo's Hula Pie.*
Dinner: 5–10 p.m., entrées $10–$20.

Fresh fish brought in directly from the boats is a specialty of this restaurant and bar (The Barefoot Bar is a happening local watering hole) on beautiful Kalapaki Beach. This '40s Hawaiian-style eatery is dedicated in memory of the father of surfing, Duke Kahanamoku (there's another Duke's on Waikiki Beach), who surfed and canoed in this area. The hostess station is made of bamboo and covered by a thatched roof. The polished koa wood-paneled walls are hung with photos, memorabilia and some of the Duke's surfboards. A 30-foot lava-rock waterfall, koi pond and a 40-foot outrigger canoe complete the picture. For those who don't like fish, there's burly prime rib with the bone still in, pork ribs glazed in plum sauce (thankfully served small or regular size), shrimp scampi, even a plate of pasta with fresh veggies. Everything comes with an "all you care to eat" salad bar, which includes Caesar salad, muffins, sourdough rolls and steamed rice. Watch out for strolling musicians, though, unless you like that sort of thing. Features: outside dining. Reservations recommended.

Hamura's Saimin $

2956 Kress Street, Lihue, ☎ *(808) 245-3271.*
Japanese cuisine. Specialties: Saimin, won ton soup, ribs, barbecue chicken and beef teriyaki sticks, lilikoi chiffon pie.
Lunch: 10 a.m.–1 p.m., entrées $1–$5.
Dinner: 4–10 p.m., entrées $1–$5.
Small, medium, large or even extra-large bowls of steaming saimin (the best in the state), are slurped day and night at this old Lihue standby. Counter seating only, and there's inevitably a wait. Soup is made to order and topped with everything from fish cake to shrimp tempura. Takeout available. Reservations not accepted.

Kauai Kitchens $ ★★

4303 Rice Street, Lihue, ☎ *(808) 245-4513.*
Specialties: Sushi, bentos, homemade fried chicken, teriyaki beef.
Breakfast: 7 a.m.–1:30 p.m., entrées $2–$6.
Lunch: 11 a.m.–1:30 p.m., entrées $2–$6.
A small local chain (with locations in Koloa and Waimea) specializing in "quick and tasty island style" cooking to eat in or take out. Dishes range from Japanese (somen salad, teriyaki beef) to Filipino (pork adobo) to American (burgers, hamburger steak).

Ma's $ ★★

4277 Halenani Street (off Rice Street), Lihue, ☎ *(808) 245-3142.*
American cuisine. Specialties: Hawaiian and American breakfasts, sandwiches, stews, fresh fish.
Breakfast: 5 a.m.–1:30 p.m., entrées $2–$5.
Lunch: 11 a.m.–1:30 p.m., entrées $2–$5.
Dinner: entrées $2–$5.
A cheerful hodgepodge and a great bargain, Ma's "decor" features bright fluorescent lighting, year-round Christmas ornaments, assorted knickknacks and stuffed animals, including a tiger and Kermit the Frog. Most of the tables are "family style," meant for at least four people. A few old red booths are placed against the wall, covered with what looks like automobile floor rugs. One woman toils behind the counter doing everything, and even comes over with a cheerful "thanks for waiting," greeting. A whole pot of free coffee or tea comes with breakfast, which is almost unheard of today. It's best for breakfast; for $5 you get a Hawaiian breakfast of laulau, kalua pig or *pipikaula* (jerky) with two eggs and rice. Burgers are less than $2, as is Spam and egg. Other items include curry, tripe and beef stews, which cost $3–5, depending on size. Open until 11:30 a.m. Saturday–Sunday. For a similar menu, try **Dani's**, owned by Ma's nephew, at *4201 Rice Street,* ☎ *(808) 245-4991,* open from 5 a.m.–1:30 p.m.; it's bigger and brighter, but more impersonal. The kalua pig with eggs is recommended. Dani's is closed on Sunday. Reservations not accepted.

Nawiliwili

JJ's Broiler   **$$$**   ★★

Anchor Cove Shopping Center, Nawiliwili, ☎ (808) 246-4422.
American cuisine. Specialties: Black-bean prawns with spicy noodle salad, "world famous" Slavonic steak.
Lunch: 11 a.m.–5 p.m., entrées $6–$9.
Dinner: 5–10 p.m., entrées $9–$23.

JJ's Broiler has occupied this prime beachfront space for 25 years—in the beginning there was the trademark Slavonic steak (the restaurant calls it "world famous"), filets of beef steeped in garlic, wine and butter, and a tableside salad bar. Both items plus prime rib and barbecue chicken are menu stalwarts, but chef Mark Sassone is trying to inch the restaurant into the regional Pacific cuisine market with such offerings as Peking chicken tacos with garlic oyster sauce (offered as an appetizer for $8.95), spicy wasabi rib-eye and black-bean prawns with spicy noodle salad. Lunch is a fun and less-expensive island melting pot of light bites, including JJ's Saimin, won ton soup, Oriental chicken salad, fish and chips, and even a pastrami and Swiss cheese sandwich. Features: outside dining. Reservations recommended. Credit cards: DC, MC, V.

Kalapaki Beach Hut   **$**   ★★

Next to Anchor Cove, Nawiliwili, ☎ (808) 246-6330.
American cuisine. Specialties: Breakfasts, Steve's famous burgers, fish and chicken sandwiches, vegetarian selections.
Breakfast: 6–10:30 a.m., entrées $4–$8.
Lunch: 10:30 a.m.–6:30 p.m., entrées $4–$8.

Burgers have meant big business for Steve and Sharon Gerald, who own this grill (not quite a hut) with a second story that's open to Kalapaki Bay views and breezes. Many people don't know that the Geralds started the legendary Ono Char Burger stand (original in Anahola, second branch in Kapaa) before there was a "Duane" connected to it. Steve and Sharon still feature the juicy beef patties piled high with fixin's, but the new specialty item at the Hut are burgers ground fresh from Hanalei-raised buffalo. Sunday hours are 11 a.m.–3 p.m. Features: outside dining.

Puhi

Fisherman's Galley   **$**   ★★

Highway 50, three minutes from Lihue, Puhi, ☎ (808) 246-4700.
Seafood cuisine. Specialties: Fresh off-the-boat seafood, lobster, burgers.
Lunch: 10 a.m.–9 p.m., entrées $4–$12.
Dinner: 4–9 p.m., entrées $4–$12. Closed: Sun.

The only thing missing at the Fisherman's Galley is the ocean view (its location is in the country side across from Kauai Community College). But the fish (usually ono, never cod, like Mrs. Paul's) in the fish and chips, fish tacos, broiled fish sandwiches, seafood melts and homemade creamy seafood chowder were all just recently hooked and cooked by the folks who own Gent-Lee Sportfishing Charters. Many people just stop with the fish and chips, but be adventurous and order from the daily blackboard menu. Reservations recommended. Credit cards: A, MC, V.

Gaylord's **$$$**

3-2087 Kaumualii Highway, Puhi, ☎ *(808) 245-9593.*
American cuisine. Specialties: Fresh fish, prime rib, pasta.
Lunch: 11 a.m.–3 p.m., entrées $8–$11.
Dinner: 5–10 p.m., entrées $17–$27.

Lunch, Sunday brunch or dinner in a covered courtyard or outdoor veranda over-looking the velvet lawns and lovingly tended flower gardens of a restored 1930s sugar plantation is a romantic affair popular with local families as well as visitors. At first glance, as expected with a major tourist attraction, the menu seems timid (except for a few items such as a delicious peppered ahi Caesar salad and blackened prime rib) and pricey ($8.95 for a Kilohana burger). But it's all a delightful experience—how many times will you get to feel like a guest at Lady Whosis' country estate? Early bird specials from 5–6:30 p.m. Sunday brunch from 9:30 a.m.–3 p.m. Features: outside dining, own baking, Sunday brunch. Reservations recommended.

Wailua

Dragon Inn **$$** ★★

4-901 Kuhio Highway, in Waipouli Plaza, Wailua, ☎ *(808) 822-3788.*
Chinese cuisine. Specialties: Sizzling platters, Hong Kong-style roast duck.
Lunch: 11 a.m.–2 p.m., entrées $6–$18.
Dinner: 4:30–9:30 p.m., entrées $6–$18.

You can come for the fairly tasty all-you-can-eat buffets (lunch daily except Monday for $5.95, dinner, Monday only for $10.95) that are popular with regular custom-ers, but don't neglect to order from the Cantonese and Szechuan menu, which is peppered with unusual specialties. It's fun to eat family-style (this place caters to them) in a pleasant but nondescript room, served by waiters in bow ties. You might try sizzling shrimp balls with black-bean sauce, pot roast chicken, or perhaps order the Peking duck for two (a day in advance, please). Lighter appetites will delight in Chinese chicken salad. Old standbys such as sweet and sour spareribs, mu shu pork and egg fu yung are here, too. The kitchen does not stint on portions—there'll be equal amounts of starch as well as meat on your plate. Credit cards: A, CB, DC, D, MC, V.

North Shore

Hanalei

Bali Hai Restaurant **$$$** ★★★

5380 Honoiki Road, Hanalei, ☎ *(808) 826-6522. Associated hotel: Hanalei Bay Resort.*
International cuisine. Specialties: Salmon Bali Hai, coconut breaded shrimp, Pacific ciop-
pino.
Breakfast: 7 a.m.–11 p.m., entrées $5–$13.
Lunch: 11:30 a.m.–2 p.m., entrées $5–$14.
Dinner: 5:30–10 p.m., entrées $21–$26.

A romantic and quiet restaurant, with high ceilings and bilevel seating, Bali Hai is where the greatest jazz musicians on the island come to jam in the cocktail lounge on Saturdays and Sundays. Views from the open-air dining room are outstanding, so when it's raining, you might want to eat elsewhere. Service is unfailingly gracious and polite, but it can be slow. The cuisine features inventive twists on old favorites, especially at breakfast (poi pancakes). There are quite a few eclectic Pacific Rim selections, but most are familiar items that the meat and 'taters crowd will like. Among the former is the blackened ahi sashimi appetizer with sweetened wasabi soy sauce (ubiquitous with this cuisine), baked boursin cheese lightly crusted with macadamia nuts and blackened sesame seeds, served with papaya coulis, and pork medallions grilled and served with a raspberry shiitake sauce. Some folks think it all sounds better on paper than it tastes on the plate. Features: outside dining, own baking. Reservations recommended. Credit cards: A, CB, DC, D, MC, V.

Hanalei Dolphin $$$ ★★

5-5016 Kuhio Highway, Hanalei, ☎ (808) 826-6113.
Seafood cuisine. Specialties: Fresh fish, steaks, chicken.
Dinner: 5:30–10 p.m., entrées $13–$25.

The Hanalei Dolphin has a schizoid reputation. Some people rave that it has the finest seafood on the north shore, others say the fish is overcooked, undercooked, whatever. Service is either friendly and leisurely or the worst in the state, with attitude to match. In either case, the Dolphin is ALWAYS jammed, so expect a wait (there's decent window-shopping outside). Partially destroyed by Hurricane Iniki and now rebuilt, the rustic dining room features soft lighting, louvered windows and lanterns. Entrées are served with tasty, family style salad (choice of dressings, homemade garlic croutons), steak fries (best choice) or rice and hot homemade bread (from somebody else's bakery). Interesting choices include ceviche, artichoke crowns, fresh fish and chips, calamari, or the cholesterol-laden Dolphin shrimp baked in butter and wine, special seasonings, plus a sour-cream topping. You can have one of the "light" dinners, such as broccoli and mushroom casserole with a cheddar cheese sauce, a bowl of seafood chowder or just salad and bread ($8.50). Homemade desserts. Wines are surprisingly good and presented with a certain degree of finesse. Children's menu available. If you don't want to wait (and you will wait), there's a fish market behind the restaurant that's open from 11 a.m.–6 p.m. It has prepared items to take home, or fresh fish and shellfish to barbecue at your condo or on the beach. On a different note, you won't have to wait long for a fresh fish taco at Tropical Taco's green van, which parks next to the Dolphin daily except Mondays from 11 a.m.–3 p.m. Features: non-smoking area. Reservations not accepted. Credit cards: MC, V.

Hanalei Wake Up Café $$ ★★

Aku Road, Hanalei, ☎ (808) 826-5551.
American cuisine. Specialties: Omelettes, French toast, salads, fish tacos, mesquite-smoked Huli-Huli chicken.
Breakfast: 5:30–11:30 a.m., entrées $7.
Lunch: noon–2:30 p.m., entrées $7–$12.
Dinner: 5:30–9 p.m., entrées $7–$12.

This ultra-casual, surf-themed café is a trip. Decor features photos, trophies and constantly running videos glorifying the sport. The family that runs it is a mom and three sons who go by their first names only—Kainoa is a hunky, blond godlet who's also a champion surfer and canoer. Open surfer-hours for breakfast, the thing to order is the dessert-like custard French toast, a high-intensity alternative to eggs for breakfast. You'll need to paddle faster to work off the calories. A lunch and dinner (same menu) highlight is the mesquite smoked "huli-huli" chicken. Features: own baking. Reservations not accepted.

Tahiti Nui   **$$$**   ★★

Kuhio Highway, Hanalei, ☎ *(808) 826-6277.*
American cuisine. Specialties: Fresh fish, steaks, prime rib, chicken, scampi, plate lunches, sandwiches.
Breakfast: 7 a.m.–11:30 a.m., entrées $2–$8.
Lunch: 11:30 a.m.–4 p.m., entrées $6–$9.
Dinner: 5–10 p.m., entrées $12–$20.

This North Shore legend and party place in the heart of Hanalei just celebrated its 30th-year anniversary. Actually a glorified shack with six tables, it's crammed with nautical and South Pacific Style artifacts. The bar/lounge is almost as popular (maybe more) than the restaurant. Beat up pretty badly by Iniki, it was rebuilt exactly the same, with a slightly larger porch area. The dining room has also been brightened up some. The cheerful proceedings are still supervised by owner "Auntie" Louise Marston. Regular happenings include impromptu music sessions, hula dances or potlucks. The menu is awfully big for the size of the place, and the food better than it has to be. Tahiti Nui touts its breakfasts, an eclectic mix of things such as banana pancakes, eggs Florentine, loco moco and a three-egg "Iniki Construction Omelet," which you can fill with anything from bacon to surimi krab. At lunch, the daily soups are often flavorful and good, and the hamburgers are recommended. Also, plate lunches such as hamburger steak, or fried chicken with rice and potato salad. A nice dinner appetizer is Tahitian poisson cru, fresh fish cooked in lime juice seasoned with coconut milk and spices. Follow that with the trademark dish, calamari stuffed and sautéed in a garlic butter sauce with diced tomatoes. Many folks think that the generous portions of prime rib and steaks are the only thing to order. Desserts are on the order of homemade cream pie, hula pie or rainbow sherbet. No dinner on Friday when the luau moves in. Children's menu. Features: outside dining, own baking, private dining rooms. Reservations required. Credit cards: DC, D, MC, V.

The Hanalei Gourmet   **$$**   ★★

5161 Kuhio Highway, Hanalei, ☎ *(808) 826-2524.*
American cuisine. Specialties: Breakfasts, pastries, fresh seafood, salads, sandwiches.
Breakfast: 8 a.m.–2 p.m., entrées $2–$7.
Lunch: 10 a.m.–4 p.m., entrées $5–$19.
Dinner: 4–10 p.m., entrées $5–$19.

This small, bustling, deli-style café is housed in a converted classroom located in the Old School Building in Hanalei Center. The cheerful room consists of a bread oven, a two-burner stove, a long counter, hanging plants, Tiffany-style lamps and ceiling fans. Breakfast prices are rather bizarre; it costs just as much for half a papaya (an absurd $5.25) than it does for a breakfast sandwich with eggs tomato, lettuce and mayonnaise (if you add Canadian bacon, the price jumps up to $6.95—where's the nearest McDonalds?) Other items include a bowl of Meusli made from their own recipe, Huevos Santa Cruz, a bagel with lox and cream cheese or pastries (homemade danish, muffins, croissants). The Hanalei Gourmet has a good reputation for its sandwiches, served all day, which people like to take out to the beach. Some choices are Oregon bay shrimp made on the restaurant's own rye bread, open-face bay shrimp with melted jack cheese and New Orleans remoulade sauce. The best of the bunch is roasted eggplant with roasted red peppers, provolone, lime, cilantro, sour-cream sauce and onions on French bread. Also generous salads, including a pasta version that changes each week, pupus, fresh fish or a light meal of soup of the day and bread. Early bird specials served from 5:30–9:30 p.m., priced from $6.95–$13.95. Children's menu. The Hanalei Gourmet features live music nightly (see listing). Features: own baking.

Kilauea

Casa di Amici $$$ ★★★

2484 Keneke Street & Lighthouse Road, Kilauea, ☎ *(808) 828-1555.*
Italian cuisine. Specialties: Boursin cheese wrapped in phyllo, zuppe of mussels with fresh tomatoes, capers and white wine.
Lunch: 11:30 a.m.–2 p.m., entrées $12–$23.
Dinner: 6–9 p.m., entrées $12–$23.

One of Kauai's most popular Italian restaurants, Casa di Amici is situated in the Kong Lung Center in quiet Kilauea. Surprisingly casual in appearance, the plain latticed wood building is sort of al fresco, protected from the elements by a plastic drop. Ordinary tables surround a grand piano (its ivories are tickled Thursday–Sunday evenings) in the center of the room. Closed for a time, it was reopened recently with a new owner/chef, Randall Yates. Cuisine is traditional Italian, featuring tasty, choice ingredients at reasonable prices. Many regulars start with bacio, which is boursin cheese baked in phyllo, served with tomato sauce. There's also antipasto for two, gorgonzola mushroom polenta, caesar salad with fresh Kilauea romaine, or *zuppa di cozze* (New Zealand green-lipped mussels with fresh tomatoes, capers, three kinds of bell peppers and leeks in rich fish fumet). It's lots of fun to play with your food here, especially the mix-and-match pasta selection (bowtie, fettuccine, penne, angel hair, etc.) in light ($12) and regular ($15) portions. Choose your sauce (pesto genovese, arrabiata or a combination). You'll need to shell out a buck more for tortellini, though. If you like lasagne, the Casa's version features chopped sirloin and homemade sausage melded together with grilled zucchini, eggplant and five cheeses. Non-meat-eaters will like the vegetarian linguine. Other entrées include veal prepared three ways, chicken cacciatore, tournedos rossini, scampi and filet mignon. These dishes are also served in light ($17) or regular ($23) portions. Reasonably priced, well-chosen wine list. Seating is limited, so be sure to reserve. Features: own baking, rated wine cellar. Reservations required. Credit cards: A, MC, V.

Kilauea Bakery/Pau Hana Pizza $$$ ★★★

Kong Lung Center, Kilauea, ☎ *(808) 828-2020.*
American cuisine. Specialties: Specialty pizzas, tropical pastries and baked goods, breadsticks.
Breakfast: 6:30 a.m.–11 a.m., entrées $8–$25.
Lunch: 11 a.m.–9 p.m., entrées $8–$25.
Dinner: 5–9 p.m., entrées $8–$25. Closed: Sun.

Tucked into the Kong Lung Center in Kilauea, this small but renowned bakery and pizza place features a display counter with a couple of tables inside, plus additional garden seating. Stop by for one of its sourdough breads (try it with guava baked in!), tropical pastries and fantastic breadsticks made from pizza dough. The garlic-butter-flavored kind is made with garlic from Gilroy, California, the "Garlic Capital of the World." People have become so addicted to them (including us) that owners Tom and Katie Pickett are now selling them off island via mail order. You'll also see them in resort honor bars. These folks are smart! Wash your pastry down with rich, organically grown coffee. They start serving crispy crust pizza from 11 a.m. Both classic-style (plain cheese, pepperoni, etc.) and specialty (roasted eggplant, red onion, goat cheese, roasted garlic or tiger prawns, smoked ahi, etc.) are available, with a choice of white or whole-wheat dough, as well as six different cheeses. By the slice, too. Another recommended eatery within the Center is the Kilauea Farmer's Market (next to Casa de Amici) a full-service, gourmet grocery store with local produce, herbs, homemade soups, excellent sandwiches, salads, fine wines, microbrewery beers, spices, pastas and rice. Features: outside dining, own baking. Reservations not accepted.

Roadrunner Bakery and Café $ ★★★

2430 Oka Street, off Kilauea Road, Kilauea, ☎ (808) 828-8226.
Specialties: Mexican and vegan dishes, fresh-baked breads and desserts.
Breakfast: 7-11:30 a.m., entrées $6.
Lunch: 11:30 a.m.–8 p.m., entrées $6–$8.
Dinner: 11:30 a.m.–8 p.m., entrées $6–$8.

This Mexican café and bakery started life as an electricity transfer station for the North Shore. The large, two-story building has a unique sand floor, and mural block walls painted by two local artists. Recently opened, it's owned by Dennis Johnson of the famed O'Hana Kauai Bakery (which moved out of the woebegone Princeville Center). Johnson is up before the *moas* (roosters) are, baking goodies such as fresh baguettes, bagels, coconut rolls, taro buns, mango-coconut coffee cake and macadamia-nut shortbread cookies. Afterward, he and wife Dawn start preparing the super-fresh, lard-free Mexican food, without the aid of freezers or microwaves. Californians and Texans will be familiar with their version of burritos, called "burras" here. At breakfast, the flour tortillas are stuffed with scrambled eggs, onions, cheese, salsa fresca and cilantro. Burras appear for lunch and dinner too, including the unfortunately named "Black Dog" (ugh), which is roast pork, grilled Hanalei taro and black beans, covered with garlic anchoa sauce. Other items include tostadas, torta sandwiches on their crusty bread, plus special low-fat eggplant enchiladas, or grilled veggie salad with Kilauea mixed greens, jicama, white beans and lime vinaigrette. Roadrunners makes a concession to local tastes by serving an ahi salad and ahi burrito. There's a vegan menu too. This ain't your father's Mexican restaurant. Our one quibble with this place is the order of chips and salsa for $4.75 (!) and guacamole for $5.25 (!) You couldn't get away with that in California or Texas, no sir! Oh...celebrity watchers might want to know that Bette Midler and Harrison Ford are regulars. Open until 8:30 p.m. Saturdays; Sundays from 8 a.m.–1:30 p.m. Features: own baking.

Princeville

KAUAI

Café Hanalei $$$ ★★★★

5520 Ka Haku Road, Princeville, ☎ (808) 826-2760. Associated hotel: Princeville Hotel.

Pacific Rim cuisine. Specialties: Grilled sirloin steak with grilled Kauai onions and shiitake mushrooms.

Breakfast: 6:30-11 a.m., entrées $20–$20.

Lunch: 11 a.m.–2:30 p.m., entrées $9–$19.

Dinner: 6–9:30 p.m., entrées $20–$32.

Situated well below the lobby of the tiered, cliffside Princeville Hotel, the Café Hanalei is cleverly designed to make you feel like you're dining over water. A series of black-marble reflecting pools gurgle quietly below your feet. The terrace of this indoor-outdoor restaurant has the feel of a villa on the Italian Riviera, with its oversize Roman urns bursting with flowers. It almost comes as a shock that the sweeping seascape ahead is of Hanalei Bay and "Bali Hai" instead of the Amalfi Coast. The hotel claims that the views from here are some of the most spectacular in Hawaii—the answer to that is a resounding YES! Oh, and the food? Executive Chef Daniel Delbrel has conceived a people-pleasing blend of Pacific Rim cuisine, a number of Japanese dishes and tropical-French sweets and concoctions that include a tangy/creamy rainbow-striped circlet of mousse cake flavored with fresh lilikoi and almond paste, or ginger mango creme brulee. Specialty buffets are a big feature at Café Hanalei. A breakfast spread is available daily until 10:30 a.m. (regular menu until 11 a.m.). For Sunday brunch, you might head straight for the made-to-order crepes and omelettes so you can save the heavy decisions for the elaborate dessert bar. The seafood buffet on Friday evenings may start with sashimi, tako poki salad, or crab or shrimp on a bed of ice, and end with fresh fish grilled, sautéed or barbecued before your eyes. On the regular menu, the corn and clam chowder with Thai curry and coconut milk is a fine starter, while the stir-fried chicken salad with mixed greens, papaya and orange ginger dressing is one of their most popular items for lunch. On a more mundane note, a tuna salad sandwich with chips ($9.50) and a cheeseburger with grilled Maui onion and fries ($12.50) are also available. At dinner, there is always at least one special meal prepared nightly, as is a complete three-course feast for $39.50 per person. Features: outside dining, own baking, Sunday brunch. Reservations recommended. Credit cards: A, CB, DC, D, MC, V.

La Cascata $$$ ★★★

5520 Ka Haku Road, Princeville, ☎ (808) 826-2761. Associated hotel: Princeville Hotel.

Mediterranean cuisine. Specialties: Homemade pastas, grilled fish and meat.

Dinner: 6–9:30 p.m., entrées $20–$30.

Situated below the Princeville Hotel's Living Room lounge, La Cascata beckons you through a lacy iron doorway. Interior temptations are its terra-cotta floors and walls and trompe l'oeil murals. Dining here is a dressy affair, with candlelit tables, flowers and all the accoutrements. Sunset views are heartbreaking in summer. Servers bring you addictive home-baked foccacia and breads served with olive oil instead of butter and garlic dip or tomatoes and basil. If you need a starter course after that, choose from crisp calamari cakes with tomato compote and toasted pinenut vinaigrette, Tuscany-style white-bean soup with sliced Asiago cheese, or a daily pasta special. You might enjoy spicy penne amatriciana (with panchetta, dried tomatoes, fresh rosemary and crushed red pepper flakes) or cioppino with kona lobster over spaghettini. Follow that taste-tempter with the fresh fish of the evening, perhaps grilled island ahi with roasted garlic polenta and mushroom medley. Don't care for fish? How about duck, lamb chops, beef tenderloin or veal chop? Desserts are the fruity (chilled lemon souffle with Kauai fruit garnish) and chocolate (tiramisu or chocolate bourbon pecan tart) kind. Also offered are complete three-course dinners for $43.90 per person, which includes dessert and coffee or tea ($5 additional for foie gras terrine). Vintages from Chateau St. Jean and Robert Mondavi figure heavily on the wine list. Children's menu. Features: own baking, non-smoking area. Reservations recommended. Credit cards: A, DC, MC, V.

South Shore

Koloa

Beach House $$$ ★★★★

5022 Lawai Road, Koloa, ☎ *(808) 742-1424.*
Specialties: Incredible appetizers and inventive desserts.
Dinner: 5:30–10 p.m., entrées $17–$24.

No wet bathing suits at this beach house, please. Located across from Lawai Beach Resort, it was destroyed twice by hurricanes, like so many on the island. Not as close to the sea as it once was (with good reason), the sunsets are still spectacular (arrive half an hour before). Rebuilt on three tiers, and breezy from open windows and ceiling fans, the Beach House is now under the wing of Jean Marie Josselin of A Pacific Café fame, and is only open for dinner (it used to be a popular breakfast spot). That's the only regret, as the old place served forgettable food and rested on the laurels of its setting. Entrées are great but the appetizers and desserts really shine. Graze on them if you like. How about sizzling mussels with cashew lemon butter and balsamic vinegar syrup, deep-fried sashimi with wasabi soy beurre blanc, or ono firecracker (ono wrapped in a rice paper wrapper and deep-fried) with hot-and-sour vinaigrette and cucumber kim chee? Then you'll have room for such elaborate constructions as misu misu, a lavish take on tiramisu with espresso creme anglaise and chocolate sauce, or warm chocolate bread pudding topped with a banana crisp—that is if you can pass up the Toasted Hawaiian, a white-chocolate cake layered with haupia, and white chocolate toasted nut mousse, finished with caramel sauce. Wash it down with Kona coffee or Maui tea. Features: own baking, rated wine cellar. Reservations required. Credit cards: A, CB, DC, D, MC, V.

Sueoka's Market $

Koloa Road, Koloa, ☎ *(808) 742-1611.*
American cuisine. Specialties: Hamburgers, plate lunches.
Lunch: 10 a.m.–3 p.m., entrées $2–$5. Closed: Sun.

Primarily a takeout window adjacent to Sueoka Market in Old Koloa Town (no seating, unless you want to squat in the parking lot or eat in your car), Sueoka's makes great mahi-mahi sandwiches and laulau. Great for a picnic on Poipu Beach Park, which is just a short drive away. Reservations not accepted.

Tomkats Grill $$ ★

Koloa Road, Koloa, ☎ *(808) 742-8887.*
American cuisine. Specialties: Salads, charbroiled burgers, steaks, seafood and steak kabobs, sandwiches.
Lunch: 11 a.m.–10 p.m., entrées $7–$15.
Dinner: 11 a.m.–10 p.m., entrées $7–$15.

Although the setting is pleasant, on a covered porch facing a courtyard of bamboo trees, the food at Tomkats is distinctly average. The teriyaki burger and chicken sandwiches were nothing special; the sauce was a mite sweet; the pile of long, skinny fries that accompanied them were distinctly better. Service is nice and friendly, but rather addled. A decent choice if nothing else in open in the neighborhood. Features: outside dining.

Poipu Beach

Brennecke's $$$ ★★★

2100 Hoone Road, Poipu Beach, ☎ *(808) 742-7588.*
American cuisine. Specialties: Scampi, Hawaiian spiny lobster, prime rib.
Lunch: 11 a.m.–10 p.m., entrées $7–$26.
Dinner: 11 a.m.–10 p.m., entrées $7–$26.

Totally rebuilt after Hurricane Iniki, Brennecke's is back in a two-story building across from Poipu Beach Park. Former patrons will be glad to learn that it looks just the same as it did. The menu hasn't changed much, either. The place specializes in meat and fish that's usually served broiled on kiawe wood. At lunch and dinner, start with that island stalwart, fresh sashimi, or a "local"—or Oriental-style pupu platter. Follow up with one of the three cuts of prime rib (from seven to 20 ounces), or in a sandwich on sourdough. Brennecke's also has veggie burgers and fresh island fish selections that change daily. All entrées come with a trip to the salad bar, chef Luigi's sourdough bread, steamed rice or herbed pasta, and veggies. Features: outside dining, Sunday brunch. Reservations recommended. Credit cards: A, D, MC, V.

Keoki's Paradise $$$ ★★

Poipu Shopping Village, Poipu Beach, ☎ *(808) 742-7534.*
Seafood cuisine. Specialties: Fresh island fish, Koloa pork ribs, pesto shrimp macadamia, prime rib.
Dinner: 5:30–10 p.m., entrées $18–$20.

Lushly landscaped with hanging tropical plants and flowers, flowing waterfalls, rushing streams and tropical fishponds, all Keoki's Paradise needs is an ocean view. For that, you can visit its brother restaurant, Duke's Canoe Club (see listing). Keoki's has a coterie of regular patrons (both residents and travelers) who appreciate the convenient parking in its shopping center location. The nightly menu offers the fresh catch of the day prepared at least five different ways, koloa pork ribs glazed with plum sauce, and pesto shrimp macadamia with white wine. Keoki's is generous with side dishes; Caesar salad, a basket of fresh-baked bread and carrot muffins and steamed herb rice should keep you carbo-loaded for the evening. Oh, and don't forget hula pie (like mud pie) for dessert. Enjoy the same romantic atmosphere for even less money in the bar from 4:30–11:30 p.m., where lighter fare is served daily. Live local entertainment on Thursday and Friday nights. Reservations recommended. Credit cards: A, MC, V.

Roy's Poipu Bar and Grill $$$ ★★★★

2360 Kiahuna Plantation Drive, Poipu Beach, ☎ *(808) 742-5000.*
Asian cuisine. Specialties: Fresh fish in sauces, chocolate soufflé.
Dinner: 5:30–9:30 p.m., entrées $15–$26.

Roy's Poipu Bar and Grill, located in the undistinguished Poipu Beach Shopping Center, is entertaining, loud, lively and serves simply incredible food. Actually, the din is not so bad in the front room, and because it faces the open windows, is quite breezy, and you get an oceanfront effect from the flaming tiki torches out front. There's a glassed-in exhibition kitchen that you can go into and talk to chefs and watch pizzas and such being made. Servers receive a daily orientation on the changing specials and can give you the skinny on every ingredient in the complex sauces. The array of appetizers are expensive, and the skimpy portions keep you wanting more. Nori-seared shrimp sticks with wasabi aioli are nose-clearingly good. Seafood pot-stickers with mango lemongrass sauce are milder, but no less delicious. We stuck with the seafood theme throughout dinner and were glad we did. Fresh ono was served pan-seared with jalapeno shrimp sauce, and mahi-mahi was prepared the same way, with a touch of fresh ginger and a Thai coconut-milk curry plum sauce. The trademark chocolate soufflé with liquid chocolate center really lives up to its name. Roy's clientele is young, prosperous, showy and excessively trim—this is the place to bring your trophy mate. A trip to the rest room may be hazardous to your health, as you've got to dodge a lot of tiny tables crammed together, as well as servers, schmoozing clients, etc. If you can stand the noise and possess a bottomless wallet and a hollow leg, you may want to eat at Roy's every night. Note: there's always a wait, even with reservations. Features: own baking, rated wine cellar. Credit cards: A, MC, V.

The House of Seafood $$$ ★★★

1941 Poipu Kai Road, Poipu Beach, ☎ *(808) 742-6433. Associated hotel: Poipu Kai Resort.*
Seafood cuisine. Specialties: Fresh fish in parchment paper, shrimp luau, Hawaiian spiny lobster tail.
Dinner: 5:30–9:30 p.m., entrées $18–$38.

More than a dozen varieties of island fish are available on a single night at this high-ceilinged, plant-festooned restaurant that overlooks the tennis courts of the Poipu Kai Resort. Preparations change depending on the chef's whim and whatever's fresh, and are likely to include onaga baked in parchment paper, or papio sautéed with macadamia nut sauce. Abalone appears on the regular menu, and along with Hawaiian spiny lobster, are the most expensive items you'll find. Enticing starters run hot and cold, from oysters on the half shell to sashimi and crab-stuffed mushrooms to Wailua taro clam chowder. Meat-eating friends can tag along, too (surf-and-turf combos are available), for broiled center-cut pork chops or New York steak. The dessert menu is a trip: since when have you had baked Alaska? Also, on advance notice, you can order one or more items from the kitchen's repertoire of *en*

flambe concoctions, including crepes suzette, cherries jubilee and bananas Foster. Features: own baking. Reservations recommended.

West Shore
Hanapepe

Hanapepe Espresso Bar Café   **$$**   ★★★

3830 Hanapepe Road, Hanapepe, ☎ (808) 335-5011.
American cuisine. Specialties: Gourmet vegetarian and Italian suppers, salads, minestrone soup, croissants, espresso.
Breakfast: 8 a.m.–11 p.m., entrées $5.
Lunch: 11 a.m.–2 p.m., entrées $5–$8.
Dinner: 6:30–9:30 p.m., entrées $8–$15. Closed: Mon., Sun.

Located on Hanapepe's main drag, this is a former drugstore turned into a neo-bohemian coffee house/restaurant/bookstore/gallery. The original lunch counter and soda fountain was converted into a black-and-white-tiled espresso bar, and is the center of the action on most days. Vegetarian suppers are served Thursday–Saturday evenings, and are highly acclaimed by local residents. On the changing weekly menu might be an appetizer of a whole head of garlic for $1.75, gaspacho, grilled portabella mushrooms, pasta primavera, veggie lasagna or zucchini marinara. Otherwise, enjoy good conversation with regulars and owners Chris Ayers and Larry Reisor (a master carpenter, among other things). The regular menu features breakfast pastries, waffles, fresh salads, minestrone soup, or a daily pasta washed down by single or double espresso, cappuccino, café latte or hot chocolate. Reservations required for dinner only. Features: own baking. Reservations required.

Kalaheo

Brick Oven Pizza   **$$**   ★★

2-2555 Kaumualii Highway, Kalaheo, ☎ (808) 332-8561.
American cuisine. Specialties: Pizza, sandwiches.
Lunch: 11 a.m.–10 p.m., entrées $8–$11.
Dinner: 11 a.m.–10 p.m., entrées $8–$11. Closed: Mon.

Serving "hearth-baked" pizzas since 1977, Brick Oven Pizza has a reputation for "brok' da mouth" (means delicious in pidgin) pizza, but friends describe it as over-rated. You can watch pizza being spinned in the air. Crust choices include garlic whole-wheat or white, traditional meat or veggie toppings. Also huge sandwiches, some made with homemade sausage. Features: own baking, wine and beer only, non-smoking area. Reservations not accepted.

Camp House Grill   **$**   ★★

Kaumualii Highway, Kalaheo, ☎ (808) 332-9755.
American cuisine. Specialties: Burgers, barbecued huli chicken, ribs, fresh fish, salads, steaks, homemade pies.
Breakfast: 6:30 a.m.–1 p.m., entrées $4–$7.
Lunch: 11 a.m.–5 p.m., entrées $5–$9.
Dinner: 5–9 p.m., entrées from $5.

A worthwhile stop if you're on the way to Waimea Canyon. Great burgers and ribs, and prices are reasonable. Big-breakfast eaters might need to eat before they come. Pies are good, about three or four made daily. Features: own baking.

Kalaheo Coffee Co. and Café $ ★★★

2-2436 Kaumualii Highway, Kalaheo, ☎ (808) 332-5858.
American cuisine. Specialties: Breakfast specials, sandwiches, espresso, cappuccino,
Hawaiian coffees.
Breakfast: 6 a.m.–5 p.m., entrées $4–$7.
Lunch: 6 a.m.–5 p.m., entrées $5–$6.

Chef John Ferguson, late of the shuttered Stouffer Waiohai Beach Resort, has
opened this coffee store that's also a great breakfast and lunch place. Located across
from the Camp House Grill, it's tiny and always packed, primarily with local residents. It features omelettes, veggie bagels, salads, deli or fresh-off-the-grill sandwiches. Homemade bread and yummy macadamia nut rolls hail from the terrific
Bread Box Bakery. Coffee drinks are called "warmers" and "java jolts." Flavors
change daily and are priced from $1–$1.30; refills 50–70 cents. Coffee beans from
all over the state (Kona dark roast, Kauai estate, Molokai estate, etc.) are sold by the
pound or half-pound. If you like flavored coffees, try the "Sexual Chocolate," if you
dare. Features: own baking. Reservations not accepted. Credit cards: MC, V.

Kalaheo Steak House $$$ ★★

4444 Papalina Road, Kalaheo, ☎ (808) 332-9780.
American cuisine. Specialties: Steaks, prime rib, Kalaheo shrimp, combination platters.
Dinner: 6–10 p.m., entrées $12–$23.

Generous steaks (Midwestern-grain fed, aged and shipped) and monstrous, heart-
stopping cuts of prime rib (the 24-ounce slab is the priciest item on the menu) and
other choice meats are the specialty of this casual, upcountry restaurant. Fish dishes
are offered, too, and are mostly fresh—except for the imported ono. Lemon butter
is the usual sauce with this fare, but there are other choices. Can't decide? Combo
platters give you a choice of half meat and half seafood. Sides include fresh tossed
salad, steamed rolls from the Bread Box Bakery, Maui sweet wheat bread, plus
baked potato and rice. Desserts are the steak house variety: cheesecake, rum cake
and ice cream. Features: non-smoking area. Reservations not accepted. Credit cards:
D, MC, V.

Kokee State Park

Kokee Lodge Restaurant $ ★★

3600 Kokee Road, Kokee State Park, ☎ (808) 333-6061.
American cuisine. Specialties: Homemade cornbread, sandwiches, salads, desserts.
Breakfast: 9 a.m.–3:30 p.m., entrées $3–$7.
Lunch: 9 a.m.–3:30 p.m., entrées $3–$7.

A small, homey café with white-painted chairs and rust-red walls decorated with old
photos, Kokee Lodge provides comfort food and sustenance to hikers, campers and
passers-by exploring Kokee State Park. Light breakfasts are served as well as sand-
wiches on 12-grain bread; try the homemade pineapple mustard. Other items
include a hot dog for $2.95, Greek salad and, best of all, rich desserts ranging from
$3.25–$3.50. For a quick energy boost, there's nothing better than a slice of lilikoi
pie, Alakai swamp pie (Kona coffee ice cream with an oreo crust, ice cream, macad-
amia nuts and whipped cream) or "killer" fudge cake. The lodge's blend coffee

comes with a special mug to take home. Another interesting beverage is Lehua blossom honey wine for $3.50. There's also a gift shop attached. Credit cards: D, MC, V.

Waimea

Wrangler's Restaurant   **$$**

Highway 50, Waimea, ☎ *(808).*
American cuisine. Specialties: Mexican food, plate lunches, burgers.
Lunch: 10:30 a.m.–5 p.m., entrées $5–$15.
Dinner: 5–9 p.m., entrées $5–$15.

Local residents and visitors saddened by the Grove Dining Room's (at the Waimea Plantation Cottages) closure have been comforted somewhat by the reappearance of the Wrangler, a longtime favorite rendered supine by Hurricane Iniki. Once a rustic little place, the space has been expanded to include a patio, private dining room and even a country store that's an outlet for area artists and craftspeople. Like in the old days, Mexican food is still offered, as well as fresh fish and plate lunches, and it's certainly worth a special trip out here for one of the excellent burgers.

Nightlife

Traditional Hawaiian entertainment is the main focus on Kauai, with luaus, island music and the like—though you'll be able to find some discos, karaoke clubs, taverns, sports bars and one or two comedy clubs. Most of the action takes place at resort and hotel lounges, with the more "neighborhood" venues centered around Lihue, Kapaa and other island towns. **Kauai Community Players** presents theatrical productions several times yearly at venues in Lihue and, occasionally, the **Honolulu Symphony Orchestra** comes to town.

East Shore

Kalapaki Beach

Duke's Canoe Club Barefoot Bar   ★★★

Kauai Marriott, Kalapaki Beach, ☎ *(808) 822-7447.*
Hours: 11:30 a.m.–midnight.

Live music accompanies pupus, cocktails, sandwiches and light meals Friday through Sunday.

Lihue

Gilligan's   ★★

4331 Kauai Beach Drive, Outrigger Kauai Beach, Lihue, ☎ *(808) 245-1955.*
Hours: 8 p.m.–2 a.m.

There's dancing nightly at this popular hotel hot-spot to the left of the main lobby. On Thursday night, Gilligan's turns into the Kauai Comedy Club (there's one on almost every island) with guest comics. General admission: $12.

Hap's Hideaway ★★

4347 Rice Street, Lihue, ☎ (808) 245-3473.
Hours: 11 a.m.–2 a.m.
Sporting events on satellite TV, dart boards, a CD jukebox playin' primarily country western tunes are featured at this Lihue hangout, where "every hour is happy hour."

North Shore
Hanalei

Tahiti Nui ★★★

Kuhio Highway, Hanalei, 96714, ☎ (808) 826-6277.
Hours: 7 a.m.–10 p.m.
Live and surprisingly varied entertainment emanate from two lounges in this long-established restaurant and bar. On Sunday afternoons, from 2–5 p.m., there's a regular jazz jam session; Mondays, it's country-western night with line dancing; and rock and roll rears its shaggy head after the famous luau is over every Friday from 9:30 p.m. to 1:30 a.m. Saturday, special guest entertainers (Hawaiian, blues, pop, whatever) perform, followed by dancing until "closing."

Tahiti Nui Luau ★★★

Kuhio Highway, Hanalei, ☎ (808) 826-6277.
Hours: 6–8:30 p.m.
Closed: Mon., Tues., Wed., Thurs., Sat., Sun.
Held once a week at the wonderfully funky Tahiti Nui restaurant/lounge/show-room. Arguably Kauai's best luau (inarguably the best priced), with Tahitian themed-entertainment. The ample feast includes one drink, coffee and punch, and features an all-you-can-eat buffet of Kalua pig, baked fish, Hawaiian chicken, poi and other starches, salads, garlic bread and several desserts, including chocolate cake. Folks who don't want to eat pay $15 per person. The show is great for the kids, since everyone is outta there early. Also on Friday and Saturday nights, join in with regulars who come by to play ukuleles and other instruments, for an informal jam session. It won't be long before you, too, will be dancing on the bar. General admission: $38.

The Hanalei Gourmet ★★★

Kuhio Highway, in the Old School Building, Hanalei, ☎ (808) 826-2524.
Hours: 8 a.m.–10 p.m.
This spiffy deli offers nightly entertainment that runs the gamut from jazz to light rhythm and blues during the week, a Hawaiian jam session Sundays from 5 to 9 p.m., and rock'n' roll Friday and Saturday nights.

Princeville

The Living Room Lounge ★★★★

5520 Ka Haku Road, in the Princeville Hotel, Princeville, 96756, ☎ (808) 826-9644.
Hours: 7–11 p.m.

The rosy sunset at this sublime locale is entertainment enough, but if you need more, Hawaiian music is provided by a duo nightly.

Poipu Beach

Keoki's Paradise   ★★★
Poipu Shopping Village, Poipu Beach, ☎ *(808) 742-7534.*
Hours: 4:30 p.m.–midnight.
Live local entertainment on Thursday and Friday nights in an open-air setting; other nights waterfalls, lush foliage and streams will have to do.

Kuhio's   ★★★
1571 Poipu Road, at the Hyatt Regency Kauai, Poipu Beach, 96756, ☎ *(808) 742-1234.*
Hours: 9 p.m.–1 a.m. Closed: Mon.
Plush seating, lighting and camera tricks and a sunken dance floor make for classy surroundings at this disco with a DJ (Thursday–Saturday) and karaoke on Wednesdays from 7:30 p.m. In the same hotel is Stevenson's Library, a cocktail lounge designed like a real library, with tons of gleaming koa wood, old books, comfy couches and wing chairs, chess and backgammon boards and a couple of billiard tables. Delicious pupus (fondue, guacamole seafood cocktail) are served with drinks. Try the Tai Chi, a combination mai tai and chi chi—after a few you'll be t'ai chiing all the way to your room. A cozy place to snuggle up and listen to jazz on Friday and Saturday nights. Musicians can play almost any obscure standard you can think of—but please don't ask for "Cat Scratch Fever" or "Stairway to Heaven."

West Shore
Hanapepe

Hanapepe Espresso Bar Café   ★★★
3830 Hanapepe Road, Hanapepe, ☎ *(808) 335-5011.*
Hours: 6:30–9:30 p.m.
Closed: Mon., Tues., Wed., Sun.
Hawaiian slack key/contemporary and classical guitar music accompanies the vegetarian offerings at this bookstore/gift shop/espresso bar/restaurant.

Shopping

The **Kukui Grove Center**, four miles from the Lihue airport, is a huge new mall that sells just about everything you could want. Kauai is loaded with small specialty shops and family-owned retail outlets—much more fun than hitting the mall you just left back home—where you'll find scads of both high-quality and schlock souvenirs, aloha fashions, beachwear, T-shirts, fruit, flowers, etc. Outdoor markets and resort concessions are other shopping options. Book-lovers will enjoy the Hawaiiana selection at **Hanapepe Bookstore** in Hanapepe.

East Shore

Kapaa

Kela's A Glass Gallery ★★★

4-1354 Kuhio Highway, Kapaa, ☎ (808) 822-4527.
Hours: 10 a.m.–6 p.m.
Special hours: Sat. to 7 p.m. Closed: Sun.
You won't find anything kitschy here—Larry and Sandi Barton feature beautiful and unique glassware that would grace any home, and they ship worldwide. Choose among a wide assortment of handblown sculpture, vases, bowls, wine and champagne glasses, paperweights, perfume bottles and more. More than 50 glass artists are represented here. Prices range from $10 to $2000. The selection of hand-painted and hand-carved flowers are a standout.

M. Miura Store ★★

4-1419 Kuhio Highway, Kapaa, ☎ (808) 822-4401.
Hours: 9 a.m.–5 p.m.
This fourth-generation, family-owned shop started life 90 years ago selling Chinese crack seed from big glass jars. Now you can purchase all your surf- and beach-related attire, plus surfboards and bodyboards.

Sunny Side Farmers Market ★★★

4-1345 Kuhio Highway, Kapaa, ☎ (808) 822-0494.
Hours: 8 a.m.–8 p.m.
Special hours: Sun., 9 a.m.–8 p.m.
Unlike a lot of farmers markets, Sunny Side is open daily. This open-air affair features fresh local fruits, flowers and veggies (pineapple and watermelon are especially choice), crafts, clothing and jewelry (even Niihau shell leis).

Tin Can Mailman ★★★

1353 Kuhio Highway, Kapaa, ☎ (808) 822-3009.
Well-regarded bookseller. Features new and used books, Hawaiiana, South Pacific literature, stamps, coins, tapa cloth, botanical prints, maps.

William & Zimmer Furniture ★★★

1383 Kuhio Highway, Kapaa, ☎ (808) 822-2850.
Hours: 10 a.m.–6 p.m.
A showroom for handcrafted solid koa furniture (rockers from $1300) and gift items from $5 and up. The workshop is located at 951 Kipuni Way, Kapaa.

Lihue

Borders Books and Music ★★★

Kukui Grove Center Phase II, next to Kmart, Lihue, ☎ (808) 246-0862.
Hours: 8:30 a.m.–10 p.m.
Special hours: Friday-Saturday to 11 p.m., Sunday to 8 p.m.
Okay, it's a chain store, but there's a good Hawaiiana section (with 900 book titles for adults and children and a fine selection of contemporary and traditional music

CDs and cassettes) the air conditioning works great, it's open late, and the café is a welcoming spot to rest your dogs and have a specialty coffee and/or a pastry. Story hour for the kiddies every Saturday at 10 a.m. and at the same time on the first and third Tuesdays of the month.

Kapaia Stitchery ★★★

Kuhio Highway, half-mile north of Lihue ☎ *(808) 245-2281.*
Hours: 10 a.m.–4:30 p.m.

A terrific resource for hand-painted needlepoint canvases, Hawaiian and Oriental quilts and quilting kits, bags, patterns, books, kits, fabrics, batting, hoops and needles. Also Aloha apparel.

Kukui Grove Center ★★★

3-2600 Kaumualii Highway, Lihue, ☎ *(808) 245-7784.*
Hours: 9:30 a.m.–5:30 p.m.
Special hours: Fri. to 9 p.m., Sun., 10 a.m.–5 p.m.

Where residents go to shop, Kukui Grove is home to all the familiar chains such as Kmart, Woolworth, Sears, Longs, Liberty House, a plethora of fashion and specialty stores, 11 restaurants, a four-plex cinema and a free Polynesian entertainment on Fridays. A free shuttle takes guests of nearby hotels to and from the center.

Puhi

Kilohana Plantation Shops ★★★

Highway 50, 1.7 miles south of Lihue, Puhi, ☎ *(808) 245-5608.*
Hours: 9:30 a.m.–9:30 p.m.
Special hours: Sundays to 5 p.m.

A number of galleries, craft shops and a restaurant (Gaylord's) fill the courtyard, various rooms and bedchambers (even a cloak room!) in the main house and guest cottages of this restored 1930s-era estate. Among them are: Kilohana Galleries' The Artisan's Room, with handcrafted ceramics, wood carvings, glass, jewelry and cards. Don't miss the hand-cast paper designs (also engraved glassware) inspired by Hawaiian quilts created by Molokai's Jule Patten, one of Hawaii's unique artists; The Hawaiian Collection Room for Niihau shell leis, coins, stamps and Monarchy documents, Kauai scrimshaw, and antique ivory; The Country Store in the old library, featuring mostly made-in-Kauai gifts and collectibles; Dolls & Furrie Critters live in the Sun Room and study, and although there's an emphasis on bears, this shop specializes in antique dolls in elegant, made-to-order costumes. Within the old camphouse is Kilohana Clayworks, where you can glaze and fire your own Raku ceramic bowl or vase in just 30 minutes. Note: It might take several visits (and a map) just to find your way around the complex.

Waipouli

The Coconut Marketplace ★★

4-484 Kuhio Highway, Waipouli.
Hours: 9 a.m.–9 p.m.

Gift shops, restaurants, cinemas and hokum galore in this large resort shopping center set amid a coconut grove and conveniently located next to hotels and condos. Fun for an evening stroll. The best shop in the complex is Collector's Corner,

☎ *(808) 822-3333*, featuring vintage Hawaiiana, ukuleles, fabric, dinnerware, collectibles, even insects (!). Free hula show Mondays, Wednesdays, Fridays and Saturdays at 4:30 p.m.

North Shore
Hanalei

Yellowfish Trading Company ★★★
Hanalei Center, across from Ching Young Village, Hanalei, ☎ *(808) 826-1227.*
Hours: 10 a.m.–7 p.m.
Plenty of '40s and '50s Hawaiiana, furniture, clothing, collectibles, antiques and locally produced arts and crafts (koa paddles for your wall by artist Ray Nitta).

Kilauea

Kong Lung Center ★★★
Lighthouse Road, Kilauea, ☎ *(808) 828-1822.*
Hours: 9 a.m.–6 p.m.
Special hours: Sun., 10 a.m.–5 p.m.
Small but stylish shopping center out in the sticks is clustered around a historic building that was once a (you guessed it) plantation store. It was recently placed on the list of the National Register of Historic Places. The center consists of two clothing stores, a gift shop, an excellent bakery/pizza restaurant and one of Kauai's finest Italian eateries, Casa di Amici. Within the Kong Lung Building is the Kong Lung Co., ☎ *(808) 828-1822.* It has a talented buyer—here you'll find whimsical gifts, furnishings, accessories and clothing. Ascend the stairs to Reinventions, ☎ *(808) 828-0126*, where "gently used" fashions await. I found the selection lovely, but a tad overpriced, except for the costume jewelry (good stuff for under $10). Gifts and photographs created by local artists plus an exhibition of flora and fauna indigenous to the region are on offer at The Booby Trap, ☎ *(808) 828-1822.*

West Shore
Hanapepe

Hanapepe Bookstore and Espresso Bar Café ★★★
3830 Hanapepe Road, Hanapepe, ☎ *(808) 335-5011.*
Hours: 8 a.m.–2 p.m.
Also a highly regarded vegetarian restaurant and popular espresso bar. We didn't see many books here, but you can pick up locally made jewelry, candles, cards and even a Hawaiian Sovereignty Movement T-shirt.

Kauai Fine Arts
Hanapepe Road, Hanapepe, ☎ *(808) 335-3778.*
Special hours: by appointment only.
Fine collection of original antique maps and prints relating to exploration and travel from the 16th–19th century.

The Kauai Coffee and Gift Centre ★★
3734 Hanapepe Road, Hanapepe, 96716, ☎ *(808) 639-8629.*
Hours: 9:30 a.m.–6 p.m.

Situated in the old Ueoka Store in Hanapepe, the center was opened shortly after
Hurricane Iniki struck in 1992 to support and promote local businesses (they also
have a mail-order concern). Its specialty, of course, is island-grown coffee; free samples are given when you walk in. New flavors include Chocolate and Vanilla Macadamia Nut. Other interesting cottage industries touted here are several yummy fudge
creations from the Kauai Tropical Fudge Company. Or forget chocolate—how
about Pina Colada, Ginger Banana Macadamia or Kona Coffee and Cream? There
are also bags of Taro Ko chips made at the factory down the street. Non-food items
include polished coconut jewelry, soaps, lovely lauhala baskets and hats, quilted pillows, flowers, plants and Hawaiian music.

Uncle Eddie's Aloha Angels ★★

3905 Hanapepe Road, Hanapepe, ☎ (808) 335-0713.
Hours: 9:30 a.m.–4:30 p.m.
Angels in grass skirts, Christmas angels, angel suncatchers, angel T-shirts, angel
books, angel pins—need we say more? Mail-order catalog available.

Village Gallery ★★

3890 Hanapepe Road, Hanapepe, 96716, ☎ (808) 335-0343.
Hours: 9:30 a.m.–4:30 p.m.
Special hours: Sun., 11 a.m.–4:30 p.m. Closed: Mon.
Open since November 1995, the Village Gallery, owned by artist Lew Shortridge,
is the only gallery in Kauai dedicated to modern and experimental works by mostly
local painters, sculptors and photographers. Another notable gallery in Hanapepe is
Lele Aka Studio-Gallery, 3876 Hanapepe Road, ☎ *(808) 335-5267*, featuring
ethereal images of Hawaiian women on oversize canvases, plus African and Hawaiian handcrafted drums and local and exotic woods. Open Monday–Saturday from
10 a.m.–6 p.m.

Kalaheo

Cane Field Clothing ★★★

2488 Kaumuali'i Highway (Highway 50), Kalaheo, ☎ (808) 332-0267.
Hours: 10 a.m.–5 p.m.
Special hours: Sat. to 3 p.m. Closed: Sun.
Recently moved from historic Hanapepe to elegant new digs in Kalaheo, this distinctive store features fashionable (but not outre) clothing, accessories, '40s and
'50s English jewelry, picture frames, potpourri-filled bath oils and aromatherapy
candles.

Lawai

Old Hawaiian Trading Post ★★★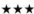

Highway 50 and Koloa Road, Lawai, ☎ (808) 332-7404.
Hours: 10:30 a.m.–5:30 p.m.
Special hours: Sun., 2–5:30 p.m.
One of the best sources for the rare (and expensive) Niihau shell leis and jewelry.
Owner Akiko Coleman has been selling these painstakingly hand-gathered and
hand-strung pieces for 25 years, directly from families on the "Forbidden Isle."
Once made as a form of barter and sold for as low as $10, some are now worth

thousands of dollars. A dying art form, each one takes as much as six months to make. There are more than 100 varieties of shells, ranging in color from pink, green, black and chocolate brown; the fuschia-toned, minuscule kahelelani shells are the rarest and priciest. In ancient times, royalty were buried with them—*kahelelani*, loosely translated, means "pathway to heaven."

Fielding's Fascinating Kauai Facts

A.k.a.	The Garden Isle
Main city	Lihue
Flower	Mokihana
Color	Purple
Area	549 square miles
Length	33 miles
Width	25 miles
Population	50,947
Highest point	Kawaikiki Peak (5243 feet)

Kauai Survival Guide

Getting There

Lihue Airport, about two miles from central Lihue, serves interisland traffic and is Kauai's principal airport. The gleaming, new terminal features a gift shop, car-rental booths, a restaurant and cocktail lounge, and various other concessions. Airlines are **Hawaiian** *(☎ (808) 245-1813)*, **Aloha** *(☎ (808) 245-3691)* and **Mahalo Air** *(☎ (808) 246-3500)*.

Tiny one-terminal Princeville Airport, just east of Princeville, is used mainly for commuter, charter and sightseeing flights. The basic amenities consist of a café and lounge, a couple of car-rental desks and rest rooms. The primary interisland commuter airline is **Island Air** *(☎ (808) 826-7969)*.

Getting Around

Iniki Express *(☎ (808) 241-6410)* is a post-hurricane bus service that operates between Kilauea and Kekaha from 6 a.m. to 6 p.m., every day except Sunday. Fare is just 50 cents. You can take it from Lihue Airport into either Kilauea or Kekaha. Otherwise the only transportation from Lihue or Princeville airports is by taxi or rental car. Rental car agencies with booths at Lihue Airport are **Alamo** *(☎ (808) 46-0646)*, **Avis** *(☎ (808) 245-3512)*, **Budget** *(☎ (808) 245-1901)*, **Hertz** *(☎ (808) 245-3356)* and **National** *(☎ (808) 245-5636)*. The main road along the coastline is **Kuhio Highway** (Highway 56) north of Lihue, changing to **Kaumualii Highway** (Highway 50) when traveling west of town. Roads are generally good throughout the island and parking is rarely a problem. Impatient drivers should avoid rush-hour traffic between Lihue and Kapaa.

Metered **taxis** are always on hand at Lihue Airport. The fare into town is about $6, but it gets expensive to other destinations ($35 from Lihue to Poipu, $65 from Lihue to Princeville, etc.). Taxi companies include **Kauai Cab**, in Lihue *(☎ (808) 246-9554)*, **A-1**, in Poipu *(☎ (808) 742-1390)*, **North Shore Taxi**, in Hanalei *(☎ (808) 826-6189)* and **Akiko's**, in Wailua *(☎ (808) 82-3613)*. Be prepared to wait—if you're headed for the airport, allow *plenty* of time (*Hawaiian* time).

Kauai is a great ride for **cyclists**, except for the steep road up to Kokee State Park and some of the narrow bits along the North Shore. Also, the roads tend to get very crowded during high season. Bring your own or rent from local shops such as **Bicycle Kauai**, Kapaa *(☎ (808) 822-3315)*, **Pedal and Paddle**, Hanalei *(☎ (808) 826-9069)*, **Bicycle John's**, Lihue *(☎ (808) 245-7579)* and Kapaa *(☎ (808) 822-3495)*; or **Outfitters Kauai**, Poipu Beach *(☎ (808) 742-9667)*. For **mopeds and scooters**, try **Pedal and Paddle** (above) or **South Shore Activities**, Poipu Beach *(☎ (808) 742-6873)*.

Visitor Information

Get local information at the local **Hawaii Visitors Bureau**, *3016 Umi Street, Lihue 96766 (☎ (808) 245-3971)*.

MOLOKAI

Aerial view of Molokai

Lovely Molokai—congenial offspring of Wakea and his goddess Hina—is probably best known as home to both the now-defunct Dole Plantation and the nearly defunct leper colony. "The Friendly Isle" (once known as "The Lonely Isle," then "The Forgotten Isle") is—aside from that "forbidden" Niihau—the "most Hawaiian" isle with the highest amount of pure- or part-Hawaiian blood flowing through the veins of its approximately 6700 inhabitants. This is the spot where other Hawaii residents come to escape the rat race on *their* islands. It's a place where time—the commodity that seems to continually *fly* for everyone else—barely seems to budge. The "No Pressure" isle.

156°50'

Molokai

| 0 | 3 mi. | 6 mi. |
| 0 | 3 km. | 6 km. |

Molokai Lighthouse

Kalaupapa
Peninsula

Kalaupapa
Airport

Father Damien Monument,
Siloama Church

Kalaupapa

iau
te Park

Haupu   Pelekunu
Bay   Bay

Wailau

Kahiwa
Falls

Halawa Valley

Halawa
Bay

alae

Waimanu
Falls

World's
Highest Cliffs

Moaula
Falls

Puuo Hoku
Ranch

Sacred Kukui
Grove

Molokai Museum
& Cultural Center

Mokuhooniki
Island

Kanaha
Rock

Keaina Bay

Malahini
Cave

Kamakou
Preserve

Waialua

Iliiliopae
Heiau

Hokukano
Heiau

Pauwalu

Pukoo

450

wela Place
of Refuge

Kakahaia Nat.
Wildlife

Kaluaaha

Pailolo Channel

Ancient Hawaiian
Fishponds

Pakuhiwa
Battleground

Kaluaaha

450

Ualapue

Kamalo

Smith-Bronte
Landing

Kalae Loa
Harbor

PACIFIC OCEAN

Molokai was revered by the ancient Hawaiians whose kahunas dubbed it *"Moloka'i pule o'o"* (translation: place of the potent prayer) and turned it into a sublime refuge filled with chanting, spirituality, sorcery and mysticism. It was the *kahunas*, in fact, who held out there. They were so wise and power-ful that even combating chiefs stayed away, decreeing Molokai "The Lonely Isle." Even the intrepid Captain Cook backed off, though there was abso-lutely *no* stopping King Kamehameha the Great. In the late 1700s, the king—determined to conquer all the islands—blasted in with his fierce en-tourage and pretty much made shark meat out of Molokai's valiant warriors. Once the island had been conquered, the king lost interest, and what was left of the islanders were left alone to fish and tend farmlands. In the 1830s, the Protestant missionaries cruised in, making *their* presence known, then—in the 1850s—humongous Molokai Ranch was established.

In the 1800s, Molokai—*still* lonely—apparently seemed like the ideal loca-tion in which to get rid of those "untouchable"—and *definitely* unwanted—leprosy (or Hansen's disease) victims. The place was hardly very "friendly" then—it was a harsh, isolated wilderness that turned its diseased inhabitants into a bunch of crazed animals with no food, no scruples and no hope. At first the victims were dumped in the remote bay at Kalawao, then later were "upgraded" to the village of Kalaupapa. Their lives were a virtual hell until in came the good Samaritan of Good Samaritans, Father Damien, a Catholic priest from Belgium who devoted his life to caring for the lepers and bring-ing them a modicum of dignity. Damien, himself, died from the disease and was beatified for his efforts (*much* later, in 1994). After Damien (now known as Blessed Damien) came and passed, various other nuns, priests and mis-sionaries carried on with his work. In the 1940s, sulfonate drugs were intro-duced and given a *much* bigger welcome than any God-worker or overseer, for the miraculous chemicals finally put a halt to the disease. Two decades later, the disease had been rendered noncontagious and today, only about 60 patients remain, some of them acting as tour guides for visitors.

Meanwhile, the Hawaiian Homes Act had been passed by Congress in 1921. This effectively freed up 43,000 acres of Molokai's land (not the best land, of course), to be doled out in 40-acre parcels, to state residents with at least 50-percent pure Hawaiian blood coursing through their veins. Many natives grabbed the ring and went to settle on Molokai, thereby rendering it "the most Hawaiian" of the islands.

Most-Hawaiian or not, Molokai's future—like so many of the "last remain-ing" special places—is probably going to be left in the vulturous claws of the developers. The economy that flourished while the pineapple plantations were in full swing has, with the closing of Dole and Del Monte in the 1980s, gone to the dogs. The workers, who previously had steady jobs and incomes, now try to make ends meet on welfare. Unfortunately, this doesn't provide a good argument for nondevelopment.

Developers would no doubt like to see more resorts, condos, restaurants, at least *one* good mall, requisite fast-food joints and the like. "Bring in the tourists!" they cry. They're butting heads with various "Save Molokai" groups, including the OHA (Office of Hawaiian Affairs), as well as cloutless, poverty-struck locals who don't want their island turned into a tourist mecca *nor* do they want the jobs associated with serving and cleaning up after them. Aside from other interested parties, the Molokai Ranch Development Corporation—controlled by Cooke & Castle, one of the Big Five and owner of about one-fourth of the island—is hot to see the place become a "destination." Is there any doubt as to who will win?

In the meantime, Molokai continues to maintain its public relations image as "The Friendly Isle." It's the place to come (come quickly!) for a glimpse of "real" Hawaii," coupled with absolutely nothing to do and no one to answer to except the call of sweet nature. Don't come for the shopping (there isn't much), the planned activities (ditto) or the restaurant and nightlife scene (ditto ditto). And *definitely* don't come with an attitude. You don't own the place—*yet*.

Bird's-Eye View

Hawaii's fifth-largest island lies just 22 miles from Oahu, yet—for now—it may as well be light years away. Measuring 260 square miles (38 miles long and 10 miles wide), most of Molokai's usable agricultural land is part and parcel of the 70,000-acre Molokai Ranch on the western edge and the comparatively minuscule 14,000-acre Puu O Hoku Ranch on the eastern edge. The hilly, pastoral west side of the island is where you'll find the luxe Kaluakoi Resort, Hawaii's largest sand beach, prairie lands, Molokai Ranch Wildlife Park and the old pineapple plantation town of Maunaloa. The east, green and lush, harbors Halawa Valley (thought to be Hawaii's oldest settlement, dating from the 7th century) and its 300-foot waterfalls, the world's highest sea cliffs (up to 3000 feet), Molokai Forest Reserve and Mount Kamakou (4961 high), Molokai's highest peak. The main town, Kaunakakai, situated about mid-island on the south side, has been likened to a circa-1930s, Hollywood-style, Old West movie set—easy to see why with its hitching posts, wooden facades, and a three-block-long main street. North of Kaunakakai, you'll hit Kualapuu Reservoir (the world's largest), Palaau State Park, with its Kalaupapa Lookout and enticing Phallic Rock, and—on the northern coast—the old leper colony at Kalaupapa.

Nature Guide

Bicyclists enjoy the Molokai coast.

Birders will be able to find a number of introduced game birds, as well as species such as the *pueo* (Hawaiian owl), *alae ke'oke'o* (Hawaiian coot), and *ae'o* (Hawaiian stilt). The *kukui* (candlenut tree)—prevalent around the mountainsides at lower elevations—is Hawaii's state tree, while its blossom holds reign as Molokai's official flower. Kapuaiwa Coconut Grove, west of Kaunakakai, still shelters several hundred of the palms planted back in the 1860s by King Kamehameha V, when he was but a prince.

As for animals, all were imported over centuries. Goats came in from the Mediterranean, axis deer were sent over from India, pigs arrived from wherever. Around the 1960s, Molokai Ranch imported hundreds of animals from Africa and, today, about a thousand of them—from antelopes and giraffes to ostriches and zebras—roam the grounds at Molokai Ranch Wildlife Park.

Fielding's Beach Finder

Molokai has a distinctive range of beaches. Some have soft white sand and wade-in-me water, others are narrow with treacherous waves and rip currents. Ask locals or the **Department of Parks, Land and Natural Resources** *(☎ (808) 567-6083)* before you hit the surf.

Onealii Beach Park

Just several miles east of Kaunakakai.
This centrally located beach will appeal to most families. The swimming is relatively safe, plus there's a run-around meadow, pavilion, picnic facilities, outdoor showers, and rest rooms (no lifeguards, though). Expect crowds, especially on weekends.

On the western side of the island

Papohaku Beach

Below the Kaluakoi Resort.
This is Hawaii's longest beach—three miles long and 100-feet wide—with lots of white sand and mean rip currents. Winter months see huge swells (and surfers) but, come summer, the beach is generally safe for swimming. Outdoor showers, rest rooms, picnic facilities and no lifeguards.

Kepuhi Beach

Also in front of Kaluakoi Resort.
Another white-sand beauty. It comes with the same warnings as Papohaku, plus year-round winds that hamper swimming (and hair-dos). Outdoor showers, no lifeguards.

Kawakiu Beach

North of Kapuhi Bay.
Offers excellent swimming (when the water is calm) and is also a designated archeological site. Free weekend camping, no facilities, no lifeguards.

Moomomi Beach

At the northwest shore.
A favorite with residents for swimming (best in front of the community recreation center) and snorkeling. Visitors must get permission from the Hawaiian Home Lands *(☎ (808) 567-6104)*.

Halawa Bay

Over on the east side at the far end.
Features waterfalls, a freshwater pool, snorkeling, fishing and excellent summer swimming and winter surfing.

MOLOKAI

Adventure Guide

Rock formations along the Molokai coast

With no shopping or nightlife, face it—you either came to Molokai to do absolutely nothing and forget everything, *or* to have a memorable adventure.

One of the island's best **treks** is into the lush **Halawa Valley**, on the eastern side. The well-marked (albeit occasionally muddy) trail presses through fruit-tree groves, fern grottos and ancient archeological sites until it reaches the magnificent 250-foot **Moaula Falls**. The icy mountain pool, at the bottom of the falls, is an excellent place to wash off your mud and sweat, though you should beware of the mythical lizard, *mo'o*, that supposedly resides in the pool.

Follow in the footsteps of the Molokai Mule Ride on the **trail to Kalaupapa**. The recently restored trail is fit for mules or hikers who are in good condition. You must have a permit from the **National Park Service** (☎ *(808) 567-6102)* as well as a confirmed reservation with Damien Tours for the leper-colony extravaganza.

If you have a four-wheel-drive vehicle and are a somewhat stalwart hiker, you can access trails at Molokai Forest Reserve (where you'll be rewarded with glorious views and valleys) and Pepeopae Bog in the Kamakou Preserve, an almost-unbelievable isolated ecosystem protected by the **Nature Conservancy of Hawaii** *(☎ (808) 553-5236)*.

Camping is allowed at **Palauu State Park**, where you'll get a view of Kalaupapa Peninsula and be close to the shameless Phallic Rock. It's a free rest but permits are required from the **Department of Land and Natural Resources** in Hoolehua *(☎ (808) 567-6618)*. Another free site is at **Moomomi Beach**, over on the northwest coast. More **beach camping** can be found at **Papohaku Beach Park** and **Onealii Beach Park**, both near Kaunakakai and both with all the necessary facilities (and both with all the expected noise and crowds). Permits cost a few bucks a day and are issued by the **Kaunakakai office of County Parks and Recreation** *(☎ (808) 553-3204)*. If you don't mind the risk of having your brains bonked by falling coconuts, you might try the royal coconut grove at **Kioea Park**, also near Kaunakakai. Get a permit from the **Hawaiian Home Lands Department** in Hoolehua *(☎ (808) 567-6104)*. **Molokai Ranch** *(☎ (808) 552-2767)* offers camping at various sites on the property for around $10 per night.

For more information on **hiking**, **trails** and **camping** on Molokai, contact **Hawaii State Department of Land and Natural Resources** *(Palauu Park Office, Kalae 96757; ☎ (808) 567-6083)*, **Hawaiian Home Lands Department** *(P.O. Box 198, Hoolehua, 96729; ☎ (808) 567-6104)*, **Maui County Department of Parks and Recreation** *(P.O. Box 526, Kaunakakai, 96748; ☎ (808) 553-5141)* and the **Nature Conservancy of Hawaii** *(1116 Smith Street, Suite 201, Honolulu 96817; ☎ (808) 553-5136)*.

Diving and snorkeling are easy—when the water is calm, that is—and you'll be able to view everything from manta rays to angel fish. Diving at **Makuhooniki Rock**, an old bombing target on the eastern side of the island, is apt to turn up World War II artifacts as well as black coral, gray reef sharks and barracuda. Best **snorkeling spots** are, on the eastern side, **Fagans**, **Murphy**, **Honouli Wai**, **Honouli Maloo** and **Sandy**. And out west: **Kaupoa**, **Kapukahehu**, **Moomomi**, **Poolau** and **Kaunala**. A variety of operators will take you out or just rent you some equipment and point out the way (see "Sports" below). **Ocean kayaking** on the island during the summer months is truly superb. Experienced kayakers will be able to explore isolated valleys and remote hideaways. Kayaks can be rented, or tours arranged, through **Fun Hogs at Kaluakoi Resort** *(☎ (808) 567-9292)*. **Surfers** will find good waves at **Halawa Beach**, **Kawaaloa Bay**, **Kepuhi Beach**, **Kanalukaha Beach**, **Kaunakakai Wharf** and **Hale O Lono Beach**, but bring your own board (rentals aren't available on the island).

MOLOKAI

What Else to See

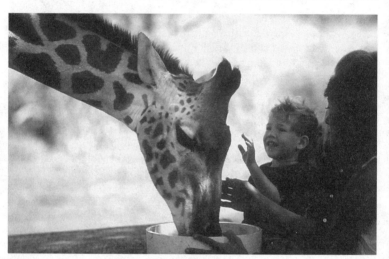

Children visit the giraffe at Molokai Wildlife Park.

You'll get a good idea of what Molokai is all about when you explore **Kaunakakai**, the main town. The atmosphere is decidedly "laid back," and you can load up on provisions, shop for some local crafts and souvenirs, and soak up the local ambiance. Everything is slow as proverbial molasses—even the local teens as they cruise up and down the nearby wharf (by Los Angeles standards, anyway). West of Kaunakakai is the **Kapualwa Coconut Grove**, planted back in the mid-1800s for King Kamehameha V. Thankfully, hundreds of the trees are still standing and you can parade around the grove like royalty—just watch out for falling coconuts. **Church Row**, across the way, is an exercise in side-by-side religion with just about all the major denominations represented in churches built under a Hawaiian Home Lands' grant (you're welcome to join islanders for Sunday services). North is **Kualapuu Reservoir** (the world's largest), the mini-town of **Hoolehua** (renowned for cockfights, and site of Hawaiian Homes allotments) and **Purdy's All Natural Macadamia Nut Farm** (learn everything you never wanted to know about macadamias, then buy a sack and eat them all). **Palaau State Park** is where you'll find knockout views from **Kalaupapa Lookout** and *at* **Phallic Rock**. Re-live the horrors of leprosy (Hansen's disease in kinder, gentler language) at **Kalaupapa**, but sign up in advance for a tour with **Damien Tours**. A resident of the colony will lead you around his home-turf and sit you down for a picnic lunch.

On the western side of the island, **Maunaloa** affords a good view of a plantation town, albeit without the plantation. Stop in at **Maunaloa General Store**, **Big Wind Kite Factory**, **The Plantation Gallery** and a variety of other crafts/gallery/gift shops in the area. You have to sign up in advance for a tour of **Molokai Ranch Wildlife Park**, one of the country's most esteemed game preserves where you can check out imported exotic beasts in some of their glory. (Tours leave from Kaluakoi Resort several times daily.) **Hale o Lono Harbor**, one mile west of Halena, is especially interesting in October, when the annual outrigger canoe competition sets off for Oahu.

Venturing eastward, you'll come to **St. Joseph Church** and then **Our Lady of Sorrows Church**, both built by Father Damien in the 1870s. Get a dose of Hawaiian-style entertainment, a barbecue and a wagon tour at **Molokai Horse & Wagon Ride**, then make your way to the lush **Halawa Valley**, site of a 7th-century settlement—thought to be Hawaii's oldest. Ooh and aah over the views, then take a swim in the (safe) bay or cool stream and pretend you have time-traveled back to the really good old days.

MOLOKAI

Father Damien Statue in Molokai pays tribute to the Catholic priest from Belgium who devoted his life to caring for the island's leprosy colony.

Central Molokai

Hoolehua

Fun For Free

Purdy's Natural Macadamia Nut Farm ★★

P.O. Box 84, Hoolehua, From Highway 470, turn left to Farrington Avenue; one mile to Lihi Pali Avenue, turn right, 96729, ☎ (808) 567-6601.
Hours: 9:30 a.m.–3:30 p.m.
Special hours: Saturday, 10 a.m.–2 p.m., Sun. by appointment only. Closed: Sun.

A family enterprise since 1980, this 70-year-old, one-acre grove of 50 mac-nut trees is located in Hoolehua, an agricultural community in Central Molokai. The Purdy family acquired the grove through the Hawaiian Homestead Act. This law has provided opportunity for some people of Hawaiian ancestry to return to the land. The entire family helps maintain the trees and gather and prepare the nuts. A visit here is a must, especially for kids who love to crack open the nuts. Best of all, it's free, and Tuddie Purdy is a marvelous raconteur who is nutty about nuts. His partner Kammy might give you her recipe for macadamia nut cookies. Preservative- and pesticide-free macs and mac-nut honey are available for purchase.

Tours

Molokai Air Shuttle ★★

Hoolehua, ☎ (808) 567-6847.

If a long, fairly strenuous hike or the popular but expensive Mule Ride doesn't turn your crank, you can wing it to the Kalaupapa Peninsula on the Molokai Air Shuttle—and at a reasonable price. This company offers daily round-trip airfare from the Molokai Airport to the peninsula, coupled with a ground tour of the settlement by Damien Tours. Weather permitting, Molokai Air Shuttle will also throw in a free aerial tour of Molokai's North Shore. Air transport to and from Kalaupapa is $49.90 per person; ground tour is $25 per person. If you just want an aerial tour of the North Shore, the price is $49.90 per person.

Kalae

City Celebrations

Molokai Music Festival ★★

Molokai Museum and Cultural Center, Highway 470, Kalae, Four miles north of Highway 460, two miles past Kualupuu, 96748, ☎ (808) 567-6436.

The creme de la creme of the Hawaiian music world appears at this outdoor music festival held annually on the third Sunday in August. For more information, write: PO Box 84, Kaunakakai, HI 96748.

Tours

Molokai Museum at R.W. Meyer Sugar Mill ★★★

Four miles north of Highway 460, Kalae, Two miles past Kualupuu, ☎ (808) 567-6436.
Hours: 10 a.m.–2 p.m.

Even if you think you're not interested in sugarcane processing, a visit to this museum and cultural center adjacent to a lovingly restored sugar mill is a must. The mill, which is on the National Register of Historic Places, was built in the 1870s by

German immigrant Rudolph W. Meyer. The simple wooden building with a metal roof houses a boiler and a fully operative, stationary steam engine, with copper evaporators for the separation of the molasses, and a flat belt-driven centrifuge for the separation of the sugar from the molasses. Outside is the original stone-lined, mule-driven, cane-crushing pit. The accessory building and research center, which is only the first phase of an ambitious project (two more buildings are expected to be added) is located about 50 yards from the mill. It was built by Honolulu architect Paul Morgan, and contains a gift shop and the mill archives. It's used for an amazing number of special community events, including the annual Moloka'i Music Festival, a taro and sweet potato festival, and monthly talks by archeologists who have worked on Molokai sites. Classes held here include loom-weaving, coconut-frond-weaving, making ukuleles from scratch (also how to play them), Hawaiian quilt-making and much more. It's run by Barbara Schonley, formerly with the Molokai Visitors Association; she's one of the most knowledgeable people on the island. General admission: $2.50.

Molokai's North Coast offers wilderness tours for hikers.

Kalaupapa

Historical Sites

Kalaupapa Peninsula ★★★★

Damien Tours, c/o Richard Marks, P.O. Box 1, Kalaupapa, 96742, ☎ *(808) 567-6171.* Designated a National Historic Park in 1980, Kalaupapa, located on the Kalaupapa/Makanalua Peninsula on Molokai's northern coast, was the home to sufferers of leprosy, now called Hansen's Disease. After the first instances of the disease appeared in Hawaii in 1835, it became a raging epidemic. Victims were forcibly "quarantined" here in 1866, arriving on the eastern end, at Kalawao, with little food, no materials for shelter and almost no hope of escape, except through a merciful death. Newcomers had to face treacherous seas, and the peninsula's formidable 3300-foot cliffs. Already weakened by the journey and the spiritual pain of being separated from loved ones forever, they had to fight off physical attacks by the afflicted who had come before them. This hardscrabble existence continued until Father Damien de Veuster, a Belgian priest, arrived for a short visit in 1873. Almost a one-man army, Father Damien stayed on to nurse the sick, help build their homes and dig their graves. He died of leprosy himself in 1889. Others who were overshadowed by Father Damien's larger-than-life career were Mother Marianne Cope, who lived in Kalaupapa for 30 years and founded a home for women; she is largely credited with founding the hospice movement. Although by the 1940s the development of sulfonate drugs brought the disease under control, health policies forbade residents to leave the colony until 1969. Ironically, we now know that leprosy is one of the least communicable diseases. At its height, the colony counted some 8000 people. Today, there are fewer than 100, all 50 years or older. They choose to remain, as it is the only life they've ever known. Visitors can enter the peninsula by mule, or choose to hike or fly in. Permission is required to visit the settlement itself; contact Damien Tours (for more information, see "Tours").

Tourists view the Molokai coast.

Tours

Hike Kalaupapa Trail ★★★★

Damien Tours, c/o Richard Marks, P.O. Box 1, Kalaupapa, On the right side of Highway 470 between the stables and Kalaupapa Overlook, 96742, *(808) 567-6171. Hours: 8:15 a.m.–3:30 p.m.*

Participants should be on the trail by 8:15 a.m. before the mules leave the Kalae stables; although you set your own pace, you should time yourself to get to the mule tie-up spot by 10:15 a.m. You might meet a mule(s) on the trail, do not attempt to pass or weave through them. Just stay on the side at a safe place and allow the mules to pass you. The tour bus will pick you up with the mule riders at the same time. You must have a reservation; wandering around the beach or the settlement on your own is strictly *kapu* (forbidden). The trail has been upgraded recently, but locals say the new steps on the trail make it hard on your legs going both ways. It helps to have a reliable pair of sturdy shoes and to be in good physical condition. Minimum age is 16 years. Includes: settlement tour. Bring your own lunch (and cold water), as there is no food available for sale in Kalaupapa. Cameras OK. Damien Tours' office hours are 7–9 a.m.; and 5–7 p.m. General admission: $38.

Kualupu'u

Hiking

Nature Conservancy of Hawaii Hikes ★★★

P.O. Box 220, Kualupu'u, About 1/3 of a mile before Highway 470 west from Kaunaka-kai, 96757, ☎ (808) 553-5236.
Hours: 8 a.m.–3 p.m.
Conservancy guides lead hikes to Molokai's Mo'omomi and Kamakou preserves one day every month. Guides are experienced naturalists. Mo'omomi (means "Jeweled Reptile") Preserve, which is near a small beach on Hawaiian Home Lands popular with islanders on the northwest coast of Molokai and was created to protect five endangered-plant species. The Keonelele coastal dunes west of Mo'omomi are of great cultural and scientific significance to geologists and experts in Hawaiian history and paleontology; it was once a native Hawaiian burial site. Kamakou Preserve, near the Waikolou Lookout, is a remote and spectacular 2774-acre native rainforest. After a ride to the entrance of the reserve via four-wheel-drive vehicle, Conservancy guides lead hikes from the Pepeopae Trail (a raised wooden boardwalk) through the forest, to an untrammeled Hawaiian montane bog, and onto a dizzying point overlooking the preserve in Pelekunu Valley. The valley's 4000-foot seacliffs are reportedly the tallest in the world. The preserve has more than 250 species of plants and ferns and five rare bird species. These hikes are popular with residents of other islands who come down for the day; Molokai staff and volunteers meet hikers at the airport, serve as guides and return hikers to the airport in the afternoon. To reserve a spot way in advance (there is always a two-month waiting list) and to confirm dates, call the number above. (On Oahu, ☎ (808) 524-0779.) Donations made to help defray costs are appreciated. For a donation of $25, nonmembers will receive a one-year membership in the Conservancy, including all benefits. General admission: $25.

Tours

Coffees of Hawaii Wagon Tour ★★★

P.O. Box 160, Kualupu'u, 96757, ☎ (808) 567-9241.
Hours: 10 a.m.–3 p.m.
The hilly area of Kualupu'u is a perfect environment for the locally grown coffee—called Muleskinner, after the hardy guys who led their animals down the switchbacks of the 3300-foot North Shore seacliffs to the Kalaupapa peninsula below on a daily basis. This is strong joe—a natural dry dark roast, which may be richer than

the brands you're used to. Another aromatic blend is Malulani Estate Coffee (Malulani means "heavenly aroma"), which is premium Arabica coffee made from select beans. In this interesting tour, you can sample the coffee for yourself and learn the history of the island's only working coffee plantation while riding in a mule-drawn wagon. The original trees were planted by an Argentinian immigrant (who has since left the island). He left behind a promising industry, as well as teaching the local youth some of the finer points of world-class soccer. You'll also tour the mill and possibly purchase a bag of beans and a coffee mug just like the one you drank from. The gift shop is also a showcase for local arts and crafts (island artists are highly skilled in woodworking, jewelry, quilting and more). There's also a new Espresso Bar serving a variety of specialty brews and snacks. Morning tour, 10 a.m.; afternoon tour, 1 p.m. No afternoon tour on Saturday. Reservations required. General admission: $14.

Palaau

Tours

Kalaupapa Mule Ride

25 Mule Barn Parkway, on Highway 470 in Palaau State Park, Palaau, ☎ (808) 567-6088.

Hours: 8 a.m.–3:30 p.m.

Special hours: closed Christmas and New Year's Day.

Closed down for about two years, the original Kalaupapa Mule Ride is once more alive and kicking. You're in good hands with the new owner, Eldon "Buzzy" Sproat, a fixture on the statewide rodeo circuits; he was the original trainer of most of the surefooted mules more than 20 years ago. Sproat even shoes each of his mules six times a year. The three-mile-long trail, which is maintained by the National Park Service, was recently upgraded. The tour begins with a check-in, signing of waivers, tour briefing and riding "instruction," although no experience is necessary; you'll also learn your mule's name. After that it's downhill all the way (about 1800 feet) with 26 switchbacks—bring your camera for some spectacular coast views (east of the trail are the world's tallest sea cliffs, according to the Guinness Book of World Records). The ground tour, conducted by Richard Marks of Damien Tours (and sheriff of Kalaupapa) commences at 10:15 a.m., when you'll board an old yellow school bus, and for the next couple of hours, Marks will engage your heart and mind with the history and background of the former leper colony (leprosy is now called Hansen's disease). Highlights include St. Philomena's Church, built by Belgian priest (recently beatified by Pope John Paul), Blessed Damien de Veuster, who was afflicted with the disease after selflessly caring for the patients when no one else dared. Although his remains have been returned to his native land, his right hand is buried in the church graveyard. You'll also see the small museum, the post office, the simple, white-washed homes of the residents, the general store, medical facility and dock. Included is a simple lunch at Judd Park in Kalawao. The ride back (at 2 p.m.) is just as viewfully astounding as the downward trek. Important note: Richard Marks is basically a one-man operation. Unfortunately, when Marks is off the island, less-qualified guides may take his place. Check status the night before your trip. It makes a BIG difference and may severely affect what should be an unforgettable experience. In any event, Kalaupapa Mule Rides, Inc., is a totally SEPARATE entity from Damien Tours, and is therefore not responsible for any of the aspects of the ground tour. Souvenirs of the visit include a rider-completion certificate and a bumper sticker. Minimum age is 16 years, weight limitation is 240 pounds. Covered shoes, slacks or jeans, sunvisor/hat and light windbreakers are recommended. Reservations required. For more information, write: *100 Kalae Highway, Suite 104, Molokai, HI 96757-0200; toll free ☎ (800) 567-7550*, or after hours, *(800) 567-7717*. General admission: $120.

East Molokai

Halawa Valley

Beaches

Halawa Beach Park   ★★★

Highway 450 (Kamehameha V Highway), Halawa Valley, At the eastern end of Highway 450.

Probably the most lush and beautiful setting on the island, this black-sand beach is a prime surfing spot. The downside is the usual nasty currents in winter, but the swimming is fine in summer, and many use the beach as a kick-off point for north shore kayaking trips. Bring a picnic and bottled water (water here is not potable). Outdoor showers, pavilion, barbecue grills, parking.

Kaluaaha

Historical Sites

Iliiliopae Heiau   ★★

Highway 450, 1/2 mile past the 15-mile marker, Kaluaaha.

Listed on the National Register of Historic Places, this is one of the largest *heiaus* in Hawaii–320 feet long and 120 feet wide (longer than a football field) and was the site of human sacrifice. What remains today is the foundation, and it is believed to have been three times that size in its heyday. Legends relate that the stones to build the temple were hauled to Molokai over the mountains by *Menehune*, a mystical race of "little people" (somewhat akin to Ireland's leprechauns). Why such a large temple in Molokai? Long ago, the island was a center of religious learning and mysticism, where the highest priests trained acolytes to follow in their footsteps. The *heiau* is on private property, but if you take the Molokai Horse and Wagon Tour (see "Tours") the *heiau* is included in the itinerary.

Kamalo

St. Joseph's Church   ★

Highway 450, Kamalo, 10 miles east of Kaunakakai.

Built in 1876 by Kalaupapa's Father Damien and restored in 1971, this is the second-oldest church on the island, although it is no longer used for services. Father Damien, who counted carpentry among his many other skills and gifts, built four churches outside of the Peninsula.

Mapulehu

Tours

Molokai Horse and Wagon Ride ★

At the Mapulehu Mango Grove, Mapulehu, Just past mile marker 15 on Route 450 (east end), ☎ (808) 558-8380.
Hours: 10:30 a.m.–12:30 p.m.

These friendly folks invite you to experience "old Hawai'i...Molokai style." This informal and informative two-hour tour in a real wagon drawn by two horses combines Hawaiian music, stories, legends, hula lessons, coconut husking, net throwing and more. Places you'll see include the huge Mapulehu Mango Grove (the meeting point) and the sacred Iliiliopae *Heiau* (temple). The whole shebang is either $35 for the ride only, or $40 with lunch. Children's fare is $18.50 for ages 6–12; under five, free. This tour can also be arranged through Colony's Kaluakoi Hotel, ☎ (808) 552-2555; ask for Kiku at the tour desk. General admission: $35–$40.

Papohaku Beach is three miles long and 100 feet wide.

Twenty Mile Beach

Beaches

No Name Beach at 20 Mile Marker ★★

Highway 450, Twenty Mile Beach, Go east on Highway 450 for about seven miles to 20-mile marker.

This intimate circlet of white-sand beach is number one on the East side of the island, locals say, especially in winter, when other beaches are dangerous to swim in. Bring your snorkeling gear. Rest rooms, roadside parking. Rocky Point at the 21-mile marker is the best surfing spot in the summer; you'll see a lot of young people there.

Kaunakakai

City Celebrations

Aloha Festivals   ★★★

Downtown Kaunakakai ☎ (808) 944-8857.

Celebrating its 50th anniversary in 1996, the statewide Aloha Festival is a two-month-long cultural fete featuring traditional music and dance, historical ceremonies, contests and ho'olaule'a, or block parties. It was begun in 1946 (then called Aloha Week) to honor the Makahiki, a period of time in the ancient Hawaiian calendar where war was not permitted. Special events in Molokai include the Molokai Parade and Mule Drag. In 1996, Molokai was the kickoff point of the festival, with the investiture of the Royal Court. Usually held in late September-early October.

Bankoh Moloka'i Hoe/Outrigger Canoe Race   ★★★

Hale O Lono Harbor, Kaunakakai.

The 41-mile Molokai to Oahu world championship outrigger canoe race has been a big deal for 45 years running (rowing?). Starting from the Hale O Lono Harbor on Molokai Ranch property, the race crosses Kaiwi channel to a finish at Fort DeRussy Beach, in Waikiki. Owned, organized and produced by the Oahu Hawaiian Canoe Racing Association, the race is sponsored by the Bank of Hawaii, which built two fiberglass canoes for visiting and home teams in 1991, although traditional koa (wood) canoes are also used. Participants usually include world-class teams from the United States, Australia, Canada, Tahiti and Europe; 1995 was a record year—95 teams in all (that's a lot of elbow grease). Women's race: September; men's race: October. The event usually begins at 7:30 a.m.; first team finishes at around 1 p.m. By the way, outrigger canoe racing is Hawaii's official team sport.

Moloka'i Makahiki   ★★

Kaunakakai Park and Manae Canoe Club, Kaunakakai, ☎ (808) 553-3876.
Hours: 7:30 a.m.–Sunset.

Long after the stale champagne memories and unkept resolutions have faded on the mainland, Molokaians are just celebrating their own New Year's festival—the Molokai Makahiki, observed annually (established in 1980) in mid-January. Actually a festival of peace, it's a sunrise-to-sunset party in Kaunakakai, where everyone chows down on *ono grinds* (good eats) while listening to traditional music and watching dancers from various hula schools. Other activities include canoe races and arts and crafts. Makahiki is also a chance to play native games such as *'o'oihe*, (spear throwing), *'ulu maika* and *konane* (ancient forms of bowling and checkers, respectively).

Tours

Kukui Tours & Limousines   ★★

P.O. Box 1985, Kaunakakai, 96748, ☎ (808) 553-5133.
Hours: 8 a.m.–5 p.m.

Offers half-day (three hours) and full-day (seven hours) tours of the island in air-conditioned comfort; you may request a custom stretch-limo (minimum six passengers, $294 half-day, $514 full-day). The shorter tour encompasses the West end of Molokai, including the Kaluakoi resort area, Papohaku Beach and the old plantation town of Maunaloa. You'll also experience an eagle-eye view of the craggy North

Shore and Kalaupapa settlement from the Kalae lookout, as well as a visit to Phallic Rock. When spirits start to flag, a java break at Coffees of Hawaii is in order for some home-grown brew. If weather permits, a detour to Purdy's Macadamia Nut Farm is an added bonus. The full-day tour takes you to the east end of the island and includes lunch at a local restaurant or hotel. Rate is per person; all tours based on a minimum of three passengers. The company also provides an airport shuttle and 24-hour taxi service. General admission: $22.76 –$40.34.

Mapulehu Glass House   ★★

P.O. Box 500, Kaunakakai, East of the 15-mile marker on Highway 450, 15 miles East of Kaunakakai, 96748, ☎ (808) 558-8160.
Hours: 7 a.m.–noon
Special hours: tours at 10:30 a.m. Closed: Sat., Sun.

Sorry, this isn't your local Waterford crystal outlet, but a historic greenhouse built in the 1920s that specializes in exotic tropical blooms. What may be the state's largest glass house is attached to a working nine-acre certified cut-flower farm that offers free tours. After the tour, you may purchase pink and white ginger, heliconia and more to perfume your condo or hotel room; the Glass House also ships flowers by Federal Express to your friends languishing on the mainland. Sigh. A nice stop while touring the Halawa Valley area.

Scenic view of Molokai

Molokai Off-Road Tours & Taxi   ★★

P.O. Box 747, Kaunakakai, 96748, ☎ (808) 553-3369.

As long as it isn't raining, this company's guides will take you to the entrance of the Molokai Forest Preserve (also known as Kamakou) west of Kaunakakai by four-wheel-drive vehicle, usually an air-conditioned Jeep Cherokee. From here, you do the hike yourself, and arrange a pickup time with your driver. Here you'll find a primeval, dense wonderland of giant ferns, eucalyptus and pine, and some 500 native

MOLOKAI

plant species. The daylong hike (about seven hours) ends at the Waikolou Overlook, where you can picnic (bring your own bag) while gazing at waterfalls and plunge pools in the valley below and offshore islands in the distance. Dress in layers as the climate changes quickly from hot to mighty nippy, dry to humid in a heartbeat; discuss the particulars when you make a reservation. This tour requires a minimum of three people and a max of 10. Molokai Off-Road also conducts a Grand Tour of the island for $40 per person; minimum three persons, maximum 10; there are 10 additional tours and activities available.

The Maui Princess ★★

Kaunakakai, ☎ *(808) 661-8397.*

Used both as an excursion yacht and daily mode of transportation for Molokai commuters working in Maui, the *Maui Princess* sails daily from Lahaina Harbor Maui's Pier 3 to Kaunakakai Harbor in Molokai. The comfortable yacht has an air-conditioned main cabin, but for those wishing to travel al fresco, it provides a capacious upper-level observation deck. Snacks and beverages for sale on board. The sailing schedule is as follows: depart Lahaina Pier 3 at 7 a.m.; arrive Kaunakakai at 8:45 a.m.; depart Kaunakakai at 3:55 p.m.; arrive Lahaina at 5:45 p.m. The fare is $50 for adults, $25 for children. The company also offers tour packages to Molokai, including four cruise/drive deals ranging from $74 to $109; a Molokai Grand Tour, which includes a local guide; a golf package; hotel overnighters; and three Kalaupapa Tours. The Trail Hike and Settlement Tour is $139; Fly-in and Settlement Tour; $189; and Guided Mule Tour; $225 (available Monday-Friday only). Passengers must be at least 16 years of age to tour Kalaupapa. General admission: $50.

West Molokai

Maunaloa

Beaches

Kepuhi Beach ★★★

Kaluakoi Road, Maunaloa, 96770.

Unless you're an experienced bodysurfer, this lovely white sand beach in front of Colony's Kaluakoi Resort's golf course is better for long strolls, beachcombing and sun worshiping. Dangerous swimming conditions, even on calm days, due to strong currents. A favorite winter surfing spot (experienced only!). Facilities at the resort, parking.

Children's Activities

Kite Making/Kite Flying Classes ★★

120 Maunaloa Highway, Maunaloa, 96770, ☎ *(808) 552-2364.*
Hours: 8:30 a.m.–5 p.m.
Special hours: Sundays, 10 a.m.–2 p.m.

For more than 15 years, the Big Wind Kite Factory, purveyor of colorful handmade kites and windsocks, has been giving kite-making classes to the children on Molokai. Proprietor "Uncle Jonathan" Socher calls his surefire technique "20 Kids, 20 Kites, 20 Minutes." What this means is, if he can get 20 kids, he can have them each finish a kite in 20 minutes! The materials list includes brightly colored typing paper and barbecue sticks. Child impersonators (that's you and me) can also drop by and take one of Socher's daily kite-flying lessons; no strings attached (his pun, not ours). Factory tours daily. Call the store for lesson times.

City Celebrations

Moloka'i Ka Hula Piko

Papohaku Beach Park, Maunaloa, In the Kaluakoi Resort, ☎ *(808) 553-3876.*
Contrary to the image presented by corny old Hollywood movies, Hula is a highly refined form of artistic expression. It's an ancient dance, a language, that speaks of the history and aspirations of a people. Molokai is the birthplace of the hula. At Ka'ana on the slopes of Maunaloa in west Molokai, there was once a famous hula school. Here tradition holds, the goddess Laka first danced the hula, then traveled throughout the islands teaching others the graceful movements and chants that have been passed on through generations to today's *kumu hula.* Each year, on the third Saturday in May, Molokai celebrates the birth of hula, attracting visitors from all over the world; festivities include music, food, arts and crafts, and of course, demonstrations by hula *halaus,* or schools. The day-long program is preceded by a week of lectures on hula and Hawaiian history, as well as guided tours to historic sites celebrated in hula chants. Rooms sell out for this event; contact the Molokai Visitors Association ☎ *(808) 553-3876,* for special travel packages.

Theme/Amusement Parks

Molokai Ranch Wildlife Conservation Park

P.O. Box 259, Maunaloa, 96770, ☎ *(808) 552-2773.*
Special hours: 10 a.m. and 1 p.m. Closed: Mon., Sun.
Open-air safari vans allow visitors to observe and photograph more than 800 rare (and not so rare) animals from Africa and Asia such as Barbary sheep, kudu, Indian black buck, giraffe, zebras, eland and oryx, who seem to thrive in West Molokai's pleasing, arid climate. The park encompasses 350 acres of the 53,000-acre Molokai Ranch, which many participants compare with Africa's Serengeti plain. Afterward, the kids can take turns feeding the graceful (and grateful) giraffes in the popular "giraffe picnic." Reservations required. $15 for ages 13–18; $5 for ages three–12; under three free. May be cancelled in event of rain. General admission: $35.

Sports

Choose from two golf courses: the flashy par-72 with all accoutrements at **Kaluakoi Golf Course,** or the relatively Spartan, nine-hole course at **Ironwood Hills Golf Club.** Guests play **tennis** for free at Kaluakoi Resort (with the best facilities), Wavecrest Condos and Ke Nani Kai Condos. Nonguests can play at Kaluakoi for a fee, or try the public courts at Molokai High School or the Kaunakakai Community Center.

Fishermen usually luck out in Molokai's fish-filled waters, reeling in big favorites such as marlin, ahi, mahi-mahi, ono, onaga and uku. Cast your line from the shore for ulua and ama ama, or head for the south shore's fishpond sites for squid. Charter excursions will take you to the best sportfishing locations. Sailing, snorkeling, kayaking and scuba-diving excursions are all available. If you'd rather stay on land, Molokai Ranch Outfitters Center offers a variety of **horseback rides**. One tour—the Saturday Lunch Adventure—includes swimming, kayaking, snorkeling, lunch *and* the horse.

Central Molokai

Kalae

Ironwood Hills Golf Course ★

P.O. Box 182, Kalae, Just south of Molokai Museum/Meyer Sugar Mill, 96757, ☎ (808) 567-6000.
Hours: 7 a.m.–5 p.m.
This is the "people's" golf course—no membership required. Only nine holes, but you can pay a little extra to play the course all over again. No frills or facilities other than cart rental ($14 power cart, $2.50 pull it yourself). Ironwood also has superior ocean views (it has a 1200-foot elevation) and a few challenging holes. General admission: $7–$14.

Palaau

Palaau State Park ★★

Highway 470, Palaau, Highway 460 south to Kaunakakai, left (North) to Highway 470 to the park, ☎ (808) 567-6083.
This 223-acre, refreshingly cool (and somewhat damp) North Shore park is abundant with eucalyptus, pine and plenty of green stuff. About 2000 foot above sea level, it rains a lot here—at least an inch or more per month. Quiet and uncrowded, this is the least-used state campground in the district. Rest rooms, but no showers, no electricity. Water, picnic tables, tentsites. Kaunakakai is 10 miles away. Best for hiking, there's a trail leading to Phallic Rock, which legends credit with granting childless women fertility. Camping is free; seven-day limit. Permits from the Division of Parks, PO Box 153, Kaunakakai, HI 96748.

East Molokai

Halawa Valley

Chris' Adventures Bike or Hike ★★★

P.O. Box 869, Kula, HI 96790, Halawa Valley, ☎ (800) 224-5344.
Hours: 8 a.m.–6 p.m.
Special hours: Saturdays, 8-10 a.m. Closed: Sun.
Chris and his associates offer hiking or cycling (on- and off-road) tours of Molokai's lush Halawa Valley every Thursday from 6:30 a.m.–6 p.m. You can bike along

ancient Hawaiian fish ponds to the valley. They used to offer hiking trips through the valley to Moaula Falls, but the trail is now closed to visitors. Tour includes breakfast, and island-style picnic lunch, 21-speed TREK bicycles, helmets, gloves, weather gear, day packs, maps, safety briefings. This tour is recommended for all levels of experience. Also offered are Maui-Lanai-Molokai "inn-to-inn vacations," (three to eight days) which combines hiking/biking with a kayak or raft adventure. Most tours are tailored to accommodate occasional practitioners of these sports, but can be geared to more-advanced levels. Price is $200–$275 per day; includes meals, transportation, equipment, lodging, extras. Call Chris' Adventures tour planner for details, dates and trip itineraries. General admission: $160–$275.

Halawa Valley/Moaula Falls ★★★

Halawa Valley, After the 21-mile marker on Highway 450.

This popular trail to Moaula Falls begins near Jerusalema Hou Church. The wet, slippery, two-mile trail (two hours both ways) punctuated by tropical fruit trees and lava-rock terraces, is a hardy climb through primeval jungle up to the 250-foot waterfall and pool, where the traveler is rewarded by a freezing dip in the crystal-clear water. Before doing so, people followed local legend by throwing a ti leaf into the pool; only if it floated to the surface was it safe to swim. Unfortunately, the trail to the falls is closed to hikers for the foreseeable future, due to a lawsuit.

Waikolou Valley

Waikolu Valley ★★★

Highway 460 south towards Kaunakakai, Waikolu Valley, From Highway 460, turn left at Maunahui Road 10 miles to Waikolu Valley Lookout, ☎ (808) 553-5019.

Access to the valley is difficult; after a relatively smooth beginning, the last seven miles are extremely rough; recommendation is to park your vehicle and hike. It has the best views on the island (maybe the world) from a 4000-foot lookout to Waikolu Valley and numerous waterfalls. The downside is a persistent cloud cover; 50 percent chance of overcast, especially in winter. No water, picnic tables or grills. Pit toilet (one). Pretty cold camping, but gorgeous and wild, and close to the Kamakou Forest Preserve trails. Better bring all supplies in, no facilities for miles. Permit required; five-day limit. Contact State Department of Forestry (located in Maui) at the phone number above. There's also a ranger station, where you might be able to obtain permits in person, on Oloolo Street, one mile west of Kaunakakai off Highway 460. Call ☎ (808) 553-5019.

Kaunakakai

Alyce C. ★

P.O. Box 825, Kaunakakai, 96748, ☎ (808) 558-8377.

Alyce C. is Joe "Captain" Reich's baby, a 31-foot diesel-powered fishing vessel available for a full- or half-day charter; Reich provides the equipment and bait; all you have to do is show up. He'll take you and your party off the coast of Molokai to catch plenty of ahi, mahi-mahi, ono ulua, kawakawa and perhaps a Pacific blue marlin, if you're lucky. Reich has 20 years' experience. Whale-watching in season.

Bill Kapuni's Snorkel and Dive Adventure ★

Kaunakakai, 96748, ☎ *(808) 553-9867.*
Let Bill, a native Hawaiian and professional PADI instructor, take you on a snorkeling adventure to a secluded, unspoiled barrier reef, with warm tropical waters teeming with colorful marine life. It also has one of the most dense populations of turtles and eagle rays in Hawaii. Includes gear, soda and chips. Air fills and tank rentals, scuba instruction. Morning tour: 7:30 and 10:30 a.m.; afternoon tour: 1 p.m. General admission: $85.

Kioea Park ★

Highway 460, one mile west of Kaunakakai ☎ *(808) 567-6296.*
This beach park is adjacent to Kamehameha V's royal Kapuaiwa Coconut Grove, where you risk being dive-bombed by errant nuts (a sign says, "Beware of Falling Coconut"). Administered by the Department of Hawaiian Homelands, it is available to visitors only if it isn't in use by native Hawaiians; otherwise, you have the whole site to yourself for $5 a night. Entrance is through a locked gate—you have to obtain a key from the Department to get in. Facilities include ample tentsites, a beach pavilion with electricity, picnic tables and barbecue grills, toilets and showers. The beach is too silty for swimming or snorkeling. For permits call the number above, or write to the Department of Hawaiian Homelands, Box 198, Hoolehua, HI 96729. General admission: $5.

Ma'a Hawaii: Molokai Action Adventures ★★★

Kaunakakai, 96748, ☎ *(808) 558-8184.*
Hunt axis deer, wild boar or Spanish goats using bows ($150 per day) or rifles ($250 per day) with Walter "Crocodile" Naki (as he is known on Molokai). Trips take all day; 10 hunters maximum. Naki, a decathlon champion and renowned spear fisherman and free diver, also takes people on snorkeling, diving, kayaking, reef trolling and hiking trips. (See appropriate sections.) He'll also take the less-intrepid on cultural/historical tours to sites such as the Ili'ili'opa'e Heiau and the Kawela petroglyphs, which are on private lands. Price: $150–$450. Even if you've never done it before, attempt a spear-fishing adventure with Walter "Crocodile" Naki, who has won statewide contests in the sport. Many novices report on awesome experiences with the gregarious Naki, who likes to cook the catch on the beach for the ultimate "local-style" experience. His snorkeling trips are also renowned. Price: $50. Although he'll take you hunting, spear-fishing, hiking and more, snorkeling with sportsman Walter "Crocodile" Naki is an exhilarating experience. He knows where all the octopus holes are; you might get to pet one. Tip: after putting up with you for a while, the octopus likes to spurt you with harmless ink before taking off. Price: $50.

Molokai Bicycle

P.O. Box 379, Kaunakakai, 96748, ☎ *(808) 553-3931.*
Hours: 4–7 p.m.
Special hours: Sat. from 9 a.m.–2 p.m. Closed: Tue., Thurs., Sun.
Philip Kikukawa's shop is the only bicycle repair shop on the island; he also rents mountain bikes for $19 a day; if you rent two bikes the price is $17 a day. He also

MOLOKAI

conducts informal bike tours of the island (including one to the forest reserve) when he's not busy. If you fall in love with your bike, he'll sell it to you, as well as accessories. Other cycling adventures: Molokai Ranch Outfitters Center, ☎ (800) 254-8871 or (808) 552-2681, offers mountain bike trail riding on the 53,000-acre ranch (unguided). Full day is $75, including drop-off service, gourmet picnic lunch and shuttle back to the Center. Fun Hogs, ☎ (808) 552-2555, rents mountain bikes for $6 hour, or $20 day, including helmets and gloves. General admission: $17–$19 per day.

Molokai Charters ★★

P.O. Box 1207, Kaunakakai, 96748, ☎ *(808) 553-5852.*

Billing itself as Molokai's original charter service since 1975, Richard and Doris Reed's Molokai Charters is practically the only charter service on the island. After piloting *Satan's Doll* a rakishly named 42-foot sloop, around the world for the past four years, the couple has returned to roost once more at Kaunakakai Harbor. Packages include a two-hour sunset sail at $30 per person, a half-day sail and whale-watching (in season) excursion for $40 per person that includes soft drinks and *haole pupus*; a full-day sail to Lanai for $75 with swimming, snorkeling and whale-watching; they promise to anchor at an isolated spot. The full-day sail includes a picnic lunch and soft drinks; snorkeling gear is available for rental. All trips are based on a minimum party of four.

One Ali'i Park ★

Highway 450, three miles east of Kaunakakai., Kaunakakai, Take Highway 460 from the airport, go south to Kaunakakai, where road becomes Highway 450, ☎ *(808) 553-5141.*

This family beach and county park on Molokai's south shore isn't worth going out of your way for, but it's close to town (and stores, in case you get a snack attack) and lack of rainfall ensures a lot of sunny, dry days. Although the sea is calm, the water is silty and murky, which is typical for the area. Swimming, snorkeling and fishing, therefore, are not advised. There are two campgrounds (one for 40, another for about 100), both a few yards from the beach. Picnic tables, no open fires allowed. Showers and rest rooms for men and women, but bring your own toilet paper just in case. No lifeguard on duty. On the west end of the island is Papohaku Beach Park, also a sunny, dry area about 40 minutes from Kaunakakai and 25 minutes from the airport. It has broad, golden sand (nearly three miles long) that is usually uncrowded, wonderful for beachcombing. On the downside, surf is hazardous (surfers like this) and currents strong in the winter. There are about 100 tentsites with picnic tables and grills. Clean rest rooms. It's seven miles from the town of Maunaloa, where there's a grocery store and restaurant. Directions: From the airport, take Highway 460 west to Maunaloa. Before Maunaloa, turn right at Kaluakoi Road and follow signs to the park. Both require permits; $3 per person, three-day limit. Contact Department of Parks and Recreation, P.O. Box 153, Kaunakakai, HI 96748; see phone number above. General admission: $3.

Shon-A-Lei II

Kaunakakai, ☎ *(808) 553-5242.*

Skipper Steve Schonley (the "Shon" in Shon-A-Lei) takes groups on half-day, full-day or overnight sport fishing trips; the 35-foot twin-diesel Bertrum is fully equipped. Whale-watching (December-March) and bottom fishing...who knows, you might find a school of lawyers down there. From mainland United States and Canada, call ☎ *(800) 998-FISH*.

West Molokai
Maunaloa

Fun Hogs ★★

At Colony's Kaluakoi Hotel and Golf Club, Maunaloa, 96770, ☎ (808) 552-2555.
Hours: 9 a.m.–5 p.m.
Closed: Mon.
Specializing in guided shoreline kayaking/snorkeling trips that venture about a mile and a half to Kawakiu Bay and back, this recreational company is located in the beach shack at Colony's Kaluakoi Hotel and Golf Club. The hogs are actually Mike and Maria Holmes, Honolulu escapees who've been leading these trips for about two years. Usually offered in the summer months, participants can choose a one- or two-person kayak; children under 10 must ride with a parent. Snorkeling gear is included (or you can bring your own) for $40 per person. Other activities include a snorkeling/catamaran sailing/whale-watching package (2.5 hours, whale watching in December–April) for $50 per person. You can also rent mountain bikes, body boards, kayaks, camping/snorkeling equipment. Guided tours daily, kayaking from 8-10:30 a.m.; other activities from 1 p.m. For more information, write: *PO Box 424, Hoolehua, HI 96729*.

Kaluakoi Golf Course

P.O. Box 26, Maunaloa, At Colony's Kaluakoi Hotel and Golf Club, 96770, ☎ (808) 552-2739.
Hours: 7:30 a.m.–6:30 p.m.
Special hours: weekends, holidays from 7 a.m.
With five holes facing the oceanfront and others in a wooded setting replete with deer and other wildlife wandering by, this 18-hole (par-72) championship course designed by Ted Robinson is one of the most picturesque in Hawaii. It's also relatively uncrowded. Pro shop, driving range, practice green, lessons available. General admission: $55–$75.

Molokai Ranch Campsites

C/o Molokai Ranch, P.O. Box 259, Maunaloa, 96770, ☎ (808) 552-2681.
Camping is free at Kawakiu, north of Colony's Kaluakoi Hotel (on a red dirt road past the resort's golf course). It's fairly accessible, by four-wheel-drive or on foot, and no permit is required. Swimming conditions here are usually good (except when the surf gets rough in winter), and there's lots of white sand to stroll on. No drinking water or facilities. A favorite locals beach is Mo'omomi on the western edge of the Hoolehua Plains (see Nature Conservancy Hikes). To get there, take Highway 460 east of the airport until it branches out to Highway 480. Turn left onto Farrington Avenue and head west. Paved road turns into red dirt (people in rental cars are not supposed to go off paved roads) which is not always in good

shape. But it's a rewarding experience, as the three-mile-long coast is full of unexpected, uncrowded coves. Swimming is fine here most of the year (dangerous in winter months). No facilities. West of the Mo'omomi are the Keonelele Dunes (see Nature Conservancy Hikes), rare plant forms and an ancient Hawaiian burial site. Foot access allowed without a permit, required for vehicles. Contact the phone number and address above for more information.

Molokai Ranch Outfitters Center

P.O. Box 259, Maunaloa, 96770, ☎ *(808) 552-2681.*
Special hours: 9 a.m. and 12:30 p.m. Closed: Mon., Sun.

Accompanied by a Molokai *paniolo* (cowboy) guide well versed in the history and culture of the island, these popular trail rides (about two hours) meander through ancient Hawaiian cultural sites and probably the world's highest sea cliffs for views of the neighbor island of Lanai. Two rides, 9 a.m. and 12:30 p.m. Age limit: 12 years. General admission: $40.

Molokai Ranch Outfitters Center/Malihini Rodeo ★★★

P.O. Box 259, Maunaloa, 96770, ☎ *(808) 552-2681.*
Closed: Mon., Tue., Thurs., Sat., Sun.

Molokai is big on horses and rodeos—it has its own Junior Roping Club, and now with the newly completed, state-of-the art rodeo arena, the folks at Molokai Ranch (a 53,000-acre working cattle ranch for more than 100 years) Outfitters Center offer visitors an exciting, one-of-a-kind experience—anyone (as long as they're 16 and over) can be a "Cowboy (all right, person) for a Day." The fun includes traditional rodeo games such as barrel-racing and pole-bending, roping cattle (at your own pace, of course) with Ranch *paniolos* (the real thing, podner) to guide your every shaky move. Go for it! The Malihini Rodeo takes place every Wednesday and Friday; reservations required. General admission: $50.

Where to Stay

You won't find a lot of choices and, if locals have anything to say about it, things will stay that way. Don't come expecting a lot of flash and fanfare, though the trade-off is a lot of peace and good Hawaiian hospitality. For those who can't live without the vestiges of posh, you'd best aim for **Colony's Kaluakoi Hotel and Golf Club**, at Kaluakoi Resort, or the luxurious condos nearby at **Kaluakoi Villas** or **Ke Nani Kai Resort**. A smattering of other inns and condos are sprinkled about, with a couple of B&Bs tossed in. **Hotel Molokai**, a couple of miles from Kaunakakai, is a Polynesian-style favorite for the good-value-for-money set, while budget-travelers (who aren't camping) usually hide out at **Pau Hana Inn**, Molokai's oldest hotel.

East Molokai

Kamalo

Bed-and-Breakfasts

Kamalo Plantation $55–$75 ★★

HC1, Box 300, Kamalo, 96748, Highway 460 to Highway 450 (past Kaunakakai), go east 10.5 miles, ☎ (808) 558-8236, FAX (808) 558-8236.
Single: $55–$75. Double: $55–$75.

Glenn and Akiko Foster's five-acre, tropical, park-like property is at the foot of Mount Kamakou on the island's east side, just in front of Father Damien's St. Joseph's Church. Archaeology and history buffs may be interested to know that the foundations of an ancient *heiau* (temple) are on the plantation. Your choice of accommodations include a self-contained cottage set far enough away from the main house to ensure total privacy. It sleeps two to four with a king-size bed, queen-size sleeper couch, shower and a fully equipped kitchen (including oils and spices). Home-baked bread and fruit from the plantation's orchard, which is just steps away from the cottage, are supplied for "do it yourself" breakfasts. Lounging chairs are provided for relaxing on the outside lanai; nearby is a hammock strung between two lauhala trees. When you bestir yourself from all this languor, beach towels, mats, a cooler and ice are on hand for your use. More sociable types may opt to lodge in the two rooms in the main house; here guests are served an "Aloha" breakfast in the dining room. The Kukui Room features a king or twin beds, microwave, refrigerator and outside lanai; it shares a bath with the Hibiscus Room (twin waterbeds, hot pot, refrigerator, outside lanai). The Kukui Room has a private entrance, and guests staying here have the option of requesting a private bath for $10 extra per night. (The Fosters will then not rent out the Hibiscus Room.) All accommodations have tape decks and radios, but no television or telephones. No smoking indoors. Children allowed in the cottage only; no pets. Amenities: balcony or patio. 3 rooms. Credit cards: not accepted.

Kawela

Ka Hale Mala $60–$70 ★★★

In the Kawela area, about five miles from Kaunakakai, Kawela, ☎ (808) 553-9009, FAX (808) 553-9009.
Single: $60–$70. Double: $60–$70.

Ka Hale Mala ("The Garden House") is a two-story Polynesian pole house on a 12,000-square-foot lot across from the ocean and about a five-mile walk to the beach. But you're also in the country—deer often use a trail behind the property. The vivacious owners, Cheryl Corbiell and Jack Pugh, live upstairs; the entire ground floor is rented to guests. The four-room guest suite is 840 square feet with a four-sided lanai providing views of the tropical garden and orchard where you're free to pick and eat your fill of pomelos, tangerines, tangelos or whatever exotic fruit may be growing at the time. Not only that, but as Cheryl says, her Hawaiian tomatoes grow like weeds; the vegetable and herb garden is a good source of fresh greens for your salad bowl. The four-room guest suite features a bedroom with two single beds (two more on request), combination bath, living room with entertainment center (television, stereo, VCR on request), and two twin day beds. The fully equipped kitchen features a microwave, stove/oven, refrigerator, coffee maker and more. Washer/dryer. Included in the rate are two mountain bikes and snorkel gear. All this for $70 per day! You can also opt for preparing your own breakfast; rates then drop $10 less. But you wouldn't want to miss Cheryl's hearty, country repasts (besides, you're on vacation) consisting of taro sourdough waffles, cheesy egg pie, banana fritters and sometimes a breakfast pizza with tomatoes, eggs, bacon, chopped apple, apricots, cheddar cheese and fresh garden herbs. Your hosts will respect your privacy if you wish, but will also arrange guided tours, suggest outdoor activities, snorkel trips, visits to artists' studios and more. If you want to learn how to make laulau (steamed fish and chicken cooked in ti leaves and taro leaves) the couple will be more than glad to instruct you. The apartment can also be rented for $420 per week (without breakfast). For more than two people, there's a $10 charge. Amenities: balcony or patio. 1 rooms. Credit cards: not accepted.

Uluapue

Cottage

Beach Cottage at Ualupue Pond   **$80**

Past the 13-mile marker in Ualapue, Uluapue, 13.5 miles east of Kaunakakai in front of Ualapue Fishpond, ☎ *(808) 576-9146.*
Single: $80. Double: $80.

Located in peaceful, low-key East Molokai, this private, solar-heated cottage overlooks the historic Ualupue Fishpond, which was constructed around the 13th century; it has recently been restored. The Polynesian-style, one-bedroom dwelling (with two queen beds) was built to look old (although it was actually completed in 1993) and is surrounded by a rock wall and has its own lush garden. Amenities include a color TV and fully equipped kitchen with granite counter-tops. If you're looking for a private retreat, this is a good value; it can also be rented for $500 per week or $1500 per month ($10 additional person). Supplies? Try the nearby Wavecrest Resort's general store. 1 room. Credit cards: not accepted.

Kaunakakai

Condos

Molokai Shores Suites   **$125–$159**

Kamehameha Highway, P.O. Box 1037, Kaunakakai, 96748, One mile from Kaunakakai between the Pau Hana and Hotel Molokai, ☎ *(800) 535-0085, (808) 553-5954.*
Single: $125–$159. Double: $125–$159.

This three-story condo is for those who can't quite face the down-home virtues of the nearby Pau Hana and Hotel Molokai. The pleasant but unprepossessing chocolate-brown structure houses units that are like the equivalent of a pasta dinner—comfort food for the tired body. The Molokai Shores Suites offers one- and two-bedroom suites with separate living areas, fully equipped kitchens, ceiling fans and color cable TV. Wooden louvers let as much sunshine in as you like. If you like that

Molokai Wildlife Park

Papohaku Beach, Molokai

Mule ride to Kalaupapa

Pohakuloa Beach, West Molokai

Halawa Beach Park

top-of-the-world feel, ask for a loft suite with airy, cathedral ceilings. All have lanais where you can dine ál fresco, each overlooking the pretty grounds lit with tiki torches come nightfall. Diversions on the premises include a beachfront swimming pool, barber/beauty shop, guest laundry, shuffleboard and barbecue area. Amenities: balcony or patio. 102 rooms. Credit cards: A, DC, MC, V.

Wavecrest Resort $109–$169 ★

HC01, Box 541, Kaunakakai, 96748, At the 13-mile marker in Ualupue, ☎ (800) 367-2980, (808) 558-8101, FAX (808) 553-8206.
Single: $109–$169. Double: $109–$169.
A breezy, five-acre oceanfront property in East Molokai with a lot of swaying palms and bright tropical blooms in the well-tended yard. Recently renovated one- and two-bedroom suites are pleasantly but not spectacularly furnished and have a separate bedroom, fully equipped kitchen, sofa bed, color TV and spacious lanai, but no telephones. Swimming pool, shuffleboard, laundry facility, barbecue grills, free parking. A small but decently stocked "general store" (how quaint!) on the premises comes in handy, since this secluded property is miles from anything. Three-night minimum stay, substantial discounts for two-week stays. Amenities: tennis, balcony or patio, family plan. Credit cards: MC, V.

Hotels

Hotel Molokai $59–$125 ★

P.O. Box 546, Kamehameha Highway, Kaunakakai, 96748, Two miles east of Kaunakakai on Highway 450, ☎ (800) 423-6656, (808) 553-5347, FAX (808) 553-5047.
Single: $59–$125. Double: $59–$125.
The Hotel Molokai is what people used to come to Hawaii for before the days of self-contained mega-resorts where attendants spray you with Evian water at poolside every five minutes. Many travelers might consider the brown-shingled, two-story, A-frame cottage buildings a little rustic and funky, but for old-timers, the place just cries out "nostalgia." Lower-level rooms are small, dark and gloomy, and soundproofing isn't the greatest, but the deluxe upstairs rooms and studios are quite nice and spacious, with cathedral ceilings, and best of all, a breezy lanai with a rattan porch swing where you can cozy up to your honey (or read a good book). All rooms with portable fan, refrigerator. Some with air conditioning. TVs on request. Facilities include a gift shop, swimming pool and poolside bar. Unfortunately, the popular restaurant, Holo Holo Kai, is closed, so guests have to drive into town to eat. Amenities: balcony or patio. 55 rooms. Credit cards: CB, DC, MC, V.

West Molokai

Maunaloa

Condos

Blair's Original Molokai Vacation Rentals $89–$109 ★★

At the Kaluakoi Resort, Maunaloa, Off Highway 460 at the 15-mile marker, take road to resort, ☎ (800) 228-HANA, (808) 248-7868, FAX (808) 248-8240.
Single: $89–$109. Double: $89–$109.
These two deluxe adjoining beachfront condos in the Kaluakoi Resort front the first hole of the golf course. Decorated with a Hawaiiana theme, both are large studios

with 20-foot-high ceilings and lanais almost directly facing the ocean. Condominium One, or Beachfront, features a king-size bed and full kitchen; Condominium Two or Beachfront Adjoining has a queen bed and a kitchenette; both have sleeper sofas. The units can be opened up for two couples traveling together. Amenities include color TVs with VCR, and stereo systems with CD player. Pool. On the premises (shared with the resort) are a restaurant, lounge and snack bar, barbecues and shops. Condo One is available for weekly rental at $625; Condo Two for $575. Amenities: balcony or patio. 2 rooms. Credit cards: A, MC, V.

Kaluakoi Villas $120–$195 ★★

1131 Kaluakoi Road, Maunaloa, 96770, ☎ *(800) 525-1470, (808) 552-2721, FAX (808) 552-2201.*
Single: $120–$195. Double: $120–$195.
A secluded oceanfront condominium retreat on the grounds of Colony's Kaluakoi Hotel and Golf Club (but under separate management); guests here are free to use the resort's pool, 18-hole golf course, four lighted tennis courts, restaurants and other facilities at no extra charge. The units consist of studios and one-bedroom suites with kitchenettes (refrigerator, counter-top range, microwave, cooking utensils) or the more-deluxe cottages with full kitchens. Price depends on where you're situated—you pay more for a golf course or full ocean view. All have a private lanai and color TV. Living and sleeping areas have generic-tropical art, teal carpets in good repair and attractive, light rattan furniture with floral upholstery. Amenities: balcony or patio, family plan. 95 rooms. Credit cards: A, MC, V.

Ke Nani Kai $95–$135 ★★★

P.O. Box 289, Maunaloa, 96770, At the entrance to Colony's Kaluakoi Resort, ☎ *(800) 888-2791, (808) 552-2761.*
Single: $95–$135. Double: $95–$135.
Popular with families (a one-bedroom unit sleeps up to four persons) and golfers (it's set between Kaluakoi resort's eighth and 17th fairways), these two-story, one- and two-bedroom condos boast all the comforts of home (if your home is a tropical island). Bright white walls and carpeting set off handsome, high-quality, open-work rattan furniture, including glass-topped oval dining tables and ecru and taupe upholstered seating areas opening onto spacious lanais draped with berry-colored bougainvillea. Artwork and lighting is subtle and soothing. In the bedrooms, built-in, mirrored bookshelves come in handy; lots of drawer space. The modern kitchens are fully equipped with dishwasher, coffee maker and refrigerator with automatic ice maker. Units also come with washer and dryer. Maid service every three days. Fax facilities. Although it's on Kaluakoi resort property, Ke Nani Kai has its own free-form pool and spa, and two tennis courts. Book early, as only a few condos (these are privately owned) are available at a time. Two-night minimum stay, four-night December 15–January 4. Amenities: tennis, Jacuzzi, balcony or patio, business services. 120 rooms. Credit cards: A, DC, MC, V.

Paniolo Hale $95–$195 ★★★

Lio Place, P.O. Box 190, Maunaloa, 96770, Adjacent to Colony's Kaluakoi Hotel and Golf Club, ☎ *(800) 367-2984, (808) 552-2731, FAX (808) 552-2288.*
Single: $95–$195. Double: $95–$195.

Although individually decorated (mostly in wicker and rattan and chic floral fabrics), all the studio and one- or two-bedroom units in this fairly luxurious condo resort are built in true Hawaiian style with large and spacious living areas, screened lanais, open-beam ceilings, hardwood floors with area rugs, and ceiling fans. Practicalities include color TV and washer-dryer. Kitchens are equipped with refrigerator with ice maker; one- and two-bedroom units have microwaves. Most two-bedroom units have private Jacuzzi tubs on lanais (set-up fee $35, plus $25 per day with three-day minimum). If you have the extra cash, we recommend going for this romantic idea. Facilities on the property include a pool, paddle tennis, picnic tables, barbecues. Kepuhi Beach is behind the property; as the hotel puts it, "a mere fairway away." Management provides an airport shuttle ($8), but as with all properties on the west side, a rental car is a must for exploring. Amenities: Jacuzzi, balcony or patio. 77 rooms. Credit cards: A, MC, V.

Resorts

Colony's Kaluakoi Hotel & Golf Club   **$95–$195**   ★★★

P.O. Box 1977, Maunaloa, 96770, Off Highway 460 at the 15-mile marker; follow road to resort, ☎ *(800) 777-1700, (808) 552-2555, FAX (808) 552-2821. Rated Restaurant: Ohia Lodge*

Single: $95–$195. Double: $95–$195.

The only full-fledged resort on Molokai, the Kaluakoi is one of the most relaxing hotels we've ever visited. It has an old-fashioned, gracious air, incorporating 33 low-rise, Polynesian-style buildings on sweeping, nicely landscaped and maintained grounds, with a huge and sandy stretch of beach that's ideal for strolling, they say. We wouldn't know, as we spent most of our time in languid contentment pool-side, old-fashioned mai tais (complete with paper umbrellas) in hand. The thatched-roof theme is carried into the Ohia Lodge, where birds flew blissfully about at meals; dinner here is not haute cuisine, but nicely prepared and presented. And the evening meal is a romantic affair; ask for one of the tables-for-two on the terrace, overlooking the dark sea and the twinkling lights of Oahu. Foodwise, breakfast is totally delightful, and in our opinion, the best meal in the restaurant. The guest rooms, which include studios, deluxe two-bedroom ocean-view units and one-bedroom cottages, have been nicely refurbished in wood and rattan, and upholstered with island-style floral fabrics. Second-story quarters feature high-beamed ceilings. All have private lanais and big picture windows. Amenities include a refrigerator, phone and color TV with VCR. Some units come equipped with kitchens, coffee makers and utensils. Irons and non-smoking rooms on request. But the resort beckons you to leave your room with plenty of activities such as golf on the 18-hole Ted Robinson-designed course, tennis (four courts lit for night play), volleyball, bicycling (rental available from Fun Hogs activity center, as is snorkeling equipment, boogie boards and more) and craft demonstrations on Saturdays. The resort's activity desk is excellent, with a knowledgeable and helpful staff; ask for Kiku. When your energy level starts to flag, you can rent a video and pop it into your own machine. All in all, this isn't a place where the staff will peel grapes for you (you have to do your own laundry, machines provided), but that's not what you came to Molokai for in the

MOLOKAI

first place. Amenities: tennis, Jacuzzi, balcony or patio, family plan. 170 rooms.
Credit cards: A, CB, DC, D, MC, V.

Where to Eat

Foodies will be miserable on Molokai—this is just not the spot for the big wine-and-dine. You *will* find a gaggle of "fun" places—little diners and cafés that have been around for ages, serve good unpretentious food, and give you a chance to hobnob with the locals. Pizza, natural foods, fresh-baked breads, spicy Filipino dishes, fresh fish, American favorites and plate lunches are the norm. **Ohia Lodge**, on the western side, is probably as good as you're going to get, with the dining rooms at **Hotel Molokai** and **Kaluakoi Resort** reasonable follow-ups. If you're super fussy, you'd better rent a room or condo with kitchen facilities and cook your own.

Central Molokai

Kualupu'u

Kualupuu Cookhouse $$ ★★

P.O. Box 174, Kualupu'u, 96757, From Kalae Road turn left to Farrington Road, across from Kualupuu Market, ☎ *(808) 567-6185.*

American cuisine. Specialties: Burgers, plate lunches, chicken stir-fry, mahi-mahi, home-made pies and cakes.

Breakfast: 7–11 a.m., entrées $5–$9.

Lunch: 11 a.m.–5 p.m., entrées $6–$9.

Dinner: 5–8 p.m., entrées $9–$17. Closed: Sun.

Terrific things are issuing out of this vintage wooden plantation cottage with lace valances and hand-carved booths that served as the cookhouse of the Del Monte plantation. This spiffy restaurant, with one chef working nonstop in the open kitchen, is obviously giving people what they want; a lot of good food, at very fair prices. Every day, almost a dozen house-baked pies in unusual flavors are available, many made with local fruit and served with real whipped cream, including fresh Molokai lime, or orange with passion fruit. The brownie-like chocolate macadamia nut pie is almost impossible to finish, it's so rich. Meat is hand-ground for the delectable hamburgers, which many folks say wins hands down for the best on the island; try the Mexi-Chicken burger. Breakfast items include steak and eggs, a mahi-mahi omelette and loco moco. Plate lunches are accompanied with a choice of green salad as well as the usual potato-mac salad or rice. Teriyaki steak and fresh seafood and the specialty, chicken stir-fry, are recommended for dinner. Recently, owner Nanette Yamashita, who also made the pies, sold the restaurant to staff members Penny and

Pat Talini. Friends have written to say that although the menu is still the same, the counter has been taken out, much to the dismay of singles who liked to eat there for breakfast. Service is still slow. The restaurant closes at 4 p.m. on Saturdays. Features: outside dining, own baking.

Kaunakakai

Banyan Tree Terrace Restaurant   **$$**   ★

Seaside Place, P.O. Box 546, Kaunakakai, 96748, ☎ (808) 553-5342. Associated hotel: Pau Hana Inn.
American cuisine. Specialties: Prime rib, short ribs, fresh fish, Boston cream pie.
Breakfast: 6:30 a.m.–10:30 a.m., entrées $6.
Lunch: 11 a.m.–2 p.m., entrées $6–$7.
Dinner: 6–9 p.m., entrées $11–$18.
Hearty breakfasts, including French toast made from Kanemitsu Bakery bread, and prime rib dinners for under $18 are the best bets at this atmospheric, local-style restaurant in the Pau Hana Inn. The fireplace in the open-to-the-breezes dining room looks big enough to roast a whole wild boar in, but it's rarely used these days. The height of the action is under the spreading banyan tree outside (it has easily passed the century mark) facing the beach. Features: outside dining. Reservations recommended. Credit cards: A, DC, MC, V.

Kamoi Snack-n-Go   **$**   ★

P.O. Box 558, Kaunakakai, 96748, In the Kamoi Professional Center, ☎ (808) 553-3742.
American cuisine. Specialties: Dave's ice cream.
Basically a snack bar where you get it and go, Kamoi's is notable for featuring at least a dozen sorbets and ice creams from Dave's of Oahu every day. Exotic flavors include lilikoi, lychee and the top-seller, green tea. Many consider these frozen treats the best in the state. Kamoi's also has frozen yogurt, candy, icees and other evil things to make your fillings sizzle. A favored local hot spot, there are wooden benches outside in the shade to eat your cone and talk story. Open daily from 9 a.m.–9 p.m.; from noon on Sundays. Features: outside dining. Reservations not accepted.

Kanemitsu Bakery & Coffee Shop   **$**

Ala Malama Street, Kaunakakai, 96748, ☎ (808) 553-5855.
American cuisine. Specialties: Specialty breads, hamburgers, plate lunches.
Breakfast: 5:30 a.m.–6:30 p.m., entrées $2–$4.
Lunch: 10 a.m.–6:30 p.m., entrées $2–$4. Closed: Tue.
Fresh bread from this old-fashioned bakery conjures up memories of Molokai many years after one has left the islands. The fresh, round loaves are truly special, especially the onion cheese and the long-standing favorite, Molokai French. Tropical fruit and nut varieties include pineapple, papaya, coconut and passion fruit (yum!). Although you can buy packaged bread (in plastic bags) to go, the fresh from the oven varieties usually sell out early in the morning. To prevent this from happening, you can buy hot loaves from the eatery's back alley from 9:30 p.m. every day except Monday (baking takes place until 3 a.m.); just knock at the double door and place your order. These treats are served halved with a choice of plain butter, cinnamon

raspberry jelly, cream cheese or all three, if you can't decide. It's been a local tradition for teens to pick up a loaf before going home from their dates and calling it "pau." New additions to the baking slate include bread-making kits and Molokai Lavosh (an Armenian flatbread). Lavosh is available in three varieties: Original Sesame, Macadamia and Brown Wheat. The coffee shop area serves hearty breakfasts, hamburgers for under $2, and plate lunches. The bread is also sold at the airport—great for gift giving ideas. The bakery closes at 11 a.m. on Sundays. Features: own baking. Reservations not accepted.

Molokai Drive Inn   **$**

Highway 450, Kaunakakai, 96748, Just out of downtown near the Visitor's Association,
☎ *(808) 553-5655.*
American cuisine. Specialties: Plate lunches, breakfasts.
Breakfast: 6 a.m.–1 p.m., entrées $3–$5.
Lunch: 10 a.m.–10 p.m., entrées $3–$5.
Dinner: 5–10 p.m., entrées $3–$5.

More of a "dive inn," this down-home eatery has been a center of Molokai life since 1960. It's worth a look for people-watching; everyone stops in here after ball games, Sunday services and all kinds of social occasions. You have a choice of air-conditioned indoor dining, picnic-style tables under an awning, or takeout. Inexpensive breakfasts, served all day, rely heavily on Spam (which we happen to like), but there are decent daily specials and plate lunches. Open until 10:30 p.m. on Fridays; 6:30 a.m.–10:30 p.m. on Saturdays and Sundays. Features: outside dining.

Molokai Pizza Café   **$$**   ★

15 Kaunakakai Place, Kaunakakai, 96748, Behind the tourist office, ☎ *(808) 553-3288.*
American cuisine. Specialties: Pizza, salads, fresh fish, pasta, ribs.
Lunch: 11 a.m.–10 p.m., entrées $6–$22.
Dinner: 5–10 p.m., entrées $6–$22.

Probably the most mainland-like eatery in town, the Molokai Pizza Café is the only place to order a pie with everything on it since the Mid Nite Inn burned down. For about $22 you can pig out on a monstrous creation called the "Big Island Pizza" loaded with three kinds of meat, including bacon. But come here even if you don't like pizza; there's crisp salads, pasta and even frozen yogurt. Local kids love the place; pizzas here are offered as prizes in school contests. Delivery and takeout available. Open until 11 p.m. on Fridays and Saturdays. Features: own baking.

Outpost Natural Foods   **$**   ★

70 Makaena Place, Kaunakakai, 96748, Near Kalama's Service Station, next to the Civic Center, ☎ *(808) 553-3377.*
American cuisine. Specialties: Vegetarian lunch bar, low-fat specials, organic produce.
Breakfast: 9 a.m.–6 p.m., entrées $5–$6.
Lunch: 10 a.m.–6 p.m., entrées $5–$6. Closed: Sat.

Actually a health food store and juice bar, Outpost is an outlet for the best homegrown produce in town, and you can be sure that the greens in your pita sandwich or salad bowl are of the highest quality. Not only are the vegetarian dishes served here low-fat, they are also low-priced. Complete meals, stir-fries or veggie burritos, served with salad, are under $5. You can eat here, but there's only one picnic table outside. A good place to recover from a Spam overdose. Closes at 3:30 p.m. on Fridays. Features: outside dining.

Oviedo's $ ★

Ala Malama Street, Kaunakakai, 96748, ☎ *(808) 553-5014.*
Asian cuisine. Specialties: Chicken and green papaya, pigs feet.
Breakfast: 10 a.m.–1 p.m., entrées $8–$10.
Lunch: 10 a.m.–6:30 p.m., entrées $8–$10.
Dinner: 5 a.m.–6:30 p.m., entrées $8–$10.
Oviedo's is just a counter-type operation in an old and funky location with a surfeit of plastic, but the Filipino food is tasty and sticks to the ol' ribs. The mongo bean soup is comforting and Oviedo's makes a great chicken with green papaya. Reservations not accepted.

Rabang's Restaurant $ ★

Ala Malama Street, Kaunakakai, Next door to Molokai Fish and Dive, ☎ *(808) 553-5014.*
Asian cuisine. Specialties: Chicken or pork adobo, halohalo, plate lunch.
Breakfast: 6–10 a.m., entrées $4–$7.
Lunch: 10 a.m.–9 p.m., entrées $4–$7.
Dinner: 5–9 p.m., entrées $4–$7.
Mrs. Rabang cooks up quite a diverse ethnic stew for such a small restaurant— (there are only five tables) Hawaiian plate lunches on Fridays, Chinese dishes, Filipino adobo, *halohalo* (sort of an ice cream sundae with purple yam, preserved coconut, garbanzo beans and more) and burgers and sandwiches for the timid palate. Takeout available. The Rabangs also own the deli/grocery next door. Reservations not accepted.

West Molokai
Maunaloa

Jojo's Café $$ ★★

P.O. Box 44, Maunaloa, 96770, Highway 460, past the 10-mile marker, go to the end of the road, ☎ *(808) 552-2803.*
Seafood cuisine. Specialties: Indian-style curries, fresh fish, desserts.
Lunch: Noon–2 p.m., entrées $7–$15.
Dinner: 5–7:45 p.m., entrées $7–$15. Closed: Wed., Sun.
The ONLY place to eat in Maunaloa town besides the resort, Jojo's gets many local (and visitor) votes for a romantic restaurant, mostly because of the Old West-style saloon doors, vintage photographs, cozy tables and the long, dark, antique wooden bar. Jojo is actually Girish Patel, who cooks up a mean Indian curry along with the fresh fish the restaurant is known for. Most of the menu is a potpourri of international dishes such as Korean kalbi ribs, Southern fried chicken and Portuguese bean soup. Sandwiches are good at lunch, especially the mahi burgers. Desserts are remarkably original for a small restaurant, including the passion-fruit ice cream. Features: own baking. Reservations not accepted. Credit cards: MC, V.

Ohia Lodge $$$ ★★

Kepuhi Beach, P.O. Box 1977, Maunaloa, 96770, Off Highway 460 at the 15-mile marker, ☎ *(808) 552-2555. Associated hotel: Colony's Kaluakoi Hotel & Golf.*

American cuisine. Specialties: Fresh fish prepared three ways, ribs, pasta, steaks.

Breakfast: 6:30–10:30 a.m., entrées $11–$11.

Dinner: 6–8:45 p.m., prix fixe $22–$24.

The Ohia Lodge at Colony's Kaluakoi Hotel and Golf Club is one of the most romantic spots to dine in Molokai, whether for breakfast or dinner (no lunch is served). The wide, high-ceilinged dining room, with an open setting, is built on several levels, and has a airy feel. There are several choice tables for two on the terrace, which are ideal for sunset suppers and star-gazing. The menu is a fairly straightforward assembly of well-prepared broiled and grilled steaks and fish, with some adventurous items thrown in such as Kalua pork pot-stickers, sate sticks and Cajun pasta. Although the restaurant ran out of bread the evening we dined there, you won't go hungry. An order of tasty baby back pork ribs will get you an entire rack that literally falls off the plate; my portion was so humongous that I was almost embarrassed to be seen with it. Features: outside dining. Reservations recommended. Credit cards: A, CB, DC, MC, V.

Nightlife

Huh? *What* nightlife? The "scene," by most standards, is nonexistent on Molokai. On Friday and Saturday nights you can do the dance-to-Top-40s routine and hear the local band FIBRE (Friendly Isle Band Rhythmic Experience) on the **Banyan Tree Terrace** at the Pau hana Inn near Kaunakakai. **Hotel Molokai** and **Ohia Lodge** (at the Kaluakoi Hotel) usually host live entertainment on the weekends. Other than that, the choices are nil unless you happen to fall into some impromptu local entertainment.

Kaunakakai

Banyan Tree Terrace ★

P.O. Box 546, Kaunakakai, A short walk from town, 96748, ☎ *(808) 553-5342.*

Hours: 9 a.m.–1 p.m. Fri. and Sat. only.

A local tradition for umpteen years is to dance and party to the Top 40 and Hawaiian band FIBRE, who have been playing under the 100-year-old banyan tree for as long as some Broadway shows have been running. Note: The Banyan Tree Terrace is located in the Pau Hana Inn, which has been sold recently. Check status upon arrival. General admission: $3.

West Molokai
Maunaloa

Ohia Lounge ★★

Colony's Kaluakoi Hotel and Golf Club, Kepuhi Beach, Maunaloa, 96770, ☎ (808) 552-2555.
Hours: 6:30–9:30 p.m. Fri. and Sat. only.

Hawaiian trios or a top 40 dance band will get you up off your feet for some mild rug cuttin' every Friday and Saturday at this nightspot-lounge off the Ohia Lodge restaurant.

Shopping

The good news is that you won't ever see a mall during your stay on Molokai. The bad news is there's not much shopping of *any* sort. The big shopping "center" is along **Ala Malama Street** in Kaunakakai where you'll find a smattering of craft- and souvenir shops, as well as natural and other foods. Some of the hotels and condos have tiny shops on site, and over at **Maunaloa** (the old plantation town on the western end) there are some interesting crafts outlets and galleries.

Kaunakakai

Carol Klein-Jewelry Designer ★★★

P.O. Box 1018, Kaunakakai, 96748, ☎ (808) 558-8569.
Special hours: by appointment.

From her studio, Carol Klein creates such fascinating work as petroglyph-inspired jewelry in gold and silver. She also does custom work.

Designs Pacifica/Jule Patten ★★★★

P.O. Box 1365, Kaunakakai, 96748, ☎ (808) 553-5725.
Special hours: by Appointment only.

Primarily a watercolorist, artist Jule Patten creates hand-painted paper castings that incorporate traditional Hawaiian *kapa* (quilt) designs. The complex patterns resemble a large snowflake and frequent themes include native flowers, fruit, waterfalls, crowns and the royal feather *kahili* (a tall pole used by *ali'i* to announce their presence). The designs appear on T-shirts and clothing and are a wonderful gift or souvenir of your trip. A favorite T-shirt with kids incorporates a Molokai spider with a marking that looks like a "happy face," whether you look at it right side up or upside-down. She also features cloissone painting, hand-etched glassware, embossed art cards, bookbags, aprons and pot holders. Patten, originally from Michigan, has a studio in Molokai and has exhibited in galleries all over the islands.

She's sold more than 75 *kapa* paintings to the Hyatt Regency Kauai resort, where they're on display. Although her work is featured in several local boutiques, you must visit her studio as prices are better there (call for appointment). She loves to explain the meaning of her designs; she studied for many years with traditional *kapa* artists.

Haunani's Flowers   ★

P.O. Box 2038, Kaunakakai, 96748, ☎ *(808) 553-9019.*
Hours: 8:30 a.m.–5:30 p.m.
Special hours: Saturday, 9 a.m.– 1 p.m. Closed: Sun.
Haunani's will ship and wire flower orders, including a lovely selection of cut anthuriums, worldwide. (for more flowers, see "Mapulehu Glass House").

He Ki'i Kapa (The Picture Quilt)   ★★★

P.O. Box 102, Kaunakakai, 96748, ☎ *(808) 553-5408.*
Special hours: by appointment only.
Sadly, Molokai has lost two of its best-loved practitioners of the art of *kapa lau* (traditional Hawaiian quilt-making)—Mrs. Kewano, who passed away, and Ginger LaVoie, who taught popular quilt making-classes at Colony's Kaluakoi Resort, has since moved to Oregon. On the up side, Yvonne Friel, Mrs. Kewano's protegee, and a fine artist in her own right, is teaching others as well as selling *kapa* pillow kits and framed handmade quilts by appointment only.

Imports Gift Shop

P.O. Box 828, Kaunakakai, Across from the post office, 96748, ☎ *(808) 553-5734.*
Hours: 9 a.m.–6 p.m.
Where locals go for a varied selection of casual and what passes for dressy clothing on Molokai, as well as jewelry and accessories.

Imports Gift Shop   ★★

125-C Puali Place, Kaunakakai, East of the Credit Union, across Ala Malama Street from the post office, 96748, ☎ *(808) 553-5734.*
Hours: 9 a.m.–6 p.m.
This gift shop is easy to find—it always has a bright orange "Sale" sign in the window. Among the quilts, jewelry and Hawaiiana is a witty souvenir, a "Molokai Night Life" T-shirt, featuring a quarter moon set in a black box.

Molokai Craft Fairs   ★

Various locations, Kaunakakai.
Starting in November and running right up to Christmas, there are dozens of local crafts fairs—the biggest ones are at the high school and various locations in town, but many large, extended families hold them at their homes. You'll find handmade Christmas ornaments and *ono* festive foods. Watch the local paper and bulletin boards downtown for announcements—this is also a good source for news on the Saturday morning yard sales year-round where you can purchase one-of-a-kind antiques and memorabilia. (There are no antique shops or thrift stores in Molokai.)

Molokai Farmer's Market   ★

Ala Malama Street, Kaunakakai, In front of American Savings Bank, across from the library.
Hours: 8 a.m.–noon. Sat. only.

Fresh produce and crafts by local artists are featured at this lively farmer's market. If you haven't had enough, meander over to a similar market in the Credit Union parking lot (also on Ala Malama Street, across from the post office), which has an extensive selection of veggies and fruits.

Molokai Fish and Dive ★

Ala Malama Street, P.O. Box 567, Kaunakakai, 96748, ☎ *(808) 553-5926.*
Hours: 9 a.m.–6 p.m.
Special hours: Saturday from 8 a.m., Sunday until 2 p.m.
Jim Brocker carries what might be the largest selection of Molokai T-shirts and souvenirs in town, as well as fishing, snorkeling and outdoor paraphernalia. He'll also rent you underwater equipment, in case you forgot yours. Complete rental (snorkel, mask, fins) for $7.98 per day.

Take's Variety Store

P.O. Box 1890, Kaunakakai, 96748, ☎ *(808) 553-5442.*
Hours: 9 a.m.–6 p.m.
Special hours: Friday 8:30 a.m.–5:30 p.m.; Saturday 7–9 p.m.
This general variety store is Molokai's best source for practical, everyday stuff. If no one else has what you want, Take's will. Also open on Sunday from 8:30 a.m. to 5:30 p.m.

West Molokai

Maunaloa

Big Wind Kite Factory ★★

120 Maunaloa Highway, Maunaloa, 96770, ☎ *(808) 552-2364.*
Hours: 8:30 a.m.–5 p.m.
Special hours: Sunday, 10 a.m.–2 p.m.
This world-famous kite store features handmade kites and windsocks made in the shop incorporating owner Jonathan Socher's and his son Zachariah's designs. Also factory tours, kite-making and kite-flying lessons (see Children's Activities). Next door is the Plantation Gallery (same ownership), with a wide variety of items from all over the Pacific, including batik (I still have a pareo I bought there five years ago) fabrics, T-shirts, wood carvings, quilt patterns, a good selection of Hawaiian music, and Pacific Rim arts and crafts. It also has one of the best selection of books on the island.

MOLOKAI

Fielding's Fascinating Molokai Facts

A.k.a.	**The Friendly Island**
Main city	**Kaunakakai**
Flower	**White kuku blossom**
Color	**Green**
Area	**260 square miles**
Length	**38 miles**
Width	**10 miles**
Population	**7000**
Highest point	**Kamakou Peak (4961 feet)**

Molokai Survival Guide

Getting There

You'll most likely fly into Hoolehua Airport, a one-terminal operation about eight miles west of Kaunakakai. You won't find much except a lounge, souvenir shop, lunch counter, information booth and a couple of car rental desks. Airlines are **Hawaiian** (☎ *(808) 553-3644*), **Island Air** (☎ *(808) 567-6115*), **Mahalo Air** (☎ *(808) 567-6515*) and **Air Molokai** (☎ *(808) 553-3636*). Air Molokai's low-flying commuter craft provides an especially exhilarating ride.

If you're coming from Maui, you can **ferry** over on the **Maui Princess** (☎ *(808) 553-5736*)—a once-daily shuttle between Lahaina and Kaunakakai; cost is about $50 round trip.

Getting Around

There is no public transport on Molokai, so you'll either have to rent a car from **Budget** (☎ *(808) 567-6877)* or **Dollar** (☎ *(808) 567-6156)*, or take a taxi. Most of the roads are paved and parking is as-you-please.

Taxis are usually on hand to meet flights (fare into town is about $6), and can be also be hired for tours. Contact **Kukui Tours and Limousines** (☎ *(808) 553-5133)*, **Molokai Style Services** (☎ *(808) 553-9090)*, or **Molokai Off-Road Tours and Taxi** (☎ *(808) 553-9046)*, or—for tours of Kalaupapa (the leper colony)—**Damien Tours** (☎ *(808) 567-6171)*.

Cyclists can rent bicycles at **Colony's Kaluakoi Hotel and Golf Club** (☎ *(808) 552-2555)*.

Visitor Information

Contact the **Molokai Visitors Association** (☎ *(808) 533-3876 or 800-553-0404)* for helpful information. Call ahead and they'll send you a brochure with lists of accommodations, car rentals, restaurants, airlines and other island services.

MOLOKAI

MOLOKAI

LANAI

Snorkeling near Shark Fin Rock, Lanai

This pineapple paradise has not yet been hammered to death by developers or the tourist crunch (which seem to go hand-in-hand), so hurry over for the chance to see everything. Hardly anyone comes to this isle of 2426 occupants, but the ones who *do* are formidable—celebrities, high hogs, the exu-

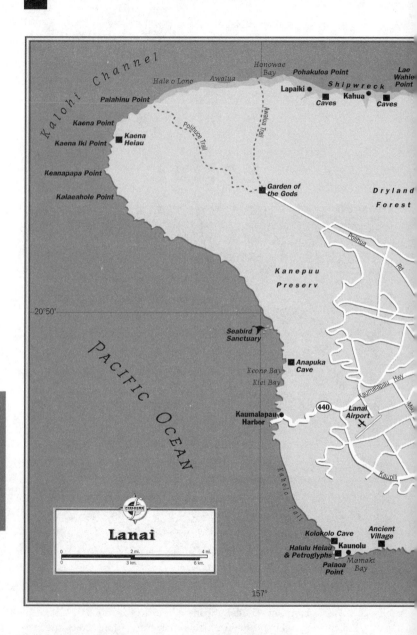

Kalohi Channel

Honowae Bay

Pohakuloa Point

Lae Wahle Point

Hale o Lono

Awalua

Shipwreck

Lapaiki

Kahua

Caves

Caves

Palahinu Point

Kaena Point

Polihuoe Trail

Awalua Trail

Kaena Iki Point

Kaena Heiau

Keanapapa Point

Kalaeahole Point

Garden of the Gods

Dryland Forest

Polihua Rd

Kanepuu Preserv

20°50'

Seabird Sanctuary

Keone Bay

Kiei Bay

Anapuka Cave

Kaumalapau Hwy

Lanai Airport

PACIFIC OCEAN

440

Kaumalapau Harbor

Kaupili

Kaholo Palii

LANAI

FIELDING

Lanai

Kolokolo Cave

Ancient Village

Halulu Heiau & Petroglyphs

Kaunolu

Palaoa Point

Mamaki Bay

0   2 mi.   4 mi.
0   3 km.   6 km.

157°

berantly rich and famous (Bill Gates chose this island for his wedding site)—those seeking luxury along with privacy. Good choice, because "The Private Island" is Lanai's current title. Not so, always, Lanai, in past years, was known as "The Forbidden Island" and not too many natives even wanted to set foot there, let alone the likes of Master Gates.

Lanai's history is hardly filled with images of peace and luxury. According to legend the place was a feeding frenzy for evil spirits and other-worlders with a penchant for human flesh and blood. Sound like the perfect getaway? Somehow along the way these spirits met their match when courageous and crafty Prince Kaululaau (who'd been banished from Maui by his father, who was sick of his son's spoiled behavior) outwitted them and drove them away (but *where?*). Anyway, Lanai was suddenly on the map for those who wanted to come over and settle down.

Fiendish spirits or not, settlement took awhile. By and by, a few thousand people cruised over to fish and farm, setting up camp mostly along the shore facing Maui. During the 1700s, Lanai was fraught with the ravages of war, taking a particularly nasty hit from Big Island warriors. Sea captains steered their vessels clear of the island, passing on tales of dangerous waters ("Shipwreck Beach" was not bequeathed that name for nothing). Lanai received only a short-lived boost when Hawaii-unifier King Kamehameha the Great began to summer over on the south shore. However, the population began to dwindle yet again there were a few (failed) attempts to establish commercial sugar enterprises, a valiant (and scandalous) effort by Mormon missionaries to set up a colony and work the land, and a stint at cattle raising. But, all in all, the island languished until 1922, when pineapple king James D. Dole bought the entire shebang.

Dole paid $1.1 million for Lanai, planted the "golden fruit" on about 18,000 of his 89,000 acres, and turned the place into "The Pineapple Island." Lanai Plantation became the world's largest pineapple plantation, and the Dole Food Company held reign on every worker and resident—all whom were in some way connected to the pineapple business. Lanai City sprung up as the plantation town and community center, and life went on. When pineapple production in the Philippines and Malaysia took off in the 1990s, the Lanai industry was no longer profitable. But something else *was*—almighty tourism.

Dole's corporate heirs, the Big Five members, Castle & Cooke, fairly jumped on the tourist bandwagon, building two luxury resorts on the island with which to lure the rich and famous. Workers who once toiled in the fields now work in the hotel industry, catering to well-heeled visitors (for the workers, their only other choice was to leave the island). Recognizing that the resorts are not going to run themselves, Castle & Cooke is trying to keep the employees content by building housing projects and refurbishing the downtown area (particularly some of the family-owned shops). It remains to be seen whether Castle & Cook will play fair with the locals, and whether the locals can adhere to all these "improvements." Most tourists, no doubt, will welcome the "upscale" change.

Most of Lanai's residents are Filipinos—originally recruited for the pineapple fields—followed by lesser numbers of Japanese, Hawaiians, Caucasians and a smattering of Chinese. The community is basically tight and supportive, going all out to help one another, and visitors will be impressed by how relaxed everyone is. Lanai City, the hub of the island, is an exercise in civility and laid-back living.

Don't be put off if you're not a wealthy, corporate type (or just not wealthy)—there *are* a few other options for overnighters (but *just* a few), and a day-trip from one of the other islands is another possibility. However, if you're rolling in big bucks and searching for a hideaway that could even please a billionaire, Lanai is waiting for you.

Bird's-Eye View

The least-visited of the six major islands, 140-square-mile Lanai also measures in as the smallest (18 miles long and 13 miles wide). Shaped like a fat gourd, the island's eastern coast is just eight miles from Maui and its northern shore is a mere nine miles south of Molokai (at one time the three were most likely connected). If you think of Lanai as one gigantic pineapple plantation, you're right *and* wrong. True, the island harbors the world's largest pineapple fields; however, the golden fruit actually accounts for less than one-fifth of the land. The rest of the space is serene, remote and yours to hike, swim or adventure upon. Only three main roads traverse the island though unpaved roads (and a four-wheel-drive vehicle) will put you all over the place. Mountain ridges run north to south along the eastern side, which is cut by the Munroe Trail which offers exquisite views of neighboring islands. Assorted beaches curve from the northern shore at Polihua, around the east coast and down to Hulope and Manele bays in the south. Mount Lanaihale—also on the eastern side—is the island's highest point (3366 feet). Most of the western region is open rugged land—sunbaked, barren and covered in a sort of rust-colored dirt (which turns to dust on your skin and clothing), and just perfect for growing those pineapples (around Palawi). Dramatic sea cliffs—some climbing to 1500 feet— protect the western coast, an area that can be reached only by boat. Lanai City—located about dead center in the island, at an altitude of 1700 feet with Mount Lanaihale in the distance—is home to most of the island's residents. Lined with the breezy Norfolk pines planted by New Zealander George Munro (former manager of the failed cattle ranch), the old plantation town is characterized by its colorful tin-roof houses and cheerful, laid-back locals.

LANAI

The rugged coastline of Lanai

Nature Guide

Lanai, *au natural*, was pretty barren. Consequently much of the island's flora and fauna has been introduced over the years, either as deliberate imports or as gifts from visiting dignitaries and others.

The native bird population is dwindling. You'll have to really search to find the *apapane*, *amakahi* and Hawaiian petrel. You'll have a lot better luck locating pheasants, quails, turkeys, chukar and doves.

It won't be difficult to spot the perfectly conical Norfolk pines—they're all over Lanai City and up along the Munro Trail, along with silver oaks, eucalyptus, ironwoods and koa. Fragrant gardenias also waft along the ridges. The *kaunaoa* (Lanai's official flower) and *pohuehue* are easy finds around the beaches.

Axis deer from India, Moulton sheep from Corsica and Sardinia, pronghorn (sort-of) antelopes from North America and feral goats are common to see.

Fielding's Beach Finder

Lanai's western coast is fortressed by enormous sea cliffs, but a few good beaches curve from the north shore, around the eastern side, down to the southern bays at Hulopoe and Manele. For more information, ask at your hotel (if you're staying at one) or contact **Destination Lanai** (☎ *(808) 565-7600)*.

Hulopoe Beach

About eight miles away from Lanai City, at the southern end of Highway 440.
The island's only easy-to-get-to white-sand beach. The protected beach is excellent for swimming, bodysurfing, surfing and boogie-boarding, as well as snorkeling and diving. Locals favor this spot for swims and picnics. Facilities include barbecue pits, showers, rest rooms, picnic areas and permit-only camping.

Polihua Beach

On the northwest shore some 11 miles from Lanai City.

If you have a four-wheel-drive, you might try this beach, an isolated white-sand beach. Although you'll find plenty of privacy (and good fishing) here, strong currents and trade winds put it on the danger list for swimming. Experienced—and fearless—surfers and bodysurfers often head in anyway. No facilities (bring your own water).

Shipwreck Beach

At the end of Keomuku Highway on the north shore (about 10 miles north of Lanai City).

You can view **petroglyphs** as well as the carnage of offshore wrecks on this eight-mile stretch of sand. This is yet another no-swim beach, but it's an excellent spot for wading, beach combing, shoreline fishing and hunting out relics that keep washing onto shore.

Adventure Guide

You can either do nothing on Lanai, or head to the great outdoors for some action.

The **Munro Trail** is a "must" for **hikers**. Follow in the footsteps of New Zealander George Munro who, around the turn of the century, imported and planted Lanai's trademark Norfolk pines, believing (correctly!) they would collect moisture from the passing mist-filled trade winds. The trail runs from about a mile beyond the Lodge at Koele and ends at Manele Road. It's not an easy trek, but you'll see exquisite scenery—particularly from the lookout at **Mount Lanaihale**, the island's highest spot.

Other **good hikes** are into the magical **Garden of the Gods** and out to **Polihua Beach** or **Kaena Point**, up in the northern area. Adventurers will find plenty of interesting trails, or trail-blazing opportunities, on Lanai. Make sure you have good maps and directions, and take plenty of water when you venture out. Contact **Destination Lanai**, or ask at your hotel, before heading into uncharted territory.

Camping on Lanai *could* be fantastic—if it were allowed. There are plenty of gorgeous possibilities, particularly on the remote beaches, but, unfortunately, use of them is allocated only to island residents. The only official campground is a six-space site at **Hulopoe Bay**, where reservations and permits must be issued in advance by Castle & Cooke's sibling, the Lanai Land Company.

Cost is about $5 per person per night, with a seven-day maximum stay. Contact **Lanai Land Company**, *Box L, Lanai City, HI 96763* (☎ *(808) 565-7400)*.

Divers love Lanai's south shore **Cathedrals**, so-named because of the cathedral-like effect of the sunlight as it bounces around the deep pinnacles, through vast caverns and delicate sheets of coral. Lobster, ghost shrimp and spotted moray eels are some of the parishioners to be encountered. Other fine dives on the south shore are at **Sergeant Major Reef** (with a cave, archway, lava ridges and sergeant major fish), **Menpachi Cave**, **Lobster Rock** and **Monolith**.

The most popular area for both **diving and snorkeling** is near **Hulopole and Manele bays**. Clear-and-calm Hulopoe Bay—a protected Marine Life Conservation Area—affords close-ups of lava formations, coral and an abundance of colorful tropical fish. Bring your own equipment, rent it on another island, buy it in town (expensive!) or sign on for one of the organized excursions that tosses gear into the deal. Guests of either The Lodge at Koele or Manele Bay Hotel are bestowed with complimentary snorkeling equipment. **Sailing excursions** and **private boat charters** can also be arranged through local operators, or your hotel. **Hulopoe Beach** is also a good **surfing and bodysurfing** site, though experienced surfers often hit the rough waters up at **Polihua Beach**.

What Else to See

Lanai is delightfully devoid of common stuff to do. There are no malls, traffic lights, no theme parks (thank God!), and absolutely no glitz or glitter. Pretty much "all" there is to see is sweet, beautiful nature (both on the land and in its people).

Lanai City is not exactly what most people think of when the word "city" pops up. The 1920s plantation town is more like a "mountain village gone troppo." Tall Norfolk pines shelter multi-colored, boxy houses with corrugated tin roofs, assorted business offices and rustic shops and buildings, the air breezy with the scent of blossoms and the relaxed chatter of "talk stories." Most of the stores hover around **Dole Park**, a sort of town square where locals pass the time. **Kaumalapau Harbor**, Lanai's major seaport—constructed in 1926 by the Hawaiian Pineapple Company—is at the western end of Kaumalapau Highway.

Pineapples on Lanai

Venturing north, you'll hit the **Lodge at Koele** and, a couple of miles later, the beginning of the **Munro Trail** and the "road" to **Mount Lanaihale**. Head up the Kanepuu Highway to visit **Garden of the Gods**, a magical canyon with other-worldly rocks and boulders in a variety of shapes and sizes, all changing colors and shades as the sun rises and sets. Various turnoffs near Garden of the Gods will lead you to **Shipwreck Beach**, **Polihua Beach**, **Kaena Point** and **Kaenaiki**, the island's largest (and very remote) *heiau*.

From Lanai City, go south along Manele Road (Highway 440) and a couple of unmarked dirt roads for a look at the ancient **Luahiwa Petroglyphs**. Back on the highway, keep going to the coastal fishing village at **Kaunolu**, and the former retreat of King Kamehameha the Great. You can explore the village site as well as the sacred **Halulu Heiau** ruins and **Kahekili's Leap** (a bluff where Kamehameha's warriors once jumped into the sea below, purportedly as a test of courage). Back on Manele Road, travel downhill to **Manele Bay** (location of the small boat and "tourist" harbor). Nearby are the **Manele Bay Hotel** and **Hulopoe Beach**.

Take Keomuku Road, again from Lanai City, to reach the eastern shore. Sightsee your way through **Keomuku Village** (which really has only the Hawaiian church), **Halepaloa Landing** (where sugar cane was shipped from in other days), **Lopa** and **Naha**.

East Lanai

Keomoku

Historical Sites

Keomoku Village ★★

At the end of Keomoku Road, 8 miles from Lanai City, Keomoku, Turn right at the end of road; site is 6 miles ahead.

There was once a lot of commercial activity in this old ghost town on the northeast coast; in the 1890s, it was the site of the Maunalei Sugar Company. Unfortunately, what was once sweet turned sour, including subsequent efforts to make a go of cotton and alfalfa farming; there just wasn't enough water. You can still see the Ka Lanakila O Ka Malamala Church, built in 1903 to serve workers, and its adjacent cemetery. As early as the 1950s, the area was the coastal headquarters for the Gay family's cattle and sheep ranch. In 1956, the company folded operations, and workers looked to the greener (and rust-red) pastures of Jim Dole's pineapple plantation. Continue about two miles to Kahalepalaoa, an old wharf used to ship sugarcane to Maui. Nearby is Lopa, a picnic site and beach good for sunbathing (used by Club Lanai).

Lanai City

Children's Activities

Children's Ride ★★

Stables at Koele, P.O. Box L, Lanai City, 96763, ☎ (808) 565-4424.

This is a gentle way to instill a love of things equine in your youngster—an experienced instructor will slowly lead him or her around the stable at Koele's protected corral for 15 minutes on a "child-friendly" mount.

City Celebrations

Aloha Festivals ★★★

Lanai City and various locations, Lanai City, ☎ (808) 944-8857.

Annual statewide cultural festival (begun in 1946), featuring traditional music and dance, contests, parades and *ho'olaule'a*, or block parties. Special events in Lanai include Aloha Beach Day and an Aloha Street Dance. Usually held in mid-October.

Fun For Free

Lanai Visiting Artist Program ★★★★

Lodge at Koele, Lanai City, At the Lodge at Koele, past Cavendish Golf Course, just above Lanai City, 96763, ☎ (808) 565-7300.

The idea of the grand salon has come to Lanai—and it's open to all at no charge. These special events include cooking demonstrations by some of the country's most innovative chefs (Bradley Ogden of Lark Creek Inn in Marin County was a recent guest) musical concerts, lectures and author readings (Peter Schickele, the musical satirist, who is also known as the expert on the works of "PDQ Bach," movie mogul David Wolper and Brazilian pianist Ciao Pagano were all featured early this year within one week of each other). Hours and locations vary; evenings, usually at 8:30 p.m.; call for schedule.

Historical Sites

Munro Trail   ★★★

Off Keomoku Road, Lanai City, Take Keomoku Road toward the Lodge, after about 1 mile turn right.

The dirt road to George Munro's famous Norfolk pine-lined ridge trail begins just past the colorful cemetery above the Lodge at Koele. The former ranch manager of the Lanai Ranch Co., Munro, a native of New Zealand, and sort of the Johnny Appleseed of Lanai, planted the trees by hand as part of a reforestation project. Although many travelers like to make the bumpy trip via four-wheel-drive vehicle, it's equally popular with hikers and off-road cyclists. The high point (literally) of the journey is standing atop the 3370-foot elevation of Mt. Lanaihale (also called the Hale), which affords a five-island view (all but Kauai) on a clear day.

Museums and Exhibits

Kaupe Cultural and Heritage Museum   ★★

7th Street, Lanai City, Across from Dole Park, *(808) 565-4545.*
Special hours: call for hours.

Lanai's first historical museum, opened in the summer of 1995, is proudly installed within the old Dole plantation administration building, which was renovated to the tune of $50,000. The 1300-square-foot museum houses photographs and memorabilia from pre- to post-pineapple days. The Bishop Museum has donated a substantial collection of rare Hawaiian artifacts to the collection.

Lanai Art Program Complex   ★★

339 7th Street, north side of Dole Park, Lanai City, North side of Dole Park, 96763, *(808) 565-7503.*
Hours: 9 a.m.–4 p.m.
Special hours: occasionally open Saturday. Closed: Sun.

The Lanai Art Program Complex features an artists co-op, gallery and studio, and art instruction for residents and guests.

The Shows

Lanai Playhouse   ★

465 7th Street, Lanai City, *(808) 565-7500.*

Catch a current feature film for a reasonable price at this new, 150-seat theatrical venue/movie house in Lanai City; from time to time you can see Lanai City denizens take to the boards and strut their stuff. General admission: $5.

Tours

Carriage Rides   ★★★

Stables at Koele, P.O. Box L, Lanai City, 96763, ☎ *(808) 565-4424.*

Along with a plethora of horseback-riding adventures, the Stables at the Lodge at Koele offers a one- or two-hour ride on a Cheyenne carriage, an intricately crafted rig pulled by a Belgian Draft horse, guided by an local driver who knows where all the great sights are. This is the first horse-drawn carriage to be licensed in Maui County. Blankets and snacks provided; participants can plan their own itineraries.

Lanai City Service ★★

P.O. Box N, Lanai Avenue between 10th-11th Streets, Lanai City, 96763, ☎ *(808) 565-7227.*

Hours: 7 a.m.–7 p.m.

Lanai City Service, which is also the Dollar Rent-a-Car franchise, offers the only guided, half-day four-wheel-drive van tour (four passengers minimum, 12 passengers maximum) of some of Lanai's hard-to-get-to sites; including the Munro Trail (conditions permitting) and Shipwreck Beach. The tour leaves from two locations, at 6:45 a.m. from the Lodge at Koele (return at 1 p.m.) and 7:15 a.m. at the Manele Bay Hotel (return at 1:30 p.m.). Included are a lei greeting, coffee, breakfast rolls, mineral water, juices and sodas, a box lunch on the beach (choice of tuna, egg salad, corned beef, turkey or veggie sandwich with potato salad). The company recommends stain-resistant clothing (but nothing can resist that rich red dirt) and a good pair of broken-in footwear. Chartered tours are available, minimum 10 passengers. Reservations at least 12 hours in advance; however, if seats are available, last-minute bookings are possible on a "first-come, first-served" basis. Tours must be paid for at the company's office in Lanai City on Lanai Avenue, but reservations can be made from the concierge desks at either of the above hotels. American Express, Visa, MasterCard and Diner's Club accepted. General admission: $59.

Spinning Dolphin Charters ★★

P.O. Box 491, Lanai City, 96763, ☎ *(808) 565-6613.*

In addition to private deep-sea fishing and light-tackle fishing charters, Captain Jeff Menze, a commercial fisherman and master diver, takes parties of three to six maximum on exciting, three-hour whale-watching excursions from late December through April. Captain Jeff's 28-foot, diesel-powered Omega sportfisher (called, appropriately, the *Spinning Dolphin*) is equipped with an underwater microphone that amplifies the whales' songs. He says, "A new song is started where the old songs left off." Soda, juice, water and ice are provided. All sailing times are flexible, and can be arranged at time of booking. Menze also offers a three-hour sightseeing charter tour of Lanai from the water. You'll cruise to Nanahoa, an islet off west Lanai, one of the island's most impressive landmarks. Local lore contends that Nanahoa, a cruel wife beater, was turned into one of the two pillar stones; inexplicably, the other one is his long-suffering spouse. Other tour highlights include Kaunolu, an ancient royal summer camp and former fishing community and also the site of a heiau (place of worship). Snorkeling can be included in the trip; this requires an additional hour, plus an additional $100. Soda, juice and water are provided. Hours are open; arrangements made at time of booking. General admission: $300.

Northeast Lanai

Shipwreck Beach

Beaches

Shipwreck Beach (Kaiolohia Bay) ★★

On the northeast shore of Lanai, Shipwreck Beach, North on Lanai Avenue, right to Keomuku Road to its end, turn left.

Although the highway to this sometimes incredibly windy beach (watch out for stinging sands—ouch) is paved, you'll need a four-wheel-drive vehicle (or your own two feet) to get here. Sights along the eight-mile sands include "Federation Camp," a moniker given to describe the rustic structures used by Filipino immigrants in the 1930s (they hung out here to fish and socialize), primitive rock carvings, or petroglyphs (look for the "Do Not Deface" sign), and the rusted-out hulk of a Liberty ship towed to these shores after World War II. If you want to decorate your own beach shack with pieces of driftwood (plentiful) or glass fishing-floats, this is the place to come. Otherwise, forget about watersports—conditions are too rocky and the Kalohi channel (between Lanai and Molokai) is treacherous. Hikers in good condition can follow the coastline 10 miles north to Polihua Beach.

Offshore wrecks and petroglyphs are found at Shipwreck Beach, Lanai.

Northwest Lanai

Kanepu'u

Historical Sites

Kanepu'u Preserve and Garden of the Gods   ★★

Fraser Avenue north to Polihua Road, turn right, Kanepu'u.

The remnants of what was once a vast native dryland forest are located in the northwest section of Lanai, six miles out of town on a dirt road (four-wheel-drive vehicle only). More than 400 acres have been fenced in by the Nature Conservancy of Hawaii, which manages the dryland forest, to keep feral axis deer out. Native dryland forests are one of the fastest disappearing ecosystems in the world. Kanepuu encloses some extremely rare species of plants including *iliahi*, or Hawaiian sandalwood, native versions of olive and persimmon, and a kind of dryland gardenia tree, called *nau*. To take a monthly Nature Conservancy Hike (two hours), call the Oahu office at ☎ *(808) 537-4508*, or contact Gaylien Kaho'ohalahala, the Kanepuu field technician, at ☎ *(808) 565-7430*. Donations of $25 are requested; nonmembers receive a one-year membership in the conservancy, including all benefits. About six miles farther is the somewhat awe-inspiringly named Garden of the Gods. The deities in question are rocks, stones and mounds in hues reminiscent of a Georgia O'Keeffe canvas, all shaped by howling winds, then baked in the sun and left to set and dry in an almost rain-starved climate. With some imagination, the rocks appear most godlike at sunrise and sunset.

Palawai Basin

Luahiwa Petroglyphs ★★

Manele Road south to Hoike Road, left to water tank, Palawai Basin.

Lanai's largest concentration of ancient rock drawings—crude but distinctive figures of animals, canoes and humans—are found on 34 boulders on a steep slope overlooking the Palawai Basin (agricultural and grazing land that was a Mormon colony in 1854).

South Lanai

Hulopoe Beach

Beaches

Hulopoe Beach ★★★★

Manele Road, Hulopoe Beach.

Lanai's most user-friendly and all-around best beach, Hulopoe Bay (and nearby Manele Bay) was once an ancient Hawaiian village dating from A.D. 900. A marine life conservation district, Hulopoe is home to cavorting spinner dolphins in season. Swimming, boogie-boarding and snorkeling are usually all very good here, but high surf conditions exist, so use caution. The artificial tide pools around the bay are full of interesting marine life (again a caveat: some of the beasties may be hazardous to your health). Best exploration time is at low tide. A minor quibble: Although the beach is for the most part uncrowded, the passenger ferry from Maui brings in day-trippers and weekenders, so sometimes things can get a little crazy. Top-of-the-line facilities include rest rooms, showers (outdoor), picnic areas, barbecue pits. And oh my goodness—a lifeguard.

City Celebrations

Pineapple Festival ★★

End of Manele Road, Hulopoe Beach, ☎ *(808) 565-7600.*

Held in early May. Fourth annual event honoring the late (un) lamented crop. Live entertainment, food, craft booths, tastings. Times vary.

Historical Sites

Sweetheart Rock (Pu'upehe) ★★

South Lanai, Hulopoe Beach, 15 minutes walk from Hulopoe Beach.

A rock islet off the southwest point of Manele Bay, Sweetheart Rock actually has a bittersweet story. Its Hawaiian name—*Pu'upehe*—means Pehe's Hill. Pehe was the beautiful but unfortunate wife of a jealous cad who hid her in a cave so no other man could set eyes on her. Inevitably, she was drowned during a storm while her husband was away. After burying Pehe atop Sweetheart Rock, he later fell to his death.

Tours

Expeditions

P.O. Box 10, Lahaina, HI 96767-0010, Hulopoe Beach, ☎ *(808) 661-3756.*

Expeditions is the Lahaina- (Maui) Lanai Passenger ferry departing daily from either Manele Harbor (8 and 10:30 a.m., and 2, 4:30 and 8:45 p.m.) or Lahaina Harbor at the public loading dock in front of the Pioneer Inn (6:45 and 9:15 a.m., and 12:45, 3:15 and 5:45 p.m.). Trips each way take approximately one hour. Special tour packages include snorkeling tours (round trip to Manele Harbor included, bring your own gear and lunch), Jeep expeditions (approximately $100 per day, plus fuel, optional insurance and pickup charge), shoreline cruises (two hours round trip, whale watching in season). For $199 per person with round-trip transportation from Lahaina you can play golf at the Experience at Koele or Challenge at Manele championship courses or stay overnight at one of the two luxury hotels (from $320 for two, with round-trip fare from Lahaina). The company will also help you tailor your own expedition. General admission: $25 each way.

Southwest Lanai

Kaunolu

Historical Sites

Kaunolu

Kaumalapau Highway, left on Kaupili Road, Kaunolu.

Two miles to the trail past Kaupili Road. An active archaeological site and ancient fishing village, Kaunolou is sometimes closed to visitors. Located on the south shore of the island, its beginnings are in shadow, but scholars in the mid-'20s catalogued the remains of the Halulu *Heiau*, a place of refuge and temple that was still in use until the early 19th century. The temple platform is still standing, plus petroglyphs and remains of house sites (although hard to find, unless you know where to look). Kaunolou was also a fishing community and later Kamehameha I's summer home; northwest of the heiau is Kahekili's Leap—the king often dared errant chiefs to jump off this break in the towering sea cliffs into the roiling waves below.

Sports

Golfers can play the Greg Norman-designed 18-hole, par-72, championship course at **Experience at Koele** (at the Lodge at Koele), or the Jack Nicklaus-designed 18-hole, par-72 course at Manele Bay Hotel (called **Challenge at Manele**). Both guests and non-guests can play, though high greens fees get even higher for nonguests. Or play nine holes in the Norfolk pines, for free, at the public **Cavendish Golf Course**. Each of the "Big Two" resorts offers three **tennis courts** apiece.

Shipwreck Beach offers good **fishing** for *papio*, *ulua* and other types. Kamehameha the Great used to hit Kaunolu on the south shore when he had the fishing urge. **Kaumalapau Harbor** is a top choice for shore fishing. For the best advice on fishing holes, try befriending one of the locals. Only one charter fishing operation runs on the island, with a few more choices for **scuba diving** and **snorkeling**. Contact the Lodge at Koele if you're interested in **horseback riding**—a variety of excursions are offered for all riding levels, plus you can take lessons or arrange for a private ride.

A wide variety of exotic sea life thrills snorkelers at Manele Bay.

East Lanai

Kahalepalaoa Landing

Club Lanai   ★ ★

355 Hukilike Street, Suite 211, Kahului, Maui 96732, Kahalepalaoa Landing, ☎ *(808) 871-1144.*

This company takes day-trippers from Maui to its own isolated and pretty beach in east Lanai (by Kahalepalaoa Harbor) for a day of snorkeling, kayaking over a turtle reef and bicycling to remote beaches. Other choices include volleyball, croquet, or visiting a sea turtle sanctuary or a whale research center. You can also opt to swing in a hammock and do nothing at all. The fare includes an all-you-can-eat buffet lunch and open bar, plus massage therapy (extra). Club Lanai also offers scuba diving; all levels welcome. The boat leaves Lahaina Harbor daily at Slip 4 at 7:30 a.m., returning at 3:30 p.m. Reservations required. General admission: $89.

Lanai City

Cavendish Golf Course   ★

On the north side of Lanai City, Lanai City, ☎ (808) 565-6979.

For those of you who can't see paying $99 and up to play at the Manele Bay Hotel and the Lodge at Koele's five-star courses, how about this freebie? Cavendish Golf Course is a pleasant, local 9-hole, par-36 course, which has the distinction of being the only free golf course in the state, but visitors are asked to leave a $5 donation for upkeep. No dress code, no carts, club rental or club house.

Chris' Adventures   ★★★

P.O. Box 869, Kula, HI 96790, Lanai City, ☎ (800) 224-5344.
Hours: 8 a.m.–6 p.m.
Special hours: Saturdays, 8-10 a.m. Closed: Sun.

Chris and his associates offer cycling on- and off-road and hiking day tours (6:30 a.m.–5:30 p.m.) of Lanai's picturesque (and rugged) Munro Trail every Wednesday. Travelers leave by boat from Maui, or meet your guide at an arranged location if you're already on the island. These are for experienced cyclists only. Cost is $110 per person; includes breakfast and "island-style" picnic lunch. Also available are "Inn-to-Inn Vacations," three- to eight-day multiple day biking and/or hiking trips for all levels, with options for the more advanced (or masochistic) participants. Maui-Molokai-Lanai combo trips last eight days, and include a kayak or raft adventure. Included are all meals, transportation, equipment, lodging and all extras; price ranges from $200–$275 per day. Call Chris' Adventures tour planner for details, dates and trip itineraries. General admission: $110–$275.

Hunting in Lanai   ★★

c/o The Lanai Co. P.O. Box L, Lanai City, 96763, ☎ (808) 565-7233.

Hunting axis deer, Mouflon sheep, ring-necked pheasant, partridge and other game birds has always been a popular activity in Lanai, before it became a tourist destination and pineapple was king. Permission must be "granted" from the Lanai Company, who can provide guides (about $750 per day). Since most of the hunting grounds are on company land, the guides will probably tell you where the best spots are. They will also issue you a permit ($275 per day). If you're an experienced hunter, you'll have no trouble passing a special two-hour course (required) or obtaining a license (mandatory). A nonresident license, good for one year, costs $95. Information and applications from the Forestry and Wildlife Division of the State Department of Land and Natural Resources on Oahu, at 1151 Punchbowl, Room 325, Honolulu, HI 96813.

Spinning Dolphin Charters   ★★

P.O. Box 491, Lanai City, 96763, ☎ (808) 565-6613.

Captain Jeff Menze offers sport-fishing (deep-sea fishing and light tackle) charter trips aboard the *Spinning Dolphin II*, his 28-foot diesel-powered Omega sportfisher. On these four-hour trips (three-person minimum, six maximum) fish for marlin, ahi, mahi-mahi, barracuda and ono, and "fight" Hawaii's best loved game fish, the papio. There's also a share-boat option offered, also for four hours, for $300. Soda, juice, water and ice are provided. Hours are flexible; arrangements can be made at time of booking. General admission: $400.

Stables at Koele ★★★

P.O. Box L, Lanai City, 96763, ☎ (808) 565-4424.

The Lodge at Koele offers a wide range of different horseback riding trips, from a 15-minute children's ride to a four-hour "private adventure" for the experienced rider. (Unfortunately, no high jinks—these are sedate "walking" rides only.) The Plantation Trail Ride is perfect for beginners or those wishing to polish old skills. For the experienced equestrian, there are several private rides for one or two guests; larger groups are accommodated by arrangement. These are tailored to the individ- uals' needs, itineraries may include trips to Kanepu'u, the island's rare dryland forest ecosystem. Many rides offer sweeping views of the neighbor islands with glimpses of axis deer, quail and other wildlife. Lessons available, both Western and English. Dress code, limited boot rental. Maximum weight is 250 pounds, children must be nine years old and at least four feet high. Safety helmets provided. All riders must be able to mount and dismount on their own. Backpack lunch rides available. General admission: $35–$50.

The lodge at Koele offers a variety of horseback riding trips through Lanai.

The Experience at Koele ★★★★★

Lodge at Koele, P.O. Box L, Lanai City, 96763, ☎ (808) 565-4653.
Special hours: tee times from 8 a.m.

This championship 18-hole, par-72 golf course, opened in May 1991, is a collaboration between designer and Australian golf pro Greg Norman and architect Ted Robinson. Almost immediately, it was lauded by Fortune magazine, Andrew Harper's Hideaway Report and Golf Magazine as the best new golf course. Built on

163 acres of natural island terrain, it features the challenging Number 8 hole, where players contend with a 250-foot drop from tee to fairway, battling some formidable headwinds blowing in daily from a wooded ravine in the process. Higher greens fee is for nonguests, includes cart. Club rental $35, shoe rental, $10. Pro shop, driving range, restaurant and putting green. General admission: $99–$140.

South Lanai

Hulopoe Beach

Challenge at Manele ★★★★

Manele Road, Hulopoe Beach, 96763, ☎ (808) 565-2222.
Hours: 7:30 a.m.–5 p.m.
Special hours: Tuesday-Friday from 8 a.m.

A relative newcomer to the golfing world, the seaside, 18-hole, par-72 Challenge at Manele course opened at the Manele Bay Hotel on Christmas Day 1993. Designed by Jack Nicklaus, it's built on natural lava outcroppings overlooking the hotel, the bay and the Pacific Ocean. The course features three holes constructed on the cliffs of Hulopoe Bay that use the Pacific Ocean as a water hazard. The par-3, Number 12 "signature hole" plays from a cliff 150 feet above the surf below, requiring a demanding 200-yard tee shot across the ocean. Higher prices are for nonguests. Full-service clubhouse with a good restaurant, driving range, putting green. Club rental, $35; shoe rental, $10. General admission: $99–$140.

Manele Bay Hotel Tennis Center ★★★

P.O. Box 310, Manele Road, Hulopoe Beach, 96763, ☎ (808) 565-7700.

Tennis with ocean views are the ticket here at Manele Bay Hotel's Tennis Center, with six lighted Plexipaved courts, a fully equipped pro shop and tournament facilities. Free to guests, fee above is for nonguests. Private instruction for guests and nonguests is $30 (half-hour) and $50 (hour). General admission: $9.

Trilogy Ocean Sports Lanai ★★★

P.O. Box 1119, Lahaina, Maui, 96767-1119, Hulopoe Beach, Leaves from the Manele Bay Hotel, ☎ (800) 874-2666.

Whether you're a seasoned scuba diver or a neophyte, Trilogy Excursions of Maui will do the right thing by you, with a group of experienced instructors intimately familiar with Lanai's famous and spectacular southern coast (rated by *Skin Diver* Magazine as one of the top 10 diving sites in the world). Explore underwater coral grottos and lava caves, and have a close encounter of the safe kind with moray eels and white tip sharks. Two-tank dives: Wednesdays, Saturdays, Sundays; One-tank dives: daily. Newbies will start with a complimentary lesson at the Manele Bay Hotel pool (given daily at 2:30 p.m.); learn the basics before venturing off to one of the southern coast's numerous protected coves and bays before swimming with the sharks. The company also offers PADI open-water certification (which requires a minimum of four days; included are all materials, lessons, pool sessions, catamaran dives, beach dives and dive equipment) and advanced openwater certification (includes navigation, night diving, plus two custom elective dives). For reservations, contact the concierge at the Manele Bay Hotel.

LANAI

Trilogy Ocean Sports Sailing-Snorkel ★★★

P.O. Box 1119, Lahaina, Maui, 96767-1119, Hulopoe Beach, Leaves from the Manele Bay Hotel, ☎ *(800) 874-2666.*

Hours: 8:30 a.m.–1 p.m.

This well-regarded and popular Maui company takes groups on daily four-hour sailing and snorkeling adventures along the southern coast of Lanai aboard one of its luxury sailing catamarans. The awesome southern coast is home to spinner dolphins, flying fish and green turtles. Leaving every morning from the Manele Bay Hotel, the tours are priced to include continental breakfast, gourmet lunch, snorkeling lessons and equipment. For reservations and prices, see the hotel concierge.

Manele Bay

Hulopoe Beach Campsites ★★

Manele Road, Manele Bay, ☎ *(808) 565-6661.*

Lanai offers six overnight camping sites (about 200 yards inland from Hulopoe Beach) which must be the cheapest accommodations in town for $5 per person per night (plus a $5 registration fee). Length of stay is one week maximum. Facilities include picnic tables and barbecue grills, rest rooms, outdoor shower (one!). Permits must be obtained from the Koele Company, P.O. Box L, Lanai City, HI 96763 or by calling the number above. General admission: $5.

Where to Stay

The handful of choices consists of the two ritzy (and very expensive) resorts (**Lodge at Koele** and **Manele Bay Hotel**), the vintage-1920s **Hotel Lanai**, a couple of B&Bs and the half-dozen campsites (reservations and permit required) at Hulopoe Bay.

Lanai City

Bed-and-Breakfasts

Dreams Come True $55–$75 ★★

P.O. Box 525, Lanai City, 96763, A five-minute walk from the center of town, ☎ *(800) 566-6961, (808) 565-6961, FAX (808) 565-7056.*

Single: $55. Double: $75.

Susan and Michael Hunter have remodeled a spacious plantation manager's house into a bed-and-breakfast about five minutes' walk from the center of town. The property, surrounded by tropical fruit gardens, is quietly tucked away within high lava-stone walls. The Hunters, who have an adjacent jewelry studio, rent out three rooms (there are a total of six bedrooms), two of which have private baths. They are furnished quite attractively with polished, antique four-poster beds. The house is decorated throughout with hand-carved screens, rare and colorful textiles and one-of-a-kind treasures collected by the couple on various Asian travels. Amenities include cable TV in the living room. Breakfast consists of homemade bread and fresh fruits from the garden. Children are welcome ($10 each additional child); the Hunters have two of their own. Also offered are four-wheel-drive rentals and massage services, and both in-house and out calls. If you are traveling with a large party, the Hunters will rent out an additional two-bedroom house with an attached cottage with one large bedroom. Called the Jasmine Garden House, it can accommodate up to eight people. Amenities include linens, washer-dryer, cable TV, fan, full kitchen, outside shower and beach gear. Rate is $190 per night or $960 per week. 3 rooms. Credit cards: not accepted.

Hotels

Hotel Lanai   **$95–$135**   ★★

828 Lanai Avenue, Lanai City, 96763, ☎ *(800) 321-4666, (808) 565-7211. Rated Restaurant: Hotel Lanai Dining Room*
Single: $95–$135. Double: $95–$135.
Built in 1923 as a guesthouse for Dole executives and VIPs, the Hotel Lanai was once the only lodging on the island. We remember waking up to the 4 a.m. plantation whistle and the subsequent rumblings of the workers' Jeeps as they headed off to work. Rooms were simply furnished and a little on the dowdy side, small and anything but soundproofed. After a thorough refurbishment in 1992, the 10 units in the main building are much the same size, but the new country decor is a marked improvement, with light, knotty-pine furniture, natural wood floors and patchwork quilts in rose, cream and blue shades. There's also a self-contained, plantation-style cottage with a four-poster canopy bed and period furnishings. Perfect for families, the suite has a separate entrance and sitting room with sofa bed. Management thoughtfully retained the veranda, where everyone met to "talk story," though the simple wooden furniture has been replaced with white wicker sofas and loveseats with striped pillows to set your bum down on. A fire still burns nightly in the dining room (see restaurants) which has been gussied up with local artwork, vintage light fixtures and plenty of fresh tropical flowers. Surprisingly, rates have only gone up about 5 percent more from the old days. And that's a minor miracle. Facilities include a private garden with picnic and barbecue areas. Amenities: balcony or patio. 11 rooms. Credit cards: A, MC, V.

Resorts

The Lodge at Koele   **$295–$1100**   ★★★★★

P.O. Box 310, Lanai City, 96763, ☎ *(800) 321-4666, (808) 565-7300, FAX (808) 565-4561. Rated Restaurant: Koele Terrace.*
Single: $295–$1100. Double: $295–$1100.

Once upon a time, Lanai had only one very small hotel (the Hotel Lanai) and was devoted to the cultivation of pineapples. In April 1990, a sprawling, luxurious mountain retreat in the best old plantation-style was opened with quiet fanfare, and tourism replaced pineapple picking forever. Local artists were coaxed into hand-painting the ceilings and floors in the sprawling public areas and guest rooms. The results are stunning indeed. Two guest wings are connected by large porches with wicker furniture to the high-beamed Great Hall with its 30-foot ceilings and enormous stone fireplaces. Guests can meet and greet in a series of unique chambers, including the Music Room, a modern-day version of a Paris salon where visiting artists, writers and musicians of world-renown perform, lecture and read their works to the public free of charge. Special outdoor features include an ornamental glass house filled with exotic orchids, a Japanese and Hawaiian fruit garden (feel free to indulge) and an executive putting green. Guest rooms, decorated in shades of carnelian and pale blue, feature huge four poster beds crowned with carved pineapples (lest you forget where you are), loveseats and dark-stained wicker armchairs. Pillowed bay window seats overlook the lawns and surrounding countryside. You can't help but notice the colorful, multi-striped carpets with more than 100 colors custom-woven into them. The marble-floored baths have deep, hand-tiled tubs, and pampering products include thick robes, plenty of towels, custom toiletries, hair dryer, slippers and makeup mirror. There's even a walking stick in the closet. All rooms have color TVs with remote control, video player, in-room safe and wet bar. When you get hunger pangs, you have a choice of two dining rooms plus an English tea room and bar, and The Experience at Koele clubhouse. Other activities include lawn bowling, horseback riding, tennis, croquet, game room, pool, hiking trails, The Experience at Koele 18-hole golf course and access to all facilities of the beachfront Manele Bay Hotel; a shuttle between the two properties runs regularly. Amenities: tennis, horseback riding, Jacuzzi. 102 rooms. Credit cards: A, DC, MC, V.

South Lanai

Hulopoe Beach

Manele Bay Hotel view from the beach

LANAI

The Manele Bay Hotel   **$250–$2000**   ★★★★

    Box 310, Hulopoe Beach, 96763, Manele Road 20 minutes from Lanai City, ☎ *(800) 321-4666, (808) 565-7700, FAX (808) 565-2483. Rated Restaurant: Ihilani. Single: $250–$2000. Double: $250–$2000.*

The Manele Bay Hotel, completed in 1991, offers luxurious rooms and suites, all with verandas and ocean and coastline views. The resort is situated on a promontory above the island's most beautiful white-sand beach, Hulopoe Bay. Its exterior is a blend of Mediterranean and traditional Hawaiian design. The interior, however, is crammed with Oriental statuary, porcelains, art and antiques; walls are painted with Chinese court scenes. Sometimes it's hard to decide where to look—the vistas of the beach from the lobby are literally jaw-dropping from any angle. Landscape schemes include five theme gardens, waterfalls, koi ponds and lush tropical flowers. Incorporated into the scheme of things is an ancient archaeological site. The spacious accommodations, in nine buildings, are all individually decorated; but the ones we saw combined dark Chippendale-style armoires and nightstands with Chinoiserie vases and lamps. King-size beds, covered with thick floral quilts, have carved headboards. All rooms have sliding louvered doors opening to lanais. There are 13 suites that come with your veddy own local-born, but British-trained, butler. Amenities include wet bars and entertainment center with color TV and video player. Luxurious marble baths you can live in contain deep-soaking tubs, double sinks, vanity, shower for two, custom toiletries, hair dryer, slippers and terry robes. Other facilities include a health spa, tennis complex, pool, gift shop, pool table, game room, The Challenge at Manele golf course, three dining rooms, lounge and clubhouse. In addition, the resort shares the facilities at the Lodge at Koele; a regular shuttle service is provided between the properties. Amenities: tennis, health club, exercise room, Jacuzzi, sauna, balcony or patio. 250 rooms. Credit cards: A, CB, DC, MC, V.

Where to Eat

    Again, the choices are limited. Try the two resorts for upmarket, gourmet dining, but keep in mind that the dining room at the Lodge at Koele requires men to wear a jacket and tie. Locals head for the dining room at **Hotel Lanai** for simple preparations of such favorites as omelettes, pancakes, sandwiches, steak and chicken. For your funky, local diner/café experience, don't miss either **Blue Ginger Café** or **S & T Properties**.

Lanai City

Blue Ginger Café   **$**   ★

    407 7th Street, Lanai City, 96763, ☎ *(808) 565-.636.*

cuisine. Specialties: Fresh fish, saimin, mahimahi.
Breakfast: 6:30 a.m.–2 p.m., entrées $6–$8.
Lunch: 6:30 a.m.–2 p.m., entrées $6–$8.
Dinner: 3:30–9 p.m., entrées $6–$8.

A down-home café (some might call it a dump) and local hangout that does double
duty as a bakery; the *bento* (Japanese box lunches) are recommended, as are the
breakfast waffles. Hint: tourists should keep a low profile and dress down, as some
of the regulars resent outsiders. Features: outside dining, own baking. Reservations
not accepted. Credit cards: not accepted.

Hotel Lanai Dining Room $$$ ★★

828 Lanai Avenue, Lanai City, 96763, ☎ (808) 565-7211. Associated hotel: Hotel
Lanai.
American cuisine. Specialties: Steaks, fresh fish, sashimi.
Breakfast: 7-9:30 a.m., entrées $15–$18.
Lunch: 11:30 a.m.–1 p.m., entrées $15–$18.
Dinner: 6–8 p.m., entrées $15–$18.

For a long time the only place open after 1 p.m. for meals on the island, the Hotel
Lanai is still a welcome respite for eyes dazzled by the new resorts and their high
prices. Sink into a comfortable seat at a white cloth-covered table by the fire in the
cozy, pine-paneled dining room and chow down on well-prepared steaks, local fish
and chicken dishes. Afterward, an after-dinner drink and a chat with other guests on
the veranda is de rigueur. For lunch, we think the cheeseburgers here are mighty
fine and a great alternative to the $6 hot dogs at the Manele Bay Hotel. Reserva-
tions not accepted. Credit cards: A, MC, V.

Lodge at Koele Great Hall is warm and friendly.

Koele Terrace Restaurant $$ ★★★★

Box 774, Lanai City, 96763, Just outside Lanai City, ☎ (808) 565-7300. Associated
hotel: Lodge at Koele.

International cuisine. Specialties: Roast Lanai Venison with Molokai sweet pepper puree.
Breakfast: 7 a.m.–11 p.m., entrées $9–$20.
Lunch: 11 a.m.–6 p.m., entrées $9–$20.
Dinner: 6–9 p.m., entrées $9–$20.

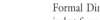

Extra-wide and comfy cushioned Craftsman-style chairs invite lingering in this lovely, sun-filled dining room with floor-to-ceiling windows overlooking the Lodge at Koele's picture-postcard hillside gardens. After a sufficient period of woolgathering over cocktails, prepare to be impressed by executive chef Edwin Goto's imaginatively prepared culinary creations, which utilize local produce, fish and wild game. Your breakfast omelette may be garnished with fresh basil grown on the hotel grounds: in the tradition of fine English country house hotels (which the Lodge is clearly trying to emulate), the Lodge at Koele maintains an organic vegetable and herb farm. Venison plays a decided role on Chef Goto's menus; in a robust chili with black beans and spicy Jack cheese, or carpaccio with shaved reggiano, or a signature roast loin partnered with either a fried and mashed puree of sweet Molokai potatoes or sage polenta. For dessert try an exotic red banana soufflé or raspberry sorbet with blueberries and fresh-baked macaroons. The Lodge's fireplace-warmed Formal Dining Room (yes, that is its name) offers a similar menu, but requires a jacket for gentlemen in the evening. Features: own baking. Jacket requested. Reservations recommended. Credit cards: A, MC, V.

S & T Property, Inc. $ ★

419 7th Street, Lanai City, 96763, Next to the Blue Ginger Café, ☎ *(808) 565-6537.*
American cuisine. Specialties: Breakfast, burgers and sandwiches.
Breakfast: 6:30 a.m.–1 p.m., entrées $3–$5.
Lunch: 6:30 a.m.–1 p.m., entrées $3–$5. Closed: Wed.

Sounding more like a real estate office than the soda fountain/general store it is, S & T Properties is a must for visitors seeking a glimpse of the Lanai of yore. Hormel is king here, and the cholesterol-packed menu features eggs with Spam or Vienna sausages. We like the big, juicy hamburgers and Filipino-style plate lunches. Reservations not accepted.

South Lanai

Hulopoe Beach

Hulopoe Court $$ ★★★

P.O. Box 310, Hulopoe Beach, 96763, Manele Road, 20 minutes from Lanai City, ☎ *(808) 565-7700. Associated hotel: Manele Bay Hotel.*
cuisine. Specialties: Seared ahi with green papaya salad, Hunan-style lamb chops.
Breakfast: 6 a.m.–11 a.m., entrées $4–$18.
Lunch: 11 a.m.–5 p.m., entrées $7–$20.
Dinner: 5–9 p.m., entrées $7–$20.

The Mediterranean-themed Hulopoe Court offers gorgeous ocean views and Hawaiian-Regional cuisine with a distinct Asian flavor for breakfast, lunch and dinner. Dishes are on the light and healthful side, with a focus on fresh seafood and "Lanai grown" produce. Chances are you've never had taro hashbrowns for breakfast—this is a good place to try them. If the great outdoors calls you, repair to the Pool Grill, located adjacent to the…(three guesses). Specialty sandwiches, grilled dishes and local favorites (most under $20) are featured. The grill is open from 11 a.m.–5 p.m. daily. Features: own baking. Reservations recommended. Credit cards: A, DC, MC, V.

Ihilani   **$$$**   ★ ★ ★ ★

P.O. Box 310, Hulopoe Beach, 96763, Manele Road, 20 minutes from Lanai City,
☎ *(808) 565-7700. Associated hotel: Manele Bay Hotel.*
Mediterranean cuisine. Specialties: Broiled onaga in a seaweed/seafood sauce, salmon confit in virgin olive oil.
Dinner: 6–9 p.m., entrées $16–$45.
Philippe Padovani, who nurtured the kitchens at the Halekulani Hotel (La Mer and Orchids) and the Ritz Carlton Mauna Lani (now the Orchid) to greatness, has turned his talents to the Manele Bay Hotel's three restaurants. But the jewel in the beachside beauty's crown is Ihilani ("Heavenly Splendor" in Hawaiian), the hotel's specialty dining room. Open only for dinner, the Mediterranean-style menu strives to accentuate the rich bounty of the state's oceans, forests and farms. Entrées may include broiled onaga (deepwater snapper) in an elemental seaweed sauce, and the exquisite chocolate desserts are made exclusively with cocoa beans grown on the black lava slopes of Kilauea volcano in Kona; the taste is likened to that of great vintage wines. But Padovani's reach also extends to Hawaii's Pacific Rim neighbors; witness an appetizer of fresh ravioli with Manila clams. Excellent selection of wines, both French and domestic, available by the glass. Features: own baking, rated wine cellar. Jacket requested. Reservations recommended. Credit cards: A, CB, D, MC, V.

Nightlife

It's slim pickings. The **Lodge at Koele** offers occasional live entertainment and performances by local residents. The landmark 1930s **Lanai Theater and Playhouse** is a 153-seat venue featuring films, theatrical performances and other events. Or, hang with the locals at **Hotel Lanai** and swap "talk-stories" (gossip).

Shopping

The shopping scene is pretty basic and is centered in **Lanai City**. You'll find a few old-fashioned, general-type stores with everything from food to clothing, plus a sprinkling of specialty outlets and arts-and-crafts galleries. The two **resorts** house swankier shops and boutiques.

Lanai City

Akamai Trading & Gifts   ★

408 8th Street, Lanai City, Near the post office, 96763, ☎ *(808) 565-6587.*
Hours: 9 a.m.–5:30 p.m.
Special hours: Sun. until noon.
Pick up a Lanai logo T-shirt here as well as handmade Hawaiian flower-dyed gourds, koa wood boxes, Norfolk pine tree bowls and Lanai potpourri.

Island Collections Gallery   ★ ★

7th Street, Lanai City, North side of Dole Park, 96763, ☎ *(808) 565-6405.*
Hours: 9 a.m.–7 p.m.
Special hours: sometimes open at 10 a.m.
Local artisans, woodworkers, jewelers, painters and more showcase and sell their work here. Also offered are classes for both residents and guests.

Richard's Shopping Center   ★

434 8th Street, Lanai City, Next to the post office, 96763, ☎ *(808) 565-6047.*
Hours: 8:30 a.m.–5:30 p.m.
A combination general store and food market, Richard's was established in 1946. Locals shop here for groceries, fresh meats, liquor and snacks, as well as clothing, athletic shoes and distinctive Lanai T-shirts. Also Hawaiian jewelry and souvenirs.

Fielding's Fascinating Lanai Facts

A.k.a.	The Private Island
Main city	**Lanai City**

LANAI

Flower	Kaunaoa
Color	Orange
Area	140 square miles
Length	18 miles
Width	13 miles
Population	2426
Highest point	Lanaihale (3366 feet)

Lanai Survival Guide

Getting There

Lanai Airport, about four miles southwest of Lanai City, now has a new passenger terminal with a few food concessions and shops. Everything you need to know is posted on a bulletin board. (Don't go looking for the first-class lounge.) Airlines are **Hawaiian** *(☎ (808) 565-6977)*, **Island Air** *(☎ 800-323-3345)* and **Mahalo Air** *(☎ 800-277-8333)*. Hawaiian Air flies DC-9 jets, the others use small commuter planes such as Twin Otters and Dornier 228s.

Expeditions *(☎ (808) 661-3756)* operates **ferry service** five times daily from Lahaina, Maui; cost is about $50 round trip.

Getting Around

There is no public transport on Lanai. Hotel Lanai provides guests with **shuttle service** to most of the major spots. The island has only 30 miles of paved road, so it's best to rent a four-wheel-drive vehicle for some real exploration. **Lanai City Service**, **Dollar Rent A Car** *(☎ (808) 565-7227)*—one and the same company—rents a variety of vehicles and provides airport pickup. You can call for an airport shuttle even if you don't rent from them; cost is about $5 from the terminal into Lanai City. Hotel Lanai and both resorts provide complimentary shuttle service for guests. Lanai City Service also operates a **taxi service** to paved parts of the island.

Guests staying at The Lodge at Koele or Manele Bay Hotel are provided with free mountain bikes—a great way to hit the back country.

Visitor Information

For maps, brochures, and other information, contact **Destination Lanai**, *P.O. Box 700, Lanai City, HI 96763* (☎ *(808) 565-7600*). If possible, call or write ahead of your visit.

HAWAIIAN ITINERARIES

Island of Lanai view of rocky coastline

One-Day Itinerary

You're only in Hawaii for one day. *One* day?! Okay, maybe it's a stopover between the mainland and Australia or Indonesia or somewhere.

You'll definitely want to stay on **Oahu**. Explore **downtown Honolulu**. Check out the beautiful Eastern and Western collections at the **Honolulu Academy of Arts** and then pay a visit to **Iolani Palace**, the United States' only royal residence (this is where Queen Liliuokalani lived out her house arrest after the coup forced her out of power). The **Hawaii State Capitol**, nearby, is an interesting bit of architecture with palm-tree-shaped columns and other kitschy- and dramatic features.

Zoom in on early Hawaiian culture at the **Bishop Museum**, where you can get a close look at magnificent featherwork capes, an outrigger canoe, petroglyphs, weapons, carvings, rare jewelry and other artifacts and exhibitions. Eat lunch in **Chinatown**, then work it off on a walk through the **historic district**, where you'll pass the venerable **Oahu Market**, the **Chinese Cultural Plaza**, the art-deco **Hawaii Theatre** and the **Kuan Yin Buddhist Temple**. If you weren't bestowed with a lei at the airport, pick one up on Maunakea Street.

Hit **Waikiki Beach** and work on your tan with the multitudes or, for something a bit more active, take a walk over to **Kapiolani Park**—maybe check out the rose garden, or just keep ogling the view of **Diamond Head**. Dinner? Why a **luau**, of course! Sign up for one of the commercial feasts, for which you'll be bused to a beach with a crowd of others to pig your way into oblivion.

Back at the airport, pick up a boxed take-home **pineapple** or a package of **macadamia nuts** and get on the plane. There, you've done Hawaii.

Three-Day Itinerary

Motocross races are frequently held in scenic Oahu.

Ah, *three* whole days.

See some more of Honolulu's attractions. If you're interested in how those 19th-century missionaries operated, you can voyeur your way into their lives at **Mission Houses Museum**. The **Hawaii Maritime Center** offers plenty of non-boring exhibits related to Hawaii's long maritime history—dioramas, canoes and displays galore highlighting the various groups who arrived in the islands, from the first Polynesian settlers to the tourists like you.

Time for lunch? Backtrack over to **Restaurant Row** (bounded by Ala Moana Boulevard and Punchbowl, Pohukaina and South streets) and pick out one of Honolulu's trendy spots. Since you won't get to see all of the islands' exotic flowers, trees and plants, get a mini-view at the **Foster Botanical Garden**, with 14 acres of some of the most superb specimens in the South Pacific.

You *know* the **USS *Arizona* Memorial** is calling, so head over to **Pearl Harbor** for a sobering, but well-worthwhile experience. The **USS *Bowfin***, a World War II submarine, and its related museum are conveniently located next to the *Arizona* Memorial.

Drive up the **Pali Highway** to see **Queen Emma's Summer Palace**, grand former hideaway for Queen Emma and King Kamehameha IV and, since 1915, a museum. Farther up the road, the **Nuuanu Pali Lookout** will give you a knockout view the entire length of the windward coast. Back down toward Honolulu, round out your memorial day at **Punchbowl Crater** (or **National Memorial Cemetery of the Pacific**), burial place for 37,000 American troops—marked by row upon row of white gravestones—who died in the Pacific during conflicts this century.

Ready for something cheerier? **The Contemporary Museum** offers five galleries-worth of paintings, sculpture and other works by top international artists. The posh café serves gourmet sandwiches, salads and desserts. Then take windy **Tantalus Drive** up nearly to the top of 2013-foot Mount Tantalus for a thrill—and a great view. Up at the top, you'll find a variety of trails—good for that island hike you won't get in otherwise. **Round Top Drive** will lead you back into Honolulu. Do some shopping at **Ward Warehouse**, on Ala Moana Boulevard, where you'll find better-quality souvenirs, clothing and arts and crafts than the usual tourist schlock. For a real island fashion statement, go directly to **Bailey's Antique Clothes** outlet and choose from thousands of vintage aloha shirts (lots of celebrities buy here).

Time to watch the sunset. **House Without A Key**, at the Halekulani Hotel, serves great pupu platters and exotic drinks, plus affords a postcard view of the Pacific and Diamond Head. Most evenings there's live entertainment. For dinner, how about **Keo's Thai Cuisine** (another celebrity favorite)? Try "Naked Shrimp" or "Evil Jungle Prince"—how can you *not*? The place is so popular, it has expanded to three locations. The one on Kapahulu Avenue is the original, with photos of famous Keo-aficionados adorning the walls. After dinner, take in some **nightlife**: **Scruples**, in the Waikiki Marketplace, for the dance-your-socks-off-crowd; **Studebaker's**, on Ala Moana Boulevard (in Restaurant Row), for '50s retro; the Majaraja, in the Waikiki Trade Center, for dress-code disco; **Anna Bannana's**, on King Street, for live reggae, blues and experimental music (and darts); **Sand Island Restaurant and Bar**, on Sand Island Access Road, for great blues jams; **Java Café**, for coffeehouse culture; or one of the large-hotel lounges for quiet island sounds and a couple of drinks—make it the **Paradise Lounge**, at the Hilton Hawaiian Village.

On **Day Three**, do the leisurely **Circle-Island tour**. Heading to **Diamond Head** to the Windward side, you can breeze right past the'burbs of Hawaii Kai around to **Koko Head** and **Hanauma Bay**. Stop for a look at the **Blow Hole**, then do a quick explore of **Sandy** and **Makapuu beach parks** (yes, those *are* daredevil surfers out there).

Visit **Sea Life Park Hawaii** (especially if you've got kids with you), for all the fishy theme park activities plus a good look at some endangered creatures. You'll pass plenty of good **beaches** before reaching the **Byodo-In Temple** in the **Valley of the Temples Memorial Park**. Anyone who is in the least sparked by Eastern religion or culture should kick off their shoes and check out this replica of a 900-year-old Japanese temple. The gardens and grounds are pretty inspiring, as well. Do lunch at **Paniolo Café**, a laid-back burger and mason-jar-margarita joint (you've come for the atmosphere, not the food).

Continuing north, it's one fantastic drive along the Pacific Ocean. The **Polynesian Cultural Center** is another sprawling theme-type attraction that provides a good bead on the lifestyles of the ancient ones (and it's another good stop for the kids). Just beyond the Turtle Bay Hilton and Country Club are famous **Sunset Beach** and **Waimea Bay**. If you've come in winter, you'll catch top surfers thumbing their toes at monster waves. Drive up **Pupukea Road** to see an ancient temple *(heiau)* as well as a spectacular North Shore view. Hop on an open-air minibus (or do the self-guided walk) at **Waimea Falls Park** with its 1800 lush acres, 30-plus botanical gardens and 45-foot falls (with cliff divers). **Haleiwa** is your old hippie- and New Age-experience town, with the associated galleries, shops and crafts emporiums (everything is organic). Slurp the ultimate shave ice at **Matsumoto's Grocery** and—if you're running short on time—head back to Honolulu via Kamehameha Road and H2 (and through the **pineapple plantations** and **military installations**), which will put you back near Pearl Harbor. Otherwise, continue around the island to more beaches, view points and small communities.

Back in Honolulu, pick a restaurant for your goodbye-Hawaii splurge. We recommend **Orchids** at the Halekulani Hotel for Pacific Rim cuisine in absolutely stunning surroundings (yes, it has wonderful ocean views).

Aloha.

Five-Day Itinerary

For those extra two days, hop over to one of the other islands. How about a visit to old **Lahaina**, on Maui, and maybe a hair-raising drive on the **Hana Highway**? Then on to **Molokai**, for a look at some 300-foot waterfalls and the world's highest sea cliffs? Or **Kauai**, for a romantic interlude and eye-pop at

Kaunolu Bay, Lanai

Garden of the Gods, Lanai

Manele Bay snorkelers

Hiking Munro Trail, Lanai

Waimea Canyon? The **Big Island**, to ski down a volcano and take in a rodeo? Or **Lanai**, for a couple of days of absolutely nothing....

Mauna Kea Volcano can be viewed from an observatory 27 miles from Hilo.

FIELDING'S FAVORITE HIDEAWAYS

Halawa Valley (Molokai)	Waterfalls, jungle, a lagoon and beach all hidden away in a lush (mosquito-filled) valley.
Waikamoi Ridge Trail (Maui)	Pools, waterfalls, bamboo forests and a superbly isolated picnic setting for those willing to hike up the (mosquito-filled) ridge.
Swinging Bridges (Maui)	Man-made waterfall, swimming hole, fruit trees, bamboo forests and a couple of swinging bridges, tucked away on the windward side of the West Maui Mountains. Beware of flash floods!
Green Sand Beach (the Big Island)	Grab a four-wheel-drive vehicle to frolic in the secluded (green) sand on Mahana Bay.
Waikiki Beach (Oahu)	For those who believe that hiding away is only a state of mind.

FIELDING'S FAVORITE VIEWS

Wailuku River State Park (the Big Island)	Head for the path adjacent to the parking lot to look out over **Rainbow Falls**. Come at sunrise to catch the rainbows form.

FIELDING'S FAVORITE VIEWS

Onomea Bay Scenic Route (the Big Island)
A four-mile drive (off Mamalahoa Highway Scenic Drive) above the bay.

Pololu Valley Lookout (the Big Island)
The scenic valley below is filled with taro farms.

Waimea Canyon Overlook (Kauai)
Ooh and aah at the canyon's often mist-shrouded colors—red, green, amber and purple.

Keanae Lookout (Maui)
Hana Highway twists and turns, bridges, fruit trees, pools and forests.

Kalaupapa Lookout (Molokai)
View the settlement of Kalaupapa from 1500 feet above.

Phallic Rock (Molokai)
Look *at* it, not *from* it!

Nuuanu Pali Lookout (Oahu)
The view is really supposed to be of windward Oahu, but it's just as much fun to watch the tourists battle with the gusty winds.

Diamond Head (Oahu)
Climb to the top for a great gander at Honolulu.

Waikiki Beach (Oahu)
A rare opportunity to see mounds of (pale) jiggling flesh, cavorting as one.

Sea Life Park in Waimanalo features a number of exhibits including whales, dolphins, seals, sharks, stingrays, sea lions and penguins. It's open daily.

FIELDING'S FAVORITE PLACES FOR KIDS

Sea Life Park
(Oahu)

Kids will be fascinated by the dolphins, penguins, tropical fish and other displays, plus the Touch Pool will wow them with starfish, giant worms and other sea creatures.

Diamond Head
(Oahu)

The hike to the top is kid-friendly—though the tunnel might be a little freaky for delicate types.

Aloha Tower Marketplace
(Oahu)

Of course, they'll love the mall. This one has stage entertainers plus a roving troupe of magicians and clowns.

Whale-watching
(Maui)

Between November and April, humpback whales can be spotted off the coast.

Astronaut Ellison S. Onizuka
Space Center
(the Big Island)

Everyone will want to play with the computer interactive exhibits, launch a mini-space shuttle and watch space-related films.

Molokai Ranch Wildlife Park
(Molokai)

Lots of wild animals to irritate.

Searching for seashells
(Maui)

Free, and it will keep them (and you) busy for *hours.*

Waikiki Beach
(Oahu)

Sign them (and you?) up for surfing lessons. One day they may be riding the 30-footers on the North Shore.

SPEAKING
HAWAIIAN

Once, as I was passing through a parking lot outside a hotel in Kauai, I overheard a mainlander struggling to extract a piece of information from a tour bus driver. "Is this the bus to Wammy?" she asked. When he replied, "Where?" and she repeated her question, his face remained perplexed. Finally she snapped in indignant annoyance, "Wammy Canyon, I said!" She seemed to think that the driver should have known immediately that what she meant was "Waimea (why-*may*-ah) Canyon." This woman was like the proverbial Ugly American who visits Italy and raises her voice—in English—when an Italian does not understand her. If she had paid any attention to the spelling of the word and taken a few moments to bone up on the pronunciation of Hawaiian, she would have been showing respect and staving off hassles at the same time. A local joke tells of a tourist on his way to a *luau* (feast) who ends up at a *lua* (toilet).

The credit for first putting Hawaiian on paper goes to the New England missionaries, who arrived in the islands in 1820. As they created an alphabet, their Western ears had a tough time sorting through the language's dozens of different sounds. Unable to hear the distinction between *t* and *k*, or *l* and *r*, or *b* and *p*, for instance, the missionaries whittled the language down to a mere **12 letters**. *Honoruru* turned into *Honolulu; Ranai* became *Lanai; Mauna Roa* was transformed into *Mauna Loa;* and *taboo* into *kapu.* Although missionaries forever altered the way island tongues would move, Hawaiians learned to read with voracious speed. *Within a little more than two decades, they were among the most literate people in the world.* Today, one of the few arenas where the legacy of Hawaii's ancient Polynesians lives on in full force is in the state's street signs and place names, the vast majority of which are Hawaiian. Familiarizing yourself with the pronunciation of the

SPEAKING HAWAIIAN

605

language will make it easier for you to ask directions, get around, and remember where you've been (or even the name of your hotel).

Duke Kahanamoku Statue, Oahu, honors the championship surfer who used a 16 ft. koa wood board that weighed 114 pounds. He's a legend among surfers.

Since it's phonetic, Hawaiian is not nearly as difficult to pronounce as it appears to the uninitiated. It consists of only seven consonants *(h, k, l, m, n, p, w)* and five vowels *(a, e, i, o, u)*, and no letter is silent. Each syllable ends with a vowel. The accent is usually on the next to last syllable of a word.

Consonants sound just as they do in English, with the exception of *w*. This letter is pronounced like a *v* when it precedes the last vowel of a word (such as *ewa* or *Kahoolawe*). Vowels sound like those in Spanish: *a* as in *around; e* like the *a* in *day; i* like the *ee* in *see; o* as in *so;* and *u* as in *sue*. When two or three vowels are together, they each get their own syllable (unless they are part of a diphthong). The double *o* in *Kahoolawe* sounds like "oh-oh" and the double *a* in *Kapaa* sounds like "ah-ah." The four diphthongs are *au,* pronounced *ow; ae* and *ai,* both pronounced like the *y* in *sky;* and *ei,* which rhymes with *hay.*

A mark like an apostrophe was once commonly used in many words to signal a sharp pause between syllables. This punctuation is rarely seen in writing anymore and pronunciations have changed accordingly. To purists, however, Hawaii (Hawai'i) will always be "Hah- *vy* ee." You'll also hear some people correctly pronounce the names of Neighbor Islands: "cow-*wah*'ee" (Kaua'i), "*mole*-oh-*kah*'ee" (Moloka'i), and "lah-*nah*'ee" (Lana'i) instead of "cow-*why,*" "*mole-* oh-kye," and "lah-*nye.*" In this book, I've used this mark only when two letters might otherwise appear to be a diphthong, to indicate the difference between *pau* ("pow"—finished) and *pa'u* ("*pah*-oo"—a long skirt), for instance.

You'll notice that even though quite a few names are long, in many cases syllables are simply repeated. Take, for example, one of the rainiest places in the world, *Mount Waialeale* (why *ah*-lay *ah*-lay) on Kauai, or the historic valley on the Big Island of Hawaii called *Pohakuhaku* (poh *hah*-koo *hah*-koo). Wrapping your tongue around *humuhumunukunukuapuaa* (a small trigger fish with a shark-sized name) may appear an impossible feat at first. But if you look closely, you'll see that the trick is to sound redundant: *hoo*-moo *hoo*-moo *noo*-koo *noo*-koo *ah*-poo *ah*-ah.

Most residents today will greet you with "aloha" and say "mahalo" instead of "thank you." Knowing other common Hawaiian words can prevent you from going places you shouldn't, such as into a men's room (many of which are marked *kane*) if you're a *wahine* (woman). When you don't understand what people are saying, the Hawaiian language will rarely be the reason. Among others, Japanese, Korean, Tagalog, Cantonese, and Pidgin, the local dialect, are far more widely spoken. Sometimes referred to as "lazy English," Pidgin is used with a real flourish among young Hawaiians and other locals. Originating with the laborers who came to work on Hawaii's plantations, it is a colorful blend of Hawaiian, English, Cantonese, Portuguese and a chop suey of other tongues. Its vocabulary and pronunciation can vary from island to island and even region to region.

When Hawaiian residents speak English, their accent tends to be sing-songy, elevating in pitch at the end of a sentence. Someone who answers your telephone call might ask you to "Hold on, yeh?" A person who gives you directions might end with, "Simple, yeh?" Be sure to spend some time "talking story" (chatting or gossiping) with locals.

Not all communication in Hawaii is either oral or written. When someone raises his hand with the three middle fingers down and the thumb and pinky extended and gives it a couple of quick shakes, this is a greeting or a good-natured signal to "hang loose" ("relax" or "cool out").

COMMON HAWAIIAN AND PIDGIN WORDS AND EXPRESSIONS

Term	Pronunciation	Meaning
aa	(*ah*-ah)	the rough kind of lava
ae	(eye)	yes
ahi	(*ah*-hee)	yellowfin tuna; or sometimes albacore or big-eye tuna
aikane	(eye-*kah*-nay)	friend
alii	(ah-*lee*-ee)	Hawaiian chief, royalty, person or people of high rank
aloha	(ah-*low*-ha)	welcome, hello, good-bye, love, friendship ...
aole	(ah-*oh*-lay)	no
brah	(bra)	bro' (brother), friend
cockroach		to steal something or take something in an underhanded manner
da kine	(dah kyne)	thingamajig, whatchamacallit
diamondhead		east (toward Diamond Head on Oahu)
ewa	(*ay*-vah—as in Eva Gabor)	west (toward Oahu's Ewa Plantation)
hale	(*hah*-lay)	house
haole	(*how*-lee)	Caucasian, mainlander, foreigner

COMMON HAWAIIAN AND PIDGIN WORDS AND EXPRESSIONS

Term	Pronunciation	Meaning
hapa	(*hah*-pah)	**half**
hapa-haole	(*hah*-pah *how*-lee)	**part Caucasian and part Hawaiian; not authentically Hawaiian**
hauoli la hanau	(how-*oh*-lee lah hah-*now*)	**Happy Birthday**
hauoli makahiki hou	(how-*oh*-lee mahkah*hee*-key *ho*-oo)	**Happy New Year**
heiau	(hey-ee-ow)	**ancient Hawaiian temple**
holo holo	(*hoe*-low *hoe*-low)	**to cruise, bar hop, go from place to place, visit**
hono	(*hoe*-know)	**bay**
hoolaulea	(ho-oh-lau-*lay*-ah)	**gathering, celebration, street party**
Howzit?		**How goes it? What's happening?**
hula	(*who*-lah)	**traditional Hawaiian dance**
imu	(*ee*-moo)	**underground oven still used in luaus**
kahuna	(kah-*who*-nah)	**Hawaiian priest**
kai	(kye)	**ocean**
kamaaina	(kah-mah-*eye*-nah)	**longtime resident**
kane	(*kah*-nay)	**man**
kapu	(kah-*poo*)	**taboo, forbidden, off-limits, keep out**
kau kau	(cow cow)	**food**
keiki	(*kay*-kee)	**child**
kiawe	(key-*ah*-vay)	**mesquite tree or wood**
koa	(*ko*-ah)	**an increasingly scarce tree prized for its wood**

COMMON HAWAIIAN AND PIDGIN WORDS AND EXPRESSIONS

Term	Pronunciation	Meaning
kokua	(ko-*koo*-ah)	help
lanai	(lah-*nye*)	terrace, balcony, patio, porch
lauhala	(low-*hah*-lah)	pandanus leaves (used for weaving)
lei	(lay)	long necklace made of flowers
li' dat	(lie dat)	like that
li' dis	(lie dis)	like this
lilikoi	(*lee*-lee-koy)	passion fruit
lua	(*loo*-ah)	toilet
luau	(*loo*-ow)	feast, celebration
mahalo	(mah-*hah*-low)	thank you
mahi mahi	(*mah*-hee *mah*-hee)	dolphin fish (not the mammal)
makai	(mah-*kye*)	in the direction of the sea
malihini	(*mah*-lee-*hee*-nee)	visitor, newcomer
malo	(*mah*-low)	loincloth once worn by Hawaiian men
mauka	(*mow*-kah)	toward the mountains, inland
mauna	(*mow*-nah)	mountain
mele kalikimaka	(*may*-lay keh-*lee*-keymah-kah)	Merry Christmas
muumuu	(moo-moo or moo-oo-moo-oo)	roomy, full-length dress
ohana	(oh-*hah*-nah)	clan, family
okole	(oh-*ko*-lay)	buttocks
onago	(oh-*nah*-go)	snapper
ono	(*oh*-no)	a fish similar to mackerel; also meaning that something tastes delicious

COMMON HAWAIIAN AND PIDGIN WORDS AND EXPRESSIONS

Term	Pronunciation	Meaning
opakapaka	(oh-*pah*-kah-*pah*-kah)	pink snapper
pahoehoe	(pah-*hoy*-hoy)	smooth or ropy lava
pakalolo	(pah-kah-*low*-low)	marijuana
pali	(*pah*-lee)	cliff
paniolo	(pah-nee-*oh*-low)	cowboy in Hawaii
pau	(pow)	finished
pau hana time	(pow*hah*-nah time)	when the work day is over
pa'u	(*pah*-oo)	a long skirt once worn by Hawaiian women
poi	(poy)	gooey, porridge-like food made from cooked and pounded taro root
puka	(*poo*-kah)	hole
pupu	(*poo*-poo)	hors d'oeuvres
shaka!	(*shah*-kah)	All right! Great! Excellent!
suck 'em up		go drinking
talk story		chew the cud, chat, gossip
tutu or tutu whanine	(too-too wah-*hee*-nee)	grandmother
ukulele	(oo-koo-*lay*-lay)	small, guitar-like instrument with four strings; literally "leaping flea"
wahine	(wah-*hee*-nee)	woman
wikiwiki	(*wee*-kee-*wee*-kee)	fast, quick

INDEX

I

FIELDING'S BAJA

The most complete guidebook to Baja for the outdoor adventurer.

This new Fielding guide, by Jack Williams, a recognized expert on Baja California, who has driven more than 20,000 miles of its roads and highways and twice sailed around the peninsula in his yacht, is filled with valuable insider information. Everything is covered—from sportfishing, watersports, beaches and deserts, to the best resorts, seaside getaways, camping spots and restaurants.

With 78 maps, tour guides and b/w photos.

- *Practical tips:* What to know before you go, plus insurance and customs info, and helpful glossary.
- *Watersports:* Where to find the best swimming holes, surfing and dive spots, windsurfing, and boating—plus a special sportfishing section.
- *Rated accommodations:* In-depth reviews of first-class resorts, modest motels, campsites and trailer parks.
- *Tips on shopping:* From Tijuana to Cabo San Lucas, where to find the best buys on leather, ceramics, silver, perfume, and more.

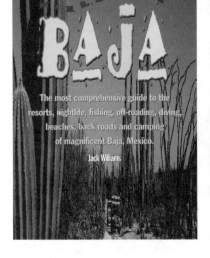

400 pages, 5" x 7-1/4", 30 b/w photos, 78 maps, 3-D tour guides

October 1996

$18.95

UK £9.95 CAN $21.95 AUS$24.95

ISBN 1-56952-106-9

Order Your Guide to Travel and Adventure

Title	Price	Title	Price
Fielding's Alaska Cruises and the Inside Passage	$18.95	Fielding's London Agenda	$14.95
Fielding's The Amazon	$16.95	Fielding's Los Angeles	$16.95
Fielding's Asia's Top Dive Sites	$19.95	Fielding's Malaysia & Singapore	$16.95
Fielding's Australia	$16.95	Fielding's Mexico	$18.95
Fielding's Bahamas	$16.95	Fielding's New Orleans Agenda	$16.95
Fielding's Baja	$18.95	Fielding's New York Agenda	$16.95
Fielding's Bermuda	$16.95	Fielding's New Zealand	$16.95
Fielding's Borneo	$18.95	Fielding's Paris Agenda	$14.95
Fielding's Budget Europe	$17.95	Fielding's Portugal	$16.95
Fielding's Caribbean	$18.95	Fielding's Paradors, Pousadas and Charming Villages	$18.95
Fielding's Caribbean Cruises	$18.95	Fielding's Rome Agenda	$14.95
Fielding's Disney World and Orlando	$18.95	Fielding's San Diego Agenda	$14.95
Fielding's Diving Indonesia	$19.95	Fielding's Southeast Asia	$18.95
Fielding's Eastern Caribbean	$17.95	Fielding's Southern Vietnam on 2 Wheels	$15.95
Fielding's England	$17.95	Fielding's Spain	$18.95
Fielding's Europe	$18.95	Fielding's Surfing Indonesia	$19.95
Fielding's European Cruises	$18.95	Fielding's Sydney Agenda	$16.95
Fielding's Far East	$18.95	Fielding's Thailand, Cambodia, Laos and Myanmar	$18.95
Fielding's France	$18.95	Fielding's Vacation Places Rated	$19.95
Fielding's Freewheelin' USA	$18.95	Fielding's Vietnam	$17.95
Fielding's Hawaii	$18.95	Fielding's Western Caribbean	$18.95
Fielding's Italy	$18.95	Fielding's The World's Most Dangerous Places	$19.95
Fielding's Kenya	$16.95	Fielding's Worldwide Cruises '97	$19.95
Fielding's Las Vegas Agenda	$14.95		

To place an order: call toll-free 1-800-FW-2-GUIDE
(VISA, MasterCard and American Express accepted)
or send your check or money order to:
Fielding Worldwide, Inc., 308 S. Catalina Avenue, Redondo Beach, CA 90277
http://www.fieldingtravel.com
Add $2.00 per book for shipping & handling (sorry, no COD's), allow 2–6 weeks for delivery

FIELDING'S MEXICO

"Among the very best."
—*Library Journal*

Authors Lynn and Lawrence Foster, both with a background in Mesoamerican archaeology and a Ph.D. in philosophy, have traveled throughout Mexico for 15 years, exploring major cities as well as hidden ruins and remote villages. What they bring to the reader is an educated insider's guide—with a real understanding of the history and the culture.

Including 2292 reviews, extensive coverage of ruins, shopping and food—plus detailed maps, 3-D tour guides, b/w photos.

- *Tips on places off the beaten track:* Such as the Temple of the Jaguars and Eagles in the town of Malinalco; the village of Cuetzalan, reminiscent of a legendary lost city; and the unusual little fishing village of Rio Lagartos, with its thousands of flamingos.
- *Advice on the best spots for watersports:* Including water-skiing, sailing, snorkeling and diving.
- *Fascinating background information:* On history and ancient civilizations.
- *Shopping ideas:* In this shopper's nirvana, where to find fabulous crafts, gorgeous silver, ceramic and glass pieces, serapes, rebozos and leather goods.

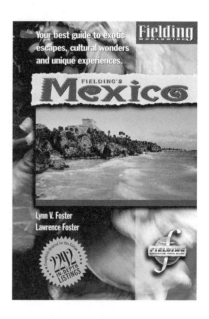

800 pages, 5" x 7-1/4", b/w photos, 54 maps, 3-D tour guides

October 1996

$18.95

UK £10.95 CAN $23.95 AUS $24.95

ISBN 1-56952-118-2

Replaces ISBN#1-56952-092-5

FIELDING'S
WORLDWIDE CRUISES '97

"Recommended without reservation."

—Philadelphia Inquirer

This totally new, encyclopedic volume is the definitive guide for choosing the perfect cruise. It's really two books in one, with ratings of 178 ships and profiles of 58 cruise lines, as well as the lowdown on the 220 most visited ports around the world. Written by Shirley Slater and Harry Basch, a husband-and-wife travel-writing team whose work has been published internationally, the text is both urbane and engaging and packed with valuable insider information.

Reviews of 178 ships, and 220 ports of call, with 200 b/w photos and 23 helpful maps.

- *Essential data:* All the facts the reader needs to choose the right ship and the right destination; supplemented with maps, charts and tables.
- *Important info to know beforehand:* What to wear, how to select a cabin, how to book a table, how to avoid seasickness, and more.
- *Special-interest choices:* The best cruises for families, singles, fitness fans and couch potatoes; plus descriptions of elegant sailing vessels, paddle-wheel steamers and riverboats.

1024 pages, 5-3/8" x 8-3/8",
312 b/w photos, 23 maps

August 1996

$19.95

UK £10.95 CAN $23.95 AUS $24.95

ISBN 1-56952-115-8
Replaces ISBN#1-56952-073-9

NEW FIELDINGWEAR!

Now that you own a Fielding travel guide, you have graduated from being a tourist to full-fledged traveler! Celebrate your elevated position by proudly wearing one of these heavy-duty, all-cotton shirts, selected by our authors for their comfort and durability (and their ability to hide dirt). Choose from three styles—radical "World Tour," politically correct "Do the World Right," and elegant "All-Access."

Important Note: Fielding authors have field-tested these shirts and have found that they can be swapped for much more than their purchase price in free drinks at some of the world's hottest clubs and in-spots. They also make great gifts.

WORLD TOUR

Hit the hard road with a travel fashion statement for out times. Visit all 35 of Mr. D.P.'s favorite nasty spots (listed on the back), or just look like you're going to. This is the real McCoy, worn by mujahadeen, mercenaries, UN peacekeepers and the authors of Fielding's The World's Most Dangerous Places. Black, XL, heavy-duty 100% cotton. Made in the USA. $18.00.

DO THE WORLD RIGHT

Start your next adventure wearing Fielding's policically correct "Do the World Right" shirt, complete with freaked-out red globe and blasting white type. A shirt that tells the world that within that high-mileage, overly educated body beats the heart of a true party animal. Only for adrenline junkies, hard-core travelers and seekers of knowledge. Black, XL, heavy-duty 100% cotton. Made in the USA. $18.00.

ALL ACCESS

Strike terror into the snootiest maitre'd, make concierges cringe, or just use this elegant shirt as the ultimate party invitation. The combination of the understated red Fielding logo embroidered on a jet-black golf shirt will get you into the snobiest embassy party or jumping night spot. An elegant casual shirt for those who travel in style and comfort. Black, XL or L, 100% preshrunk cotton, embroidered Fielding Travel Guide logo on front. Made in the U.S.A. $29.00.

Name:

Address:

City:

State: Zip:

Telephone:
Shirt Name:
Quantity:

For each shirt add $4 shipping and handling. California residents add $1.50 sales tax. Allow 2 to 4 weeks for delivery.

Send check or money order with your order form to:

Fielding Worldwide, Inc.
308 South Catalina Ave.
Redondo Beach, CA 90277

or
order your shirts by phone,:
1-800-FW-2-GUIDE
Visa, MC, AMex accepted

International Conversions

TEMPERATURE

To convert °F to °C, subtract 32 and divide by 1.8. To convert °C to °F, multiply by 1.8 and add 32.

Fahrenheit		Centigrade	
230°		110°	
220°			
210°		100°	Water Boils
200°			
190°		90°	
180°		80°	
170°			
160°		70°	
150°			
140°		60°	
130°			
120°		50°	
110°			
100°		40°	
90°		30°	
80°			
70°		20°	
60°			
50°		10°	
40°		0°	Water Freezes
30°			
20°		-10°	
10°			
0°		-20°	
-10°			
-20°		-30°	
-30°			
-40°		-40°	

WEIGHTS & MEASURES

LENGTH

1 km	=	0.62 miles
1 mile	=	1.609 km
1 meter	=	1.2936 yards
1 meter	=	3.28 feet
1 yard	=	0.9144 meters
1 yard	=	3 feet
1 foot	=	30.48 centimeters
1 centimeter	=	0.39 inch
1 inch	=	2.54 centimeters

AREA

1 square km	=	0.3861 square miles
1 square mile	=	2.590 square km
1 hectare	=	2.47 acres
1 acre	=	0.405 hectare

VOLUME

1 cubic meter	=	1.307 cubic yards
1 cubic yard	=	0.765 cubic meter
1 cubic yard	=	27 cubic feet
1 cubic foot	=	0.028 cubic meter
1 cubic centimeter	=	0.061 cubic inch
1 cubic inch	=	16.387 cubic centimeters

CAPACITY

1 gallon	=	3.785 liters
1 quart	=	0.94635 liters
1 liter	=	1.057 quarts
1 pint	=	473 milliliters
1 fluid ounce	=	29.573 milliliters

MASS and WEIGHT

1 metric ton	=	1.102 short tons
1 metric ton	=	1000 kilograms
1 short ton	=	.90718 metric ton
1 long ton	=	1.016 metric tons
1 long ton	=	2240 pounds
1 pound	=	0.4536 kilograms
1 kilogram	=	2.2046 pounds
1 ounce	=	28.35 grams
1 gram	=	0.035 ounce
1 milligram	=	0.015 grain

cm 0 1 2 3 4 5 6 7 8 9 10

Inch 0 1 2 3 4